The Achievement Test Desk Reference (ATDR)

Comprehensive Assessment and Learning Disabilities

Dawn P. Flanagan
St. John's University

Samuel O. Ortiz
St. John's University

Vincent C. Alfonso
Fordham University

Jennifer T. Mascolo
St. John's University

Allyn and Bacon
Boston • London • Toronto • Sydney • Tokyo • Singapore

Executive editor: Rebecca Pascal
Manufacturing buyer: JoAnne Sweeney
Cover designer: hannusdesign.com
Production coordinator: Pat Torelli Publishing Services
Editorial-production service: TKM Productions
Electronic composition: TKM Productions

Library of Congress Cataloging-in-Publication Data
The achievement test desk reference (ATDR) : comprehensive assessment and learning disabilities / Dawn P. Flanagan ... [et al.].
    p. cm.
    Includes bibliographical references and index.
    ISBN 0-205-32547-5
    1. Achievement tests. 2. Learning disabilities. I. Title: ATDR. II. Flanagan, Dawn P.

    LB3060.3 .A28 2001
    371.26'2--dc21   2001045192

Printed in the United States of America

10 9 8 7 6 5 4 3 2 1   05 04 03 02 01

To the special people in our lives

The children who bring tremendous joy to my life:

Joel Greenbaum (10-14-93)
Nicholas Juk (11-11-94)
Bryan Greenbaum (2-2-97)
Emily Howard (6-12-99)
Ryan Flanagan (5-26-00)

DPF

*My children who taught me more about school achievement
than any book ever did:*

Carlos Ayala Ortiz (12-28-95)
Alisa Carmen Ortiz (1-15-94)
Gabriella (Bella) Marie Ortiz (12-11-90)
Samuel Benjamin Ortiz (2-16-89)
Kathryn Anne Hippe (1-7-85)

SOO

The people who have supported me throughout the years:

My parents, Mary and Alfred Alfonso
My graduate students
at Fordham University

VCA

*My husband who has provided me with unwavering love
and support and who inspires me every day:*

Michael Louis Mascolo

JTM

Contents

Foreword

The Achievement Test Desk Reference (ATDR) is one of those books that belongs on the bookshelf of every professional involved in the assessment of individuals with learning disabilities. By assisting practitioners in developing a clear understanding of exactly which abilities are being measured by specific achievement tests, evaluators will be able to select the tests that are most appropriate to the referral question and make more valid and defensible interpretations than through that usually obtained with traditional methods. Part of the reason that the *ATDR* will prove so valuable to many professionals lies in the authors' recognition of the artificial distinction that is often made between the contents of intelligence tests and academic achievement tests. In reality, all tests measure some finite set of abilities, but with few exceptions practitioners have not often seen the connection or relationship between what are commonly referred to as cognitive abilities and academic skills or achievement. Flanagan, Ortiz, Alfonso, and Mascolo have gone beyond the observations of previous researchers and formally specified the manner in which the two are related and how they may be measured more accurately and reliably, particularly when the focus of assessment is on a suspected learning disability (LD).

There are several notable and substantive contributions made by the authors in this book that will have a significant impact on the manner in which academic abilities and LD are assessed and evaluated. Perhaps the most far-reaching development is their use of the Cattell-Horn-Carroll (CHC) theory of cognitive abilities as the framework from which both cognitive and academic abilities may be understood. Flanagan and colleagues extend this framework into the practical realm by providing classifications of over 50 major test batteries and some 320 total tests in accordance with the theoretical specifications of the CHC framework. The result is an incredible compilation of achievement tests (including language batteries) classified with respect to the broad and narrow CHC abilities they measure. In addition, the authors provide information and data regarding the psychometric properties of each test to create an enormous database for practitioners, known as the *Desk Reference* component of the book. The wealth of information contained in the *Desk Reference* will provide practitioners with the information necessary to make well-informed decisions regarding test selection and interpretation.

Apart from the classification of achievement tests alongside cognitive tests within an overarching theoretical model, the authors have developed and proposed an operational definition of LD that incorporates the major elements of LD while at the same time eliminating or deemphasizing traditional concepts that are either unsupported or unnecessary. Their definition builds on the work of a long tradition of pioneering LD researchers such as Monroe (1932) and Kirk and Bateman (1962). This definition moves beyond the simplicity of sole reliance on "aptitude-achievement discrepancy" and may be used to guide practice more directly and effectively than traditional ability-achievement discrepancy models.

Another significant contribution to academic assessment and LD determination comes by way of what is known as CHC Cross-Battery assessment (Flanagan, McGrew, & Ortiz, 2000; Flanagan & Ortiz, 2001; McGrew & Flanagan, 1998). In this book, the authors are both refining and extending much of their previous work, and have developed a unique method for conducting assessment with standardized, norm-referenced tests of achievement that enhances the reliability and validity of assessment with such tools. CHC Cross-Battery assessment has begun to impact the field of cognitive assessment in many important ways—from the manner in which individual practitioners conceptualize their referrals to the way in which test developers construct their tests. It is likely that the application of CHC Cross-Battery methods described in the *ATDR* will have a similar impact on the field of academic assessment and will change the way achievement is viewed and measured.

Flanagan, Ortiz, Alfonso, and Mascolo also succeed in enlightening practitioners about the many misconceptions involved in both academic assessment and LD determination. Apart from their innovative ideas, they also take the time to dispel many erroneous notions and discredit long held, but unsupported, beliefs about LD. For example, a great deal of controversy surrounding the concept of LD stems from the myriad problems associated with the notion of ability-achievement discrepancy analysis. Throughout the text, the authors recognize and discuss the problems inherent in the use of discrepancy formulae and point out the invalidity of many of the assumptions. They note that determination of a numerical discrepancy alone reveals nothing about the etiology of the discrepancy and nothing about the ways to intervene. The authors conclude that sole reliance on any type of formula will not result in consistent, reliable, and valid diagnostic and placement decisions. As observed by Simpson and Buckhalt (1990), "Though the formula method may have some appeal because it requires less clinical competence and judgment, the fact remains that reducing an important diagnostic decision to a mathematical equation gives a false sense of objectivity to a contrived procedure that is still essentially subjective" (p. 274).

Again, Flanagan and colleagues do not merely cite the problems with notions of discrepancy but actually advance the thinking in this area. For example, in discussing limitations of discrepancy procedures, the authors note that some individuals with learning disabilities may demonstrate *consistency,* rather than discrepancy, between measures of aptitude and achievement. This is because the selected aptitude measure includes tests that are related to the area of disability and where, logically, the individual is likely to score low. Although discrepancy analysis can be conducted within the scope of the operational definition and comprehensive framework outlined by the authors, it is important to note that Flanagan and colleagues provide a well-reasoned and highly defensible method for LD determination (including compliance with LD evaluations conducted under IDEA) that does not rely on any type of discrepancy at all.

Flanagan, Ortiz, Alfonso, and Mascolo succeed in demonstrating that by overrelying on the discrepancy criterion, among other reasons, the field has lost sight of the central purpose of assessment. As the authors note, the primary purpose of assessment is to develop specific interventions that will address the referral concern. The goals of a learning disability evaluation should therefore be to (1) determine the factors, both intrinsic and extrinsic, that may have caused the student to have difficulties; (2) explain how the observed difficulties relate to academic performance; and (3) select appropriate intervention(s). In other words, assessment results are used to plan appropriate interventions. In this respect, the *ATDR* is clearly an indispensable resource. The authors remind readers of the importance of integrating test results with other types of information, including school records, observations, interviews, and work samples, and their cautions are prominently incorporated into their proposed operational definition and comprehensive assessment framework. These contributions will no doubt help practitioners increase their understanding of achievement tests and, as a result, improve the precision of learning disability evaluations.

Nancy Mather

References

Flanagan, D. P., & Ortiz, S. O. (2001). *Essentials of cross-battery assessment.* New York: Wiley Press.

Kirk, S., & Bateman, B. (1962). Diagnosis and remediation of learning disabilities. *Exceptional Children, 29,* 73–78.

Monroe, M. (1932). *Children who cannot read.* Chicago: University of Chicago Press.

Simpson, R. G., & Buckhalt, J. A. (1990). *School Psychology International, 11,* 273–279.

Preface

Overview

The Achievement Test Desk Reference (ATDR) is the first book to link the practice of academic and learning disability (LD) assessment across a wide variety of practitioners, including educational evaluators, LD specialists, school/clinical psychologists, and speech/language pathologists, and ground it in a common, well-validated theoretical framework. The primary focus is on the use of tests of academic achievement. The *ATDR* is intended to serve as a companion volume to the cognitive-focused *Intelligence Test Desk Reference (ITDR)* and provides extensions and refinements of the methods shared by each. We believe that the *ATDR* represents a unique contribution to *both* the practice of academic assessment and learning disability evaluation. It achieves this distinction by combining detailed descriptions and critical reviews of over 50 recently published achievement tests with a comprehensive, innovative framework for learning disability evaluation that incorporates a viable, modern operational definition of LD and by following state-of-the-art assessment and interpretation methods.

The *Desk Reference* section contains descriptions and reviews of comprehensive, brief/screening, and specific academic skills batteries and achievement tests, including measures of reading, math, written and oral language, and phonological processing. Using an expert consensus process, achievement tests are also classified according to contemporary Cattell-Horn-Carroll (CHC) theory. In addition, all tests were evaluated for correspondence with the seven areas of achievement listed in the federal definition of LD (IDEA; P.L. 105-17) and seven Academic Clinical Composites (ACC) were developed to allow more precision and consistency in their measurement. These classifications, along with the description of the psychometric and qualitative characteristics of each test provided in this book, can be used to assist practitioners in selecting and organizing assessments as well as interpreting academic performance.

Assessment of academic abilities, particularly as related to LD determination, is further enhanced by the delineation of an operational definition of LD that incorporates notions gleaned from the latest research in the area while bridging the wide-ranging practices that span across various professional disciplines routinely involved in LD assessment. The foundation of the assessment process rests primarily with the CHC Cross-Battery approach first introduced in the *ITDR* and now further delineated and extended in this text. The use of illustrative case studies and reproducible worksheets and data summary sheets also help to facilitate and guide practitioners in applying the methods described in the text so that evaluation of academic functioning, and especially LD, can be enhanced and made more defensible than through use of traditional assessment methods and practices.

Laying the Foundation

Chapter 1 provides the reader with a description of the prevailing definitions of LD, including the manner in which these definitions are similar, and highlights the current problems with LD assessment and the need for a theory-based operational definition to guide practice. Chapter 2 describes a well-validated psychometric theory of abilities, the Cattell-Horn-Carroll (CHC) theory, and demonstrates how this taxonomy can be used as the foundation for cross-battery methods that guide test selection and inform test interpretation. The seven areas of academic achievement, listed in the federal definition of LD, are described and linked to CHC theory, particularly through the operationalization of the Academic Clinical Composites, which correspond directly to the IDEA specifications but which are formed via CHC-specified broad and narrow abilities. Together, Chapters 1 and 2 place the practice of LD evaluation within the context of current theory and research, particularly as it applies to the measurement and interpretation of academic abilities.

The Desk Reference

Chapters 3 through 10 constitute the *Desk Reference* component of this book. Chapter 3 describes how the *Desk Reference* is organized, as well as the criteria that were used to evaluate the individual tests included therein. This section of the book provides a visual-graphic display and review of important psychometric, theoretical, and qualitative features of 50 current achievement batteries, including over 320 individual tests. Batteries are organized alphabetically within the following categories: Comprehensive Achievement Tests (Chapter 4), Brief/Screening Achievement Tests (Chapter 5), Reading Tests (Chapter 6), Math Tests (Chapter 7), Written Language Tests (Chapter 8), Oral Language Tests (Chapter 9), and Phonological Processing Tests (Chapter 10). The information contained in the *Desk Reference* is particularly useful to practitioners in their decision-making process, as it provides crucial data that assist in determining the overall suitability and appropriateness of tests for specific applications in assessment.

A Defensible Approach to LD Determination

Chapter 11 begins with a review of the many misconceptions inherent in the application of current diagnostic criteria for determining LD. Considerable emphasis is placed on the uses and misuses of data yielded by various discrepancy approaches within the context of an evaluation for LD (e.g., ability-achievement discrepancy). Next, the chapter presents a review of the past 15 years of research on the relationship between cognitive abilities and specific academic outcomes. This research is used as a guide to test selection because it allows for the tailoring of an assessment battery according to specific referral concerns. In addition, this research provides a solid foundation for interpretation using methods that are highly defensible and consistent with prevailing notions of dysfunction or LD, as appropriate. Finally, Chapter 11 describes the essential elements of a viable, modern operational definition of LD proposed by the authors and culled from the core concepts in extant conceptualizations. The various elements of this definition include measurement of specific academic skills and acquired knowledge, evaluation of exclusionary factors, measurement of broad abilities/processes and aptitudes for learning, evaluation of underachievement, and evaluation of interference with functioning. Results at each phase of data collection are evaluated within the context of contemporary CHC theory and research so that the process of LD determination is conducted within the bounds of much more scientific rigor than that which has been applied traditionally.

Chapter 12 describes the current incarnation and advancement of the CHC Cross-Battery approach to measurement and interpretation of academic abilities and cognitive abilities that were initially presented in the *ITDR*. The foundation, rationale, and application of this approach are presented and a strong case is made with regard to the need for such a theory- and research-based approach in assessment-related fields. Step-by-step guidelines on how to use the CHC Cross-Battery method to organize a thorough assessment of one or more areas of academic abilities (e.g., reading, math, etc.) or one or more areas of LD (e.g., basic reading skills, math reasoning, written expression) are provided. Several examples of how to supplement the comprehensive achievement batteries (described in Chapter 4) are presented as a means to illustrate the cross-battery method.

Chapter 13 instructs the reader in how to interpret academic test performance using the research presented in Chapter 11 as well as recent findings and developments in the cognitive psychology and learning disabilities literature. The chapter also demonstrates how to integrate the findings from both academic and cognitive assessments following the same theoretical model and research base and the utility of evaluating ability scores from a normative perspective.

Chapter 14 presents the reader with a step-by-step case study that illustrates the components of a comprehensive framework for LD determination that adheres to general best practices in assessment. The case study explains the decision-making process inherent in the comprehensive framework, which follows an hypothesis-driven approach and encompasses the operational definition of LD presented in Chapter 11. The reader is instructed in how to organize assessments according to referral concerns, generate and test hypotheses, and interpret data from a wide variety of sources and professional disciplines following contemporary theory and research. Chapter 14 also demonstrates how to organize data in the form of a written psychological report.

In sum, the final three chapters of this book focus primarily on how the operational definition of LD may be readily incorporated into everyday practice. In general, these chapters describe a process for diagnosing a learning disability following an hypothesis-generation approach to assessment and interpretation that is based on the latest research, assessment methods, and theory on the structure of cognitive and academic abilities. The information presented in these chapters encourages a transdisciplinary approach to evaluation of individuals suspected of having an LD that is wholly consistent with the nature of the disorder that is reflected by deficits across traditionally separate areas of functioning.

Intended Audience

This book is intended for a wide variety of professionals who either work with individuals who are learning disabled or evaluate students with learning difficulties, including LD specialists, educational evaluators, reading specialists, special educators, practitioners, researchers, and other scholars who seek to infuse current theory and research in their use and interpretation of academic abilities. Practitioners, university trainers, students, researchers, and other professionals in school, clinical counseling, and educational psychology as well as neuropsychology who use or interpret academic achievement tests in applied settings will find this book valuable. This text is very appropriate for courses dealing with topics such as learning disabilities or those with primary focus on beginning or advanced achievement testing, measurement, and psychoeducational assessment. However, the book is also particularly valuable for anyone who seeks an organized, systematic, and theory-based method for evaluating a wide range of academic and cognitive abilities in any individual, including those suspected of having a learning disability.

Acknowledgments

There are many people who need to be acknowledged for their special and extraordinary contributions to this book. We wish to express our deep appreciation to Randy Floyd and Barbara Read for their time and many thoughtful insights and suggestions in their review of earlier drafts of this book. We also express our most sincere gratitude to Lenny Caltabiano for his dedication and commitment to this project as well as his superb competence in handling many of the coordinating activities that tend to drive the average person insane. His contributions greatly enhanced the quality of this book and we thank him for all he did. A big thank you also goes to Jennifer Jablonski, Kevin McGrew, Taryn Wallace, Stacey Lella, Michelle Memoli, James Bowman, John Willis, and Ron Dumont for contributing significantly to various portions of the book. We also gratefully acknowledge Rebecca Pascal, the staff at Allyn and Bacon, Lynda Griffiths, and the staff at TKM Productions for their support, understanding, and most of all their patience with us. The expertise, guidance, and pleasant and cooperative working style of these individuals helped to develop what we believe is a book of the finest quality possible.

And last, but by no means least, we are deeply grateful for the contributions of the theorists, scholars, researchers, and practitioners who assisted in developing the CHC classifications of the achievement tests included in this book. These individuals are listed in Appendix H. The participation of these individuals influenced this current work and will continue to enrich and inform the research foundation upon which the CHC Cross-Battery approach was built. Your extraordinary effort and sacrifice are truly appreciated.

D. P. F.
S. O. O.
V. C. A.
J. T. M.

Chapter 1

Academic Achievement
and Learning Disabilities

Individuals associated with education in some way (e.g., students, parents, teachers, principals, guidance counselors, school psychologists, and others) are all too familiar with the terms *achievement* and *learning disability*. These words are common in the day-to-day business of education and are discussed within the school setting as if each were quite well defined and easily understood. Discussions regarding such concepts within the context of the various school-related disciplines suggest, however, that the exact meaning of each term differs markedly depending on who is being asked.

It would be safe to say that the general conceptualization of achievement, in the education arena, primarily revolves around the traditional "three *R*s" of school learning—reading, [w]riting, and [a]'rithmetic. Although there are other areas of achievement (e.g., social studies, science, history, art, physical education, etc.), it is these three subjects that form the core of what is often regarded as the hallmark measures of school-related achievement and success (in particular in elementary school-aged children). But is achievement truly so easily defined and circumscribed? Are reading and writing actually distinct abilities or do they possibly reflect a broader skill or collective ability (e.g., literacy)? Doesn't language development provide an accurate context for defining achievement because it represents both the spoken (oral) form of learning as well as the symbolic (written) form? And what about the cognitive processes that underlie development of these skills—are they not a part of achievement's ultimate definition? Are academic abilities different from cognitive abilities? As will become evident throughout the chapters of this book, the notion that academic achievement skills represent neat and tidy little packages that can easily be measured through standardized tests will be demonstrated to be untrue. Achievement, it would appear, is a much more complex subject than many have thought.

Unlike the concept of achievement, few would argue that the term *learning disability* or simply *LD,* is indeed hard to define. In general, LD, as is implied by the very term, primarily revolves around some type of dysfunction, intrinsic to the individual, that somehow prevents the individual from being able to learn "the three Rs" as well, as fast, or as efficiently as might be expected in the absence of the dysfunction. Although accurate, such a straightforward conceptualization is deceptively simple. Because the concept of LD includes issues related to achievement—in particular the development of academic skills—the very questions regarding the definition and meaning of these terms now becomes part and parcel of the LD definition problem. Moreover, the basic principles underlying LD introduce other concepts that have fared no better with respect to definition or specification than achievement. How does one determine what an individual might do if he or she had no disability? Should IQ scores be used to reflect potential, even though they were never designed for this purpose? And if so, should academic performance be necessarily discrepant from potential in order to suggest LD, or might consistency between related abilities and performance be the marker for LD? What is the relationship between academic and cognitive abilities that underlies LD and what is the theory upon which this is based? Do schools even need any tests of cognitive ability or intelligence to determine LD? The questions are many but the answers are few.

Given that the assessment and evaluation of achievement and learning disabilities, in particular under the mandate of the Individuals with Disabilities Education Act (IDEA; P.L. 105-17), represents one of the most common activities within the school setting, it seems unreasonable to proceed with any practice that cannot offer clear and defensible answers to the questions that are raised. In fact, the major problem that continues to plague practitioners in the assessment of LD revolves around the very lack of specificity in any definition of learning disability in the literature, which undermines the reliability and validity of the entire evaluative effort. Moreover, there do not exist any viable frameworks for assessment that integrate evaluation of both academic abilities and cognitive abilities, as would be necessary in the case of LD. The matter of reliable and valid LD assessment is further confounded by the unfortunately vague and ambiguous codification of various definitions (e.g., achievement, learning disability, disorder in psychological processing, severe discrepancy, substantial limitation in daily life activity, adverse effect on educational performance, etc.) directly into laws that often govern or influence the process of LD determination (e.g., IDEA, Americans with Disabilities Act [ADA], Section 504 of the Vocational and Rehabilitation Act of 1973, etc.). The lack of clear specification and the poor operationalization of the terms leaves the whole process of LD determination open to highly subjective and variable interpretation.

Clearly, the lack of any theoretical basis for specifying measurement of and the necessary relationships between academic and cognitive abilities undermines any effort toward valid and reliable assessment. The language of the statute is also noteworthy for allowing the identification of a learning disability to be completed *without* having to engage in any type of discrepancy analysis. The latter part of the wording provides that "a team may determine that a child has a specific learning disability" through use of discrepancy procedures, but the law does not in fact require that such discrepancy procedures be used. Unfortunately, the additional language provides a crude operationalization of the process of identifying learning disability and has led many states to adopt the concept of discrepancy evaluation as a necessary, if not central, component of LD determination. The problems with discrepancy models for LD notwithstanding (Badian, 1999; Finlan, 1992; Flanagan & Ortiz, 2001; Fletcher, Francis, Rourke, Shaywitz, et al., 1992; Fletcher, Francis, Shaywitz, Lyon, Foorman, Stuebing, & Shaywitz, 1998; Gaskill & Brantley, 1996; Heath & Kush, 1991; Meyer, 2000; Reynolds, 1990; Ross, 1992; Siegel, 1999; Stanovich, 1991), the wording in IDEA provides no further definition or specification as to exactly what constitutes achievement in any of the seven areas mentioned. Although reading comprehension and mathematics calculation are probably defined well enough as terms of achievement, oral expression, written expression, and basic reading skill are so vaguely specified that they do little if anything to guide appropriate evaluation.

It is largely in direct response to the problems regarding poor specificity in both the definitions of and relationship between academic achievement and learning disability that we offer this book. If the process of measuring academic achievement and one of its foremost purposes for doing so—evaluation of learning disabilities—is to be improved in any way, it must come from greater precision in virtually every facet of assessment. The remaining sections of this chapter will provide discussion regarding the development of current definitions of learning disability and the nature and definition of academic achievement as defined under IDEA. In the chapters that follow, we propose several innovations that help address the questions that remain, even in the most modern conceptualizations of academic achievement and learning disability—including application of contemporary theory, an operational definition with significantly greater specification and based on theory, and a comprehensive framework for assessment of academic achievement and LD. In this manner, we hope that the process of LD assessment can become one where professionals of all disciplines may communicate within a common language and framework that informs high-stakes educational decisions with a greater degree of reliability and validity.

Learning Disability Defined

Early Definitions: Research Based

Working in Great Britain in 1896, W. Pringle Morgan and James Hinshelwood used the term *congenital word blindness* to describe an individual's inability to learn to read fluently despite no apparent injury or illness. In describing similar unexplainable difficulties in learning to read, Samuel Orton (1937) used the terms *strephosymbolia* and later *word deafness.* In 1947, Alfred Strauss, in his study of individuals with mental retardation who suffered from brain injury, assigned behavioral criteria for the diagnosis of a biophysical phenomenon that established a basis for inferring tangible brain damage merely on the basis of behavioral signs. Researchers in LD embraced this notion and in 1966, Clemens established minimal brain dysfunction (MBD) as a behavioral concept underlying the notion of academically related learning problems. Clemens believed that MBD could be inferred as the underlying cause of learning problems and described it as a condition affecting "children of near average, average, or above average general intelligence with certain learning or behavioral disabilities ... which are associated with deviations of functions of the central nervous system" (p. 241).

Orton and other seminal researchers in the LD field tended to study absolute deficits or the total or near-total inability to associate sounds with their associated written symbols. Consequently, these early descriptions were primarily conceptual and lacked any real functional criteria specific to the condition. Nevertheless, the behaviors documented by these early researchers eventually evolved into the primary diagnostic features of learning disabilities. It is important to recognize, therefore, that the early research in LD described this condition from an exclusionary perspective more on the basis of what it was *not,* rather than what it *was* (Kavale & Forness, 2000).

Following the early developments in LD research, some of the most influential work in the field was conducted by Samuel Kirk. Recognizing the need to provide more specificity in the concept of LD, his work represents an impressive effort that provided a great deal of original thought regarding the concept. According to Kirk and Bateman (1962),

*a learning disability refers to a retardation, disorder, or delayed development in
one or more of the processes of speech, language, reading, writing, arithmetic, or
other school subjects resulting from a psychological handicap caused by a possible cerebral dysfunction and/or emotional or behavioral disturbances. It is not the
result of mental retardation, sensory deprivation, or cultural and instructional factors. (p. 263)*

In their definition, Kirk and Bateman reinforced the concept of MBD by using the term
cerebral dysfunction as the presumptive underlying cause of the learning problem. They
also seemed to affirm the idea of absolute deficit (an inability to function within normal limits) as a key feature in LD. Much like the subjects of early research, Kirk also worked with
individuals who were either unable to read or had such labored and difficult reading that they
were regarded as severely impaired, which probably influenced his adoption of presumed
organic dysfunction. And again, much like his predecessors and despite his attempts at better specification, Kirk's description of learning disability continued to rest on defining
exclusionary more than inclusionary criteria. Nevertheless, Kirk's original thinking and
clarification of the concept of LD continues to influence the many modern definitions in use
to the present day. A summary of the development of these early research-based definitions
can be found in Figure 1.1.

Transformational Definitions: Education Oriented and Discrepancy Based

During the 1960s and 1970s, the primary influence on the development of the concept of LD
shifted away from the clinical setting to the educational and legal realms. It was perhaps the
increasing number of school children who had unexplainable difficulties learning to read
fluently despite having apparently normal intelligence that led to the adoption of a more educationally oriented view of LD. Within the educational arena, LD was defined more on the
basis of educational criteria than physiological dysfunction. In addition, the educational criteria introduced the concept of *discrepancy.* Because such children seemed to be academically capable in many other respects, there emerged a notion that a discrepancy existed
between a child's *expected* level of academic functioning and *actual* academic performance.
In essence, this specification highlighted the idea that LD was responsible for a student's
underachievement in school.

In addition, educators capitalized on the popularity of IQ and derived what seemed to
be a rather simple way of operationalizing such underachievement by examining the discrepancy between IQ and actual achievement. The operationalization of underachievement
through this particular IQ-achievement comparison became so popular that not only did it
become the central criterion in learning disability identification but it has become virtually
synonymous with it. Today, the identification of school children with this and even other
types of discrepancies has provided a rationale for securing funding for remedial services
and has influenced almost every modern conceptualization of LD, including the diagnostic
criteria for the class of Learning Disorders found in the fourth edition of the *Diagnostic and
Statistical Manual of Mental Disorders,* published by the American Psychiatric Association
(APA, 1994, 2000).

FIGURE 1.1   Development and Evolution of Learning Disability Definitions

Early Definitions: Research based		
Name	**Dates**	**Salient Features**
W. Pringle Morgan and James Hinshelwood	1896	Labeled inability to learn to read "word blindness"
Samuel Orton	1925, 1937	Described unexplained difficulties in reading
Alfred Strauss	1947	Assumed brain injury on the basis of observed reading difficulties
Samuel Kirk	1962	Included: 1) assignment of cerebral dysfunction as a likely cause of inability to read; 2) affirmation of inability to function within normal limits as defining characteristic
Transformational Definitions: Education oriented and discrepancy based		
Bateman	1965	Included: 1) aptitude-achievement discrepancy; 2) introduced requirement of underachievement
Clemens	1966	Affirmed minimal brain dysfunction as cause of learning difficulties
Council on Exceptional Children Division for Children with Learning Disabilities	Late 1960s	Excluded co-morbidity as accompanying feature
National Advisory Committee on Handicapped Children Annual Report	1968	Presented underpinnings for federal Education of All Handicapped Children Act (P.L. 94-142)
Northwestern University Institute for Advanced Study	1969	Included: 1) aptitude-achievement discrepancy; 2) served as foundation for 1976 U.S. Dept. of Education definition
P.L. 94-142 (Education of All Handicapped Children Act)	1975	Included co-morbidity as a new feature
Wepman	1975	Restricted definition to perceptual process-based academic problems
U.S. Department of Education	1976	Added requirement of severe discrepancy between intellect and achievement
Consensus Definitions: Current revisions and modern conceptualizations		
Diagnostic and Statistical Manual of Mental Disorders	1994, 2000	Included: 1) aptitude/achievement discrepancy; and 2) substantial interference with academic achievement or activities of daily living
National Joint Committee on Learning Disabilities (NJCLD)	1981	Identified primary cause as CNS dysfunction; operational or descriptive criteria not clearly detailed
Interagency Committee on Learning Disabilities (ICLD)	1987	Incorporated most generally accepted descriptive characteristics of LD
Individuals with Disabilities Education Act (IDEA)	1991, 1997	Identified underlying cognitive deficit(s) as cause of language disorder

Although schools had recognized to some extent the phenomenon of learning disability prior to the 1960s and 1970s, there was no substantial impetus to serve these children in any systematic way. Moats and Lyon (1993) pointed out that the eventual disability category of LD arose out of recognition of the existence of a practical problem involving students who were encountering substantive learning difficulties despite average or above-average aptitude. Unlike students who were, for example, blind or deaf, very often these individuals were effectively "disenfranchised from any formal special education services because their cognitive and educational features did not correspond to any of the recognized categories of disability" (p. 290). The concept of underachievement remained central to the call for educational intervention and was promoted heavily by parents and advocacy groups who began to demand increased support for students who experienced difficulties in learning in spite of average or better ability and level of effort expended.

In 1975, the passage of P.L. 94-142 (i.e., the Education of All Handicapped Children Act; EHCA—later renamed the Individuals with Disabilities Education Act; IDEA) provided the first direct mandate requiring schools to identify and remediate children with learning disabilities. The concepts outlined previously by Kirk and presented as early as 1968 in the annual report of the National Advisory Committee on Handicapped Children served as the primary basis for the definition used in P.L. 94-142 (and its later reauthorizations). The section of the statute that defines a child with a disability states in part:

> *(1) Specific learning disability is defined as follows:*
>
> *(i) General. The term means a disorder in one or more of the basic psychological processes involved in understanding or in using language, spoken or written, that may manifest itself in an imperfect ability to listen, think, speak, read, write, spell, or to do mathematical calculations, including such conditions as perceptual disabilities, brain injury, minimal brain dysfunction, dyslexia, and developmental aphasia.*
>
> *(ii) Disorders not included. The term does not include learning problems that are primarily the result of visual, hearing, or motor disabilities, of mental retardation, of emotional disturbance, or of environmental, cultural, or economic disadvantage. (IDEA, Sec. 300.7b)*

The concept of *co-morbidity* is evident in this definition where use of the word *primarily* clearly indicates that the criteria stipulate LD as a condition separate from visual, hearing, and so on, but that it *may* coexist with these conditions in the same child. Nevertheless, the definition remains extremely vague and continues to rely heavily on exclusionary criteria. The concept of learning disability as defined in IDEA may have been inadvertently confounded by additional wording, included presumably to assist in the identification of LD. A section in IDEA related to the criteria for determining the existence of a specific learning disability states that:

> *(a) A team may determine that a child has a specific learning disability if—*
>
> *(1) The child does not achieve commensurate with his or her age and ability levels in one or more of the areas listed in paragraph (a)(2) of this section, if provided with learning experiences appropriate for the child's age and ability levels; and*

> *(2) The team finds that a child has a severe discrepancy between achievement and intellectual ability in one or more of the following areas:*
>> *(i)   Oral expression*
>> *(ii)   Listening comprehension*
>> *(iii) Written expression*
>> *(iv)   Basic reading skill*
>> *(v)   Reading comprehension*
>> *(vi)   Mathematics calculation*
>> *(vii) Mathematics reasoning (IDEA; Sec. 300.541)*

The statute is noteworthy with respect to the use of the word *may* as opposed to *shall* or *must.* This signifies that this specification, which revolves around the notion of discrepancy, is not the only way that LD may be identified. Yet, many state and local educational agencies seem to have interpreted this section of IDEA as requiring the identification of a discrepancy between ability and achievement to the point that discrepancy analysis has become so entrenched in LD evaluations that it is conducted in the vast majority of cases where LD is suspected. Alternative methods and conceptualizations of LD have not been completely ignored, and despite the pervasive use of discrepancy analysis, there is no consensus that discrepancy is even a necessary component of LD evaluations (Siegel, 1999). MacMillan and colleagues (1998), for example, compared school-based decisions regarding LD designations of students with the currently recognized research-based criteria. They found that children were often classified as LD on the basis of low absolute achievement, regardless of whether a discrepancy existed. Irrespective of whether discrepancy is a necessary part of LD determination, the various definitions that developed during this period generally included some type of ability-achievement discrepancy analysis as the preferred method for operationalizing underachievement. Bateman's (1965) definition of LD, for example, included the idea of *aptitude-achievement* discrepancy and reinforced the notion of underachievement as an essential component of LD. However, Bateman offered no explanation regarding why such a discrepancy is crucial to identifying LD, merely stating that "children . . . manifest an educationally significant discrepancy between their estimated intellectual potential and actual level of performance."

In January of 1968, the National Advisory Committee on Handicapped Children offered a definition conceptually similar to Kirk and Bateman's (1962) in its first annual report. The committee emphasized primarily the notion of delayed or retarded acquisition of academic skills and restricted the definition to children, reinforcing its believed developmental nature. The U.S. Department of Education later adopted the committee's definition and eventually incorporated it into IDEA. Subsequent refinements of educationally based LD definitions continued to affirm the centrality of underachievement in the identification of LD and explicitly acknowledged the notion of discrepancy as the key method for establishing it (Kass & Myklebust, 1969). In addition to this component, the educational focus of prevailing definitions was reinforced by suggestions that special education techniques were a basic requirement for enhancing performance. As such, educational definitions during this period began to omit any specification of etiology or reference to central nervous system dysfunction or minimal brain dysfunction.

As definitions of LD became widespread in the educational arena, particularly after the passage of IDEA, there seemed to be more divergence than convergence. A definition developed by the Council on Exceptional Children, for example, flatly rejected the notion of co-morbidity by excluding mentally retarded, blind, deaf, and emotionally disturbed from meeting the requirements for learning disability. Wepman and colleagues (1975) presented another highly restrictive view of LD by limiting the disorder to perceptual process-based academic problems. The notion of discrepancy was given perhaps its greatest boost when, in 1976, the U.S. Department of Education published its definition of learning disability in the *Federal Register.* In this definition and in an attempt to better operationalize the concept, the diagnostic criterion of *severe discrepancy* was added, which necessitated the development of a formula for calculating a severe discrepancy between ability and achievement.

Opposition to the use of a formula rose quickly for several reasons. Critics claimed that the formula was mathematically unsound and that its use selected students who were different from those who were already being served by special education programs. In addition, the use of a formula made the evaluation and identification of LD seem objective and impartial, and gave too much importance to a single procedure that minimized the importance of other data and indicators that might otherwise rule in or rule out LD. The problems with the use of discrepancy formulas in LD evaluation were evident in the feedback received by the U.S. Department of Education to the extent that it dropped the formula from later regulations but retained the notion of discrepancy as the primary means for identifying LD (Mercer et al., 1985).

Advances in the development of definitions of LD during the 1960s and 1970s did not completely ignore medical and clinical perspectives. Perhaps the most significant influence from the medical setting during this time came from the American Psychiatric Association, which included specific criteria for clinical diagnosis of several types of Learning Disorders in its *Diagnostic and Statistical Manual of Mental Disorders (DSM).* In the most recent version *(DSM-IV),* dysfunction in academic skill acquisition—in particular Reading Disorder, Mathematical Disorder, and Disorder of Written Expression—are included. In general, a diagnosis is made when an individual's achievement on individually administered, standardized tests is found to be substantially below that expected for age, schooling, and level of intelligence. The specification in *DSM-IV* adds an interesting but important criterion related to the fact that the learning problems must significantly interfere with academic achievement or activities of daily living that require the deficient skill. In addition, there is an attempt to operationalize the specification regarding *substantially below* by defining it as a discrepancy of at least two or more standard deviations between achievement and IQ.

There is some concession in *DSM-IV* to the use of a strict standard in identifying LD wherein the specification allows for a smaller discrepancy between achievement and IQ (i.e., between one and two standard deviations) to be used in cases where an individual's performance on an IQ test may have been compromised by an associated disorder in cognitive processing, a co-morbid medical disorder or general medical condition, or differences in the individual's ethnic, cultural, or linguistic background. The criteria do not specify, however, any particular method for calculating discrepancies, and different methods may well lead to different results (Flanagan, McGrew, & Ortiz, 2000; Flanagan & Ortiz, 2001). A final component of the *DSM-IV* definition relates to co-morbidity and specifies that if any sensory deficit is already present in the individual, then the learning difficulties must be in excess of those associated with that deficit.

In general, the *DSM-IV* definition seems to require both an ability-achievement discrepancy *and* evidence of impairment in both the specific academic skill and general life activities that require the skill. The specification related to impairment in activities that require the skill seems particularly important because it implies the need to identify absolute rather than relative deficits in performance. Certainly, the vague language of the *DSM-IV* criteria does not allow definitive interpretation of intent, but there does seem to be a clear message regarding the need to establish underachievement on the basis of both discrepancy *and* clear achievement deficits. Evaluation of individuals under this specification should be done cautiously, especially in cases where a discrepancy is identified but where there is an absence of absolute, not relative, deficits in achievement. In addition, unlike many other definitions of LD, the *DSM-IV* specification does not address whether an underlying cognitive dysfunction must be present or whether alternative reasons for academic difficulties outside of sensory impairments (e.g., noncognitive factors) must be taken into account. In this way, the *DSM-IV* definition tends to ignore important current research that supports impairment of cognitive processing functions as an underlying cause of difficulties in reading and other academic skills deficits. A summary of the development of educational-oriented and discrepancy-based definitions of LD is presented in Figure 1.1.

Consensus Definitions: Current Revisions and Modern Conceptualizations

The National Joint Committee on Learning Disabilities (NJCLD) presented a consensus definition in 1981 developed by its eight constituent member LD organizations, including Orton Dyslexia Society—now known as the International Dyslexia Association; Association for Children with Learning Disabilities (ACLD); Association on Higher Education and Disability (AHEAD); Division for Children with Communication Disorders (DCCD); Division for Children with Learning Disabilities (DCLD) of the Council for Exceptional Children (CEC); International Reading Association (IRA); American Speech, Language, and Hearing Association (ASHA); and Council for Learning Disabilities (CLD). The definition offered by the NJCLD seemed to run counter to the earlier federal definitions that described *specific* learning disabilities, because it specified LD as a rather generic disorder likely to manifest itself in a variety of symptoms. The definition made no explicit attempt to define underachievement or any related discrepancy requirement and described the level of severity in impairment quite vaguely and simply as *significant*. It did, however, acknowledge central nervous system dysfunction as the primary etiology of LD, which represented a departure from earlier transformative definitions. The rather authoritative and broad-based heritage of the NJCLD definition gave it an immediate and "high level of acceptance among multiple national associations and individuals" (Hammill, 1990, p. 83). The NJCLD definition did not, however, completely supplant other definitions and alternative conceptualizations continued to proliferate during this period.

Between 1982 and 1989, Hammill (1990) was able to identify as many as 11 different definitions in general use. None of these definitions strongly influenced developments in LD determination, mainly because they tended to focus on conceptual rather than operational issues. Of course, this was also true of the NJCLD definition, but the power and sheer numbers behind its constituent organizations involved in developing the definition helped ensure a much wider scope of acceptance. But concerns about the limitations inherent in exclusionary definitions, which included the one from NJCLD, continued to haunt conceptualizations of LD, particularly with respect to proper diagnosis. Lyon (1995), a notable and influential researcher, summarized his criticisms of both the NJCLD definition and the IDEA definition, stating that they fail to provide objective guidelines and criteria for distinguishing individuals with dyslexia from those with other generalized learning difficulties. Lyon extended his criticisms regarding LD evaluation and cautioned that there were serious negative consequences that resulted whenever inadequate definitions serve as the basis for assigning support services for children with reading problems. In short, when empirically supported criteria for determining who does and does not receive special education are absent, the entire system becomes ineffective at best and discriminatory at worst (Lyon, 1995).

Lyon's (1995) criticisms, beginning in the 1980s and extending through present day, seemed particularly biting, yet his cautions went almost totally unheeded and consensus definitions continued to emerge unabated. In 1987, the Interagency Committee on Learning Disabilities (ICLD) developed a definition and the NJCLD offered a slightly revised definition of its original specification. These consensus definitions recognized the heterogeneity of LD but still endorsed a set of common definitional characteristics that included the idea that LD is probably the result of CNS dysfunction; involves psychological processing disorders; is associated with underachievement; can be manifested in spoken language, academic, or thinking disorders; occurs across the life span; and does not result from other conditions.

The NJCLD definition represents a development that accomplished a rather high level of concordance with respect to the conceptual nature of LD. It has not, however, provided any more of a viable and practical operational definition than many of the conceptualizations that preceded it (Kavale & Forness, 2000). Problems with lack of specific criteria and measurable processes continue to undermine efforts to reliably identify individuals with LD from those without it. Even some of the central components of LD, such as ability-achievement discrepancy, seem to have very little empirical and theoretical support. For example, in studies using IQ as the operational element of ability in LD determination, IQ-achievement discrepancy revealed nothing about the etiology of the discrepancy nor did it suggest any avenue of intervention for reducing it. Brenner also noted that poor readers may have the same underlying phonological processing problem whether or not their reading achievement and IQ are discrepant, and that children may underachieve relative to Verbal IQ (VIQ) but still achieve at a near-average, average, or even above-average level (see also Aaron, 1997). Brenner's conclusions are particularly relevant to the central theme of this book in that he cautioned that, at least in the early elementary years, diagnosis of a learning disability should incorporate not only the IQ-achievement discrepancy but also such inclusionary criteria as absolute cognitive, linguistic, or psychomotor deficits shown to be related to specific academic deficits.

The popularity and widespread use of current consensus definitions has not diminished the criticisms being leveled at such specifications. Some of these criticisms are related to the problems inherent in current definitions, but others revolve more around the effect such vague definitions have had in actual practice. For example, in their investigation of the U.S. Department of Education's definition and its use in schools, McMillan, Gresham, and Bocian (1998) found that the current clinical and even educational underpinnings of the learning disability concept have largely been abandoned in favor of a pragmatic rationale for funding of remedial and support services for poorly achieving students. The emerging focus and recognition of economic realities seem to reveal that public school practices for diagnosing children with LD bear little resemblance to what is prescribed in federal and state regulations and are governed more by economic concerns than actual legal criteria. The increasing rate at which public schools identify students formerly labeled "mentally retarded" as LD is perhaps one result of the failure to adhere closely to federal and state regulations (Epps et al., 1982; MacMillan et al., 1996). In addition, it is likely that schools are also succumbing to the intense pressure from parents and advocacy organizations that seek to have services provided to the growing cadre of students who experience academic difficulty, often irrespective of the legal criteria and mandates regarding who is eligible for such services.

It seems equally plausible that schools have also resorted to use of the LD label as a socially desirable and less stigmatizing alternative to mental retardation. Between the 1976–77 and 1992–93 school years, the number of children classified as LD nationwide increased by an astonishing 198 percent. During the same period, there was a corresponding *decrease* of 41 percent in the identification of children with mental retardation and a 15.5 percent decrease in children identified as having speech and language impairments (U.S. Department of Education, 1995). Even school personnel have openly acknowledged that LD is a much more "acceptable" label to parents and children alike (MacMillan et al., 1998). The vague and nonspecific operationalization and specification of LD in prevailing consensus and legal definitions are no doubt responsible in large part for the current practice of using the label of LD as essentially a nonspecific category for public schools to serve those children who experience some type of academic difficulty but who might otherwise fail to meet state criteria for eligibility for special education services.

The lack of a clear and specific operational definition of LD has had effects that are not limited to the applied arena but that also extend to research in the field of learning disabilities. Without the benefit of commonly accepted operational definitions, methods of identifying LD remain highly variable. As a result, researchers and educational personnel may well find themselves working with populations and samples that are more dissimilar than similar. For example, there is a considerable lack of agreement among states regarding exactly what constitutes a learning disability. In a survey of 42 state departments of education, Mercer, Forgnone, and Wolking (1976) found considerable variation in state definitions (see also Mercer, King-Sears, & Mercer, 1990). Furthermore, Epps and colleagues (1982) investigated the number of students identified according to three different LD definitions—ability-achievement discrepancy, low achievement, and test profile scatter—and found that the various definitions identified significantly different numbers and groups of children. Therefore, it is easy to see that individuals who might be identified as LD in one setting may not be so identified in a different setting. What one researcher identifies as a group of individuals with LD may not share the same properties as a group identified by a different researcher (Epps et al., 1982).

In light of these findings, it is not unreasonable to suggest that many of the research studies that have been conducted on LD may have been done so with poorly defined samples obtained from inconsistently applied and ill defined criteria. Findings from such studies are likely to yield results that are difficult to interpret, replicate, and generalize, thereby hampering efforts to advance the identification of LD (Lyon, 1995). In a sense, the findings from a great many investigations into LD would thus seem to apply less and less to the actual population of children being served as learning disabled in the public schools precisely because that population is poorly defined and demarcated (MacMillan et al., 1996).

Ultimately, the vagaries of current definitions and the lack of theoretical and empirical support for many of the components central to modern definitions of learning disability continue to undermine the validity and utility of both clinical diagnosis and identification practices in the schools. Many of these components have come under considerable scrutiny and are being seriously questioned with regard to their logic and necessity in LD determination. For example, the concept of ability-achievement discrepancy has been evaluated critically with regard to its utility in LD determination. Very often, a discrepancy between ability and achievement alone (typically via the comparison between a global ability score or Wechsler Full Scale IQs and some achievement score) has been used as the primary or sole basis upon which to diagnose a learning disability. Such practices have been rendered invalid and unnecessary for the purposes of LD determination and some have suggested that the notion of consistency (between underlying cognitive deficits and academic deficits) may be a more useful way of conceptualizing the very nature of LD (Flanagan, McGrew, & Ortiz, 2000; Flanagan & Ortiz, 2001). These researchers point to the fact that the use of a discrepancy comparison between global IQ and achievement fail to recognize the extent to which IQ influences achievement and developmental skills and, conversely, the extent to which achievement and developmental skills influence IQ (e.g., Siegel, 1989, 1999). In addition, discrepancy procedures seem to take on such importance that little consideration is often given to the need to identify absolute deficits in performance. In other words, an individual may *underachieve* relative to his or her measured IQ, but still perform academically at an average or even above-average level. Thus, sole reliance on a discrepancy model frequently results in labeling *relative* weaknesses as impairments or disabling deficits despite the fact that performance is average or above average relative to age-related peers (Flanagan, McGrew, & Ortiz, 2001; Flanagan & Ortiz, 2001).

In sum, the label of LD is apparently being applied to much broader contexts than ever before. Although the concept of LD began primarily with a focus on reading difficulties, it has now come to encompass a wide array of academically related difficulties, including problems in learning to write, do math, or express thoughts and ideas orally. The medical view of LD and its presumption of underlying brain dysfunction has not been totally rejected, probably because unlike the educational view, the medical perspective seems to offer some insight into the etiology of LD. Conceptualizations of LD have often highlighted both the notion of underachievement and the presence of cerebral dysfunction as the underlying cause of such underachievement. The development of modern definitions of LD have also frequently included descriptions of behavioral manifestations that are apparently characteristic of individuals with LD but the definitions are rarely operationalized (Kavale & Forness, 2000). Not surprisingly, despite decades of research and the existence of myriad current definitions, a practical description and viable operational definition of LD to guide professionals across the many disciplines involved in determining LD has remained quite elusive. As long as LD continues to be defined in a variety of different ways in as many different contexts, the lack of an accepted or prevailing definition to guide the evaluation and diagnosis of LD will remain problematic. Not only do conceptualizations vary widely, but many of the terms used in LD evaluation do not mean the same thing when applied in one setting versus another. Moreover, the complete lack of any modern theoretical foundation to guide conceptualizations of LD means that LD will be operationalized and measured in ways that lack consistency and any semblance of reliability.

As has been discussed in this section, reliable identification of LD will remain contingent on better specification of its essential components. The concept of achievement is a critical element of any such definition and therefore merits discussion. Because the concept of a learning disability is inextricably linked to achievement and academic skills development, the following section of this chapter presents commonly accepted psychoeducational definitions of the various areas of academic achievement as the first step in moving toward a viable operational definition of LD.

Academic Achievement Defined

Additional improvement in the process of academic and LD assessment requires better specification of relatively precise definitions of achievement. When academic achievement is examined within the context of learning disabilities, as described previously, it can become subject to the interpretive whims of any and all individuals involved in the determination process. The specifications and requirements, under IDEA in particular, are vague to the point that they undoubtedly mean different things to different individuals. When these individuals (e.g., teachers, special education teachers, school psychologists, speech-language specialists, administrators, parents, etc.) come together to make decisions regarding the presence or absence of a learning disability, its effect on academic achievement, and the need for special services and instruction, it seems highly unlikely that each enters with the same conceptualization regarding achievement.

Without greater specificity in definitions regarding academic achievement, the process of learning disability evaluation is likely to remain an exercise in frustration. To that end, in this section we attempt to clearly and specifically define the major areas of academic achievement as included in IDEA. The reason for choosing to work with the wording in IDEA is twofold. First, the definition of IDEA represents the latest evolution of the definition of learning disability as borrowed from the definitions originally proposed and recently modified by organizations such as NJCLD, LDA, and so on. Therefore, the definition specified in IDEA is consistent with other extant definitions. Second, the majority of evaluations for learning disabilities are conducted under the auspices of IDEA for the provision of special education services. Therefore, use of the IDEA specifications remains directly applicable and relevant to such evaluations and provides the most widespread benefit to practitioners. As will become evident, these areas will be defined in accordance with the definitions that have begun to emerge from integration of the psychoeducational assessment literature on both academic and cognitive abilities. Our desire to improve on precision of measurement will be reflected by the inclusion of discussion that also involves the types of tests that are used typically to measure an individual's attainment of the major academic domain skills. Likewise, improving the precision of learning disabilities evaluation necessitates discussion of the literature on the relationship between cognitive abilities and functioning in specific academic domains. Because optimal achievement in any academic area requires relatively unimpaired mental processing of information, that information will also be included in the next chapter.

Reading

Palinscar and Perry (1995) note that from a cognitive perspective, reading can be conceptualized as "thinking, reasoning, and problem solving with the use of print for a broad range of purposes" (p. 332). Although this is a rather general definition, the process of reading requires two distinct but interrelated skills. The first, basic reading skills, involves decoding and sight-word recognition, whereas the second, reading comprehension, involves understanding individual word meanings and using syntactic and semantic clues to obtain meaning from written text (Mather, 1991). Basic reading is generally conceptualized as involving two rudimentary skills, sight-word recognition and word analysis. At its most basic level, *sight-word recognition* refers to an individual's ability to recognize and name the letters of the alphabet, whereas at a higher level, this skill refers to one's ability to recognize and accurately name commonly used words. Conversely, *word analysis skills* refer to an individual's ability to apply structural and phonetic analysis to unknown or less familiar words, as well as "nonsense" words. Together, these basic reading skills enable a reader to effectively decode written text; thus, they are seen to be critical in the development of reading. As noted by Glass (1973), "Decoding is at once a least important aspect of reading, and at the same time the most crucial aspect of reading. If one does not learn to decode efficiently and effectively, one will never be allowed the opportunity to read, i.e., deal with and react to meaning via the printed word" (pp. 4–5).

Commonly used measures of basic reading skills include word lists involving real words or nonsense words wherein the examinee is required to read a series of words that are presented in isolation. Examples of such measures include the Wechsler Individual Achievement Test-Second Edition (WIAT-II; Psychological Corporation, 2001) Word Reading subtest, the Woodcock-Johnson III (WJ III; Woodcock, McGrew, & Mather, 2001) Letter-Word Identification subtest, and the Woodcock Reading Mastery Test-Revised/Normative Update (WRMT-R/NU; Woodcock, 1998) Word Attack subtest. A comprehensive listing of subtests that assess basic reading skills is included in Appendix A.

Whereas basic reading requires the ability to accurately decode graphic symbols (e.g., letters, words), reading comprehension refers to the ability to both "construct meaning from graphic symbols and to project meaning onto those symbols" (Brown, Hammill, & Wiederholt, 1995, p. 1). Assessment of basic reading skills generally requires the examinee to read words in isolation. Reading comprehension subtests, on the other hand, typically require the examinee to read connected text (i.e., paragraphs). Reading comprehension skills can be assessed through either having the examinee read aloud or silently. Irrespective of the particular type of reading required (i.e., oral or silent), such tests typically require the examinee to respond to a series of questions regarding the passage or text he or she has read. Such questions can be literal (e.g., information is contained directly within the text) or inferential/predictive (e.g., information is implied within the text). Some examples of reading comprehension tests include WJ III Passage Comprehension, Test of Reading Comprehension–Third Edition (TORC-3; Brown, Hammill, & Wiederholt, 1995) Sentence Sequencing, and WIAT-II Reading Comprehension. These tests all assess reading comprehension in a distinct manner. For instance, WJ III Passage Comprehension utilizes a cloze format wherein the examinee is required to supply a missing word based on semantic and syntactic cues within a sentence. TORC-3 Sentence Sequencing requires the examinee to read a series of sentences and arrange them in a sequence that makes sense. Finally, WIAT-II Reading Comprehension requires the examinee to read a series of paragraphs and answer literal, inferential, and predictive questions regarding those paragraphs. Although the formats on these tests differ, the goal of each is to assess the examinee's ability to obtain meaning from written text. A comprehensive listing of reading comprehension subtests can be found in Appendix A.

Mathematics

Mathematics is "the science of numbers and their properties, operations, and relations and with shapes in space and their structure and measurement" (*Webster's,* 1994, p. 453). Mathematics involves not only the computation of numbers but also the ability to reason with such numbers. As such, a comprehensive assessment of mathematics generally involves evaluating both skill areas.

   Math calculation refers to the application of mathematical operations (i.e., addition, subtraction, multiplication, division) and basic axioms (e.g., commutative property, inverse operations, etc.) to solve mathematical problems (Mercer, 1997). Generally, tests of math calculation require the examinee to answer questions regarding basic math facts and rules, complete paper-and-pencil calculations for basic math problems, or perform mental computations on a series of problems requiring the use of basic math operations. Measures of math calculation are included on such tests as Hammill Multiability Achievement Tests (HAMAT; Hammill, Hresko, Ammer, Cronin, & Quinby, 1998); KeyMath-Revised/Normative Update (KM-R/NU; Connolly, 1998); and WJ III (see Appendix A for a more comprehensive listing of tests assessing math calculation). Overall, the purpose of math calculation tests, whether part of a comprehensive achievement battery or diagnostic math battery, is to assess the degree to which the examinee has acquired and can perform the basic computations required to solve math problems. Although basic skills (i.e., calculation) are an integral part of mathematics, mathematics involves more than the ability to perform calculations in isolation (e.g., compute simple addition problems). That is, mathematics also involves reasoning skills. According to Hessler (1993), this aspect of mathematics (i.e., math reasoning) involves "comprehending the nature of mathematical problems, recognizing relevant information, and identifying and applying appropriate calculations" (p. 119).

   Commonly used measures of math reasoning include such tests as the WJ III Applied Problems; Test of Mathematical Ability–Second Edition (TOMA-2; Brown, Cronin, & McEntire, 1994) Story Problems; and the Diagnostic Achievement Test for Adolescents–Second Edition (DATA-2; Newcomer & Bryant, 1993) Math Problem Solving subtest (see Appendix A for a comprehensive listing of math reasoning tests). In general, these tests, as well as other measures of math reasoning, require the examinee to apply appropriate computations or operations to a series of word problems. The specific questions presented in such tasks may differ according to the amount of information given, the specific operation required by the problem, the degree of extraneous information present in the problem, and problem content (e.g., problems regarding money, time, estimation, etc.). Despite the differing formats of such tests, the overarching goal of a mathematics reasoning test is to assess an individual's ability to appropriately *apply* his or her knowledge of basic math operations, axioms, and rules.

Writing

Writing is defined as "the act of putting ideas or feelings on paper or some other surface using a pencil, pen, word processor, stylus, or some other instrument" (McGhee, Bryant, Larsen, & Rivera, 1995, p. 1). Although this is a rather simple definition, the act of writing is a complex process that requires several abilities, including ideation, syntax, semantics, spelling, capitalization, punctuation, and legibility (McGhee et al., 1995). Although McGhee and colleagues have noted that experts differ in their categorization of writing skills, the process of writing can be conceptualized as involving two separate components—basic skills and written expression. *Basic writing skills* refer to the fundamental skills required to generate written text. An assessment of basic skills in this area can include measures that assess an individual's knowledge of syntactic rules, one's ability to use appropriate punctuation and capitalization, as well as one's ability to spell words correctly. Additionally, such an assessment may include measures of legibility (i.e., handwriting skills). An assessment of basic writing skills is an integral part of a writing assessment, as difficulties in this area can greatly impact the overall quality of one's writing (Mather, 1991). That is, if an individual is unfamiliar with commonly accepted rules of punctuation and capitalization, for instance, such a deficiency is likely to interfere with his or her ability to communicate meaningfully.

Although basic writing skills can be assessed in a number of ways, the traditional formats seen on standardized tests of achievement generally involve contrived test formats. More specifically, such measures focus on evaluation of one's spelling, capitalization, and punctuation, as well as usage abilities in isolation. Examples of tests that assess basic writing skills include the Test of Written Language–Third Edition (TOWL-3; Hammill & Larsen, 1996); the WJ III; and the Test of Early Written Language–Second Edition (TEWL-2; Hresko, Herron, & Peak, 1998) (see Appendix A for a more comprehensive listing of tests measuring basic writing skills).

Written expression, or *written language,* can be defined as the "expression of thought through the use of characters, letters, or words" (Hammill & Larsen, 1996). Whereas an assessment of basic writing skills is generally concerned with *how* an individual writes, an assessment of written expression generally focuses on *what* a writer writes. This is not to say that tests of written expression do not include an assessment of basic skills; rather, it is to say that they also focus on an additional aspect of writing—namely, the quality of one's ideas.

As McGhee and colleagues (1995) note, "The forming of ideas before and during writing is called ideation" (p. 1). Ideation is a complex aspect of writing, as it requires the writer to generate a series of ideas, analyze their appropriateness in the context of the current task, and make a decision on which ones to retain and which ones to dismiss (McGhee et al., 1995). As such, well-developed ideation skills reflect the writer's ability to generate and convey quality ideas.

Another aspect of written expression deals with the semantics of writing. Although semantics is typically measured through an assessment of an individual's vocabulary knowledge, McGhee and colleagues (1995) note that vocabulary is not the only element of semantics; rather, semantics is a broader linguistic unit that refers to a writer's ability to utilize a written medium to express meaningful thoughts in print.

Whereas basic skills assessment typically involves contrived writing formats (e.g., assessing skills in isolation), the assessment of written expression generally focuses on evaluating skills in the context of spontaneous writing. As McGhee and colleagues (1995) note, "The ability to write meaningfully in everyday life or school situations requires an integrated grasp of the components rather than mere competence in the components when they are measured in isolation" (p. 4). Typical tasks of writing ability that require writing in context (as opposed to isolated units of writing) are included on such tests as the WIAT-II Test of Written Expression (TOWE; McGhee, Bryant, Larsen, & Rivera, 1995), and the Peabody Individual Achievement Test-Revised/Normative Update (PIAT-R/NU; Markwardt, 1997) Written Expression (see Appendix A for a more complete listing of written expression measures).

Language

Language can be defined as "a socially shared code or conventional system for representing concepts through the use of arbitrary symbols and rule-governed combinations of those symbols" (Owens, 1994, p. 45, cf. Mercer, 1997). Typically, language is conceptualized as involving five distinct, interrelated components. These components include (1) phonology, (2) morphology, (3) syntax, (4) semantics, and (5) pragmatics.

Although language abilities are generally dichotomized into receptive and expressive skills, the five components of language are important for both listening and speaking (Hammill & Newcomer, 1997; Mercer, 1997). For instance, at the receptive level, phonology is concerned with one's ability to *discriminate* speech sounds, whereas at the expressive level, the focus is on one's ability to *articulate* speech sounds. Similarly, whereas syntactic abilities (e.g., one's ability to understand phrases and sentences) are important at the receptive level, they are equally important at the expressive level (e.g., one's ability to appropriately use grammar in spoken phrases and sentences). In short, the forms of language cut across both expressive and receptive abilities. That is, the ability to effectively communicate with language involves, among other things, adequate listening comprehension and oral expression abilities across all forms of language (Mercer, 1997). The following discussion presents a definition for each of these abilities (i.e., listening comprehension and oral expression) as well as describes measures that are typically used to assess them. *Receptive language* refers to "those operations by which symbolic-abstract meaning is given to spoken stimuli when they are heard or to written stimuli when they are seen" (Hammill, Brown, Larsen, & Wiederholt, 1994, p. 5). Thus, receptive language encompasses both oral and written forms of communication. In the current context, however, the focus is on the former form of communication—namely, listening comprehension. *Listening comprehension* can be defined rather simply as the ability to prescribe meaning to auditory input. Thus, expressive language is concerned with language use, whereas receptive language, or listening comprehension, is primarily concerned with language understanding (Hammill & Newcomer, 1997).

As with any academic area, there are different methods available to assess listening comprehension. For instance, some language tests that provide a comprehensive assessment of language functioning include receptive measures in the context of a larger battery that also includes measures of expressive language functioning. This is the case with the Test of Language Development: Primary–Third Edition (TOLD-P:3; Newcomer & Hammill, 1997), which assesses both expressive and receptive language skills. In terms of receptive language, the TOLD-P:3 provides receptive measures of phonology (i.e., Word Discrimination); semantics (i.e., Picture Vocabulary); and syntax (i.e., Grammatic Understanding). Similarly, the Test of Children's Language (TOCL; Barenbaum & Newcomer, 1996) contains receptive measures of listening comprehension that involve knowledge of syntax, semantics, and phonology.

While the TOLD-P:3 and other comprehensive measures (i.e., Clinical Evaluation of Language Fundamentals–Third Edition [CELF-3; Semel, Wiig, & Secord, 1995]; Oral and Written Language Scales [OWLS; Carrow-Woolfolk, 1995]; Test of Adolescent and Adult Language–Third Edition [TOAL-3; Hammill, Brown, Larsen, & Wiederholt, 1994]) cover both expressive and receptive language domains, other tests—such as the Peabody Picture Vocabulary Test–Third Edition (PPVT-3; Dunn & Dunn, 1997) and the Test for Auditory Comprehension of Language–Third Edition (TACL-3; Carrow-Woolfolk, 1999)—assess receptive functioning only (see Appendix A for a more complete listing of listening comprehension tests). As Wallace and Hammill (1994) explain, assessments of listening comprehension, such as the measures just described, often involve the examinee being presented with a stimulus word and having to point to a picture that depicts the word. Although this is a popular format, other assessments require the examinee to listen to a series of directions and carry out the actions required by the direction. Regardless of the type of format employed, the goal of listening comprehension tests is to assess the individual's ability to demonstrate an understanding of spoken stimuli when they are heard.

Expressive language, or *oral expression,* can be defined as the use of an "arbitrary vocal system to communicate ideas and thoughts to a listener" (Mercer, 1997, p. 421). Oral expression deals with the production aspect of language. Thus, whereas listening comprehension is concerned with the *understanding* of language, expressive language is concerned with language *use* (Hammill & Newcomer, 1997).

Typically, tests of expressive language, like their receptive counterparts, assess one or more of the five components of language described earlier (i.e., syntax, semantics, phonology, morphology, and pragmatics). For instance, the TOLD-P:3 assesses expressive language by measuring phonology (i.e., Word Articulation subtest), semantics (i.e., Oral Vocabulary), and syntax (i.e., Grammatic Completion), whereas the Comprehensive Receptive and Expressive Vocabulary Test (CREVT; Wallace & Hammill, 1994), as its name implies, includes expressive measures that deal primarily with semantics. In general, expressive language measures that assess syntax require the examinee to orally construct sentences or phrases that are syntactically appropriate. Measures that assess semantics typically require the examinee to complete such tasks as defining words and completing sentences using words or word combinations that are semantically appropriate (Carrow-Woolfolk, 1999). Expressive language tests also may assess an individual's ability to appropriately use functional language. Tests such as these are intended to assess pragmatics. Finally, measures that assess phonology or morphology typically include tasks that require the examinee to correctly articulate a series of speech sounds or use appropriate grammar in words (e.g., *-ed* for past tense), respectively (Mercer, 1997). A comprehensive listing of tests assessing oral expression is available in Appendix A.

Advancing Academic and Learning Disability Assessment

Although the definitions regarding the academic achievement areas related to LD can be operationalized rather well, it is clear that the ambiguity and inconsistency among the current definitions of LD simply will not allow for the identification of students with learning disability in a reliable and consistent manner. A student may or may not be labeled learning disabled solely on the basis of which definition is selected, how it is operationalized, the idiosyncratic approach to assessment used by the diagnostician, the degree of curriculum bias, or the extent to which information on exclusionary criteria is used (Epps et al., 1982). In addition, state and federal definitions used in the schools are not necessarily consistent with the clinical definition of *learning disability* found in *DSM-IV* that forms the more likely standard by which diagnosis of LD is most often made by professionals outside the school setting.

Because IDEA and state-specific regulations, the two main pieces of legislation that provide guidance for diagnosis of LD in childhood, contain no true operational definition of LD, many practitioners are confused regarding the manner in which the elements that constitute LD (achievement and cognitive abilities) are to be measured, compared, and evaluated. Given the gaps and inconsistencies between research, current definitions, and the greatly disparate school-based identification practices and goals, diagnosing LD remains an activity that defies any real degree of consistency or reliability. There is virtually no theoretical or empirically based framework for determining LD in the school setting that allows practitioners across a wide variety of settings to engage in practices that reflect a common understanding of the nature and manifestations of LD. For example, modern researchers have affirmed the notion that the concept of learning disability transcends underachievement alone yet it still remains an important part of the definition (Kavale & Forness, 2000). This concept leads to a dilemma across disciplines: How is educational underachievement defined, identified, or measured? The concept of underachievement is based primarily on an understanding of the developmental process—that children generally grow and mature according to recognizable physical, social, and psychological milestones. Even when underachievement is defined and identified via some accepted standard, it is unlikely to be enough by itself to establish LD, and other data will need to be considered as well so that in the final analysis, there is a convergence of indicators to support any conclusions regarding the presence or absence of LD.

In the subsequent chapters of this text, we present a discussion of the main issues involved in advancing both academic assessment and LD determination, which includes a desk reference section of academic tests. These components, along with the accompanying discussions in the text, form the basis for the development of both a viable operational definition and comprehensive framework for assessment that are designed specifically to address problems with current definitions and procedures. The operational definition we propose incorporates the concepts of (1) inter-academic ability analysis of specific school-related skills and acquired knowledge; (2) evaluation of exclusionary factors; (3) analysis of inter-cognitive abilities, processes, and aptitudes for learning; (4) integrated ability analysis of achievement and measured aptitude; and (5) evaluation of degree of interference with learning. We believe this definition and the comprehensive assessment framework within which it is embedded provides a systematic and practical solution for LD determination that is well suited for children and adults. We assert that reliable evaluation of LD should be predicated on definitions and frameworks that are research based and that provide clear specifications and criteria for measurement and identification of the processes underlying the concept of LD.

C h a p t e r   2

Achievement and the Cattell-Horn-Carroll Theory of Cognitive Abilities

Assessment of academic abilities or achievement in areas such as reading, mathematics, written expression, oral expression, and listening comprehension is typically accomplished through the use of one or more individually administered, standardized, norm-referenced tests of achievement. Yet, depending on the specific instruments chosen for assessment, certain *academic* abilities appear to be measured by *intelligence* tests, whereas certain *cognitive* abilities appear to be measured by *achievement* tests. For example, it is common to find tests that measure an individual's knowledge of vocabulary—an "ability" that is typically associated with schooling and therefore considered an academic achievement, rather than a cognitive ability per se—*comfortably located within the context of a major cognitive battery*. Similarly, it is not unusual to find tests that measure an individual's ability to reason contained in comprehensive batteries of achievement. For example, many applied problems or math reasoning tests require an individual to reason both inductively and deductively using numbers. This type of quantitative reasoning ability is typically considered to be more cognitively intrinsic than academic in nature. Thus, there is considerable confusion surrounding the precise definitions of *ability* and *achievement* and indeed controversy with regard to which tests ought to be used (i.e., intelligence or achievement) in the assessment of individuals suspected of having a learning disability.

In order to provide more clarity regarding the nature of abilities measured by intelligence and achievement tests, this chapter will describe a comprehensive theory of abilities called the Cattell-Horn-Carroll theory (or CHC theory) that encompasses both cognitive and academic abilities. Next, more precise theoretical and operational definitions of cognitive ability and academic ability (or achievement) will be offered in an attempt to better distinguish the differences between these two constructs. With a better understanding of the nature of and relationship between cognitive and academic abilities within the context of CHC theory, evaluation of individuals with learning difficulties can focus more on measuring the *specific abilities* germane to the referral, rather than on questions related to the *type of test* to be used (i.e., intelligence or achievement).

Conceptualizing Cognitive Abilities and Academic Achievement from Contemporary Theory

The phrase *cognitive ability* is most often associated with intelligence tests (e.g., the Wechsler Intelligence Scale for Children–Third Edition [WISC-III]; Wechsler, 1991), whereas the phrase *academic achievement* is generally linked mainly to achievement tests (e.g., the Woodcock-Johnson Tests of Achievement–Third Edition [WJ III]; Woodcock, McGrew, & Mather, 2001). If asked to provide a definition of each of these terms, many practitioners would likely offer two relatively distinct descriptions. Yet, cognitive ability and academic achievement need not be conceptualized as dichotomous concepts at all. In fact, an ability-achievement dichotomy is seldom recognized or supported in the cognitive psychology literature. The differences that are often made between cognitive ability and academic achievement are the result of popular *verbal* distinctions that are not supported from either an empirical or theoretical standpoint.

According to Horn (1988), "Cognitive abilities are measures of achievements, and measures of achievements are just as surely measures of cognitive abilities" (p. 655). Carroll (1993) echoed this conceptualization when he stated,

> *It is hard to draw the line between . . . cognitive abilities and . . . cognitive achievements. Some will argue that* all *cognitive abilities are in reality learned achievements of one kind or another. Such an argument is difficult to counter, because it is obvious that the performances required on even the most general tests of intelligence depend on at least some learnings—learnings of language and its uses, of commonly used symbols such as numbers and digits, or of procedures for solving various kinds of problems. (p. 510; emphasis in original)*

Thus, rather than conceiving of cognitive abilities and academic achievements as mutually exclusive, they may be better thought of as lying on an *ability continuum* that has the most general types of abilities at one end and the most specialized types of knowledge at the other (Carroll, 1993). Prior to articulating such a continuum, however, it is necessary to specify a validated theoretical framework from which to clearly understand general and specific cognitive abilities and academic achievement.

There are numerous theories of the structure of cognitive and academic capabilities, such as Gardner's theory of multiple intelligences (Chen & Gardner, 1997; Gardner, 1987a, 1987b), Sternberg's triarchic theory of intelligence (Sternberg, 1985, 1997), Greenspan's model of personal competence (Greenspan, 1991; Greenspan & Driscoll, 1997), contemporary *Gf-Gc* theory (or the Cattell-Horn *Gf-Gc* theory; Horn, 1991, 1994; Horn & Noll, 1997), and the three-stratum theory of cognitive abilities (Carroll, 1993, 1997), to name a few (see Flanagan, Genshaft, & Harrison, 1997, for a comprehensive review). Despite the popularity of Gardner's theory among the lay public, it is the last two theories that have received the most attention in the psychoeducational assessment literature and that are among the most well-validated and best established within the psychometric tradition. These two theories have been integrated recently into a comprehensive theory called the Cattell-Horn-Carroll theory of cognitive abilities (or simply CHC theory; see Flanagan, McGrew, & Ortiz, 2000; Flanagan & Ortiz, 2001; Woodcock, McGrew, & Mather, 2001). Because CHC theory is well validated and because its structure is particularly well suited for the organization and interpretation of psychometric instruments (such as cognitive and achievement tests), it is the theoretical framework around which this book is organized. Following is a description of the evolution of CHC theory.

CHC Theory Defined

The Cattell-Horn-Carroll theory represents the most recent evolution and integration of the original and widely influential works of Raymond Cattell, John Horn, and John Carroll. In comparison to other well-known theories of intelligence and cognitive abilities, CHC theory is the most comprehensive and empirically supported psychometric theory of the structure of cognitive and academic abilities (Carroll, 1993). Given its impressive level of empirical support and contemporary representation of cognitive abilities, it is our contention that CHC theory should serve as a foundation for the selection and interpretation of both intelligence and achievement batteries. Although CHC theory has been used recently as the foundation for selecting, organizing, and interpreting tests of intelligence and cognitive abilities (e.g., Flanagan, McGrew, & Ortiz, 2000; Flanagan & Ortiz, 2001; McGrew & Flanagan, 1998), to date, there have been few attempts to apply this theoretical framework to the understanding of academic achievement with regard to how academic abilities should be defined and measured. In order to implement a CHC-based approach to assessing and interpreting academic achievement, it is necessary to understand how the theory evolved as well as the major components of the theory.

Gradual and Progressive Changes in Fluid-Crystallized Theory: A Brief Historical Perspective

In 1941, Cattell postulated a dichotomous fluid-crystallized (or *Gf-Gc*) theory of cognitive abilities. Fluid intelligence (*Gf*) encompassed inductive and deductive reasoning abilities that were thought to be influenced by both biological and neurological factors and incidental learning through interaction with the environment (Taylor, 1994). Crystallized intelligence (*Gc*) consisted primarily of abilities (especially acquired knowledge) that were thought to reflect the influences of acculturation (namely, verbal-conceptual knowledge; Gustafsson, 1994; Taylor, 1994). Thus, the original *Gf-Gc* theory was a dichotomous conceptualization of human cognitive ability, but quite distinct from the prevailing verbal-performance dichotomy that was ushered in by the Wechsler scales and that remains in use to the present day. Although *Gf-Gc* theory has not been conceived of as a dichotomy since the 1960s (Gustafsson & Undheim, 1996; Horn & Noll, 1997; Woodcock, 1993), the *Gf-Gc* label was retained as the acronym for this theory until just recently. As a result, *Gf-Gc* theory was often misunderstood to be a two-factor model, rather than multiple-factor model, of the structure of abilities.

In the mid-1960s, Horn (1965) expanded the *Gf-Gc* model to include four additional abilities, including visual perception or processing (*Gv*), short-term memory (Short-term Acquisition and Retrieval—SAR or *Gsm*), long-term storage and retrieval (Tertiary Storage and Retrieval—TSR or *Glr*), and speed of processing (*Gs*). By 1968, additional analyses led Horn to add auditory processing ability (*Ga*) to the theoretical model and refine the definitions of *Gv*, *Gs*, and *Glr*. More recently, a factor representing a person's quickness in reacting (reaction time) and making decisions (decision speed) (called *Gt* by Horn, 1991, and Correct Decision Speed [CDS] by Carroll, 1993) was added to the *Gf-Gc* model. In addition, factors representing a person's quantitative ability or knowledge (*Gq*) and facility with reading and writing (*Grw*) (Horn, 1985, 1988, 1991; Woodcock, 1994) emerged from further research and were added to the model, resulting in a 10-factor ability structure. Noteworthy is the fact that these last two abilities (i.e., *Gq* and *Grw*) are often conceived of by practitioners, who routinely conduct psychoeducational assessments, as academic achievements rather than cognitive abilities.

The Hierarchical Structure of Abilities

In his review of the extant factor analytic research literature, Carroll (1993) differentiated factors or abilities into three strata that varied according to the "relative variety and diversity of variables" (Carroll, 1997, p. 124) included at each level. The various *G* abilities are the most prominent and recognized abilities of the model. They are classified as broad or stratum II abilities and include abilities such as *Gf* and *Gc*, the two original factors. According to Carroll (1993), *broad* abilities represent "basic constitutional and long standing characteristics of individuals that can govern or influence a great variety of behaviors in a given domain" and they vary in their emphasis on process, content, and manner of response (p. 634). Broad abilities, like *Gf* and *Gc*, subsume a large number of narrow or stratum I abilities of which approximately 70 have been identified (Carroll, 1993, 1997). *Narrow* abilities "represent greater specializations of abilities, often in quite specific ways that reflect the effects of experience and learning, or the adoption of particular strategies of performance" (Carroll, 1993, p. 634). The hierarchical structure of *Gf-Gc* theory is demonstrated for the domain of crystallized intelligence (*Gc*) in Figure 2.1.

In the *Gf-Gc* taxonomy, *Gc* is classified as a broad stratum II cognitive ability. The 11 narrow or stratum I crystallized abilities that comprise *Gc* demonstrate the "broadness" or breadth of this factor. Figure 2.1 shows that 11 different narrow or specialized crystallized abilities have been identified in the literature. The broad *Gc* ability and the narrow abilities it encompasses are defined later in this chapter, as are the remaining *Gf-Gc* broad and narrow abilities that comprise CHC theory. The significant, moderate to high intercorrelations displayed by the narrow (*Gc*) abilities suggest the presence of a broader factor or construct that

FIGURE 2.1   Hierarchical Structure of Crystallized Intelligence (*Gc*)

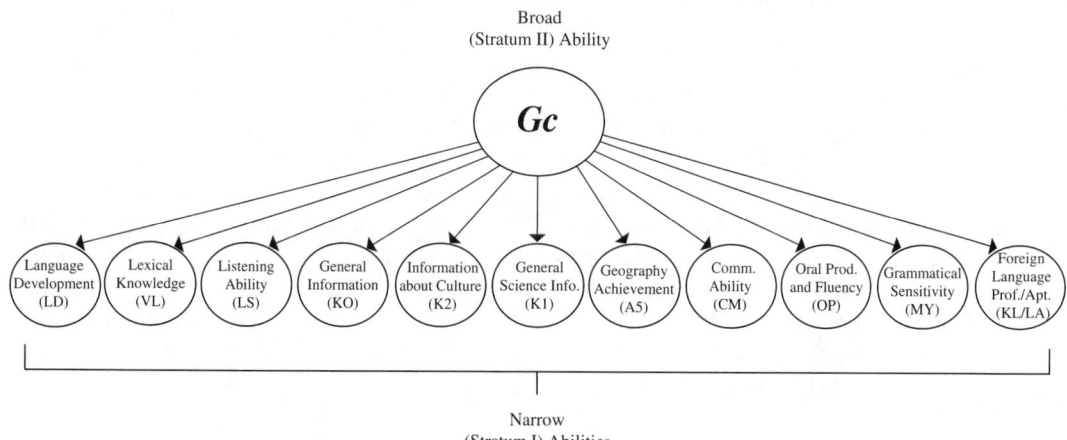

accounts for this shared and (as depicted in Figure 2.1) supposed "crystallized" intelligence variance. The broad *Gc* factor is hypothesized to represent this higher-order explanatory construct and is believed to exert a significant common effect (reflected by the direction of the arrows in Figure 2.1) on the narrow abilities. When this concept is extended to the 9 other broad ability domains, each of which also subsumes a number of narrow abilities, it is clear that *Gf-Gc* theory is quite comprehensive.

Even without the benefit of a thorough understanding of *Gf-Gc* theory and the information presented in subsequent chapters of this book, after reflecting on Figure 2.1, it is likely that practitioners who use individual tests of achievement are able to identify relations between narrow *Gc* abilities and certain subtests included on popular achievement batteries, such as the Wechsler Individual Achievement Test–Second Edition (WIAT-II; Psychological Corporation, 2001) and the WJ III Tests of Achievement (Woodcock et al., 2001). For example, WIAT-II Oral Expression appears to be primarily a measure of Communication Ability (CM); WJ III Humanities, a subtest within the Academic Knowledge Cluster, is likely a measure of Information about Culture (K2); WJ III Editing is a good measure of Grammatical Sensitivity (MY); and WJ III Story Recall seems to correspond very closely to a measure of Listening Ability (LS). Practitioners who are familiar with the WIAT-II and WJ III, for example, will also observe that these achievement batteries measure only a subset of the entire *Gc* domain. Such observations should set the stage for practitioners to recognize the breadth (or narrowness) of coverage of certain *Gf-Gc* abilities by the achievement batteries they use routinely. Knowledge of the breadth of abilities specified in contemporary theory, coupled with an understanding of what abilities are specifically measured (and conversely, not measured) by certain achievement batteries, can directly inform the selection and organization of tests around the specific abilities to be assessed in any given evaluation vis-à-vis referral concerns. The manner in which achievement tests can be selected and organized in deliberate and systematic fashion according to specific ability constructs and academic skill domains will be discussed in detail in subsequent chapters.

The broadest or most general level of ability in the *Gf-Gc* model is represented by stratum III, located at the apex of Carroll's (1993) hierarchy. This single cognitive ability, which subsumes both broad (stratum II) and narrow (stratum I) abilities, is interpreted as representing a general factor (i.e., *g*) that is involved in complex higher-order cognitive processes (Gustafsson & Undheim, 1996; McGrew & Woodcock, 2001).

It is important to understand that the abilities within each level of the hierarchical *Gf-Gc* model typically display non-zero positive intercorrelations (Carroll, 1993; Gustafsson & Undheim, 1996). For example, similar to the *Gc* discussion above, the different stratum I (narrow) abilities that define the various *Gf-Gc* domains are correlated positively and to varying degrees. These intercorrelations give rise to and allow for the estimation of the stratum II (broad) ability factors. Likewise, the positive non-zero correlations among the stratum II (broad) *Gf-Gc* abilities allows for the estimation of the stratum III (general) *g* factor. The positive factor intercorrelations within each level of the *Gf-Gc* hierarchy indicate that the different *Gf-Gc* abilities do not reflect completely independent (uncorrelated or orthogonal) traits. However, they can, as is evident from the vast body of literature that supports their existence, be reliably distinguished from one another and therefore represent unique, albeit related, abilities.

Similarities and Differences between the Cattell-Horn Model and the Carroll Model

Simplified versions of the Cattell-Horn and the Carroll models of the structure of abilities (i.e., where the narrow abilities are omitted) are presented together in Figure 2.2. A review of Figure 2.2 shows a number of important similarities and differences between the two models. In general, these models are similar in that they both include some form of fluid intelligence (*Gf*), crystallized intelligence (*Gc*), short-term memory and learning (*Gsm* or *Gy*), visual perception or processing (*Gv*), auditory perception or processing (*Ga* or *Gu*), long-term retrieval (*Glr* or *Gr*), processing speed (*Gs*), and decision and reaction time speed (*CDS* or *Gt*) abilities. Although there are some differences in the broad-ability definitions, as well as in the specific narrow abilities that are subsumed by the respective broad *Gf-Gc* abilities, the major structural differences between the two models are primarily fourfold (McGrew, 1997).

First, the Cattell-Horn and the Carroll models differ in their inclusion of g (global or general ability) at stratum III. According to Carroll (1993, 1997), the general intelligence

FIGURE 2.2 Comparison of Cattell-Horn *Gf-Gc* and Carroll Three-Stratum Models

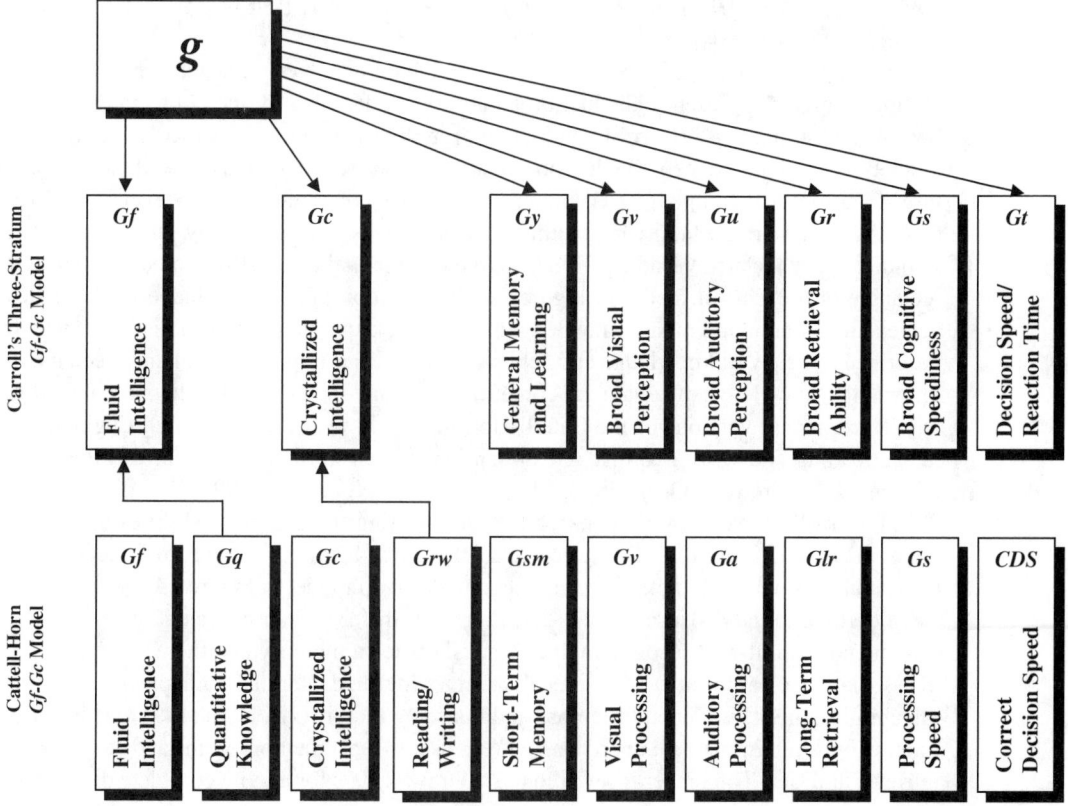

factor at the apex of his three-stratum theory is analogous to Spearman's *g*. The off-center placement of *g* (to the left side of Figure 2.2) in the Carroll model is intended to reflect the strength of the relations between *g* and the respective broad *Gf-Gc* abilities. As represented in Carroll's model in Figure 2.2 (i.e., the top half of the figure), *Gf* has the strongest association with *g,* followed next by *Gc,* and continuing on through the remaining abilities to the two broad abilities that are weakest in association with *g* (i.e., *Gs* and *Gt*). [1]

Although Carroll (1997) has stated that the evidence for *g* is "overwhelming," Horn disagrees strongly, believing *g* to be primarily a statistical artifact (see Horn, 1991; Horn & Noll, 1997). Accordingly, Horn posits a *truncated hierarchical model*—that is, a model that does not contain a single *g* factor at the apex (Jensen, 1998). Debates about the nature and existence of *g* have waxed and waned for decades and have been some of the liveliest debates in differential psychology (Gustafsson & Undheim, 1996; Jensen, 1997). Much of the debate has been theoretical in nature, with definitions of *g* ranging from an index of neural cognitive efficiency, general reasoning ability, or mental energy to a mere statistical irregularity (Neisser et al., 1996). After being "more or less banned from the scientific scene" (Gustafsson & Undheim, 1996), the prominent position of *g* in contemporary psychometric models of the structure of abilities (e.g., Carroll's three-stratum model and Jensen's [1998] "*g* factor" treatise) has helped it to take center stage once again in intelligence research and dialogue. Interested readers are directed to the writings of Carroll (1993, 1997), Horn (1991), Horn and Noll (1997), and Jensen (1997, 1998) for further discussion of *g*-related issues and research.

Second, in the Cattell-Horn model, quantitative knowledge and quantitative reasoning abilities together represent a distinct broad ability, as depicted by the *Gq* rectangle in the bottom half of Figure 2.2. Carroll (1993), however, views quantitative ability as "an inexact, unanalyzed popular concept that has no scientific meaning unless it is referred to the structure of abilities that compose it. It cannot be expected to constitute a higher-level ability" (p. 627). As such, Carroll classified quantitative reasoning as a narrow ability subsumed by *Gf,* as indicated by the arrow leading from the *Gq* rectangle in the Cattell-Horn model to the *Gf* rectangle in the Carroll model in Figure 2.2. Furthermore, Carroll included mathematics achievement and mathematics knowledge factors in a separate chapter in his book, which described a variety of knowledge and achievement abilities (e.g., technical and mechanical knowledge, knowledge of behavioral content) that are not included in his theoretical model.

Third, recent versions of the Cattell-Horn model have included a broad English-language reading and writing ability (*Grw*) that is depicted in the bottom half of Figure 2.2 (Flanagan, McGrew, & Ortiz, 2000; McGrew, 1997; Woodcock, 1993; Woodcock et al., 2001). Carroll, however, considers reading and writing to be narrow abilities subsumed under the broad ability of *Gc,* as reflected by the arrow leading from the *Grw* rectangle in the Cattell-Horn model to the *Gc* rectangle in the Carroll model in Figure 2.2.

Fourth, the Cattell-Horn and the Carroll models differ in their treatment of certain narrow memory abilities. Carroll combined both short-term memory and the narrow abilities of associative, meaningful, and free recall memory (defined later in this chapter) with learning abilities under his General Memory and Learning factor (*Gy*). Horn (1991) made a distinction between immediate apprehension (e.g., short-term memory span) and storage and retrieval abilities. The reader is referred to McGrew (1997) for a more complete discussion of these differences.

Notwithstanding the important differences between the Cattell-Horn and the Carroll models, in order to realize the practical benefits of using theory to guide test selection, organization, and interpretation, it is necessary to define a single taxonomy—one that can be used to classify the individual tests of pyschoeducational batteries, including tests of cognitive ability and tests of academic achievement. A first effort to create a single taxonomy for this purpose was an integrated Cattell-Horn and Carroll model proposed by McGrew (1997). McGrew and Flanagan (1998) subsequently presented a slightly revised integrated model, which was further refined by Flanagan, McGrew, and Ortiz (2000). The model presented in Flanagan, McGrew, and Ortiz (i.e., the Cattell-Horn-Carroll theory of cognitive abilities [or CHC theory]) is described briefly in the following section.

A Taxonomy for Understanding Specific Cognitive Abilities and Academic Achievements: CHC Theory

The integration of the Cattell-Horn and the Carroll models, or CHC theory, is presented in Figure 2.3. This figure depicts the current structure of contemporary CHC theory and reflects the manner in which the Cattell-Horn and Carroll models have been integrated.[2] In this figure, CHC theory includes 10 broad cognitive abilities, which are subsumed by over 70 narrow abilities. The abilities printed in italic in Figure 2.3 are those that were not included in Carroll's three-stratum model but that were included by Carroll in his definitions of *knowledge* and *achievement* (Carroll, 1993). The abilities printed in bold in Figure 2.3 are those that were placed under CHC broad abilities in a differing manner than that proposed by Carroll (1993). These changes (or otherwise integrations of the Cattell-Horn and the Carroll models) are based on the most recent developments of and refinements to the Cattell-Horn model (e.g., Horn & Noll, 1997) and recent factor-analysis research (e.g., Woodcock et al., 2001; see also Flanagan, McGrew, & Ortiz, 2000; McGrew, 1997; McGrew & Flanagan, 1998, for a review). The interested reader is referred to Flanagan, McGrew, and Ortiz (2000) for a more comprehensive description of the specific ways in which CHC theory represents an integration of the Cattell-Horn and Carroll models.

The exclusion of *g* in Figure 2.3 does not mean that the integrated model used in this text does not subscribe to a separate general human ability or that *g* does not exist. Rather, *g* was omitted by McGrew (1997) and Flanagan, McGrew, and Ortiz (2000) because it was judged to have little practical relevance to the selection and organization of tests around referral concerns and the interpretation of cognitive and academic capabilities via cross-battery principles and procedures. That is, the CHC Cross-Battery approach espoused by these researchers (e.g., Flanagan & Ortiz, 2001; McGrew & Flanagan, 1998) was designed specifically to improve psychoeducational assessment practice by describing the unique patterns of cognitive and academic capabilities of individuals. This approach to assessment is presented later in this book.

CHC theory represents the culmination of more than 60 years of factor-analysis research in the psychometric tradition. However, in addition to structural evidence, there are other sources of validity evidence, some quite substantial, that support CHC theory. Prior to defining the broad and narrow abilities that comprise CHC theory, a brief overview of the validity evidence in support of this structure of cognitive abilities is presented.

FIGURE 2.3 The Cattell-Horn-Carroll Theory of Cognitive Abilities (CHC Theory)

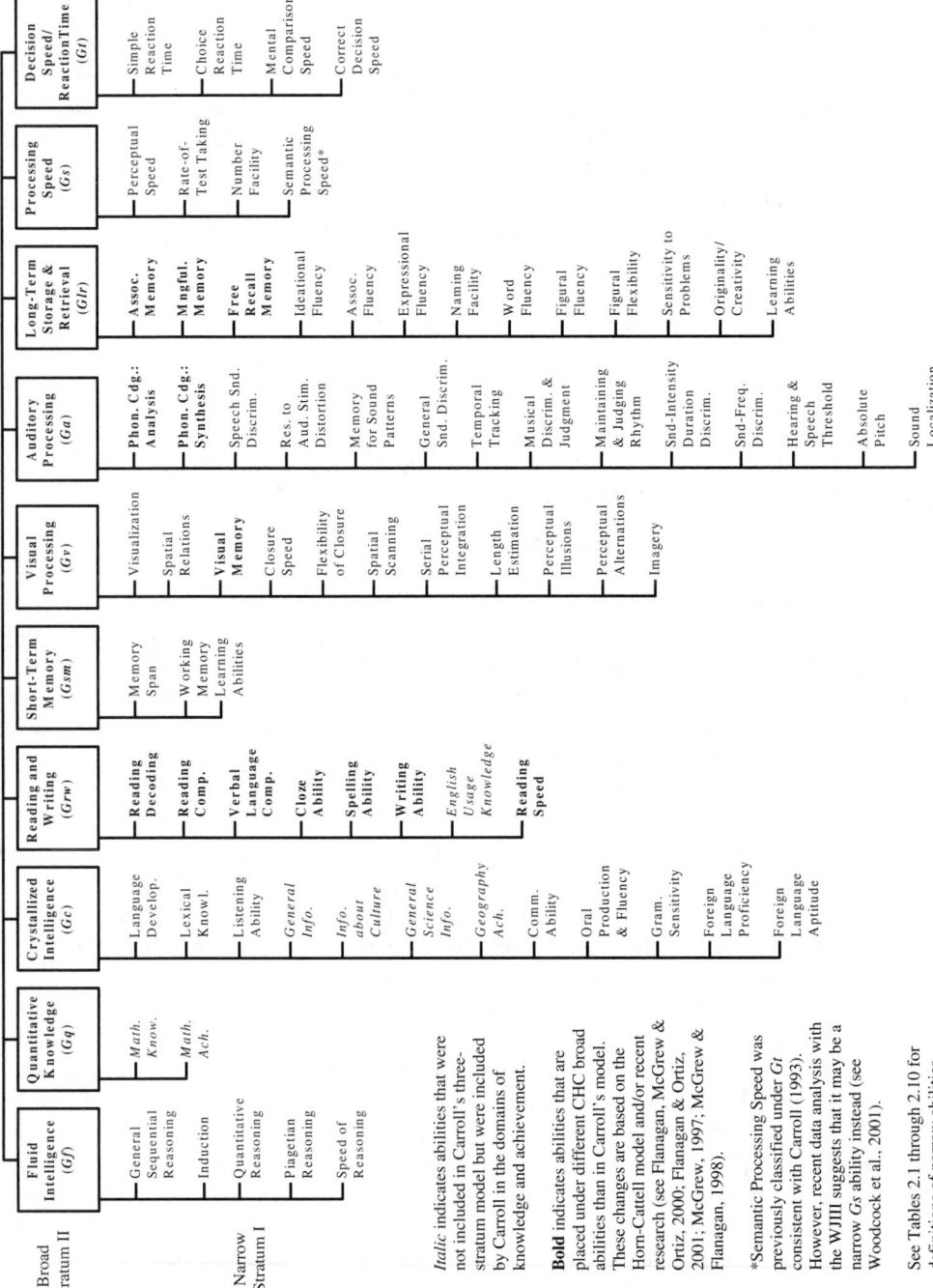

Italic indicates abilities that were not included in Carroll's three-stratum model but were included by Carroll in the domains of knowledge and achievement.

Bold indicates abilities that are placed under different CHC broad abilities than in Carroll's model. These changes are based on the Horn-Cattell model and/or recent research (see Flanagan, McGrew & Ortiz, 2000; Flanagan & Ortiz, 2001; McGrew, 1997; McGrew & Flanagan, 1998).

*Semantic Processing Speed was previously classified under *Gt* consistent with Carroll (1993). However, recent data analysis with the WJIII suggests that it may be a narrow *Gs* ability instead (see Woodcock et al., 2001).

See Tables 2.1 through 2.10 for definitions of narrow abilities.

A Network of Validity Evidence in Support of CHC Theory

It is beyond the scope of this chapter to provide a fully detailed account and review of all the validity evidence currently available in support of the CHC structural model as well as the broad- and narrow-ability constructs it encompasses. The interested reader is referred to Carroll (1993), Flanagan, McGrew, and Ortiz (2000), Horn and Noll (1997), and McGrew (1997) for a more thorough discussion.

Briefly, the CHC structure of abilities is supported by factor-analytic (i.e., structural) evidence as well as developmental, neurocognitive, and heritability evidence (see Flanagan, McGrew, & Ortiz, 2000, and Horn & Noll, 1997, for a summary). Additionally, there is a mounting body of research available on the relations between the broad cognitive CHC abilities and many academic outcomes (summarized later in this chapter) as well as occupational outcomes (Ackerman & Heggestad, 1997; McGrew & Flanagan, 1998). Furthermore, studies have shown that the factor structure of CHC theory is invariant across the lifespan (Bickley, Keith, & Wolfe, 1995; Woodcock et al., 2001) and across gender, ethnic, and cultural groups (e.g., Carroll, 1993; Gustafsson & Balke, 1993; Keith, 1997, 1999). In general, CHC theory is based on a more extensive network of validity evidence than other contemporary multidimensional ability models (see Daniel, 1997; Kranzler & Keith, 1999; McGrew & Flanagan, 1998; Messick, 1992; Sternberg & Kaufman, 1998).

Given the breadth of empirical support for the CHC structure of intelligence, it provides one of the most useful frameworks for designing and evaluating psychoeducational batteries, including intelligence and achievement tests (Carroll, 1997, 1998; Flanagan, 2000; Flanagan & McGrew, 1997; Kaufman, 2000; Keith & Kranzler, 1999; Keith, Kranzler, & Flanagan, 2000; Keith & Witta, 1997; Kranzler, Keith, & Flanagan, 2000; McGrew, 1997; Woodcock, 1990; Ysseldyke, 1990). Moreover, in light of the well-established structural validity of CHC theory, external validity support for the various CHC constructs, derived through sound research methodology, can be used confidently to guide test interpretation (see Benson, 1998; Flanagan, 2000).

It is important to recognize that research related to CHC theory is not static. Rather, research on the hierarchical structure of abilities (within the *Gf-Gc* and now CHC framework) has been systematic, steady, and mounting for decades. Even within the context of this book, the attempt to fully integrate academically related abilities within the CHC theoretical framework has necessitated significant rethinking of the model (e.g., differences in types of abilities subsumed under *Gc* and the nature of *Grw* as a broad variable representing distinct academic skills) and forced decisions to be made that previously were either not relevant or not considered.

Broad and Narrow CHC Ability Definitions

In this section the definitions of the broad and narrow abilities included in the CHC model are presented. These definitions are consistent with those presented in Flanagan, McGrew, and Ortiz (2000), Flanagan and Ortiz (2001), and McGrew and Flanagan (1998). They were derived from an integration of the writings of Carroll (1993), Gustafsson and Undheim

(1996), Horn (1991), McGrew (1997), McGrew, Werder, and Woodcock (1991), and Woodcock (1994). The narrow-ability definitions are presented in Tables 2.1 through 2.10.

Fluid Intelligence *(Gf)*.   *Fluid intelligence* refers to mental operations that an individual uses when faced with a relatively novel task that cannot be performed automatically. These mental operations may include forming and recognizing concepts, perceiving relationships among patterns, drawing inferences, comprehending implications, problem solving, extrapolating, and reorganizing or transforming information. Inductive and deductive reasoning are generally considered to be the hallmark narrow-ability indicators of *Gf*. Although most practitioners would agree that this ability is typically not measured directly by individually administered achievement batteries, some tests of achievement clearly involve the use of specific *Gf* abilities. For example, many tests of reading comprehension require individuals to draw inferences from the text.

Aside from general inductive and deductive reasoning abilities, *Gf* also subsumes more specific types of reasoning, most notably Quantitative Reasoning (RQ). Unlike the other narrow *Gf* abilities, RQ is more directly related to formal instruction and classroom related experiences. In many ways, RQ can be seen as a measure of learning, and in fact, tests like the Mathematics Reasoning subtest of the WIAT-II appear to measure RQ directly. As such, RQ—perhaps more than the other *Gf* abilities—seems to lie well within the overlap of the continuum of cognitive and academic abilities referred to earlier. At the very least, it represents a good example of one of those abilities that is often measured by both cognitive and achievement tests. This issue is discussed further in Chapter 12 and definitions of the narrow abilities subsumed by *Gf* are presented in Table 2.1.

Crystallized Intelligence *(Gc)*.   *Crystallized intelligence* refers to the breadth and depth of a person's acquired knowledge of a culture and the effective application of this knowledge. This store of primarily verbal or language-based knowledge represents those abilities that have been developed largely through the "investment" of other abilities during educational and general life experiences (Horn & Noll, 1997).

Gc includes both declarative (static) and procedural (dynamic) knowledge. Declarative knowledge is held in long-term memory and is activated when related information is in working memory *(Gsm)*. Declarative knowledge includes factual information, comprehension, concepts, rules, and relationships, especially when the information is verbal in nature. *Declarative knowledge* refers to knowledge "that something is the case, whereas procedural knowledge is knowledge of how to do something" (Gagne, 1985, p. 48). *Procedural knowledge* refers to the process of reasoning with previously learned procedures in order to transform knowledge. For example, a child's knowledge of his or her street address would reflect declarative knowledge, whereas a child's ability to find his or her way home from school would require procedural knowledge (Gagne, 1985). As mentioned earlier, most comprehensive academic achievement batteries measure many different aspects of *Gc*. For example, the Test of Written Language–Third Edition (TOWL-3; Hammill & Larson, 1996) includes a Vocabulary subtest, which is a measure of Lexical Knowledge (VL; i.e., a narrow *Gc* ability). The breadth of *Gc* is apparent from the number of narrow abilities (12) it subsumes (see Table 2.2).

A rather unique aspect of *Gc* not seen in the other broad abilities is that it appears to be both a store of acquired knowledge (e.g., lexical knowledge, general information, informa-

TABLE 2.1 Narrow *Gf* Stratum I Ability Definitions and Task Examples

Narrow Stratum I Name (code)	Definition	Task Example
Fluid Intelligence (Gf)		
General Sequential Reasoning (RG)	Ability to start with stated rules, premises, or conditions, and to engage in one or more steps to reach a solution to a novel problem (also called "deduction")	An examinee is required to attend to logical premises presented visually and aurally, and then to respond to a question by making use of the logical premise.
Induction (I)	Ability to discover the underlying characteristic (e.g., rule, concept, process, trend, class membership) that governs a problem or a set of materials	An examinee is required to read a short story and select, from among four scenarios, what is likely to happen next.
Quantitative Reasoning (RQ)	Ability to inductively and deductively reason with concepts involving mathematical relations and properties	An examinee is presented with an incomplete series of related numbers and must select the number(s) that best complete the series.
Piagetian Reasoning (RP)	Seriation, conservation, classification, and other cognitive abilities as defined by Piaget's developmental theory	An examinee must demonstrate knowledge of conservation of mass or volume when presented with transformations of either the actual state of the object or items extraneous to the object, such as a container holding the object (e.g., When 5 ounces of water are transformed to ice, is there a change in the amount of water?).
Speed of Reasoning (RE)	(Not clearly defined by existing research.)	Not applicable.

Note: Most all definitions were derived from Carroll (1993). Two-letter factor codes (e.g., RG) are from Carroll (1993).

tion about culture, etc.) as well as a collection of processing abilities (e.g., oral production and fluency, listening ability). Although *Gc* is most often conceptualized much like *Gq* and *Grw* as an ability that is highly dependent on learning experiences (especially formal, classroom type experiences), it also seems to encompass abilities that are more process oriented. The narrow ability of General Information (K0), for example, is clearly a repository of learned information, whereas the narrow Listening Ability (LS) appears to represent the ability to effectively comprehend and process information presented orally. Although comprehension is of course dependent on knowledge of the words being presented, the nature of these two *Gc* abilities is clearly not identical. Although research is needed to discern the nature of acquired knowledge versus processing abilities within the *Gc* domain, assessment of *Gc* should pay close attention to the nature of the narrow abilities that define this broad domain. Despite the interrelatedness of all narrow abilities under *Gc*, there may well be

TABLE 2.2   Narrow *Gc* Stratum I Ability Definitions and Task Examples

Narrow Stratum I Name (code)	Definition	Task Example
	Crystallized Intelligence (Gc)	
Language Development (LD)	General development, or the understanding of words, sentences, and paragraphs (*not* requiring reading), in spoken native language skills	An examinee is presented with two words and must describe the common relation or similarity between them.
Lexical Knowledge (VL)	Extent of vocabulary that can be understood in terms of correct word meanings	An examinee must provide oral definitions for words of increasing difficulty.
Listening Ability (LS)	Ability to listen and comprehend oral communications	An examinee is presented with a series of tape-recorded instructions and must perform the action specified in the instructions.
General (verbal) Information (K0)	Range of general knowledge	An examinee must provide specific responses to questions of general factual information (e.g., Who was Benjamin Franklin?).
Information about Culture (K2)	Range of cultural knowledge (e.g., music, art)	An examinee is presented with pictures of major artistic works (e.g., Picasso) and must correctly identify the name of the work and/or the artist.
General Science Information (K1)	Range of scientific knowledge (e.g., biology, physics, engineering, mechanics, electronics)	An examinee must correctly respond to questions demonstrating general knowledge of basic scientific ideas or facts (e.g., What is the largest planet in our solar system?).
Geography Achievement (A5)	Range of geographic knowledge	An examinee must identify capitals of countries around the world.
Communication Ability (CM)	Ability to speak in "real-life" situations (e.g., lecture, group participation) in an adult-like manner	An examinee is required to view a picture of a small town with stores and streets and must describe the scene and give directions from one store in the picture to another.
Oral Production and Fluency (OP)	More specific or narrow oral communication skills than reflected by Communication Ability (CM)	An examinee is presented with a starting stimulus word and must use the word properly in a sentence.
Grammatical Sensitivity (MY)	Knowledge or awareness of the grammatical features of the native language	An examinee must correctly label the parts of speech contained in a sentence and/or correct those parts of speech that are utilized incorrectly (e.g., disparate tenses in a sentence).

TABLE 2.2 *Continued*

Narrow Stratum I Name (code)	Definition	Task Example
	Crystallized Intelligence (Gc)	
Foreign Language Proficiency (KL)	Similar to Language Development (LD) but for a foreign language	An examinee is presented with two words in a foreign language and must describe the common relation or similarity between them.
Foreign Language Aptitude (LA)	Rate and ease of learning a new language	An examinee is presented with several foreign words that are paired with pictorial stimuli and must pair the words with the pictures following a single presentation.

Note: Most all definitions were derived from Carroll (1993). Two-letter factor codes (e.g., LD) are from Carroll (1993).

times when focus on the abilities that are more process oriented as opposed to those that are knowledge oriented, is most important, and vice versa.

Quantitative Knowledge *(Gq)*. *Quantitative knowledge* represents an individual's store of acquired quantitative declarative and procedural knowledge. The *Gq* store of acquired knowledge represents the ability to use quantitative information and manipulate numeric symbols. *Gq* abilities are typically measured by achievement tests. For example, most comprehensive tests of achievement include measures of math calculation, applied problems, and general math knowledge. Some specialized achievement batteries measure *Gq* exclusively, such as KeyMath–Revised/Normative Update (KM-R/NU; Connolly, 1998). Although some intelligence batteries measure aspects of *Gq* (e.g., Arithmetic on the Wechsler Scales and Quantitative on the Stanford Binet–IV) they typically do not measure this ability comprehensively.

It is important to understand the difference between *Gq* and the Quantitative Reasoning (RQ) ability that is subsumed by *Gf*. On the whole, *Gq* represents an individual's store of acquired mathematical knowledge, including the ability to perform mathematical calculations (i.e., procedural knowledge). Quantitative Reasoning represents only the ability to reason inductively and deductively when solving quantitative problems. Recall that RQ is a narrow ability that is typically found to fall under *Gf*. However, because RQ, as discussed previously, is dependent on possession of basic mathematical concepts and knowledge, it seems to be as much related to *Gq* as it is related to *Gf*. *Gq* is most evident when a task requires mathematical skills (e.g., addition, subtraction, multiplication, division) and general mathematical knowledge (e.g., knowing what the square root symbol means). RQ, on the other hand, would be required to solve for a missing number in a number series task (e.g., 3, 6, 9, ___). Although most achievement batteries measure specific math skills and general math knowledge (i.e., *Gq*), some also require individuals to solve quantitative problems through inductive or deductive reasoning (i.e., RQ). Therefore, at least for purposes of assessing overall mathematics ability, which includes mathematics reasoning, it may be best to conceptualize RQ as being a narrow ability that falls under both *Gf* and *Gq* broad abilities (see Chapter 12). Consequently, three narrow abilities are listed and defined under *Gq* in Table 2.3.

Reading/Writing Ability *(Grw).* *Reading/Writing ability* is an acquired store of knowledge that includes basic reading and writing skills required for the comprehension of written language and the expression of thought via writing. It includes both basic abilities (e.g., reading decoding, spelling) and complex abilities (e.g., comprehending written discourse and writing a story). Like *Gq*, *Grw* is considered to be an "achievement" domain, and therefore has been measured traditionally and almost exclusively by tests of academic achievement. In Carroll's (1993) three-stratum model, eight narrow reading and writing abilities are subsumed by *Gc* in addition to other abilities. In the CHC model, these eight narrow abilities define the broad *Grw* ability. These *Grw* narrow abilities are defined in Table 2.4.

A closer review of the nature of *Grw* presents a rather curious finding. Although reading and writing are often thought of as distinct academic abilities, the research underlying the classification of these narrow abilities suggests that they are very closely related abilities (Woodcock, 1994). The strong relationship seems to imply that a measure of reading is an accurate measure of writing ability, just as a measure of writing ability is an accurate measure of reading ability. Without question, reading and writing go hand in hand, and for good reason—they are the basic elements of proficiency with the symbolic aspect of language. Lan-

TABLE 2.3   Narrow *Gq* Stratum I Ability Definitions and Task Examples

Narrow Stratum I Name (code)	Definition	Task Example
	Quantitative Knowledge (Gq)	
Mathematical Knowledge (KM)	Range of general knowledge about mathematics	An examinee is asked to demonstrate knowledge of basic mathematical facts and operations.
Mathematical Achievement (A3)	Measured mathematics achievement	An examinee is required to perform simple mathematical calculations using pencil and paper.
Quantitative Reasoning (RQ)[1]	Ability to inductively and deductively reason with concepts involving mathematical relations and properties	An examinee is presented with an incomplete series of related numbers and must select the number(s) that best complete(s) the series.

[1] Although RQ is a narrow *Gf* ability, it is included here because its measurement is relevant to the comprehensive assessment of overall mathematics ability.
Note: Most all definitions were derived from Carroll (1993). Two-letter factor codes (e.g., KM) are from Carroll (1993).

TABLE 2.4   Narrow *Grw* Stratum I Ability Definitions and Task Examples

Narrow Stratum I Name (code)	Definition	Task Example
	Reading/Writing (Grw)	
Reading Decoding (RD)	Ability to recognize and decode words or pseudowords in reading	An examinee is required to accurately pronounce a list of real words or nonsense words.
Reading Comprehension (RC)	Ability to comprehend connected discourse during reading	An examinee is required to read a short passage and respond to questions about the passage.
Verbal (printed) Language Comprehension (V)	General development, or the understanding of words, sentences, and paragraphs in native language, as measured by *reading* vocabulary and *reading* comprehension tests	An examinee must read a list of four vocabulary words and choose two of the four words that belong together in some meaningful way.
Cloze Ability (CZ)	Ability to supply words deleted from prose passages that must be read	An examinee is required to read a short passage and supply a missing word that best corresponds to the theme and/or content of the passage.
Spelling Ability (SG)	Ability to spell	An examinee must spell a series of increasingly difficult orally presented words.
Writing Ability (WA)	Ability to write with clarity of thought, organization, and good sentence structure	An examinee is given a starting stimulus and must write a well-organized story that adheres to the structural rules of writing (e.g., examinee starts a new paragraph when he or she presents a new idea).
English Usage Knowledge (EU)	Knowledge of writing in the English language with respect to capitalization, punctuation, usage, and spelling	An examinee must correct sentences that have capitalization, punctuation, spelling, and usage errors.
Reading Speed (RS)	Time required to silently read a passage or series of sentences as quickly as possible	An examinee is asked to read a list of short statements silently and as quickly as possible and indicate whether each statement is "true" or "false."

Note: Most all definitions were derived from Carroll (1993). Two-letter factor codes (e.g., RD) are from Carroll (1993).

guage abilities are clearly present in the various narrow abilities found under the broad *Gc* ability described previously, but generally are limited to those involving the receptive and expressive aspects of language. *Grw*, however, seems to represent skill in the symbolic aspect of language where facility with the written form of speech and communication are required. Reading, therefore, is the ability to decode the symbols in order to derive linguistic meaning, and writing is the production of symbols to express linguistic meaning. In this sense, reading and writing are seen to be highly interrelated components of the same fundamental construct. It is likely only a semantic issue that creates a sense of reading and writing as being more distinct than they actually are. Use of the label "*Grw*—reading and writing" reflects this semantic separation, whereas another label, reflecting a broad *literacy* factor, for example, may better capture the true essence of this variable. Because of its basis in both reading and writing skills, the term *literacy* seems to provide a better umbrella for covering the types of abilities that are currently found under the label of *Grw*. This presumes, of course, that reading and writing are indeed quite interchangeable as measures of symbolic language processing (i.e., literacy). Although current research suggests that this is true (Woodcock, 1994), it is rather preliminary and largely unreplicated. Thus, if future research reveals that reading and writing abilities can be reliably and validly distinguished as distinct constructs, then the label itself may need to be split accordingly (i.e., *Gr*—reading and *Gw*—writing). Although not supported by current research, this distinction is made later in this volume for the purpose of clarifying LD evaluation in response to referral concerns. The code *Grw-R* (reading) is used to denote narrow abilities that seem to relate more to reading skills and the code *Grw-W* (writing) is used to refer to narrow abilities that represent skills related to writing. This issue is further discussed in Chapter 12.

Short-Term Memory *(Gsm).*   *Short-term memory* is the ability to apprehend and hold information in immediate awareness and then use it within a few seconds. *Gsm* is a limited capacity system, as most individuals can retain only seven "chunks" of information (plus or minus two chunks) in this system at one time. An example of *Gsm* is the ability to remember a telephone number long enough to dial it, or the ability to retain a sequence of spoken directions long enough to complete the tasks specified in the directions. Given the limited amount of information that can be held in short-term memory, information is typically retained for only a few seconds before it is lost. As most individuals have experienced, it is difficult to remember an unfamiliar telephone number for more than a few seconds unless one consciously uses a cognitive learning strategy (e.g., continually repeating or rehearsing the numbers) or other mnemonic device. When a new task requires an individual to use his or her *Gsm* abilities to store new information, the previous information held in short-term memory is either lost or must be stored in the acquired stores of knowledge (i.e., *Gc*, *Gq*, *Grw*) through the use of *Glr*.

In the CHC model, *Gsm* subsumes the narrow ability of working memory, which has received considerable attention recently in the cognitive psychology literature. Working memory is considered to be the "mechanism responsible for the temporary storage and processing of information" (Richardson, 1996, p. 23). It has been referred to as the "mind's scratchpad" (Jensen, 1998, p. 220) and most models of working memory postulate a number of subsystems or temporary "buffers." The phonological or articulatory loop processes auditory-linguistic information, where-as the visuospatial sketch/scratchpad (Baddeley, 1986,

1992; Logie, 1996) is the temporary buffer for visually processed information. Most working memory models also posit a central executive or processor mechanism that coordinates and manages the activities and subsystems in working memory.

Carroll (1993) is skeptical of the working memory construct, as reflected in his conclusion that "although some evidence supports such a speculation, one must be cautious in accepting it because as yet there has not been sufficient work on measuring working memory, and the validity and generality of the concept have not yet been well established in the individual differences research" (p. 647). Notwithstanding, the working memory construct has been related empirically to a variety of different outcomes, including many specific reading and math skills (presented later in this chapter). Therefore, despite the questions that have been raised regarding its validity as a measurable construct, Flanagan, McGrew, and Ortiz (2000) and Woodcock, McGrew, and Mather (2001) included working memory in the CHC taxonomy in light of the current literature that argues strongly for its predictive utility. Nevertheless, given that Carroll has raised questions about the validity of the construct of working memory, it is important to remember that this construct was included in current CHC theory primarily for practical application and ease of communication. Additional research is necessary before definitive decisions can be reached about the inclusion or exclusion of working memory in CHC theory. The narrow *Gsm* abilities are defined in Table 2.5.

TABLE 2.5 Narrow *Gsm* Stratum I Ability Definitions and Task Examples

Narrow Stratum I Name (code)	Definition	Task Example
Short-Term Memory (Gsm)		
Memory Span (MS)	Ability to attend to and immediately recall temporally ordered elements in the correct order after a single presentation	An examinee is presented with a sequence of digits and must retain them long enough to repeat them verbatim.
Working Memory (MW)	Ability to temporarily store and perform a set of cognitive operations on information that requires divided attention and the management of the limited capacity of short-term memory	An examinee is presented with a series of numbers and words in a mixed-up order and is then required to reorder the information by first saying the numbers in the order they were presented followed by the words in order.
Learning Abilities (L1)	A number of factors that are specific to particular kinds of learning situations and memory (Also listed under *Glr*; not clearly defined by existing research.)	Not applicable.

Note: Most all definitions were derived from Carroll (1993). Two-letter factor codes (e.g., MS) are from Carroll (1993).

Visual Processing (Gv).   *Visual processing* (Gv) is the ability to generate, perceive, analyze, synthesize, store, retrieve, manipulate, transform, and think with visual patterns and stimuli (Lohman, 1994). These abilities are measured frequently by tasks that require the perception and manipulation of visual shapes and forms, usually of a figural or geometric nature (e.g., a standard block design task). An individual who can mentally reverse and rotate objects effectively, interpret how objects change as they move through space, perceive and manipulate spatial configurations, and maintain spatial orientation would be regarded as having a strength in *Gv* abilities. Most widely recognized achievement batteries do not measure *Gv* abilities directly, although these abilities have been found to be related significantly to higher-level mathematics achievement (e.g., geometry and trigonometry). The various narrow abilities subsumed by *Gv* are listed and defined in Table 2.6.

TABLE 2.6   Narrow *Gv* Stratum I Ability Definitions and Task Examples

Narrow Stratum I Name (code)	Definition	Task Example
Visual Processing (Gv)		
Spatial Relations (SR)	Ability to rapidly perceive and manipulate relatively simple visual patterns or to maintain orientation with respect to objects in space	An examinee is required to reproduce a design using blocks or cubes while viewing a stimulus pattern or design.
Visual Memory (MV)	Ability to form and store a mental representation or image of a visual stimulus and then recognize or recall it later	An examinee is required either to reproduce or to recognize a previously presented visual stimulus.
Closure Speed (CS)	Ability to quickly combine disconnected, vague, or partially obscured visual stimuli or patterns into a meaningful whole, *without knowing in advance* what the pattern is	An examinee is required to identify objects from line drawings that have portions of the line missing under timed conditions.
Flexibility of Closure (CF)	Ability to find, apprehend, and identify a visual figure or pattern embedded in a complex visual array, *when knowing in advance* what the pattern is	An examinee must find all the triangles that are embedded in a complex figure or design.
Spatial Scanning (SS)	Ability to accurately and quickly survey a spatial field or pattern and identify a path through the visual field or pattern	An examinee is required to complete a series of increasingly difficult mazes within a specified time period.
Serial Perceptual Integration (PI)	Ability to apprehend and identify a pictorial or visual pattern when parts of the pattern are presented rapidly in serially or successive order	An examinee is required to correctly identify or name a stimulus when portions of the stimuli are presented serially (e.g., portions of a line drawing of a cat are passed through a small "window").

TABLE 2.6   *Continued*

Narrow Stratum I Name (code)	Definition	Task Example
	Visual Processing (Gv)	
Length Estimation (LE)	Ability to accurately estimate or compare visual lengths and distances without using measurement instruments	An examinee is presented with a series of paired double-arrow lines of differing orientations and must determine whether they are the same length or different.
Perceptual Illusions (IL)	Ability to resist being affected by perceptual illusions involving geometric figures	An examinee is presented with a series of geometric shapes and lines that have been altered in terms of specific features (e.g., color, orientation) and determine whether the shapes and/or lines are the same or different on the basis of size alone.
Perceptual Alternations (PN)	Consistency in the rate of alternating between different visual perceptions	An examinee is asked to sort a series of cards along one visual dimension (e.g., color) and then, in midstream, sort on the basis of a different dimension (e.g., shape).
Visualization (Vz)	Ability to mentally manipulate objects or visual patterns and to "see" how they would appear under altered conditions	The examinee is presented with a visual image and must draw how the image would look upside down.
Imagery (IM)	Ability to vividly mentally manipulate abstract spatial forms (Not clearly defined by existing research.)	Not applicable.

Note: Most all definitions were derived from Carroll (1993). Two-letter factor codes (e.g., SR) are from Carroll (1993).

Auditory Processing (Ga).   In the broadest sense, auditory abilities "are cognitive abilities that depend on sound as input and on the functioning of our hearing apparatus" (Stankov, 1994, p. 157) and reflect "the degree to which the individual can cognitively control the perception of auditory stimulus inputs" (Gustafsson & Undheim, 1996, p. 192). *Auditory processing* is the ability to perceive, analyze, and synthesize patterns among auditory stimuli, and to discriminate subtle nuances in patterns of sound (e.g., complex musical structure) and speech when presented under distorted conditions. Although *Ga* abilities do not require the comprehension of language (*Gc*) per se, they are important in the development of language skills (Liberman, Shankweiler, Fischer, & Carter, 1974; Wagner & Torgesen, 1987). *Ga* subsumes most of those abilities referred to as "phonological awareness/processing." Tests that measure these abilities (e.g., phonetic coding tests) are found typically on achievement batteries, such as the Comprehensive Test of Phonological Processing (CTOPP; Wagner, Torgesen, & Rashotte, 1999). In fact, the number of tests specifically designed to measure phonological processing has increased significantly in recent years, presumably as a result of the consistent finding that phonological awareness/processing appears to be the core deficit in individuals with reading difficulties (e.g., Morris et al., 1998; Vellutino, Scanlon, & Lyon, 2000). However, as can be seen from the list of narrow abilities subsumed by *Ga* (Table 2.7), this domain is very broad, extending far beyond phonetic coding ability.

In CHC theory, Carroll's Phonetic Coding (PC) narrow ability was split into separate analysis (PC:A) and synthesis (PC:S) abilities. Support for two different PC abilities comes from a growing number of sources. First, in a sample of kindergarten students, Yopp (1988) reported evidence in favor of two phonemic awareness factors: simple phonemic awareness (required one operation to be performed on sounds) and compound phonemic awareness (required holding sounds in memory while performing another operation on them). Second, in what appears to be the most comprehensive *Ga* factor-analytic study to date, Stankov and Horn (1980) presented evidence for seven different auditory abilities, two of which had tests of sound blending (synthesis) and incomplete words (analysis) as factor markers. Third, the WJ Sound Blending and Incomplete Words tests (which are almost identical in format to the tests used by Stankov and Horn) correlated only moderately (.37 and .46 and 13.7 percent and 21 percent shared variance) across the kindergarten to adult WJ-R and WJ III norm samples, respectively, a correlation range that suggests that these tests are measuring different aspects of PC. Fourth, using confirmatory factor-analytic methods, Wagner, Torgesen, Laughton, Simmons, and Rashotte (1993) presented a model of phonological processing that included separate auditory analysis and synthesis factors.

Although the features of these different auditory factors across respective studies are not entirely consistent, there are many similarities. For example, Yopp's (1988) simple phonemic factor appears to be analogous to Wagner and colleagues' (1993) synthesis factor and the factor Stankov and Horn (1980) identified with the aid of sound blending tasks. Also, Yopp's (1988) compound phonemic factor bears similarities to Wagner and colleagues' analysis factor and the Stankov and Horn factor identified, in part, by an incomplete words task. Presently, it appears that Wagner and colleagues' analysis-synthesis distinction is likely the most useful. According to Wagner and associates, analysis and synthesis can be defined as "the ability to segment larger units of speech into smaller units" and "the ability to blend smaller units of speech to form larger units" (p. 87), respectively. The analysis-synthesis distinction continues to be empirically supported as demonstrated by the separate Phonetic Coding: Analysis and Phonetic Coding: Synthesis tests included in the new WJ III (Woodcock, McGrew, & Mather, 2001).

Long-Term Storage and Retrieval *(Glr).* *Long-term storage and retrieval* is the ability to store information in and fluently retrieve new or previously acquired information (e.g., concepts, ideas, items, names) from long-term memory. *Glr* abilities have been prominent in creativity research, where they have been referred to as idea production, ideational fluency, or associative fluency. It is important not to confuse *Glr* with *Gc, Gq,* and *Grw,* which represent to a large extent an individual's stores of acquired knowledge.

TABLE 2.7   Narrow *Ga* Stratum I Ability Definitions and Task Examples

Narrow Stratum I Name (code)	Definition	Task Example
Auditory Processing (Ga)		
Phonetic Coding: Analysis (PC:A)	Ability to segment larger units of speech sounds into smaller units of speech sounds	An examinee is presented with the pronunciation of a word and must identify the beginning and ending sounds.
Phonetic Coding: Synthesis (PC:S)	Ability to blend smaller units of speech together into larger units of speech	An examinee is presented with the isolated sounds for a word and must blend the sounds together and identify the word.
Speech Sound Discrimination (US)	Ability to detect differences in speech sounds under conditions of little distraction or distortion	An examinee is presented with a series of regular phonemic sounds via a tape recorder and must identify whether the sounds are the same or different.
Resistance to Auditory Stimulus Distortion (UR)	Ability to understand speech and language that has been distorted or masked in one or more ways	An examinee must identify mono- and multisyllabic words that are presented orally while listening to an increasing level of noise.
Memory for Sound Patterns (UM)	Ability to retain on a short-term basis auditory events such as tones, tonal patterns, and voices	An examinee is presented with a series of tonal patterns and later must identify whether these patterns were heard previously.
General Sound Discrimination (U3)	Ability to discriminate tones, tone patterns, or musical materials with regard to pitch, intensity, duration, and rhythm	An examinee is presented with two short musical patterns and must identify whether the patterns are similar or different. If they differ in pitch, intensity, etc., then the response will be "different."
Temporal Tracking (UK)	Ability to track auditory temporal events so as to be able to count, rearrange, or anticipate them	An examinee is presented with a steady pattern of musical beats and must identify the note that is to come next after the music has stopped.
Musical Discrimination and Judgment (U1, U9)	Ability to discriminate and judge tonal patterns in music with respect to melodic, harmonic, and expressive aspects (e.g., phrasing, tempo, and intensity variations)	An examinee is presented with tape-recorded samples of musical pieces from different musical genres presented in either major or minor and must describe the differences in the music in terms of its harmonic complexity and mood.

Continued

TABLE 2.7 *Continued*

Narrow Stratum I Name (code)	Definition	Task Example
Auditory Processing (Ga)		
Maintaining and Judging Rhythm (U8)	Ability to recognize and maintain a musical or equal time beat	An examinee is presented with a tape-recorded metronome keeping 4/4 time (i.e., one measure) that is comprised of quarter notes and must demonstrate knowledge of equal time beat by tapping out eighth notes.
Sound-Intensity/Duration Discrimination (U6)	Ability to discriminate sound intensities and to be sensitive to the temporal/rhythmic aspects of tonal patterns	An examinee must listen to a series of tape-recorded sounds and indicate by raising his or her right hand when one sound becomes more intense than the previously presented sound.
Sound-Frequency Discrimination (U5)	Ability to discriminate frequency attributes (pitch and timbre) of tones	An examinee is presented with random tape-recorded notes played on the high, middle, and low ends of a piano key board and must describe the relationship of the second note played to the first note played (e.g., higher, lower).
Hearing and Speech Threshold factors (UA, UT, UU)	Ability to hear pitch and varying sounds over a range of audible frequencies	An examinee is presented with a series of 15 tape-recorded sounds and must indicate by writing a check mark in a response booklet whenever he or she hears a sound.
Absolute Pitch (UP)	Ability to perfectly name or identify the pitch of tones	An examinee is presented with a tape-recorded note of a piano key (e.g., C or F sharp) and is required to name the note.
Sound Localization (UL)	Ability to localize heard sounds in space	An examinee is presented with earphones and must indicate whether a presented sound was heard in the left, right, or both sides of the headset.

Note: Most all definitions were derived from Carroll (1993). Two-letter factor codes (e.g., PC:A) are from Carroll (1993).

Specifically, *Gc*, *Gq*, and *Grw* represent *what* is stored in long-term memory, whereas *Glr* is the *efficiency* by which this information is initially stored in and later retrieved from long-term memory.

It is also important to note that different processes are involved in *Glr* and *Gsm*. Although the word *long-term* frequently carries with it the connotation of days, weeks, months, and years in the clinical literature, long-term storage processes can begin within a few minutes or hours of performing a task. Therefore, the time lapse between the initial task performance and the recall of information related to that task is not necessarily of critical importance in defining *Glr*. More important is the occurrence of an intervening task that engages short-term memory during the interim before the attempted recall of the stored information (e.g., *Gc*; Woodcock, 1993). Although *Glr* is measured more consistently and directly by intelligence, rather than achievement batteries, some achievement tests measure *Glr*. For example, the WJ III Tests of Achievement include Story Recall-Delayed, a measure of *Glr*—namely, Meaningful Memory. One *Glr* ability that has been receiving increased attention in the literature is Naming Facility or the ability to produce names for concepts rapidly. This ability, often referred to as *Rapid Automatic Naming (RAN),* has been found to predict reading achievement significantly (this research is summarized later in this chapter). However, Naming Facility or RAN is measured only by a select few achievement tests, such as Rapid Object Naming on the Comprehensive Test of Phonological Processing (CTOPP; Wagner, Torgesen, & Rashotte, 1999) (see CHC worksheets in Appendix A for other examples). In the present CHC model, 13 narrow memory and fluency abilities are included under *Glr* (see Table 2.8).

Processing Speed *(Gs).* *Processing speed* or mental quickness is often mentioned when talking about intelligent behavior (Nettelbeck, 1994). Processing speed is the ability to fluently and automatically perform cognitive tasks, especially when under pressure to maintain focused attention and concentration. "Attentive speediness" encapsulates the essence of *Gs*. *Gs* is measured typically by fixed-interval timed tasks that require little in the way of complex thinking or mental processing (e.g., the Wechsler Animal Pegs, Symbol Search, and Digit Symbol/Coding tests).

Recent interest in information processing models of cognitive functioning has resulted in a renewed focus on *Gs* (Kail, 1991; Lohman, 1989). A central construct in information processing models is the idea of limited processing resources (e.g., the limited capacities of short-term and working memory): "Many cognitive activities require a person's deliberate efforts and . . . people are limited in the amount of effort they can allocate. In the face of limited processing resources, the speed of processing is critical because it determines in part how rapidly limited resources can be reallocated to other cognitive tasks" (Kail, 1991, p. 152). Woodcock (1993) likens *Gs* to a valve in a water pipe. The rate in which water flows in the pipe (i.e., *Gs*) increases when the valve is opened wide and it decreases when the valve is partially closed. Although *Gs* is not measured directly by commonly used achievement tests, it seems clear that many specific achievement tests rely, sometimes heavily, on the ability to process information quickly. For example, the WJ III Tests of Achievement include Reading, Math, and Writing Fluency tests, all of which rely on quick, accurate processing of information (Woodcock, McGrew, & Mather, 2001). Four different narrow speed of processing abilities are subsumed by *Gs* in the present CHC model (see Table 2.9).

TABLE 2.8 Narrow *Glr* Stratum I Ability Definitions and Task Examples

Narrow Stratum I Name (code)	Definition	Task Example
Long-Term Storage and Retrieval (Glr)		
Associative Memory (MA)	Ability to recall one part of a previously learned but unrelated pair of items when the other part is presented (i.e., paired-associative learning)	An examinee is presented with a set of visual stimuli paired with nonsense words and must correctly identify the nonsense word that had been presented with a certain visual stimulus.
Meaningful Memory (MM)	Ability to recall a set of items where there is a meaningful relation between items or the items comprise a meaningful story or connected discourse	An examinee is presented with a short story and must retell the story as accurately as possible immediately following a single presentation.
Free Recall Memory (M6)	Ability to recall as many unrelated items as possible, in any order, after a large collection of items is presented	An examinee is presented with a series of objects and, after they are removed, must recall as many of the objects as possible in any order.
Ideational Fluency (FI)	Ability to rapidly produce a series of ideas, words, or phrases related to a specific condition or object (Quantity not quality is emphasized.)	An examinee must rapidly name as many kitchen utensils/appliances as possible within a specified time limit.
Associational Fluency (FA)	Ability to rapidly produce words or phrases associated in meaning (semantically associated) with a given word or concept	An examinee must name as many examples of objects that fit into a specified category (e.g., name as many fruits as you can think of) within a specified time limit.
Expressional Fluency (FE)	Ability to rapidly think of and organize words or phrases into meaningful complex ideas under high general or more specific cueing conditions	An examinee must rapidly name a category that bests represents a series of presented words (e.g., Pattern, material, thread . . . things to make clothing).
Naming Facility (NA)	Ability to rapidly produce names for concepts when presented with a pictorial or verbal cue (sometimes called Rapid Automatic Naming [RAN] in the literature)	An examinee must rapidly name a series of objects printed on consecutive pages as quickly as possible.
Word Fluency (FW)	Ability to rapidly produce words that have specific phonemic, structural, or orthographic characteristics (independent of word meanings)	An examinee must name as many words as he or she can think of that start with the "sh" sound within a specified time limit.
Figural Fluency (FF)	Ability to rapidly draw or sketch several examples or elaborations when given a starting visual or descriptive stimulus	An examinee must draw as many things as possible when presented with a nonmeaningful starting visual stimulus.

TABLE 2.8   *Continued*

Narrow Stratum I Name (code)	Definition	Task Example
Long-Term Storage and Retrieval (Glr)		
Figural Flexibility (FX)	Ability to quickly change set in order to generate new and different solutions to figural problems	An examinee is presented with five geometric shapes and must manipulate those shapes to create objects described by the examiner (e.g., build a house, build a car).
Sensitivity to Problems (SP)	Ability to identify and state practical problems in a given situation and/or rapidly think of and state various solutions to, and/or consequences of, such problems	An examinee is required to answer questions such as, "What is the thing to do if you lock your keys in the car?"
Originality/Creativity (FO)	Ability to rapidly produce original, clever, or uncommon verbal or ideational responses to specified tasks	An examinee is given a starting stimulus word, such as *car* and must construct as many words as possible using those three letters in the word (e.g., carrot, care, carton, cartoon, racecar, macaroon).
Learning Abilities (L1)	A number of factors that are specific to particular kinds of learning situations and memory (Also listed under *Gsm*; not clearly defined by existing research.)	Not applicable.

Note: Most all definitions were derived from Carroll (1993). Two-letter factor codes (e.g., MA) are from Carroll (1993).

Decision Speed/Reaction Time *(Gt).* In addition to *Gs*, both Carroll and Horn included a second broad speed ability in their respective models of the structure of abilities. Processing Speed or Decision Speed/Reaction Time (*Gt*), as proposed by Carroll, subsumes narrow abilities that reflect an individual's quickness in reacting (reaction time) and making decisions (decision speed). Correct Decision Speed (CDS), proposed by Horn as a second speed ability (*Gs* being the first), is typically measured by recording the time an individual requires to provide an answer to problems on a variety of tests (e.g., letter series, classifications, vocabulary; Horn, 1988, 1991). Because Correct Decision Speed appeared to be a much narrower ability than *Gt*, it is subsumed by *Gt* in Cattel-Horn-Carroll theory.

It is important not to confuse *Gt* with *Gs*. *Gt* abilities reflect the immediacy with which an individual can react to stimuli or a task (*typically* measured in seconds or parts of seconds), whereas *Gs* abilities reflect the ability to work quickly over a longer period of time

TABLE 2.9   Narrow *Gs* Stratum I Ability Definitions and Task Examples

Narrow Stratum I Name (code)	Definition	Task Example
Processing Speed (Gs)		
Perceptual Speed (P)	Ability to rapidly search for and compare known visual symbols or patterns presented side-by-side or separated in a visual field	An examinee must rapidly view rows of stimuli and cross out those stimuli that are similar in each row within a specified time limit.
Rate-of-Test-Taking (R9)	Ability to rapidly perform tests that are relatively easy or that require very simple decisions	An examinee is shown a key with a series of symbols, each paired with a specific letter. The examinee is then presented with rows of letters and must use the key to quickly draw the matching symbol.
Number Facility (N)	Ability to rapidly and accurately manipulate and deal with numbers, from elementary skills of counting and recognizing numbers to advanced skills of adding, subtracting, multiplying, and dividing numbers	An examinee is required to rapidly complete a series of arithmetic problems using paper and pencil in a specified time limit.
Semantic Processing Speed (R4)	Ability to rapidly make decisions that require some encoding and mental manipulation of stimulus content	An examinee is required to quickly determine which two pictures in an array of pictures are most similar conceptually.

Note: Most all definitions were derived from Carroll (1993). Two-letter factor codes (e.g., P) are from Carroll (1993).

(typically measured in intervals of 2 to 3 minutes). Being asked to read a passage (on a self-paced scrolling video screen) as quickly as possible and, in the process, touch the word *the* with a stylus pen each time it appears on the screen, is an example of *Gs*. The individual's *Gs* score would reflect the number of correct responses (taking into account errors of omission and commission). In contrast, *Gt* may be measured by requiring a person to read the same text at his or her normal rate of reading and press the space bar as quickly as possible whenever a light is flashed on the screen. In this latter paradigm, the individual's score is based on the average response latency or the time interval between the onset of the stimulus and the individual's response. Table 2.10 includes descriptions of the narrow abilities subsumed by *Gt*.

Although the preceding discussion is admittedly not an exhaustive description of CHC abilities, by now it should be clear from the definitions presented that CHC theory is comprehensive, encompassing a wide range of abilities, many of which are regarded as "academic" rather than "cognitive" in nature. In order to circumvent confusion and the tendency

TABLE 2.10   Narrow *Gt* Stratum I Ability Definitions and Task Examples

Narrow Stratum I Name (code)	Definition	Task Example
Decision Speed/Reaction Time (Gt)		
Simple Reaction Time (R1)	Reaction time to the presentation of a single visual or auditory stimulus	An examinee is required to quickly depress a computer key when presented with a specific geometric shape (e.g., a square) that appears intermittently in a series of other shapes on the computer screen.
Choice Reaction Time (R2)	Reaction time to one of two or more alternative stimuli, depending on which alternative is signaled	An examinee is required to quickly depress one of two computer keys depending on the type of stimulus presented (e.g., press the green key when the square is presented and the red key when the circle is presented).
Mental Comparison Speed (R7)	Reaction time where the stimuli must be compared for a particular attribute	An examinee is required to quickly depress a key when presented with two identical geometric shapes and refrain from pressing the key when the shapes differ.

Note: Most all definitions were derived from Carroll (1993). Two-letter factor codes (e.g., R1) are from Carroll (1993).

to think of intelligence (or cognitive ability) and achievement (or academic ability) as dichotomous constructs, more precise definitions of these terms are presented in the next section.

Ability and Achievement: How Are They Different?

Conceptualizing a structure of *abilities* (e.g., CHC theory) that encompasses both "cognitive" abilities and "academic" abilities (or achievements) may seem counterintuitive to some, perhaps many. After all, it is commonly believed that one's level of overall cognitive ability (e.g., global IQ; *g*) represents his or her *potential* for academic achievements (or academic success). So, it would appear that "cognitive ability" and "academic achievement," although highly correlated, represent two distinct and separate constructs. We do not, however, subscribe strictly to this point of view. Rather, we are of the opinion that cognitive and academic abilities lie on a continuum of human mental abilities, as described by Horn (1988) at the beginning of this chapter and as illustrated in Figure 2.4. However, in order to properly understand the relations between cognitive ability and academic achievement, it is necessary to settle on definitions of these terms. We will begin by defining the term *ability*.

According to Snow (1994), "an ability is a power to perform some specified act or task, either physical or mental" (p. 3). When this definition is applied to the tasks on intelligence and academic achievement batteries, it seems clear that both types of batteries measure ability (see Figure 2.4). However, a more precise definition of ability than the one offered by Snow seems necessary to shed light on the difference between that which is measured by cognitive or intelligence tests and that which is measured by academic or achievement tests.

According to Carroll (1993), *"As used to describe an attribute of individuals,* ability *refers to the possible variations over individuals in the liminal* [threshold] *levels of task difficulty (or in derived measurements based on such liminal levels) at which on any given occasion in which all conditions appear favorable, individuals perform successfully on a defined class of tasks"* (p. 8). Within the context of this definition, Carroll defined *task* as *"an activity in which a person engages, given an appropriate setting, in order to achieve a specifiable class of objectives, final results, or terminal states of affairs"* (p. 8; emphasis in original). He used the phrase *class of tasks* to imply "a group or series of possible tasks that have at least some identical or similar attributes" (p. 8). According to Carroll, tasks, of course, vary in their level of *difficulty* and in their *parameters* (i.e., defining characteristics). When tasks differ in their parameters but are related to the same ability, an estimate of an individual's ability can be obtained through aggregating the measurements on the various tasks. For example, on the WJ III, the Reading Vocabulary and Passage Comprehension tests, two different tasks related to the same ability (i.e., reading) are combined or aggregated to yield a Reading Comprehension Cluster.

Indeed, Carroll's definition of ability is more precise than most, such as the one offered by Snow. However, even when Carroll's definition is used to evaluate the tasks on intelligence and achievement batteries, it remains clear that both types of instruments measure an individual's *ability*. Thus, the definition of ability, however precise in this case, does not appear to assist in discerning the differences between *cognitive* ability and *academic* ability. Moreover, the definition of ability offered by Carroll appears to be applicable to a wide range of individual attributes, seemingly extending far beyond that which is measured by

FIGURE 2.4 Definition and Continuum of Ability

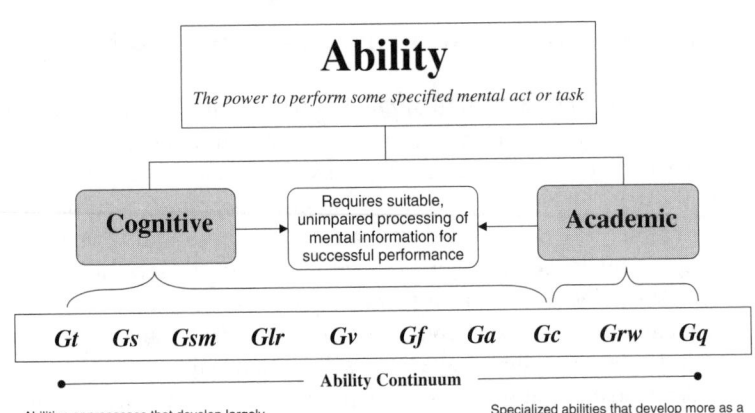

intelligence and achievement tests (e.g., weight-lifting ability, athletic ability, musical ability, etc.).

Recognizing that the definition of ability could encompass a seemingly endless number of attributes of the individual, Carroll (1993) used the adjective *cognitive* "to limit the range of cognitive tasks to those that centrally involve mental functions not only in the understanding of the intended end results but also in the performances of the task, most particularly in the *processing of mental information*" (p. 10; emphasis in original). He stated further, "A cognitive task is one in which suitable processing of mental information is the major determinant of whether the task is successfully performed" (p. 10).

Again, even when the definition of ability is defined more narrowly to include performances that require processing of mental information, it is evident that tests found on both intelligence *and* achievement batteries measure *ability,* and because they require the processing of mental information (see Figure 2.4), in accordance with Carroll's definition, indeed, *cognitive* ability. Given these definitions, the question as to why there are separate batteries of ability tests—intelligence and achievement—seems a rather curious one. Why is it that test developers have made and continue to make this distinction instead of developing batteries called "Test of Abilities" or "Tests of Cognitive Abilities" or "Tests of CHC Abilities"? Why do test developers persist in calling the abilities measured by intelligence tests *cognitive abilities* and the abilities measured by achievement tests *academic abilities* or *academic achievements*? We propose that the answer to these questions lies in understanding the differences among the specific environmental factors that govern the development of the particular abilities.

Cognitive and academic abilities can be differentiated to some extent by the manner in which their development is influenced by different types of learning (e.g., formal school-based instruction versus informal real-life experience), achievements (e.g., level of education, opportunities to cultivate unique strengths), and experiences (e.g., cultural, linguistic). Carroll (1993), for example, conceptualized cognitive and academic abilities as lying on a continuum that extends from "the most general abilities to the most specialized types of knowledges" (p. 510), the latter of which develops more through an individual's instructional and educational experiences. Through an examination of the broad CHC ability definitions presented earlier, it is likely that most practitioners would agree that *Gq* and *Grw* abilities are more influenced by school-based, experiential factors (such as direct classroom instruction) than *Gv* or *Gf* abilities, for example. Likewise, it is also likely that practitioners would agree that *Gq* and *Grw* represent specialized types of knowledge bases, whereas *Gv* and *Gf* represent processing or thinking abilities. Therefore, rather than being mutually exclusive, academic and cognitive abilities may best be conceived of as lying on a continuum with those abilities that develop largely as a function of formal education and direct learning and instruction (i.e., abilities that reflect more specialized types of knowledges) at one end and abilities that develop largely independent of formal education and school-related experiences (i.e., processing or thinking abilities) at the other end (see Figure 2.4).

We propose, then, that the abilities specified in CHC theory can be roughly characterized as either cognitive or academic, depending primarily on the extent to which their development is influenced by experiential factors. Figure 2.4 shows the placement of the CHC broad abilities along a continuum, with those abilities that are most influenced by formal instruction and school-based educational experiences at one end (i.e., *Gq, Grw*) and those that are least influenced by direct classroom instruction and schooling at the other end (e.g.,

Gt, Gs, Gsm). Although the precise order of these abilities along such a continuum has not been well validated, an examination of the developmental growth curves of the broad CHC abilities (McGrew, Werder, & Woodcock, 1991; McGrew & Woodcock; 2001) provides some empirical evidence that can be used to guide placement of abilities on the continuum in Figure 2.4.[3] A growth curve is essentially a graphical representation of the phase or phases in development that occur for a particular cognitive ability as a function of age. Examination of growth curves related to the stores of acquired knowledge that typically reflect achievement abilities (e.g., *Gq, Grw*) are seen to be distinct from the growth curves of the process-oriented abilities that are more maturationally related (e.g., *Gv, Glr*, etc.). For example, CHC ability growth curves that are characterized by relatively little change with age represent those abilities that are believed to be much less influenced by formal educational training, acculturation, and learning, with the exception of *Gs* (McGrew, Werder, & Woodcock, 1991). An example of this type of growth curve for *Glr* is illustrated in Figure 2.5. Abilities that tend to show similar and rather characteristically flat growth patterns, particularly during the schooling years, are depicted on the left side of the ability continuum in Figure 2.4. Conversely, those abilities that tend to show a marked increase in the rate of developmental change coinciding roughly with the school-aged years, are depicted as falling to the right side of the ability continuum in Figure 2.4. An example of this type of growth curve for *Grw* is also illustrated in Figure 2.5. As is evident in the illustration, the rate of growth for these types of abilities is generally greater than the rate of development associated with the abilities that fall to the left side precisely because of the introduction of formal, school-based training, education, and classroom learning experiences.

FIGURE 2.5   Developmental Growth Curve for Long-Term Storage and Retrieval (*Glr*) and Reading (*Grw-R*)

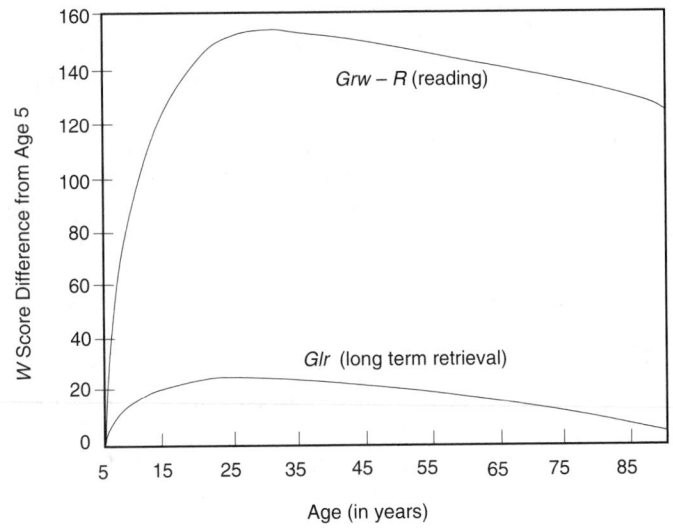

Source: Adapted from K. S. McGrew and R. W. Woodcock, *WJ III Technical Manual* (Itasca, IL: Riverside Publishing, 2001), pp. 55–58. Used by permission. (See copyright page of this text for full credit citation.)

Because abilities such as *Gq* and *Grw* represent more specialized types of knowledges that have been accumulated primarily through formal educational experiences, they are logically referred to as *academic abilities* (or achievements) rather than "cognitive" abilities. Conversely, because the abilities at the opposite end of this continuum reflect those that develop more through real-world learning or informal, general life experiences, they are more appropriately referred to as *cognitive abilities.* However, Figure 2.4 shows that the distinction is not discrete, especially as it applies to the abilities that fall toward the center of the continuum. Interestingly, it is precisely these abilities (e.g., *Gc*) that are measured consistently by both intelligence and achievement batteries. As such, there are times that specific *Gc* abilities, for example, are in fact conceived of as cognitive in nature (e.g., verbal ability as represented by a Wechsler Verbal IQ) and, at other times, academic (e.g., lexical knowledge). It is important to remember that the differentiation in factors within the CHC model (e.g., 10 different broad stratum II abilities) is evident, in part, because of the varying experiences of individuals. However, this does not rule out the possibility that genetic factors also influence this differentiation (see Carroll, 1993). Indeed, "most abilities develop from extensive experience across learning history. . . . And ability differences are influenced by genetic factors as well as by experience" (Snow, 1994, p. 4).

The Relationship between Cognitive Abilities and Achievement

A useful and practical theoretical model of cognitive abilities does not end with specification of its various constructs. Indeed, CHC theory in and of itself would be of little use in assessment if it did not extend further than simply providing categories for different abilities. A useful theory needs to specify the relationships between such constructs in order to provide a suitable vehicle for deriving meaning. Without knowing the relationships between the composite elements, the ability to test hypotheses is negated and it becomes impossible to provide any rationale for decisions involved in assessment. Therefore, it is not surprising that CHC theory is discussed herein because this is precisely another area in which it distinguishes itself from alternative theoretical models. Not only are such specifications provided in the model but there is also considerable research in most cases to support them. Next is a discussion of the relationship between the various cognitive abilities and processes that underlie the major areas of achievement—namely, reading, math, and writing.[4]

Cognitive Abilities and Reading Achievement

Although achievement batteries are generally the preferred instrument for assessing basic reading and reading comprehension skills, cognitive batteries are often used to assess abilities and processes that are related to reading. Table 2.11 lists CHC-designed studies, independent research studies, and reviews on the relationship between cognitive abilities or processes and reading achievement. A review of the studies included in this table suggests a number of conclusions regarding the relations between CHC abilities and reading achievement. First, narrow abilities subsumed by *Ga*, *Gc*, *Glr*, *Gsm*, and *Gs* displayed the most consistent significant relations with reading achievement. Measures of phonological processing

TABLE 2.11   Research on the Relations Between CHC Abilities and Reading Achievement

Type of Research	Fluid Intelligence (*Gf*)	Crystallized Intelligence(*Gc*)	Short-Term Memory(*Gsm*)
Key CHC Studies	McGrew (1993)	Flanagan et al. (2000) Garcia & Stafford (2000) McGrew (1993) McGrew et al. (1997)	McGrew (1993)
Reviews		Aaron (1995) Johnson (1993) Joshi (1995) Just & Carpenter (1992) Kintsch (1988) Lohman (1989) Palinscar & Perry (1995)	Daneman & Merikle (1996) Felton & Pepper (1995) Just & Carpenter (1992) Torgensen (1988) Torgesen & Wagner (1998)
Individual Studies	Santos (1989)	Badian (1988) Booth & Hall (1994) Bowey et al. (1992) Bowey & Patel (1988) Bryant et al. (1989) Carnine et al. (1984) Das & Siu (1982) Engle et al. (1990) Griswold et al. (1987) Jackson et al. (1988) Leather & Henry (1994) MacDonald & Cornwall (1995) McGuinness et al. (1995) Metsala (1997) Mills & Jackson (1990) Sears & Keogh (1993) Snider (1989) Snider & Tarver (1987) Stanovich et al. (1984) Wagner et al. (1997)	Berninger et al. (1994) Bowey et al. (1992) Bowey & Patel (1988) Cormier & Dea (1997) Daneman et al. (1995) Daneman & Carpenter (1980) DeJong & van der Leij (1999) Das & Siu (1982) Engle et al. (1990) Engle et al. (1992) Jackson et al. (1988) John (1998) John & Rattan (1991) Mann & Liberman (1984) Montgomery (1995) Shankweiler et al. (1979) Stahl & Murray (1994) Swanson (1992) Swanson (1994) Swanson & Berninger (1995) Swanson & Berninger (1996) Turner & Engle (1989) Vellutino et al. (1996) Wagner et al. (1993) Wagner et al. (1994) Watson & Willows (1995) Yuill et al. (1989)

TABLE 2.11 *Continued*

Visual Processing (*Gv*)	Auditory Processing (*Ga*)	Long-Term Retrieval (*Glr*)	Processing Speed (*Gs*)
	Flanagan et al. (2000) Garcia & Stafford (2000) McGrew (1993) McGrew et al. (1997)	McGrew (1993)	Flanagan et al. (2000) McGrew (1993) McGrew et al. (1997)
Kavale (1982)	Aaron (1995) Ball (1993) Farmer & Klein (1995) Felton & Pepper (1995) Hoskyn & Swanson (2000) Johnson (1993) Joshi (1995) Lyon (1995) McBride-Chang (1995) Palinscar & Perry (1995) Snyder & Downey (1997) Torgesen et al. (1994) Torgesen & Wagner (1998) Wagner & Torgesen (1987)	Aaron (1995) Denckla & Cutting (1999) Felton & Pepper (1995) Johnson (1993) Just & Carpenter (1992) Kavale (1982) Snyder & Downey (1997) Torgesen & Wagner (1998)	Aaron (1995) Greene & Royer (1994)
Eden et al. (1996) Gupta & Garg (1996) Jackson et al. (1988)	Berninger et al. (1994) Berninger et al. (1999) Bowers et al. (1999) Bowey (1995) Bowey et al. (1992) Bowey & Patel (1988) Brady et al. (1983) Bryant et al. (1989) Byrne et al. (1995) Catts (1993) Cormier & Dea (1997) Cronin & Carver (1998) DeJong & van der Leij (1999) Gupta & Garg (1996) Iversen & Tunmer (1993) Leather & Henry (1994) Lennon & Slesinski (1999) Levy et al. (1999) MacDonald & Cronwall (1995) Mann & Liberman (1984) Margolese & Kline (1999) McGuinness et al. (1995) Metsala (1997) O'Connor et al. (1995) Shankweiler et al. (1979) Spector (1992) Stahl & Murray (1994) Stanovich et al. (1984) Swanson et al. (1999) Torgesen et al. (1999) Uhry (1993) van Daal & van der Leij (1999) Vellutino et al. (1996) Wagner et al. (1993) Wagner et al. (1994) Wagner et al. (1997) Wimmer et al. (1998) Yopp (1988)	Abbott & Berninger (1999) Badian et al. (1991) Bear & Barone (1991) Berninger et al. (1997) Berninger et al. (1999) Catts (1993) Cronin & Carver (1998) Das & Siu (1982) DeJong & van der Leij (1999) Fletcher et al. (1994) Jackson et al. (1988) Joshi & Aaron (2000) Levy et al. (1999) Manis et al. (1999) McGuinness et al. (1995) Meyer et al. (1998) Mills & Jackson (1990) O'Connor et al. (1995) Scarborough (1998) Sinatra & Royer (1993) Stanovich & Siegel (1994) Swanson (1982) Swanson (1986) Torgesen et al. (1997) van Daal & van der Leij (1999) Vellutino et al. (1996) Wagner et al. (1993) Wagner et al. (1994) Wagner et al. (1997) Watson & Willows (1995) Wolf (1991) Young & Bowers (1995)	Baker et al. (1984) Decker & DeFries (1980) LaBada & DeFries (1988) Watson & Willows (1995)

or awareness (e.g., Phonetic Coding [PC], which is subsumed by *Ga*) showed strong and consistent relations with reading achievement across many studies, especially during the early elementary school years (mainly, kindergarten through third grade). *Gc* abilities, which were typically represented by measures of Lexical Knowledge (VL), Listening Ability (LS), and Language Development (LD), were also significantly related to reading achievement. As reported in some of the key CHC studies (e.g., Garcia & Stafford, 2000; McGrew, 1993; McGrew et al., 1997), the significant effects of *Ga* and *Gc* on reading were present even after the powerful effect of *g* was accounted for in the analyses. That is, specific CHC abilities contributed significantly to the explanation of reading above and beyond the significant and large effect of *g*.

The importance of *Gsm* for reading achievement (as suggested by the number of studies listed under *Gsm* in Table 2.11) needs qualification. Most of the studies listed under *Gsm* in Table 2.11 used measures of working memory (WM). The studies that reported significant relationships between measures of working memory and reading indicate that *Gsm* abilities most likely contribute to reading achievement through their involvement during the working memory processes. Support for a significant relation between *Gsm* and reading achievement independent of the working memory literature was present in the significant *Gsm* (Memory Span) and reading achievement relations reported by McGrew (1993). Taken as a whole, the research studies listed in Table 2.11 suggest that *Gsm*, particularly working memory, contributes significantly to the prediction of reading achievement.

The significant studies listed under *Glr* in Table 2.11 are predominantly from investigations that examined the relations between Rapid Automatic Naming (RAN) (i.e., Naming Facility [NA], which is subsumed by *Glr*) and reading achievement, especially during the early elementary school years (e.g., Geary, 1993; Marjoribanks, 1976; Rasanen & Ahonen, 1995). McGrew's (1993) key CHC study reported significant relations between measures of Associative Memory (MA) (another narrow ability subsumed by *Glr*) and reading at only a small number of age levels (i.e., age 6 with reading decoding, late adulthood with reading comprehension). Thus, the preponderance of the significant *Glr* literature reviewed suggests that Naming Facility or RAN is an important predictor of early reading achievement (e.g., Johnson, 1993; Scarborough, 1998; Young & Bowers, 1995).

Although no reviews and only a handful of individual studies were listed under *Gs* in Table 2.11, the strength of the *Gs* effects found in the key CHC studies cannot be ignored. For example, McGrew (1993) and McGrew and colleagues (1997) found a strong relation between Perceptual Speed (P), a narrow *Gs* ability, and reading achievement throughout the elementary school years. The effect of *Gs* was present even after the effect of *g* was accounted for in the McGrew and colleagues' (1997) study. Thus, as with *Ga* and *Gc*, *Gs* explains significant variance in reading achievement above and beyond the variance explained by *g*.

The small number of studies listed under *Gf* and *Gv* in Table 2.11 indicates that these two broad abilities are related less to reading achievement than are the other broad abilities. The significant *Gf* findings reported by McGrew (1993) were only for reading comprehension, not reading decoding. This suggests that the comprehension of text may draw on an individual's deductive and inductive reasoning abilities, depending on the demands of the comprehension task. With regard to *Gv*, only two studies reported a significant relation between *Gv* and reading achievement. No relation between *Gv* and reading achievement was found in the key CHC studies. Therefore, it appears that *Gv* abilities do not play a significant role in reading achievement. This does not mean that visual processing abilities are not involved during reading. The lack of significant *Gv*/reading research findings indicates that the contribution of *Gv* abilities (as measured by the major intelligence batteries) to the explanation and prediction of reading achievement is so small that, when compared to other abilities (e.g., *Ga*), it is of little practical significance. However, it is important not to overgeneralize this conclusion to all visual abilities. As pointed out by Berninger (1990), visual perceptual abilities should not be confused with abilities that are related to the coding of visual information in printed words (i.e., orthographic code processing)—visual processes thought to be important during reading.

In summary, narrow abilities in five broad CHC domains appear to be related significantly to reading achievement. The literature reviewed here suggests that abilities subsumed by *Gc* (Language Development, Lexical Knowledge, General Information), *Gsm* (Memory Span, Working Memory), *Ga* (Phonetic Coding), *Glr* (Associative Memory, Naming Facility), and *Gs* (Perceptual Speed) are related significantly to reading achievement (see Tables 2.2., 2.5, 2.7, 2.8, and 2.9, respectively, for definitions of these narrow abilities). Furthermore, the developmental results reported in the key CHC studies suggest that the *Ga*, *Gs*, and *Glr* relations with reading are strongest during the early elementary school years, after which they systematically decrease in strength (e.g., McGrew, 1993). In contrast, the strength of the relations between *Gc* abilities and reading achievement increases with age. *Gf* abilities appear related primarily to reading comprehension from childhood to young adulthood. Finally, *Gv* abilities appear largely unrelated to reading achievement in school-aged children. Given the importance of linking assessments to academic outcomes, additional studies are needed that are designed to investigate specifically the relations between valid measures of CHC abilities and reading achievement. Such research would elucidate the nature of the relations between broad and narrow CHC abilities and reading at different developmental periods.

Cognitive Abilities and Math Achievement

Although there were fewer research studies that investigated the relations between CHC abilities and math achievement (see Table 2.12), as compared to reading achievement (Table 2.11), the relatively equal distribution of studies listed under the respective CHC abilities for math achievement suggests that a greater breadth of CHC abilities is related significantly to this skill, as compared to reading. Similar to reading, evidence from all three types of research (i.e., key CHC studies, reviews, and individual studies) suggests that *Gc*, *Gsm* (particularly working memory), and *Gs* are related significantly to math achievement. In contrast to reading, evidence was also found for the importance of *Gf* and *Gv* abilities in predicting and explaining math achievement.

In the key CHC study of McGrew and Hessler (1995), *Gf*, *Gc*, and *Gs* abilities correlated consistently and significantly with mathematics achievement. However, there were developmental differences. The *Gc* relation with mathematics achievement increased monotonically with age, whereas the *Gs* relation was strongest during the elementary school years, after which it decreased (although the relationship remained significant well into

TABLE 2.12 Research on the Relations between CHC Abilities and Mathematics Achievement

Type of Research	Fluid Intelligence (*Gf*)	Crystallized Intelligence (*Gc*)	Short-Term Memory (*Gsm*)	Visual Processing (*Gv*)	Long-Term Retrieval (*Glr*)	Processing Speed (*Gs*)
Key CHC Studies	McGrew et al. (1997) McGrew & Hessler (1995)	McGrew et al. (1997) McGrew & Hessler (1995)	McGrew & Hessler (1995)			McGrew et al. (1997) McGrew & Hessler (1995)
Reviews	Carroll & Maxwell (1979)	Carroll & Maxwell (1979) Friedman (1995)	Geary (1993) Snow & Swanson (1992)	Bishop (1980) Carroll & Maxwell (1979) Friedman (1995) Geary (1993) Snow & Swanson (1992)	Geary (1993)	Carroll & Maxwell (1979) Geary (1993)
Individual Studies	Benbow (1992) Benbow & Arjmand (1990) Hakstian & Bennet (1977) Manger & Eikeland (1996) Taylor et al. (1976)	Benbow (1992) Hale (1981) Marjoribanks (1976) Rasanen & Ahonen (1995) Taylor et al. (1976)	Cooney & Swanson (1990) DeJong & van der Leij (1999) Hitch (1978) Kail & Hall (1999) Lehto (1995) Lemaire et al. (1996) Rasanen & Ahonen (1995) Swanson (1994) Swanson (1996) Webster (1979)	Casey et al. (1997) Hakstian & Bennet (1977) Hegarty & Kozhevni-kov (1999) Marjoribanks (1976) Stevenson et al. (1976) Swanson (1996) Taylor et al. (1976)	Marjoribanks (1976) Rasanen & Ahonen (1995) Stevenson et al. (1976)	Ackerman et al. (1986) Hakstain & Bennett (1977) Kail & Hall (1999) Kirby & Becker (1988) McGrew & Pehl (1988) Rasanen & Ahonen (1995) Stevenson et al. (1976)

adulthood). *Gf* was related consistently to mathematics achievement at levels higher than all other CHC abilities (except *Gc*) across all ages. As in the reading achievement research just mentioned, certain specific abilities (*Gf, Gs, Gc*) were found to be related significantly to mathematics achievement above and beyond the contribution of *g* (McGrew et al., 1997).

It is interesting to note that when the reading and math achievement results are compared, *Ga* and *Gf* abilities appear to be differentially important for the prediction of each achievement domain, respectively. *Ga* abilities are related significantly to reading achievement but not to math achievement, whereas *Gf* abilities are related significantly to math achievement and less so to reading achievement. This finding has implications for the design of assessments that seek to address specific referral questions (see Flanagan, McGrew, & Ortiz, 2000; Flanagan & Ortiz, 2001; McGrew & Flanagan, 1998).

No significant relations between *Gv* and *Glr* and mathematics achievement were found in the key CHC studies and only one review reported a significant correlation between *Glr* and math achievement (Geary, 1993). This suggests that, until further research examines the relations between *Glr* abilities and mathematics achievement more completely, the importance of *Glr* for math achievement remains in question. In contrast, a review of the *Gv* studies suggest that *Gv* abilities are not significantly related to basic math achievement (e.g., addition, subtraction), but, instead, may be related to performance on tasks that require advanced and higher-level math skills and thinking (e.g., geometry, calculus, and trigonometry). As is the case for reading, additional research with validated CHC measures is needed to clarify the nature of the relations between broad and narrow cognitive abilities and math achievement.

Cognitive Abilities and Writing Achievement

A review of Table 2.13 demonstrates that several CHC domains are related to writing achievement. Specifically, researchers have documented relations between cognitive abilities and writing achievement across the seven CHC domains listed in Table 2.13 (*Gf, Gc, Gsm, Gv, Ga, Glr,* and *Gs*). However, the limited number of studies in certain CHC domains clearly suggests that the consistency of relations differs markedly across areas. For instance, only one key CHC study demonstrated a relation between *Gf* abilities and writing achievement. Specifically, McGrew and Knopik (1993) found that fluid reasoning abilities (i.e., induction and general sequential reasoning) were significantly related to basic writing skills primarily during the elementary school years (i.e., ages 6 to 13) and significantly related to written expression across all ages.

Similarly, the study by McGrew and Knopik (1993) provided evidence for the role of *Gs* abilities in writing. More specifically, this study demonstrated that the *Gs* cluster (comprised of measures of perceptual speed) "was significantly related to Basic Writing Skills during the school years . . . after which it decreased in strength of association" (p. 690) with age. The relations between *Gs* and written expression were more consistent in strength across ages. As explained by McGrew and Knopik, "Given the timed nature of the Writing Fluency tests that comprises one-half of the Written Expression cluster, the finding of consistently significant associations between Processing Speed and this writing achievement criterion was not surprising" (p. 692).

TABLE 2.13 Research on the Relations between CHC Abilities and Writing Achievement

Type of Research	Fluid Intelligence (*Gf*)	Crystallized Intelligence (*Gc*)	Short-Term Memory (*Gsm*)	Visual Processing (*Gv*)	Auditory Processing (*Ga*)	Long-Term Retrieval (*Glr*)	Processing Speed (*Gs*)
Key CHC Studies	McGrew & Knopik (1993)	McGrew & Knopik (1993)				McGrew & Knopik (1993)	McGrew & Knopik (1993)
Reviews		Johnson (1993)	Johnson (1993)		Johnson (1993) Joshi (1995)	Johnson (1993)	
Individual Studies		McCutchen et al. (1997)	Berninger et al. (1994) Cormier & Dea (1997) Lehto (1996) McCutchen et al. (1994) Steffler et al. (1998) Swanson & Berninger (1996) Treiman et al. (1993)	Aaron (1995)	Aaron (1995) Abbott & Berninger (1993) Ball & Blachman (1991) Berninger et al. (1994) Cormier & Dea (1997) Leong (1999) Stahl & Murray (1994) Steffler et al. (1998) Treiman et al. (1993) Vernon & Ferreiro (1999)	McCutchen et al. (1994)	Williams et al. (1993)

Similar to McGrew and Knopik's (1993) findings, Williams and associates (1993) also reported significant relations between *Gs* and writing abilities. Specifically, their study demonstrated relations between the WISC-III Coding subtest (a measure of perceptual speed) and the WJ-R Writing Fluency test. Given these findings, it seems likely that perceptual speed is important in terms of writing automaticity, rather than writing mechanics or writing quality. Although no reviews and only one individual study are listed under *Gs* in Table 2.13, the strength of the *Gs* effects demonstrated in McGrew and Knopik (1993) is significant and warrants further investigation.

Research on the relations between *Gv* and writing achievement is extremely sparse, suggesting the need for continued investigation. Because only one study reported a significant relation between *Gv* and writing achievement (see Table 2.13) and no key CHC studies or reviews substantiated this finding, it may be that *Gv* abilities as assessed by the major intelligence batteries do not play a significant role in writing achievement. This is not to say that *Gv* abilities are unimportant for writing. In fact, an ability known as *orthographic processing* is particularly influential in basic writing tasks (e.g., spelling). As explained by Aaron (1995), *orthography* refers to the visual patterns of the written language. However, "orthographic processing ability is not the same as visual memory even though visual memory may play a role in it" (Aaron, 1995, p. 347). Specifically, some researchers have indicated that a certain type of memory for orthographic units may play a role in spelling words that cannot be accurately spelled using the rules of pronunciation alone. (See Kreiner and Gough [1990] for a more in-depth discussion.) Despite the role that orthographic knowledge plays in basic writing tasks, this relation is not evident in Table 2.13, primarily because CHC theory does not have a narrow-ability category corresponding to this type of knowledge and few, if any, standardized tests exist that measure orthographic processing. The *Gv* abilities that comprise CHC theory (e.g., visualization, spatial relations, visual memory, etc.; see Table 2.6) appear to be minimally related to writing achievement. Perhaps *Gv*-type abilities, such as orthographic processing, that may be related to writing achievement have not been identified in the literature because they have not yet been properly or accurately incorporated within the CHC theoretical framework. Clearly, this is an area where there is considerable room for research on expanding the range of abilities specified under CHC theory.

The research on the relations between *Glr* and *Gc* and writing achievement is also sparse, as may be seen in Table 2.13. The fact that only two studies documented a significant relation between *Glr* and writing suggests that either *Glr* abilities are of limited importance to the writing process or the importance of *Glr* in writing ability has not been investigated thoroughly. Accordingly, definitive conclusions regarding the role that *Glr* may or may not play in the development of writing achievement cannot be made at this time and await further empirical investigation. In terms of *Gc*, McGrew and Knopik (1993) found significant relations among language development (LD), lexical knowledge (VL), general information (K0), and writing abilities (i.e., basic writing skills and written expression).

Despite the limited research on the relations between CHC abilities and writing achievement, Table 2.13 shows that *Ga* and *Gsm* displayed the most consistent significant relations with overall writing achievement. Additionally, Phonetic Coding, a narrow *Ga* ability, was found to have a strong and consistent relation with writing achievement across many studies, especially during the early elementary school years (kindergarten through third grade) (e.g., Berninger et al., 1994; Johnson, 1993; Joshi, 1995; McGrew & Knopik,

1993). Finally, the majority of studies listed under *Gsm* in Table 2.13 investigated the relations between memory span (MS) and writing achievement. Findings from these studies were consistent and suggested that memory span is an important predictor of early writing achievement.

Overall, several CHC abilities are related significantly to writing achievement. Among these, the most consistent relations appear to be with *Ga* (phonetic coding), *Gsm* (memory span), and *Gs* (perceptual speed). Although *Gc* abilities (lexical knowledge, language development, and general information) were also found to predict writing achievement significantly, more research is needed to replicate the existing research in this area. The limited research on the relations between cognitive abilities and writing achievement may be related, in part, to the fact that writing research has taken a tertiary position compared to reading and math research. That is, although the early pioneering literature on learning disabilities emphasized both writing and reading disabilities, the subsequent learning disabilities literature has given more attention to reading than writing (Berninger, 1997). Given the importance of writing throughout one's educational (and often, professional) careers, the field would benefit from additional research within this domain.

In summary, Tables 2.11 through 2.13 presented the available literature on the relations between cognitive abilities and reading, math, and writing achievement, respectively. Table 2.14 provides a summary of the specific or narrow CHC abilities that emerged from the literature as the most important in explaining academic achievement. For example, narrow abilities subsumed by *Gc* (lexical knowledge, language development, listening ability), *Gsm* (working memory), *Ga* (phonetic coding), *Glr* (naming facility), and *Gs* (perceptual speed) were found to be significantly related to reading achievement. Similarly, narrow abilities within these same broad abilities were found to be related to writing achievement. With the exception of *Glr*, *Ga*, and *Gv*, narrow abilities within the areas of *Gf*, *Gc*, *Gsm*, and *Gs* were found to relate significantly to math achievement, with *Gf* (induction and general sequential reasoning) showing a stronger relation to this academic area than either reading or writing. The information in this table can be used to identify those CHC abilities that should receive primary consideration in the design of assessments for individuals referred for reading, math, and writing difficulties.

Conclusions

CHC theory represents a well-validated structure of abilities. Measurement of these abilities requires an individual to perform some specified mental act or task, and such performance requires suitable processing of mental information for success (see Figure 2.4). Although the tasks included on intelligence and achievement batteries reflect a broad range of an individual's abilities, use of the adjectives *academic* and *cognitive* assist in distinguishing those abilities that develop more or less as a function of formal, school-based learning, educational experiences, and acculturation, respectively.

There are several advantages to conceptualizing academic and cognitive abilities within a comprehensive theoretical framework. For example, such a framework provides professionals with a standard nomenclature (i.e., a common set of terms and definitions) that will facilitate communication and may yield the ultimate benefit of reducing or eliminating

TABLE 2.14 Summary of Findings on Relations between CHC Abilities and Academic Achievement

CHC Ability	Reading Achievement	Math Achievement	Writing Achievement
Gf	Inductive (I) and general sequential reasoning (RG) abilities play a moderate role in reading comprehension.	**Inductive (I) and general sequential (RG) reasoning abilities are consistently very important at all ages.**	Inductive (I) and general sequential reasoning abilities are related to basic writing skills primarily during the elementary school years (e.g., 6 to 13) and consistently related to written expression at all ages.
Gc	**Language development (LD), lexical knowledge (VL), and listening ability (LS) are important at all ages. These abilities become increasingly more important with age.**	**Language development (LD), lexical knowledge (VL), and listening ability (LS) are important at all ages. These abilities become increasingly more important with age.**	**Language development (LD), lexical knowledge (VL), and general information (K0) are important primarily after age 7. These abilities become increasingly more important with age.**
Gsm	**Memory span (MS) is important especially when evaluated within the context of working memory.**	Memory span (MS) is important especially when evaluated **within the context of working memory.**	Memory span (MS) is important to writing, especially spelling skills whereas working memory has shown relations with advanced writing skills (e.g., written expression).
Gv		May be important primarily for higher level or advanced mathematics (e.g., geometry, calculus).	
Ga	**Phonetic coding (PC) or "phonological awareness/processing" is very important during the elementary school years.**		**Phonetic coding (PC) or "phonological awareness/processing" is very important during the elementary school years for both basic writing skills and written expression (primarily before age 11).**
Glr	**Naming facility (NA) or "rapid automatic naming" is very important during the elementary school years.** Associative memory (MA) may be somewhat important at select ages (e.g., age 6).		Naming facility (NA) or "rapid automatic naming" has demonstrated relations with written expression, primarily the fluency aspect of writing.
Gs	**Perceptual speed (P) is important during all school years, particularly the elementary school years.**	**Perceptual speed (P) is important during all school years, particularly the elementary school years.**	**Perceptual speed (P) is important during all school years for basic writing and related to all ages for written expression.**

Note: The absence of comments for a particular CHC ability and achievement area (e.g., *Ga* and mathematics) indicates that the research reviewed either did not report any significant relations between the respective CHC ability and the achievement area, or if significant findings were reported, they were weak and were for only a limited number of studies. Comments in bold represent the CHC abilities that showed the strongest and most consistent relations with the respective achievement domain. Information in this table is from McGrew and Flanagan (1998) and Flanagan, McGrew, and Ortiz (2000), reprinted by permission from Allyn & Bacon.

miscommunication and misinterpretation. In addition, the extant validity research on the relations between and among the abilities specified in the CHC model can be used to (1) organize assessments that are closely in line with referral information, (2) guide interpretation, and (3) provide data that can be more readily linked to appropriate intervention. A comprehensive and well-validated theoretical framework, therefore, like CHC theory, guides the selection of tests and specification of abilities that are germane and unique to the individual case and allows for interpretations to follow directly from what is known about the theory. Evaluations of individuals with learning difficulties that are *theory focused* and grounded in current research are more psychometrically respectable and have more accountability than those that are *test-kit focused* or devoid of a firm grounding in contemporary theory and research.

Endnotes

1. It is important not to conceive of abilities that have low correlations with *g* (i.e., abilities located furthest to the right in Carroll's model) as unimportant. For example, abilities such as *Gs* appear to be important in understanding reading, math, and writing achievement. The reader is referred to Flanagan, McGrew, and Ortiz (2000) for a discussion.

2. Recently, John Horn and John Carroll agreed that "modern *Gf-Gc* theory," which encompasses both their models, should be referred to as the "Cattell-Horn-Carroll theory of cognitive abilities" or "CHC theory" (R. Woodcock, personal communication, July 16, 1999).

3. Growth curves are based on cross-sectional data, not longitudinal data. They show the rise and decline of median performance across age for the general population (see McGrew, Werder, & Woodcock, 1991; McGrew & Woodcock, 2001).

4. Studies included in this literature review were identified via several methods. First, research studies that investigated the relations between cognitive, reading, math, and writing achievement that were cited in the electronic database PSYC INFO were identified and reviewed. Second, an ancestral search strategy (i.e., locating key studies cited in other studies) was used to identify other potentially relevant studies. Third, the previous literature reviews conducted by McGrew and Flanagan (1998) were reviewed and incorporated into the current presentation of results. Studies included in Tables 2.11 through 2.13 were classified according to whether they were *key CHC studies* (studies designed expressly to examine the relations between multiple CHC abilities and school achievement across a wide age range), *reviews* (narrative or meta-analytic review of literature), or *individual investigations* (single research studies not considered to be "key" studies).

Introduction to the ATDR

Chapter 2 presented a discussion of a comprehensive theoretical framework for conceptualizing cognitive and academic abilities, called the Cattell-Horn-Carroll theory of cognitive abilities (or CHC theory). This well-validated theory is particularly useful to practitioners who engage in assessment-related activities, because it serves to guide measurement and interpretation better than that which can be accomplished through the application of most existing theories and methods. Not only does the practice of firmly grounding assessment-related activities in contemporary theory and research help to advance the science of assessment, but knowledge of the characteristics of the tests themselves can also guide test selection and interpretation. For example, in addition to understanding what construct(s) a test measures from the perspective of contemporary theory, knowledge of a test's psychometric properties (e.g., reliability, floors and ceilings) and qualitative characteristics (e.g., length of test, type of response required) can significantly inform the decisions that are made about the appropriateness of a specific test for a select population (e.g., dual language learners). The psychometric and qualitative characteristics of individual tests also guide interpretation, for example, because the reliability of a test determines, in part, whether the instrument should be used for screening or diagnostic purposes. The primary purpose of this chapter is to describe the most important characteristics of new and commonly used achievement tests and their relevance to various decisions inherent in the assessment process. This information will be presented and evaluated in the *Desk Reference* section of this book (i.e., Chapters 4 through 10).

Chapters 4 through 10 provide a comprehensive description of the critical features of individually administered *achievement* tests, and are referred to collectively as the *Achievement Test Desk Reference (ATDR)*. The information contained in the *Desk Reference* section of this book (Chapters 4–10) is presented in a visual, easy-to-read, graphic format. Similar to McGrew and Flanagan's (1998) *Intelligence Test Desk Reference (ITDR),* this *Desk Reference* evaluates tests from a wide range of academic achievement and related processing batteries (as opposed to tests of cognitive processes and abilities) according to a set of common criteria. The test batteries included in this Desk Reference are listed in Table 3.1.

The achievement batteries in this table are organized into three broad categories: (1) comprehensive batteries (2) brief or screening instruments, and (3) specific academic skills tests (i.e., reading, math, written language, oral language, and phonological processing). Achievement tests were placed into one of these three categories according to their intended purpose as expressed by the test's author(s) and publisher. For example, some achievement batteries are intended to be *comprehensive* in that they are designed to assess a wide range of academic abilities (e.g., reading, math, written expression, and listening comprehension). Table 3.1 shows that the Wechsler Individual Achievement Test–Second Edition (WIAT–II; Psychological Corporation, 2001) and Woodcock-Johnson Tests of Achievement III (WJ III: ACH; Woodcock, McGrew, & Mather, 2001) fit into this category. Other tests are intended to be used as *brief* or *screening* instruments. These tests are significantly shorter than the comprehensive tests and were not expressly designed to provide an in-depth assessment of achievement in any given domain. Table 3.1 shows that the Mini-Battery of Achievement (MBA; Woodcock, McGrew, & Werder, 1994) and Wide Range Achievement Test 3 (WRAT 3; Wilkinson, 1993) fit into this category. Finally, some achievement tests were developed to measure only one *specific academic skill,* such as reading or math, or a specific *processing ability* that underlies specific academic skill development. These tests vary in length and some provide a more in-depth assessment of a given domain than others. Table 3.1 shows that tests such as the KeyMath-Revised/Normative Update (KM-R/NU; Connolly, 1998) and the Woodcock Diagnostic Reading Battery (WDRB; Woodcock, 1997) fall into this category. A total of 50 complete achievement batteries and their individual subtests are listed in Table 3.1.

Inclusion of tests and test batteries in the *ATDR* was based on the following specific criteria:

1. Tests must have been published no later than 1993. Tests that were published prior to 1993 were not included because their respective normative data would be considered outdated (i.e., more than 10 years old) about the time of this book's publication.
2. Tests must be designed specifically as or considered an appropriate measure of an area of achievement corresponding to one or more of the areas of academic functioning specifically listed in the definition of learning disability (LD) contained in the Individuals with Disabilities Education Act (IDEA).
3. Tests had to be normed on a sample taken from the United States.
4. Tests had to include age-based norms in order to allow for the application and use of CHC Cross-Battery assessment methods and procedures. Tests that contained only grade-based norms were therefore not included in the *ATDR.*

For tests that met each of these criteria, the psychometric properties, qualitative descriptions, and theoretical classifications of each battery (and component subtests within the battery) listed in Table 3.1 are presented on "summary pages" in the *Desk Reference* using a standard nomenclature and a uniform format (see Chapters 4 through 10). The third column in Table 3.1 provides the page number that corresponds to each individual subtest's summary page. The last column in this table provides the page number that corresponds to each individual subtest's task characteristics (e.g., task demands, nature of test stimuli, type of response required, etc.).

The remainder of this chapter is organized into four main sections. First, psychometric test characteristics are described and the procedures for reporting and evaluating these characteristics are presented. Second, pertinent theoretical information for the tests comprising the major achievement batteries is reviewed. Third, qualitative information for the major achievement batteries is presented. Fourth, the achievement test summary pages of the *Desk Reference* are described.

(text continues on page 73)

TABLE 3.1 Test Batteries and Component Subtests Included in the *ATDR*

Comprehensive Test Batteries	Component Subtests	Summary Page #	Task Characteristic Page #
1. Diagnostic Achievement Battery–Third Edition (DAB–3)	Story Comprehension	98	519
	Characteristics	98	519
	Synonyms	99	522
	Grammatic Completion	99	522
	Alphabet/Word Knowledge	100	508
	Reading Comprehension	100	511
	Capitalization	101	513
	Punctuation	101	513
	Spelling	102	513
	Contextual Language	102	513
	Story Construction	103	513
	Math Reasoning	103	517
	Math Calculation	104	516
	Phonemic Analysis	104	508
2. Diagnostic Achievement Test for Adolescents–Second Edition (DATA–2)	Receptive Vocabulary	106	519
	Receptive Grammar	106	519
	Expressive Grammar	107	519
	Expressive Vocabulary	107	522
	Word Identification	108	508
	Reading Comprehension	108	511
	Math Calculation	109	516
	Math Problem Solving	109	517
	Spelling	110	513
	Writing Composition	110	513
	Science	111	
	Social Studies	111	
	Reference Skills	112	
3. Kaufman Test of Educational Achievement-Revised/ Normative Update (KTEA-R/ NU)	Mathematics Applications	114	517
	Reading Decoding	114	508
	Spelling	115	513
	Reading Comprehension	115	511
	Mathematics Computation	116	516
4. Peabody Individual Achievement Test-Revised/ Normative Update (PIAT-R/ NU)	General Information	118	
	Reading Recognition	118	508
	Reading Comprehension	119	511
	Mathematics	119	516
	Spelling	120	513
	Written Expression (Level I)	120	513
	Written Expression (Level II)	121	513

Continued

TABLE 3.1   *Continued*

5. Wechsler Individual Achievement Test–Second Edition (WIAT–II)	Word Reading	123	508
	Numerical Operations	123	516
	Reading Comprehension	124	511
	Spelling	124	513
	Pseudoword Decoding	125	508
	Mathematics Reasoning	125	517
	Written Expression	126	513
	Listening Comprehension	126	519
	Oral Expression	127	522
6. Woodcock-Johnson Tests of Achievement III (WJ III)	Letter-Word Identification	129	508
	Reading Fluency	129	508
	Story Recall	130	519
	Understanding Directions	130	519
	Calculation	131	516
	Math Fluency	131	516
	Spelling	132	513
	Writing Fluency	132	513
	Passage Comprehension	133	511
	Applied Problems	133	517
	Writing Samples	134	513
	Story Recall-Delayed	134	519
	Word Attack	135	508
	Picture Vocabulary	135	
	Oral Comprehension	136	519
	Editing	136	513
	Reading Vocabulary	137	508
	Quantitative Concepts	137	516
	Academic Knowledge	138	
	Spelling of Sounds	138	513
	Sound Awareness	139	508
	Punctuation and Capitalization	139	513

Brief/Screening Tests	Component Subtests	Summary Page #	Task Characteristic Page #
1. Hammill Multiability Achievement Test (HAMAT)	Reading	141	511
	Writing	141	513
	Arithmetic	142	516
	Facts	142	
2. Kaufman Functional Academic Skills Test (K-FAST)	Arithmetic	146	516
	Reading	146	511
3. Kaufman Survey of Early Academic and Language Skills (K-SEALS)	Vocabulary	148	
	Numbers, Letter, & Words	148	508, 516
4. Mini-Battery of Achievement (MBA)	Reading	150	508
	Writing	150	513
	Mathematics	151	517
	Factual Knowledge	151	

TABLE 3.1 *Continued*

5. Test of Academic Achievement Skills–Revised (TAAS–R)	Spelling	153	513
	Letter/Word Reading	153	508
	Listening Comprehension	154	519
	Arithmetic (Oral)	154	517
	Arithmetic (Written)	155	516
	Oral Reading Accuracy (Stories)	155	508
	Story Comprehension	156	511
6. Test of Children's Language (TOCL)	Spoken Language	158	519
	Knowledge of Print	158	508
	Word Recognition	159	508
	Reading Comprehension	159	511
	Writing Skills	160	513
	Writing from Memory	160	513
	Original Writing	161	513
7. Wide Range Achievement Test 3 (WRAT 3)	Reading	163	508
	Spelling	163	513
	Arithmetic	164	516
8. Young Children's Achievement Test (YCAT)	General Information	167	
	Reading	167	508
	Mathematics	168	516
	Writing	168	513
	Spoken Language	169	519

Specific Academic Skills— Reading Tests	Component Subtests	Summary Page #	Task Characteristic Page #
1. Gray Oral Reading Tests– Fourth Edition (GORT–4)	Rate	171	508
	Accuracy	171	508
	Fluency	172	508
	Comprehension	172	511
2. Gray Silent Reading Test (GSRT)	Silent Reading Comprehension	176	511
3. Standardized Reading Inventory–Second Edition (SRI–2)	Vocabulary in Context	178	511
	Word Recognition Accuracy	178	508
	Passage Comprehension	179	511
4. Test of Early Reading Ability– Third Edition (TERA–3)	Alphabet	182	508
	Conventions	182	508
	Meaning	183	511
5. Test of Reading Comprehension–Third Edition (TORC–3)	General Vocabulary	186	511
	Syntactic Similarities	186	511
	Paragraph Reading	187	511
	Sentence Sequencing	187	511
	Mathematics Vocabulary	188	
	Social Studies Vocabulary	188	
	Science Vocabulary	189	
	Reading the Directions of Schoolwork	189	511

Continued

TABLE 3.1   *Continued*

6. Test of Word Reading Efficiency (TOWRE)	Sight Word Efficiency	191	508
	Phonemic Decoding Efficiency	191	508
7. Woodcock Diagnostic Reading Battery (WDRB)	Letter-Word Identification	193	508
	Word Attack	193	508
	Reading Vocabulary	194	509
	Passage Comprehension	194	511
	Memory for Sentences	195	519
	Visual Matching	195	
	Incomplete Words	196	509
	Sound Blending	196	509
	Oral Vocabulary	197	522
	Listening Comprehension	197	519
8. Woodcock Reading Mastery Tests–Revised/Normative Update (WRMT–R/NU)	Visual-Auditory Learning	199	
	Letter Identification	199	509
	Supplementary Letter Checklist	200	509
	Word Identification	200	509
	Word Attack	201	509
	Word Comprehension	201	509
	Passage Comprehension	202	511

Specific Academic Skills— Math Tests	Component Subtests	Summary Page #	Task Characteristic Page #
1. KeyMath-Revised/Normative Update (KM-R/NU)	Numeration	205	516
	Rational Numbers	205	516
	Geometry	206	516
	Addition	206	516
	Subtraction	207	516
	Multiplication	207	516
	Division	208	516
	Mental Computation	208	516
	Measurement	209	516
	Time and Money	209	516
	Estimation	210	516
	Interpreting Data	210	517
	Problem Solving	211	517
2. Slosson-Diagnostic Math Screener (S-DMS)	Math Concepts	213	516
	Math Problem Solving	213	517
	Math Calculation	214	516
3. Test of Mathematical Abilities– Second Edition (TOMA–2)	Vocabulary	216	
	Computation	216	516
	General Information	217	516
	Story Problems	217	517
	Attitude Toward Math	218	

TABLE 3.1   *Continued*

Specific Academic Skills—Written Language Tests	Component Subtests	Summary Page #	Task Characteristic Page #
1. Oral and Written Language Scales: Written Expression (OWLS:WE)	Written Expression Scale	220	514
2. Test of Early Written Language–Second Edition (TEWL–2)	Basic Writing	222	514
	Contextual Writing	222	514
3. Test of Written Expression (TOWE)	Items	225	514
	Essay	225	514
4. Test of Written Language–Third Edition (TOWL–3)	Vocabulary	227	514
	Spelling	227	514
	Style	228	514
	Logical Sentences	228	514
	Sentence Combining	229	514
	Contextual Conventions	229	514
	Contextual Language	230	514
	Story Construction	230	514
5. Test of Written Spelling–Fourth Edition (TWS–4)		236	514

Specific Academic Skills—Oral Language Tests	Component Subtests	Summary Page #	Task Characteristic Page #
1. Clinical Evaluation of Language Fundamentals–Third Edition (CELF–3)	Sentence Structure	239	519
	Word Structure	239	519
	Concepts and Directions	240	519
	Formulated Sentences	240	522
	Word Classes	241	519
	Recalling Sentences	241	519
	Sentence Assembly	242	522
	Semantic Relationships	242	519
	Word Associations	243	522
	Listening to Paragraphs	243	519
	Rapid, Automatic Naming	244	

Continued

TABLE 3.1   *Continued*

2. Comprehensive Assessment of Spoken Language (CASL)	Comprehension of Basic Concepts	246	519
	Antonyms	246	522
	Synonyms	247	519
	Sentence Completions	247	519
	Idiomatic Language	248	519
	Syntax Construction	248	522
	Paragraph Comprehension of Syntax	249	519
	Grammatical Morphemes	249	522
	Sentence Comprehension of Syntax	250	519
	Grammaticality Judgment	250	519
	Nonliteral Language	251	522
	Meaning from Context	251	522
	Inference	252	519
	Ambiguous Sentences	252	522
	Pragmatic Judgment	253	522
3. Comprehensive Receptive & Expressive Vocabulary Test (CREVT)	Receptive Vocabulary	255	520
	Expressive Vocabulary	255	522
4. Comprehensive Receptive & Expressive Vocabulary Test–Adult (CREVT–A)	Receptive Vocabulary	258	520
	Expressive Vocabulary	258	522
5. Expressive One-Word Picture Vocabulary Test (EO-WPVT)	Expressive Vocabulary	261	522
6. Expressive Vocabulary Test (EVT)		263	522
7. Illinois Test of Psycholinguistic Abilities–Third Edition (ITPA–3)	Spoken Analogies	265	523
	Spoken Vocabulary	265	523
	Morphological Closure	266	523
	Syntactic Sentences	266	523
	Sound Deletion	267	509
	Rhyming Sequences	267	523
	Sentence Sequencing	268	511, 514
	Written Vocabulary	268	509
	Sight Decoding	269	509
	Sound Decoding	269	509
	Sight Spelling	270	514
	Sound Spelling	270	514
8. Language Processing Test–Revised (LPT–R)	Pretest 1	272	
	Pretest 2	272	523
	Associations	273	523
	Categorization	273	523
	Similarities	274	523
	Differences	274	523
	Multiple Meanings	275	523
	Attributes	275	523

TABLE 3.1   *Continued*

9. Oral and Written Language Scales–List. Comp/Oral Express. (OWLS: LC/OE)	Listening Comprehension Scale	277	520
	Oral Expression Scale	277	523
10. Peabody Picture Vocabulary Test III (PPVT III)	Form III	279	520
11. Receptive One-Word Picture Vocabulary Test (RO-WPVT)	Receptive Vocabulary	281	520
12. Test of Adolescent & Adult Language–Third Edition (TOAL–3)	Listening/Vocabulary	283	520
	Listening/Grammar	283	514, 520
	Speaking/Vocabulary	284	523
	Speaking/Grammar	284	520
	Reading/Vocabulary	285	509
	Reading/Grammar	285	511
	Writing/Vocabulary	286	514
	Writing/Grammar	286	514
13. Test of Early Language Development–Third Edition (TELD–3)	Receptive Language	288	520
	Expressive Language	288	523
14. Test of Language Development–Intermediate: Third Edition (TOLD–I:3)	Sentence Combining	291	514
	Picture Vocabulary	291	520
	Word Ordering	292	523
	Generals	292	523
	Grammatic Comprehension	293	520
	Malapropisms	293	520
15. Test of Language Development–Primary: Third Edition (TOLD–P:3)	Picture Vocabulary	295	520
	Relational Vocabulary	295	523
	Oral Vocabulary	296	523
	Grammatic Understanding	296	514, 520
	Sentence Imitation	297	520
	Grammatic Completion	297	514, 520
	Word Discrimination	298	
	Phonemic Analysis	298	509
	Word Articulation	299	523

Continued

TABLE 3.1 *Continued*

Specific Academic Skills—Phonological Processing Tests	Component Subtests	Summary Page #	Task Characteristic Page #
1. Comprehensive Test of Phonological Processing (CTOPP)	Elision	301	509
	Blending Words	301	509
	Sound Matching	302	509
	Memory for Digits	302	520
	Nonword Repetition	303	520
	Rapid Color Naming	303	522
	Rapid Object Naming	304	522
	Rapid Digit Naming	304	522
	Rapid Letter Naming	305	522
	Blending Nonwords	305	509
	Phoneme Reversal	306	509
	Segmenting Words	306	509
	Segmenting Nonwords	307	509
2. SCAN-C Test for Auditory Processing Disorders in Children–Revised (SCAN-C–R)	Filtered Words	309	
	Auditory Figure-Ground	309	
	Competing Words	310	
	Competing Sentences	310	
3. Test for Auditory Comprehension of Language–Third Edition (TACL–3)	Vocabulary	312	520
	Grammatical Morphemes	312	520
	Elaborated Phrases & Sentences	313	520
4. Test of Auditory-Perceptual Skills–Revised (TAPS–R)	Auditory Number Memory-Forward	315	520
	Auditory Number Memory-Reversed	315	520
	Auditory Sentences Memory	316	520
	Auditory Word Memory	316	520
	Auditory Interpretation of Directions	317	520
	Auditory Word Discrimination	317	
	Auditory Processing	318	
5. Test of Auditory-Perceptual Skills–Upper Level (TAPS–UL)	Auditory Number Memory-Forward	320	520
	Auditory Number Memory-Reversed	320	520
	Auditory Sentences Memory	321	520
	Auditory Word Memory	321	520
	Auditory Interpretation of Directions	322	520
	Auditory Word Discrimination	322	
	Auditory Processing	323	
6. Test of Phonological Awareness (TOPA)	Initial Sound	325	509
	Ending Sound	325	

Psychometric Characteristics of Achievement Batteries

In their *Ethical Principles of Psychologists and Code of Conduct,* the American Psychological Association (1992) indicated, "Psychologists who perform interventions or administer, score, interpret, or use assessment techniques are familiar with the reliability, validation, and related standardization or outcome studies of, and proper applications and uses of, the techniques they use" (APA, Standard 2.04). Taken as a whole, the explicit requirement of this standard is that practitioners possess knowledge of the *psychometric properties* of test batteries.

Building a knowledge base of the psychometric characteristics of commonly used tests is important not only for test selection but also for test interpretation. For example, it is imperative that practitioners' interpretations of test performance be guided by "careful analyses of the statistical properties of test scores, the internal psychometric characteristics of the test, and the data regarding its relationship to external factors" (Reynolds & Kaufman, 1990, p. 131). Failure to use psychometric information to inform test interpretation threatens the validity of the conclusions that are drawn about test performance.

Because many achievement batteries allow for interpretation at both the composite and individual subtest score level, it is essential that practitioners understand the psychometric properties of *each individual* subtest comprising the battery. The achievement test summary pages provide practitioners with the necessary information about the psychometric characteristics of individual achievement subtests. The criteria used to evaluate the psychometric characteristics of subtests and the batteries themselves were based on the *Standards for Educational and Psychological Testing* (AERA et al., 1999*), A Consumer's Guide to Tests in Print* (Hammill, Brown, & Bryant, 1992), *The Intelligence Test Desk Reference* (McGrew & Flanagan, 1998), and a review of recent literature (e.g., Flanagan, Mascolo, & Genshaft, 2000). Note, however, that evaluation of every important component related to the psychometric properties of a test cannot always be accomplished. Sometimes the necessary information is simply not available and other times the information given is ambiguous at best. In some cases, such as with validity issues or adequacy of norm sample representation, there are far too many variables and complex considerations that preclude simple or quick evaluative judgments. To that end, where evaluation is impossible or impractical, we have endeavored to provide descriptive information that may assist practitioners in reaching conclusions of their own appropriate to the purpose for which an assessment is being conducted. The results of our evaluation of the psychometric characteristic of achievement subtests and batteries are reported in the *Desk Reference* section of this book.

Five main psychometric characteristics of each test are included on the summary pages of the *Desk Reference,* including (1) derived score information, (2) norming information, (3) types of validity evidence reported in the test manual, (4) test reliability, and (5) test floors and ceilings. Although not an exhaustive list, these characteristics are among the most important for the purpose of evaluating the psychometric integrity of an instrument. The presentation and evaluation of the psychometric properties of individual achievement tests are intended to provide practitioners with the requisite knowledge for proper test selection and interpretation. The following section describes each of these test characteristics as well as its relevance to and bearing on particular decisions in the assessment process.

Derived Score Information

Because the overall purpose of score transformations is to "help the test user make sense out of one individual's score in relation to an appropriate comparison group" (Gregory, 2000, p. 69), test authors and publishers typically provide two or three (or more) types of derived scores in their test manuals. The *Desk Reference* lists the types of derived scores that are available in each achievement battery. Practitioners are well advised to understand the exact meaning behind each and every score transformation prior to communicating the results of an individual's test performance. One or more of the following six types of derived scores are typically reported in test manuals: (1) standard scores, (2) percentiles, (3) stanines, (4) normal curve equivalents, (5) age equivalents, and (6) grade equivalents. Although some test manuals may provide other types of score transformations, the ones listed here are among the most popular. Standard scores and percentiles appear to be used most frequently by practitioners for the purpose of communicating test results to colleagues, whereas age and grade equivalents appear to be used most frequently to communicate test performance to teachers and parents. Unfortunately, some types of derived scores, such as grade equivalents, can be easily misinterpreted and are often misleading. Grade equivalents are typically misinterpreted for tests that have items with a limited range of difficulty. On these types of tests, a student's score "is more a reflection of the student's accuracy level than the grade level of task difficulty that this student can perform" (McGrew & Woodcock, 2001, p. 73). Despite their popularity, in the vast majority of cases, grade equivalents do not represent a desirable metric for discussions revolving around relative standing or performance in comparison to peers in the general population (Hishinuma & Tadaki, 1997; Sattler, 2001).

Standard scores express the score difference from the mean in standard deviation units and retain "the relative magnitudes of distances between successive values found in the original raw scores [and] exemplify the most desirable psychometric properties" (Gregory, 2000, p. 65). *Percentiles* indicate the percentage of individuals in the normative sample who scored below a particular standard score when the distribution of scores is normal. Although percentiles are among the more popular and useful standard score transformations, caution should be used because they can be distorted when they fall at the extreme ends of the score range. That is, although individuals may have the same absolute difference in percentile points, the standard score differences can vary greatly. For example, a 14-point difference in percentile ranks exists between the 43rd and 57th percentiles as well as between the 84th and 98th percentiles. However, in the former case, the difference in equivalent standard scores (with a mean of 100 and standard deviation of 15) is only 6 points (97–103), just over a third of a standard deviation. The latter example, however, falls at the upper end of the normal distribution, where the difference in equivalent standard scores is 15 (115–130), or one full standard deviation.

Stanines are based on a single-digit score system (ranging from 1 to 9) from which raw scores are transformed and essentially reflect a categorical classification (Crocker & Algina, 1986). Given that some information is lost in this transformation (e.g., standard scores ranging from 111 to 119 are converted to a stanine of 7), this type of score does not provide much precision. Nevertheless, stanines are used regularly in academic assessment-related fields. *Normal curve equivalents (NCE)* are standard scores that are based on a raw score's percentile and that indicate "the raw score's standard-deviation distance from a distribution's mean if the distribution had been normal" (Popham, 2000, p. 179). These scores represent "a standardized scale of scores developed by the U.S. Department of Education. Test takers scoring at the mean get an NCE of 50; persons scoring in the 1st percentile get a score of 1; those in the 99th percentile, a score of 99. The standard deviation for the NCE is 21.06" (Vogt, 1993, p. 155). *Grade equivalents* are scores that reflect an individual's "performance in terms of the grade level in the norming sample at which the average score is the same as the subject's score" (Mather & Woodcock, 2001, p. 68). *Age equivalents* are similar to grade equivalents except that they reflect "performance in terms of the age level in the norming sample at which the average score is the same as the subject's score" (Mather & Woodcock, 2001, p. 69).

Among the various types of scores reported in test manuals, normal curve equivalents, age equivalents, and grade equivalents are notoriously more difficult to interpret correctly, let alone explain accurately to nonprofessionals. Age and grade equivalents in particular are developmentally based scores that tend to have extremely broad "confidence intervals" that may tend to exaggerate impressions of performance. In some cases, a confidence band of only one standard error of measurement (SEM) can result in ranges that appear alarming (e.g., grade equivalent range of 1.6 to 11.3 or age equivalent of 6.5 to 17.4). Thus, it would seem that under most circumstances, these scores are probably best avoided when trying to communicate information regarding performance to nonprofessionals, especially parents and teachers who may not be familiar with the exact nature of these scores (see McGrew & Woodcock, 2001).

Norming Information

In general, test developers seek to draw individuals from the population on whom the test will be used in an effort to create a sample that is representative of the larger population. Evaluation of the demographics and characteristics of the norm sample in comparison to the demographics and characteristics of the population provides an indication regarding the success of the sampling procedure. When there is correspondence along the various descriptive indices between the sample and the population, it can be inferred that representation is adequate. Adequacy of the standardization sample of any given test is crucial because it forms the basis for making accurate comparisons of performance to the general population. Accurate representation is not, however, the only measure of norm sample adequacy. Beyond simple demographic matching lies issues related to sampling methods and psychometric procedures for deriving norms that also play a significant role in determining the overall quality of a given standardization group. As stated previously, the wide range of specific information necessary to make evaluative judgments regarding norm sample adequacy is all too often unavailable—making efforts toward evaluation impossible and impractical. We have, therefore, endeavored in the *ATDR* to provide as much information as possible regarding the most salient and critical characteristics necessary to assist practitioners in making their own judgments about the quality and suitability of a given norm sample. Typically, the adequacy of the standardization sample of any given test can be effectively gauged through an examination of the following particular characteristics: (1) size of the norm group sample, (2) recency of the normative data as reflected by the date when collected, (3) average number of individuals per age/grade interval included in the standardization sample, (4) size of the age blocks used in the norm tables across the entire age range of the test, (5) number and types of variables included in the norming plan and (6) whether any special features, such as continuous norming procedures were used (Bracken, 1987; Flanagan & Alfonso, 1995; Hammill et al., 1992; McGrew & Woodcock, 2001).

Size of Normative Group.   The adequacy of the size of the normative group of each achievement test is dependent on the adequacy of its component parts—namely, (1) the average number of individuals included at each age/grade interval, (2) the size of age blocks in the norm table, and (3) the number and type of variables in the norming plan. Therefore, information regarding these specific standardization sample characteristics are provided in the *Desk Reference* component of this book. Although it is true that the larger the sample size, the more likely it is to be a better estimate of performance of the population as a whole, it is important to note that size alone is an insufficient indicator of norm sample adequacy. A carefully constructed small sample may in fact provide a closer match or correspondence with the population than a larger sample that is collected with less care or attention. Thus, evaluation of a standardization sample's component parts provides additional important indicators regarding the appropriateness of the overall sample size. In general, it is reasonable to assume that when these component characteristics are adequate, the size of the normative sample is probably large enough to ensure stable values that are representative of the population under consideration (Anastasi & Urbina, 1997, p. 69).

Recency of Normative Data.   Including information about the *recency* of the normative data for the tests included in the *Desk Reference* seems unnecessary, primarily because of the decision to include only tests that were published recently (i.e., 1993 or later). This was done to ensure that practitioners could safely assume that the respective normative information for the tests included in this book is not outdated (i.e., gathered within the past 10 years). In the vast majority of cases, normative information for any given test is gathered typically within two to three years of the test's date of publication. However, in spite of the implications of publication dates, this is not always the case for every achievement test included in the *Desk Reference.* For example, normative information for some achievement tests was gathered at different times, spanning more than 10 years. For example, the Test of Adolescent and Adult Language–Third Edition (TOAL–3; Hammill, Brown, Larson, & Wiederholt, 1994) has a total sample size of 3,057 individuals. Of the total number comprising this sample, 1,512 persons were tested in 1980, 957 in 1986–1987, and 587 in 1993. Therefore, only a small percentage of the TOAL–3's standardization data is actually recent. Furthermore, although the TOAL–3 is appropriate for individuals between the ages of 12 years, 0 months, to 24 years, 11 months, the most recent normative information was gathered on individuals between the ages of 18 years, 0 months, to 24 years, 11 months. Thus, not all normative data are as recent as might be implied by the publication date of the test. The tests that do not contain updated normative data, despite the recency of publication, are noted clearly on the summary pages in the *Desk Reference,* under the "Sample Collection Date(s)" heading.

Average Number of Individuals per Age/Grade Interval.   Review of the average number of participants at each age/grade interval in the normative sample provides important information about the generalizability of the sample. For instance, suppose that a particular battery was normed on 6,000 individuals ages 2 to 85 years. Relative to the size of most norm groups of achievement tests, 6,000 is quite large and therefore would appear to represent adequately the true performance of the general population of individuals from ages 2 to 85. However, careful examination of the number of individuals included at every one-year age interval reveals that only 50 individuals comprised the "3 years, 0 months, to 3 years, 11 months" interval, whereas all other one-year age intervals include 200 individuals through age 18, for example. The small number of 3-year-olds in this example suggests that this test does not adequately represent all of the 3-year-olds who might be given this test. This example again demonstrates that practitioners cannot evaluate the adequacy of a test's normative sample on the basis of overall sample size alone because the adequacy of the sample size is related, in part, to the number of individuals included within each age/grade interval for which the test was normed. Therefore, in order to ensure that norms at a particular age (e.g., age 3 in the preceding example) can be validly generalized to all individuals of that same age, practitioners should ensure that the average number of participants at the age level corresponding to the age of the individual being tested is adequate.

Size of Age Blocks in Norm Table.   An age block in a norm table contains the data from a selected age range of the normative sample against which an individual's performance is compared. Age blocks can range from one-month intervals to 1-, 5-, or even 10-year intervals. Although it might be desirable to provide actual norms for every specific age or grade level for all examinees (e.g., 5 years, 1 month or 3rd grade, 2nd month), the dramatic increase in the number of individuals needed to develop such norms makes this impractical. Therefore, test authors and publishers generally attempt to ensure that the age block divisions are small enough to yield valid estimates of an individual's functioning relative to similar, but not necessarily identical, same-aged peers in the general population. Norms for ages or grades that were not directly sampled are derived by interpolation. Naturally, age blocks at the youngest age range of the test should typically be quite small (e.g., one-month intervals) due to the rapid rate of growth along the ability dimensions measured by the instrument at this age level. Conversely, age blocks at the upper end of the test's age range may be rather large (e.g., $\geq$ one-year age blocks) due to slower and less variable growth rates along the ability dimensions measured by the test for older individuals.

Number and Types of Variables Included in the Norming Plan.   According to the *Standards for Educational and Psychological Testing,* the demographic characteristics of a standardization sample are important variables that play a role in the test selection process. Specifically, "selecting a test with demographically appropriate normative groups relevant for the [individual] being tested is important to the generalizability of the inferences that the [practitioner] seeks to make" (AERA, APA, NCME, 1999, p. 120). Therefore, the variables included in the norming plan provide information about the *representativeness of the norm sample,* or how well the characteristics of the norm sample reflect the characteristics of the general population. Evaluation of the variables included in the norming plan, and hence the representativeness of the norm sample relative to the general population, is particularly important because "the validity of norm-referenced interpretations depends in part on the appropriateness of the reference group to which test scores are compared" (AERA et al., 1999,

p. 51). Therefore, the standardization sample on which the norms of a test are based should be appropriately representative of the individuals on whom the test will be used. Appropriate representation is achieved primarily through consideration of both the *number* and *type* of variables included in the norming plan.

Although age and grade represent important characteristics in the norm sample, given the intended purpose of academic achievement tests, these variables are not necessarily stratified in most norm samples. That is, test developers rarely attempt to match the proportion of first-graders or 6-year-olds to that of twelfth-graders or 18-year-olds as it may exist in the general population. As long as enough individuals from each age or grade are adequately represented, the performance of each group is unlikely to be poorly estimated simply on the basis of not matching the true proportion that exists in the population. Thus, generalizability is largely unaffected. The same could be said for other demographic variables; however, in many cases there is more concern that failure of the norm sample to closely match the characteristics of the population along certain variables carries greater implications for generalizability that may affect the validity of comparisons of performance. As such, test developers look to establish as much correspondence between their norm sample and the general population on the basis of stratification of a wide variety of characteristics that typically include gender, race, ethnicity, socioeconomic status (SES), geographic region, and residence location. Other common variables in norm samples include disability status, educational placement or program, and type of school or institution. The greater the stratification of a norm sample on the basis of these and other variables, assuming a close correspondence with the true percentage and proportion of these variables in the general population was achieved, the more likely the norm sample provides a reliable and accurate estimate of the performance of the population as a whole, and establishes a valid basis for reliable interpretation of performance of any given individual from that population. For example, SES may be represented by a single variable, such as parental income. But more frequently, it is represented by a combination of subcategories in addition to parental income that might include occupation, occupational status, and educational attainment. Going to such lengths to represent SES, or any other variable for that matter, is important because this variable has been found to be a strong predictor of a number of outcomes, including overall cognitive ability and academic achievement (Collier, 1992; Gould, 1981; Neisser et al., 1996; Thomas & Collier, 1997).

Because it is impractical to achieve an exact match between the standardization sample and the U.S. population characteristics through a purely random sampling method, weighting procedures have become routine. In general, tests that have relatively large standardization samples (e.g., 1,000 to 2,000 participants or greater) and that possess adequate component characteristics will likely have norm groups that closely match the general population characteristics. This will not, of course, be true in every case, and practitioners should therefore pay close attention to the number and type of demographic variables included in the norming plan, as discussed previously.

Use of Continuous Norming Procedures. A test developer may generate an adequate norm sample yet fail to provide accurate norms depending on how the data are analyzed. For example, suppose there are two tests that each use 200 subjects for the 10-year-old age range. In developing the norms for one of the tests, the test developer simply calculated the average (median) score and the standard deviation for all subjects collectively. This would mean that performance for an individual aged 10 years, 1 month, would be compared against the same median score and standard deviation for an individual aged 10 years, 11 months. In contrast, the developer of the other test chose to sort the 200 subjects into smaller groups or blocks, with the first block containing the youngest 50 subjects, the second block containing the next 50 youngest, and so forth. Then, the median scores and standard deviations from all four blocks were calculated and fitted with a smoothed curve. From this smoothed curve, the average (median) score and standard deviation to be used for any age (10 years, 1 month; 10 years, 2 months; etc.) is taken from the smoothed curve and used for a subject of that exact age. In the norms of this test, there will be a gradual and noticeable change in what is expected (as reflected by the median score) as age and schooling increase. Moreover, the standard deviations will change slightly, either increasing or decreasing, depending on the trait that was measured. Thus, although both tests used an equal amount of subjects for this age interval, the norms for the second test will likely be much more accurate than the norms of the first test primarily because it is more sensitive to the short-term effects of schooling or maturation.

Grouping subjects on the basis of one-year age or grade intervals, as was done in the first test, produces norms that tend to underestimate the ability of younger subjects (or students just beginning the school year) and overestimate the ability of older subjects (or students about to complete the school year). Likewise, use of these norms will also reflect rather large jumps between age groups, which is not an accurate picture of human development. The procedure used for the second test in this example is referred to as *continuous norming* and represents an important consideration in evaluating the adequacy of a given norm sample (Zachary & Gorsuch, 1985). Where use of this procedure is specifically stated in the test manual, it has been noted in the *ATDR* under the heading of "Special Features" on the summary pages.

Types of Validity Evidence Reported in the Test Manual

Much like the variable and complex nature of norm samples, validity is not an "all-or-nothing" condition, and the validity of one test is dependent on the validity of the criterion measure to which it is being compared (Bracken, 1987, p. 317). Therefore, an acceptable validity criterion is difficult to establish. Because the concept of validity itself is more abstract than the concept of reliability, for example, it is difficult to agree on specific criteria that are appropriate for evaluating the adequacy of any given test (Hammill et al., 1992). The criteria that currently exist for specifying the conditions under which an instrument is determined to be valid are rather arbitrary and confusing (Flanagan & Alfonso, 1995). Therefore, in lieu of providing some type of overall evaluation of the validity evidence that exists for achievement tests (e.g., good, adequate, inadequate), reporting the presence or absence of three types of validity data—including content, criterion, and construct validity—seems more appropriate. These three types of validity were chosen because they are among the traditional validity categories most often used in establishing the validity of psychometric instruments (Anastasi & Urbina, 1997; AERA et al., 1999). In order to determine the validity evidence that exists for each of the achievement tests included in the *Desk Reference*, each test's examiner's manual and technical manual was reviewed. Furthermore, a thorough search of the literature was conducted to identify additional validation evidence available for achievement tests. These additional sources of validity evidence are reported in Appendix C of this text.

The *Standards for Educational and Psychological Testing* state that practitioners are responsible for familiarizing themselves with the validity evidence "for the intended use and purposes of the tests and inventories selected" (AERA et al., 1999, p. 120). Therefore, it is incumbent on practitioners to review the types of validity evidence that are available for the achievement tests that they use. In addition to the individual test manuals, Appendix C can serve as a quick reference for identifying the types of validity evidence that have been published for any given achievement test in the extant literature. For further discussion of validity concepts, the reader is referred to AERA and associates (1999), Aiken (2000), Anastasi and Urbina (1997), Gregory (2000), Salvia and Ysseldyke (1991), and Sattler (2001).

Test Reliability

Reliability refers to "the consistency of scores obtained by the same persons when they are reexamined with the same test on different occasions, or with different sets of equivalent items, or under other variable examining conditions" (Anastasi & Urbina, 1997, p. 84). The reliability of a scale affects practitioners' interpretations of the test results because it guides decisions regarding the range of scores (i.e., standard error of measurement) likely to occur as the result of factors that are not directly relevant to actual ability or performance (e.g., measurement error, chance, etc.). Test reliability, in its broadest sense, indicates the extent to which individual differences can be attributed to true differences in the characteristics under investigation or to error or chance (Anastasi & Urbina, 1997). The degree of confidence a practitioner can place in the precision of a test score is related directly to the estimated reliability of the test score. Unreliable test scores can contribute to misdiagnosis and inappropriate placement and treatment. This potential problem can be significantly reduced by selecting tests that have good reliability and thus less error associated with their scores or by combining individual test scores into composite scores. In the latter case, measurement of the same or highly related abilities provides information that converges toward true performance, thereby increasing reliability. For in-depth treatment of reliability concepts, the reader is referred to Anastasi and Urbina (1997), AERA and associates (1999), Crocker and Algina (1986), Lord and Novick (1968), Nunnally (1978), Salvia and Ysseldyke (1991), and Sattler (2001).

Given the singular importance of this characteristic as related to both test selection and interpretation, the individual internal consistency and test-retest (or stability) reliability coefficients for each test of each achievement battery were evaluated. The reliabilities for the individual achievement tests reported in the *Desk Reference* were taken from their respective technical manuals. All reported internal consistency reliabilities reflect estimates of how consistently examinees performed across items or subsets of items in a single test administration. All test-retest reliabilities reflect estimates of how stable individual test scores are over time.

Achievement subtests were categorized as having either *high* (coefficients of .90 and above), *medium* (coefficients of .80 to .89), or *low* (coefficients less than .80) reliability.

These evaluations provide the practitioner with an indication of the degree of confidence that can be placed in test score interpretation. Specifically, tests with high reliability yield scores that are sufficiently reliable for use in diagnostic decision making when supported with convergent data sources. Tests with medium reliability yield scores that are moderately reliable and therefore are most appropriately used to make screening decisions only. It is possible, however, to combine tests with medium reliability with other similar measures to form a more reliable and stable composite. Tests with low reliability yield scores that are insufficiently reliable for most purposes and therefore should not be used to make either screening or diagnostic decisions.

Although the criteria for evaluating the reliability of psychometric tests described here are used widely, they are most appropriate for evaluating a test's *internal consistency* reliability and should not be confused with test-retest reliability coefficients. As with internal consistency coefficients, higher is generally better. However, whereas internal consistency coefficients provide information about a test's reliability or, conversely, unreliability (i.e., measurement error), it must be remembered that a test's stability not only reflects measurement error but also systematic changes, such as those due to development or prior exposure to test materials, and nonsystematic changes, such as unpredictable variations in trait level (e.g., verbal ability) over time (McGrew et al., 1991). Because test-retest reliability coefficients are confounded by trait stability (or conversely, instability), they may be *lower* than internal consistency coefficients (Cattell, 1957; McGrew et al., 1991). In such cases, they are often interpreted inappropriately as reflective of the quality of the instrument (for a more detailed discussion, see Flanagan & Alfonso, 1995, and McGrew et al., 1991).

In addition to evaluating the magnitude of test-retest reliability coefficients, other factors related to the quality of test-retest studies should be considered prior to using test-retest findings to inform interpretation. There are three factors in particular that directly affect the magnitude of test-retest reliability coefficients: (1) the size and representativeness of the test-retest sample, (2) the age range of the sample, and (3) the length of the test-retest interval. First, the size of the sample on which the stability coefficient is calculated should be sufficiently large to ensure that adequate representation is possible. It should be noted that the overwhelming majority of achievement test manuals include test-retest samples that are not sufficiently large and therefore do not meet this criterion. Second, because achievement tests span a wide age and ability range, test-retest coefficients should be provided for the various age levels at which the test was normed (Anastasi & Urbina, 1997). For example, if a test was normed on individuals between the ages of 3 and 12 years, interpretations regarding a 4-year-old's expected performance based on stability information from a sample ranging in age from 3 to 10 years (mean age = 6.5 years) is likely to be misleading (Flanagan & Alfonso, 1995). Generalizations regarding this child's expected performance would be most accurate if they were based on stability estimates that were calculated on a representative sample of *4-year-olds only*. However, most test-retest samples include individuals of varying ages, spanning 5 or more years, rendering stability information of questionable utility. Third, because progressive developmental changes are discernible at early ages over a period of a month or less, the test-retest interval "should rarely exceed six months" (Anastasi & Urbina, 1997, p. 92). Naturally, stability coefficients decrease steadily as the time between test-retest intervals lengthens. Although most test-retest samples meet this criterion, they fail to meet the first two criteria, resulting in poor test-retest sample characteristics for most of the batteries included in the *Desk Reference.* Therefore, when practitioners are interested in expected stability of test performance, they should evaluate carefully the test-retest sample characteristics of the test prior to using stability coefficients to inform interpretation.

Test Floors and Ceilings

Tests with adequate floors and ceilings will yield scores that effectively discriminate among various degrees of functioning at the extremes of an ability continuum. A test with an *inadequate floor,* or an insufficient number of easy items, may not distinguish adequately between individuals functioning in the average, low average, and borderline ranges of ability. Likewise, a test with an *inadequate ceiling,* or an insufficient number of difficult items, may not distinguish adequately between individuals who function in the average, high average, and superior ranges of ability. Thus, a test that does not have adequate floors or ceilings may not provide information with sufficient precision for diagnostic classification or placement decisions, especially with individuals functioning at or near the extreme ranges of the ability continuum.

Information about individual achievement test floors and ceilings is therefore reported in the *Desk Reference* to assist practitioners in evaluating this component of tests. This information was derived from the published norm tables of each achievement battery. A simple raw score to standard score conversion for each norm table age grouping was used to examine the adequacy of individual test floors and ceilings across the age range of all individual achievement tests in a manner similar to that of Bracken (1987), Flanagan and Alfonso (1995), and McGrew and Flanagan (1998).

For test floors, subtests in which a raw score of 1 was associated with a standard score that was *more than* 2 standard deviations below the normative mean of the test was considered adequate. If this condition was not met, the subtest floor was rated as inadequate. Similarly, for test ceilings, the maximum raw score for the test had to be associated with a standard score that was *more than* 2 standard deviations above the normative mean of the test to be considered adequate. Failure to meet this criterion resulted in an inadequate rating for the test ceiling. In order to simplify the presentation of this information, the *Desk Reference* lists only those age ranges for which the subtest floor or ceiling was rated as *inadequate.* Therefore, if the *Desk Reference* summary pages include the word *none* in the "floors and ceilings" section, then the practitioner can assume that these psychometric characteristics are adequate for the entire age range of the test.

Theoretical Characteristics of Achievement Batteries

Although psychometric characteristics aid practitioners in making sound judgments about test selection and interpretation, the meaningfulness of such judgments is enhanced greatly when it is grounded in an empirically supported theoretical model of the structure of intelligence (Flanagan, McGrew, & Ortiz, 2000). As discussed in Chapter 2, knowledge of the breadth of abilities specified in contemporary theory, coupled with an understanding of what abilities are measured (and conversely, not measured) by certain achievement batteries, will inform the selection and organization of tests around the specific abilities to be assessed in any given evaluation vis-à-vis referral concerns (see Chapters 12–14). As such, the individual subtests of each achievement battery have been classified according to the CHC taxonomy of abilities described in Chapter 2. These classifications are also reported in the *Desk Reference* component of this book.

The CHC broad-ability classifications assigned to the subtests in the *Desk Reference* (and in other sources, e.g., McGrew & Flanagan, 1998) were derived either empirically or logically. Empirical classifications are generally derived from theory-driven conjoint factor analyses, whereas logical classifications are based on an expert consensus process (see McGrew, 1997, and McGrew & Flanagan, 1998). Due to the paucity of factor-analytic studies that included tests from one or more *achievement* batteries (as opposed to cognitive batteries; see McGrew & Flanagan, 1998), with few exceptions (e.g., WJ III), most of the CHC classifications in the *Desk Reference* section of this book were derived logically (i.e., through expert consensus). A brief description of the procedures employed to classify individual achievement tests according to the CHC abilities they measure follows.

Upon reviewing the broad CHC ability definitions as well as the content, stimuli, and task demands of the tests included on any general achievement battery, it appears quite reasonable to conclude that achievement batteries tend to measure primarily various aspects of Reading and Writing (*Grw*), Quantitative Knowledge (*Gq*), Auditory Processing (*Ga*), and Crystallized Intelligence (*Gc*). On occasion, however, achievement batteries appear to include tests of Short-Term Memory (*Gsm*), Processing Speed (*Gs*), and perhaps other broad CHC abilities. For example, some achievement batteries contain a memory for words or memory for sentences test (e.g., Woodcock Diagnostic Reading Battery), which are measures of *Gsm*, and math and reading tests are often timed. Other achievement batteries include measures of Fluid Intelligence (*Gf*), such as tests of quantitative reasoning (e.g., WJ III). However, the overwhelming majority of achievement batteries include tests that can be classified at the CHC broad-ability level primarily as either a measure of *Grw, Gq, Ga,* or *Gc*.

Classifying individual achievement tests at the CHC *narrow*-ability level is more difficult. This is because *Grw, Ga,* and *Gc,* in particular, are quite broad, subsuming approximately 8 to 14 narrow abilities each. Furthermore, the match between a particular narrow-ability definition and a given set of test stimuli and task demands is made difficult by subtle or ambiguous distinctions between certain narrow abilities within or across broad-ability domains. For example, Grammatical Sensitivity (MY), a narrow ability subsumed by *Gc*, measures one's knowledge or awareness of the grammatical features of the native language. English Usage Knowledge (EU), a narrow ability subsumed by *Grw,* measures one's knowledge of writing in the English language with respect to capitalization, punctuation, usage, and spelling. Although similar, Grammatical Sensitivity (MY) pertains to the ability to identify incorrect grammar in spoken prose or written discourse. English Usage Knowledge (EU) pertains to the ability to use grammar correctly when writing. Also, as noted in Chapter 2, *Gc* tends to be both a variable that represents a store of acquired knowledge (like *Grw* and *Gq*) as well as a variable that reflects language-based abilities (much like *Ga*). These examples make it clear that the process of mapping the CHC ability taxonomy (as presented in Chapter 2) to the tests in achievement batteries is not a straightforward process. Ideally, the classifications should be made on the basis of research that reveals the empirically based loadings of these narrow abilities along the broad CHC ability dimensions (e.g., through factor analysis). However, given the sheer number of narrow abilities subsumed even by just *Gc* and *Ga*, for example (a total of 26), the task of providing such empirically based analysis is quite daunting and has yet to be undertaken, let alone completed. Therefore, until and unless such research emerges in the literature, classification of tests through an expert consensus process remains the most practical method available for making decisions at this time to guide practice.

CHC Expert Consensus Classification Process

Given the lack of empirical data involving the broad- and narrow-ability classifications of the vast majority of achievement tests, it was necessary to undertake a formal expert consensus process in order to derive some idea regarding what abilities achievement tests are measuring. We recognize, of course, the inherent limitations of such a method of classification and we do not suggest that the classifications contained in the *ATDR* are definitive by any means. Rather, we propose these classifications on the basis of expert consensus to serve as both an initial guide for practitioners looking to apply a theoretical framework in their assessments and as a starting point for researchers who may seek to explore the actual classifications and relationships among the constructs in some empirical fashion. Not all achievement tests in the *ATDR*, however, needed to be subjected to the expert consensus classification. The WJ III, for example, was developed specifically to operationalize CHC theory and the standardization data of this battery fit the theory well, and better than competing theoretical models. Therefore, the results of these analyses provided empirical support for the CHC classifications of the WJ III tests of achievement contained in the *ATDR*.

In order to participate in the classification process of the tests of achievement included in the *Desk Reference* according to CHC theory, individuals needed to possess a thorough understanding of (1) CHC theory, including recent developments and refinements; (2) the definitions of the broad and narrow abilities that comprise CHC theory; and (3) the empirical research in support of CHC theory, including the specific conjoint factor analyses that led to previous classifications of ability tests (e.g., Flanagan, McGrew, & Ortiz, 2000; Flanagan & Ortiz, 2001; McGrew & Flanagan, 1998). In addition to this information, knowledge of the results of recent confirmatory factor analyses conducted with the WJ III tests of cognitive and academic ability (McGrew & Woodcock, 2001), in particular, was required.

Participants who identified themselves as having sufficient knowledge of CHC theory and research (as outlined earlier) received a complete manual consisting of all the CHC broad- and narrow-ability definitions (i.e., not just *Grw*, *Gq*, *Gc*, or *Ga* but also *Gf*, *Gv*, *Gsm*, etc.), which included a task example of each narrow ability. The broad- and narrow-ability definitions and task examples included in the manual were identical to those presented in Chapter 2 of this text. In addition, each participant received a packet containing approximately 40 test descriptions that were selected randomly from the total of 323 tests contained in the *Desk Reference*. Participants were not provided with the name of the battery from which the tests were drawn nor were they provided with the name of the test. The descriptions of each test were taken directly from the test manuals. Participants were instructed to select only *one* broad ability that they believed the test most likely measured. Next, each participant was instructed to select only *one* narrow ability from the broad-ability domain identified in the previous step that provided the most probable description of what the test measured more specifically. In this manner, each test was classified independently and blindly by each participant in the consensus study.

Selection of more than one broad and narrow ability was deliberately constrained for several reasons. First, doing so greatly facilitated interpretation of the meaning of the results. Second, it allowed the data to "speak" more clearly without being muddled by the potentially numerous permutations and combinations of ratings. And third, it provided a means for developing criteria that would more objectively indicate and specify the presence of mixed or dual loadings. Thus, requiring that participants select only one broad ability and one corresponding narrow ability for classification resulted in a more straightforward and viable basis for determining consensus while still yielding sufficient information with which to identify and classify tests with probable mixed or dual measures of ability. Ultimately, the methods used in the present study are consistent with prior methodology and criteria about how CHC and other theoretical classifications should be determined (e.g., Carroll, 1993; Flanagan, McGrew, & Ortiz, 2000; Flanagan & Ortiz, 2001; Horn, 1991; McGrew & Flanagan, 1998).

The nature of this consensus process represents a variation of inter-rater reliability procedures and the data were analyzed and interpreted in accordance with specific criteria set by the authors consistent with prevailing guidelines for evaluating inter-rater agreement. Ordinarily, reliability of raters rests on agreement regarding estimates of the degree or quantity of some observable phenomena. In other cases, reliability refers to agreement on the basis of a dichotomous (yes or no, right or wrong) choice. In the present case, agreement rested on the extent to which raters believed that a particular test description measured a particular broad- or narrow-ability attribute as represented by the percentage of raters selecting the same attribute for each test. Agreement is often evaluated statistically (e.g., through chi-square analyses) in order to establish a minimum number of ratings that need to converge so that it can be attributed to intent (reliability) and not chance. However, given the number of raters and total number of ratings completed, along with the fact that there were nine choices for classifying broad ability and over 70 choices for classifying narrow ability, it was deemed highly unlikely that any type of "agreement" might be reached in this particular study solely on the basis of chance. In addition, adoption of relatively strict and conservative standards (criteria) for agreement also helped to reinforce the reliability of the ratings obtained through this expert consensus process.

The specific criteria used to determine agreement among participants relative to the broad- and narrow-ability classifications of tests is presented in Table 3.2. Note that examination of agreement was accomplished first through examination of the classifications of broad ability. Once so classified, the data were then examined for agreement on the basis of narrow-ability classifications. In general, when the percentage of agreement among participants for either the broad- or narrow-ability test classifications was greater than or equal to 80 percent, then the test was classified as measuring a single broad- or narrow-ability corresponding to the consensus classification. Similarly, when the percentage of agreement among participants for either the broad- or narrow-ability test classifications fell between 60 to 80 percent *and* there was less than 40 percent agreement on any other broad- or narrow-ability classification, then the test was also classified as measuring a single broad or narrow ability in accordance with the consensus classification. In cases where there was at least 40 percent agreement on two different broad- or narrow-ability classifications for a given test, then the test was classified as being a mixed measure of those two broad or narrow abilities,

TABLE 3.2   Evaluative Criteria and Classification Guidelines for CHC Broad and Narrow Abilities

Evaluative Criteria	Classification
Broad Abilities	
Agreement of 80% or higher on a single broad ability	Single broad-ability classification
Agreement of ≥ 60% on a single broad ability and no agreement of ≥ 40% on any other broad ability	Single broad-ability classification
Agreement of ≥ 40% on two different broad abilities	Mixed broad-ability classification
Pattern of agreement not meeting any of the above criteria	Classified by authors
Narrow Abilities[1]	
Agreement of 80% or higher on a single narrow ability[2]	Single narrow-ability classification
Agreement of ≥ 60% on a single narrow ability and no agreement of ≥ 40% on any other narrow ability[2]	Single narrow-ability classification
Agreement of ≥ 40% on two different narrow abilities[3]	Mixed narrow-ability classification
Pattern of agreement not meeting any of the above criteria	Classified by authors

[1] Narrow-ability classifications were dependent on the corresponding broad-ability classifications.
[2] Classification was based only on the ratings for the single corresponding broad ability for which agreement was reached.
[3] Classification was based only on the ratings for the two corresponding mixed broad abilities that were identified.

respectively. And in cases where the results of the classifications showed a pattern of agreement that did not meet any of the above three conditions, tests were classified by the authors using any available, empirically based classifications of tests with similar task characteristics and demands.

A summary of the results of the expert consensus procedure along with additional descriptive information is presented in Figure 3.1. Of particular note is the fact that of the 323 tests subjected to the classification process, 309 (96 percent) were successfully classified in accordance with the one of the first three criteria specified in Table 3.2. Only 14 tests (4 percent) required logical classification by the authors. It should be noted that in both the *Desk Reference* section of this book and the CHC Cross-Battery worksheets contained in Appendix A, any test that was classified logically by the authors is marked clearly to distinguish it from tests that were classified through the consensus procedure. Table 3.2 also shows that agreement on classification of tests with respect to measurement of a single broad ability was reached in 92 percent (297 of 323 tests) of the cases, with an additional 4 percent (12 tests) agreement on classification of tests that are believed to measure two different broad abilities, resulting in 96 percent agreement at the broad-ability level.

A similar pattern of results was obtained for classifications relative to narrow abilities, although the percentages were slightly lower than that found for the broad-ability classifications. Agreement on classification of tests with respect to measurement of a single narrow

FIGURE 3.1   Summary Statistics for CHC Achievement Test Expert Consensus Classifications

General Information

Total number of tests evaluated: 323

Total number of raters: 57

Total number of ratings: 8,824

Average number of raters per test: 15 (range = 11 – 18)

Average number of ratings per test: 31 (range = 22 – 36)

Inter-rater Agreement

Percentage of tests classified according to Broad (Stratum II) criteria[1]: 96% (309 of 323 tests)

Percentage of tests classified as single Broad (Stratum II) ability: 92% (297 of 323 tests)

Percentage of tests classified as mixed Broad (Stratum II) ability: 4% (12 of 323 tests)

Percentage of tests classified according to Narrow (Stratum I) criteria[2]: 87% (281 of 323 tests)

Percentage of tests classified as single Narrow (Stratum I) ability: 73% (236 of 323 tests)

Percentage of tests classified as mixed Narrow (Stratum I) ability: 14% (45 of 323 tests)

Validity Check

Total number of ratings for WJ III tests[3]: 726

Percent agreement with WJ III Broad-ability classifications: 92% (668 of 726 ratings)

Percent agreement with WJ III Narrow-ability classifications: 87% (632 of 726 ratings)

[1] This percentage indicates the degree to which agreement between raters was reached for all tests as specified by the criteria in Table 3.2 at the broad ability level. If a test could not be classified at the broad ability level, no further classification (i.e., of narrow abilities) was conducted.

[2] This percentage reflects the loss of 9% of the tests where agreement was reached on the broad ability level but was not subsequently obtained at the narrow ability level.

[3] This number represents the subsample of the total number of blind ratings that were conducted on the WJ III tests included in the classification process.

ability (only for those tests in which agreement at the broad-ability level was obtained) was 73 percent (236 tests) with an additional 14 percent (45 tests) agreement on classification of tests that are believed to measure two different narrow abilities, resulting in 87 percent agreement at the narrow-ability level. Lower percentages of agreement on the narrow abilities is not unexpected and is likely due to the fact that in most cases there are more choices regarding narrow abilities than broad abilities (e.g., 9 choices for broad and as many as 13 choices for narrow). Narrow abilities also tend to be very closely related because they share a great deal of common variance. Thus, making distinctions among test classifications with respect to particular narrow abilities is inherently more difficult than making classifications relative to broad abilities.

The CHC broad- and narrow-ability classifications of achievement tests based on the results of this expert consensus process represent one component of the information that is specified in the *Desk Reference* section of this book and also served as the guide for grouping tests according to measured broad and narrow abilities as presented in the CHC Cross-Battery worksheets that appear in Appendix A. For those subtests in which consensus was not reached, classifications reflect our own judgments following an in-depth examination of test materials. These latter subtest classifications are clearly marked as having been derived from our own efforts in the *Desk Reference.* For additional information regarding the percentage of agreement across the entire set of 323 tests included in the expert consensus process, the reader is referred to Appendix H. For those tests in which no agreement or consensus was reached, the classifications made by the authors are listed in the last two columns while the preceding columns by definition contain no data. The names of the participants in the study are also provided. For a more extensive description of this expert consensus process and study findings, see Caltabiano, Flanagan, Ortiz, and Alfonso (2002).

Overall, the results of the expert consensus process appear to indicate that the reliability of the ratings is rather good. The percentages of agreement with respect to classification are reasonable and in line with standards and criteria for evaluating the success of the consensus process. Additional evidence that tends to support the reliability and accuracy of the ratings can be seen in data presented in Figure 3.1, which involves ratings made in comparison to an empirically established standard. Because tests from the WJ III have been subjected to careful factor analysis and their classifications determined on the basis of results obtained with a very large sample, these classifications have an extremely high degree of reliability and are likely as valid as can be achieved. As such, by comparing the classifications made by raters on those tests from the WJ III that were included in the expert consensus process with the extant classifications published in the WJ III Technical Manual (McGrew & Woodcock, 2001), an additional method for evaluating the success of the classifications can be achieved. The data in the third section of Figure 3.1 show that of the 726 total ratings made on WJ III tests through the expert consensus process, agreement with the extant WJ III classifications was 92 percent (668 ratings) for the broad abilities and 87 percent (632 ratings) for the narrow abilities. Although this is only a subsample of the total number of ratings, these data nevertheless indicate a high level of consistency between the classifications of the WJ III tests generated in the current consensus study and the empirically based classifications of the WJ III (McGrew & Woodcock, 2001).

Although by no means definitive, the results of the expert consensus process described here represent a form of CHC *content validity* (AERA et al., 1999) for the individual tests of the achievement batteries included in this text. It is important to realize that some, perhaps many, of the CHC broad- and narrow-ability classifications that resulted from this initial consensus process will likely undergo modification as a result of future research and scholarly dialogue. It is also possible that future research will simply serve to confirm the nature of many of the classifications made herein. As stated previously, in the absence of any research that demonstrates otherwise, we believe the classification of tests contained in this book, and derived from the expert consensus process just described, represents a reasonable starting point in regard to understanding what each test may measure according to CHC theory. Only when practitioners have a base that provides both a comprehensive framework for measuring abilities and a foundation for interpretation of those abilities is the science of assessment advanced in accordance with contemporary theory. We believe that the CHC classifications that resulted from this expert consensus process provides a base that may serve to improve current assessment practice.

The classifications of tests at the broad- and narrow-ability level in accordance with CHC theory allows practitioners to ground their interpretations in sound theory and research in a manner that is unattainable through any other current methods. Chapters 11–14 will provide practitioners with a systematic, practical method for putting these classifications into practice. These chapters present a complete and detailed description of CHC Cross-Battery assessment and how such a framework aids practitioners in the selection and interpretation of tests by taking advantage specifically of the broad- and narrow-ability test classifications listed in the *Desk Reference*. An operational definition of learning disability (LD) and an illustrative case study that uses the proposed comprehensive framework for LD determination and integrates CHC Cross-Battery measurement of both academic and cognitive abilities will also be presented.

Qualitative Characteristics of Achievement Batteries

In addition to the psychometric and theoretical characteristics of tests, knowledge of qualitative characteristics also informs appropriate test selection and interpretation. Three general categories of qualitative test characteristics were deemed important for consideration prior to selecting an achievement battery, including composite measure information, learning disability assessment area(s) covered, and special features highlighted in the examiner or technical manual. First, composite measure information is listed in the *Desk Reference* for each battery in order to provide practitioners with a brief overview of the battery's content. Second, the achievement areas represented on each battery that were judged by the authors to correspond to one or more of the seven academic areas of learning disability, as outlined in IDEA (Individuals with Disabilities Education Act Amendments of 1997; P.L. 105-17, 20 U.S.C. 1400 et seq.), were reported to assist practitioners in selecting relevant achievement tests for their assessments of individuals with learning difficulties in keeping with the applicable state and federal guidelines governing such practice. Third, the important or special features of each achievement battery were highlighted to provide information that may not be immediately accessible to practitioners. For example, information regarding the availability of computer scoring, the use of manipulatives or engaging materials for younger examinees, the addition of new subtests or composites (for revised batteries), the availability of alternate forms, and so forth, are reported by battery in the *Desk Reference*.

Clearly, test selection should not be based solely on psychometric or theoretical characteristics of a test. The qualitative aspects of each test may form a significant and defensible basis for selecting one test versus another. As such, qualitative characteristics cannot be ignored and should play a rightful part in influencing a practitioner's decision regarding which test is most appropriate for a given situation. We believe that the qualitative test characteristics that are included in the *Desk Reference* (i.e., composite measure information, learning disability assessment area(s) covered, and special features) will assist practitioners in making sound judgments in the practice of assessment. In addition, the valuable qualitative information presented in Appendix F (i.e., description of differing test demands and characteristics for tests that purport to measure the same ability, such as reading comprehension) will assist practitioners in testing hypotheses about disparate test performance on seemingly similar measures. The following section provides an example of how to locate and interpret the test characteristic information available for each individual subtest included in the *Desk Reference*.

The ATDR *Summary Pages*

Proper interpretation of academic achievement tests is a complex activity that often has significant implications (e.g., diagnosis, treatment, placement) for the individual being evaluated. Therefore, it is incumbent on those who use achievement batteries to consider all available information about each test in the assessment and interpretation process. Knowledge of this type of information as well as mastery and use of the wide range of psychometric, theoretical, and qualitative test characteristic information described in this chapter for the individual tests of all achievement batteries may seem at first to be a daunting task for practitioners. Yet, we believe it to be essential. To facilitate the infusion of this critical test characteristic information into the day-to-day assessment practices of practitioners, the next seven chapters present easy-to-read summary pages for each individual subtest of each individually administered achievement battery included in the *Desk Reference*. A sample summary page for the Test of Language Development–Primary: Third Edition (TOLD–P:3; Newcomer & Hammill, 1997) is presented in Figure 3.2 and is used here to explain how practitioners can quickly and easily identify all the necessary psychometric, theoretical and qualitative characteristics of any and all achievement batteries (and their individual subtests) included in the *Desk Reference*.

As shown in Figure 3.2, a general summary page providing information relevant to each achievement battery (in this case, the TOLD–P:3) precedes the individual subtest summary pages. The first section of the general summary page is labeled "General Information" and includes the following:

- Author(s)
- Publisher
- Publication Date(s)
- Age Range
- Administration Time

The next section of the general summary page is labeled "Composite Measure Information." Figure 3.2 shows that the TOLD–P:3 provides six composite scores: listening, speaking, syntax, organizing, semantics, and spoken language. Following is a section labeled "Score Information." Figure 3.2 shows that the TOLD–P:3 provides five of the six listed score transformations as indicated by the shaded boxes in this section. Therefore, raw scores obtained on this battery can be expressed as either standard scores, percentiles, stanines, NCEs, or age equivalents.

In the middle of the general battery summary page in Figure 3.2 is a section labeled "Norming Information." A review of the norming information of the TOLD–P:3 indicates that 1,000 individuals were included in the standardization sample; the normative data were collected in 1996; the average number of participants per age/grade interval was 200 per year for ages 4-0 to 8-11; the age blocks included in the norm tables are divided into 6-month blocks for ages 4-0 to 8-11; eight demographic variables were included in the norming plan (gender [males and females], geographic region, residence, race/ethnicity, SES [which included two subcategories—parent education level and income]; and other [disability status]).

Following the Norming Information is a section labeled "Validity." In this section, all three validity boxes are shaded (see Figure 3.2), indicating that content, criterion, and construct validity evidence for the TOLD–P:3 is reported in the examiner/technical manual.

The next section in Figure 3.2 is labeled "Contains at Least One Indicator Consistent with the Following Learning Disability Assessment Areas." The two shaded boxes in this section indicate that the TOLD–P:3 contains at least one measure of two of the seven LD assessment areas of achievement specified in IDEA—namely, oral expression and listening comprehension. The final section of the general summary page is labeled "Special Features." This section lists four salient features of the TOLD–P:3 that are related to scoring, stimulus materials, and test content. Specifically, the TOLD–P:3 offers computer scoring, its stimulus materials are presented in color, and it offers two new subtests (Phonemic Analysis and Relational Vocabulary) and one new composite over and above those offered by its predecessor (i.e., TOLD–P:2).

In addition to information related to the test battery as a whole, the summary sheets provide information for each subtest comprising the battery. In this example, Figure 3.2 displays the Picture Vocabulary and Relational Vocabulary subtests from the TOLD–P:3. As may be seen from this individual subtest summary page, the name of the battery and individual subtest name, as well as the age range for which norms are provided, are located at the top of the summary page. A brief description of the subtest follows. Next, the individual test summary pages provide a rating (high, medium, low) of the individual subtest reliabilities (i.e., internal consistency and test-retest) across the entire age range of the subtest. Specifically, reliability information is presented by age in a visual-graphic format. The evaluation of each subtest's reliability, according to the psychometric criteria presented earlier, is determined by locating the appropriate age level and inspecting the percent of gray shading in the small square associated with that age using the key at the top, left side of the summary page. For example, at age 5, the TOLD–P:3 Picture Vocabulary subtest is classified as having *medium* internal consistency and *medium* test-retest reliability.

The next section of the summary page provides information on the adequacy of test floors and ceilings. For example, Figure 3.2 shows that the TOLD–P:3 Picture Vocabulary subtest has *inadequate* test floors at ages 4-0 to 5-5. As such, practitioners should use cau-

FIGURE 3.2   Achievement Summary Pages (TOLD–P:3 Battery and Picture Vocabulary and Relational Vocabulary Subtests)

Test of Language Development-Primary: Third Edition (TOLD-P:3)

GENERAL INFORMATION

Author(s): Phyllis L. Newcomer and Donald D. Hammill   *Age Range*: 4-0 to 8-11
Publisher: PRO-ED   *Administration Time*: 30 to 60 minutes
Publication Date(s): 1977, 1982, 1988, 1997

COMPOSITE MEASURE INFORMATION

Spoken Language   Listening
Organizing   Speaking
Semantics   Syntax

SCORE INFORMATION

Standard scores	Percentiles	Stanines	Normal curve equivalents	Age equivalents	Grade equivalents

NORMING INFORMATION

Standardization Sample Size: 1,000   *Sample Collection Date(s): 1996*

Avg. Number per Age/Grade Interval: *Demographic Variables:*
  200 per year: 4-0 to 8-11   *Gender   - male; female*
          Geographic region   - 4 regions; 28 states
Age Blocks in Norm Table: *Residence   - urban; rural*
  6 months: 4-0 to 8-11   *Race/ethnicity   - White; Black; Native American; Hispanic; Asian;*
          other
          SES   - parent education; family income
          Other   - disability status (none, LD, SLD, MR, other)

VALIDITY

Types of Validity Evidence Reported in the Test Manual:

Content	Criterion	Construct

Test Review(s) and Validity Evidence Reported in Extant Literature: See Appendix C

CONTAINS AT LEAST ONE INDICATOR CONSISTENT WITH THE FOLLOWING LEARNING DISABILITY ASSESSMENT AREA(S)

Oral Expression	Listening Comprehension	Written Expression	Basic Reading Skill	Reading Comprehension	Mathematics Calculation	Mathematics Reasoning

SPECIAL FEATURES

- Provides computer scoring and interpretive profiling report
- Includes two new subtests (i.e., Phonemic Analysis and Relational Vocabulary) that measure important linguistic abilities not measured on previous editions
- Includes a new composite (i.e., Organizing) that represents linguistic abilities that mediate between receptive and expressive modes of communication
- Pictures are in color to present a more contemporary and appealing look to children

FIGURE 3.2   *Continued*

| *Battery:* TOLD-P:3 | **Picture Vocabulary** | *Age Range:* **4-0 to 8-11** |

DESCRIPTION

The examinee is required to select from four pictures the one that best represents the meaning of a word stated by the examiner.

RELIABILITY [1]

☐ - Low   ■ - Medium   ■ - High   ☐ - No Information Available

	2	3	4	5	6	7	8	9	10	11	12	13	14	15	16	17	18	19 24	25 29	30 34	35 39	40 44	45 49	50 54	55 59	60 64	65 69	70 74	75 79	80 84	85 90+
Internal consistency																															
Test-retest*																															

*Interval between testings: 4 months

FLOORS AND CEILINGS

	Test Floor	**Test Ceiling**
Inadequate at ages:	4-0 to 5-5	none

CHC CLASSIFICATIONS (**Broad: stratum II** / *Narrow: stratum I*)

Crystallized Intelligence (*Gc*): *Lexical Knowledge (VL)* - Extent of vocabulary that can be understood in terms of correct word meanings.

| *Battery:* TOLD-P:3 | **Relational Vocabulary** | *Age Range:* **4-0 to 8-11** |

DESCRIPTION

The examinee is required to express orally the relationship between two words stated by the examiner.

RELIABILITY [1]

☐ - Low   ■ - Medium   ■ - High   ☐ - No Information Available

	2	3	4	5	6	7	8	9	10	11	12	13	14	15	16	17	18	19 24	25 29	30 34	35 39	40 44	45 49	50 54	55 59	60 64	65 69	70 74	75 79	80 84	85 90+
Internal consistency																															
Test-retest*																															

*Interval between testings: 4 months

FLOORS AND CEILINGS

	Test Floor	**Test Ceiling**
Inadequate at ages:	4-0 to 5-5	none

CHC CLASSIFICATIONS (**Broad: stratum II** / *Narrow: stratum I*)

Crystallized Intelligence (*Gc*): *Language Development (LD)* - General development, or the understanding of words, sentences, and paragraphs (not requiring reading), in spoken native language skills.

[1]Test-retest coefficients were reported by grade in the test manual. Therefore, corresponding ages were estimated by this text's authors.

tion when administering this measure to children ages 6 and younger, as there is unlikely a sufficient number of easy items to distinguish adequately between individuals at this age level who function in the average, low average, and borderline ranges of ability.

The last section of the summary page, labeled "CHC Classifications," provides information about how to interpret the test from CHC theory and research. This section shows that the TOLD-P:3 Picture Vocabulary subtest measures Crystallized Intelligence (*Gc*)—specifically, the narrow ability of Lexical Knowledge (VL). As may be seen in Figure 3.2, definitions of these CHC abilities are provided on the summary page.

Overall, it is clear from the Figure 3.2 example that the battery and subtest summary pages provide practitioners with a wealth of information critical to the appropriate selection of tests and concomitant interpretation of test results. Use of the information contained in the summary pages can be extremely valuable in advancing the science of assessment of academic and cognitive abilities for virtually any purpose in which standardized testing is deemed necessary.

Conclusions

The information presented in this chapter was intended to provide practitioners with a means for systematically identifying and evaluating the important characteristics of academic achievement batteries and their constituent subtests. Through examination of psychometric, theoretical, and qualitative characteristics, practitioners are able to make better, more informed decisions regarding test selection and are able to generate interpretations that are defensible psychometrically as well as from the standpoint of contemporary theory on the structure of academic and cognitive abilities. The presentation of such information in an easy-to-read format facilitates the practitioner's task of selecting batteries and organizing an academic skills assessment according to specific referral concerns. It is hoped that this chapter will serve to simplify practitioners' assessment-related tasks and strengthen their psychometric, theoretical, and qualitative knowledge base of achievement batteries, thereby improving the overall science and practice of academic achievement assessment as it relates to test selection and interpretation.

Given the vast range of test features that may be necessary to consider for the appropriate selection, use, and interpretation of achievement tests, it was not possible to include each and every factor that might play a role in these activities. For instance, factors such as the ease of subtest administration and the background/ environmental and individual/situational variables that influence test performance were not included. This is not to say that these factors are unimportant. In fact, there may well be cases in which such factors play a pivotal role in either test selection, test interpretation, or both. Notwithstanding, this chapter included only those psychometric, theoretical, and qualitative test characteristics that were judged to be most important and most common in the day-to-day selection, use, and interpretation of academic achievement batteries.

Overall, use of the battery and subtest characteristic information presented in the *Desk Reference* is intended to inform test selection and facilitate psychometrically and theoretically defensible interpretations of academic achievement performance. Chapters 12–14 of this book will illustrate how the information presented in the *Desk Reference* can aid in organizing cross-battery assessments that are psychometrically and theoretically sound and that are consistent with current research regarding the relationships between academic skill areas and cognitive abilities and processes.

ATDR *Summary Pages*
Comprehensive Achievement Tests

Diagnostic Achievement Battery-Third Edition (DAB-3)

GENERAL INFORMATION

Author(s): Phyllis L. Newcomer
Publisher: PRO-ED
Publication Date(s): 1984, 1990, 2001

Age Range: 6-0 to 14-11
Administration Time: 90 to 120 minutes

COMPOSITE MEASURE INFORMATION

Listening
Reading
Math
Written Language Quotient

Speaking
Writing
Spoken Language Quotient
Total Achievement Quotient

SCORE INFORMATION

Standard scores	Percentiles	Stanines	Normal curve equivalents	Age equivalents	Grade equivalents

NORMING INFORMATION

Standardization Sample Size: 1,094

Sample Collection Date(s): 1997-2000

Avg. Number per Age/Grade Interval:
122 per year: 6-0 to 14-11

Age Blocks in Norm Table:
6 months: 6-0 to 14-11

Demographic Variables:
Gender   *- male; female*
Geographic region   *- 4 regions; 16 states*
Residence   *- urban; rural*
Race/ethnicity   *- White; Black; Native American; Hispanic; Asian; other*
SES   *- parent education; family income*
Other   *- disability status (none, LD, SLD, ADD, other)*

VALIDITY

Types of Validity Evidence Reported in the Test Manual:

Content	Criterion	Construct

Test Review(s) and Validity Evidence Reported in Extant Literature: See Appendix C

CONTAINS AT LEAST ONE INDICATOR CONSISTENT WITH THE FOLLOWING LD ASSESSMENT AREA(S)

Oral Expression	Listening Comprehension	Written Expression	Basic Reading Skill	Reading Comprehension	Mathematics Calculation	Mathematics Reasoning

SPECIAL FEATURES

- Provides for some individual and small group administration
- New subtest, Phonemic Analysis, added to help examiners identify deficits related to spoken language and reading problems
- Writing Composition subtest has been divided into two subtests: Contextual Language and Story Construction
- Capitalization and Punctuation subtests have been redeveloped, shortened, and reordered for easier administration
- Story Comprehension subtest has been recorded on audiotape for easier test administration
- Entry items, basals, and ceilings have been clarified and made easier

DESCRIPTION

The examinee is required to listen to a passage read by the examiner or played on audiotape and then answer a question about the item or story.

RELIABILITY

☐ - Low   ◼ - Medium   ◼ - High   ☐ - No Information Available

	2	3	4	5	6	7	8	9	10	11	12	13	14	15	16	17	18	19 24	25 29	30 34	35 39	40 44	45 49	50 54	55 59	60 64	65 69	70 74	75 79	80 84	85 90+
Internal consistency Test-retest*																															

*Interval between testings: 2 weeks

FLOORS AND CEILINGS

	Test Floor	Test Ceiling
Inadequate at ages:	none	12-0 to 14-11

CHC CLASSIFICATIONS (Broad: stratum II / Narrow: stratum I)

Crystallized Intelligence (Gc): Listening Ability (LS) - Ability to listen and comprehend oral communications.

DESCRIPTION

The examinee is required to listen to a sentence read by the examiner and decide whether the statement is true or false.

RELIABILITY

☐ - Low   ◼ - Medium   ◼ - High   ☐ - No Information Available

	2	3	4	5	6	7	8	9	10	11	12	13	14	15	16	17	18	19 24	25 29	30 34	35 39	40 44	45 49	50 54	55 59	60 64	65 69	70 74	75 79	80 84	85 90+
Internal consistency Test-retest*																															

*Interval between testings: 2 weeks

FLOORS AND CEILINGS

	Test Floor	Test Ceiling
Inadequate at ages:	6-0 to 7-5	11-0 to 14-11

CHC CLASSIFICATIONS (Broad: stratum II / Narrow: stratum I)

Crystallized Intelligence (Gc): Listening Ability (LS) - Ability to listen and comprehend oral communications.

DESCRIPTION

The examinee is required to state a word similar in meaning to the word spoken by the examiner.

RELIABILITY

☐ - Low   ■ - Medium   ■ - High   ☐ - No Information Available

	2	3	4	5	6	7	8	9	10	11	12	13	14	15	16	17	18	19 24	25 29	30 34	35 39	40 44	45 49	50 54	55 59	60 64	65 69	70 74	75 79	80 84	85 90+
Internal consistency																															
Test-retest*																															

Interval between testings: 2 weeks

FLOORS AND CEILINGS

	Test Floor	Test Ceiling
Inadequate at ages:	6-0 to 7-11	none

CHC CLASSIFICATIONS (Broad: stratum II / *Narrow: stratum I*)

Crystallized Intelligence (*Gc*): *Lexical Knowledge (VL)* - Extent of vocabulary that can be understood in terms of correct word meanings.

DESCRIPTION

The examinee is required to supply the missing morphological form to unfinished sentences read by the examiner.

RELIABILITY

☐ - Low   ■ - Medium   ■ - High   ☐ - No Information Available

	2	3	4	5	6	7	8	9	10	11	12	13	14	15	16	17	18	19 24	25 29	30 34	35 39	40 44	45 49	50 54	55 59	60 64	65 69	70 74	75 79	80 84	85 90+
Internal consistency																															
Test-retest*																															

Interval between testings: 2 weeks

FLOORS AND CEILINGS

	Test Floor	Test Ceiling
Inadequate at ages:	6-0 to 7-11	10-6 to 14-11

CHC CLASSIFICATIONS (Broad: stratum II / *Narrow: stratum I*)

Crystallized Intelligence (*Gc*): *Grammatical Sensitivity (MY)* - Knowledge or awareness of the grammatical features of the native language.

DESCRIPTION

The examinee is required to read aloud letters/words.

RELIABILITY

☐ - Low   ■ - Medium   ■ - High   ☐ - No Information Available

	2	3	4	5	6	7	8	9	10	11	12	13	14	15	16	17	18	19-24	25-29	30-34	35-39	40-44	45-49	50-54	55-59	60-64	65-69	70-74	75-79	80-84	85-90+
Internal consistency Test-retest*					■	■	■	■	■	■	■	■	■																		

Interval between testings: 2 weeks

FLOORS AND CEILINGS

	Test Floor	Test Ceiling
Inadequate at ages:	none	10-6 to 14-11

CHC CLASSIFICATIONS (Broad: stratum II / Narrow: stratum I)

Reading/Writing (Grw): *Reading Decoding (RD) - Ability to recognize and decode words or pseudowords in reading.*

DESCRIPTION

The examinee is required to read short passages silently and respond to comprehension questions asked by the examiner.

RELIABILITY

☐ - Low   ■ - Medium   ■ - High   ☐ - No Information Available

	2	3	4	5	6	7	8	9	10	11	12	13	14	15	16	17	18	19-24	25-29	30-34	35-39	40-44	45-49	50-54	55-59	60-64	65-69	70-74	75-79	80-84	85-90+
Internal consistency Test-retest*					■	■	■	■	■	■	■	■	■																		

Interval between testings: 2 weeks

FLOORS AND CEILINGS

	Test Floor	Test Ceiling
Inadequate at ages:	6-0 to 7-11	11-0 to 14-11

CHC CLASSIFICATIONS (Broad: stratum II / Narrow: stratum I)

Reading/Writing (Grw): *Reading Comprehension (RC) - Ability to comprehend connected discourse during reading.*

Battery: DAB-3	Capitalization	Age Range: 6-0 to 14-11

DESCRIPTION

The examinee is required to rewrite sentences making appropriate capitalization corrections.

RELIABILITY

▨ - Low   ▦ - Medium   ■ - High   ☐ - No Information Available

	2	3	4	5	6	7	8	9	10	11	12	13	14	15	16	17	18	19 24	25 29	30 34	35 39	40 44	45 49	50 54	55 59	60 64	65 69	70 74	75 79	80 84	85 90+
Internal consistency																															
Test-retest*																															

Interval between testings: 2 weeks

FLOORS AND CEILINGS

	Test Floor	**Test Ceiling**
Inadequate at ages:	6-0 to 9-5	11-0 to 14-11

CHC CLASSIFICATIONS (Broad: stratum II / *Narrow: stratum I*)

Reading/Writing (*Grw*): *English Usage Knowledge (EU)* - Knowledge of writing in the English language with respect to capitalization, punctuation, usage, and spelling.

Battery: DAB-3	Punctuation	Age Range: 6-0 to 14-11

DESCRIPTION

The examinee is required to rewrite sentences making appropriate punctuation corrections.

RELIABILITY

▨ - Low   ▦ - Medium   ■ - High   ☐ - No Information Available

	2	3	4	5	6	7	8	9	10	11	12	13	14	15	16	17	18	19 24	25 29	30 34	35 39	40 44	45 49	50 54	55 59	60 64	65 69	70 74	75 79	80 84	85 90+
Internal consistency																															
Test-retest*																															

Interval between testings: 2 weeks

FLOORS AND CEILINGS

	Test Floor	**Test Ceiling**
Inadequate at ages:	6-0 to 8-5	none

CHC CLASSIFICATIONS (Broad: stratum II / *Narrow: stratum I*)

Reading/Writing (*Grw*): *English Usage Knowledge (EU)* - Knowledge of writing in the English language with respect to capitalization, punctuation, usage, and spelling.

Battery: DAB-3	Spelling	Age Range: 6-0 to 14-11

DESCRIPTION

The examinee is required to spell phonetically regular words.

RELIABILITY

■ - Low   ■ - Medium   ■ - High   ☐ - No Information Available

	2	3	4	5	6	7	8	9	10	11	12	13	14	15	16	17	18	19 24	25 29	30 34	35 39	40 44	45 49	50 54	55 59	60 64	65 69	70 74	75 79	80 84	85 90+
Internal consistency																															
Test-retest*																															

Interval between testings: 2 weeks

FLOORS AND CEILINGS

	Test Floor	Test Ceiling
Inadequate at ages:	6-0 to 7-5	11-0 to 14-11

CHC CLASSIFICATIONS (Broad: stratum II / Narrow: stratum I)

Reading/Writing (*Grw*): *Spelling Ability (SG)* - Ability to spell.

Battery: DAB-3	Contextual Language	Age Range: 7-0 to 14-11

DESCRIPTION

The examinee is required to write a short story with a beginning, middle, and ending based on three stimulus pictures.

RELIABILITY

■ - Low   ■ - Medium   ■ - High   ☐ - No Information Available

	2	3	4	5	6	7	8	9	10	11	12	13	14	15	16	17	18	19 24	25 29	30 34	35 39	40 44	45 49	50 54	55 59	60 64	65 69	70 74	75 79	80 84	85 90+
Internal consistency																															
Test-retest*																															

Interval between testings: 2 weeks

FLOORS AND CEILINGS

	Test Floor	Test Ceiling
Inadequate at ages:	7-0 to 8-5	none

CHC CLASSIFICATIONS (Broad: stratum II / Narrow: stratum I)

Reading/Writing (*Grw*): *Writing Ability (WA)* - Ability to write with clarity of thought, organization, and good sentence structure.

DESCRIPTION

The examinee is required to write a short story with a beginning, middle, and ending based on three stimulus pictures.

RELIABILITY

☐ - Low　　■ - Medium　　■ - High　　☐ - No Information Available

	2	3	4	5	6	7	8	9	10	11	12	13	14	15	16	17	18	19-24	25-29	30-34	35-39	40-44	45-49	50-54	55-59	60-64	65-69	70-74	75-79	80-84	85-90+
Internal consistency Test-retest*																															

Interval between testings: 2 weeks

FLOORS AND CEILINGS

	Test Floor	Test Ceiling
Inadequate at ages:	7-0 to 9-11	none

CHC CLASSIFICATIONS (Broad: stratum II / Narrow: stratum I)

Reading/Writing (Grw): *Writing Ability (WA)* - Ability to write with clarity of thought, organization, and good sentence structure.

DESCRIPTION

The examinee is required to answer general mathematics questions that are presented orally by the examiner.

RELIABILITY

☐ - Low　　■ - Medium　　■ - High　　☐ - No Information Available

	2	3	4	5	6	7	8	9	10	11	12	13	14	15	16	17	18	19-24	25-29	30-34	35-39	40-44	45-49	50-54	55-59	60-64	65-69	70-74	75-79	80-84	85-90+
Internal consistency Test-retest*																															

Interval between testings: 2 weeks

FLOORS AND CEILINGS

	Test Floor	Test Ceiling
Inadequate at ages:	none	12-0 to 14-11

CHC CLASSIFICATIONS (Broad: stratum II / Narrow: stratum I)

Quantitative Knowledge (Gq): *Mathematical Knowledge (KM)* - Range of general knowledge about mathematics.

DESCRIPTION

The examinee is required to calculate mathematics problems.

RELIABILITY

☐ - Low   ■ - Medium   ■ - High   ☐ - No Information Available

	2	3	4	5	6	7	8	9	10	11	12	13	14	15	16	17	18	19 24	25 29	30 34	35 39	40 44	45 49	50 54	55 59	60 64	65 69	70 74	75 79	80 84	85 90+
Internal consistency Test-retest*					■	■	■	☐	☐	■	■	■	■																		

Interval between testings: 2 weeks

FLOORS AND CEILINGS

	Test Floor	Test Ceiling
Inadequate at ages:	6-0 to 8-5	none

CHC CLASSIFICATIONS (Broad: stratum II / Narrow: stratum I)

Quantitative Knowledge (*Gq*): *Mathematical Achievement (A3)* - Measured mathematics achievement.

DESCRIPTION

The examinee is required to repeat a compound word stated by the examiner, and then restate the word without one word as indicated by the examiner. The examinee is then required to repeat a word stated by the examiner, then state the word without a particular phoneme as indicated by the examiner.

RELIABILITY

☐ - Low   ■ - Medium   ■ - High   ☐ - No Information Available

	2	3	4	5	6	7	8	9	10	11	12	13	14	15	16	17	18	19 24	25 29	30 34	35 39	40 44	45 49	50 54	55 59	60 64	65 69	70 74	75 79	80 84	85 90+
Internal consistency Test-retest*					■	■	■	■	■	■	☐	■	■																		

Interval between testings: 2 weeks

FLOORS AND CEILINGS

	Test Floor	Test Ceiling
Inadequate at ages:	6-0 to 6-11	6-6 to 14-11

CHC CLASSIFICATIONS (Broad: stratum II / Narrow: stratum I)

Auditory Processing (*Ga*): *Phonetic Coding: Analysis (PC:A)* - Ability to segment larger units of speech sounds into smaller units of speech sounds.

Diagnostic Achievement Test for Adolescents-Second Edition (DATA-2)

GENERAL INFORMATION

Author(s): Phyllis L. Newcomer and Brian R. Bryant
Publisher: PRO-ED
Publication Date(s): 1986, 1993

Age Range: 12-0 to 18-11
Administration Time: 1 to 2 hours

COMPOSITE MEASURE INFORMATION

Listening
Reading
Writing
Written Language Quotient
Total Achievement Quotient

Speaking
Math
Spoken Language Quotient
Achievement Screener Quotient

SCORE INFORMATION

Standard scores	Percentiles	Stanines	Normal curve equivalents	Age equivalents	Grade equivalents

NORMING INFORMATION

Standardization Sample Size: 2,085

Sample Collection Date(s): 1985-1986; 1990-1991

Avg. Number per Age/Grade Interval:
298 per year: 12-0 to 18-11

Age Blocks in Norm Table:
6 months: 12-0 to 17-5
18 months: 17-6 to 18-11

Demographic Variables:
Gender   *- male; female*
Geographic region   *- 4 regions; 19 states*
Residence   *- urban; rural*
Race/ethnicity   *- White; Black; American Indian; Asian;*
Hispanic; other

VALIDITY

Types of Validity Evidence Reported in the Test Manual:

Content	Criterion	Construct

Test Review(s) and Validity Evidence Reported in Extant Literature: See Appendix C

CONTAINS AT LEAST ONE INDICATOR CONSISTENT WITH THE FOLLOWING LD ASSESSMENT AREA(S)

Oral Expression	Listening Comprehension	Written Expression	Basic Reading Skill	Reading Comprehension	Mathematics Calculation	Mathematics Reasoning

SPECIAL FEATURES

- Provides computer scoring program with interpretive profiling report
- Includes pronunciation guides for Word Identification and Spelling subtests

DESCRIPTION

The examinee is required to determine whether two words spoken by the examiner are synonyms, antonyms, or unrelated to one another.

RELIABILITY

☐ - Low   ■ - Medium   ■ - High   ☐ - No Information Available

	2	3	4	5	6	7	8	9	10	11	12	13	14	15	16	17	18	19 24	25 29	30 34	35 39	40 44	45 49	50 54	55 59	60 64	65 69	70 74	75 79	80 84	85 90+
Internal consistency											■	■	■	■	■	■	■														
Test-retest*																															

Interval between testings: not applicable

FLOORS AND CEILINGS

	Test Floor	Test Ceiling
Inadequate at ages:	none	none

CHC CLASSIFICATIONS (Broad: stratum II / *Narrow: stratum I*)

Crystallized Intelligence (*Gc*): *Language Development (LD)* - General development, or the understanding of words, sentences, and paragraphs (not requiring reading), in spoken native language skills.

DESCRIPTION

The examinee is required to determine whether two sentences spoken by the examiner are grammatically correct.

RELIABILITY

☐ - Low   ■ - Medium   ■ - High   ☐ - No Information Available

	2	3	4	5	6	7	8	9	10	11	12	13	14	15	16	17	18	19 24	25 29	30 34	35 39	40 44	45 49	50 54	55 59	60 64	65 69	70 74	75 79	80 84	85 90+
Internal consistency											☐	■	■	■	☐	■	■														
Test-retest*																															

Interval between testings: not applicable

FLOORS AND CEILINGS

	Test Floor	Test Ceiling
Inadequate at ages:	12-0 to 16-11	none

CHC CLASSIFICATIONS (Broad: stratum II / *Narrow: stratum I*)

Crystallized Intelligence (*Gc*): *Grammatical Sensitivity (MY)* - Knowledge or awareness of the grammatical features of the native language.

DESCRIPTION

The examinee is required to repeat verbatim a sentence that is stated by the examiner.

RELIABILITY

☐ - Low   ■ - Medium   ■ - High   ☐ - No Information Available

	2	3	4	5	6	7	8	9	10	11	12	13	14	15	16	17	18	19 24	25 29	30 34	35 39	40 44	45 49	50 54	55 59	60 64	65 69	70 74	75 79	80 84	85 90+
Internal consistency											■	■	■	■	■	■	■														
Test-retest*																															

Interval between testings: not applicable

FLOORS AND CEILINGS

	Test Floor	Test Ceiling
Inadequate at ages:	none	none

CHC CLASSIFICATIONS (Broad: stratum II / *Narrow: stratum I*)

Short-Term Memory (*Gsm*): *Memory Span (MS)* - Ability to attend to and immediately recall temporally ordered elements in the correct order after a single presentation.

DESCRIPTION

The examinee is required to use a stimulus word stated by the examiner in a sentence.

RELIABILITY

☐ - Low   ■ - Medium   ■ - High   ☐ - No Information Available

	2	3	4	5	6	7	8	9	10	11	12	13	14	15	16	17	18	19 24	25 29	30 34	35 39	40 44	45 49	50 54	55 59	60 64	65 69	70 74	75 79	80 84	85 90+
Internal consistency											■	■	■	■	■	■	■														
Test-retest*																															

Interval between testings: not applicable

FLOORS AND CEILINGS

	Test Floor	Test Ceiling
Inadequate at ages:	12-0 to 13-5	none

CHC CLASSIFICATIONS (Broad: stratum II / *Narrow: stratum I*)

Crystallized Intelligence (*Gc*): *Oral Production and Fluency[a] (OP)* - More specific or narrow oral communication skills than reflected by communication ability (CM).

[a]The narrow CHC classification for this test was determined by the authors because no agreement was reached through the group consensus process.

Battery: DATA-2	Word Identification	Age Range: 12-0 to 18-11

DESCRIPTION

The examinee is required to read words.

RELIABILITY

▨ - Low	■ - Medium	■ - High	☐ - No Information Available

	2	3	4	5	6	7	8	9	10	11	12	13	14	15	16	17	18	19 24	25 29	30 34	35 39	40 44	45 49	50 54	55 59	60 64	65 69	70 74	75 79	80 84	85 90+
Internal consistency											■	■	■	■	■	▨	■														
Test-retest*																															

Interval between testings: not applicable

FLOORS AND CEILINGS

	Test Floor	Test Ceiling
Inadequate at ages:	none	12-6 to 18-11

CHC CLASSIFICATIONS (Broad: stratum II / Narrow: stratum I)

Reading/Writing (Grw): *Reading Decoding (RD) - Ability to recognize and decode words or pseudowords in reading.*

Battery: DATA-2	Reading Comprehension	Age Range: 12-0 to 18-11

DESCRIPTION

The examinee is required to read short passages silently and respond to six comprehension questions per passage.

RELIABILITY

▨ - Low	■ - Medium	■ - High	☐ - No Information Available

	2	3	4	5	6	7	8	9	10	11	12	13	14	15	16	17	18	19 24	25 29	30 34	35 39	40 44	45 49	50 54	55 59	60 64	65 69	70 74	75 79	80 84	85 90+
Internal consistency											▨	■	■	■	■	■	■														
Test-retest*																															

Interval between testings: not applicable

FLOORS AND CEILINGS

	Test Floor	Test Ceiling
Inadequate at ages:	12-0 to 18-11	15-6 to 18-11

CHC CLASSIFICATIONS (Broad: stratum II / Narrow: stratum I)

Reading/Writing (Grw): *Reading Comprehension (RC) - Ability to comprehend connected discourse during reading.*

DESCRIPTION

The examinee is required to calculate math problems that pertain to general mathematics, algebra, or geometry.

RELIABILITY

☐ - Low   ■ - Medium   ■ - High   ☐ - No Information Available

	2	3	4	5	6	7	8	9	10	11	12	13	14	15	16	17	18	19/24	25/29	30/34	35/39	40/44	45/49	50/54	55/59	60/64	65/69	70/74	75/79	80/84	85/90+
Internal consistency											■	■	■	■	■	■	■														
Test-retest*																															

Interval between testings: not applicable

FLOORS AND CEILINGS

	Test Floor	Test Ceiling
Inadequate at ages:	12-0 to 13-5	16-0 to 18-11

CHC CLASSIFICATIONS (Broad: stratum II / *Narrow: stratum I*)

Quantitative Knowledge (*Gq*): *Mathematical Achievement (A3)* - Measured mathematics achievement.

DESCRIPTION

The examinee is required to solve math word problems read by the examiner.

RELIABILITY

☐ - Low   ■ - Medium   ■ - High   ☐ - No Information Available

	2	3	4	5	6	7	8	9	10	11	12	13	14	15	16	17	18	19/24	25/29	30/34	35/39	40/44	45/49	50/54	55/59	60/64	65/69	70/74	75/79	80/84	85/90+
Internal consistency											■	■	■	■	■	■	■														
Test-retest*																															

Interval between testings: not applicable

FLOORS AND CEILINGS

	Test Floor	Test Ceiling
Inadequate at ages:	12-0 to 13-5	17-6 to 18-11

CHC CLASSIFICATIONS (Broad: stratum II / *Narrow: stratum I*)

Quantitative Knowledge (*Gq*): *Mathematical Achievement (A3)* - Measured mathematics achievement.

DESCRIPTION

The examinee is required to spell phonetically regular and phonetically irregular words.

RELIABILITY

■ - Low   ■ - Medium   ■ - High   ☐ - No Information Available

	2	3	4	5	6	7	8	9	10	11	12	13	14	15	16	17	18	19 24	25 29	30 34	35 39	40 44	45 49	50 54	55 59	60 64	65 69	70 74	75 79	80 84	85 90+
Internal consistency											■	■	■	■	■	■	■														
Test-retest*																															

Interval between testings: not applicable

FLOORS AND CEILINGS

	Test Floor	**Test Ceiling**
Inadequate at ages:	12-0 to 18-11	16-6 to 18-11

CHC CLASSIFICATIONS (Broad: stratum II / *Narrow: stratum I*)

Reading/Writing (*Grw*): *Spelling Ability (SG)* - Ability to spell.

DESCRIPTION

The examinee is required to write a short story based on three stimulus pictures that are presented in such a manner to elicit a story that has a beginning, a middle, and an end.

RELIABILITY

■ - Low   ■ - Medium   ■ - High   ☐ - No Information Available

	2	3	4	5	6	7	8	9	10	11	12	13	14	15	16	17	18	19 24	25 29	30 34	35 39	40 44	45 49	50 54	55 59	60 64	65 69	70 74	75 79	80 84	85 90+
Internal consistency											■	■	■	■	■	■	■														
Test-retest*																															

Interval between testings: not applicable

FLOORS AND CEILINGS

	Test Floor	**Test Ceiling**
Inadequate at ages:	12-0 to 12-11	15-6 to 18-11

CHC CLASSIFICATIONS (Broad: stratum II / *Narrow: stratum I*)

Reading/Writing (*Grw*): *Writing Ability (WA)* - Ability to write with clarity of thought, organization, and good sentence structure.

DESCRIPTION

The examinee is required to answer questions pertaining to earth, science, biology, and chemistry that are read by the examiner.

RELIABILITY

☐ - Low   ■ - Medium   ■ - High   ☐ - No Information Available

	2	3	4	5	6	7	8	9	10	11	12	13	14	15	16	17	18	19 24	25 29	30 34	35 39	40 44	45 49	50 54	55 59	60 64	65 69	70 74	75 79	80 84	85 90+
Internal consistency											■	■	■	■	■	■	■														
Test-retest*																															

Interval between testings: not applicable

FLOORS AND CEILINGS

	Test Floor	Test Ceiling
Inadequate at ages:	12-0 to 12-5	none

CHC CLASSIFICATIONS (Broad: stratum II / Narrow: stratum I)

Crystallized Intelligence (Gc): *General Science Information (K1)* - Range of scientific knowledge (e.g., biology, physics, engineering, mechanics, electronics).

DESCRIPTION

The examinee is required to answer questions pertaining to economics, geography, world history, and civics that are read by the examiner.

RELIABILITY

☐ - Low   ■ - Medium   ■ - High   ☐ - No Information Available

	2	3	4	5	6	7	8	9	10	11	12	13	14	15	16	17	18	19 24	25 29	30 34	35 39	40 44	45 49	50 54	55 59	60 64	65 69	70 74	75 79	80 84	85 90+
Internal consistency											■	■	■	■	■	■	■														
Test-retest*																															

Interval between testings: not applicable

FLOORS AND CEILINGS

	Test Floor	Test Ceiling
Inadequate at ages:	12-0 to 16-5	none

CHC CLASSIFICATIONS (Broad: stratum II / Narrow: stratum I)

Crystallized Intelligence (Gc): *General (verbal) Information (K0)* - Range of general knowledge.

DESCRIPTION

The examinee is required to respond to questions regarding reference skills relating to guide words use, alphabetizing, encyclopedia use, table of contents use, library cataloging use, and dictionary use.

RELIABILITY

☐ - Low   ■ - Medium   ■ - High   ☐ - No Information Available

	2	3	4	5	6	7	8	9	10	11	12	13	14	15	16	17	18	19 24	25 29	30 34	35 39	40 44	45 49	50 54	55 59	60 64	65 69	70 74	75 79	80 84	85 90+
Internal consistency Test-retest*											■	■	■	■	■	■	■														

Interval between testings: not applicable

FLOORS AND CEILINGS

	Test Floor	Test Ceiling
Inadequate at ages:	none	12-6 to 18-11

CHC CLASSIFICATIONS (Broad: stratum II / *Narrow: stratum I*)

Crystallized Intelligence (*Gc*): *General (verbal) Information (K0)* - Range of general knowledge.

Kaufman Test of Educational Achievement/Normative Update (K-TEA/NU)

GENERAL INFORMATION

Author(s): Alan S. Kaufman and Nadeen L. Kaufman
Publisher: American Guidance Service
Publication Date(s)*: 1985, 1997

Age Range: 6-0 to 22-11
Administration Time: 20 to 65 minutes

COMPOSITE MEASURE INFORMATION

Reading Composite
Battery Composite

Mathematics Composite

SCORE INFORMATION

Standard scores	Percentiles	Stanines	Normal curve equivalents	Age equivalents	Grade equivalents

NORMING INFORMATION

Standardization Sample Size: 2,057-2,089

Sample Collection Date(s): 1995-1996

Avg. Number per Age/Grade Interval:
  100-199 per grade: K-12
  245-345 per five years: 18-0 to 22-11

Demographic Variables:
  Gender   *- male; female*
  Geographic region   *- 4 regions; 39 States and the District of Columbia; 129 communities*

Age Blocks in Norm Table:
  3 months: 6-0 to 18-11
  1 year: 19-0 to 22-11

  Race/ethnicity   *- African American; Hispanic; White; other*
  SES   *- parent education*
  Other   *- educational placement (special education: 6 categories; gifted)*

VALIDITY

Types of Validity Evidence Reported in the Test Manual:

Content	Criterion	Construct

Test Review(s) and Validity Evidence Reported in Extant Literature: See Appendix C

CONTAINS AT LEAST ONE INDICATOR CONSISTENT WITH THE FOLLOWING LD ASSESSMENT AREA(S)

Oral Expression	Listening Comprehension	Written Expression	Basic Reading Skill	Reading Comprehension	Mathematics Calculation	Mathematics Reasoning

SPECIAL FEATURES

- Provides computer scoring and interpretive profiling report
- Includes a sample report to parents in English and Spanish
- Includes an error analysis form to assist in identifying remediation needs for writing an Individualized Education Program
- Available in a brief form that includes mathematics, reading, and spelling subtests
- Provides standard scores by grade (fall and spring)

[*]All reliability and validity data reported in the test manual and thus in these summary pages pertain to the 1985 standardization sample.

DESCRIPTION

The examinee is required to solve math problems stated by the examiner while attending to visual stimuli such as pictures and graphs.

RELIABILITY [1]

☐ - Low   ◼ - Medium   ◼ - High   ☐ - No Information Available

	2	3	4	5	6	7	8	9	10	11	12	13	14	15	16	17	18	19–24	25–29	30–34	35–39	40–44	45–49	50–54	55–59	60–64	65–69	70–74	75–79	80–84	85/90+
Internal consistency																															
Test-retest*																															

Interval between testings: 1 to 35 days

FLOORS AND CEILINGS

	Test Floor	**Test Ceiling**
Inadequate at ages:	none	none

CHC CLASSIFICATIONS (Broad: stratum II / *Narrow: stratum I*)

Quantitative Knowledge (*Gq*): *Mathematical Achievement (A3)* - Measured mathematics achievement.

DESCRIPTION

The examinee is required to identify letters and pronounce words of increasing difficulty.

RELIABILITY [1]

☐ - Low   ◼ - Medium   ◼ - High   ☐ - No Information Available

	2	3	4	5	6	7	8	9	10	11	12	13	14	15	16	17	18	19–24	25–29	30–34	35–39	40–44	45–49	50–54	55–59	60–64	65–69	70–74	75–79	80–84	85/90+
Internal consistency																															
Test-retest*																															

Interval between testings: 1 to 35 days

FLOORS AND CEILINGS

	Test Floor	**Test Ceiling**
Inadequate at ages:	none	18-0 to 22-11

CHC CLASSIFICATIONS (Broad: stratum II / *Narrow: stratum I*)

Reading/Writing (*Grw*): *Reading Decoding (RD)* - Ability to recognize and decode words or pseudowords in reading.

[1]Split-half coefficients were reported as estimates of internal consistency rather than coefficient alpha. Test-retest coefficients were reported by grade in the test manual. Therefore, corresponding ages were estimated by the authors.

| Battery: K-TEA/NU | Spelling | Age Range: 6-0 to 22-11 |

DESCRIPTION

The examinee is required to spell words that are stated by the examiner.

RELIABILITY [1]

☐ - Low   ▨ - Medium   ■ - High   ☐ - No Information Available

	2	3	4	5	6	7	8	9	10	11	12	13	14	15	16	17	18	19 24	25 29	30 34	35 39	40 44	45 49	50 54	55 59	60 64	65 69	70 74	75 79	80 84	85 90+
Internal consistency					▨	■	■	■	■	■	■	■	■	■	■	■	■	■													
Test-retest*					■	■	■	■	■	■	■	■	■	■	■	■	■	■													

Interval between testings: 1 to 35 days

FLOORS AND CEILINGS

	Test Floor	Test Ceiling
Inadequate at ages:	6-0 to 8-2	none

CHC CLASSIFICATIONS (Broad: stratum II / *Narrow: stratum I*)

Reading/Writing (*Grw*): *Spelling Ability (SG)* - Ability to spell.

| Battery: K-TEA/NU | Reading Comprehension | Age Range: 6-0 to 22-11 |

DESCRIPTION

The examinee is required to read a passage, read one or two questions about the passage, and respond orally to these questions.

RELIABILITY [1]

☐ - Low   ▨ - Medium   ■ - High   ☐ - No Information Available

	2	3	4	5	6	7	8	9	10	11	12	13	14	15	16	17	18	19 24	25 29	30 34	35 39	40 44	45 49	50 54	55 59	60 64	65 69	70 74	75 79	80 84	85 90+
Internal consistency				■	■	■	■	■	■	■	■	■	■	■	■	▨	■	■													
Test-retest*				■	■	■	■	■	■	■	■	■	■	■	■	▨	■	■													

Interval between testings: 1 to 35 days

FLOORS AND CEILINGS

	Test Floor	Test Ceiling
Inadequate at ages:	6-0 to 8-8	22-0 to 22-11

CHC CLASSIFICATIONS (Broad: stratum II / *Narrow: stratum I*)

Reading/Writing (*Grw*): *Reading Comprehension (RC)* - Ability to comprehend connected discourse during reading.

[1]Split-half coefficients were reported as estimates of internal consistency rather than coefficient alpha. Test-retest coefficients were reported by grade in the test manual. Therefore, corresponding ages were estimated by the authors.

DESCRIPTION

The examinee is required to solve written computational problems using the four basic operations as well as solve algebra problems.

RELIABILITY [1]

| | - Low | ■ - Medium | ■ - High | ☐ - No Information Available |

	2	3	4	5	6	7	8	9	10	11	12	13	14	15	16	17	18	19 24	25 29	30 34	35 39	40 44	45 49	50 54	55 59	60 64	65 69	70 74	75 79	80 84	85 90+
Internal consistency																															
Test-retest*																															

Interval between testings: 1 to 35 days

FLOORS AND CEILINGS

	Test Floor	**Test Ceiling**
Inadequate at ages:	6-0 to 6-2	22-0 to 22-11

CHC CLASSIFICATIONS (Broad: stratum II / *Narrow: stratum I*)

Quantitative Knowledge (*Gq*): *Mathematical Achievement (A3)* - Measured mathematics achievement.

[1]Split-half coefficients were reported as estimates of internal consistency rather than coefficient alpha. Test-retest coefficients were reported by grade in the test manual. Therefore, corresponding ages were estimated by the authors.

Peabody Individual Achievement Test-Revised/Normative Update (PIAT-R/NU)

GENERAL INFORMATION

Author(s): Frederick C. Markwardt, Jr.
Publisher: American Guidance Service
Publication Date(s)*: 1978, 1989, 1998

Age Range: 5-0 to 22-11
Administration Time: 60 minutes

COMPOSITE MEASURE INFORMATION

Total Reading
Total Test

Written Language

SCORE INFORMATION

Standard scores	Percentiles	Stanines	Normal curve equivalents	Age equivalents	Grade equivalents

NORMING INFORMATION

Standardization Sample Size: 1,285-2,809

Sample Collection Date(s): 1995-1996

Avg. Number per Age/Grade Interval:
  <100-199 per grade: K-12
  168-345 per five years: 18-0 to 22-11

Demographic Variables:
  Gender   - male; female
  Geographic region - 4 regions; 39 States and the District of Columbia; 129 communities

Age Blocks in Norm Table:
  3 months: 5-0 to 18-11
  1 year: 19-0 to 22-11

  Race/ethnicity - African American; Hispanic; White; other
  SES   - parent education
  Other   - educational placement (special education: 6 categories; gifted)

VALIDITY

Types of Validity Evidence Reported in the Test Manual:

Content	Criterion	Construct

Test Review(s) and Validity Evidence Reported in Extant Literature: See Appendix C

CONTAINS AT LEAST ONE INDICATOR CONSISTENT WITH THE FOLLOWING LD ASSESSMENT AREA(S)

Oral Expression	Listening Comprehension	Written Expression	Basic Reading Skill	Reading Comprehension	Mathematics Calculation	Mathematics Reasoning

SPECIAL FEATURES

- Provides computer scoring and interpretive profiling report
- Includes an Optional Pronunciation Guide cassette for accepted pronunciation of words in the Reading Recognition and Spelling subtests
- Provides standard scores by grade (fall, winter, and spring)

---

[*]All reliability and validity data reported in the test manual and thus in these summary pages pertain to the 1989 standardization sample.

DESCRIPTION

The examinee is required to provide oral responses to general information questions that are read by the examiner.

RELIABILITY [1]

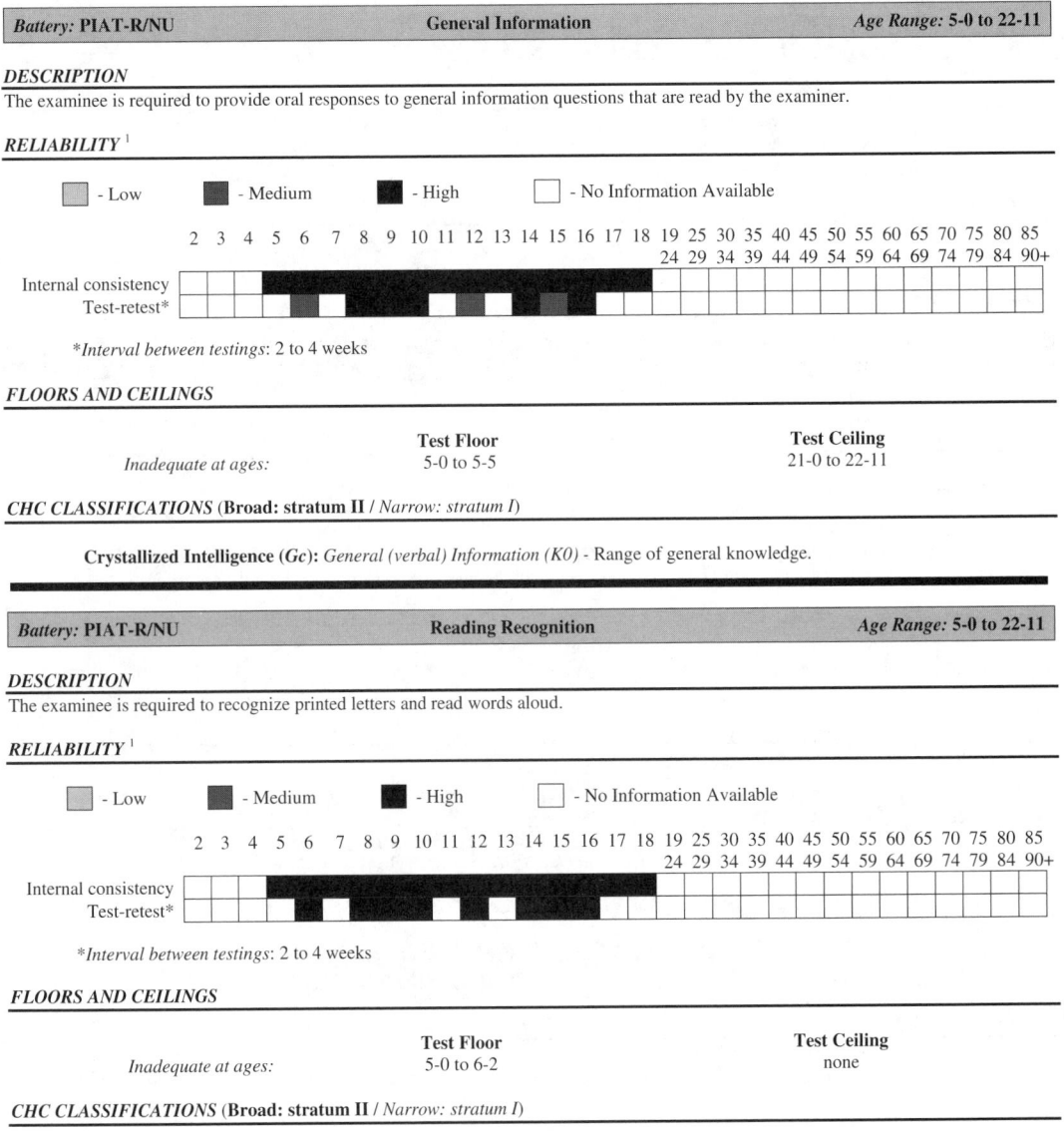

- Low   - Medium   - High   - No Information Available

Internal consistency
Test-retest*

*Interval between testings: 2 to 4 weeks

FLOORS AND CEILINGS

	Test Floor	Test Ceiling
Inadequate at ages:	5-0 to 5-5	21-0 to 22-11

CHC CLASSIFICATIONS (Broad: stratum II / *Narrow: stratum I*)

Crystallized Intelligence (*Gc*): *General (verbal) Information (K0)* - Range of general knowledge.

DESCRIPTION

The examinee is required to recognize printed letters and read words aloud.

RELIABILITY [1]

- Low   - Medium   - High   - No Information Available

Internal consistency
Test-retest*

*Interval between testings: 2 to 4 weeks

FLOORS AND CEILINGS

	Test Floor	Test Ceiling
Inadequate at ages:	5-0 to 6-2	none

CHC CLASSIFICATIONS (Broad: stratum II / *Narrow: stratum I*)

Reading/Writing (*Grw*): *Reading Decoding (RD)* - Ability to recognize and decode words or pseudowords in reading.

---

[1]Split-half coefficients were reported as estimates of internal consistency rather than coefficient alpha.

DESCRIPTION

The examinee is required to read a sentence silently and then select one of four pictures that best represents the meaning of that sentence.

RELIABILITY [1]

☐ - Low ☐ - Medium ☐ - High ☐ - No Information Available

	2	3	4	5	6	7	8	9	10	11	12	13	14	15	16	17	18	19 24	25 29	30 34	35 39	40 44	45 49	50 54	55 59	60 64	65 69	70 74	75 79	80 84	85 90+
Internal consistency																															
Test-retest*																															

Interval between testings: 2 to 4 weeks

FLOORS AND CEILINGS

	Test Floor	Test Ceiling
Inadequate at ages:	5-0 to 6-2	22-0 to 22-11

CHC CLASSIFICATIONS (Broad: stratum II / *Narrow: stratum I*)

Reading/Writing (Grw): *Reading Comprehension (RC)* - Ability to comprehend connected discourse during reading.

DESCRIPTION

The examinee is required to listen as the examiner reads aloud a math question (and for later items, read silently while the examiner reads aloud). Then the examinee is required to use a multiple-choice format to provide answers to the questions or problems.

RELIABILITY [1]

☐ - Low ☐ - Medium ☐ - High ☐ - No Information Available

	2	3	4	5	6	7	8	9	10	11	12	13	14	15	16	17	18	19 24	25 29	30 34	35 39	40 44	45 49	50 54	55 59	60 64	65 69	70 74	75 79	80 84	85 90+
Internal consistency																															
Test-retest*																															

Interval between testings: 2 to 4 weeks

FLOORS AND CEILINGS

	Test Floor	Test Ceiling
Inadequate at ages:	none	none

CHC CLASSIFICATIONS (Broad: stratum II / *Narrow: stratum I*)

Quantitative Knowledge (Gq): *Mathematical Knowledge (KM)* - Range of general knowledge about mathematics.

[1] Split-half coefficients were reported as estimates of internal consistency rather than coefficient alpha.

DESCRIPTION

The examinee is required to discriminate letters visually, select the letter that corresponds to a given sound, identify the word that begins with a given sound, and select the correct spelling for a word from four choices that the examiner states.

RELIABILITY [1]

☐ - Low   ■ - Medium   ■ - High   ☐ - No Information Available

	2	3	4	5	6	7	8	9	10	11	12	13	14	15	16	17	18	19 24	25 29	30 34	35 39	40 44	45 49	50 54	55 59	60 64	65 69	70 74	75 79	80 84	85 90+
Internal consistency																															
Test-retest*																															

Interval between testings: 2 to 4 weeks

FLOORS AND CEILINGS

	Test Floor	**Test Ceiling**
Inadequate at ages:	5-0 to 5-8	none

CHC CLASSIFICATIONS (**Broad: stratum II** / *Narrow: stratum I*)

Reading/Writing (*Grw*): *Spelling Ability (SG)* - Ability to spell. **Auditory Processing (*Ga*):** *Phonetic Coding: Analysis (PC:A)* - Ability to segment larger units of speech sounds into smaller units of speech sounds.

DESCRIPTION

The examinee is required to write his/her first and last name, copy letters or words, and write letters, words, and sentences dictated by the examiner.

RELIABILITY [2]

☐ - Low   ■ - Medium   ■ - High   ☐ - No Information Available

	2	3	4	5	6	7	8	9	10	11	12	13	14	15	16	17	18	19 24	25 29	30 34	35 39	40 44	45 49	50 54	55 59	60 64	65 69	70 74	75 79	80 84	85 90+
Internal consistency																															
Test-retest*																															

Interval between testings: 2 to 4 weeks

FLOORS AND CEILINGS

	Test Floor	**Test Ceiling**
Inadequate at ages:	none	none

CHC CLASSIFICATIONS (**Broad: stratum II** / *Narrow: stratum I*)

Reading/Writing (*Grw*): *Spelling Ability (SG)* - Ability to spell.

---

[1]Split-half coefficients were reported as estimates of internal consistency rather than coefficient alpha.
[2]Test-retest coefficients were reported by grade in the test manual. Therefore, corresponding ages were estimated by the authors.

DESCRIPTION

The examinee is required to write a story related to a picture.

RELIABILITY [1]

☐ - Low   ■ - Medium   ■ - High   ☐ - No Information Available

	2	3	4	5	6	7	8	9	10	11	12	13	14	15	16	17	18	19 24	25 29	30 34	35 39	40 44	45 49	50 54	55 59	60 64	65 69	70 74	75 79	80 84	85 90+
Internal consistency																															
Test-retest*																															

*Interval between testings: not applicable

FLOORS AND CEILINGS

	Test Floor	Test Ceiling
Inadequate at ages:	none	none

CHC CLASSIFICATIONS (Broad: stratum II / Narrow: stratum I)

Reading/Writing (Grw): *Writing Ability (WA)* - Ability to write with clarity of thought, organization, and good sentence structure.

DESCRIPTION

The examinee is required to write a story related to a picture.

RELIABILITY [1]

☐ - Low   ■ - Medium   ■ - High   ☐ - No Information Available

	2	3	4	5	6	7	8	9	10	11	12	13	14	15	16	17	18	19 24	25 29	30 34	35 39	40 44	45 49	50 54	55 59	60 64	65 69	70 74	75 79	80 84	85 90+
Internal consistency																															
Test-retest*																															

*Interval between testings: not applicable

FLOORS AND CEILINGS

	Test Floor	Test Ceiling
Inadequate at ages:	none	none

CHC CLASSIFICATIONS (Broad: stratum II / Narrow: stratum I)

Reading/Writing (Grw): *Writing Ability (WA)* - Ability to write with clarity of thought, organization, and good sentence structure.

[1]Coefficients were reported by grade in the test manual. Therefore, corresponding ages were estimated by the authors.

Wechsler Individual Achievement Test-Second Edition (WIAT-II)

GENERAL INFORMATION

Author(s): The Psychological Corporation
Publisher: The Psychological Corporation
Publication Date(s): 1992, 2001

Age Range: 4-0 to 19-11
Administration Time: 30 to 75 minutes

COMPOSITE MEASURE INFORMATION

Reading
Written Language
Total

Mathematics
Oral Language

SCORE INFORMATION

Standard scores	Percentiles	Stanines	Normal curve equivalents	Age equivalents	Grade equivalents

NORMING INFORMATION

Standardization Sample Size: 2,950

Sample Collection Date(s): 1999-2001

Avg. Number per Age/Grade Interval:
184 per age: 4-0 to 19-11

Demographic Variables:
  Gender   *- male; female*
  Geographic region   *- 4 regions*

Age Blocks in Norm Table:
4 months: 4-0 to 13-11
1 year: 14-0 to 16-11
3 years: 17-0 to 19-11

  Race/ethnicity   *- White; African-American; Hispanic; Asian; other*
  SES   *- parent education*

VALIDITY

Types of Validity Evidence Reported in the Test Manual:

Content	Criterion	Construct

Test Review(s) and Validity Evidence Reported in Extant Literature: See Appendix C

CONTAINS AT LEAST ONE INDICATOR CONSISTENT WITH THE FOLLOWING LD ASSESSMENT AREA(S)

Oral Expression	Listening Comprehension	Written Expression	Basic Reading Skill	Reading Comprehension	Mathematics Calculation	Mathematics Reasoning

SPECIAL FEATURES

- Provides computer scoring and interpretive profiling report
- Includes comprehensive coverage of the areas of learning disability specified in IDEA
- Includes a new subtest called Pseudoword Decoding
- Linked with the Wechsler Intelligence Scale for Children-Third Edition, Wechsler Preschool and Primary Scale of Intelligence-Revised, and Wechsler Adult Intelligence Scale-Third Edition.
- Developed in conjunction with the Process Assessment of the Learner: Test Battery for Reading and Writing
- Provides standard scores by grade (fall and spring)
- Normative information for the college and adult standardization sample is available in the WIAT-II Supplement for College Students and Adults
- Includes a detachable parent report as part of the test protocol

Battery: WIAT-II	Word Reading	Age Range: 4-0 to 19-11

DESCRIPTION

The examinee is required to name all of the letters of the alphabet, identify and generate rhyming words, identify the beginning and ending sounds of words, match sounds with letters and letter blends, and read aloud from a graded word list.

RELIABILITY [1]

☐ - Low ■ - Medium ■ - High ☐ - No Information Available

	2	3	4	5	6	7	8	9	10	11	12	13	14	15	16	17	18	19 24	25 29	30 34	35 39	40 44	45 49	50 54	55 59	60 64	65 69	70 74	75 79	80 84	85 90+
Internal consistency Test-retest*																															

*Interval between testings: 7 to 45 days

FLOORS AND CEILINGS

	Test Floor	Test Ceiling
Inadequate at ages:	4-0 to 5-11	14-0 to 19-11

CHC CLASSIFICATIONS (Broad: stratum II / Narrow: stratum I)

Reading/Writing (Grw): *Reading Decoding (RD)* - Ability to recognize and decode words or pseudowords in reading.

Battery: WIAT-II	Numerical Operations	Age Range: 5-0 to 19-11

DESCRIPTION

The examinee is required to identify and write numbers, count using 1:1 correspondence, solve written calculation problems and simple equations involving all basic operations.

RELIABILITY [1]

☐ - Low ■ - Medium ■ - High ☐ - No Information Available

	2	3	4	5	6	7	8	9	10	11	12	13	14	15	16	17	18	19 24	25 29	30 34	35 39	40 44	45 49	50 54	55 59	60 64	65 69	70 74	75 79	80 84	85 90+
Internal consistency Test-retest*																															

*Interval between testings: 7 to 45 days

FLOORS AND CEILINGS

	Test Floor	Test Ceiling
Inadequate at ages:	5-0 to 5-7	15-0 to 19-11

CHC CLASSIFICATIONS (Broad: stratum II / Narrow: stratum I)

Quantitative Knowledge (Gq): *Mathematical Achievement (A3)* - Measured mathematics achievement.

[1]Split-half coefficients were reported as estimates of internal consistency rather than coefficient alpha.

DESCRIPTION

The examinee is required to match a written word with its representative picture, read different types of passages and answer questions involving the comprehension of content, and read short sentences aloud and respond to comprehension questions.

RELIABILITY [1]

■ - Low   ■ - Medium   ■ - High   □ - No Information Available

	2	3	4	5	6	7	8	9	10	11	12	13	14	15	16	17	18	19/24	25/29	30/34	35/39	40/44	45/49	50/54	55/59	60/64	65/69	70/74	75/79	80/84	85/90+
Internal consistency																															
Test-retest*																															

Interval between testings: 7 to 45 days

FLOORS AND CEILINGS

	Test Floor	Test Ceiling
Inadequate at ages:	none	none

CHC CLASSIFICATIONS (Broad: stratum II / *Narrow: stratum I*)

Reading/Writing (*Grw*): *Reading Comprehension (RC)* - Ability to comprehend connected discourse during reading.

DESCRIPTION

The examinee is required to write dictated letters, letter blends, and words.

RELIABILITY [1]

■ - Low   ■ - Medium   ■ - High   □ - No Information Available

	2	3	4	5	6	7	8	9	10	11	12	13	14	15	16	17	18	19/24	25/29	30/34	35/39	40/44	45/49	50/54	55/59	60/64	65/69	70/74	75/79	80/84	85/90+
Internal consistency																															
Test-retest*																															

Interval between testings: 7 to 45 days

FLOORS AND CEILINGS

	Test Floor	Test Ceiling
Inadequate at ages:	5-0 to 6-7	17-0 to 19-11

CHC CLASSIFICATIONS (Broad: stratum II / *Narrow: stratum I*)

Reading/Writing (*Grw*): *Spelling Ability (SG)* - Ability to spell.

[1]Split-half coefficients were reported as estimates of internal consistency rather than coefficient alpha.

Battery: WIAT-II	Pseudoword Decoding	Age Range: 4-0 to 19-11

DESCRIPTION

The examinee is required to read aloud from a list of nonsense words designed to mimic the phonetic structure of words in the English language.

RELIABILITY [1]

■ - Low ■ - Medium ■ - High □ - No Information Available

	2	3	4	5	6	7	8	9	10	11	12	13	14	15	16	17	18	19/24	25/29	30/34	35/39	40/44	45/49	50/54	55/59	60/64	65/69	70/74	75/79	80/84	85/90+
Internal consistency																															
Test-retest*																															

Interval between testings: 7 to 45 days

FLOORS AND CEILINGS

	Test Floor	Test Ceiling
Inadequate at ages:	6-0 to 9-7	8-8 to 19-11

CHC CLASSIFICATIONS (Broad: stratum II / Narrow: stratum I)

Reading/Writing (Grw): *Reading Decoding (RD)* - Ability to recognize and decode words or pseudowords in reading.

Battery: WIAT-II	Mathematics Reasoning	Age Range: 4-0 to 19-11

DESCRIPTION

The examinee is required to count, identify geometric shapes, solve single and multi-step word problems, interpret graphs, identify mathematical patterns, and to solve problems related to statistics and probability.

RELIABILITY [1]

■ - Low ■ - Medium ■ - High □ - No Information Available

	2	3	4	5	6	7	8	9	10	11	12	13	14	15	16	17	18	19/24	25/29	30/34	35/39	40/44	45/49	50/54	55/59	60/64	65/69	70/74	75/79	80/84	85/90+
Internal consistency																															
Test-retest*																															

Interval between testings: 7 to 45 days

FLOORS AND CEILINGS

	Test Floor	Test Ceiling
Inadequate at ages:	4-0 to 4-11	13-4 to 19-11

CHC CLASSIFICATIONS (Broad: stratum II / Narrow: stratum I)

Fluid Reasoning (Gf): *Quantitative Reasoning (RQ)* - Ability to inductively and deductively reason with concepts involving mathematical relations and properties.

[1]Split-half coefficients were reported as estimates of internal consistency rather than coefficient alpha.

Battery: WIAT-II	Written Expression	Age Range: 4-0 to 19-11

DESCRIPTION

The examinee is required to write the alphabet, write words fluently, and combine and generate sentences to produce a rough-draft paragraph (grades 3-6) or persuasive essay (grade 7 and above).

RELIABILITY

☐ - Low   ■ - Medium   ■ - High   ☐ - No Information Available

	2 3 4 5 6 7 8 9 10 11 12 13 14 15 16 17 18 19 25 30 35 40 45 50 55 60 65 70 75 80 85
	24 29 34 39 44 49 54 59 64 69 74 79 84 90+
Internal consistency	
Test-retest*	

*Interval between testings: 7 to 45 days

FLOORS AND CEILINGS

	Test Floor	Test Ceiling
Inadequate at ages:	6-0 to 7-11	none

CHC CLASSIFICATIONS (Broad: stratum II / *Narrow: stratum I*)

Reading/Writing (*Grw*): *Writing Ability (WA)* - Ability to write with clarity of thought, organization, and good sentence structure.

Battery: WIAT-II	Listening Comprehension	Age Range: 4-0 to 19-11

DESCRIPTION

The examinee is required to select a picture that matches a word or sentence, and to generate a word that matches a picture and oral description.

RELIABILITY [1]

☐ - Low   ■ - Medium   ■ - High   ☐ - No Information Available

	2 3 4 5 6 7 8 9 10 11 12 13 14 15 16 17 18 19 25 30 35 40 45 50 55 60 65 70 75 80 85
	24 29 34 39 44 49 54 59 64 69 74 79 84 90+
Internal consistency	
Test-retest*	

*Interval between testings: 7 to 45 days

FLOORS AND CEILINGS

	Test Floor	Test Ceiling
Inadequate at ages:	4-0 to 4-7	14-0 to 19-11

CHC CLASSIFICATIONS (Broad: stratum II / *Narrow: stratum I*)

Crystallized Intelligence (*Gc*): *Listening Ability (LS)* - Ability to listen and comprehend oral communications.

[1] Split-half coefficients were reported as estimates of internal consistency rather than coefficient alpha.

DESCRIPTION

The examinee is required to name targeted words, repeat sentences, and generate stories from visual cues and directions from visual or verbal cues.

RELIABILITY

| ☐ - Low | ■ - Medium | ■ - High | ☐ - No Information Available |

	2	3	4	5	6	7	8	9	10	11	12	13	14	15	16	17	18	19 24	25 29	30 34	35 39	40 44	45 49	50 54	55 59	60 64	65 69	70 74	75 79	80 84	85 90+
Internal consistency																															
Test-retest*																															

Interval between testings: 7 to 45 days

FLOORS AND CEILINGS

	Test Floor	**Test Ceiling**
Inadequate at ages:	4-0 to 4-7	none

CHC CLASSIFICATIONS (Broad: stratum II / *Narrow: stratum I*)

Crystallized Intelligence (*Gc*): *Communication Ability (CM)* - Ability to speak in "real life" situations (e.g., lecture, group participation) in an adult-like manner.

Woodcock-Johnson Tests of Achievement III (WJ III)[1]

GENERAL INFORMATION

Author(s): Richard W. Woodcock, Kevin S. McGrew, and
Nancy Mather
Publisher: Riverside Publishing
Publication Date(s): 1977, 1989, 2001

Age Range: 2-0 to 90+
Administration Time: 60 to 70 minutes (Standard Battery)

COMPOSITE MEASURE INFORMATION

Broad Reading
Reading Comprehension
Oral Language-Extended
Oral Expression
Math Calculation Skills
Broad Written Language
Written Expression
Academic Skills
Academic Applications
Total Achievement

Basic Reading Skills
Oral Language-Standard
Listening Comprehension
Broad Math
Math Reasoning
Basic Writing Skills
Academic Knowledge
Academic Fluency
Phoneme/Grapheme Knowledge

SCORE INFORMATION

Standard scores	Percentiles	Stanines	Normal curve equivalents	Age equivalents	Grade equivalents

NORMING INFORMATION

Standardization Sample Size: 8,818

Sample Collection Date(s): 1999-2000

Avg. Number per Age/Grade Interval:
  351 per year: 2-0 to 19-11
  313 per ten years: 20-0 to 90-11

Age Blocks in Norm Table:
  1 month: 2-0 to 19-11
  1 year: 20-0 to 89-11
  >1 year: 90+

Demographic Variables:
  Gender   *- male; female*
  Geographic region *- 4 regions; 27 states; 100 communities*
  Residence   *- central city and urban fringe; larger and smaller communities and associated rural areas*
  Race/ethnicity *- White; Black; American Indian; Asian and Pacific Islander; Hispanic*
  SES   *- parent/examinee education; occupation*
  Other   *- type of school/college/university*

VALIDITY

Types of Validity Evidence Reported in the Test Manual:

Content	Criterion	Construct

Test Review(s) and Validity Evidence Reported in Extant Literature: See Appendix C

CONTAINS AT LEAST ONE INDICATOR CONSISTENT WITH THE FOLLOWING LD ASSESSMENT AREA(S)

Oral Expression	Listening Comprehension	Written Expression	Basic Reading Skill	Reading Comprehension	Mathematics Calculation	Mathematics Reasoning

SPECIAL FEATURES

- Provides alternate forms (A and B)
- Provides computer scoring and interpretive profiling report
- Provides standard scores by age and grade using a continuous norming procedure
- Includes comprehensive coverage of the areas of learning disability specified in IDEA
- Includes seven new subtests and eight new clusters

[1]The broad and narrow CHC classifications reported for the WJ III here and in Appendix A are based on the empirical analyses provided in McGrew and Woodcock (2001). These classifications, therefore, may differ from those obtained through the expert consensus process reported in Appendix H.

Battery: WJ III	Letter-Word Identification (Form A or B)	Age Range: 2-0 to 90+

DESCRIPTION

The examinee is required to identify letters and words correctly.

RELIABILITY [1]

☐ - Low   ■ - Medium   ■ - High   ☐ - No Information Available

	2	3	4	5	6	7	8	9	10	11	12	13	14	15	16	17	18	19 24	25 29	30 34	35 39	40 44	45 49	50 54	55 59	60 64	65 69	70 74	75 79	80 84	85 90+
Internal consistency																															
Test-retest*																															

Interval between testings: 1 year

FLOORS AND CEILINGS

	Test Floor	Test Ceiling
Inadequate at ages:	2-0 to 4-0	18-0 to 90+

CHC CLASSIFICATIONS (Broad: stratum II / *Narrow: stratum I*)

Reading/Writing (*Grw*): *Reading Decoding (RD)* - Ability to recognize and decode words or pseudowords in reading.

Battery: WJ III	Reading Fluency (Form A or B)	Age Range: 6-0 to 90+

DESCRIPTION

The examinee is required to read simple sentences quickly and decide if the statement is true.

RELIABILITY [2]

☐ - Low   ■ - Medium   ■ - High   ☐ - No Information Available

	2	3	4	5	6	7	8	9	10	11	12	13	14	15	16	17	18	19 24	25 29	30 34	35 39	40 44	45 49	50 54	55 59	60 64	65 69	70 74	75 79	80 84	85 90+
Internal consistency																															
Test-retest*																															

Interval between testings: 1 year

FLOORS AND CEILINGS

	Test Floor	Test Ceiling
Inadequate at ages:	6-0 to 7-0	none

CHC CLASSIFICATIONS (Broad: stratum II / *Narrow: stratum I*)

Reading/Writing (*Grw*): *Reading Speed (RS)* - Time required to silently read a passage or series of sentences as quickly as possible.

[1]Split-half coefficients were reported as estimates of internal consistency rather than coefficient alpha.
[2]Item response theory coefficients were reported as estimates of internal consistency rather than coefficient alpha.

DESCRIPTION

The examinee is required to recall increasingly complex stories that are presented using an audio recording.

RELIABILITY [1]

☐ - Low   ■ - Medium   ■ - High   ☐ - No Information Available

	2	3	4	5	6	7	8	9	10	11	12	13	14	15	16	17	18	19-24	25-29	30-34	35-39	40-44	45-49	50-54	55-59	60-64	65-69	70-74	75-79	80-84	85-90+
Internal consistency																															
Test-retest*																															

Interval between testings: 1 year

FLOORS AND CEILINGS

	Test Floor	Test Ceiling
Inadequate at ages:	2-0 to 5-6	none

CHC CLASSIFICATIONS (Broad: stratum II / *Narrow: stratum I*)

Crystallized Intelligence (*Gc*): *Listening Ability (LS)* - Ability to listen and comprehend oral communications. **Long-Term Retrieval (*Glr*):** *Meaningful Memory (MM)* - Ability to recall a set of items where there is a meaningful relation between items or the items comprise a meaningful story or connected discourse.

DESCRIPTION

The examinee is required to listen to a sequence of audio-recorded instructions and then follow the directions by pointing to various objects in a colored picture.

RELIABILITY [2]

☐ - Low   ■ - Medium   ■ - High   ☐ - No Information Available

	2	3	4	5	6	7	8	9	10	11	12	13	14	15	16	17	18	19-24	25-29	30-34	35-39	40-44	45-49	50-54	55-59	60-64	65-69	70-74	75-79	80-84	85-90+
Internal consistency																															
Test-retest*																															

Interval between testings: not applicable

FLOORS AND CEILINGS

	Test Floor	Test Ceiling
Inadequate at ages:	2-0 to 3-6	none

CHC CLASSIFICATIONS (Broad: stratum II / *Narrow: stratum I*)

Crystallized Intelligence (*Gc*): *Listening Ability (LS)* - Ability to listen and comprehend oral communications. **Short-Term Memory (*Gsm*):** *Working Memory (MW)* - Ability to temporarily store and perform a set of cognitive operations on information that requires divided attention and the management of the limited capacity of short-term memory.

---

[1]Item response theory coefficients were reported as estimates of internal consistency rather than coefficient alpha.
[2]Split-half coefficients were reported as estimates of internal consistency rather than coefficient alpha.

DESCRIPTION

The examinee is required to perform mathematical operations (addition, subtraction, multiplication, division, and combinations of these basic operations, as well as geometric, trigonometric, logarithmic, and calculus operations) involving decimals, fractions, and whole numbers.

RELIABILITY [1]

☐ - Low   ■ - Medium   ■ - High   ☐ - No Information Available

	2	3	4	5	6	7	8	9	10	11	12	13	14	15	16	17	18	19 24	25 29	30 34	35 39	40 44	45 49	50 54	55 59	60 64	65 69	70 74	75 79	80 84	85 90+
Internal consistency																															
Test-retest*																															

*Interval between testings: 1 year

FLOORS AND CEILINGS

	Test Floor	Test Ceiling
Inadequate at ages:	5-0 to 6-6	none

CHC CLASSIFICATIONS (Broad: stratum II / *Narrow: stratum I*)

Quantitative Knowledge (*Gq*): *Mathematical Achievement (A3)* - Measured mathematics achievement.

DESCRIPTION

The examinee is required to solve simple addition, subtraction, and multiplication facts quickly.

RELIABILITY [2]

☐ - Low   ■ - Medium   ■ - High   ☐ - No Information Available

	2	3	4	5	6	7	8	9	10	11	12	13	14	15	16	17	18	19 24	25 29	30 34	35 39	40 44	45 49	50 54	55 59	60 64	65 69	70 74	75 79	80 84	85 90+
Internal consistency																															
Test-retest*																															

*Interval between testings: 1 year

FLOORS AND CEILINGS

	Test Floor	Test Ceiling
Inadequate at ages:	7-0	none

CHC CLASSIFICATIONS (Broad: stratum II / *Narrow: stratum I*)

Processing Speed (*Gs*): *Number Facility (N)* - Ability to rapidly and accurately manipulate and deal with numbers, from elementary skills of counting and recognizing numbers to advanced skills of adding, subtracting, multiplying, and dividing numbers. **Quantitative Knowledge (*Gq*):** *Mathematical Achievement (A3)* - Measured mathematics achievement.

[1] Split-half coefficients were reported as estimates of internal consistency rather than coefficient alpha.
[2] Item response theory coefficients were reported as estimates of internal consistency rather than coefficient alpha.

| Battery: WJ III | Spelling (Form A or B) | Age Range: 2-0 to 90+ |

DESCRIPTION

The examinee is required to write orally presented words correctly.

RELIABILITY [1]

☐ - Low   ■ - Medium   ■ - High   ☐ - No Information Available

	2	3	4	5	6	7	8	9	10	11	12	13	14	15	16	17	18	19 24	25 29	30 34	35 39	40 44	45 49	50 54	55 59	60 64	65 69	70 74	75 79	80 84	85 90+
Internal consistency Test-retest*																															

Interval between testings: 1 year

FLOORS AND CEILINGS

	Test Floor	Test Ceiling
Inadequate at ages:	2-0 to 3-6	none

CHC CLASSIFICATIONS (Broad: stratum II / Narrow: stratum I)

Reading/Writing (Grw): *Spelling Ability (SG)* - Ability to spell.

| Battery: WJ III | Writing Fluency (Form A or B) | Age Range: 7-0 to 90+ |

DESCRIPTION

The examinee is required to formulate and write a simple sentence by using a set of three words that relates to a given stimulus picture.

RELIABILITY [2]

☐ - Low   ■ - Medium   ■ - High   ☐ - No Information Available

	2	3	4	5	6	7	8	9	10	11	12	13	14	15	16	17	18	19 24	25 29	30 34	35 39	40 44	45 49	50 54	55 59	60 64	65 69	70 74	75 79	80 84	85 90+
Internal consistency Test-retest*																															

Interval between testings: 1 year

FLOORS AND CEILINGS

	Test Floor	Test Ceiling
Inadequate at ages:	7-0 to 8-0	none

CHC CLASSIFICATIONS (Broad: stratum II / Narrow: stratum I)

Reading/Writing (Grw): *Writing Ability (WA)* - Ability to write with clarity of thought, organization, and good sentence structure. **Processing Speed (Gs):** *Rate of Test Taking (R9)* - Ability to rapidly perform tests which are relatively easy or that require very simple decisions.

[1]Split-half coefficients were reported as estimates of internal consistency rather than coefficient alpha.
[2]Item response theory coefficients were reported as estimates of internal consistency rather than coefficient alpha.

DESCRIPTION

The examinee is required to point to pictures represented by a phrase and read a short passage to identify a missing key word that makes sense in the context of that passage.

RELIABILITY [1]

| | - Low | | - Medium | | - High | | - No Information Available |

| | 2 3 4 5 6 7 8 9 10 11 12 13 14 15 16 17 18 19 25 30 35 40 45 50 55 60 65 70 75 80 85 |
| | 24 29 34 39 44 49 54 59 64 69 74 79 84 90+ |

Internal consistency
Test-retest*

*Interval between testings: 1 year

FLOORS AND CEILINGS

	Test Floor	**Test Ceiling**
Inadequate at ages:	2-0 to 5-6	none

CHC CLASSIFICATIONS (Broad: stratum II / *Narrow: stratum I*)

Reading/Writing (*Grw*): *Reading Comprehension (RC)* - Ability to comprehend connected discourse during reading; *Cloze Ability (CZ)* - Ability to supply words deleted from prose passages that must be read.

DESCRIPTION

The examinee is required to analyze and solve practical problems in mathematics by deciding on the appropriate mathematical operations to use.

RELIABILITY [1]

| | - Low | | - Medium | | - High | | - No Information Available |

| | 2 3 4 5 6 7 8 9 10 11 12 13 14 15 16 17 18 19 25 30 35 40 45 50 55 60 65 70 75 80 85 |
| | 24 29 34 39 44 49 54 59 64 69 74 79 84 90+ |

Internal consistency
Test-retest*

*Interval between testings: 1 year

FLOORS AND CEILINGS

	Test Floor	**Test Ceiling**
Inadequate at ages:	2-0 to 3-0	none

CHC CLASSIFICATIONS (Broad: stratum II / *Narrow: stratum I*)

Fluid Reasoning (*Gf*): *Quantitative Reasoning (RQ)* - Ability to inductively and deductively reason with concepts involving mathematical relations and properties. **Quantitative Knowledge (*Gq*):** *Mathematical Achievement (A3)* - Measured mathematics achievement; *Mathematical Knowledge (KM)* - Range of general knowledge about mathematics.

[1]Split-half coefficients were reported as estimates of internal consistency rather than coefficient alpha.

Battery: WJ III	Writing Samples (Form A or B)	Age Range: 5-0 to 90+

DESCRIPTION

The examinee is required to phrase and present written sentences that are evaluated with respect to quality of expression.

RELIABILITY [1]

☐ - Low   ■ - Medium   ■ - High   ☐ - No Information Available

	2	3	4	5	6	7	8	9	10	11	12	13	14	15	16	17	18	19 24	25 29	30 34	35 39	40 44	45 49	50 54	55 59	60 64	65 69	70 74	75 79	80 84	85 90+

Internal consistency
Test-retest*

Interval between testings: 1 year

FLOORS AND CEILINGS

	Test Floor	Test Ceiling
Inadequate at ages:	5-0 to 6-0	none

CHC CLASSIFICATIONS (Broad: stratum II / Narrow: stratum I)

Reading/Writing (Grw): *Writing Ability (WA)* - Ability to write with clarity of thought, organization, and good sentence structure.

Battery: WJ III	Story Recall-Delayed (Form A or B)	Age Range: 3-0 to 90+

DESCRIPTION

The examinee is required to recall, after 30 or more minutes on the same day or up to 8 days after the administration, the story elements presented in Story Recall.

RELIABILITY [1]

☐ - Low   ■ - Medium   ■ - High   ☐ - No Information Available

	2	3	4	5	6	7	8	9	10	11	12	13	14	15	16	17	18	19 24	25 29	30 34	35 39	40 44	45 49	50 54	55 59	60 64	65 69	70 74	75 79	80 84	85 90+

Internal consistency
Test-retest*

Interval between testings: not applicable

FLOORS AND CEILINGS

	Test Floor	Test Ceiling
Inadequate at ages:	none	none

CHC CLASSIFICATIONS (Broad: stratum II / Narrow: stratum I)

Long-Term Retrieval (Glr): *Meaningful Memory (MM)* - Ability to recall a set of items where there is a meaningful relation between items or the items comprise a meaningful story or connected discourse.

[1]Item response theory coefficients were reported as estimates of internal consistency rather than coefficient alpha.

DESCRIPTION

The examinee is required to read aloud letter combinations that are linguistically logical in English (but that do not form actual words), or words that occur with low frequency in the English language.

RELIABILITY [1]

☐ - Low   ■ - Medium   ■ - High   ☐ - No Information Available

	2	3	4	5	6	7	8	9	10	11	12	13	14	15	16	17	18	19–24	25–29	30–34	35–39	40–44	45–49	50–54	55–59	60–64	65–69	70–74	75–79	80–84	85–90+
Internal consistency																															
Test-retest*																															

*Interval between testings: 1 year

FLOORS AND CEILINGS

	Test Floor	Test Ceiling
Inadequate at ages:	4-0 to 6-0	12-0 to 90+

CHC CLASSIFICATIONS (Broad: stratum II / Narrow: stratum I)

Reading/Writing (Grw): *Reading Decoding (RD)* - Ability to recognize and decode words or pseudowords in reading.
Auditory Processing (Ga): *Phonetic Coding: Analysis (PC:A)* - Ability to segment larger units of speech sounds into smaller units of speech sounds

DESCRIPTION

The examinee is required to identify pictured objects.

RELIABILITY [1]

☐ - Low   ■ - Medium   ■ - High   ☐ - No Information Available

	2	3	4	5	6	7	8	9	10	11	12	13	14	15	16	17	18	19–24	25–29	30–34	35–39	40–44	45–49	50–54	55–59	60–64	65–69	70–74	75–79	80–84	85–90+
Internal consistency																															
Test-retest*																															

*Interval between testings: not applicable

FLOORS AND CEILINGS

	Test Floor	Test Ceiling
Inadequate at ages:	2-0 to 2-6	none

CHC CLASSIFICATIONS (Broad: stratum II / Narrow: stratum I)

Crystallized Intelligence (Gc): *Lexical Knowledge (VL)* - Extent of vocabulary that can be understood in terms of correct word meanings; *Language Development (LD)* - General development, or the understanding of words, sentences, and paragraphs (not requiring reading), in spoken native language skills.

[1]Split-half coefficients were reported as estimates of internal consistency rather than coefficient alpha.

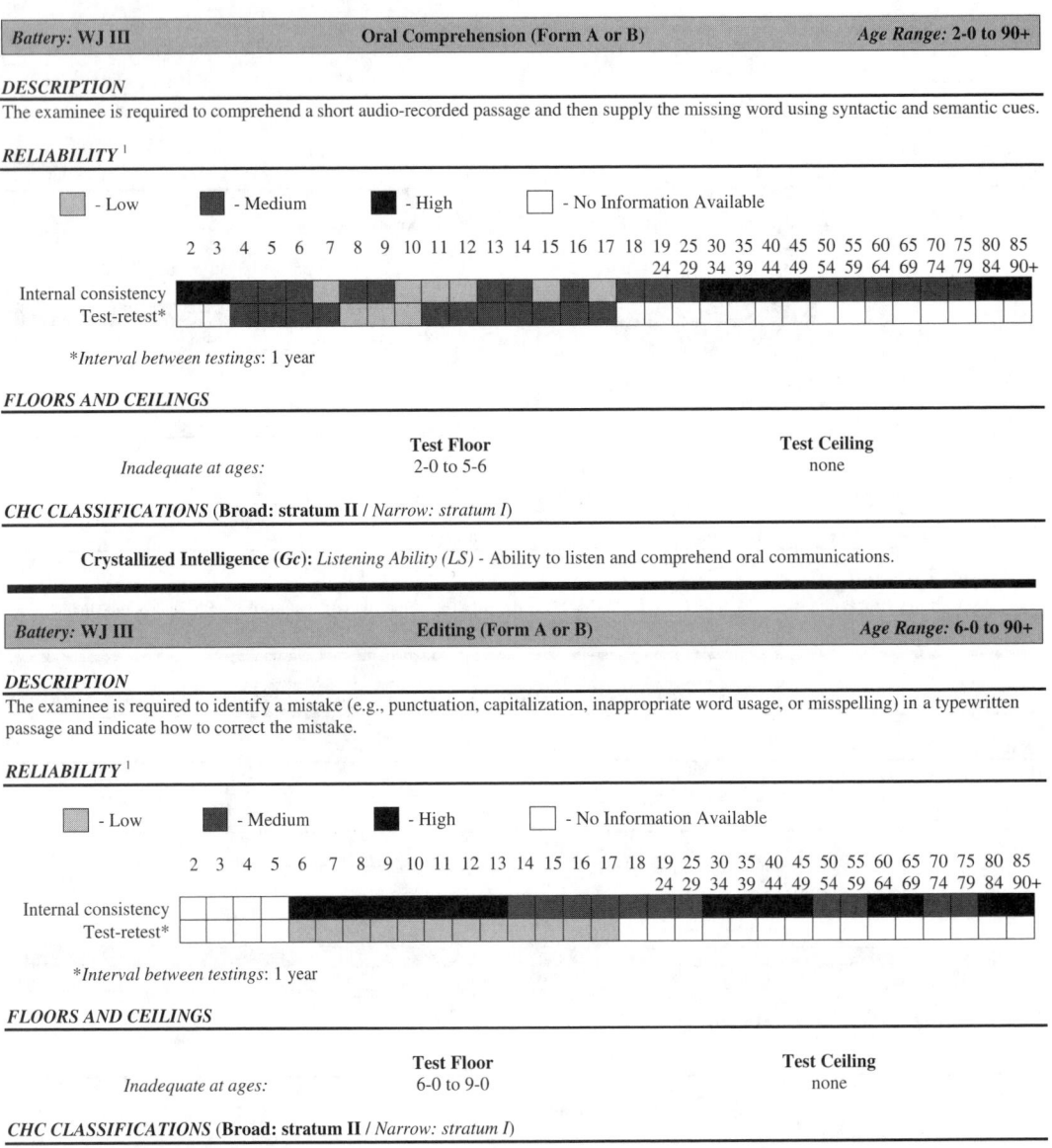

| *Battery:* **WJ III** | Oral Comprehension (Form A or B) | *Age Range:* **2-0 to 90+** |

DESCRIPTION

The examinee is required to comprehend a short audio-recorded passage and then supply the missing word using syntactic and semantic cues.

RELIABILITY [1]

| ☐ - Low | ■ - Medium | ■ - High | ☐ - No Information Available |

	2	3	4	5	6	7	8	9	10	11	12	13	14	15	16	17	18	19 24	25 29	30 34	35 39	40 44	45 49	50 54	55 59	60 64	65 69	70 74	75 79	80 84	85 90+
Internal consistency
Test-retest*

*Interval between testings: 1 year

FLOORS AND CEILINGS

	Test Floor	**Test Ceiling**
Inadequate at ages:	2-0 to 5-6	none

CHC CLASSIFICATIONS (Broad: stratum II / Narrow: stratum I)

Crystallized Intelligence (*Gc*): *Listening Ability (LS)* - Ability to listen and comprehend oral communications.

| *Battery:* **WJ III** | Editing (Form A or B) | *Age Range:* **6-0 to 90+** |

DESCRIPTION

The examinee is required to identify a mistake (e.g., punctuation, capitalization, inappropriate word usage, or misspelling) in a typewritten passage and indicate how to correct the mistake.

RELIABILITY [1]

| ☐ - Low | ■ - Medium | ■ - High | ☐ - No Information Available |

	2	3	4	5	6	7	8	9	10	11	12	13	14	15	16	17	18	19 24	25 29	30 34	35 39	40 44	45 49	50 54	55 59	60 64	65 69	70 74	75 79	80 84	85 90+
Internal consistency
Test-retest*

*Interval between testings: 1 year

FLOORS AND CEILINGS

	Test Floor	**Test Ceiling**
Inadequate at ages:	6-0 to 9-0	none

CHC CLASSIFICATIONS (Broad: stratum II / Narrow: stratum I)

Crystallized Intelligence (*Gc*): *Grammatical Sensitivity (MY)* - Knowledge or awareness of the grammatical features of the native language. **Reading/Writing (*Grw*):** *English Usage Knowledge (EU)* - Knowledge of writing in the English language with respect to capitalization, punctuation, usage, and spelling.

---

[1]Split-half coefficients were reported as estimates of internal consistency rather than coefficient alpha.

DESCRIPTION

A three-part subtest. In Part I, the examinee is required to state a one-word response similar in meaning to the word presented. In Part II, the examinee is required to state a one-word response opposite in meaning to the word presented. In Part III, the examinee is required to read three words of an analogy and provide the fourth word to complete the analogy.

RELIABILITY [1]

▨ - Low   ■ - Medium   ■ - High   □ - No Information Available

	2	3	4	5	6	7	8	9	10	11	12	13	14	15	16	17	18	19 24	25 29	30 34	35 39	40 44	45 49	50 54	55 59	60 64	65 69	70 74	75 79	80 84	85 90+
Internal consistency																															
Test-retest*																															

Interval between testings: 1 year

FLOORS AND CEILINGS

	Test Floor	Test Ceiling
Inadequate at ages:	5-0 to 8-6	none

CHC CLASSIFICATIONS (Broad: stratum II / *Narrow: stratum I*)

Reading/Writing (*Grw*): *Verbal (printed) Language Comprehension (V)* - General development, or the understanding of words, sentences, and paragraphs in native language, as measured by reading vocabulary and reading comprehension tests. **Crystallized Intelligence (*Gc*):** *Lexical Knowledge (VL)* - Extent of vocabulary that can be understood in terms of correct word meanings.

DESCRIPTION

The examinee is required to demonstrate knowledge of mathematical concepts and vocabulary.

RELIABILITY [1]

▨ - Low   ■ - Medium   ■ - High   □ - No Information Available

	2	3	4	5	6	7	8	9	10	11	12	13	14	15	16	17	18	19 24	25 29	30 34	35 39	40 44	45 49	50 54	55 59	60 64	65 69	70 74	75 79	80 84	85 90+
Internal consistency																															
Test-retest*																															

Interval between testings: not applicable

FLOORS AND CEILINGS

	Test Floor	Test Ceiling
Inadequate at ages:	2-0 to 4-6	none

CHC CLASSIFICATIONS (Broad: stratum II / *Narrow: stratum I*)

Quantitative Knowledge (*Gq*): *Mathematical Knowledge (KM)* - Range of general knowledge about mathematics. **Fluid Reasoning (*Gf*):** *Quantitative Reasoning (RQ)* - Ability to inductively and deductively reason with concepts involving mathematical relations and properties.

[1]Split-half coefficients were reported as estimates of internal consistency rather than coefficient alpha.

| Battery: WJ III | Academic Knowledge (Form A or B) | Age Range: 2-0 to 90+ |

DESCRIPTION

The examinee is required to answer questions in the sciences, history, geography, government, economics, art, music, and literature.

RELIABILITY [1]

■ - Low ■ - Medium ■ - High ☐ - No Information Available

	2	3	4	5	6	7	8	9	10	11	12	13	14	15	16	17	18	19 24	25 29	30 34	35 39	40 44	45 49	50 54	55 59	60 64	65 69	70 74	75 79	80 84	85 90+

Internal consistency
Test-retest*

*Interval between testings: 1 year

FLOORS AND CEILINGS

	Test Floor	Test Ceiling
Inadequate at ages:	2-0 to 2-6	none

CHC CLASSIFICATIONS (Broad: stratum II / Narrow: stratum I)

Crystallized Intelligence (Gc): *General (verbal) Information (K0)* - Range of general knowledge; *Information about Culture (K2)* - Range of cultural knowledge (e.g., music, art).

| Battery: WJ III | Spelling of Sounds (Form A or B) | Age Range: 6-0 to 90+ |

DESCRIPTION

The examinee is required to write single letters of sounds and to listen to an audio recording to spell letter combinations that are regular patterns in English spelling.

RELIABILITY [2]

■ - Low ■ - Medium ■ - High ☐ - No Information Available

	2	3	4	5	6	7	8	9	10	11	12	13	14	15	16	17	18	19 24	25 29	30 34	35 39	40 44	45 49	50 54	55 59	60 64	65 69	70 74	75 79	80 84	85 90+

Internal consistency
Test-retest*

*Interval between testings: not applicable

FLOORS AND CEILINGS

	Test Floor	Test Ceiling
Inadequate at ages:	6-0	none

CHC CLASSIFICATIONS (Broad: stratum II / Narrow: stratum I)

Reading/Writing (Grw): *Spelling Ability (SG)* - Ability to spell. **Auditory Processing (Ga):** *Phonetic Coding: Analysis (PC:A)* - Ability to segment larger units of speech sounds into smaller units of speech sounds.

---

[1]Split-half coefficients were reported as estimates of internal consistency rather than coefficient alpha.
[2]Item response theory coefficients were reported as estimates of internal consistency rather than coefficient alpha.

Battery: WJ III	Sound Awareness (Form A or B)	Age Range: 4-0 to 90+

DESCRIPTION

The examinee is required to provide a word that rhymes with a stimulus word that is presented orally, remove part of a compound word or a letter sound from a word to make a new word, substitute a word, a word ending, or a letter sound to create a new word, and to reverse parts of compound words as well as reverse letter sounds of words to create new words.

RELIABILITY [1]

☐ - Low   ■ - Medium   ■ - High   ☐ - No Information Available

	2	3	4	5	6	7	8	9	10	11	12	13	14	15	16	17	18	19 24	25 29	30 34	35 39	40 44	45 49	50 54	55 59	60 64	65 69	70 74	75 79	80 84	85 90+
Internal consistency																															
Test-retest*																															

*Interval between testings: not applicable

FLOORS AND CEILINGS

	Test Floor	Test Ceiling
Inadequate at ages:	4-0 to 5-6	none

CHC CLASSIFICATIONS (Broad: stratum II / Narrow: stratum I)

Auditory Processing (Ga): *Phonetic Coding: Analysis (PC:A)* - Ability to segment larger units of speech sounds into smaller units of speech sounds; *Phonetic Coding: Synthesis (PC:S)* - Ability to blend smaller units of speech together into larger units of speech.

Battery: WJ III	Punctuation and Capitalization (Form A or B)	Age Range: 6-0 to 90+

DESCRIPTION

The examinee is required to punctuate or capitalize items correctly.

RELIABILITY [2]

☐ - Low   ■ - Medium   ■ - High   ☐ - No Information Available

	2	3	4	5	6	7	8	9	10	11	12	13	14	15	16	17	18	19 24	25 29	30 34	35 39	40 44	45 49	50 54	55 59	60 64	65 69	70 74	75 79	80 84	85 90+
Internal consistency																															
Test-retest*																															

*Interval between testings: 1 year

FLOORS AND CEILINGS

	Test Floor	Test Ceiling
Inadequate at ages:	6-0	none

CHC CLASSIFICATIONS (Broad: stratum II / Narrow: stratum I)

Reading/Writing (Grw): *English Usage Knowledge (EU)* - Knowledge of writing in the English language with respect to capitalization, punctuation, usage, and spelling.

[1]Item response theory coefficients were reported as estimates of internal consistency rather than coefficient alpha.
[2]Split-half coefficients were reported as estimates of internal consistency rather than coefficient alpha.

ATDR *Summary Pages*
Brief/Screening Achievement Tests

Hammill Multiability Achievement Test (HAMAT)

GENERAL INFORMATION

Author(s): Donald D. Hammill, Wayne P. Hresko, Jerome J. Ammer, Mary E. Cronin, and Sally S. Quinby
Publisher: PRO-ED
Publication Date(s): 1998

Age Range: 7-0 to 17-11

Administration Time: 30 to 60 minutes

COMPOSITE MEASURE INFORMATION

General Achievement Quotient

SCORE INFORMATION

Standard scores	Percentiles	Stanines	Normal curve equivalents	Age equivalents	Grade equivalents

NORMING INFORMATION

Standardization Sample Size: 1,672

Avg. Number per Age/Grade Interval:
  152 per year: 7-0 to 17-11

Age Blocks in Norm Table:
  6 months: 7-0 to 17-11

Sample Collection Date(s): 1996-1997

Demographic Variables:
  Gender - *male; female*
  Geographic region - *4 regions; 5 states and District of Columbia*
  Residence - *urban; rural*
  Race/ethnicity - *White; Black; Native American; Hispanic; Asian;*
      - *other*
  SES - *parent education; family income*
  Other - *disability status (none, LD, MR, other)*

VALIDITY

Types of Validity Evidence Reported in the Test Manual:

Content	Criterion	Construct

Test Review(s) and Validity Evidence Reported in Extant Literature: None currently available

CONTAINS AT LEAST ONE INDICATOR CONSISTENT WITH THE FOLLOWING LD ASSESSMENT AREA(S)

Oral Expression	Listening Comprehension	Written Expression	Basic Reading Skill	Reading Comprehension	Mathematics Calculation	Mathematics Reasoning

SPECIAL FEATURES

- Provides alternate forms (A and B)
- Linked with the Hammill Multiability Intelligence Test

DESCRIPTION

The examinee is required to read a passage in which three words are omitted from three of its sentences and then select from a group of four words the one word that is needed to complete the sentence correctly.

RELIABILITY [1]

☐ - Low   ■ - Medium   ■ - High   ☐ - No Information Available

	2	3	4	5	6	7	8	9	10	11	12	13	14	15	16	17	18	19 24	25 29	30 34	35 39	40 44	45 49	50 54	55 59	60 64	65 69	70 74	75 79	80 84	85 90+
Internal consistency																															
Test-retest*																															

Interval between testings: 2 weeks

FLOORS AND CEILINGS

	Test Floor	Test Ceiling
Inadequate at ages:	none	14-0 to 17-11

CHC CLASSIFICATIONS (Broad: stratum II / *Narrow: stratum I*)

Reading/Writing (*Grw*): *Cloze Ability (CZ)* - Ability to supply words deleted from prose passages that must be read.

DESCRIPTION

The examinee is required to write sentences from dictation.

RELIABILITY [1]

☐ - Low   ■ - Medium   ■ - High   ☐ - No Information Available

	2	3	4	5	6	7	8	9	10	11	12	13	14	15	16	17	18	19 24	25 29	30 34	35 39	40 44	45 49	50 54	55 59	60 64	65 69	70 74	75 79	80 84	85 90+
Internal consistency																															
Test-retest*																															

Interval between testings: 2 weeks

FLOORS AND CEILINGS

	Test Floor	Test Ceiling
Inadequate at ages:	7-0 to 10-5	15-0 to 17-11

CHC CLASSIFICATIONS (Broad: stratum II / *Narrow: stratum I*)

Reading/Writing (*Grw*): *English Usage Knowledge[a] (EU)* - Knowledge of writing in the English language with respect to capitalization, punctuation, usage, and spelling.

[1]Test-retest coefficients were reported by grade in the test manual. Therefore, corresponding ages were estimated by the authors.
[a]The narrow ability CHC classification for this test was determined by the authors because no agreement was reached through the group consensus process.

Battery: HAMAT	**Arithmetic (Form A)**	**Age Range: 7-0 to 17-11**

DESCRIPTION

The examinee is required to perform calculations to solve mathematical problems.

RELIABILITY [1]

- ☐ - Low   ■ - Medium   ■ - High   ☐ - No Information Available

	2	3	4	5	6	7	8	9	10	11	12	13	14	15	16	17	18	19 24	25 29	30 34	35 39	40 44	45 49	50 54	55 59	60 64	65 69	70 74	75 79	80 84	85 90+

Internal consistency
Test-retest*

Interval between testings: 2 weeks

FLOORS AND CEILINGS

	Test Floor	**Test Ceiling**
Inadequate at ages:	7-0 to 7-11	16-0 to 17-11

CHC CLASSIFICATIONS (Broad: stratum II / *Narrow: stratum I*)

Quantitative Knowledge (*Gq*): *Mathematical Achievement (A3)* - Measured mathematics achievement.

Battery: HAMAT	**Facts (Form A)**	**Age Range: 7-0 to 17-11**

DESCRIPTION

The examinee is required to answer a series of factual questions about science, social studies, health, and language arts.

RELIABILITY [1]

- ☐ - Low   ■ - Medium   ■ - High   ☐ - No Information Available

	2	3	4	5	6	7	8	9	10	11	12	13	14	15	16	17	18	19 24	25 29	30 34	35 39	40 44	45 49	50 54	55 59	60 64	65 69	70 74	75 79	80 84	85 90+

Internal consistency
Test-retest*

Interval between testings: 2 weeks

FLOORS AND CEILINGS

	Test Floor	**Test Ceiling**
Inadequate at ages:	7-0 to 11-11	14-6 to 17-11

CHC CLASSIFICATIONS (Broad: stratum II / *Narrow: stratum I*)

Crystallized Intelligence (*Gc*): *General (verbal) Information (K0)* - Range of general knowledge.

[1] Test-retest coefficients were reported by grade in the test manual. Therefore, corresponding ages were estimated by the authors.

DESCRIPTION

The examinee is required to read a passage in which three words are omitted from three of its sentences and then select from a group of four words the one word that is needed to complete the sentence correctly.

RELIABILITY [1]

☐ - Low   ▧ - Medium   ■ - High   ☐ - No Information Available

	2	3	4	5	6	7	8	9	10	11	12	13	14	15	16	17	18	19 24	25 29	30 34	35 39	40 44	45 49	50 54	55 59	60 64	65 69	70 74	75 79	80 84	85 90+
Internal consistency Test-retest*						■	■	■	■	■	■	■	■	■	■	■															

Interval between testings: 2 weeks

FLOORS AND CEILINGS

	Test Floor	Test Ceiling
Inadequate at ages:	none	14-0 to 17-11

CHC CLASSIFICATIONS (Broad: stratum II / Narrow: stratum I)

Reading/Writing (Grw): *Cloze Ability (CZ)* - Ability to supply words deleted from prose passages that must be read.

DESCRIPTION

The examinee is required to write sentences from dictation.

RELIABILITY [1]

☐ - Low   ▧ - Medium   ■ - High   ☐ - No Information Available

	2	3	4	5	6	7	8	9	10	11	12	13	14	15	16	17	18	19 24	25 29	30 34	35 39	40 44	45 49	50 54	55 59	60 64	65 69	70 74	75 79	80 84	85 90+
Internal consistency Test-retest*						▧	▧	▧	▧	▧	■	■	▧	▧	▧	▧															

Interval between testings: 2 weeks

FLOORS AND CEILINGS

	Test Floor	Test Ceiling
Inadequate at ages:	7-0 to 10-5	15-0 to 17-11

CHC CLASSIFICATIONS (Broad: stratum II / Narrow: stratum I)

Reading/Writing (Grw): *English Usage Knowledge[a] (EU)* - Knowledge of writing in the English language with respect to capitalization, punctuation, usage, and spelling

---

[1]Test-retest coefficients were reported by grade in the test manual. Therefore, corresponding ages were estimated by the authors.
[a]The narrow ability CHC classification for this test was determined by the authors because no agreement was reached through the group consensus process.

DESCRIPTION

The examinee is required to perform calculations to solve mathematical problems.

RELIABILITY [1]

☐ - Low   ■ - Medium   ■ - High   ☐ - No Information Available

	2	3	4	5	6	7	8	9	10	11	12	13	14	15	16	17	18	19 24	25 29	30 34	35 39	40 44	45 49	50 54	55 59	60 64	65 69	70 74	75 79	80 84	85 90+
Internal consistency																															
Test-retest*																															

*Interval between testings: 2 weeks

FLOORS AND CEILINGS

	Test Floor	Test Ceiling
Inadequate at ages:	7-0 to 7-11	16-0 to 17-11

CHC CLASSIFICATIONS (Broad: stratum II / Narrow: stratum I)

Quantitative Knowledge (Gq): *Mathematical Achievement (A3)* - Measured mathematics achievement.

DESCRIPTION

The examinee is required to answer a series of factual questions about science, social studies, health, and language arts.

RELIABILITY [1]

☐ - Low   ■ - Medium   ■ - High   ☐ - No Information Available

	2	3	4	5	6	7	8	9	10	11	12	13	14	15	16	17	18	19 24	25 29	30 34	35 39	40 44	45 49	50 54	55 59	60 64	65 69	70 74	75 79	80 84	85 90+
Internal consistency																															
Test-retest*																															

*Interval between testings: 2 weeks

FLOORS AND CEILINGS

	Test Floor	Test Ceiling
Inadequate at ages:	7-0 to 11-11	14-6 to 17-11

CHC CLASSIFICATIONS (Broad: stratum II / Narrow: stratum I)

Crystallized Intelligence (Gc): *General (verbal) Information (K0)* - Range of general knowledge.

[1] Test-retest coefficients were reported by grade in the test manual. Therefore, corresponding ages were estimated by the authors.

Kaufman Functional Academic Skills Test (K-FAST)

GENERAL INFORMATION

Author(s): Alan S. Kaufman and Nadeen L. Kaufman
Publisher: American Guidance Service
Publication Date(s): 1994

Age Range: 15-0 to 85+
Administration Time: 15 to 25 minutes

COMPOSITE MEASURE INFORMATION

Functional Academic Skills

SCORE INFORMATION

Standard scores	Percentiles	Stanines	Normal curve equivalents	Age equivalents	Grade equivalents

NORMING INFORMATION

Standardization Sample Size: 1,424

Sample Collection Date(s): 1988-1991

Avg. Number per Age/Grade Interval:
  51 per year: 15-0 to 19-11
  161 per five years: 20-0 to 24-11
  183 per ten years: 25-0 to 64-11
  139 per ten years: 65-0 to 85+

Demographic Variables:
  Gender   *- male; female*
  Geographic region   *- 4 regions; 27 states; 60 communities*
  Race/ethnicity   *- Black; Hispanic; White; other (5 categories)*
  SES   *- parent/examinee education*

Age Blocks in Norm Table
  1 year: 15-0 to 20-11
  2 years: 21-0 to 24-11
  10 years: 25-0 to 44-11; 75-0 to 85+
  5 years: 45-0 to 74-11

VALIDITY

Types of Validity Evidence Reported in the Test Manual:

Content	Criterion	Construct

Test Review(s) and Validity Evidence Reported in Extant Literature: See Appendix C

CONTAINS AT LEAST ONE INDICATOR CONSISTENT WITH THE FOLLOWING LD ASSESSMENT AREA(S)

Oral Expression	Listening Comprehension	Written Expression	Basic Reading Skill	Reading Comprehension	Mathematics Calculation	Mathematics Reasoning

SPECIAL FEATURES

- Allows stable measurement at very low ability levels as well as at above average and superior ability levels
- Assesses the strengths of normal elderly individuals and many clinical groups

DESCRIPTION

The examinee is required to respond to a question while looking at a visual stimulus such as a graph, the key facts to remember in a problem, a numerical symbol, a picture, an advertisement, a pie chart, or the actual words to the problem.

RELIABILITY [1]

☐ - Low   ◼ - Medium   ◼ - High   ☐ - No Information Available

	2	3	4	5	6	7	8	9	10	11	12	13	14	15	16	17	18	19 24	25 29	30 34	35 39	40 44	45 49	50 54	55 59	60 64	65 69	70 74	75 79	80 84	85 90+
Internal consistency																															
Test-retest*																															

*Interval between testings: 1 to 12 weeks

FLOORS AND CEILINGS

	Test Floor	**Test Ceiling**
Inadequate at ages:	none	20-0 to 59-11

CHC CLASSIFICATIONS (**Broad: stratum II** / *Narrow: stratum I*)

Quantitative Knowledge[a] (*Gq*): *Mathematical Achievement[a] (A3)* - Measured mathematics achievement; *Mathematical Knowledge[a] (KM)* - Range of general knowledge about mathematics.

| *Battery:* **K-FAST** | **Reading** | *Age Range:* **15-0 to 85+** |

DESCRIPTION

The examinee is required to interpret the meaning of rebuses, abbreviations, or words, phrases, sentences, and paragraphs that are seen frequently in commonplace situations. Some rebuses and abbreviations appear in isolation, while many others are embedded in familiar contexts such as recipes, newspaper ads, drug labels, or doors.

RELIABILITY [1]

☐ - Low   ◼ - Medium   ◼ - High   ☐ - No Information Available

	2	3	4	5	6	7	8	9	10	11	12	13	14	15	16	17	18	19 24	25 29	30 34	35 39	40 44	45 49	50 54	55 59	60 64	65 69	70 74	75 79	80 84	85 90+
Internal consistency																															
Test-retest*																															

*Interval between testings: 1 to 12 weeks

FLOORS AND CEILINGS

	Test Floor	**Test Ceiling**
Inadequate at ages:	none	20-0 to 34-11

CHC CLASSIFICATIONS (**Broad: stratum II** / *Narrow: stratum I*)

Reading/Writing (*Grw*): *Reading Comprehension (RC)* - Ability to comprehend connected discourse during reading.
Crystallized Intelligence (*Gc*): *Information About Culture[b] (K2)* - Range of cultural knowledge (e.g., music, art).

[1]Split-half coefficients were reported as estimates of internal consistency rather than coefficient alpha.
[a]The broad and narrow ability CHC classifications for this test were determined by the authors because no agreement was reached through the group consensus process.
[b]The narrow Gc ability CHC classification for this test was determined by the authors because no agreement was reached through the group consensus process.

Kaufman Survey of Early Academic and Language Skills (K-SEALS)

GENERAL INFORMATION

Author(s): Alan S. Kaufman and Nadeen L. Kaufman
Publisher: American Guidance Service
Publication Date(s): 1993

Age Range: 3-0 to 6-11
Administration Time: 15 to 25 minutes

COMPOSITE MEASURE INFORMATION

Expressive Skills
Number Skills
Early Academic and Language Skills

Receptive Skills
Letter and Word Skills

SCORE INFORMATION

Standard scores	Percentiles	Stanines	Normal curve equivalents	Age equivalents	Grade equivalents

NORMING INFORMATION

Standardization Sample Size: 1,000

Sample Collection Date(s): 1987-1988

Avg. Number per Age/Grade Interval:
 250 per year: 3-0 to 6-11

Age Blocks in Norm Table
 3 months: 3-0 to 6-11

Demographic Variables:
 Gender   *- male; female*
 Geographic region *- 4 regions; 28 states; 42 communities*
 Race/ethnicity   *- Black; Hispanic; White; other (4 categories)*
 SES   *- parent education*
 Other   *- school district size*

VALIDITY

Types of Validity Evidence Reported in the Test Manual:

Content	Criterion	Construct

Test Review(s) and Validity Evidence Reported in Extant Literature: See Appendix C

CONTAINS AT LEAST ONE INDICATOR CONSISTENT WITH THE FOLLOWING LD ASSESSMENT AREA(S)

Oral Expression	Listening Comprehension	Written Expression	Basic Reading Skill	Reading Comprehension	Mathematics Calculation	Mathematics Reasoning

SPECIAL FEATURES

- Includes a sample report to parents
- Includes analysis of children's articulation errors

DESCRIPTION

The examinee is required to identify by pointing or by naming, pictures of objects or actions based on the specific attributes stated by the examiner.

RELIABILITY [1]

■ - Low   ■ - Medium   ■ - High   □ - No Information Available

	2	3	4	5	6	7	8	9	10	11	12	13	14	15	16	17	18	19/24	25/29	30/34	35/39	40/44	45/49	50/54	55/59	60/64	65/69	70/74	75/79	80/84	85/90+
Internal consistency		High	Med	High	High																										
Test-retest*																															

Interval between testings: 1 to 4 weeks

FLOORS AND CEILINGS

	Test Floor	Test Ceiling
Inadequate at ages:	none	none

CHC CLASSIFICATIONS (Broad: stratum II / *Narrow: stratum I*)

Crystallized Intelligence (Gc): *Lexical Knowledge[a] (VL)* - Extent of vocabulary that can be understood in terms of correct word meanings; *Language Development[a] (LD)* - General development, or the understanding of words, sentences, and paragraphs (not requiring reading), in spoken native language skills.

DESCRIPTION

The examinee is required to select or name numbers, letters, or words, count, indicate knowledge of number concepts, and solve number problems.

RELIABILITY [1]

■ - Low   ■ - Medium   ■ - High   □ - No Information Available

	2	3	4	5	6	7	8	9	10	11	12	13	14	15	16	17	18	19/24	25/29	30/34	35/39	40/44	45/49	50/54	55/59	60/64	65/69	70/74	75/79	80/84	85/90+
Internal consistency		High	High	High	High																										
Test-retest*																															

Interval between testings: 1 to 4 weeks

FLOORS AND CEILINGS

	Test Floor	Test Ceiling
Inadequate at ages:	3-0 to 4-8	none

CHC CLASSIFICATIONS (Broad: stratum II / *Narrow: stratum I*)

Quantitative Knowledge (Gq): *Mathematical Knowledge (KM)* - Range of general knowledge about mathematics.

---

[1]Split-half coefficients were reported as estimates of internal consistency rather than coefficient alpha.
[a]The narrow ability CHC classifications for this test were determined by the authors because no agreement was reached through the group consensus process.

Mini-Battery of Achievement (MBA)

GENERAL INFORMATION

Author(s): Richard W. Woodcock, Kevin S. McGrew, and Judy K. Werder

Age Range: 4-0 to 95-11

Publisher: Riverside Publishing Company

Administration Time: 30 minutes

Publication Date(s): 1994

COMPOSITE MEASURE INFORMATION

Basic Skills

SCORE INFORMATION

Standard scores	Percentiles	Stanines	Normal curve equivalents	Age equivalents	Grade equivalents

NORMING INFORMATION

Standardization Sample Size: 6,026

Sample Collection Date(s): 1986-1988

Avg. Number per Age/Grade Interval:
   256 per year: 4-0 to 19-11
   240 per ten years: 20-0 to 95-11

Demographic Variables:
   Gender   *- male; female*
   Geographic region   *- 4 regions; 100 communities*
   Residence   *- central city; urban fringe; outside urban; rural*

Age Blocks in Norm Table
   1 month: 4-0 to 18-11
   1 year: 19-0 to 90-11
   5 years: 91-0 to 95-11

   Race/ethnicity   *- White; Black; American Indian; Asian and Pacific Islander; Hispanic*
   SES   *- parent/examinee education; occupation*
   Other   *- funding/type of college/university*

VALIDITY

Types of Validity Evidence Reported in the Test Manual:

Content	Criterion	Construct

Test Review(s) and Validity Evidence Reported in Extant Literature: See Appendix C

CONTAINS AT LEAST ONE INDICATOR CONSISTENT WITH THE FOLLOWING LD ASSESSMENT AREA(S)

Oral Expression	Listening Comprehension	Written Expression	Basic Reading Skill	Reading Comprehension	Mathematics Calculation	Mathematics Reasoning

SPECIAL FEATURES

- Provides computer scoring program with interpretive profiling report

DESCRIPTION

The examinee is required to identify letters and words, provide antonyms to printed words, and read a short passage and identify a missing word.

RELIABILITY [1]

■ - Low   ■ - Medium   ■ - High   ☐ - No Information Available

	2	3	4	5	6	7	8	9	10	11	12	13	14	15	16	17	18	19 24	25 29	30 34	35 39	40 44	45 49	50 54	55 59	60 64	65 69	70 74	75 79	80 84	85 90+

Internal consistency

Test-retest*

*Interval between testings: 1 week

FLOORS AND CEILINGS

	Test Floor	Test Ceiling
Inadequate at ages:	4-0 to 6-0	none

CHC CLASSIFICATIONS (Broad: stratum II / Narrow: stratum I)

Reading/Writing (Grw): *Reading Decoding[a] (RD)* - Ability to recognize and decode words or pseudowords in reading; *Reading Comprehension[a] (RC)* - Ability to comprehend connected discourse during reading; *Verbal (printed) Language Comprehension[a] (V)* - General development, or the understanding of words, sentences, and paragraphs in native language, as measured by reading vocabulary and reading comprehension tests.

DESCRIPTION

The examinee is required to provide a written response or written responses to questions requiring knowledge of letter forms, spelling, punctuation, capitalization, and word usage. The examinee also is required to identify mistakes in typewritten passages and then indicate how to correct the mistakes.

RELIABILITY [1]

■ - Low   ■ - Medium   ■ - High   ☐ - No Information Available

	2	3	4	5	6	7	8	9	10	11	12	13	14	15	16	17	18	19 24	25 29	30 34	35 39	40 44	45 49	50 54	55 59	60 64	65 69	70 74	75 79	80 84	85 90+

Internal consistency

Test-retest*

*Interval between testings: 1 week

FLOORS AND CEILINGS

	Test Floor	Test Ceiling
Inadequate at ages:	4-0 to 6-0	none

CHC CLASSIFICATIONS (Broad: stratum II / Narrow: stratum I)

Reading/Writing (Grw): *English Usage Knowledge (EU)* - Knowledge of writing in the English language with respect to capitalization, punctuation, usage, and spelling.

[1] Split-half coefficients were reported as estimates of internal consistency rather than coefficient alpha.
[a] The narrow ability CHC classifications for this test were determined by the authors because no agreement was reached through the group consensus process.

Battery: MBA	Mathematics	Age Range: 4-0 to 95-11

DESCRIPTION

The examinee is required to perform basic mathematical operations such as addition, subtraction, multiplication, and division, as well as some geometry, trigonometry, logarithm, and calculus problems. The examinee also is required to analyze and solve practical problems in mathematics and demonstrate knowledge of mathematical concepts and vocabulary.

RELIABILITY [1]

☐ - Low   ■ - Medium   ■ - High   ☐ - No Information Available

	2	3	4	5	6	7	8	9	10	11	12	13	14	15	16	17	18	19–24	25–29	30–34	35–39	40–44	45–49	50–54	55–59	60–64	65–69	70–74	75–79	80–84	85–90+
Internal consistency																															
Test-retest*																															

Interval between testings: 1 week

FLOORS AND CEILINGS

	Test Floor	Test Ceiling
Inadequate at ages:	none	none

CHC CLASSIFICATIONS (Broad: stratum II / *Narrow: stratum I*)

Quantitative Knowledge (*Gq*): *Mathematical Achievement (A3)* - Measured mathematics achievement; *Mathematical Knowledge (KM)* - Range of general knowledge about mathematics.

Battery: MBA	Factual Knowledge	Age Range: 4-0 to 95-11

DESCRIPTION

The examinee is required to answer general information items in science, social studies, and the humanities.

RELIABILITY [1]

☐ - Low   ■ - Medium   ■ - High   ☐ - No Information Available

	2	3	4	5	6	7	8	9	10	11	12	13	14	15	16	17	18	19–24	25–29	30–34	35–39	40–44	45–49	50–54	55–59	60–64	65–69	70–74	75–79	80–84	85–90+
Internal consistency																															
Test-retest*																															

Interval between testings: 1 week

FLOORS AND CEILINGS

	Test Floor	Test Ceiling
Inadequate at ages:	none	none

CHC CLASSIFICATIONS (Broad: stratum II / *Narrow: stratum I*)

Crystallized Intelligence (*Gc*): *General (verbal) Information (K0)* - Range of general knowledge.

---

[1]Split-half coefficients were reported as estimates of internal consistency rather than coefficient alpha.

Test of Academic Achievement Skills-Revised (TAAS-R)

GENERAL INFORMATION

Author(s): Morrison F. Gardner
Publisher: Psychological and Educational Publications, Inc.
Publication Date(s): 1989, 1994

Age Range: 5-0 to 14-11
Administration Time: 15 to 30 minutes

COMPOSITE MEASURE INFORMATION

Arithmetic

Reading and Comprehension

SCORE INFORMATION

Standard scores	Percentiles	Stanines	Normal curve equivalents	Age equivalents	Grade equivalents

NORMING INFORMATION

Standardization Sample Size: 1,054

Sample Collection Date(s): 1989-1990

Avg. Number per Age/Grade Interval:
  105 per year: 5-0 to 14-11

Age Blocks in Norm Table
  4 months: 5-0 to 14-11

Demographic Variables:
  Gender   - male; female
  Geographic region   - 25 states
  Race/ethnicity   - Black; White; Hispanic; other
  Other   - type of school (public, private, parochial)

VALIDITY

Types of Validity Evidence Reported in the Test Manual:

Content	Criterion	Construct

Test Review(s) and Validity Evidence Reported in Extant Literature: See Appendix C

CONTAINS AT LEAST ONE INDICATOR CONSISTENT WITH THE FOLLOWING LD ASSESSMENT AREA(S)

Oral Expression	Listening Comprehension	Written Expression	Basic Reading Skill	Reading Comprehension	Mathematics Calculation	Mathematics Reasoning

SPECIAL FEATURES

- Includes a new subtest (i.e., Oral Reading Stories and Comprehension) which measures the accuracy of oral and reading comprehension abilities
- Provides age specific directions and scoring for each subtest

Battery: TAAS-R	Spelling	Age Range: 5-0 to 14-11

DESCRIPTION

The examinee is required to write letters or words after the letters or words are presented orally by the examiner.

RELIABILITY [1]

☐ - Low	■ - Medium	■ - High	☐ - No Information Available

	2	3	4	5	6	7	8	9	10	11	12	13	14	15	16	17	18	19 24	25 29	30 34	35 39	40 44	45 49	50 54	55 59	60 64	65 69	70 74	75 79	80 84	85 90+
Internal consistency						■	■	■	■	■	■	☐	☐	☐																	
Test-retest*																															

Interval between testings: not applicable

FLOORS AND CEILINGS

	Test Floor	Test Ceiling
Inadequate at ages:	none	9-4 to 14-11

CHC CLASSIFICATIONS (Broad: stratum II / *Narrow: stratum I*)

Reading/Writing (*Grw*): *Spelling Ability (SG) - Ability to spell.*

Battery: TAAS-R	Letter/Word Reading	Age Range: 5-0 to 14-11

DESCRIPTION

The examinee is required to name letters and read words presented by the examiner on a separate plastic reading card.

RELIABILITY [1]

☐ - Low	■ - Medium	■ - High	☐ - No Information Available

	2	3	4	5	6	7	8	9	10	11	12	13	14	15	16	17	18	19 24	25 29	30 34	35 39	40 44	45 49	50 54	55 59	60 64	65 69	70 74	75 79	80 84	85 90+
Internal consistency				☐	■	☐	☐	■	☐	☐	☐																				
Test-retest*																															

Interval between testings: not applicable

FLOORS AND CEILINGS

	Test Floor	Test Ceiling
Inadequate at ages:	5-0 to 5-3	9-8 to 14-11

CHC CLASSIFICATIONS (Broad: stratum II / *Narrow: stratum I*)

Reading/Writing (*Grw*): *Reading Decoding (RD) - Ability to recognize and decode words or pseudowords in reading.*

[1]Kuder-Richardson 20 coefficients were reported as estimates of internal consistency rather than coefficient alpha.

DESCRIPTION

The examinee is required to provide an oral response to questions asked by the examiner after the examiner reads aloud passages.

RELIABILITY [1]

☐ - Low   ■ - Medium   ■ - High   ☐ - No Information Available

	2	3	4	5	6	7	8	9	10	11	12	13	14	15	16	17	18	19-24	25-29	30-34	35-39	40-44	45-49	50-54	55-59	60-64	65-69	70-74	75-79	80-84	85-90+
Internal consistency				▒	▒	▒	▒	▒	▒	▒	▒	▒	▒																		
Test-retest*																															

Interval between testings: not applicable

FLOORS AND CEILINGS

	Test Floor	Test Ceiling
Inadequate at ages:	5-0 to 5-11	11-4 to 14-11

CHC CLASSIFICATIONS (Broad: stratum II / *Narrow: stratum I*)

Crystallized Intelligence (*Gc*): *Listening Ability (LS)* - Ability to listen and comprehend oral communications.

DESCRIPTION

The examinee is required to identify numbers, smaller or larger numbers, and compute problems orally in response to oral questions stated by the examiner.

RELIABILITY [1]

☐ - Low   ■ - Medium   ■ - High   ☐ - No Information Available

	2	3	4	5	6	7	8	9	10	11	12	13	14	15	16	17	18	19-24	25-29	30-34	35-39	40-44	45-49	50-54	55-59	60-64	65-69	70-74	75-79	80-84	85-90+
Internal consistency				■	▒																										
Test-retest*																															

Interval between testings: not applicable

FLOORS AND CEILINGS

	Test Floor	Test Ceiling
Inadequate at ages:	none	none

CHC CLASSIFICATIONS (Broad: stratum II / *Narrow: stratum I*)

Quantitative Knowledge (*Gq*): *Mathematical Knowledge (KM)* - Range of general knowledge about mathematics.

---

[1] Kuder-Richardson 20 coefficients were reported as estimates of internal consistency rather than coefficient alpha.

| *Battery:* TAAS-R | **Arithmetic (Written Component)** | *Age Range:* 5-0 to 14-11 |

DESCRIPTION

The examinee is required to solve addition, subtraction, multiplication, and division problems printed in the test protocol.

RELIABILITY [1]

▨ - Low   ▨ - Medium   ■ - High   ☐ - No Information Available

	2	3	4	5	6	7	8	9	10	11	12	13	14	15	16	17	18	19 24	25 29	30 34	35 39	40 44	45 49	50 54	55 59	60 64	65 69	70 74	75 79	80 84	85 90+
Internal consistency																															
Test-retest*																															

Interval between testings: not applicable

FLOORS AND CEILINGS

	Test Floor	**Test Ceiling**
Inadequate at ages:	none	12-0 to 14-11

CHC CLASSIFICATIONS (Broad: stratum II / *Narrow: stratum I*)

Quantitative Knowledge (*Gq*): *Mathematical Achievement (A3)* - Measured mathematics achievement.

| *Battery:* TAAS-R | **Oral Reading Accuracy (Stories)** | *Age Range:* 5-0 to 14-11 |

DESCRIPTION

The examinee is required to read aloud some passages. Any word that the examinee does not or cannot read is an error.

RELIABILITY [1]

▨ - Low   ▨ - Medium   ■ - High   ☐ - No Information Available

	2	3	4	5	6	7	8	9	10	11	12	13	14	15	16	17	18	19 24	25 29	30 34	35 39	40 44	45 49	50 54	55 59	60 64	65 69	70 74	75 79	80 84	85 90+
Internal consistency																															
Test-retest*																															

Interval between testings: not applicable

FLOORS AND CEILINGS

	Test Floor	**Test Ceiling**
Inadequate at ages:	5-0 to 6-7	11-8 to 14-11

CHC CLASSIFICATIONS (Broad: stratum II / *Narrow: stratum I*)

Reading/Writing (*Grw*): *Reading Decoding (RD)* - Ability to recognize and decode words or pseudowords in reading.

[1]Kuder-Richardson 20 coefficients were reported as estimates of internal consistency rather than coefficient alpha.

DESCRIPTION

The examinee is required to respond to questions read by the examiner that pertain to each story read previously by the examinee.

RELIABILITY [1]

- Low   - Medium   - High   ☐ - No Information Available

	2	3	4	5	6	7	8	9	10	11	12	13	14	15	16	17	18	19 24	25 29	30 34	35 39	40 44	45 49	50 54	55 59	60 64	65 69	70 74	75 79	80 84	85 90+
Internal consistency																															
Test-retest*																															

*Interval between testings: not applicable

FLOORS AND CEILINGS

	Test Floor	Test Ceiling
Inadequate at ages:	5-0 to 6-7	none

CHC CLASSIFICATIONS (Broad: stratum II / Narrow: stratum I)

Reading/Writing (Grw): Reading Comprehension (RC) - Ability to comprehend verbal discourse during reading.

[1]Kuder-Richardson 20 coefficients were reported as estimates of internal consistency rather than coefficient alpha.

Test of Children's Language (TOCL)

GENERAL INFORMATION

Author(s): Edna Barenbaum and Phyllis Newcomer
Publisher: PRO-ED
Publication Date(s): 1996

Age Range: 5-0 to 8-11
Administration Time: 30 to 40 minutes

COMPOSITE MEASURE INFORMATION

Spoken Language Quotient
Writing Quotient

Reading Quotient
Total Language Quotient

SCORE INFORMATION

Standard scores	Percentiles	Stanines	Normal curve equivalents	Age equivalents	Grade equivalents

NORMING INFORMATION

Standardization Sample Size: 908

Sample Collection Date(s): 1993-1994

Avg. Number per Age/Grade Interval:
227 per year: 5-0 to 8-11

Age Blocks in Norm Table
6 months: 5-0 to 5-11
6 months: 6-0 to 8-11

Demographic Variables:
Gender   - *male; female*
Geographic region - *4 regions; 15 states*
Residence   - *urban; rural*
Race/ethnicity   - *White; Black; Hispanic; Asian; Native American; other*
Other   - *disability status (none, LD, other)*

VALIDITY

Types of Validity Evidence Reported in the Test Manual:

Content	Criterion	Construct

Test Review(s) and Validity Evidence Reported in Extant Literature: None currently available

CONTAINS AT LEAST ONE INDICATOR CONSISTENT WITH THE FOLLOWING LD ASSESSMENT AREA(S)

Oral Expression	Listening Comprehension	Written Expression	Basic Reading Skill	Reading Comprehension	Mathematics Calculation	Mathematics Reasoning

SPECIAL FEATURES

DESCRIPTION

The examinee is required to employ correct syntax and semantics in speech in the context of reading a story with the examiner.

RELIABILITY [1]

■ - Low   ■ - Medium   ■ - High   ☐ - No Information Available

	2	3	4	5	6	7	8	9	10	11	12	13	14	15	16	17	18	19–24	25–29	30–34	35–39	40–44	45–49	50–54	55–59	60–64	65–69	70–74	75–79	80–84	85–90+
Internal consistency			■	■	■	■	■																								
Test-retest*			■	■	■	■	■																								

*Interval between testings: 2 to 3 weeks

FLOORS AND CEILINGS

	Test Floor	Test Ceiling
Inadequate at ages:	5-0 to 6-5	7-0 to 8-11

CHC CLASSIFICATIONS (Broad: stratum II / *Narrow: stratum I*)

Crystallized Intelligence (*Gc*): *Grammatical Sensitivity (MY)* - Knowledge or awareness of the grammatical features of the native language. **Reading/Writing (*Grw*):** *English Usage Knowledge[a] (EU)* - Knowledge of writing in the English language with respect to capitalization, punctuation, usage, and spelling.

DESCRIPTION

The examinee is required to demonstrate an awareness of the internal phonological structure of words by pointing to letters, parts of words, etc. in the context of a short story read by the examiner.

RELIABILITY [1]

■ - Low   ■ - Medium   ■ - High   ☐ - No Information Available

	2	3	4	5	6	7	8	9	10	11	12	13	14	15	16	17	18	19–24	25–29	30–34	35–39	40–44	45–49	50–54	55–59	60–64	65–69	70–74	75–79	80–84	85–90+
Internal consistency			■	■	■	■	■																								
Test-retest*			■	■	■	■	■																								

*Interval between testings: 2 to 3 weeks

FLOORS AND CEILINGS

	Test Floor	Test Ceiling
Inadequate at ages:	5-0 to 5-5	7-0 to 8-11

CHC CLASSIFICATIONS (Broad: stratum II / *Narrow: stratum I*)

Auditory Processing (*Ga*): *Phonetic Coding: Analysis (PC:A)* - Ability to segment larger units of speech sounds into smaller units of speech sounds.

---

[1]Test-retest coefficients were reported by grade in the test manual. Therefore, corresponding ages were estimated by the authors.
[a]The narrow Grw ability CHC classification for this test was determined by the authors because no agreement was reached through the group consensus process.

Battery: TOCL	Word Recognition	Age Range: 5-0 to 8-11

DESCRIPTION

The examinee is required to identify words on a page and answer questions about passages read both silently and by the examiner.

RELIABILITY [1]

■ - Low   ■ - Medium   ■ - High   ☐ - No Information Available

	2	3	4	5	6	7	8	9	10	11	12	13	14	15	16	17	18	19 24	25 29	30 34	35 39	40 44	45 49	50 54	55 59	60 64	65 69	70 74	75 79	80 84	85 90+
Internal consistency Test-retest*																															

Interval between testings: 2 to 3 weeks

FLOORS AND CEILINGS

	Test Floor	Test Ceiling
Inadequate at ages:	5-0 to 7-5	6-0 to 8-11

CHC CLASSIFICATIONS (Broad: stratum II / *Narrow: stratum I*)

Reading/Writing (*Grw*): *Reading Decoding (RD)* - Ability to recognize and decode words or pseudowords in reading; *Reading Comprehension (RC)* - Ability to comprehend connected discourse during reading.

Battery: TOCL	Reading Comprehension	Age Range: 5-0 to 8-11

DESCRIPTION

The examinee is required to read a passage and respond to questions stated by the examiner.

RELIABILITY [1]

■ - Low   ■ - Medium   ■ - High   ☐ - No Information Available

	2	3	4	5	6	7	8	9	10	11	12	13	14	15	16	17	18	19 24	25 29	30 34	35 39	40 44	45 49	50 54	55 59	60 64	65 69	70 74	75 79	80 84	85 90+
Internal consistency Test-retest*																															

Interval between testings: 2 to 3 weeks

FLOORS AND CEILINGS

	Test Floor	Test Ceiling
Inadequate at ages:	5-0 to 8-11	5-0 to 8-11

CHC CLASSIFICATIONS (Broad: stratum II / *Narrow: stratum I*)

Reading/Writing (*Grw*): *Reading Comprehension (RC)* - Ability to comprehend connected discourse during reading.

[1]Test-retest coefficients were reported by grade in the test manual. Therefore, corresponding ages were estimated by the authors.

DESCRIPTION

The examinee is required to write letters and sentences dictated by the examiner and copy words and sentences written in the workbook.

RELIABILITY [1]

☐ - Low   ◼ - Medium   ◼ - High   ☐ - No Information Available

	2	3	4	5	6	7	8	9	10	11	12	13	14	15	16	17	18	19 24	25 29	30 34	35 39	40 44	45 49	50 54	55 59	60 64	65 69	70 74	75 79	80 84	85 90+
Internal consistency				◼	◼	◼	◼																									
Test-retest*				◼	◼	◼	◼																									

*Interval between testings: 2 to 3 weeks

FLOORS AND CEILINGS

	Test Floor	**Test Ceiling**
Inadequate at ages:	5-0 to 6-8	7-0 to 8-11

CHC CLASSIFICATIONS (Broad: stratum II / *Narrow: stratum I*)

Reading/Writing (*Grw*): *English Usage Knowledge (EU)* - Knowledge of writing in the English language with respect to capitalization, punctuation, usage, and spelling; *Spelling Ability (SG)* - Ability to spell.

DESCRIPTION

The examinee is shown the pictures from the story that was read earlier and is required to write down as much of the story as can be remembered.

RELIABILITY [1]

☐ - Low   ◼ - Medium   ◼ - High   ☐ - No Information Available

	2	3	4	5	6	7	8	9	10	11	12	13	14	15	16	17	18	19 24	25 29	30 34	35 39	40 44	45 49	50 54	55 59	60 64	65 69	70 74	75 79	80 84	85 90+
Internal consistency				◼	◼	◼	◼																									
Test-retest*				◼	◼	◼	◼																									

*Interval between testings: 2 to 3 weeks

FLOORS AND CEILINGS

	Test Floor	**Test Ceiling**
Inadequate at ages:	5-0 to 8-11	none

CHC CLASSIFICATIONS (Broad: stratum II / *Narrow: stratum I*)

Long-Term Retrieval (*Glr*): *Meaningful Memory (MM)* - Ability to recall a set of items where there is a meaningful relation between items or the items create a meaningful story or connected discourse.

---

[1]Test-retest coefficients were reported by grade in the test manual. Therefore, corresponding ages were estimated by the authors.

DESCRIPTION

The examinee is required to write an original story about animal friends that contains a beginning, middle, and end.

RELIABILITY [1]

☐ - Low   ■ - Medium   ■ - High   ☐ - No Information Available

	2	3	4	5	6	7	8	9	10	11	12	13	14	15	16	17	18	19–24	25–29	30–34	35–39	40–44	45–49	50–54	55–59	60–64	65–69	70–74	75–79	80–84	85–90+
Internal consistency				■	■	■	■																								
Test-retest*				■	■	■	■																								

*Interval between testings: 2 to 3 weeks

FLOORS AND CEILINGS

	Test Floor	Test Ceiling
Inadequate at ages:	5-0 to 8-11	none

CHC CLASSIFICATIONS (Broad: stratum II / Narrow: stratum I)

Reading/Writing (Grw): *Writing Ability (WA)* - Ability to write with clarity of thought, organization, and good sentence structure.

---

[1]Test-retest coefficients were reported by grade in the test manual; corresponding ages were estimated by this text's authors.

Wide Range Achievement Test 3 (WRAT 3)

GENERAL INFORMATION

Author(s): Gary S. Wilkinson
Publisher: Wide Range, Inc.
Publication Date(s): 1936, 1946, 1965, 1976, 1978, 1984, 1993

Age Range: 5-0 to 74-11
Administration Time: 15 to 30 minutes

COMPOSITE MEASURE INFORMATION

SCORE INFORMATION

Standard scores	Percentiles	Stanines	Normal curve equivalents	Age equivalents	Grade equivalents

NORMING INFORMATION

Standardization Sample Size: 4,433

Sample Collection Date(s): 1992-1993

Avg. Number per Age/Grade Interval:
220 per year: 5-0 to 19-11
190 per five years: 20-0 to 24-11
190 per ten years: 25-0 to 74-11

Demographic Variables:
Gender — male; female
Geographic region — 4 regions
Race/ethnicity — White; Black; Hispanic; other
SES — parent/examinee occupation

Age Blocks in Norm Table:
3 months: 5-0 to 7-11
6 months: 8-0 to 11-11
1 year: 12-0 to 16-11
3 years: 17-0 to 19-11
5 years: 20-0 to 24-11
10 years: 25-0 to 74-11

VALIDITY

Types of Validity Evidence Reported in the Test Manual:

Content	Criterion	Construct

Test Review(s) and Validity Evidence Reported in Extant Literature: See Appendix C

CONTAINS AT LEAST ONE INDICATOR CONSISTENT WITH THE FOLLOWING LD ASSESSMENT AREA(S)

Oral Expression	Listening Comprehension	Written Expression	Basic Reading Skill	Reading Comprehension	Mathematics Calculation	Mathematics Reasoning

SPECIAL FEATURES

- Provides alternate forms (Blue and Tan)
- Includes word lists on plastic cards for both forms of the Reading and Spelling subtests
- Includes an item map for graphic representation of subjects' skills
- Contains a word pronunciation guide for the dictation of the spelling test
- Can be administered individually or in a group

DESCRIPTION

The examinee is required to recognize and name letters and pronounce printed words.

RELIABILITY

☐ - Low   ■ - Medium   ■ - High   ☐ - No Information Available

	2	3	4	5	6	7	8	9	10	11	12	13	14	15	16	17	18	19-24	25-29	30-34	35-39	40-44	45-49	50-54	55-59	60-64	65-69	70-74	75-79	80-84	85-90+

Internal consistency

Test-retest*

*Interval between testings: 4 to 6 weeks

FLOORS AND CEILINGS

	Test Floor	Test Ceiling
Inadequate at ages:	5-0 to 5-5	16-0 to 74-11

CHC CLASSIFICATIONS (Broad: stratum II / Narrow: stratum I)

Reading/Writing (Grw): Reading Decoding (RD) - Ability to recognize and decode words or pseudowords in reading.

DESCRIPTION

The examinee is required to write names, letters, and words from dictation.

RELIABILITY

☐ - Low   ■ - Medium   ■ - High   ☐ - No Information Available

	2	3	4	5	6	7	8	9	10	11	12	13	14	15	16	17	18	19-24	25-29	30-34	35-39	40-44	45-49	50-54	55-59	60-64	65-69	70-74	75-79	80-84	85-90+

Internal consistency

Test-retest*

*Interval between testings: 4 to 6 weeks

FLOORS AND CEILINGS

	Test Floor	Test Ceiling
Inadequate at ages:	5-0 to 5-2	20-0 to 74-11

CHC CLASSIFICATIONS (Broad: stratum II / Narrow: stratum I)

Reading/Writing (Grw): Spelling Ability (SG) - Ability to spell.

DESCRIPTION

The examinee is required to count, read number symbols, solve oral problems, and perform written problem computations.

RELIABILITY

☐ - Low   ■ - Medium   ■ - High   ☐ - No Information Available

	2	3	4	5	6	7	8	9	10	11	12	13	14	15	16	17	18	19–24	25–29	30–34	35–39	40–44	45–49	50–54	55–59	60–64	65–69	70–74	75–79	80–84	85–90+
Internal consistency				Low	High	High	High	High	High	High	High	High	High	High	High	High	High	Med	Med	High	High	High	High	High	High	High	High			
Test-retest*				High	High	High	High	High	High	High	High	High	High	High																

Interval between testings: 4 to 6 weeks

FLOORS AND CEILINGS

	Test Floor	Test Ceiling
Inadequate at ages:	none	17-0 to 64-11

CHC CLASSIFICATIONS (Broad: stratum II / *Narrow: stratum I*)

Quantitative Knowledge (*Gq*): *Mathematical Achievement (A3)* - Measured mathematics achievement.

DESCRIPTION

The examinee is required to recognize and name letters and pronounce printed words.

RELIABILITY

☐ - Low   ■ - Medium   ■ - High   ☐ - No Information Available

	2	3	4	5	6	7	8	9	10	11	12	13	14	15	16	17	18	19–24	25–29	30–34	35–39	40–44	45–49	50–54	55–59	60–64	65–69	70–74	75–79	80–84	85–90+
Internal consistency			High	High	High	High	Med	High	High	High	High	High	High	High	High	High	High	Med	Med	High	High	High	High	High	High	High	High			
Test-retest*			High	High	High	High	High	High	High	High																				

Interval between testings: 4 to 6 weeks

FLOORS AND CEILINGS

	Test Floor	Test Ceiling
Inadequate at ages:	5-0 to 5-5	16-0 to 74-11

CHC CLASSIFICATIONS (Broad: stratum II / *Narrow: stratum I*)

Reading/Writing (*Grw*): *Reading Decoding (RD)* - Ability to recognize and decode words or pseudowords in reading.

Battery: WRAT 3	Spelling (Tan)	Age Range: 5-0 to 74-11

DESCRIPTION

The examinee is required to write names, letters, and words from dictation.

RELIABILITY

☐ - Low   ■ - Medium   ■ - High   ☐ - No Information Available

| | 2 | 3 | 4 | 5 | 6 | 7 | 8 | 9 | 10 | 11 | 12 | 13 | 14 | 15 | 16 | 17 | 18 | 19 24 | 25 29 | 30 34 | 35 39 | 40 44 | 45 49 | 50 54 | 55 59 | 60 64 | 65 69 | 70 74 | 75 79 | 80 84 | 85 90+ |

Internal consistency
Test-retest*

Interval between testings: 4 to 6 weeks

FLOORS AND CEILINGS

	Test Floor	Test Ceiling
Inadequate at ages:	5-0 to 5-2	35-0 to 74-11

CHC CLASSIFICATIONS (Broad: stratum II / *Narrow: stratum I*)

Reading/Writing (*Grw*): *Spelling Ability (SG)* - Ability to spell.

Battery: WRAT 3	Arithmetic (Tan)	Age Range: 5-0 to 74-11

DESCRIPTION

The examinee is required to count, read number symbols, solve oral problems, and perform written problem computations.

RELIABILITY

☐ - Low   ■ - Medium   ■ - High   ☐ - No Information Available

| | 2 | 3 | 4 | 5 | 6 | 7 | 8 | 9 | 10 | 11 | 12 | 13 | 14 | 15 | 16 | 17 | 18 | 19 24 | 25 29 | 30 34 | 35 39 | 40 44 | 45 49 | 50 54 | 55 59 | 60 64 | 65 69 | 70 74 | 75 79 | 80 84 | 85 90+ |

Internal consistency
Test-retest*

Interval between testings: 4 to 6 weeks

FLOORS AND CEILINGS

	Test Floor	Test Ceiling
Inadequate at ages:	none	55-0 to 64-11

CHC CLASSIFICATIONS (Broad: stratum II / *Narrow: stratum I*)

Quantitative Knowledge (*Gq*): *Mathematical Achievement (A3)* - Measured mathematics achievement

Young Children's Achievement Test (YCAT)

GENERAL INFORMATION

Author(s): Wayne P. Hresko, Pamela K. Peak, Shelley R. Herron, and Deanna L. Bridges
Publisher: PRO-ED
Publication Date(s): 2000

Age Range: 4-0 to 7-11

Administration Time: 25 to 45 minutes

COMPOSITE MEASURE INFORMATION

Early Achievement Composite

SCORE INFORMATION

Standard scores	Percentiles	Stanines	Normal curve equivalents	Age equivalents	Grade equivalents

NORMING INFORMATION

Standardization Sample Size: 1,224

Avg. Number per Age/Grade Interval:
306 per year: 4-0 to 7-11

Age Blocks in Norm Table
3 months: 4-0 to 7-11

Sample Collection Date(s): 1996-1999

Demographic Variables:
Gender - male; female
Geographic region - 4 regions; 32 states and District of Columbia
Residence - urban; rural
Race/ethnicity - White; Black; Native American; Hispanic; Asian; other
SES - parent education; family income
Other - disability status (none, LD, SLD, MR, other)

VALIDITY

Types of Validity Evidence Reported in the Test Manual:

Content	Criterion	Construct

Test Review(s) and Validity Evidence Reported in Extant Literature: None currently available

CONTAINS AT LEAST ONE INDICATOR CONSISTENT WITH THE FOLLOWING LD ASSESSMENT AREA(S)

Oral Expression	Listening Comprehension	Written Expression	Basic Reading Skill	Reading Comprehension	Mathematics Calculation	Mathematics Reasoning

SPECIAL FEATURES

- Provides a description of individual items by subtest

DESCRIPTION

The examinee is required to answer questions that focus on quantity, direction and position, sorting, categorization, time, days of the week, seasons of the year, colors, body parts, shapes, community helpers, dangers, and personal data.

RELIABILITY

▨ - Low   ▩ - Medium   ■ - High   ☐ - No Information Available

	2	3	4	5	6	7	8	9	10	11	12	13	14	15	16	17	18	19-24	25-29	30-34	35-39	40-44	45-49	50-54	55-59	60-64	65-69	70-74	75-79	80-84	85-90+
Internal consistency			■	■	▨																										
Test-retest*			■	■	■																										

*Interval between testings: 2 weeks

FLOORS AND CEILINGS

	Test Floor	Test Ceiling
Inadequate at ages:	4-0 to 5-5	4-6 to 7-11

CHC CLASSIFICATIONS (Broad: stratum II / *Narrow: stratum I*)

Crystallized Intelligence (*Gc*): *General (verbal) Information (K0)* - Range of general knowledge.

DESCRIPTION

The examinee is required to name and sound out letters of the alphabet, rhyme, read words in isolation as well as in context, and read for comprehension.

RELIABILITY

▨ - Low   ▩ - Medium   ■ - High   ☐ - No Information Available

	2	3	4	5	6	7	8	9	10	11	12	13	14	15	16	17	18	19-24	25-29	30-34	35-39	40-44	45-49	50-54	55-59	60-64	65-69	70-74	75-79	80-84	85-90+
Internal consistency			▨	■	▨	■																									
Test-retest*																															

*Interval between testings: 2 weeks

FLOORS AND CEILINGS

	Test Floor	Test Ceiling
Inadequate at ages:	4-0 to 5-8	6-0 to 7-11

CHC CLASSIFICATIONS (Broad: stratum II / *Narrow: stratum I*)

Reading/Writing (*Grw*): *Reading Decoding[a] (RD)* - Ability to recognize and decode words or pseudowords in reading.

[a]The narrow ability CHC classification for this test was determined by the authors because no agreement was reached through the group consensus process.

Battery: YCAT	Mathematics	Age Range: 4-0 to 7-11

DESCRIPTION

The examinee is required to answer questions that focus on counting, ordinal positions, number identification, calculation, concepts of relative magnitude, time, money, and problem solving.

RELIABILITY

☐ - Low   ■ - Medium   ■ - High   ☐ - No Information Available

	2	3	4	5	6	7	8	9	10	11	12	13	14	15	16	17	18	19 24	25 29	30 34	35 39	40 44	45 49	50 54	55 59	60 64	65 69	70 74	75 79	80 84	85 90+
Internal consistency																															
Test-retest*																															

*Interval between testings: 2 weeks

FLOORS AND CEILINGS

	Test Floor	Test Ceiling
Inadequate at ages:	4-0 to 5-11	5-9 to 7-11

CHC CLASSIFICATIONS (Broad: stratum II / Narrow: stratum I)

Quantitative Knowledge (Gq): *Mathematical Achievement (A3)* - Measured mathematics achievement.

Battery: YCAT	Writing	Age Range: 4-0 to 7-11

DESCRIPTION

The examinee is required to write the alphabet, his/her name, and elementary spelling words and sentences.

RELIABILITY

☐ - Low   ■ - Medium   ■ - High   ☐ - No Information Available

	2	3	4	5	6	7	8	9	10	11	12	13	14	15	16	17	18	19 24	25 29	30 34	35 39	40 44	45 49	50 54	55 59	60 64	65 69	70 74	75 79	80 84	85 90+
Internal consistency																															
Test-retest*																															

*Interval between testing: 2 weeks

FLOORS AND CEILINGS

	Test Floor	Test Ceiling
Inadequate at ages:	4-0 to 4-11	5-6 to 7-11

CHC CLASSIFICATIONS (Broad: stratum II / Narrow: stratum I)

Reading/Writing (Grw): *Spelling Ability (SG)* - Ability to spell.

DESCRIPTION

The examinee is required to point to pictures, repeat numbers and sentences, define words, and discriminate among letter sounds.

RELIABILITY

☐ - Low   ◼ - Medium   ■ - High   ☐ - No Information Available

	2	3	4	5	6	7	8	9	10	11	12	13	14	15	16	17	18	19 24	25 29	30 34	35 39	40 44	45 49	50 54	55 59	60 64	65 69	70 74	75 79	80 84	85 90+
Internal consistency			■	■	◼																										
Test-retest*			■	■	■																										

Interval between testings: 2 weeks

FLOORS AND CEILINGS

	Test Floor	**Test Ceiling**
Inadequate at ages:	4-0 to 5-2	6-3 to 7-11

CHC CLASSIFICATIONS (**Broad: stratum II** / *Narrow: stratum I*)

Crystallized Intelligence (*Gc*): *Lexical Knowledge (VL)* - Extent of vocabulary that can be understood in terms of correct word meanings; *Language Development (LD)* - General development, or the understanding of words, sentences, and paragraphs (not requiring reading), in spoken native language skills.

ATDR *Summary Pages*
Specific Academic Skills—Reading Tests

Gray Oral Reading Tests-Fourth Edition (GORT-4)

GENERAL INFORMATION

Author(s): J. Lee Wiederholt and Brian R. Bryant
Publisher: PRO-ED
Publication Date(s): 1963, 1986, 1992, 2001

Age Range: 6-0 to 18-11
Administration Time: 15 to 45 minutes

COMPOSITE MEASURE INFORMATION

Oral Reading Quotient

SCORE INFORMATION

Standard scores	Percentiles	Stanines	Normal curve equivalents	Age equivalents	Grade equivalents

NORMING INFORMATION

Standardization Sample Size: 1,677

Avg. Number per Age/Grade Interval:
140 per year: 7-0 to 18-11

Age Blocks in Norm Table:
6 months: 6-0 to 13-11
1 year: 14-0 to 18-11

Sample Collection Date(s): 1999-2000

Demographic Variables:
Gender - *male; female*
Geographic region - *4 regions; 28 states and District of Columbia*
Residence - *urban; rural*
Race/ethnicity - *White; Black; Native American; Hispanic; Asian;*
  - *other*
SES - *parent education; family income*
Other - *disability status (none, LD, SLD, ADD, other)*

VALIDITY

Types of Validity Evidence Reported in the Test Manual:

Content	Criterion	Construct

Test Review(s) and Validity Evidence Reported in Extant Literature: See Appendix C

CONTAINS AT LEAST ONE INDICATOR CONSISTENT WITH THE FOLLOWING LD ASSESSMENT AREA(S)

Oral Expression	Listening Comprehension	Written Expression	Basic Reading Skill	Reading Comprehension	Mathematics Calculation	Mathematics Reasoning

SPECIAL FEATURES

- Provides alternate forms (A and B)
- Includes one new story at the beginning of the test to provide additional information on younger children and children experiencing reading difficulties
- The Passage Score has been renamed Fluency Score in line with current terminology
- Includes an error analysis system

DESCRIPTION

The examinee is required to read aloud each passage as quickly as possible after listening to a corresponding prompt presented orally by the examiner. The examinee is then required to answer multiple-choice questions aloud as presented orally by the examiner. The rate score is a converted value that is based on the time it takes the child to read the story.

RELIABILITY

☐ - Low   ■ - Medium   ■ - High   ☐ - No Information Available

```
        2  3  4  5  6  7  8  9  10 11 12 13 14 15 16 17 18 19 25 30 35 40 45 50 55 60 65 70 75 80 85
                                                              24 29 34 39 44 49 54 59 64 69 74 79 84 90+
Internal consistency
Test-retest*
```

Interval between testings: 2 weeks

FLOORS AND CEILINGS

	Test Floor	Test Ceiling
Inadequate at ages:	6-0 to 7-11	13-6 to 18-11

CHC CLASSIFICATIONS (Broad: stratum II / *Narrow: stratum I*)

Reading/Writing (*Grw*): *Reading Speed (RS)* - Time required to silently read a passage or series of sentences as quickly as possible.

DESCRIPTION

The examinee is required to read aloud each passage as quickly as possible after listening to a corresponding prompt presented orally by the examiner. The examinee is then required to answer multiple-choice questions aloud as presented orally by the examiner. The accuracy score is a converted value that is based on the number of errors made by the child while reading the story.

RELIABILITY

☐ - Low   ■ - Medium   ■ - High   ☐ - No Information Available

```
        2  3  4  5  6  7  8  9  10 11 12 13 14 15 16 17 18 19 25 30 35 40 45 50 55 60 65 70 75 80 85
                                                              24 29 34 39 44 49 54 59 64 69 74 79 84 90+
Internal consistency
Test-retest*
```

Interval between testings: 2 weeks

FLOORS AND CEILINGS

	Test Floor	Test Ceiling
Inadequate at ages:	6-0 to 7-5	16-0 to 18-11

CHC CLASSIFICATIONS (Broad: stratum II / *Narrow: stratum I*)

Reading/Writing (*Grw*): *Reading Decoding (RD)* - Ability to recognize and decode words or pseudowords in reading.

DESCRIPTION

The examinee is required to read aloud each passage as quickly as possible after listening to a corresponding prompt presented orally by the examiner. The examinee is then required to answer multiple-choice questions aloud as presented orally by the examiner. The fluency score is the sum of the rate and accuracy scores.

RELIABILITY

☐ - Low   ■ - Medium   ■ - High   ☐ - No Information Available

	2	3	4	5	6	7	8	9	10	11	12	13	14	15	16	17	18	19-24	25-29	30-34	35-39	40-44	45-49	50-54	55-59	60-64	65-69	70-74	75-79	80-84	85-90+
Internal consistency																															
Test-retest*																															

*Interval between testings: 2 weeks

FLOORS AND CEILINGS

	Test Floor	**Test Ceiling**
Inadequate at ages:	6-0 to 7-5	18-0 to 18-11

CHC CLASSIFICATIONS (Broad: stratum II / *Narrow: stratum I*)

Reading/Writing (*Grw*): *Reading Speed (RS)* - Time required to silently read a passage or series of sentences as quickly as possible; *Reading Decoding (RD)* - Ability to recognize and decode words or pseudowords in reading.

DESCRIPTION

The examinee is required to read aloud each passage as quickly as possible after listening to a corresponding prompt presented orally by the examiner. The examinee is then required to answer multiple-choice questions aloud as presented orally by the examiner. The comprehension score is the sum of correct answers given by the examinee to the comprehension questions.

RELIABILITY

☐ - Low   ■ - Medium   ■ - High   ☐ - No Information Available

	2	3	4	5	6	7	8	9	10	11	12	13	14	15	16	17	18	19-24	25-29	30-34	35-39	40-44	45-49	50-54	55-59	60-64	65-69	70-74	75-79	80-84	85-90+
Internal consistency																															
Test-retest*																															

*Interval between testings: 2 weeks

FLOORS AND CEILINGS

	Test Floor	**Test Ceiling**
Inadequate at ages:	6-0 to 7-11	14-0 to 18-11

CHC CLASSIFICATIONS (Broad: stratum II / *Narrow: stratum I*)

Reading/Writing (*Grw*): *Reading Comprehension (RC)* - Ability to comprehend connected discourse during reading.

DESCRIPTION

The examinee is required to read aloud each passage as quickly as possible after listening to a corresponding prompt presented orally by the examiner. The examinee is then required to answer multiple-choice questions aloud as presented orally by the examiner. The rate score is a converted value that is based on the time it takes the child to read the story.

RELIABILITY

■ - Low   ■ - Medium   ■ - High   ☐ - No Information Available

	2	3	4	5	6	7	8	9	10	11	12	13	14	15	16	17	18	19/24	25/29	30/34	35/39	40/44	45/49	50/54	55/59	60/64	65/69	70/74	75/79	80/84	85/90+
Internal consistency Test-retest*																															

*Interval between testings: 2 weeks

FLOORS AND CEILINGS

	Test Floor	Test Ceiling
Inadequate at ages:	6-0 to 7-11	13-6 to 18-11

CHC CLASSIFICATIONS (Broad: stratum II / Narrow: stratum I)

Reading/Writing (Grw): *Reading Speed (RS)* - Time required to silently read a passage or series of sentences as quickly as possible.

DESCRIPTION

The examinee is required to read aloud each passage as quickly as possible after listening to a corresponding prompt presented orally by the examiner. The examinee is then required to answer multiple-choice questions aloud as presented orally by the examiner. The accuracy score is a converted value that is based on the number of errors made by the child while reading the story.

RELIABILITY

■ - Low   ■ - Medium   ■ - High   ☐ - No Information Available

	2	3	4	5	6	7	8	9	10	11	12	13	14	15	16	17	18	19/24	25/29	30/34	35/39	40/44	45/49	50/54	55/59	60/64	65/69	70/74	75/79	80/84	85/90+
Internal consistency Test-retest*																															

*Interval between testings: 2 weeks

FLOORS AND CEILINGS

	Test Floor	Test Ceiling
Inadequate at ages:	6-0 to 7-11	15-0 to 18-11

CHC CLASSIFICATIONS (Broad: stratum II / Narrow: stratum I)

Reading/Writing (Grw): *Reading Decoding (RD)* - Ability to recognize and decode words or pseudowords in reading.

DESCRIPTION

The examinee is required to read aloud each passage as quickly as possible after listening to a corresponding prompt presented orally by the examiner. The examinee is then required to answer multiple choice questions aloud as presented orally by the examiner. The fluency score is the sum of the rate and accuracy scores.

RELIABILITY

■ - Low ■ - Medium ■ - High ☐ - No Information Available

| | 2 3 4 5 6 7 8 9 10 11 12 13 14 15 16 17 18 19 25 30 35 40 45 50 55 60 65 70 75 80 85 |
| | 24 29 34 39 44 49 54 59 64 69 74 79 84 90+ |

Internal consistency
Test-retest*

*Interval between testings: 2 weeks

FLOORS AND CEILINGS

| | **Test Floor** | **Test Ceiling** |
| *Inadequate at ages:* | 6-0 to 7-11 | 17-0 to 18-11 |

CHC CLASSIFICATIONS (Broad: stratum II / *Narrow: stratum I*)

Reading/Writing (*Grw*): *Reading Speed (RS)* - Time required to silently read a passage or series of sentences as quickly as possible; *Reading Decoding (RD)* - Ability to recognize and decode words or pseudowords in reading.

| *Battery:* GORT-4 | Comprehension (Form B) | *Age Range:* 6-0 to 18-11 |

DESCRIPTION

The examinee is required to read aloud each passage as quickly as possible after listening to a corresponding prompt presented orally by the examiner. The examinee is then required to answer multiple choice questions aloud as presented orally by the examiner. The comprehension score is the sum of correct answers given by the examinee to the comprehension questions.

RELIABILITY

■ - Low ■ - Medium ■ - High ☐ - No Information Available

| | 2 3 4 5 6 7 8 9 10 11 12 13 14 15 16 17 18 19 25 30 35 40 45 50 55 60 65 70 75 80 85 |
| | 24 29 34 39 44 49 54 59 64 69 74 79 84 90+ |

Internal consistency
Test-retest*

*Interval between testings: 2 weeks

FLOORS AND CEILINGS

| | **Test Floor** | **Test Ceiling** |
| *Inadequate at ages:* | 6-0 to 8-11 | 14-0 to 18-11 |

CHC CLASSIFICATIONS (Broad: stratum II / *Narrow: stratum I*)

Reading/Writing (*Grw*): *Reading Comprehension (RC)* - Ability to comprehend connected discourse during reading.

Gray Silent Reading Tests (GSRT)

GENERAL INFORMATION

Author(s): J. Lee Wiederholt and Ginger Blalock
Publisher: PRO-ED
Publication Date(s): 2000

Age Range: 7-0 to 25-11
Administration Time: 15 to 30 minutes

COMPOSITE MEASURE INFORMATION

Silent Reading Quotient

SCORE INFORMATION

Standard scores	Percentiles	Stanines	Normal curve equivalents	Age equivalents	Grade equivalents

NORMING INFORMATION

Standardization Sample Size: 1,400

Sample Collection Date(s): 1996-1998

Avg. Number per Age/Grade Interval:
  120 per year: 7-0 to 17-11
  53 per five years: 18-0 to 25-11

Age Blocks in Norm Table:
  6 months: 7-0 to 13-11
  1 year: 14-0 to 17-11
  8 years: 18-0 to 25-11

Demographic Variables:
  Gender   *- male; female*
  Geographic region   *- 4 regions; 32 states*
  Residence   *- urban; rural*
  Race/ethnicity   *- White; Black; Native American; Hispanic; Asian; other*
  SES   *- parent education*
  Other   *- disability status (none, LD, SLD, other)*

VALIDITY

Types of Validity Evidence Reported in the Test Manual:

Content	Criterion	Construct

Test Review(s) and Validity Evidence Reported in Extant Literature: None currently available

CONTAINS AT LEAST ONE INDICATOR CONSISTENT WITH THE FOLLOWING LD ASSESSMENT AREA(S)

Oral Expression	Listening Comprehension	Written Expression	Basic Reading Skill	Reading Comprehension	Mathematics Calculation	Mathematics Reasoning

SPECIAL FEATURES

- Provides alternate forms (A and B)
- Can be administered individually or in a group

| Battery: GSRT | Silent Reading Comprehension (Form A) | Age Range: 7-0 to 25-11 |

DESCRIPTION

The examinee is required to read passages silently and respond orally to five questions for each passage read.

RELIABILITY

☐ - Low   ■ - Medium   ■ - High   ☐ - No Information Available

	2	3	4	5	6	7	8	9	10	11	12	13	14	15	16	17	18	19 24	25 29	30 34	35 39	40 44	45 49	50 54	55 59	60 64	65 69	70 74	75 79	80 84	85 90+
Internal consistency																															
Test-retest*																															

*Interval between testings: 2 weeks

FLOORS AND CEILINGS

	Test Floor	Test Ceiling
Inadequate at ages:	7-0 to 8-5	18-0 to 25-11

CHC CLASSIFICATIONS (Broad: stratum II / Narrow: stratum I)

Reading/Writing (Grw): *Reading Comprehension (RC)* - Ability to comprehend connected discourse during reading.

| Battery: GSRT | Silent Reading Comprehension (Form B) | Age Range: 7-0 to 25-11 |

DESCRIPTION

The examinee is required to read passages silently and respond to five questions for each passage read.

RELIABILITY

☐ - Low   ■ - Medium   ■ - High   ☐ - No Information Available

	2	3	4	5	6	7	8	9	10	11	12	13	14	15	16	17	18	19 24	25 29	30 34	35 39	40 44	45 49	50 54	55 59	60 64	65 69	70 74	75 79	80 84	85 90+
Internal consistency																															
Test-retest*																															

*Interval between testings: 2 weeks

FLOORS AND CEILINGS

	Test Floor	Test Ceiling
Inadequate at ages:	7-0 to 8-5	none

CHC CLASSIFICATIONS (Broad: stratum II / Narrow: stratum I)

Reading/Writing (Grw): *Reading Comprehension (RC)* - Ability to comprehend connected discourse during reading.

Standardized Reading Inventory-Second Edition (SRI-2)

GENERAL INFORMATION

Author(s): Phyllis L. Newcomer
Publisher: PRO-ED
Publication Date(s): 1986, 1999

Age Range: 6-0 to 14-6
Administration Time: 30 to 90 minutes

COMPOSITE MEASURE INFORMATION

Reading Quotient

SCORE INFORMATION

Standard scores	Percentiles	Stanines	Normal curve equivalents	Age equivalents	Grade equivalents

NORMING INFORMATION

Standardization Sample Size: 1,099

Sample Collection Date(s): 1996-1998

Avg. Number per Age/Grade Interval:
122 per year: 6-0 to 14-6

Age Blocks in Norm Table
6 months: 6-0 to 14-6

Demographic Variables:
Gender   *- male; female*
Geographic region   *- 4 regions; 28 states and District of Columbia*
Residence   *- urban; rural*
Race/ethnicity   *- White; Black; other*
SES   *- parent education; family income*
Other   *- disability status (none, LD, SLD, MR, other)*

VALIDITY

Types of Validity Evidence Reported in the Test Manual:

Content	Criterion	Construct

Test Review(s) and Validity Evidence Reported in Extant Literature: See Appendix C

CONTAINS AT LEAST ONE INDICATOR CONSISTENT WITH THE FOLLOWING LD ASSESSMENT AREA(S)

Oral Expression	Listening Comprehension	Written Expression	Basic Reading Skill	Reading Comprehension	Mathematics Calculation	Mathematics Reasoning

SPECIAL FEATURES

- Provides alternate forms (A and B)
- Includes a worksheet for recording different types of word recognition errors, word recognition irregularities, passage comprehension errors, word attack skills, and other reading behaviors

DESCRIPTION

The examinee is required to read a series of sentences each containing one underlined word. The examinee is then required to pick from an array of words the one that has the same meaning as the underlined word.

RELIABILITY [1]

☐ - Low   ■ - Medium   ■ - High   ☐ - No Information Available

	2	3	4	5	6	7	8	9	10	11	12	13	14	15	16	17	18	19 24	25 29	30 34	35 39	40 44	45 49	50 54	55 59	60 64	65 69	70 74	75 79	80 84	85 90+
Internal consistency																															
Test-retest*																															

*Interval between testings: 2 weeks

FLOORS AND CEILINGS

	Test Floor	Test Ceiling
Inadequate at ages:	6-0 to 8-11	10-0 to 14-6

CHC CLASSIFICATIONS (Broad: stratum II / Narrow: stratum I)

Reading/Writing (Grw): Verbal (printed) Language Comprehension (V) - General development, or the understanding of words, sentences, and paragraphs in native language, as measured by reading vocabulary and reading comprehension tests.

DESCRIPTION

The examinee is required to read aloud a list of words.

RELIABILITY [2]

☐ - Low   ■ - Medium   ■ - High   ☐ - No Information Available

	2	3	4	5	6	7	8	9	10	11	12	13	14	15	16	17	18	19 24	25 29	30 34	35 39	40 44	45 49	50 54	55 59	60 64	65 69	70 74	75 79	80 84	85 90+
Internal consistency																															
Test-retest*																															

*Interval between testings: 2 weeks

FLOORS AND CEILINGS

	Test Floor	Test Ceiling
Inadequate at ages:	6-0 to 7-11	11-6 to 14-6

CHC CLASSIFICATIONS (Broad: stratum II / Narrow: stratum I)

Reading/Writing (Grw): Reading Decoding (RD) - Ability to recognize and decode words or pseudowords in reading.

[1]No indication of the age or grade range of the test-retest sample was provided in the manual; thus, no rating was made.

[2]Test-retest coefficients were reported by grade in the test manual. Therefore, corresponding ages were estimated by the authors.

DESCRIPTION

The examinee is required to read some passages, first out loud and then silently. The examinee is then required to answer some questions about the passages.

RELIABILITY [1]

	- Low		- Medium		- High		- No Information Available

	2	3	4	5	6	7	8	9	10	11	12	13	14	15	16	17	18	19 24	25 29	30 34	35 39	40 44	45 49	50 54	55 59	60 64	65 69	70 74	75 79	80 84	85 90+

Internal consistency
Test-retest*

*Interval between testings: 2 weeks

FLOORS AND CEILINGS

	Test Floor	**Test Ceiling**
Inadequate at ages:	6-0 to 7-11	12-6 to 14-6

CHC CLASSIFICATIONS (Broad: stratum II / *Narrow: stratum I*)

Reading/Writing (*Grw*): *Reading Comprehension (RC)* - Ability to comprehend connected discourse during reading.

DESCRIPTION

The examinee is required to read aloud a list of words.

RELIABILITY [1]

	- Low		- Medium		- High		- No Information Available

	2	3	4	5	6	7	8	9	10	11	12	13	14	15	16	17	18	19 24	25 29	30 34	35 39	40 44	45 49	50 54	55 59	60 64	65 69	70 74	75 79	80 84	85 90+

Internal consistency
Test-retest*

*Interval between testings: 2 weeks

FLOORS AND CEILINGS

	Test Floor	**Test Ceiling**
Inadequate at ages:	6-0 to 7-11	11-6 to 14-6

CHC CLASSIFICATIONS (Broad: stratum II / *Narrow: stratum I*)

Reading/Writing (*Grw*): *Reading Decoding (RD)* - Ability to recognize and decode words or pseudowords in reading.

[1]Test-retest coefficients were reported by grade in the test manual. Therefore, corresponding ages were estimated by the authors.

DESCRIPTION

The examinee is required to read some passages, first out loud and then silently. The examinee is then required to answer some questions about the passages.

RELIABILITY [1]

| ■ - Low | ■ - Medium | ■ - High | ☐ - No Information Available |

	2	3	4	5	6	7	8	9	10	11	12	13	14	15	16	17	18	19 24	25 29	30 34	35 39	40 44	45 49	50 54	55 59	60 64	65 69	70 74	75 79	80 84	85 90+
Internal consistency																															
Test-retest*																															

Interval between testings: 2 weeks

FLOORS AND CEILINGS

	Test Floor	**Test Ceiling**
Inadequate at ages:	6-0 to 7-11	13-0 to 14-6

CHC CLASSIFICATIONS (**Broad: stratum II** / *Narrow: stratum I*)

Reading/Writing (*Grw*): *Reading Comprehension (RC)* - Ability to comprehend connected discourse during reading.

---

[1]Test-retest coefficients were reported by grade in the test manual. Therefore, corresponding ages were estimated by the authors.

Test of Early Reading Ability-Third Edition (TERA-3)

GENERAL INFORMATION

Author(s): D. Kim Reid, Wayne P. Hresko, and Donald D. Hammill

Publisher: PRO-ED

Publication Date(s): 1981, 1989, 2001

Age Range: 3-6 to 8-6

Administration Time: 15 to 45 minutes

COMPOSITE MEASURE INFORMATION

Reading Quotient

SCORE INFORMATION

Standard scores	Percentiles	Stanines	Normal curve equivalents	Age equivalents	Grade equivalents

NORMING INFORMATION

Standardization Sample Size: 875

Avg. Number per Age/Grade Interval:
175 per year: 3-6 to 8-6

Age Blocks in Norm Table:
6 months: 3-6 to 4-11
3 months: 5-0 to 6-11
6 months: 7-0 to 7-11
7 months: 8-0 to 8-6

Sample Collection Date(s): 1999-2000

Demographic Variables:
Gender — male; female
Geographic region — 4 regions; 22 states
Residence — urban; rural
Race/ethnicity — White; Black; other
SES — parent education; family income
Other — disability status (none, LD, SLD, MR, other)

VALIDITY

Types of Validity Evidence Reported in the Test Manual:

Content	Criterion	Construct

Test Review(s) and Validity Evidence Reported in Extant Literature: See Appendix C

CONTAINS AT LEAST ONE INDICATOR CONSISTENT WITH THE FOLLOWING LD ASSESSMENT AREA(S)

Oral Expression	Listening Comprehension	Written Expression	Basic Reading Skill	Reading Comprehension	Mathematics Calculation	Mathematics Reasoning

SPECIAL FEATURES

- Provides alternate forms (A and B)
- Includes standardized manipulatives

DESCRIPTION

The examinee is required to correctly identify letters and words as visually presented by the examiner using the Picture Book with verbal prompting.

RELIABILITY

■ - Low   ■ - Medium   ■ - High   ☐ - No Information Available

	2	3	4	5	6	7	8	9	10	11	12	13	14	15	16	17	18	19/24	25/29	30/34	35/39	40/44	45/49	50/54	55/59	60/64	65/69	70/74	75/79	80/84	85/90+
Internal consistency			High	High	High	High																									
Test-retest*			High	High	High	High	High																								

*Interval between testings: 2 weeks

FLOORS AND CEILINGS

	Test Floor	Test Ceiling
Inadequate at ages:	3-6 to 5-2	7-0 to 8-6

CHC CLASSIFICATIONS (Broad: stratum II / Narrow: stratum I)

Reading/Writing (Grw): *Reading Decoding (RD)* - Ability to recognize and decode words or pseudowords in reading.

DESCRIPTION

The examinee is required to identify conventions of print such as book handling, print conventions, and knowledge of punctuation, capitalization, and spelling as visually presented by the examiner using the Picture Book with verbal prompting.

RELIABILITY

■ - Low   ■ - Medium   ■ - High   ☐ - No Information Available

	2	3	4	5	6	7	8	9	10	11	12	13	14	15	16	17	18	19/24	25/29	30/34	35/39	40/44	45/49	50/54	55/59	60/64	65/69	70/74	75/79	80/84	85/90+
Internal consistency		Medium	Medium	Medium	Medium	Low																									
Test-retest*		Low	Medium	Medium	High	High																									

*Interval between testings: 2 weeks

FLOORS AND CEILINGS

	Test Floor	Test Ceiling
Inadequate at ages:	3-6 to 5-5	7-0 to 8-6

CHC CLASSIFICATIONS (Broad: stratum II / Narrow: stratum I)

Reading/Writing (Grw): *English Usage Knowledge (EU)* - Knowledge of writing in the English language with respect to capitalization, punctuation, usage, and spelling.

DESCRIPTION

The examinee is required to comprehend and identify words, sentences, and paragraphs as visually presented by the examiner using the Picture Book with verbal prompting.

RELIABILITY

■ - Low   ■ - Medium   ■ - High   ☐ - No Information Available

	2 3 4 5 6 7 8 9 10 11 12 13 14 15 16 17 18 19 25 30 35 40 45 50 55 60 65 70 75 80 85
	24 29 34 39 44 49 54 59 64 69 74 79 84 90+
Internal consistency	
Test-retest*	

*Interval between testings: 2 weeks

FLOORS AND CEILINGS

| | Test Floor | Test Ceiling |
| Inadequate at ages: | 3-6 to 3-11 | 7-6 to 8-6 |

CHC CLASSIFICATIONS (Broad: stratum II / *Narrow: stratum I*)

Reading/Writing (*Grw*): *Reading Comprehension (RC)* - Ability to comprehend connected discourse during reading; *Verbal (printed) Language Comprehension (V)* - General development, or the understanding of words, sentences, and paragraphs in native language, as measured by reading vocabulary and reading comprehension tests.

DESCRIPTION

The examinee is required to correctly identify letters and words as visually presented by the examiner using the Picture Book with verbal prompting.

RELIABILITY

■ - Low   ■ - Medium   ■ - High   ☐ - No Information Available

	2 3 4 5 6 7 8 9 10 11 12 13 14 15 16 17 18 19 25 30 35 40 45 50 55 60 65 70 75 80 85
	24 29 34 39 44 49 54 59 64 69 74 79 84 90+
Internal consistency	
Test-retest*	

*Interval between testings: 2 weeks

FLOORS AND CEILINGS

| | Test Floor | Test Ceiling |
| Inadequate at ages: | 3-6 to 5-2 | 7-0 to 8-6 |

CHC CLASSIFICATIONS (Broad: stratum II / *Narrow: stratum I*)

DESCRIPTION

The examinee is required to identify conventions of print such as book handling, print conventions, and knowledge of punctuation, capitalization, and spelling as visually presented by the examiner using the Picture Book with verbal prompting.

RELIABILITY

☐ - Low   ■ - Medium   ■ - High   ☐ - No Information Available

| | 2 3 4 5 6 7 8 9 10 11 12 13 14 15 16 17 18 19 25 30 35 40 45 50 55 60 65 70 75 80 85 |
| | 24 29 34 39 44 49 54 59 64 69 74 79 84 90+ |

Internal consistency
Test-retest*

*Interval between testings: 2 weeks

FLOORS AND CEILINGS

	Test Floor	**Test Ceiling**
Inadequate at ages:	3-6 to 5-5	7-0 to 8-6

CHC CLASSIFICATIONS (**Broad: stratum II** / *Narrow: stratum I*)

Reading/Writing (*Grw*): *English Usage Knowledge (EU)* - Knowledge of writing in the English language with respect to capitalization, punctuation, usage, and spelling.

DESCRIPTION

The examinee is required to comprehend and identify words, sentences, and paragraphs as visually presented by the examiner using the Picture Book with verbal prompting.

RELIABILITY

☐ - Low   ■ - Medium   ■ - High   ☐ - No Information Available

| | 2 3 4 5 6 7 8 9 10 11 12 13 14 15 16 17 18 19 25 30 35 40 45 50 55 60 65 70 75 80 85 |
| | 24 29 34 39 44 49 54 59 64 69 74 79 84 90+ |

Internal consistency
Test-retest*

*Interval between testings: 2 weeks

FLOORS AND CEILINGS

	Test Floor	**Test Ceiling**
Inadequate at ages:	3-6 to 3-11	7-6 to 8-6

CHC CLASSIFICATIONS (**Broad: stratum II** / *Narrow: stratum I*)

Reading/Writing (*Grw*): *Reading Comprehension (RC)* - Ability to comprehend connected discourse during reading; *Verbal (printed) Language Comprehension (V)* - General development, or the understanding of words, sentences, and paragraphs in native language, as measured by <u>reading</u> vocabulary and <u>reading</u> comprehension tests.

Test of Reading Comprehension-Third Edition (TORC-3)

GENERAL INFORMATION

Author(s): Virginia L. Brown, Donald D. Hammill, and J. Lee Wiederholt

Age Range: 7-0 to 17-11

Publisher: PRO-ED

Administration Time: 30 to 90 minutes

Publication Date(s): 1978, 1986, 1995

COMPOSITE MEASURE INFORMATION

Reading Comprehension Quotient

SCORE INFORMATION

Standard scores	Percentiles	Stanines	Normal curve equivalents	Age equivalents	Grade equivalents

NORMING INFORMATION

Standardization Sample Size: 1,962

Sample Collection Date(s): 1993-1994

Avg. Number per Age/Grade Interval:
178 per year: 7-0 to 17-11

Age Blocks in Norm Table:
6 months: 7-0 to 11-11
1 year: 12-0 to 15-11
2 years: 16-0 to 17-11

Demographic Variables:
Gender - male; female
Geographic region - 4 regions; 19 states
Residence - urban; rural
Race/ethnicity - White; Black; Native American; Hispanic; Asian; other
Other - disability status (none, LD, SLD, other)

VALIDITY

Types of Validity Evidence Reported in the Test Manual:

Content	Criterion	Construct

Test Review(s) and Validity Evidence Reported in Extant Literature: See Appendix C

CONTAINS AT LEAST ONE INDICATOR CONSISTENT WITH THE FOLLOWING LD ASSESSMENT AREA(S)

Oral Expression	Listening Comprehension	Written Expression	Basic Reading Skill	Reading Comprehension	Mathematics Calculation	Mathematics Reasoning

SPECIAL FEATURES

- Can be administered individually or in a group

DESCRIPTION

The examinee is shown a series of words and then asked to indicate which two words in these series are the most alike.

RELIABILITY

☐ - Low ■ - Medium ■ - High ☐ - No Information Available

	2	3	4	5	6	7	8	9	10	11	12	13	14	15	16	17	18	19/24	25/29	30/34	35/39	40/44	45/49	50/54	55/59	60/64	65/69	70/74	75/79	80/84	85/90+
Internal consistency						High	High	High	High	High	High	High	High	High	High	High															
Test-retest*																															

Interval between testings: 8 weeks

FLOORS AND CEILINGS

	Test Floor	**Test Ceiling**
Inadequate at ages:	7-0 to 9-5	10-0 to 17-11

CHC CLASSIFICATIONS (Broad: stratum II / *Narrow: stratum I*)

Crystallized Intelligence[a] (Gc): *Lexical Knowledge[a] (VL)* - Extent of vocabulary that can be understood in terms of correct word meanings; *Language Development[a] (LD)* - General development, or the understanding of words, sentences, and paragraphs (not requiring reading), in spoken native language skills. **Reading/Writing[a] (Grw):** *Verbal (printed) Language Comprehension[a] (V)* - General development, or the understanding of words, sentences, or paragraphs in native language, as measured by reading vocabulary and reading comprehension tests.

DESCRIPTION

The examinee is required to determine which two sentences from a series of sentences mean almost the same thing.

RELIABILITY

☐ - Low ■ - Medium ■ - High ☐ - No Information Available

	2	3	4	5	6	7	8	9	10	11	12	13	14	15	16	17	18	19/24	25/29	30/34	35/39	40/44	45/49	50/54	55/59	60/64	65/69	70/74	75/79	80/84	85/90+
Internal consistency																															
Test-retest*																															

Interval between testings: 8 weeks

FLOORS AND CEILINGS

	Test Floor	**Test Ceiling**
Inadequate at ages:	7-0 to 11-11	11-0 to 17-11

CHC CLASSIFICATIONS (Broad: stratum II / *Narrow: stratum I*)

Reading/Writing (Grw): *Verbal (printed) Language Comprehension (V)* - General development, or the understanding of words, sentences, or paragraphs in native language, as measured by reading vocabulary and reading comprehension tests.

[a]The broad and narrow ability CHC classifications for this test were determined by the authors because no agreement was reached through the group consensus process.

DESCRIPTION

The examinee is required to read different stories and then answer questions about those stories.

RELIABILITY

☐ - Low   ◼ - Medium   ◼ - High   ☐ - No Information Available

	2	3	4	5	6	7	8	9	10	11	12	13	14	15	16	17	18	19 24	25 29	30 34	35 39	40 44	45 49	50 54	55 59	60 64	65 69	70 74	75 79	80 84	85 90+
Internal consistency																															
Test-retest*																															

*Interval between testings: 8 weeks

FLOORS AND CEILINGS

	Test Floor	Test Ceiling
Inadequate at ages:	7-0 to 10-11	13-0 to 17-11

CHC CLASSIFICATIONS (Broad: stratum II / Narrow: stratum I)

Reading/Writing (Grw): *Reading Comprehension (RC)* - Ability to comprehend connected discourse during reading.

DESCRIPTION

The examinee is required to reorder written sentences so that they make sense.

RELIABILITY

☐ - Low   ◼ - Medium   ◼ - High   ☐ - No Information Available

	2	3	4	5	6	7	8	9	10	11	12	13	14	15	16	17	18	19 24	25 29	30 34	35 39	40 44	45 49	50 54	55 59	60 64	65 69	70 74	75 79	80 84	85 90+
Internal consistency																															
Test-retest*																															

*Interval between testings: 8 weeks

FLOORS AND CEILINGS

	Test Floor	Test Ceiling
Inadequate at ages:	7-0 to 10-5	none

CHC CLASSIFICATIONS (Broad: stratum II / Narrow: stratum I)

Reading/Writing[a] (Grw): *Reading Comprehension[a] (RC)* - Ability to comprehend connected discourse during reading.

[a]The broad and narrow ability CHC classifications for this test were determined by the authors because no agreement was reached through the group consensus process.

DESCRIPTION

The examinee is required to determine which two mathematically related words from a series of words are the most alike.

RELIABILITY

☐ - Low   ■ - Medium   ■ - High   ☐ - No Information Available

	2	3	4	5	6	7	8	9	10	11	12	13	14	15	16	17	18	19-24	25-29	30-34	35-39	40-44	45-49	50-54	55-59	60-64	65-69	70-74	75-79	80-84	85-90+
Internal consistency						High																									
Test-retest*														Medium																	

Interval between testings: 8 weeks

FLOORS AND CEILINGS

	Test Floor	Test Ceiling
Inadequate at ages:	7-0 to 8-11	10-0 to 17-11

CHC CLASSIFICATIONS (Broad: stratum II / Narrow: stratum I)

Quantitative Knowledge (Gq): *Mathematical Knowledge (KM)* - Range of general knowledge about mathematics.

DESCRIPTION

The examinee is required to determine which two social studies-related words from a series of words are the most alike.

RELIABILITY

☐ - Low   ■ - Medium   ■ - High   ☐ - No Information Available

	2	3	4	5	6	7	8	9	10	11	12	13	14	15	16	17	18	19-24	25-29	30-34	35-39	40-44	45-49	50-54	55-59	60-64	65-69	70-74	75-79	80-84	85-90+
Internal consistency					High																										
Test-retest*														Medium																	

Interval between testings: 8 weeks

FLOORS AND CEILINGS

	Test Floor	Test Ceiling
Inadequate at ages:	7-0 to 8-11	10-0 to 17-11

CHC CLASSIFICATIONS (Broad: stratum II / Narrow: stratum I)

Crystallized Intelligence (Gc): *Language Development (LD)* - General development, or the understanding of words, sentences, and paragraphs (not requiring reading), in spoken native language skills; *Lexical Knowledge (VL)* - Extent of vocabulary that can be understood in terms of correct word meanings.

DESCRIPTION

The examinee is required to determine which two science-related words from a series of words are the most alike.

RELIABILITY

☐ - Low ■ - Medium ■ - High ☐ - No Information Available

	2	3	4	5	6	7	8	9	10	11	12	13	14	15	16	17	18	19 24	25 29	30 34	35 39	40 44	45 49	50 54	55 59	60 64	65 69	70 74	75 79	80 84	85 90+

Internal consistency
Test-retest*

Interval between testings: 8 weeks

FLOORS AND CEILINGS

	Test Floor	Test Ceiling
Inadequate at ages:	7-0 to 11-11	12-0 to 17-11

CHC CLASSIFICATIONS (Broad: stratum II / Narrow: stratum I)

Crystallized Intelligence (Gc): *General Science Information[a] (K1)* - Range of scientific knowledge (e.g., biology, physics, engineering, mechanics, electronics).

DESCRIPTION

The examinee is required to read directions and then follow the directions.

RELIABILITY

☐ - Low ■ - Medium ■ - High ☐ - No Information Available

	2	3	4	5	6	7	8	9	10	11	12	13	14	15	16	17	18	19 24	25 29	30 34	35 39	40 44	45 49	50 54	55 59	60 64	65 69	70 74	75 79	80 84	85 90+

Internal consistency
Test-retest*

Interval between testings: 8 weeks

FLOORS AND CEILINGS

	Test Floor	Test Ceiling
Inadequate at ages:	7-0 to 8-5	8-0 to 12-11

CHC CLASSIFICATIONS (Broad: stratum II / Narrow: stratum I)

Reading/Writing (Grw): *Reading Comprehension (RC)* - Ability to comprehend connected discourse during reading.

[a]The narrow ability CHC classification for this test was determined by the authors because no agreement was reached through the group consensus process.

Test of Word Reading Efficiency (TOWRE)

GENERAL INFORMATION

Author(s): Joseph K. Torgesen, Richard K Wagner, and Carol A. Rashotte
Publisher: PRO-ED
Publication Date(s): 1999

Age Range: 6-0 to 24-11

Administration Time: 5 to 8 minutes

COMPOSITE MEASURE INFORMATION

Total Word Reading Efficiency

SCORE INFORMATION

Standard scores	Percentiles	Stanines	Normal curve equivalents	Age equivalents	Grade equivalents

NORMING INFORMATION

Standardization Sample Size: 1,507

Sample Collection Date(s): 1997-1998

Avg. Number per Age/Grade Interval:
  116 per year: 6-0 to 17-11
  80 per five years: 18-0 to 24-11

Age Blocks in Norm Table:
  6 months: 6-0 to 7-11
  1 year: 8-0 to 16-11
  8 years: 17-0 to 24-11

Demographic Variables:
  Gender   *- male; female*
  Geographic region   *- 4 regions; 30 states*
  Residence   *- urban; rural*
  Race/ethnicity   *- White; Black; Native American; Hispanic; Asian; other*
  SES   *- parent education; family income*
  Other   *- disability status (none, LD, SLD, MR, other)*

VALIDITY

Types of Validity Evidence Reported in the Test Manual:

Content	Criterion	Construct

Test Review(s) and Validity Evidence Reported in Extant Literature: None currently available

CONTAINS AT LEAST ONE INDICATOR CONSISTENT WITH THE FOLLOWING LD ASSESSMENT AREA(S)

Oral Expression	Listening Comprehension	Written Expression	Basic Reading Skill	Reading Comprehension	Mathematics Calculation	Mathematics Reasoning

SPECIAL FEATURES

- Provides alternate forms (A and B)
- Includes practice items
- Includes phonetic transcriptions for non-words in the Phonemic Decoding Efficiency subtest
- Provides standard scores by grade

DESCRIPTION

The examinee is required to read lists of words of increasing difficulty as fast as he/she can.

RELIABILITY [1]

▨ - Low ▓ - Medium ■ - High ☐ - No Information Available

	2	3	4	5	6	7	8	9	10	11	12	13	14	15	16	17	18	19 24	25 29	30 34	35 39	40 44	45 49	50 54	55 59	60 64	65 69	70 74	75 79	80 84	85 90+
Internal consistency																															
Test-retest*																															

Interval between testings: 2 weeks

FLOORS AND CEILINGS

	Test Floor	Test Ceiling
Inadequate at ages:	6-0 to 7-5	13-0 to 24-11

CHC CLASSIFICATIONS (Broad: stratum II / *Narrow: stratum I*)

Reading/Writing (*Grw*): *Reading Decoding (RD)* - Ability to recognize and decode words or pseudowords in reading; *Reading Speed (RS)* - Time required to silently read a passage or series of sentences as quickly as possible.

DESCRIPTION

The examinee is required to read lists of increasingly difficult non-words as quickly as possible.

RELIABILITY [1]

▨ - Low ▓ - Medium ■ - High ☐ - No Information Available

	2	3	4	5	6	7	8	9	10	11	12	13	14	15	16	17	18	19 24	25 29	30 34	35 39	40 44	45 49	50 54	55 59	60 64	65 69	70 74	75 79	80 84	85 90+
Internal consistency																															
Test-retest*																															

Interval between testings: 2 weeks

FLOORS AND CEILINGS

	Test Floor	Test Ceiling
Inadequate at ages:	6-0 to 8-11	13-0 to 24-11

CHC CLASSIFICATIONS (Broad: stratum II / *Narrow: stratum I*)

Reading/Writing (*Grw*): *Reading Decoding (RD)* - Ability to recognize and decode words or pseudowords in reading.

[1] Alternate-form reliability coefficients were reported as estimates of internal consistency rather than coefficient alpha.

Woodcock Diagnostic Reading Battery (WDRB)

GENERAL INFORMATION

Author(s): Richard W. Woodcock
Publisher: Riverside Publishing
Publication Date(s): 1997

Age Range: 2-0 to 95-11
Administration Time: 60 minutes

COMPOSITE MEASURE INFORMATION

Broad Reading
Reading Comprehension
Oral Comprehension
Total Reading

Basic Reading Skills
Phonological Awareness
Reading Aptitude

SCORE INFORMATION

Standard scores	Percentiles	Stanines	Normal curve equivalents	Age equivalents	Grade equivalents

NORMING INFORMATION

Standardization Sample Size: 6,026

Sample Collection Date(s): 1986-1988

Avg. Number per Age/Grade Interval:
  165 per year: 2-0 to 3-11
  256 per year: 4-0 to 19-11
  240 per ten years: 20-0 to 95-11

Age Blocks in Norm Table:
  1 month: 2-0 to 18-11
  1 year: 19-0 to 90-11
  5 years: 91-0 to 95-11

Demographic Variables:
  Gender - *male; female*
  Geographic region - *4 regions; 23 states; 100 communities*
  Residence - *central city; urban fringe; outside urban and rural*
  Race/ethnicity - *White; Black; Native American; Asian Pacific Islander; Hispanic*
  SES - *parent/examinee education; occupation*
  Other - *funding/type of college/university*

VALIDITY

Types of Validity Evidence Reported in the Test Manual:

Content	Criterion	Construct

Test Review(s) and Validity Evidence Reported in Extant Literature: None currently available

CONTAINS AT LEAST ONE INDICATOR CONSISTENT WITH THE FOLLOWING LD ASSESSMENT AREA(S)

Oral Expression	Listening Comprehension	Written Expression	Basic Reading Skill	Reading Comprehension	Mathematics Calculation	Mathematics Reasoning

SPECIAL FEATURES

- Provides computer scoring program with interpretive profiling report
- Includes suggestions on how to modify the battery for English-as-a-Second-Language (ESL) examinees and examinees with hearing, visual, or physical impairments
- Includes a flowchart of steps for learning administration of the WDRB as well as examiner training and practice exercises

DESCRIPTION

The examinee is required to identify letters and words correctly.

RELIABILITY [1]

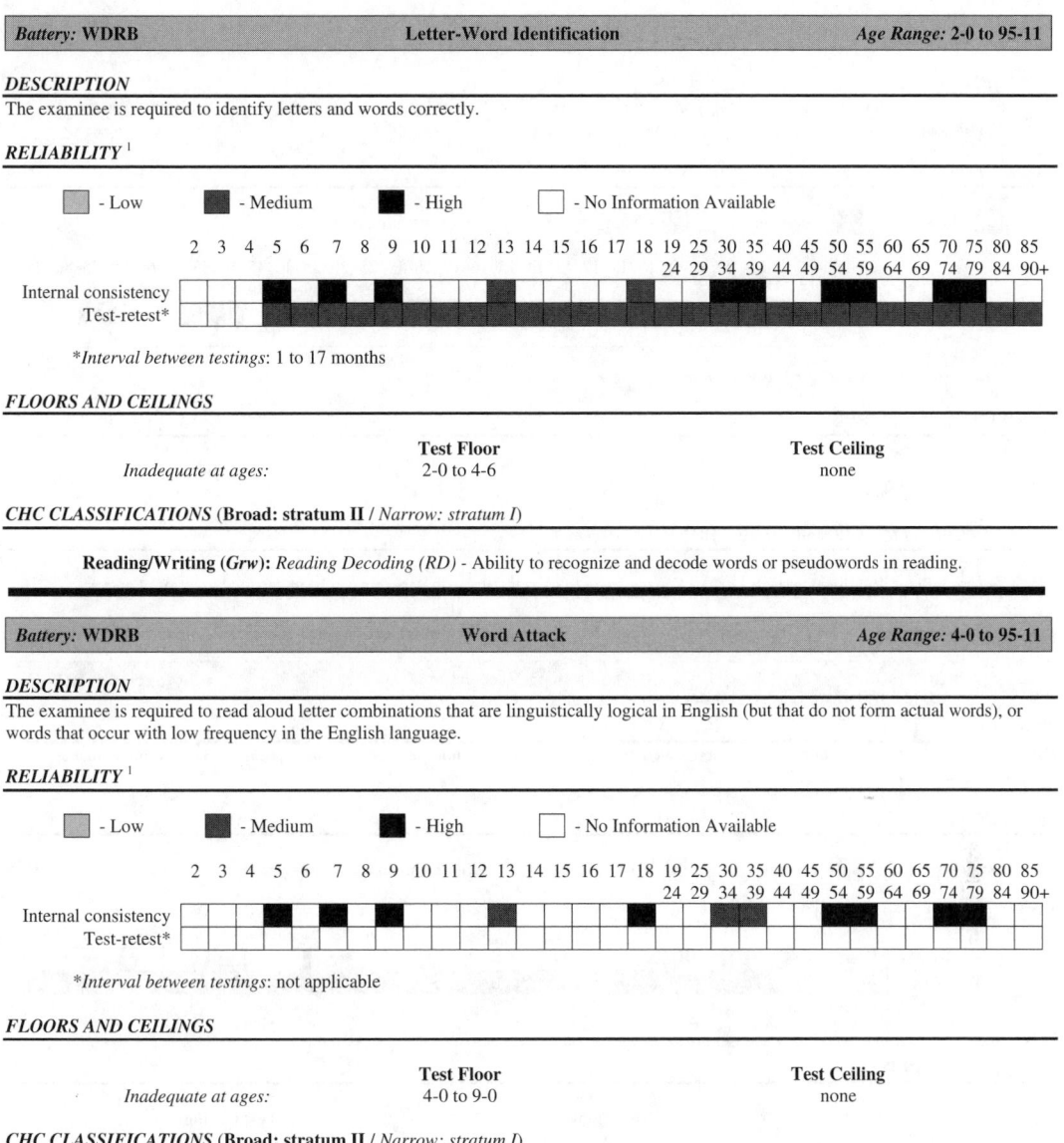

■ - Low   ■ - Medium   ■ - High   □ - No Information Available

| | 2 | 3 | 4 | 5 | 6 | 7 | 8 | 9 | 10 | 11 | 12 | 13 | 14 | 15 | 16 | 17 | 18 | 19 24 | 25 29 | 30 34 | 35 39 | 40 44 | 45 49 | 50 54 | 55 59 | 60 64 | 65 69 | 70 74 | 75 79 | 80 84 | 85 90+ |

Internal consistency
Test-retest*

Interval between testings: 1 to 17 months

FLOORS AND CEILINGS

	Test Floor	Test Ceiling
Inadequate at ages:	2-0 to 4-6	none

CHC CLASSIFICATIONS (Broad: stratum II / *Narrow: stratum I*)

Reading/Writing (*Grw*): *Reading Decoding (RD)* - Ability to recognize and decode words or pseudowords in reading.

DESCRIPTION

The examinee is required to read aloud letter combinations that are linguistically logical in English (but that do not form actual words), or words that occur with low frequency in the English language.

RELIABILITY [1]

■ - Low   ■ - Medium   ■ - High   □ - No Information Available

| | 2 | 3 | 4 | 5 | 6 | 7 | 8 | 9 | 10 | 11 | 12 | 13 | 14 | 15 | 16 | 17 | 18 | 19 24 | 25 29 | 30 34 | 35 39 | 40 44 | 45 49 | 50 54 | 55 59 | 60 64 | 65 69 | 70 74 | 75 79 | 80 84 | 85 90+ |

Internal consistency
Test-retest*

Interval between testings: not applicable

FLOORS AND CEILINGS

	Test Floor	Test Ceiling
Inadequate at ages:	4-0 to 9-0	none

CHC CLASSIFICATIONS (Broad: stratum II / *Narrow: stratum I*)

Reading/Writing (*Grw*): *Reading Decoding (RD)* - Ability to recognize and decode words or pseudowords in reading.

[1]Split-half coefficients were reported as estimates of internal consistency rather than coefficient alpha.

| Battery: WDRB | Reading Vocabulary | Age Range: 4-0 to 95-11 |

DESCRIPTION

The examinee is required to state a one-word response similar in meaning to the word presented for Part I, and in Part II, the examinee is required to state a one-word response opposite in meaning to the word presented.

RELIABILITY [1]

■ - Low   ■ - Medium   ■ - High   □ - No Information Available

	2	3	4	5	6	7	8	9	10	11	12	13	14	15	16	17	18	19 24	25 29	30 34	35 39	40 44	45 49	50 54	55 59	60 64	65 69	70 74	75 79	80 84	85 90+
Internal consistency				■		■		■				■						■		■			■				■				
Test-retest*																															

*Interval between testings: 1 to 17 months

FLOORS AND CEILINGS

	Test Floor	Test Ceiling
Inadequate at ages:	4-0 to 8-6	none

CHC CLASSIFICATIONS (Broad: stratum II / *Narrow: stratum I*)

Crystallized Intelligence (*Gc*): *Lexical Knowledge (VL)* - Extent of vocabulary that can be understood in terms of correct word meanings.

| Battery: WDRB | Passage Comprehension | Age Range: 4-0 to 95-11 |

DESCRIPTION

The examinee is required to point to pictures represented by a phrase and read a short passage to identify a missing key word that makes sense in the context of that passage.

RELIABILITY [1]

■ - Low   ■ - Medium   ■ - High   □ - No Information Available

	2	3	4	5	6	7	8	9	10	11	12	13	14	15	16	17	18	19 24	25 29	30 34	35 39	40 44	45 49	50 54	55 59	60 64	65 69	70 74	75 79	80 84	85 90+
Internal consistency			■	■	■	■	■	■				■						■		■		■			■			■			
Test-retest*			■	■	■	■	■	■	■	■	■	■	■	■	■	■	■	■	■	■	■	■	■	■	■	■	■	■	■	■	■

*Interval between testings: 1 to 17 months

FLOORS AND CEILINGS

	Test Floor	Test Ceiling
Inadequate at ages:	4-0 to 7-6	none

CHC CLASSIFICATIONS (Broad: stratum II / *Narrow: stratum I*)

Reading/Writing (*Grw*): *Cloze Ability (CZ)* - Ability to supply words deleted from prose passages that must be read.

[1]Split-half coefficients were reported as estimates of internal consistency rather than coefficient alpha.

DESCRIPTION

The examinee is required to remember and repeat phrases and sentences presented auditorily on an audiocassette or, in special cases, by an examiner.

RELIABILITY [1]

◻ - Low   ◼ - Medium   ◼ - High   ☐ - No Information Available

	2	3	4	5	6	7	8	9	10	11	12	13	14	15	16	17	18	19 24	25 29	30 34	35 39	40 44	45 49	50 54	55 59	60 64	65 69	70 74	75 79	80 84	85 90+
Internal consistency																															
Test-retest*																															

*Interval between testings: 1 to 17 months

FLOORS AND CEILINGS

	Test Floor	**Test Ceiling**
Inadequate at ages:	none	none

CHC CLASSIFICATIONS (**Broad: stratum II** / *Narrow: stratum I*)

Short-Term Memory (*Gsm*): *Memory Span (MS)* - Ability to attend to and immediately recall temporally ordered elements in the correct order after a single presentation.

DESCRIPTION

The examinee is required to locate and circle the two identical numbers in a row of six numbers. The task proceeds in difficulty from single-digit numbers to triple-digit numbers and has a 3-minute time limit.

RELIABILITY [1]

◻ - Low   ◼ - Medium   ◼ - High   ☐ - No Information Available

	2	3	4	5	6	7	8	9	10	11	12	13	14	15	16	17	18	19 24	25 29	30 34	35 39	40 44	45 49	50 54	55 59	60 64	65 69	70 74	75 79	80 84	85 90+
Internal consistency																															
Test-retest*																															

*Interval between testings: 1 to 17 months

FLOORS AND CEILINGS

	Test Floor	**Test Ceiling**
Inadequate at ages:	4-0 to 4-6	none

CHC CLASSIFICATIONS (**Broad: stratum II** / *Narrow: stratum I*)

Processing Speed (*Gs*): *Perceptual Speed (P)* - Ability to rapidly search for and compare known visual symbols or patterns presented side-by-side or separated in a visual field.

---

[1]Split-half coefficients were reported as estimates of internal consistency rather than coefficient alpha.

| Battery: WDRB | Incomplete Words | Age Range: 2-0 to 95-11 |

DESCRIPTION

The examinee is required to identify the complete word after hearing a tape-recorded word that has one or more phonemes missing.

RELIABILITY [1]

☐ - Low   ■ - Medium   ■ - High   ☐ - No Information Available

	2	3	4	5	6	7	8	9	10	11	12	13	14	15	16	17	18	19 24	25 29	30 34	35 39	40 44	45 49	50 54	55 59	60 64	65 69	70 74	75 79	80 84	85 90+
Internal consistency																															
Test-retest*																															

*Interval between testings: 1 to 17 months

FLOORS AND CEILINGS

	Test Floor	Test Ceiling
Inadequate at ages:	2-0 to 4-0	none

CHC CLASSIFICATIONS (Broad: stratum II / Narrow: stratum I)

Auditory Processing (Ga): *Phonetic Coding: Synthesis (PC:S)* - Ability to blend smaller units of speech together into larger units of speech.

| Battery: WDRB | Sound Blending | Age Range: 4-0 to 95-11 |

DESCRIPTION

The examinee is required to integrate and then say whole words after hearing part syllables and/or phonemes of the words presented on an audiocassette.

RELIABILITY [1]

☐ - Low   ■ - Medium   ■ - High   ☐ - No Information Available

	2	3	4	5	6	7	8	9	10	11	12	13	14	15	16	17	18	19 24	25 29	30 34	35 39	40 44	45 49	50 54	55 59	60 64	65 69	70 74	75 79	80 84	85 90+
Internal consistency																															
Test-retest*																															

*Interval between testings: 1 to 17 months

FLOORS AND CEILINGS

	Test Floor	Test Ceiling
Inadequate at ages:	4-0 to 4-6	none

CHC CLASSIFICATIONS (Broad: stratum II / Narrow: stratum I)

Auditory Processing (Ga): *Phonetic Coding: Synthesis (PC:S)* - Ability to blend smaller units of speech together into larger units of speech.

[1]Split-half coefficients were reported as estimates of internal consistency rather than coefficient alpha.

DESCRIPTION

The examinee is required to state a word similar in meaning to the word presented in Part A. In Part B, the examinee is required to state a word that is opposite in meaning to the word presented.

RELIABILITY [1]

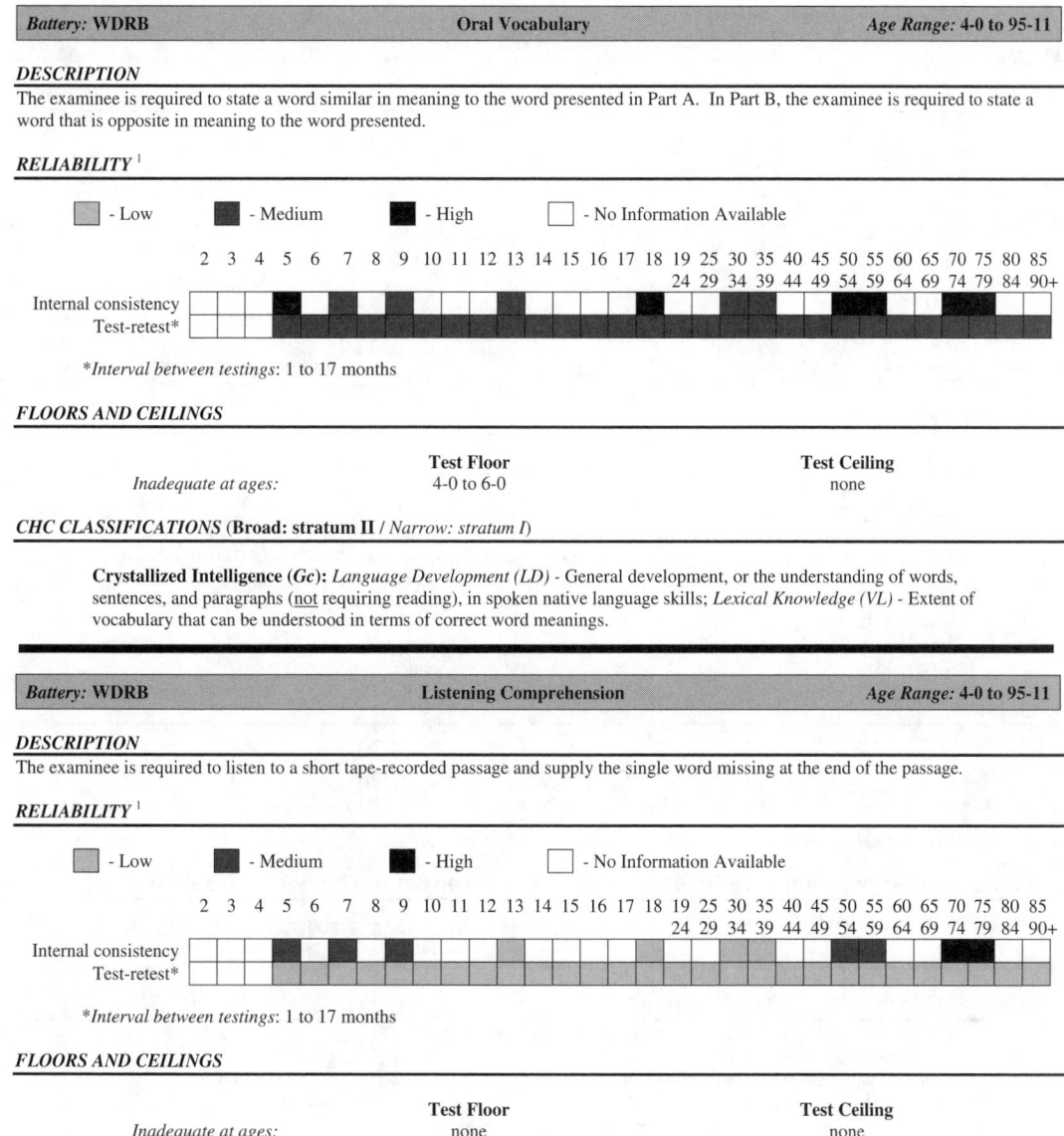

☐ - Low   ■ - Medium   ■ - High   ☐ - No Information Available

| | 2 | 3 | 4 | 5 | 6 | 7 | 8 | 9 | 10 | 11 | 12 | 13 | 14 | 15 | 16 | 17 | 18 | 19 24 | 25 29 | 30 34 | 35 39 | 40 44 | 45 49 | 50 54 | 55 59 | 60 64 | 65 69 | 70 74 | 75 79 | 80 84 | 85 90+ |

Internal consistency
Test-retest*

Interval between testings: 1 to 17 months

FLOORS AND CEILINGS

	Test Floor	Test Ceiling
Inadequate at ages:	4-0 to 6-0	none

CHC CLASSIFICATIONS (Broad: stratum II / *Narrow: stratum I*)

Crystallized Intelligence (*Gc*): *Language Development (LD)* - General development, or the understanding of words, sentences, and paragraphs (not requiring reading), in spoken native language skills; *Lexical Knowledge (VL)* - Extent of vocabulary that can be understood in terms of correct word meanings.

DESCRIPTION

The examinee is required to listen to a short tape-recorded passage and supply the single word missing at the end of the passage.

RELIABILITY [1]

☐ - Low   ■ - Medium   ■ - High   ☐ - No Information Available

| | 2 | 3 | 4 | 5 | 6 | 7 | 8 | 9 | 10 | 11 | 12 | 13 | 14 | 15 | 16 | 17 | 18 | 19 24 | 25 29 | 30 34 | 35 39 | 40 44 | 45 49 | 50 54 | 55 59 | 60 64 | 65 69 | 70 74 | 75 79 | 80 84 | 85 90+ |

Internal consistency
Test-retest*

Interval between testings: 1 to 17 months

FLOORS AND CEILINGS

	Test Floor	Test Ceiling
Inadequate at ages:	none	none

CHC CLASSIFICATIONS (Broad: stratum II / *Narrow: stratum I*)

Crystallized Intelligence (*Gc*): *Listening Ability (LS)* - Ability to listen and comprehend oral communications.

[1]Split-half coefficients were reported as estimates of internal consistency rather than coefficient alpha.

Woodcock Reading Mastery Tests-Revised/Normative Update (WRMT-R/NU)

GENERAL INFORMATION

Author(s): Richard W. Woodcock
Publisher: American Guidance Service
Publication Date(s): 1973, 1987, 1998

Age Range: 5-0 to 75+
Administration Time: 30 to 45 minutes

COMPOSITE MEASURE INFORMATION

Readiness Cluster
Reading Comprehension

Basic Skills Cluster
Total Reading-Short Scale and Full Scale

SCORE INFORMATION

Standard scores	Percentiles	Stanines	Normal curve equivalents	Age equivalents	Grade equivalents

NORMING INFORMATION

Standardization Sample Size: 721 to 2,662   *Sample Collection Date(s): 1995-1996*

Avg. Number per Age/Grade Interval:
  52-190 per grade: K-12
  68 to 327 per five years: 18-0 to 22-11

Age Blocks in Norm Table:
  1 month: 5-0 to 18-11
  1 year: 19-0 to 74-11
  >1 year: 75+

Demographic Variables:
  Gender   - *male; female*
  Geographic region   - *4 regions; 39 states and District of Columbia; 129 communities*
  Race/ethnicity   - *African American; White; Hispanic; other*
  SES   - *parent education*
  Other   - *educational placement (special education: 6 categories; gifted)*

VALIDITY

Types of Validity Evidence Reported in the Test Manual:

Content	Criterion	Construct

Test Review(s) and Validity Evidence Reported in Extant Literature: See Appendix C

CONTAINS AT LEAST ONE INDICATOR CONSISTENT WITH THE FOLLOWING LD ASSESSMENT AREA(S)

Oral Expression	Listening Comprehension	Written Expression	Basic Reading Skill	Reading Comprehension	Mathematics Calculation	Mathematics Reasoning

SPECIAL FEATURES

- Provides computer scoring program with interpretive profiling report
- Includes alternate forms (G and H)
- Includes a tape-recorded pronunciation guide to items in the Word Attack and Word Identification subtests
- Includes a sample report to parents
- Provides standard scores by grade (fall and spring)

*All reliability and validity data reported in the test manual and thus in these summary pages pertain to the 1987 standardization sample.

DESCRIPTION

The examinee is required to learn a vocabulary of unfamiliar visual symbols (rebuses) representing familiar words, and then translate sequences of rebuses that have been used to form sentences.

RELIABILITY [1]

☐ - Low ■ - Medium ■ - High ☐ - No Information Available

	2	3	4	5	6	7	8	9	10	11	12	13	14	15	16	17	18	19-24	25-29	30-34	35-39	40-44	45-49	50-54	55-59	60-64	65-69	70-74	75-79	80-84	85-90+
Internal consistency					■		■		■																						
Test-retest*																															

*Interval between testings: not applicable

FLOORS AND CEILINGS

	Test Floor	Test Ceiling
Inadequate at ages:	5-0 to 5-6	none

CHC CLASSIFICATIONS (Broad: stratum II / *Narrow: stratum I*)

Long-Term Retrieval (*Glr*): *Associative Memory (MA)* - Ability to recall one part of a previously learned but unrelated pair of items when the other part is presented (i.e., paired-associative learning).

DESCRIPTION

The examinee is required to provide either the name or the most common sound of each letter that is presented to him or her.

RELIABILITY [1]

☐ - Low ■ - Medium ■ - High ☐ - No Information Available

	2	3	4	5	6	7	8	9	10	11	12	13	14	15	16	17	18	19-24	25-29	30-34	35-39	40-44	45-49	50-54	55-59	60-64	65-69	70-74	75-79	80-84	85-90+
Internal consistency					■		■		☐																						
Test-retest*																															

*Interval between testings: not applicable

FLOORS AND CEILINGS

	Test Floor	Test Ceiling
Inadequate at ages:	5-0 to 5-6	8-6 to 75+

CHC CLASSIFICATIONS (Broad: stratum II / *Narrow: stratum I*)

Reading/Writing[a] (*Grw*): *Reading Decoding[a] (RD)* - Ability to recognize and decode words or pseudowords in reading.

---

[1]Split-half coefficients were reported as estimates of internal consistency rather than coefficient alpha. These coefficients were reported by grade in the test manual. Therefore, corresponding ages were estimated by the authors.
[a]The broad and narrow ability CHC classifications for this test were determined by the authors because no agreement was reached through the group consensus process.

DESCRIPTION

The examinee is required to give the names or the sounds of a series of capital and lowercase letters.

RELIABILITY (Not applicable)

☐ - Low ■ - Medium ■ - High ☐ - No Information Available

	2	3	4	5	6	7	8	9	10	11	12	13	14	15	16	17	18	19 24	25 29	30 34	35 39	40 44	45 49	50 54	55 59	60 64	65 69	70 74	75 79	80 84	85 90+
Internal consistency																															
Test-retest*																															

Interval between testings:

FLOORS AND CEILINGS (Not applicable)

	Test Floor	**Test Ceiling**
Inadequate at ages:		

CHC CLASSIFICATIONS (Broad: stratum II / *Narrow: stratum I*)

Reading/Writing (*Grw*): *Reading Decoding (RD)* - Ability to recognize and decode words or pseudowords in reading.

DESCRIPTION

The examinee is required to read orally a series of words and pronounce them correctly.

RELIABILITY [1]

☐ - Low ■ - Medium ■ - High ☐ - No Information Available

	2	3	4	5	6	7	8	9	10	11	12	13	14	15	16	17	18	19 24	25 29	30 34	35 39	40 44	45 49	50 54	55 59	60 64	65 69	70 74	75 79	80 84	85 90+
Internal consistency			■		■			■					■		■			■	■	■	■	■	■	■	■	■	■	■	■		
Test-retest*																															

Interval between testings: not applicable

FLOORS AND CEILINGS

	Test Floor	**Test Ceiling**
Inadequate at ages:	5-0 to 7-6	none

CHC CLASSIFICATIONS (Broad: stratum II / *Narrow: stratum I*)

Reading/Writing (*Grw*): *Reading Decoding (RD)* - Ability to recognize and decode words or pseudowords in reading.

---

[1] Split-half coefficients were reported as estimates of internal consistency rather than coefficient alpha. These coefficients were reported by grade in the test manual. Therefore, corresponding ages were estimated by the authors.

DESCRIPTION

The examinee is required to read orally a series of nonsense words and pronounce them correctly.

RELIABILITY [1]

☐ - Low ■ - Medium ■ - High ☐ - No Information Available

	2	3	4	5	6	7	8	9	10	11	12	13	14	15	16	17	18	19/24	25/29	30/34	35/39	40/44	45/49	50/54	55/59	60/64	65/69	70/74	75/79	80/84	85/90+
Internal consistency																															
Test-retest*																															

*Interval between testings: not applicable

FLOORS AND CEILINGS

	Test Floor	Test Ceiling
Inadequate at ages:	5-0 to 9-6	none

CHC CLASSIFICATIONS (Broad: stratum II / Narrow: stratum I)

Reading/Writing (Grw): Reading Decoding (RD) - Ability to recognize and decode words or pseudowords in reading.

DESCRIPTION

The examinee is required to supply antonyms for the stimulus words in Subtest 5A. In Subtest 5B, the examinee is required to supply synonyms for the stimulus words. In Subtest 5C, the examinee is required to supply appropriate words to complete analogies.

RELIABILITY [1]

☐ - Low ■ - Medium ■ - High ☐ - No Information Available

	2	3	4	5	6	7	8	9	10	11	12	13	14	15	16	17	18	19/24	25/29	30/34	35/39	40/44	45/49	50/54	55/59	60/64	65/69	70/74	75/79	80/84	85/90+
Internal consistency																															
Test-retest*																															

*Interval between testings: not applicable

FLOORS AND CEILINGS

	Test Floor	Test Ceiling
Inadequate at ages:	5-0 to 8-0	none

CHC CLASSIFICATIONS (Broad: stratum II / Narrow: stratum I)

Crystallized Intelligence (Gc): Lexical Knowledge (VL) - Extent of vocabulary that can be understood in terms of correct word meanings.

[1]Split-half coefficients were reported as estimates of internal consistency rather than coefficient alpha. These coefficients were reported by grade in the test manual. Therefore, corresponding ages were estimated by the authors.

DESCRIPTION

The examinee is required to read passages and their corresponding items silently. He/she must then respond orally to the items by providing single-word responses within 30 seconds after finishing reading the passage.

RELIABILITY [1]

☐ - Low   ■ - Medium   ■ - High   ☐ - No Information Available

	2	3	4	5	6	7	8	9	10	11	12	13	14	15	16	17	18	19 24	25 29	30 34	35 39	40 44	45 49	50 54	55 59	60 64	65 69	70 74	75 79	80 84	85 90+
Internal consistency					■		■				■						■	■	■	■	■	■	■	■	■	■	■	■	■		
Test-retest*																															

Interval between testings: not applicable

FLOORS AND CEILINGS

	Test Floor	**Test Ceiling**
Inadequate at ages:	5-0 to 7-6	none

CHC CLASSIFICATIONS (Broad: stratum II / *Narrow: stratum I*)

Reading/Writing (*Grw*): *Reading Comprehension (RC)* - Ability to comprehend connected discourse during reading.

---

[1]Split-half coefficients were reported as estimates of internal consistency rather than coefficient alpha. These coefficients were reported by grade in the test manual. Therefore, corresponding ages were estimated by the authors.

ATDR *Summary Pages*
Specific Academic Skills—Math Tests

KeyMath-Revised/Normative Update (KM-R/NU)

GENERAL INFORMATION

Author(s): Austin J. Connolly
Publisher: American Guidance Service
Publication Date(s)[*]: 1988, 1998

Age Range: 5-0 to 22-11
Administration Time: 30 to 50 minutes

COMPOSITE MEASURE INFORMATION

Basic Concepts Area
Applications Area

Operations Area
Total Test

SCORE INFORMATION

Standard scores	Percentiles	Stanines	Normal curve equivalents	Age equivalents	Grade equivalents

NORMING INFORMATION

Standardization Sample Size: 2,802 to 2,809   *Sample Collection Date(s): 1995-1996*

Avg. Number per Age/Grade Interval:
  201 per grade: K-12
  326-345 per five years: 18-0 to 22-11

Age Blocks in Norm Table:
  3 months: 5-0 to 18-11
  1 year: 19-0 to 22-11

Demographic Variables:
  Gender - *male; female*
  Geographic region - *4 regions; 39 states and The District of Columbia; 129 communities*
  Race/ethnicity - *African American; Hispanic; White; other*
  SES - *parent education*
  Other - *educational placement (special: 6 categories; gifted)*

VALIDITY

Types of Validity Evidence Reported in the Test Manual:

Content	Criterion	Construct

Test Review(s) and Validity Evidence Reported in Extant Literature: See Appendix C

CONTAINS AT LEAST ONE INDICATOR CONSISTENT WITH THE FOLLOWING LD ASSESSMENT AREA(S)

Oral Expression	Listening Comprehension	Written Expression	Basic Reading Skill	Reading Comprehension	Mathematics Calculation	Mathematics Reasoning

SPECIAL FEATURES

- Provides a computer scoring and interpretive profiling program
- Provides alternate forms (A and B)
- Provides TAP – a "teach and practice" program for children
- Includes an optional Report to Parents form
- Provides domain performance norms
- Provides standard scores by grade (fall and spring)

[*]All reliability and validity data reported in the test manual and thus in these summary pages pertain to the 1988 standardization sample.

DESCRIPTION

The examinee is required to solve problems involving concepts including correspondence, rational counting, reading and sequencing numbers, and ordinal positions. In the second domain, the examinee is required to solve problems involving the concepts of place value (tens and ones); reading, comparing, sequencing, and renaming numbers; and skip counting. In the third domain, the examinee is required to solve problems involving the concepts of place value; representing, comparing, sequencing, renaming numbers; and rounding numbers. In the fourth domain, the examinee is required to solve problems involving multi-digit numbers and advanced numeration as well as problems that require the comparing, sequencing, and rounding of multi-digit numbers.

RELIABILITY [1]

☐ - Low   ■ - Medium   ■ - High   ☐ - No Information Available

	2	3	4	5	6	7	8	9	10	11	12	13	14	15	16	17	18	19-24	25-29	30-34	35-39	40-44	45-49	50-54	55-59	60-64	65-69	70-74	75-79	80-84	85-90+
Internal consistency																															
Test-retest*																															

Interval between testings: not applicable

FLOORS AND CEILINGS

	Test Floor	**Test Ceiling**
Inadequate at ages:	5-0 to 6-5	11-6 to 22-11

CHC CLASSIFICATIONS (Broad: stratum II / *Narrow: stratum I*)

Quantitative Knowledge (*Gq*): *Mathematical Achievement (A3)* - Measured mathematics achievement; *Mathematical Knowledge (KM)* - Range of general knowledge about mathematics.

DESCRIPTION

The examinee is required to solve problems involving fractions, decimals, and percents.

RELIABILITY [1]

☐ - Low   ■ - Medium   ■ - High   ☐ - No Information Available

	2	3	4	5	6	7	8	9	10	11	12	13	14	15	16	17	18	19-24	25-29	30-34	35-39	40-44	45-49	50-54	55-59	60-64	65-69	70-74	75-79	80-84	85-90+
Internal consistency																															
Test-retest*																															

Interval between testings: not applicable

FLOORS AND CEILINGS

	Test Floor	**Test Ceiling**
Inadequate at ages:	8-9 to 13-5	14-0 to 22-11

CHC CLASSIFICATIONS (Broad: stratum II / *Narrow: stratum I*)

Quantitative Knowledge (*Gq*): *Mathematical Achievement (A3)* - Measured mathematics achievement.

[1]Split-half coefficients are reported as estimates of internal consistency rather than coefficient alpha and pertain to the fall standardization program only. See test manual for spring coefficients.

DESCRIPTION

The examinee is required to solve problems involving spatial and attribute relationships, two-dimensional shapes and their relationships, concepts of coordinate and transformational geometry, and three-dimensional shapes and their relationships.

RELIABILITY [1]

☐ - Low   ■ - Medium   ■ - High   ☐ - No Information Available

	2	3	4	5	6	7	8	9	10	11	12	13	14	15	16	17	18	19/24	25/29	30/34	35/39	40/44	45/49	50/54	55/59	60/64	65/69	70/74	75/79	80/84	85/90+
Internal consistency																															
Test-retest*																															

*Interval between testings: not applicable

FLOORS AND CEILINGS

	Test Floor	Test Ceiling
Inadequate at ages:	5-0 to 7-2	13-9 to 22-11

CHC CLASSIFICATIONS (Broad: stratum II / Narrow: stratum I)

Visual Processing[a] (**Gv**): *Spatial Relations*[a] *(SR)* - Ability to perceive and manipulate visual patterns rapidly or to maintain orientation with respect to objects in space; *Visualization*[a] *(VZ)* - Ability to manipulate objects or visual patterns mentally and to "see" how they would appear under altered conditions.

DESCRIPTION

The examinee is required to determine the total of two sets, count to determine a total, match representations with number sentences, and complete facts. In the second domain, the examinee is required to add two and three digit numbers without regrouping, with regrouping ones, with regrouping ones and tens, and in column addition. For one item, the examinee is required to add positive and negative integers. In the third domain, the examinee is required to add monetary values, other decimals with same and different place values, and fractions with like and unlike denominators.

RELIABILITY [1]

☐ - Low   ■ - Medium   ■ - High   ☐ - No Information Available

	2	3	4	5	6	7	8	9	10	11	12	13	14	15	16	17	18	19/24	25/29	30/34	35/39	40/44	45/49	50/54	55/59	60/64	65/69	70/74	75/79	80/84	85/90+
Internal consistency																															
Test-retest*																															

*Interval between testings: not applicable

FLOORS AND CEILINGS

	Test Floor	Test Ceiling
Inadequate at ages:	5-6 to 7-8	12-3 to 22-11

CHC CLASSIFICATIONS (Broad: stratum II / Narrow: stratum I)

Quantitative Knowledge (Gq): *Mathematical Achievement (A3)* - Measured mathematics achievement

[1] Split-half coefficients were reported as estimates of internal consistency rather than coefficient alpha and pertain to the fall standardization program only. See test manual for spring coefficients.
[a] The broad and narrow ability CHC classifications for this test were determined by the authors because no agreement was reached through the group consensus process.

DESCRIPTION

The examinee is required to solve problems involving all modalities of subtraction. The examinee is then required to solve problems involving matching representations and completing facts. In the second domain, the examinee is required to solve problems involving subtracting from two and three digit numbers without regrouping, with regrouping tens, with regrouping across hundreds, tens, and ones and with subtracting positive and negative integers. In the second domain, the examinee is required to solve problems involving subtracting monetary values, other decimals with same and different place values, and fractions with like and unlike denominators.

RELIABILITY [1]

☐ - Low   ■ - Medium   ■ - High   ☐ - No Information Available

	2	3	4	5	6	7	8	9	10	11	12	13	14	15	16	17	18	19/24	25/29	30/34	35/39	40/44	45/49	50/54	55/59	60/64	65/69	70/74	75/79	80/84	85/90+
Internal consistency																															
Test-retest*																															

Interval between testings: not applicable

FLOORS AND CEILINGS

	Test Floor	**Test Ceiling**
Inadequate at ages:	6-3 to 8-8	13-3 to 22-11

CHC CLASSIFICATIONS (Broad: stratum II / *Narrow: stratum I*)

Quantitative Knowledge (Gq): *Mathematical Achievement (A3)* - Measured mathematics achievement.

DESCRIPTION

The examinee is required to solve problems involving multiple sets and arrays associating a representation with a number sentence. In the second domain, the examinee is required to multiply two and three digit numbers by a one or two digit multiplier. In the third domain, the examinee is required to solve problems involving multiplying monetary values, other decimal values, fractions, and mixed numbers.

RELIABILITY [1]

☐ - Low   ■ - Medium   ■ - High   ☐ - No Information Available

	2	3	4	5	6	7	8	9	10	11	12	13	14	15	16	17	18	19/24	25/29	30/34	35/39	40/44	45/49	50/54	55/59	60/64	65/69	70/74	75/79	80/84	85/90+
Internal consistency																															
Test-retest*																															

Interval between testings: not applicable

FLOORS AND CEILINGS

	Test Floor	**Test Ceiling**
Inadequate at ages:	8-0 to 10-5	14-3 to 22-11

CHC CLASSIFICATIONS (Broad: stratum II / *Narrow: stratum I*)

Quantitative Knowledge (Gq): *Mathematical Achievement (A3)* - Measured mathematics achievement.

---

[1]Split-half coefficients were reported as estimates of internal consistency rather than coefficient alpha and pertain to the fall standardization program only. See test manual for spring coefficients.

DESCRIPTION

The examinee is required to solve problems involving the determination of how many equal-sized sets, the size of a given number of sets, and how many are left over after units are separated into sets of given sizes. The examinee is also required to associate a representation with a number sentence and completes facts. In the second domain, the examinee is required to divide with one and two digit divisors. In the third domain, the examinee is required to solve problems involving division with decimal values, fractions, and mixed numbers.

RELIABILITY [1]

☐ - Low   ■ - Medium   ■ - High   ☐ - No Information Available

	2	3	4	5	6	7	8	9	10	11	12	13	14	15	16	17	18	19/24	25/29	30/34	35/39	40/44	45/49	50/54	55/59	60/64	65/69	70/74	75/79	80/84	85/90+
Internal consistency							■	■	■	■	■	■																			
Test-retest*																															

Interval between testings: not applicable

FLOORS AND CEILINGS

	Test Floor	**Test Ceiling**
Inadequate at ages:	8-0 to 10-2	14-3 to 22-11

CHC CLASSIFICATIONS (Broad: stratum II / *Narrow: stratum I*)

Quantitative Knowledge (*Gq*): *Mathematical Achievement (A3)* - Measured mathematics achievement.

DESCRIPTION

The examinee is required to solve problems involving the oral presentation of computation chains. In the second domain, the examinee is required to solve problems involving visually presented items. In the third domain, the examinee is required to solve problems involving rational numbers, subtracting a fraction from a whole number, adding a whole number to a mixed number, multiplying by a decimal that can be easily converted to a fraction, determining percent, and multiplying a decimal value by tens. For all domains, the examinee is not permitted to use pencil and paper.

RELIABILITY [1]

☐ - Low   ■ - Medium   ■ - High   ☐ - No Information Available

	2	3	4	5	6	7	8	9	10	11	12	13	14	15	16	17	18	19/24	25/29	30/34	35/39	40/44	45/49	50/54	55/59	60/64	65/69	70/74	75/79	80/84	85/90+
Internal consistency							■	■	■	■	■	■																			
Test-retest*																															

Interval between testings: not applicable

FLOORS AND CEILINGS

	Test Floor	**Test Ceiling**
Inadequate at ages:	8-3 to 11-2	13-9 to 22-11

CHC CLASSIFICATIONS (Broad: stratum II / *Narrow: stratum I*)

Quantitative Knowledge (*Gq*): *Mathematical Achievement (A3)* - Measured mathematics achievement.

---

[1] Split-half coefficients were reported as estimates of internal consistency rather than coefficient alpha and pertain to the fall standardization program only. See test manual for spring coefficients.

DESCRIPTION

The examinee is required to solve problems involving comparing and ordering heights, lengths, weights, sizes, temperatures, and perceived container capacity. In the second domain, the examinee is required to solve problems involving non-standard units addressing length, area, capacity, weight, and perimeters. In the third domain, the examinee is required to solve problems involving standard units associated with linear scales and progresses to area and temperature measurement. In the fourth domain, the examinee is required to solve problems involving weight and capacity.

RELIABILITY [1]

☐ - Low   ☒ - Medium   ■ - High   ☐ - No Information Available

	2	3	4	5	6	7	8	9	10	11	12	13	14	15	16	17	18	19/24	25/29	30/34	35/39	40/44	45/49	50/54	55/59	60/64	65/69	70/74	75/79	80/84	85/90+
Internal consistency																															
Test-retest*																															

*Interval between testings: not applicable

FLOORS AND CEILINGS

	Test Floor	Test Ceiling
Inadequate at ages:	5-0 to 7-11	14-6 to 22-11

CHC CLASSIFICATIONS (Broad: stratum II / Narrow: stratum I)

Quantitative Knowledge (*Gq*): *Mathematical Achievement (A3)* - Measured mathematics achievement.

DESCRIPTION

The examinee is required to solve problems involving the passage of time. In the second domain, the examinee is required to solve problems involving the measurement of time, using both digital and conventional clocks. In the third domain, the examinee is required to solve problems involving monetary values to one dollar. In the fourth domain, the examinee is required to solve problems involving the coverage of money to amounts of one hundred dollars and to business transactions.

RELIABILITY [1]

☐ - Low   ☒ - Medium   ■ - High   ☐ - No Information Available

	2	3	4	5	6	7	8	9	10	11	12	13	14	15	16	17	18	19/24	25/29	30/34	35/39	40/44	45/49	50/54	55/59	60/64	65/69	70/74	75/79	80/84	85/90+
Internal consistency																															
Test-retest*																															

*Interval between testings: not applicable

FLOORS AND CEILINGS

	Test Floor	Test Ceiling
Inadequate at ages:	6-6 to 9-11	11-3 to 22-11

CHC CLASSIFICATIONS (Broad: stratum II / Narrow: stratum I)

Quantitative Knowledge (*Gq*): *Mathematical Knowledge (KM)* - Range of general knowledge about mathematics.

[1]Split-half coefficients were reported as estimates of internal consistency rather than coefficient alpha and pertain to the fall standardization program only. See test manual for spring coefficients.

DESCRIPTION

The examinee is required to solve problems involving whole numbers, rational numbers, measurement, and computation.

RELIABILITY [1]

▨ - Low   ▦ - Medium   ■ - High   ☐ - No Information Available

	2	3	4	5	6	7	8	9	10	11	12	13	14	15	16	17	18	19/24	25/29	30/34	35/39	40/44	45/49	50/54	55/59	60/64	65/69	70/74	75/79	80/84	85/90+
Internal consistency																															
Test-retest*																															

Interval between testings: not applicable

FLOORS AND CEILINGS

	Test Floor	Test Ceiling
Inadequate at ages:	6-9 to 10-2	14-3 to 22-11

CHC CLASSIFICATIONS (Broad: stratum II / *Narrow: stratum I*)

Quantitative Knowledge (Gq): *Mathematical Achievement (A3)* - Measured mathematics achievement.

DESCRIPTION

The examinee is required to solve problems involving charts and tables, graphs, and probability and statistics, respectively.

RELIABILITY [1]

▨ - Low   ▦ - Medium   ■ - High   ☐ - No Information Available

	2	3	4	5	6	7	8	9	10	11	12	13	14	15	16	17	18	19/24	25/29	30/34	35/39	40/44	45/49	50/54	55/59	60/64	65/69	70/74	75/79	80/84	85/90+
Internal consistency																															
Test-retest*																															

Interval between testings: not applicable

FLOORS AND CEILINGS

	Test Floor	Test Ceiling
Inadequate at ages:	7-6 to 11-5	13-9 to 22-11

CHC CLASSIFICATIONS (Broad: stratum II / *Narrow: stratum I*)

Quantitative Knowledge (Gq): *Mathematical Knowledge[a] (KM)* - Range of general knowledge about mathematics; *Mathematical Achievement[a] (A3)* - Measured mathematics achievement.

---

[1] Split-half coefficients were reported as estimates of internal consistency rather than coefficient alpha and pertain to the fall standardization program only. See test manual for spring coefficients.
[a] The narrow ability CHC classifications for this test were determined by the authors because no agreement was reached through the group consensus process.

DESCRIPTION

The examinee is required to solve problems for which solutions can be readily obtained with clearly perceived operational procedures. In the second domain, the examinee is required to solve problems for which the procedures leading to solutions are not readily apparent. In the third domain, the examinee is required to solve non-routine problems by whatever means he or she chooses to employ.

RELIABILITY [1]

▨ - Low   ▨ - Medium   ■ - High   ☐ - No Information Available

	2	3	4	5	6	7	8	9	10	11	12	13	14	15	16	17	18	19 24	25 29	30 34	35 39	40 44	45 49	50 54	55 59	60 64	65 69	70 74	75 79	80 84	85 90+
Internal consistency						▨	▨	▨	■	■	■	■																			
Test-retest*																															

Interval between testings: not applicable

FLOORS AND CEILINGS

	Test Floor	**Test Ceiling**
Inadequate at ages:	7-6 to 11-5	14-6 to 22-11

CHC CLASSIFICATIONS (Broad: stratum II / *Narrow: stratum I*)

Fluid Reasoning (*Gf*): *Quantitative Reasoning (RQ)* - Ability to inductively and deductively reason with concepts involving mathematical relations and properties. **Quantitative Knowledge (*Gq*):** *Mathematical Achievement (A3)* - Measured mathematics achievement.

[1]Split-half coefficients were reported as estimates of internal consistency rather than coefficient alpha and pertain to the fall standardization program only. See test manual for spring coefficients.

Slosson-Diagnostic Math Screener (S-DMS)

GENERAL INFORMATION

Author(s): Bradley T. Erford and Rita R. Boykin
Publisher: Slosson Educational Publications
Publication Date(s): 1996

Age Range: 6-0 to 13-11
Administration Time: 50 minutes

COMPOSITE MEASURE INFORMATION

Math Composite

SCORE INFORMATION

Standard scores	Percentiles	Stanines	Normal curve equivalents	Age equivalents	Grade equivalents

NORMING INFORMATION

Standardization Sample Size: 1,699

Sample Collection Date(s): 1994

Avg. Number per Age/Grade Interval:
  212 per year: 6-0 to 13-11

Age Blocks in Norm Table:
  6 months: 6-0 to 8-11
  1 year: 9-0 to 13-11

Demographic Variables:
  Gender   *- male; female*
  Geographic region   *- Virginia; Maryland*
  Residence   *- urban/suburban; rural*
  Race/ethnicity   *- White; non-White*
  SES   *- father's education*

VALIDITY

Types of Validity Evidence Reported in the Test Manual:

Content	Criterion	Construct

Test Review(s) and Validity Evidence Reported in Extant Literature: None currently available

CONTAINS AT LEAST ONE INDICATOR CONSISTENT WITH THE FOLLOWING LD ASSESSMENT AREA(S)

Oral Expression	Listening Comprehension	Written Expression	Basic Reading Skill	Reading Comprehension	Mathematics Calculation	Mathematics Reasoning

SPECIAL FEATURES

- Includes case studies to help illustrate how to score and interpret the S-DMS.

DESCRIPTION

The examinee is required to demonstrate knowledge of math concepts such as writing numbers, clocks and telling time, money, and rounding numbers.

RELIABILITY [1]

	- Low		- Medium		- High		- No Information Available

	2	3	4	5	6	7	8	9	10	11	12	13	14	15	16	17	18	19 24	25 29	30 34	35 39	40 44	45 49	50 54	55 59	60 64	65 69	70 74	75 79	80 84	85 90+

Internal consistency
Test-retest*

*Interval between testings: 1 month

FLOORS AND CEILINGS

	Test Floor	**Test Ceiling**
Inadequate at ages:	none	7-0 to 8-5
		13-0 to 13-11

CHC CLASSIFICATIONS (**Broad: stratum II** / *Narrow: stratum I*)

Quantitative Knowledge (Gq): *Mathematical Knowledge (KM)* - Range of general knowledge about mathematics.

DESCRIPTION

The examinee is required to solve problems involving addition, subtraction, multiplication, division, decimals, and/or fractions.

RELIABILITY [1]

	- Low		- Medium		- High		- No Information Available

	2	3	4	5	6	7	8	9	10	11	12	13	14	15	16	17	18	19 24	25 29	30 34	35 39	40 44	45 49	50 54	55 59	60 64	65 69	70 74	75 79	80 84	85 90+

Internal consistency
Test-retest*

*Interval between testings: 1 month

FLOORS AND CEILINGS

	Test Floor	**Test Ceiling**
Inadequate at ages:	6-0 to 7-11	7-6 to 8-11
	9-0 to 11-11	11-0 to 13-11

CHC CLASSIFICATIONS (**Broad: stratum II** / *Narrow: stratum I*)

Quantitative Knowledge (Gq): *Mathematical Achievement (A3)* - Measured mathematics achievement.

[1] Kuder-Richardson 20 coefficients were reported as estimates of internal consistency rather than coefficient alpha.

DESCRIPTION

The examinee is required to perform a number of mathematical calculations involving addition, subtraction, multiplication, and/or division.

RELIABILITY [1]

☐ - Low   ■ - Medium   ■ - High   ☐ - No Information Available

	2	3	4	5	6	7	8	9	10	11	12	13	14	15	16	17	18	19-24	25-29	30-34	35-39	40-44	45-49	50-54	55-59	60-64	65-69	70-74	75-79	80-84	85-90+
Internal consistency					■	■	■	■	■	■	■	■																			
Test-retest*					■	■	■	■	■	■	■	■																			

Interval between testings: 1 month

FLOORS AND CEILINGS

	Test Floor	**Test Ceiling**
Inadequate at ages:	6-0 to 6-11	8-0 to 8-5
		11-0 to 11-11
		13-0 to 13-11

CHC CLASSIFICATIONS (Broad: stratum II / *Narrow: stratum I*)

Quantitative Knowledge (*Gq*): *Mathematical Achievement (A3)* - Measured mathematics achievement.

[1] Kuder-Richardson 20 coefficients were reported as estimates of internal consistency rather than coefficient alpha.

Test of Mathematical Abilities-Second Edition (TOMA-2)

GENERAL INFORMATION

Author(s): Virginia L. Brown, Mary E. Cronin, and Elizabeth McEntire
Publisher: PRO-ED
Publication Date(s): 1984, 1994

Age Range: 8-0 to 18-11

Administration Time: 75 minutes

COMPOSITE MEASURE INFORMATION

Math Quotient

SCORE INFORMATION

Standard scores	Percentiles	Stanines	Normal curve equivalents	Age equivalents	Grade equivalents

NORMING INFORMATION

Standardization Sample Size: 2,082

Avg. Number per Age/Grade Interval:
  189 per year: 8-0 to 18-11

Age Blocks in Norm Table:
  1 year: 8-0 to 18-11

Sample Collection Date(s): 1983; 1990-1992

Demographic Variables:
  Gender   - *male; female*
  Geographic region - *4 regions; 26 states*
  Race/ethnicity - *White; African American; Hispanic; Oriental/Pacific Islander;*
  Other - *disability status (none, LD, other)*

VALIDITY

Types of Validity Evidence Reported in the Test Manual:

Content	Criterion	Construct

Test Review(s) and Validity Evidence Reported in Extant Literature: None currently available

CONTAINS AT LEAST ONE INDICATOR CONSISTENT WITH THE FOLLOWING LD ASSESSMENT AREA(S)

Oral Expression	Listening Comprehension	Written Expression	Basic Reading Skill	Reading Comprehension	Mathematics Calculation	Mathematics Reasoning

SPECIAL FEATURES

- Includes an Attitudes Toward Math survey with normative comparisons
- Can be administered individually or in a group

Battery: TOMA-2	Vocabulary	Age Range: 8-0 to 18-11

DESCRIPTION

The examinee is required to write a definition for a series of math-related words.

RELIABILITY

☐ - Low   ■ - Medium   ■ - High   ☐ - No Information Available

	2	3	4	5	6	7	8	9	10	11	12	13	14	15	16	17	18	19-24	25-29	30-34	35-39	40-44	45-49	50-54	55-59	60-64	65-69	70-74	75-79	80-84	85-90+
Internal consistency																															
Test-retest*																															

*Interval between testings: 2 weeks

FLOORS AND CEILINGS

	Test Floor	Test Ceiling
Inadequate at ages:	8-0 to 16-11	18-0 to 18-11

CHC CLASSIFICATIONS (Broad: stratum II / Narrow: stratum I)

Quantitative Knowledge[a] (Gq): *Mathematical Knowledge[a] (KM)* - Range of general knowledge about mathematics.

Battery: TOMA-2	Computation	Age Range: 8-0 to 18-11

DESCRIPTION

The examinee is required to solve a series of mathematical problems involving basic operations as well as advanced fractions, decimals, money, and percentages.

RELIABILITY

☐ - Low   ■ - Medium   ■ - High   ☐ - No Information Available

	2	3	4	5	6	7	8	9	10	11	12	13	14	15	16	17	18	19-24	25-29	30-34	35-39	40-44	45-49	50-54	55-59	60-64	65-69	70-74	75-79	80-84	85-90+
Internal consistency																															
Test-retest*																															

*Interval between testings: 2 weeks

FLOORS AND CEILINGS

	Test Floor	Test Ceiling
Inadequate at ages:	none	16-0 to 18-11

CHC CLASSIFICATIONS (Broad: stratum II / Narrow: stratum I)

Quantitative Knowledge (Gq): *Mathematical Achievement (A3)* - Measured mathematics achievement.

[a]The broad and narrow ability CHC classifications for this test were determined by the authors because no agreement was reached through the group consensus process.

DESCRIPTION

The examinee is required to provide an oral or written response to a series of math-related questions read by the examiner.

RELIABILITY

■ - Low   ■ - Medium   ■ - High   ☐ - No Information Available

	2	3	4	5	6	7	8	9	10	11	12	13	14	15	16	17	18	19/24	25/29	30/34	35/39	40/44	45/49	50/54	55/59	60/64	65/69	70/74	75/79	80/84	85/90+
Internal consistency							■	■	■	■	■	■	■	■	■	■	■														
Test-retest*									■	■	■	■	■																		

Interval between testings: 2 weeks

FLOORS AND CEILINGS

	Test Floor	**Test Ceiling**
Inadequate at ages:	8-0 to 10-11	15-0 to 18-11

CHC CLASSIFICATIONS (**Broad: stratum II** / *Narrow: stratum I*)

Quantitative Knowledge (*Gq*): *Mathematical Knowledge (KM)* - Range of general knowledge about mathematics; *Mathematical Achievement (A3)* - Measured mathematics achievement.

DESCRIPTION

The examinee is required to read a series of stories and solve the math problems embedded in the stories.

RELIABILITY

■ - Low   ■ - Medium   ■ - High   ☐ - No Information Available

	2	3	4	5	6	7	8	9	10	11	12	13	14	15	16	17	18	19/24	25/29	30/34	35/39	40/44	45/49	50/54	55/59	60/64	65/69	70/74	75/79	80/84	85/90+
Internal consistency							■	■	■	■	■	■	■	■	■	■	■														
Test-retest*									■	■	■	■	■																		

Interval between testings: 2 weeks

FLOORS AND CEILINGS

	Test Floor	**Test Ceiling**
Inadequate at ages:	8-0 to 10-11	none

CHC CLASSIFICATIONS (**Broad: stratum II** / *Narrow: stratum I*)

Quantitative Knowledge (*Gq*): *Mathematical Knowledge (KM)* - Range of general knowledge about mathematics; *Mathematical Achievement (A3)* - Measured mathematics achievement. **Fluid Reasoning (*Gf*):** *Quantitative Reasoning (RQ)* - Ability to inductively and deductively reason with concepts involving mathematical relations and properties.

DESCRIPTION

The examinee reads silently and/or the examiner reads aloud a series of statements relating to attitudes towards math. The examinee is then required to respond by choosing one of the following four statements: "yes, definitely," "closer to yes," "closer to no," and "no, definitely."

RELIABILITY

☐ - Low   ■ - Medium   ■ - High   ☐ - No Information Available

	2	3	4	5	6	7	8	9	10	11	12	13	14	15	16	17	18	19–24	25–29	30–34	35–39	40–44	45–49	50–54	55–59	60–64	65–69	70–74	75–79	80–84	85–90+
Internal consistency							High	High	High	High	High	High	High	High	High	High	High														
Test-retest*								Low	Low	Low	Low	Low																			

Interval between testings: 2 weeks

FLOORS AND CEILINGS

	Test Floor	**Test Ceiling**
Inadequate at ages:	none	none

CHC CLASSIFICATIONS (**Broad: stratum II** / *Narrow: stratum I*)

Not applicable

ATDR *Summary Pages*
Specific Academic Skills—Written Language Tests

Oral and Written Language Scales: Written Expression (OWLS: WE)

GENERAL INFORMATION

Author(s): Elizabeth Carrow-Woolfolk
Publisher: American Guidance Service
Publication Date(s): 1996

Age Range: 5-0 to 21-11
Administration Time: 10 to 30 minutes

COMPOSITE MEASURE INFORMATION

SCORE INFORMATION

Standard scores	Percentiles	Stanines	Normal curve equivalents	Age equivalents	Grade equivalents

NORMING INFORMATION

Standardization Sample Size: 1,373   *Sample Collection Date(s): 1992-1993*

Avg. Number per Age/Grade Interval:
98 per year: 5-0 to 18-11
66 per 5 years: 19-0 to 21-11

Demographic Variables:
Gender   *- male; female*
Geographic region   *- 4 regions; 119 communities*
Race/ethnicity   *- Black; Hispanic; White; other*
SES   *- mother or female guardian education*

Age Blocks in Norm Table:
3 months: 5-0 to 8-11
4 months: 9-0 to 13-11
6 months: 14-0 to 18-11
1 year: 19-0 to 21-11

VALIDITY

Types of Validity Evidence Reported in the Test Manual:

Content	Criterion	Construct

Test Review(s) and Validity Evidence Reported in Extant Literature: See Appendix C

CONTAINS AT LEAST ONE INDICATOR CONSISTENT WITH THE FOLLOWING LD ASSESSMENT AREA(S)

Oral Expression	Listening Comprehension	Written Expression	Basic Reading Skill	Reading Comprehension	Mathematics Calculation	Mathematics Reasoning

SPECIAL FEATURES

- Can be administered individually or in a group
- Co-normed with the Listening Comprehension and Oral Expression Scales that together yield an overall Language Composite
- Provides standard scores by grade (fall and spring)
- Contains a chapter in the manual that discusses a well-defined theory of language to assist in test performance interpretation
- Contains descriptive analysis tables and worksheets for each of the item sets

DESCRIPTION

The examinee is required to write the appropriate letter, word, sentence, or story in response to a variety of direct writing prompts presented orally by the examiner.

RELIABILITY [1]

☐ - Low   ■ - Medium   ■ - High   ☐ - No Information Available

	2	3	4	5	6	7	8	9	10	11	12	13	14	15	16	17	18	19 24	25 29	30 34	35 39	40 44	45 49	50 54	55 59	60 64	65 69	70 74	75 79	80 84	85 90+
Internal consistency																																
Test-retest*																																

Interval between testings: 2 to 24 weeks

FLOORS AND CEILINGS

	Test Floor	**Test Ceiling**
Inadequate at ages:	5-0 to 5-5	none

CHC CLASSIFICATIONS (Broad: stratum II / *Narrow: stratum I*)

Reading/Writing (*Grw*): *Writing Ability (WA)* - Ability to write with clarity of thought, organization, and good sentence structure.

[1]Split-half coefficients were reported as estimates of internal consistency rather than coefficient alpha.

Test of Early Written Language-Second Edition (TEWL-2)

GENERAL INFORMATION

Author(s): Wayne P. Hresko, Shelley R. Herron, and Pamela K. Peak

Publisher: PRO-ED

Publication Date(s): 1996, 1998

Age Range: 3-0 to 10-11

Administration Time: 50 minutes

COMPOSITE MEASURE INFORMATION

Global Writing Quotient

SCORE INFORMATION

Standard scores	Percentiles	Stanines	Normal curve equivalents	Age equivalents	Grade equivalents

NORMING INFORMATION

Standardization Sample Size: 1,479

Sample Collection Date(s): 1993-1995

Avg. Number per Age/Grade Interval:
  185 per year: 3-0 to 10-11

Age Blocks in Norm Table:
  3 months: 3-0 to 10-11

Demographic Variables:
  Gender - male; female
  Geographic region - 4 regions; 41 states and British Columbia
  Residence - urban; rural
  Race/ethnicity - White; Black; Native American; Hispanic; Asian, Oriental, Pacific Islander; other
  Other - disability status (none, LD, SLD; MR; other)

VALIDITY

Types of Validity Evidence Reported in the Test Manual:

Content	Criterion	Construct

Test Review(s) and Validity Evidence Reported in Extant Literature: See Appendix C

CONTAINS AT LEAST ONE INDICATOR CONSISTENT WITH THE FOLLOWING LD ASSESSMENT AREA(S)

Oral Expression	Listening Comprehension	Written Expression	Basic Reading Skill	Reading Comprehension	Mathematics Calculation	Mathematics Reasoning

SPECIAL FEATURES

- Provides alternate forms (A and B)
- Authors caution use with three year olds as no psychometric information has been provided for this age
- Includes an expanded scoring guide for the Contextual subtest

Battery: TEWL-2	Basic Writing (Form A)	Age Range: 3-0 to 10-11

DESCRIPTION

The examinee is required to draw specified objects and explain the drawing after receiving a verbal prompt from the examiner and point to a correct stimulus item after a verbal prompt from the examiner.

RELIABILITY

☐ - Low   ◼ - Medium   ◼ - High   ☐ - No Information Available

	2	3	4	5	6	7	8	9	10	11	12	13	14	15	16	17	18	19-24	25-29	30-34	35-39	40-44	45-49	50-54	55-59	60-64	65-69	70-74	75-79	80-84	85-90+

Internal consistency
Test-retest*

*Interval between testings: 2 to 3 weeks

FLOORS AND CEILINGS

	Test Floor	Test Ceiling
Inadequate at ages:	3-0 to 6-5	7-9 to 10-11

CHC CLASSIFICATIONS (Broad: stratum II / Narrow: stratum I)

Reading/Writing[a] (*Grw*): *English Usage Knowledge*[a] *(EU)* - Knowledge of writing in the English language with respect to capitalization, punctuation, usage, and spelling.

Battery: TEWL-2	Contextual Writing (Form A)	Age Range: 5-0 to 10-11

DESCRIPTION

The examinee is required to write a story about a picture presented to the examinee by the examiner.

RELIABILITY

☐ - Low   ◼ - Medium   ◼ - High   ☐ - No Information Available

	2	3	4	5	6	7	8	9	10	11	12	13	14	15	16	17	18	19-24	25-29	30-34	35-39	40-44	45-49	50-54	55-59	60-64	65-69	70-74	75-79	80-84	85-90+

Internal consistency
Test-retest*

*Interval between testings: 2 to 3 weeks

FLOORS AND CEILINGS

	Test Floor	Test Ceiling
Inadequate at ages:	5-0 to 7-2	9-9 to 10-11

CHC CLASSIFICATIONS (Broad: stratum II / Narrow: stratum I)

Reading/Writing (*Grw*): *Writing Ability (WA)* - Ability to write with clarity of thought, organization, and good sentence structure.

[a]The broad and narrow ability CHC classifications for this test were determined by the authors because no agreement was reached through the group consensus process.

DESCRIPTION

The examinee is required to draw specified objects and explain the drawing after receiving a verbal prompt from the examiner and point to a correct stimulus item after a verbal prompt from the examiner.

RELIABILITY

■ - Low   ■ - Medium   ■ - High   □ - No Information Available

	2	3	4	5	6	7	8	9	10	11	12	13	14	15	16	17	18	19-24	25-29	30-34	35-39	40-44	45-49	50-54	55-59	60-64	65-69	70-74	75-79	80-84	85/90+
Internal consistency																															
Test-retest*																															

*Interval between testings: 2 to 3 weeks

FLOORS AND CEILINGS

	Test Floor	**Test Ceiling**
Inadequate at ages:	3-0 to 6-5	7-9 to 10-11

CHC CLASSIFICATIONS (Broad: stratum II / *Narrow: stratum I*)

Reading/Writing[a] (**Grw**): *English Usage Knowledge*[a] *(EU)* - Knowledge of writing in the English language with respect to capitalization, punctuation, usage, and spelling.

DESCRIPTION

The examinee is required to write a story about a picture presented to the examinee by the examiner.

RELIABILITY

■ - Low   ■ - Medium   ■ - High   □ - No Information Available

	2	3	4	5	6	7	8	9	10	11	12	13	14	15	16	17	18	19-24	25-29	30-34	35-39	40-44	45-49	50-54	55-59	60-64	65-69	70-74	75-79	80-84	85/90+
Internal consistency																															
Test-retest*																															

*Interval between testings: 2 to 3 weeks

FLOORS AND CEILINGS

	Test Floor	**Test Ceiling**
Inadequate at ages:	5-0 to 7-2	9-9 to 10-11

CHC CLASSIFICATIONS (Broad: stratum II / *Narrow: stratum I*)

Reading/Writing (Grw): *Writing Ability (WA)* - Ability to write with clarity of thought, organization, and good sentence structure.

[a]The broad and narrow ability CHC classifications for this test were determined by the authors because no agreement was reached through the group consensus process.

Test of Written Expression (TOWE)

GENERAL INFORMATION

Author(s): Ron McGhee, Brian R. Bryant, Stephan C. Larsen, and Diane M. Rivera
Publisher: PRO-ED
Publication Date(s): 1995

Age Range: 6-6 to 14-11

Administration Time: 35 to 60 minutes

COMPOSITE MEASURE INFORMATION

SCORE INFORMATION

Standard scores	Percentiles	Stanines	Normal curve equivalents	Age equivalents	Grade equivalents

NORMING INFORMATION

Standardization Sample Size: 1,355

Sample Collection Date(s): 1992-1994

Avg. Number per Age/Grade Interval:
   151 per year: 6-0 to 14-11

Age Blocks in Norm Table:
   6 months: 6-0 to 14-11

Demographic Variables:
   Gender - *male; female*
   Geographic region - *4 regions; 21 states*
   Residence - *Urban; rural*
   Race/ethnicity - *White; Black; American Indian; Asian, Hispanic; other*

VALIDITY

Types of Validity Evidence Reported in the Test Manual:

Content	Criterion	Construct

Test Review(s) and Validity Evidence Reported in Extant Literature: See Appendix C

CONTAINS AT LEAST ONE INDICATOR CONSISTENT WITH THE FOLLOWING LD ASSESSMENT AREA(S)

Oral Expression	Listening Comprehension	Written Expression	Basic Reading Skill	Reading Comprehension	Mathematics Calculation	Mathematics Reasoning

SPECIAL FEATURES

- Allows examiners to analyze item performance for ideation, semantics, syntax, capitalization, punctuation, and spelling
- Includes sample essays to practice scoring

DESCRIPTION

The examinee is required to answer a series of items that tap different skills associated with writing (i.e., capitalization, punctuation, spelling, ideation, semantics, and syntax).

RELIABILITY

☐ - Low   ■ - Medium   ■ - High   ☐ - No Information Available

	2	3	4	5	6	7	8	9	10	11	12	13	14	15	16	17	18	19-24	25-29	30-34	35-39	40-44	45-49	50-54	55-59	60-64	65-69	70-74	75-79	80-84	85 90+
Internal consistency																															
Test-retest*																															

Interval between testings: 2 weeks

FLOORS AND CEILINGS

	Test Floor	Test Ceiling
Inadequate at ages:	none	none

CHC CLASSIFICATIONS (Broad: stratum II / *Narrow: stratum I*)

Reading/Writing (*Grw*): *English Usage Knowledge (EU)* - Knowledge of writing in the English language with respect to capitalization, punctuation, usage, and spelling.

DESCRIPTION

The examinee is required to compose an essay that continues a prepared story starter (i.e., the beginning of the story is provided, and the writer continues the story to its conclusion).

RELIABILITY

☐ - Low   ■ - Medium   ■ - High   ☐ - No Information Available

	2	3	4	5	6	7	8	9	10	11	12	13	14	15	16	17	18	19-24	25-29	30-34	35-39	40-44	45-49	50-54	55-59	60-64	65-69	70-74	75-79	80-84	85 90+
Internal consistency																															
Test-retest*																															

Interval between testings: 2 weeks

FLOORS AND CEILINGS

	Test Floor	Test Ceiling
Inadequate at ages:	8-0 to 13-11	none

CHC CLASSIFICATIONS (Broad: stratum II / *Narrow: stratum I*)

Reading/Writing (*Grw*): *Writing Ability (WA)* - Ability to write with clarity of thought, organization, and good sentence structure.

Test of Written Language-Third Edition (TOWL-3)

GENERAL INFORMATION

Author(s): Donald D. Hammill and Stephen C. Larsen
Publisher: PRO-ED
Publication Date(s): 1978, 1983, 1988, 1996

Age Range: 7-0 to 17-11
Administration Time: 90 minutes

COMPOSITE MEASURE INFORMATION

Contrived Writing
Overall Writing

Spontaneous Writing

SCORE INFORMATION

Standard scores	Percentiles	Stanines	Normal curve equivalents	Age equivalents	Grade equivalents

NORMING INFORMATION

Standardization Sample Size: 2,217

Sample Collection Date(s): 1995

Avg. Number per Age/Grade Interval:
 202 per year: 7-0 to 17-11

Age Blocks in Norm Table:
 1 year: 7-0 to 15-11
 2 years: 16-0 to 17-11

Demographic Variables:
 Gender — *male; female*
 Geographic region — *4 regions; 25 states*
 Residence — *urban, rural*
 Race/ethnicity — *White; Black; Native American; Hispanic; Asian; other*
 SES — *parent education; family income*
 Other — *disability status (none, LD, SLD, MR, other)*

VALIDITY

Types of Validity Evidence Reported in the Test Manual:

Content	Criterion	Construct

Test Review(s) and Validity Evidence Reported in Extant Literature: See Appendix C

CONTAINS AT LEAST ONE INDICATOR CONSISTENT WITH THE FOLLOWING LD ASSESSMENT AREA(S)

Oral Expression	Listening Comprehension	Written Expression	Basic Reading Skill	Reading Comprehension	Mathematics Calculation	Mathematics Reasoning

SPECIAL FEATURES

- Provides alternate forms (A and B)
- Easy items have been added to all the contrived subtests and some of the most difficult items have been dropped to make the test more friendly for young writers and for poor writers
- Can be administered individually or in a group

DESCRIPTION

The examinee is required to write a sentence that includes a stimulus word.

RELIABILITY

   ■ - Low   ■ - Medium   ■ - High   □ - No Information Available

	2	3	4	5	6	7	8	9	10	11	12	13	14	15	16	17	18	19 24	25 29	30 34	35 39	40 44	45 49	50 54	55 59	60 64	65 69	70 74	75 79	80 84	85 90+
Internal consistency																															
Test-retest*																															

Interval between testings: 2 weeks

FLOORS AND CEILINGS

	Test Floor	Test Ceiling
Inadequate at ages:	7-0 to 9-11	15-0 to 17-11

CHC CLASSIFICATIONS (Broad: stratum II / *Narrow: stratum I*)

Reading/Writing (*Grw*): *Writing Ability (WA)* - Ability to write with clarity of thought, organization, and good sentence structure.

DESCRIPTION

The examinee is required to write a series of sentences dictated by the examiner taking care to spell the words as accurately as possible.

RELIABILITY

   ■ - Low   ■ - Medium   ■ - High   □ - No Information Available

	2	3	4	5	6	7	8	9	10	11	12	13	14	15	16	17	18	19 24	25 29	30 34	35 39	40 44	45 49	50 54	55 59	60 64	65 69	70 74	75 79	80 84	85 90+
Internal consistency																															
Test-retest*																															

Interval between testings: 2 weeks

FLOORS AND CEILINGS

	Test Floor	Test Ceiling
Inadequate at ages:	7-0 to 12-11	13-0 to 17-11

CHC CLASSIFICATIONS (Broad: stratum II / *Narrow: stratum I*)

Reading/Writing (*Grw*): *Spelling Ability (SG)* - Ability to spell.

DESCRIPTION

The examinee is required to write a series of sentences dictated by the examiner taking care to make the punctuation and capitalization as accurate as possible.

RELIABILITY

▨ - Low   ▨ - Medium   ■ - High   ☐ - No Information Available

	2	3	4	5	6	7	8	9	10	11	12	13	14	15	16	17	18	19/24	25/29	30/34	35/39	40/44	45/49	50/54	55/59	60/64	65/69	70/74	75/79	80/84	85/90+
Internal consistency																															
Test-retest*																															

*Interval between testings: 2 weeks

FLOORS AND CEILINGS

	Test Floor	Test Ceiling
Inadequate at ages:	7-0 to 11-11	13-0 to 17-11

CHC CLASSIFICATIONS (Broad: stratum II / Narrow: stratum I)

Reading/Writing (Grw): *English Usage Knowledge (EU)* - Knowledge of writing in the English language with respect to capitalization, punctuation, usage, and spelling.

DESCRIPTION

The examinee is required to rewrite an illogical sentence so that it makes sense.

RELIABILITY

▨ - Low   ▨ - Medium   ■ - High   ☐ - No Information Available

	2	3	4	5	6	7	8	9	10	11	12	13	14	15	16	17	18	19/24	25/29	30/34	35/39	40/44	45/49	50/54	55/59	60/64	65/69	70/74	75/79	80/84	85/90+
Internal consistency																															
Test-retest*																															

*Interval between testings: 2 weeks

FLOORS AND CEILINGS

	Test Floor	Test Ceiling
Inadequate at ages:	7-0 to 8-11	none

CHC CLASSIFICATIONS (Broad: stratum II / Narrow: stratum I)

Reading/Writing (Grw): *English Usage Knowledge (EU)* - Knowledge of writing in the English language with respect to capitalization, punctuation, usage, and spelling.

DESCRIPTION

The examinee is required to combine a few short sentences into a single grammatically correct sentence.

RELIABILITY

☐ - Low   ■ - Medium   ■ - High   ☐ - No Information Available

	2	3	4	5	6	7	8	9	10	11	12	13	14	15	16	17	18	19–24	25–29	30–34	35–39	40–44	45–49	50–54	55–59	60–64	65–69	70–74	75–79	80–84	85–90+
Internal consistency						Low	High	High	High	High	High	High	High	High	High	Medium															
Test-retest*						High										High															

*Interval between testings: 2 weeks

FLOORS AND CEILINGS

	Test Floor	Test Ceiling
Inadequate at ages:	7-0 to 13-11	14-0 to 17-11

CHC CLASSIFICATIONS (Broad: stratum II / Narrow: stratum I)

Reading/Writing (Grw): *English Usage Knowledge[a] (EU)* - Knowledge of writing in the English language with respect to capitalization, punctuation, usage, and spelling; *Writing Ability[a] (WA)* - Ability to write with clarity of thought, organization, and good sentence structure.

DESCRIPTION

The examinee is required to write a story, being careful to make the capitalization, punctuation, and spelling as accurate as possible after being presented with a stimulus picture.

RELIABILITY

☐ - Low   ■ - Medium   ■ - High   ☐ - No Information Available

	2	3	4	5	6	7	8	9	10	11	12	13	14	15	16	17	18	19–24	25–29	30–34	35–39	40–44	45–49	50–54	55–59	60–64	65–69	70–74	75–79	80–84	85–90+
Internal consistency						Low	Medium	Medium	Medium	Medium	Medium	Medium	Medium	Medium	Medium	Medium															
Test-retest*						Low										Low															

*Interval between testings: 2 weeks

FLOORS AND CEILINGS

	Test Floor	Test Ceiling
Inadequate at ages:	7-0 to 14-11	none

CHC CLASSIFICATIONS (Broad: stratum II / Narrow: stratum I)

Reading/Writing (Grw): *Writing Ability (WA)* - Ability to write with clarity of thought, organization, and good sentence structure; *English Usage Knowledge (EU)* - Knowledge of writing in the English language with respect to capitalization, punctuation, usage, and spelling.

[a]The narrow ability CHC classifications for this test were determined by the authors because no agreement was reached through the group consensus process.

DESCRIPTION

The examinee's story constructed earlier is evaluated for vocabulary, sentence construction, and grammar.

RELIABILITY

☐ - Low   ■ - Medium   ■ - High   ☐ - No Information Available

2 3 4 5 6 7 8 9 10 11 12 13 14 15 16 17 18 19 25 30 35 40 45 50 55 60 65 70 75 80 85
                                                      24 29 34 39 44 49 54 59 64 69 74 79 84 90+

Internal consistency
Test-retest*

*Interval between testings: 2 weeks

FLOORS AND CEILINGS

	Test Floor	Test Ceiling
Inadequate at ages:	7-0 to 8-11	none

CHC CLASSIFICATIONS (Broad: stratum II / Narrow: stratum I)

Reading/Writing (Grw): *Writing Ability (WA)* - Ability to write with clarity of thought, organization, and good sentence structure.

DESCRIPTION

The examinee's story constructed earlier is evaluated for the quality of its plot, prose, development of characters, and interest to the reader.

RELIABILITY

☐ - Low   ■ - Medium   ■ - High   ☐ - No Information Available

2 3 4 5 6 7 8 9 10 11 12 13 14 15 16 17 18 19 25 30 35 40 45 50 55 60 65 70 75 80 85
                                                      24 29 34 39 44 49 54 59 64 69 74 79 84 90+

Internal consistency
Test-retest*

*Interval between testings: 2 weeks

FLOORS AND CEILINGS

	Test Floor	Test Ceiling
Inadequate at ages:	7-0 to 10-11	none

CHC CLASSIFICATIONS (Broad: stratum II / Narrow: stratum I)

Reading/Writing (Grw): *Writing Ability (WA)* - Ability to write with clarity of thought, organization, and good sentence structure.

DESCRIPTION

The examinee is required to write a sentence that includes a stimulus word.

RELIABILITY

☐ - Low   ■ - Medium   ■ - High   ☐ - No Information Available

	2	3	4	5	6	7	8	9	10	11	12	13	14	15	16	17	18	19	25	30	35	40	45	50	55	60	65	70	75	80	85
																			24	29	34	39	44	49	54	59	64	69	74	79	84	90+
Internal consistency																															
Test-retest*																															

Interval between testings: 2 weeks

FLOORS AND CEILINGS

	Test Floor	**Test Ceiling**
Inadequate at ages:	7-0 to 9-11	15-0 to 17-11

CHC CLASSIFICATIONS (Broad: stratum II / *Narrow: stratum I*)

Reading/Writing (*Grw*): *Writing Ability (WA)* - Ability to write with clarity of thought, organization, and good sentence structure.

DESCRIPTION

The examinee is required to write a series of sentences dictated by the examiner taking care to spell the words as accurately as possible.

RELIABILITY

☐ - Low   ■ - Medium   ■ - High   ☐ - No Information Available

	2	3	4	5	6	7	8	9	10	11	12	13	14	15	16	17	18	19	25	30	35	40	45	50	55	60	65	70	75	80	85
																			24	29	34	39	44	49	54	59	64	69	74	79	84	90+
Internal consistency																															
Test-retest*																															

Interval between testings: 2 weeks

FLOORS AND CEILINGS

	Test Floor	**Test Ceiling**
Inadequate at ages:	7-0 to 12-11	13-0 to 17-11

CHC CLASSIFICATIONS (Broad: stratum II / *Narrow: stratum I*)

Reading/Writing (*Grw*): *Spelling Ability (SG)* - Ability to spell.

Battery: TOWL-3	Style (Form B)	*Age Range:* 7-0 to 17-11

DESCRIPTION

The examinee is required to write a series of sentences dictated by the examiner taking care to make the punctuation and capitalization as accurate as possible.

RELIABILITY

■ - Low   ■ - Medium   ■ - High   ☐ - No Information Available

| | 2 3 4 5 6 7 8 9 10 11 12 13 14 15 16 17 18 19 25 30 35 40 45 50 55 60 65 70 75 80 85 |
| | 24 29 34 39 44 49 54 59 64 69 74 79 84 90+ |

Internal consistency
Test-retest*

*Interval between testings: 2 weeks

FLOORS AND CEILINGS

	Test Floor	**Test Ceiling**
Inadequate at ages:	7-0 to 11-11	13-0 to 17-11

CHC CLASSIFICATIONS (**Broad: stratum II** / *Narrow: stratum I*)

Reading/Writing (*Grw*): *English Usage Knowledge (EU)* - Knowledge of writing in the English language with respect to capitalization, punctuation, usage, and spelling.

Battery: TOWL-3	Logical Sentences (Form B)	*Age Range:* 7-0 to 17-11

DESCRIPTION

The examinee is required to rewrite an illogical sentence so that it makes sense.

RELIABILITY

■ - Low   ■ - Medium   ■ - High   ☐ - No Information Available

| | 2 3 4 5 6 7 8 9 10 11 12 13 14 15 16 17 18 19 25 30 35 40 45 50 55 60 65 70 75 80 85 |
| | 24 29 34 39 44 49 54 59 64 69 74 79 84 90+ |

Internal consistency
Test-retest*

*Interval between testings: 2 weeks

FLOORS AND CEILINGS

	Test Floor	**Test Ceiling**
Inadequate at ages:	7-0 to 8-11	none

CHC CLASSIFICATIONS (**Broad: stratum II** / *Narrow: stratum I*)

Reading/Writing (*Grw*): *English Usage Knowledge (EU)* - Knowledge of writing in the English language with respect to capitalization, punctuation, usage, and spelling.

DESCRIPTION

The examinee is required to combine a few short sentences into a single grammatically correct sentence.

RELIABILITY

☐ - Low   ■ - Medium   ■ - High   ☐ - No Information Available

	2	3	4	5	6	7	8	9	10	11	12	13	14	15	16	17	18 19 24	25 29	30 34	35 39	40 44	45 49	50 54	55 59	60 64	65 69	70 74	75 79	80 84	85 90+
Internal consistency																														
Test-retest*																														

Interval between testings: 2 weeks

FLOORS AND CEILINGS

	Test Floor	Test Ceiling
Inadequate at ages:	7-0 to 13-11	14-0 to 17-11

CHC CLASSIFICATIONS (Broad: stratum II / Narrow: stratum I)

Reading/Writing (Grw): *English Usage Knowledge[a] (EU)* - Knowledge of writing in the English language with respect to capitalization, punctuation, usage, and spelling; *Writing Ability[a] (WA)* - Ability to write with clarity of thought, organization, and good sentence structure.

DESCRIPTION

The examinee is required to write a story, being careful to make the capitalization, punctuation, and spelling as accurate as possible after being presented with a stimulus picture.

RELIABILITY

☐ - Low   ■ - Medium   ■ - High   ☐ - No Information Available

	2	3	4	5	6	7	8	9	10	11	12	13	14	15	16	17	18 19 24	25 29	30 34	35 39	40 44	45 49	50 54	55 59	60 64	65 69	70 74	75 79	80 84	85 90+
Internal consistency																														
Test-retest*																														

Interval between testings: 2 weeks

FLOORS AND CEILINGS

	Test Floor	Test Ceiling
Inadequate at ages:	7-0 to 14-11	none

CHC CLASSIFICATIONS (Broad: stratum II / Narrow: stratum I)

Reading/Writing (Grw): *Writing Ability (WA)* - Ability to write with clarity of thought, organization, and good sentence structure; *English Usage Knowledge (EU)* - Knowledge of writing in the English language with respect to capitalization, punctuation, usage, and spelling.

[a]The narrow ability CHC classifications for this test were determined by the authors because no agreement was reached through the group consensus process.

DESCRIPTION

The examinee's story constructed earlier is evaluated for vocabulary, sentence construction, and grammar.

RELIABILITY

☐ - Low   ■ - Medium   ■ - High   ☐ - No Information Available

	2	3	4	5	6	7	8	9	10	11	12	13	14	15	16	17	18	19 24	25 29	30 34	35 39	40 44	45 49	50 54	55 59	60 64	65 69	70 74	75 79	80 84	85 90+
Internal consistency																															
Test-retest*																															

Interval between testings: 2 weeks

FLOORS AND CEILINGS

	Test Floor	Test Ceiling
Inadequate at ages:	7-0 to 8-11	none

CHC CLASSIFICATIONS (Broad: stratum II / *Narrow: stratum I*)

Reading/Writing (*Grw*): *Writing Ability (WA)* - Ability to write with clarity of thought, organization, and good sentence structure.

DESCRIPTION

The examinee's story constructed earlier is evaluated for the quality of its plot, prose, development of characters, and interest to the reader.

RELIABILITY

☐ - Low   ■ - Medium   ■ - High   ☐ - No Information Available

	2	3	4	5	6	7	8	9	10	11	12	13	14	15	16	17	18	19 24	25 29	30 34	35 39	40 44	45 49	50 54	55 59	60 64	65 69	70 74	75 79	80 84	85 90+
Internal consistency																															
Test-retest*																															

Interval between testings: 2 weeks

FLOORS AND CEILINGS

	Test Floor	Test Ceiling
Inadequate at ages:	7-0 to 10-11	none

CHC CLASSIFICATIONS (Broad: stratum II / *Narrow: stratum I*)

Reading/Writing (*Grw*): *Writing Ability (WA)* - Ability to write with clarity of thought, organization, and good sentence structure.

Test of Written Spelling-Fourth Edition (TWS-4)

GENERAL INFORMATION

Author(s): Stephen C. Larsen, Donald D. Hammill, and
Louisa C. Moats
Publisher: PRO-ED
Publication Date(s): 1976, 1986, 1994, 1999

Age Range: 6-0 to 18-11

Administration Time: 15 minutes

COMPOSITE MEASURE INFORMATION

SCORE INFORMATION

Standard scores	Percentiles	Stanines	Normal curve equivalents	Age equivalents	Grade equivalents

NORMING INFORMATION

Standardization Sample Size: 4,952

Sample Collection Date(s): 1986; 1993

Avg. Number per Age/Grade Interval:
381 per year: 6-0 to 18-11

Age Blocks in Norm Table:
3 months: 6-0 to 10-11
6 months: 11-0 to 11-11
1 year: 12-0 to 18-11

Demographic Variables:
Gender   - male; female
Geographic region - 4 regions; 23 states
Residence - urban, rural
Race/ethnicity - White; Black; Native American; Hispanic; Asian;
other

VALIDITY

Types of Validity Evidence Reported in the Test Manual:

Content	Criterion	Construct

Test Review(s) and Validity Evidence Reported in Extant Literature: See Appendix C

CONTAINS AT LEAST ONE INDICATOR CONSISTENT WITH THE FOLLOWING LD ASSESSMENT AREA(S)

Oral Expression	Listening Comprehension	Written Expression	Basic Reading Skill	Reading Comprehension	Mathematics Calculation	Mathematics Reasoning

SPECIAL FEATURES

- Provides alternate forms (A and B)

DESCRIPTION

The examinee is required to write correctly words that are stated by the examiner in isolation and in a sentence.

RELIABILITY [1]

■ - Low   ■ - Medium   ■ - High   ☐ - No Information Available

	2	3	4	5	6	7	8	9	10	11	12	13	14	15	16	17	18	19 24	25 29	30 34	35 39	40 44	45 49	50 54	55 59	60 64	65 69	70 74	75 79	80 84	85 90+
Internal consistency																															
Test-retest*																															

*Interval between testings: 2 weeks

FLOORS AND CEILINGS

	Test Floor	Test Ceiling
Inadequate at ages:	6-0 to 9-2	16-0 to 18-11

CHC CLASSIFICATIONS (Broad: stratum II / Narrow: stratum I)

Reading/Writing (*Grw*): *Spelling Ability (SG)* - Ability to spell.

DESCRIPTION

The examinee is required to write correctly words that are stated by the examiner in isolation and in a sentence.

RELIABILITY [1]

■ - Low   ■ - Medium   ■ - High   ☐ - No Information Available

	2	3	4	5	6	7	8	9	10	11	12	13	14	15	16	17	18	19 24	25 29	30 34	35 39	40 44	45 49	50 54	55 59	60 64	65 69	70 74	75 79	80 84	85 90+
Internal consistency																															
Test-retest*																															

*Interval between testings: 2 weeks

FLOORS AND CEILINGS

	Test Floor	Test Ceiling
Inadequate at ages:	6-0 to 9-2	16-0 to 18-11

CHC CLASSIFICATIONS (Broad: stratum II / Narrow: stratum I)

Reading/Writing (*Grw*): *Spelling Ability (SG)* - Ability to spell.

[1]Test-retest coefficients were reported by grade in the test manual. Therefore, corresponding ages were estimated by the authors.

ATDR *Summary Pages*

Specific Academic Skills—Oral Language Tests

Clinical Evaluation of Language Fundamentals-Third Edition (CELF-3)

GENERAL INFORMATION

Author(s): Eleanor Semel, Elisabeth H. Wiig, and Wayne A. Secord

Publisher: The Psychological Corporation

Publication Date(s): 1980, 1987, 1995

Age Range: 6-0 to 21-11

Administration Time: 30 to 45 minutes

COMPOSITE MEASURE INFORMATION

Receptive Language

Total Language

Expressive Language

SCORE INFORMATION

Standard scores	Percentiles	Stanines	Normal curve equivalents	Age equivalents	Grade equivalents

NORMING INFORMATION

Standardization Sample Size: 2,450

Sample Collection Date(s): 1994-1995

Avg. Number per Age/Grade Interval:
177 per year: 6-0 to 18-11
90 per five years: 19-0 to 21-11

Age Blocks in Norm Table:
1 year: 6-0 to 16-11
5 years: 17-0 to 21-11

Demographic Variables:
Gender   - male; female
Geographic region   - 4 regions; 47 states
Race/ethnicity   - African-American; Hispanic; White; other
SES   - parent education

VALIDITY

Types of Validity Evidence Reported in the Test Manual:

Content	Criterion	Construct

Test Review(s) and Validity Evidence Reported in Extant Literature: See Appendix C

CONTAINS AT LEAST ONE INDICATOR CONSISTENT WITH THE FOLLOWING LD ASSESSMENT AREA(S)

Oral Expression	Listening Comprehension	Written Expression	Basic Reading Skill	Reading Comprehension	Mathematics Calculation	Mathematics Reasoning

SPECIAL FEATURES

- Describes how dialectical and cultural variations can affect test performance
- Includes and explains extension testing that assists in developing instructional goals
- Includes practice in scoring Formulated Sentences and Word Associations as well as inter-rater reliability coefficients
- The Rapid, Automatic Naming subtest is criterion-referenced and does not yield standard scores
- Provides computer scoring program with interpretive profiling report
- Provides a Communications Checklist to validate CELF-3 results

DESCRIPTION

The examinee is required to point to the picture that best depicts a sentence stated by the examiner.

RELIABILITY

☐ - Low   ■ - Medium   ■ - High   ☐ - No Information Available

	2	3	4	5	6	7	8	9	10	11	12	13	14	15	16	17	18	19-24	25-29	30-34	35-39	40-44	45-49	50-54	55-59	60-64	65-69	70-74	75-79	80-84	85-90+
Internal consistency					☐	☐																									
Test-retest*						☐																									

*Interval between testings: 1 to 4 weeks

FLOORS AND CEILINGS

	Test Floor	Test Ceiling
Inadequate at ages:	none	6-0 to 8-11

CHC CLASSIFICATIONS (Broad: stratum II / *Narrow: stratum I*)

Crystallized Intelligence (Gc): *Listening Ability (LS)* - Ability to listen and comprehend oral communications.

DESCRIPTION

The examinee is required to use the contents of a picture and an incomplete sentence stated by the examiner to supply the missing word or words in that sentence.

RELIABILITY

☐ - Low   ■ - Medium   ■ - High   ☐ - No Information Available

	2	3	4	5	6	7	8	9	10	11	12	13	14	15	16	17	18	19-24	25-29	30-34	35-39	40-44	45-49	50-54	55-59	60-64	65-69	70-74	75-79	80-84	85-90+
Internal consistency				■	■	■																									
Test-retest*					☐	☐																									

*Interval between testings: 1 to 4 weeks

FLOORS AND CEILINGS

	Test Floor	Test Ceiling
Inadequate at ages:	none	8-0 to 8-11

CHC CLASSIFICATIONS (Broad: stratum II / *Narrow: stratum I*)

Crystallized Intelligence (Gc): *Listening Ability (LS)* - Ability to listen and comprehend oral communications.

DESCRIPTION

The examinee is required to point to pictures of shapes in the same order stated by the examiner.

RELIABILITY

☐ - Low   ■ - Medium   ■ - High   ☐ - No Information Available

	2	3	4	5	6	7	8	9	10	11	12	13	14	15	16	17	18	19 24	25 29	30 34	35 39	40 44	45 49	50 54	55 59	60 64	65 69	70 74	75 79	80 84	85 90+
Internal consistency																															
Test-retest*																															

*Interval between testings: 1 to 4 weeks

FLOORS AND CEILINGS

	Test Floor	**Test Ceiling**
Inadequate at ages:	6-0 to 6-11	11-0 to 21-11

CHC CLASSIFICATIONS (Broad: stratum II / *Narrow: stratum I*)

Short-Term Memory (*Gsm*): *Memory Span (MS)* - Ability to attend to and immediately recall temporally ordered elements in the correct order after a single presentation.

Battery: CELF-3   **Formulated Sentences**   *Age Range:* **6-0 to 21-11**

DESCRIPTION

The examinee is shown a picture and then is required to make up (and say out loud) a sentence about the picture using a particular word.

RELIABILITY

☐ - Low   ■ - Medium   ■ - High   ☐ - No Information Available

	2	3	4	5	6	7	8	9	10	11	12	13	14	15	16	17	18	19 24	25 29	30 34	35 39	40 44	45 49	50 54	55 59	60 64	65 69	70 74	75 79	80 84	85 90+
Internal consistency																															
Test-retest*																															

*Interval between testings: 1to 4 weeks

FLOORS AND CEILINGS

	Test Floor	**Test Ceiling**
Inadequate at ages:	6-0 to 7-11	11-0 to 21-11

CHC CLASSIFICATIONS (Broad: stratum II / *Narrow: stratum I*)

Crystallized Intelligence (*Gc*): *Oral Production and Fluency (OP)* - More specific or narrow communication skills than reflected by Communication Ability (CM).

DESCRIPTION

The examinee is required to name the two words that go together best after the examiner reads aloud three words.

RELIABILITY

☐ - Low   ■ - Medium   ■ - High   ☐ - No Information Available

	2	3	4	5	6	7	8	9	10	11	12	13	14	15	16	17	18	19/24	25/29	30/34	35/39	40/44	45/49	50/54	55/59	60/64	65/69	70/74	75/79	80/84	85/90+
Internal consistency																															
Test-retest*																															

*Interval between testings: 1 to 4 weeks

FLOORS AND CEILINGS

	Test Floor	Test Ceiling
Inadequate at ages:	6-0 to 7-11	13-0 to 21-11

CHC CLASSIFICATIONS (Broad: stratum II / Narrow: stratum I)

Crystallized Intelligence (Gc): *Language Development (LD)* - General development, or the understanding of words, sentences, and paragraphs (not requiring reading), in spoken native language skills.

DESCRIPTION

The examinee is required to repeat a sentence stated by the examiner verbatim.

RELIABILITY

☐ - Low   ■ - Medium   ■ - High   ☐ - No Information Available

	2	3	4	5	6	7	8	9	10	11	12	13	14	15	16	17	18	19/24	25/29	30/34	35/39	40/44	45/49	50/54	55/59	60/64	65/69	70/74	75/79	80/84	85/90+
Internal consistency																															
Test-retest*																															

*Interval between testings: 1 to 4 weeks

FLOORS AND CEILINGS

	Test Floor	Test Ceiling
Inadequate at ages:	none	14-0 to 21-11

CHC CLASSIFICATIONS (Broad: stratum II / Narrow: stratum I)

Short-Term Memory (Gsm): *Memory Span (MS)* - Ability to attend to and immediately recall temporally ordered elements in the correct order after a single presentation.

| Battery: CELF-3 | Sentence Assembly | Age Range: 9-0 to 21-11 |

DESCRIPTION

The examinee is required to use words stated by the examiner to make two different sentences.

RELIABILITY

☐ - Low   ■ - Medium   ■ - High   ☐ - No Information Available

	2	3	4	5	6	7	8	9	10	11	12	13	14	15	16	17	18	19 24	25 29	30 34	35 39	40 44	45 49	50 54	55 59	60 64	65 69	70 74	75 79	80 84	85 90+
Internal consistency																															
Test-retest*																															

*Interval between testings: 1 to 4 weeks

FLOORS AND CEILINGS

	Test Floor	Test Ceiling
Inadequate at ages:	9-0 to 9-11	10-0 to 21-11

CHC CLASSIFICATIONS (Broad: stratum II / Narrow: stratum I)

Crystallized Intelligence (Gc): *Language Development*[a] *(LD)* - General development, or the understanding of words, sentences, and paragraphs (not requiring reading), in spoken native language skills; *Grammatical Sensitivity*[a] *(MY)* - Knowledge or awareness of the grammatical features of the native language.

| Battery: CELF-3 | Semantic Relationships | Age Range: 9-0 to 21-11 |

DESCRIPTION

The examinee is required to select from the four choices shown in the stimulus booklet the two correct answers to a sentence stated by the examiner that contains a missing part.

RELIABILITY

☐ - Low   ■ - Medium   ■ - High   ☐ - No Information Available

	2	3	4	5	6	7	8	9	10	11	12	13	14	15	16	17	18	19 24	25 29	30 34	35 39	40 44	45 49	50 54	55 59	60 64	65 69	70 74	75 79	80 84	85 90+
Internal consistency																															
Test-retest*																															

*Interval between testings: 1 to 4 weeks

FLOORS AND CEILINGS

	Test Floor	Test Ceiling
Inadequate at ages:	9-0 to 9-11	10-0 to 21-11

CHC CLASSIFICATIONS (Broad: stratum II / Narrow: stratum I)

Crystallized Intelligence (Gc): *Listening Ability (LS)* - Ability to listen and comprehend oral communications.

[a]The narrow CHC classifications for this test were determined by the authors because no agreement was reached through the group consensus process.

Battery: CELF-3	Word Associations (Supplemental)	Age Range: 6-0 to 21-11

DESCRIPTION

The examinee is given 60 seconds to name as many things as he or she can that go with a particular topic.

RELIABILITY

◻ - Low   ◼ - Medium   ◼ - High   ☐ - No Information Available

	2	3	4	5	6	7	8	9	10	11	12	13	14	15	16	17	18	19-24	25-29	30-34	35-39	40-44	45-49	50-54	55-59	60-64	65-69	70-74	75-79	80-84	85-90+
Internal consistency																															
Test-retest*																															

Interval between testings: 1 to 4 weeks

FLOORS AND CEILINGS

	Test Floor	Test Ceiling
Inadequate at ages:	none	none

CHC CLASSIFICATIONS (Broad: stratum II / Narrow: stratum I)

Long-Term Retrieval (Glr): *Ideational Fluency (FI) -* Ability to rapidly produce a series of ideas, words, or phrases related to a specific condition or object. Quantity not quality is emphasized.

Battery: CELF-3	Listening to Paragraphs (Supplemental)	Age Range: 6-0 to 21-11

DESCRIPTION

The examinee is required to provide a response to questions about a paragraph that is read by the examiner.

RELIABILITY

◻ - Low   ◼ - Medium   ◼ - High   ☐ - No Information Available

	2	3	4	5	6	7	8	9	10	11	12	13	14	15	16	17	18	19-24	25-29	30-34	35-39	40-44	45-49	50-54	55-59	60-64	65-69	70-74	75-79	80-84	85-90+
Internal consistency																															
Test-retest*																															

Interval between testings: 1 to 4 weeks

FLOORS AND CEILINGS

	Test Floor	Test Ceiling
Inadequate at ages:	8-0 to 9-11	7-0 to 21-11

CHC CLASSIFICATIONS (Broad: stratum II / Narrow: stratum I)

Crystallized Intelligence (Gc): *Listening Ability (LS) -* Ability to listen and comprehend oral communications.

DESCRIPTION

The examinee is required to name colors, shapes, and color-shape combinations as quickly as possible.

RELIABILITY (Not applicable)

☐ - Low　　　■ - Medium　　　■ - High　　　☐ - No Information Available

	2	3	4	5	6	7	8	9	10	11	12	13	14	15	16	17	18	19 24	25 29	30 34	35 39	40 44	45 49	50 54	55 59	60 64	65 69	70 74	75 79	80 84	85 90+
Internal consistency																															
Test-retest*																															

Interval between testings: not applicable

FLOORS AND CEILINGS

	Test Floor	**Test Ceiling**
Inadequate at ages:	none	none

CHC CLASSIFICATIONS (Broad: stratum II / *Narrow: stratum I*)

Long-Term Retrieval (*Glr*): *Naming Facility (NA)* - Ability to rapidly produce names for concepts when presented with a pictorial or verbal cue; *Ideational Fluency (FI)* - Ability to rapidly produce a series of ideas, words, or phrases related to a specific condition or object. Quantity not quality is emphasized.

Comprehensive Assessment of Spoken Language (CASL)

GENERAL INFORMATION

Author(s): Elizabeth Carrow-Woolfolk
Publisher: American Guidance Service
Publication Date(s): 1999

Age Range: 3-0 to 21-11
Administration Time: 30 to 60 minutes

COMPOSITE MEASURE INFORMATION

Lexical/Semantic Index
Pragmatic
Receptive Index
Core Composite

Syntactic Index
Supralinguistic Index
Expressive Index

SCORE INFORMATION

Standard scores	Percentiles	Stanines	Normal curve equivalents	Age equivalents	Grade equivalents

NORMING INFORMATION

Standardization Sample Size: 2,750

Sample Collection Date(s): 1996-1997

Avg. Number per Age/Grade Interval:
160 per year: 3-0 to 18-11
116 per five years: 19-0 to 21-11

Demographic Variables:
Gender — male; female
Geographic region — 4 regions; 42 states and The District of Columbia; 172 communities

Age Blocks in Norm Table:
3 months: 3-0 to 8-11
4 months: 9-0 to 13-11
6 months: 14-0 to 18-11
1 year: 19-0 to 21-11

Race/ethnicity — African-American; Hispanic; White; other
Other — special education category (LD, SLD, MR, ED, other)

VALIDITY

Types of Validity Evidence Reported in the Test Manual:

Content	Criterion	Construct

Test Review(s) and Validity Evidence Reported in Extant Literature: None currently available

CONTAINS AT LEAST ONE INDICATOR CONSISTENT WITH THE FOLLOWING LD ASSESSMENT AREA(S)

Oral Expression	Listening Comprehension	Written Expression	Basic Reading Skill	Reading Comprehension	Mathematics Calculation	Mathematics Reasoning

SPECIAL FEATURES

- Includes an Examiner's Observations Checklist that allows the examiner to record observations of the examinee's oral language and test-taking behaviors

DESCRIPTION

The examinee is required to point to the picture or part of the picture that represents the correct response corresponding to the item read by the examiner.

RELIABILITY [1]

☐ - Low   ■ - Medium   ■ - High   ☐ - No Information Available

	2	3	4	5	6	7	8	9	10	11	12	13	14	15	16	17	18	19 24	25 29	30 34	35 39	40 44	45 49	50 54	55 59	60 64	65 69	70 74	75 79	80 84	85 90+
Internal consistency																															
Test-retest*																															

*Interval between testings: 1 to 15 weeks

FLOORS AND CEILINGS

	Test Floor	Test Ceiling
Inadequate at ages:	none	none

CHC CLASSIFICATIONS (Broad: stratum II / Narrow: stratum I)

Crystallized Intelligence (Gc): *Lexical Knowledge[a] (VL)* - Extent of vocabulary that can be understood in terms of correct word meanings; *Language Development[a] (LD)* - General development, or the understanding of words, sentences, and paragraphs (not requiring reading), in spoken native language skills.

DESCRIPTION

The examinee is required to respond with one word that means the opposite of the word stated by the examiner.

RELIABILITY [1]

☐ - Low   ■ - Medium   ■ - High   ☐ - No Information Available

	2	3	4	5	6	7	8	9	10	11	12	13	14	15	16	17	18	19 24	25 29	30 34	35 39	40 44	45 49	50 54	55 59	60 64	65 69	70 74	75 79	80 84	85 90+
Internal consistency																															
Test-retest*																															

*Interval between testings: 1 to 15 weeks

FLOORS AND CEILINGS

	Test Floor	Test Ceiling
Inadequate at ages:	5-0 to 5-5	none

CHC CLASSIFICATIONS (Broad: stratum II / Narrow: stratum I)

Crystallized Intelligence (Gc): *Lexical Knowledge (VL)* - Extent of vocabulary that can be understood in terms of correct word meanings.

---

[1] Split-half coefficients were reported as estimates of internal consistency rather than coefficient alpha.

[a] The narrow CHC classifications for this test were determined by the authors because no agreement was reached through the group consensus process.

DESCRIPTION

The examinee is required to choose from four options the word that means the same as the stimulus word read by the examiner who also reads the four options.

RELIABILITY [1]

■ - Low ■ - Medium ■ - High □ - No Information Available

	2	3	4	5	6	7	8	9	10	11	12	13	14	15	16	17	18	19/24	25/29	30/34	35/39	40/44	45/49	50/54	55/59	60/64	65/69	70/74	75/79	80/84	85/90+
Internal consistency																															
Test-retest*																															

*Interval between testings: 1 to 15 weeks

FLOORS AND CEILINGS

	Test Floor	Test Ceiling
Inadequate at ages:	none	none

CHC CLASSIFICATIONS (Broad: stratum II / *Narrow: stratum I*)

Crystallized Intelligence (*Gc*): *Lexical Knowledge (VL)* - Extent of vocabulary that can be understood in terms of correct word meanings.

DESCRIPTION

The examinee is required to respond with a single word that meaningfully completes the sentence that the examiner reads that is missing the last word.

RELIABILITY [1]

■ - Low ■ - Medium ■ - High □ - No Information Available

	2	3	4	5	6	7	8	9	10	11	12	13	14	15	16	17	18	19/24	25/29	30/34	35/39	40/44	45/49	50/54	55/59	60/64	65/69	70/74	75/79	80/84	85/90+
Internal consistency																															
Test-retest*																															

*Interval between testings: 1 to 15 weeks

FLOORS AND CEILINGS

	Test Floor	Test Ceiling
Inadequate at ages:	3-0 to 3-11	none

CHC CLASSIFICATIONS (Broad: stratum II / *Narrow: stratum I*)

Crystallized Intelligence (*Gc*): *Listening Ability (LS)* - Ability to listen and comprehend oral communications.

[1] Split-half coefficients are reported as estimates of internal consistency rather than coefficient alpha.

Battery: CASL	Idiomatic Language	Age Range: 11-0 to 21-11

DESCRIPTION

The examinee is required to complete the phrase with an acceptable form of the idiom that the examiner reads that is missing its final part.

RELIABILITY [1]

■ - Low　　■ - Medium　　■ - High　　☐ - No Information Available

	2 3 4 5 6 7 8 9 10 11 12 13 14 15 16 17 18 19 25 30 35 40 45 50 55 60 65 70 75 80 85
	24 29 34 39 44 49 54 59 64 69 74 79 84 90+
Internal consistency	
Test-retest*	

Interval between testings: 1 to 15 weeks

FLOORS AND CEILINGS

	Test Floor	Test Ceiling
Inadequate at ages:	11-0 to 11-3	none

CHC CLASSIFICATIONS (Broad: stratum II / *Narrow: stratum I*)

Crystallized Intelligence (*Gc*): *Language Development (LD)* - General development, or the understanding of words, sentences, and paragraphs (not requiring reading), in spoken native language skills; *Listening Ability (LS)* - Ability to listen and comprehend oral communications.

Battery: CASL	Syntax Construction	Age Range: 3-0 to 21-11

DESCRIPTION

The examinee is required to respond with a word, phrase, or sentence that is semantically and grammatically compatible with the verbal stimulus and the picture that the examiner reads and shows from a test book.

RELIABILITY [1]

■ - Low　　■ - Medium　　■ - High　　☐ - No Information Available

	2 3 4 5 6 7 8 9 10 11 12 13 14 15 16 17 18 19 25 30 35 40 45 50 55 60 65 70 75 80 85
	24 29 34 39 44 49 54 59 64 69 74 79 84 90+
Internal consistency	
Test-retest*	

Interval between testings: 1 to 15 weeks

FLOORS AND CEILINGS

	Test Floor	Test Ceiling
Inadequate at ages:	3-0 to 3-11	21-0 to 21-11

CHC CLASSIFICATIONS (Broad: stratum II / *Narrow: stratum I*)

Crystallized Intelligence (*Gc*): *Grammatical Sensitivity[a] (MY)* - Knowledge or awareness of the grammatical features of the native language; *Oral Production and Fluency[a] (OP)* - More specific or narrow oral communication skills than reflected by Communication Ability (CM).

[1]Split-half coefficients are reported as estimates of internal consistency rather than coefficient alpha.
[a]The narrow CHC classifications for this test were determined by the authors because no agreement was reached through the group consensus process.

DESCRIPTION

The examinee is required to indicate which one of four pictures corresponds with what the examiner reads (i.e., a stimulus paragraph and items in the paragraph set).

RELIABILITY [1]

■ - Low   ■ - Medium   ■ - High   ☐ - No Information Available

	2	3	4	5	6	7	8	9	10	11	12	13	14	15	16	17	18	19 24	25 29	30 34	35 39	40 44	45 49	50 54	55 59	60 64	65 69	70 74	75 79	80 84	85 90+
Internal consistency																															
Test-retest*																															

*Interval between testings: 1 to 15 weeks

FLOORS AND CEILINGS

	Test Floor	Test Ceiling
Inadequate at ages:	5-0 to 5-2	9-8 to 12-11

CHC CLASSIFICATIONS (Broad: stratum II / Narrow: stratum I)

Crystallized Intelligence (Gc): *Listening Ability (LS)* - Ability to listen and comprehend oral communications; *Language Development (LD)* - General development, or the understanding of words, sentences, and paragraphs (not requiring reading), in spoken native language skills.

DESCRIPTION

The examinee is required to complete an analogy stated by the examiner that has a grammatical relationship.

RELIABILITY [1]

■ - Low   ■ - Medium   ■ - High   ☐ - No Information Available

	2	3	4	5	6	7	8	9	10	11	12	13	14	15	16	17	18	19 24	25 29	30 34	35 39	40 44	45 49	50 54	55 59	60 64	65 69	70 74	75 79	80 84	85 90+
Internal consistency																															
Test-retest*																															

*Interval between testings: 1 to 15 weeks

FLOORS AND CEILINGS

	Test Floor	Test Ceiling
Inadequate at ages:	7-0 to 7-2	none

CHC CLASSIFICATIONS (Broad: stratum II / Narrow: stratum I)

Crystallized Intelligence (Gc): *Grammatical Sensitivity (MY)* - Knowledge or awareness of the grammatical features of the native language.

[1]Split-half coefficients are reported as estimates of internal consistency rather than coefficient alpha.

DESCRIPTION

The examinee is required to determine whether both sentences stated by the examiner mean the same.

RELIABILITY [1]

☐ - Low   ▨ - Medium   ■ - High   ☐ - No Information Available

	2	3	4	5	6	7	8	9	10	11	12	13	14	15	16	17	18	19 24	25 29	30 34	35 39	40 44	45 49	50 54	55 59	60 64	65 69	70 74	75 79	80 84	85 90+
Internal consistency																															
Test-retest*																															

Interval between testings: 1 to 15 weeks

FLOORS AND CEILINGS

	Test Floor	**Test Ceiling**
Inadequate at ages:	none	11-0 to 21-11

CHC CLASSIFICATIONS (**Broad: stratum II** / *Narrow: stratum I*)

Crystallized Intelligence (*Gc*): *Language Development (LD)* - General development, or the understanding of words, sentences, and paragraphs (<u>not</u> requiring reading), in spoken native language skills.

DESCRIPTION

The examinee is required to judge the grammatical correctness of the sentence stated by the examiner.

RELIABILITY [1]

☐ - Low   ▨ - Medium   ■ - High   ☐ - No Information Available

	2	3	4	5	6	7	8	9	10	11	12	13	14	15	16	17	18	19 24	25 29	30 34	35 39	40 44	45 49	50 54	55 59	60 64	65 69	70 74	75 79	80 84	85 90+
Internal consistency																															
Test-retest*																															

Interval between testings: 1 to 15 weeks

FLOORS AND CEILINGS

	Test Floor	**Test Ceiling**
Inadequate at ages:	none	none

CHC CLASSIFICATIONS (**Broad: stratum II** / *Narrow: stratum I*)

Crystallized Intelligence (*Gc*): *Grammatical Sensitivity (MY)* - Knowledge or awareness of the grammatical features of the native language.

[1]Split-half coefficients are reported as estimates of internal consistency rather than coefficient alpha.

DESCRIPTION

The examinee is required to answer the question by explaining the nonliteral meaning of the item stated by the examiner.

RELIABILITY [1]

| ☐ - Low | ■ - Medium | ■ - High | ☐ - No Information Available |

	2	3	4	5	6	7	8	9	10	11	12	13	14	15	16	17	18	19 24	25 29	30 34	35 39	40 44	45 49	50 54	55 59	60 64	65 69	70 74	75 79	80 84	85 90+
Internal consistency																															
Test-retest*																															

Interval between testings: 1 to 15 weeks

FLOORS AND CEILINGS

	Test Floor	Test Ceiling
Inadequate at ages:	7-0 to 8-11	none

CHC CLASSIFICATIONS (Broad: stratum II / Narrow: stratum I)

Crystallized Intelligence (Gc): *Language Development[a] (LD)* - General development, or the understanding of words, sentences, and paragraphs (not requiring reading), in spoken native language skills; *Information About Culture[a] (K2)* - Range of cultural knowledge (e.g., music, art).

DESCRIPTION

The examinee is required to derive the meaning of the uncommon word stated by the examiner by using linguistic context clues to figure it out and then provide an explanation of the word in his or her own words.

RELIABILITY [1]

| ☐ - Low | ■ - Medium | ■ - High | ☐ - No Information Available |

	2	3	4	5	6	7	8	9	10	11	12	13	14	15	16	17	18	19 24	25 29	30 34	35 39	40 44	45 49	50 54	55 59	60 64	65 69	70 74	75 79	80 84	85 90+
Internal consistency																															
Test-retest*																															

Interval between testings: 1 to 15 weeks

FLOORS AND CEILINGS

	Test Floor	Test Ceiling
Inadequate at ages:	11-0 to 12-7	21-0 to 21-11

CHC CLASSIFICATIONS (Broad: stratum II / Narrow: stratum I)

Crystallized Intelligence (Gc): *Listening Ability[a] (LS)* - Ability to listen and comprehend oral communications; *Language Development[a] (LD)* - General development, or the understanding of words, sentences, and paragraphs (not requiring reading), in spoken native language skills.

[1] Split-half coefficients are reported as estimates of internal consistency rather than coefficient alpha.
[a] The narrow CHC classifications for this test were determined by the authors because no agreement was reached through the group consensus process.

Battery: CASL	Inference	Age Range: 7-0 to 17-11

DESCRIPTION

The examinee is required to answer a question using his or her own world knowledge to infer the missing information after the examiner reads a situation with part of the information left out.

RELIABILITY [1]

■ - Low   ■ - Medium   ■ - High   ☐ - No Information Available

	2	3	4	5	6	7	8	9	10	11	12	13	14	15	16	17	18	19 24	25 29	30 34	35 39	40 44	45 49	50 54	55 59	60 64	65 69	70 74	75 79	80 84	85 90+
Internal consistency																															
Test-retest*																															

*Interval between testings: 1 to 15 weeks

FLOORS AND CEILINGS

	Test Floor	Test Ceiling
Inadequate at ages:	7-0 to 8-2	none

CHC CLASSIFICATIONS (Broad: stratum II / Narrow: stratum I)

Crystallized Intelligence (Gc): *General Information (KO)* - Range of general knowledge.

Battery: CASL	Ambiguous Sentences	Age Range: 11-0 to 21-11

DESCRIPTION

The examinee is required to respond by explaining two possible meanings for the item stated by the examiner that contains a word or phrase that has more than one meaning.

RELIABILITY [1]

■ - Low   ■ - Medium   ■ - High   ☐ - No Information Available

	2	3	4	5	6	7	8	9	10	11	12	13	14	15	16	17	18	19 24	25 29	30 34	35 39	40 44	45 49	50 54	55 59	60 64	65 69	70 74	75 79	80 84	85 90+
Internal consistency																															
Test-retest*																															

*Interval between testings: 1 to 15 weeks

FLOORS AND CEILINGS

	Test Floor	Test Ceiling
Inadequate at ages:	11-0 to 15-11	none

CHC CLASSIFICATIONS (Broad: stratum II / Narrow: stratum I)

Crystallized Intelligence (Gc): *Lexical Knowledge (VL)* - Extent of vocabulary that can be understood in terms of correct word meanings.

---

[1]Split-half coefficients are reported as estimates of internal consistency rather than coefficient alpha.

DESCRIPTION

The examinee is required to respond with the appropriate thing to say or do in the situation stated by the examiner in a vignette.

RELIABILITY [1]

■ - Low   ■ - Medium   ■ - High   ☐ - No Information Available

	2	3	4	5	6	7	8	9	10	11	12	13	14	15	16	17	18	19 24	25 29	30 34	35 39	40 44	45 49	50 54	55 59	60 64	65 69	70 74	75 79	80 84	85 90+
Internal consistency																															
Test-retest*																															

*Interval between testings: 1 to 15 weeks

FLOORS AND CEILINGS

	Test Floor	**Test Ceiling**
Inadequate at ages:	3-0 to 4-5	13-0 to 21-11

CHC CLASSIFICATIONS (Broad: stratum II / *Narrow: stratum I*)

Crystallized Intelligence (*Gc*): *Language Development (LD)* - General development, or the understanding of words, sentences, and paragraphs (<u>not</u> requiring reading), in spoken native language skills; *General Information (KO)* - Range of general knowledge.

[1]Split-half coefficients are reported as estimates of internal consistency rather than coefficient alpha.

Comprehensive Receptive and Expressive Vocabulary Test (CREVT)

GENERAL INFORMATION

Author(s): Gerald Wallace and Donald D. Hammill
Publisher: PRO-ED
Publication Date(s): 1994

Age Range: 4-0 to 17-11
Administration Time: 20 to 30 minutes

COMPOSITE MEASURE INFORMATION

General Vocabulary

SCORE INFORMATION

Standard scores	Percentiles	Stanines	Normal curve equivalents	Age equivalents	Grade equivalents

NORMING INFORMATION

Standardization Sample Size: 1,920

Avg. Number per Age/Grade Interval:
    137 per year: 4-0 to 17-11

Age Blocks in Norm Table:
    6 months: 4-0 to 12-11
    1 year: 13-0 to 17-11

Sample Collection Date(s): Unknown

Demographic Variables:
    Gender   *- male; female*
    Geographic region   *- 4 regions; 33 states*
    Residence   *- urban; rural*
    Race/ethnicity   *- White; Black; Native American; Hispanic; Asian;*
    Other   *other*
                          - disability status (none, LD, SLD, MR. other)

VALIDITY

Types of Validity Evidence Reported in the Test Manual:

Content	Criterion	Construct

Test Review(s) and Validity Evidence Reported in Extant Literature: See Appendix C

CONTAINS AT LEAST ONE INDICATOR CONSISTENT WITH THE FOLLOWING LD ASSESSMENT AREA(S)

Oral Expression	Listening Comprehension	Written Expression	Basic Reading Skill	Reading Comprehension	Mathematics Calculation	Mathematics Reasoning

SPECIAL FEATURES

- Provides alternate forms (A and B)
- A computer administered version (CREVT-CA) is available

254

DESCRIPTION

The examinee is required to select from six pictures the one that best represents the stimulus word stated by the examiner.

RELIABILITY

☐ - Low   ■ - Medium   ■ - High   ☐ - No Information Available

	2	3	4	5	6	7	8	9	10	11	12	13	14	15	16	17	18	19-24	25-29	30-34	35-39	40-44	45-49	50-54	55-59	60-64	65-69	70-74	75-79	80-84	85-90+
Internal consistency																															
Test-retest*																															

*Interval between testings: 2 to 8 weeks

FLOORS AND CEILINGS

	Test Floor	Test Ceiling
Inadequate at ages:	none	14-0 to 17-11

CHC CLASSIFICATIONS (Broad: stratum II / Narrow: stratum I)

Crystallized Intelligence (*Gc*): *Lexical Knowledge (VL)* - Extent of vocabulary that can be understood in terms of correct word meanings.

DESCRIPTION

The examinee is required to provide oral definitions for a series of words.

RELIABILITY

☐ - Low   ■ - Medium   ■ - High   ☐ - No Information Available

	2	3	4	5	6	7	8	9	10	11	12	13	14	15	16	17	18	19-24	25-29	30-34	35-39	40-44	45-49	50-54	55-59	60-64	65-69	70-74	75-79	80-84	85-90+
Internal consistency																															
Test-retest*																															

*Interval between testings: 2 to 8 weeks

FLOORS AND CEILINGS

	Test Floor	Test Ceiling
Inadequate at ages:	5-0 to 8-5	13-0 to 17-11

CHC CLASSIFICATIONS (Broad: stratum II / Narrow: stratum I)

Crystallized Intelligence (*Gc*): *Lexical Knowledge (VL)* - Extent of vocabulary that can be understood in terms of correct word meanings.

DESCRIPTION

The examinee is required to select from six pictures the one that best represents the stimulus word stated by the examiner.

RELIABILITY

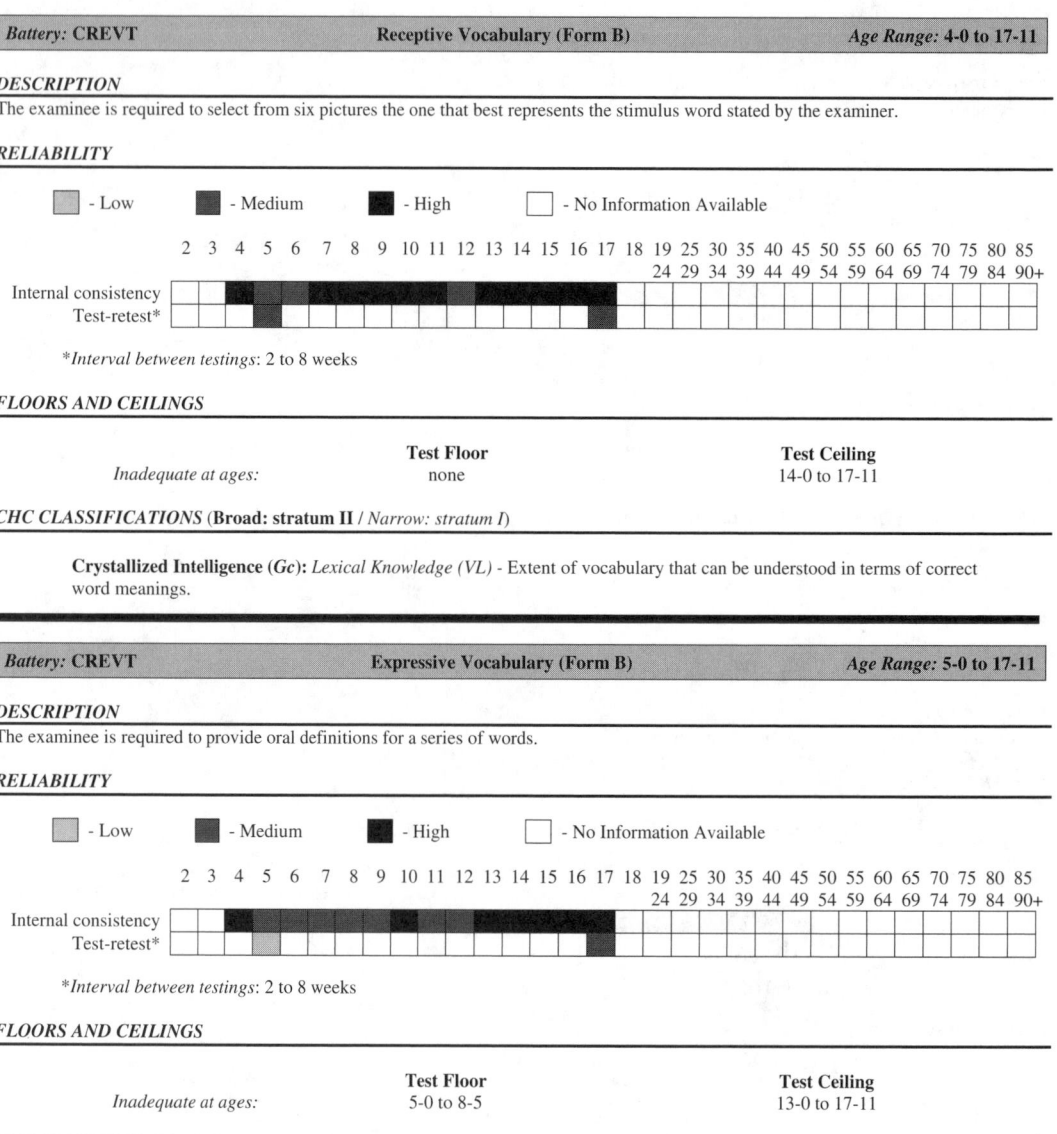

■ - Low   ■ - Medium   ■ - High   ☐ - No Information Available

	2	3	4	5	6	7	8	9	10	11	12	13	14	15	16	17	18	19 24	25 29	30 34	35 39	40 44	45 49	50 54	55 59	60 64	65 69	70 74	75 79	80 84	85 90+
Internal consistency																															
Test-retest*																															

Interval between testings: 2 to 8 weeks

FLOORS AND CEILINGS

	Test Floor	Test Ceiling
Inadequate at ages:	none	14-0 to 17-11

CHC CLASSIFICATIONS (Broad: stratum II / *Narrow: stratum I*)

Crystallized Intelligence (*Gc*): *Lexical Knowledge (VL)* - Extent of vocabulary that can be understood in terms of correct word meanings.

DESCRIPTION

The examinee is required to provide oral definitions for a series of words.

RELIABILITY

■ - Low   ■ - Medium   ■ - High   ☐ - No Information Available

	2	3	4	5	6	7	8	9	10	11	12	13	14	15	16	17	18	19 24	25 29	30 34	35 39	40 44	45 49	50 54	55 59	60 64	65 69	70 74	75 79	80 84	85 90+
Internal consistency																															
Test-retest*																															

Interval between testings: 2 to 8 weeks

FLOORS AND CEILINGS

	Test Floor	Test Ceiling
Inadequate at ages:	5-0 to 8-5	13-0 to 17-11

CHC CLASSIFICATIONS (Broad: stratum II / *Narrow: stratum I*)

Crystallized Intelligence (*Gc*): *Lexical Knowledge (VL)* - Extent of vocabulary that can be understood in terms of correct word meanings.

Comprehensive Receptive and Expressive Vocabulary Test-Adult (CREVT-A)

GENERAL INFORMATION

Author(s): Gerald Wallace and Donald D. Hammill
Publisher: PRO-ED
Publication Date(s): 1997

Age Range: 18-0 to 89-11
Administration Time: 20 to 30 minutes

COMPOSITE MEASURE INFORMATION

General Vocabulary

SCORE INFORMATION

Standard scores	Percentiles	Stanines	Normal curve equivalents	Age equivalents	Grade equivalents

NORMING INFORMATION

Standardization Sample Size: 778

Sample Collection Date(s): Unknown

Avg. Number per Age/Grade Interval:
 45 per five years: 18-0 to 29-11
 112 per ten years: 30-0 to 89-11

Age Blocks in Norm Table:
 ≥ 10 years: 18-0 to 89-11

Demographic Variables:
 Gender   *- male; female*
 Geographic region *- 4 regions; 7 states and The District of Columbia*
 Residence   *- urban; rural*
 Race/ethnicity   *- White; Black; Native American; Hispanic; Asian; other*
 SES   *- family income*

VALIDITY

Types of Validity Evidence Reported in the Test Manual:

Content	Criterion	Construct

Test Review(s) and Validity Evidence Reported in Extant Literature: None currently available

CONTAINS AT LEAST ONE INDICATOR CONSISTENT WITH THE FOLLOWING LD ASSESSMENT AREA(S)

Oral Expression	Listening Comprehension	Written Expression	Basic Reading Skill	Reading Comprehension	Mathematics Calculation	Mathematics Reasoning

SPECIAL FEATURES

- Provides alternate forms (A and B)

DESCRIPTION

The examinee is required to point to the pictures that correspond to the words stated by the examiner.

RELIABILITY

☐ - Low   ■ - Medium   ■ - High   ☐ - No Information Available

	2	3	4	5	6	7	8	9	10	11	12	13	14	15	16	17	18	19 24	25 29	30 34	35 39	40 44	45 49	50 54	55 59	60 64	65 69	70 74	75 79	80 84	85 90+
Internal consistency																															
Test-retest*																															

Interval between testings: 2 weeks

FLOORS AND CEILINGS

	Test Floor	Test Ceiling
Inadequate at ages:	none	40-0 to 59-11

CHC CLASSIFICATIONS (Broad: stratum II / *Narrow: stratum I*)

Crystallized Intelligence (Gc): *Lexical Knowledge (VL)* - Extent of vocabulary that can be understood in terms of correct word meanings.

DESCRIPTION

The examinee is required to define words orally stated by the examiner.

RELIABILITY

☐ - Low   ■ - Medium   ■ - High   ☐ - No Information Available

	2	3	4	5	6	7	8	9	10	11	12	13	14	15	16	17	18	19 24	25 29	30 34	35 39	40 44	45 49	50 54	55 59	60 64	65 69	70 74	75 79	80 84	85 90+
Internal consistency																															
Test-retest*																															

Interval between testings: 2 weeks

FLOORS AND CEILINGS

	Test Floor	Test Ceiling
Inadequate at ages:	none	18-0 to 89-11

CHC CLASSIFICATIONS (Broad: stratum II / *Narrow: stratum I*)

Crystallized Intelligence (Gc): *Lexical Knowledge (VL)* - Extent of vocabulary that can be understood in terms of correct word meanings.

DESCRIPTION

The examinee is required to point to the pictures that correspond to the words stated by the examiner.

RELIABILITY

■ - Low   ■ - Medium   ■ - High   ☐ - No Information Available

	2	3	4	5	6	7	8	9	10	11	12	13	14	15	16	17	18	19 24	25 29	30 34	35 39	40 44	45 49	50 54	55 59	60 64	65 69	70 74	75 79	80 84	85 90+
Internal consistency																															
Test-retest*																															

Interval between testings: 2 weeks

FLOORS AND CEILINGS

	Test Floor	**Test Ceiling**
Inadequate at ages:	none	40-0 to 59-11

CHC CLASSIFICATIONS (Broad: stratum II / *Narrow: stratum I*)

Crystallized Intelligence (*Gc*): *Lexical Knowledge (VL)* - Extent of vocabulary that can be understood in terms of correct word meanings.

DESCRIPTION

The examinee is required to define words orally stated by the examiner.

RELIABILITY

■ - Low   ■ - Medium   ■ - High   ☐ - No Information Available

	2	3	4	5	6	7	8	9	10	11	12	13	14	15	16	17	18	19 24	25 29	30 34	35 39	40 44	45 49	50 54	55 59	60 64	65 69	70 74	75 79	80 84	85 90+
Internal consistency																															
Test-retest*																															

Interval between testings: 2 weeks

FLOORS AND CEILINGS

	Test Floor	**Test Ceiling**
Inadequate at ages:	none	18-0 to 89-11

CHC CLASSIFICATIONS (Broad: stratum II / *Narrow: stratum I*)

Crystallized Intelligence (*Gc*): *Lexical Knowledge (VL)* - Extent of vocabulary that can be understood in terms of correct word meanings.

Expressive One-Word Picture Vocabulary Test (EO-WPVT)

GENERAL INFORMATION

Author(s): Rick Brownell
Publisher: Academic Therapy Publications
Publication Date(s): 1979, 1983, 1990, 2000

Age Range: 2-0 to 18-11
Administration Time: 10 to 15 minutes

COMPOSITE MEASURE INFORMATION

SCORE INFORMATION

Standard scores	Percentiles	Stanines	Normal curve equivalents	Age equivalents	Grade equivalents

NORMING INFORMATION

Standardization Sample Size: 2,327

Sample Collection Date(s): 1999

Avg. Number per Age/Grade Interval:
  137 per year: 2-0 to 18-11

Age Blocks in Norm Table:
  1 month: 2-0 to 4-11
  2 months: 5-0 to 10-11
  3 months: 11-0 to 18-11

Demographic Variables:
  Gender   *- male; female*
  Geographic region   *- 4 regions; 32 states; 117 cities*
  Residence   *- urban; rural*
  Race/ethnicity   *- Asian; Black; Hispanic; White; other*
  SES   *- parent education*
  Other   *- disability status (none, LD, SLD, MR, other)*

VALIDITY

Types of Validity Evidence Reported in the Test Manual:

Content	Criterion	Construct

Test Review(s) and Validity Evidence Reported in Extant Literature: See Appendix C

CONTAINS AT LEAST ONE INDICATOR CONSISTENT WITH THE FOLLOWING LD ASSESSMENT AREA(S)

Oral Expression	Listening Comprehension	Written Expression	Basic Reading Skill	Reading Comprehension	Mathematics Calculation	Mathematics Reasoning

SPECIAL FEATURES

- Includes an appendix with examples of incorrect and cued responses

DESCRIPTION

The examinee is shown a series of pictures and is asked to say the word that names each picture or group of pictures.

RELIABILITY

▨ - Low	▩ - Medium	▪ - High	☐ - No Information Available

	2	3	4	5	6	7	8	9	10	11	12	13	14	15	16	17	18	19 24	25 29	30 34	35 39	40 44	45 49	50 54	55 59	60 64	65 69	70 74	75 79	80 84	85 90+
Internal consistency																															
Test-retest*																															

*Interval between testings: 20 days

FLOORS AND CEILINGS

	Test Floor	**Test Ceiling**
Inadequate at ages:	none	none

CHC CLASSIFICATIONS (**Broad: stratum II** / *Narrow: stratum I*)

Crystallized Intelligence (*Gc*): *Lexical Knowledge (VL)* - Extent of vocabulary that can be understood in terms of correct word meanings; *Language Development (LD)* - General development, or the understanding of words, sentences, and paragraphs (not requiring reading), in spoken native language skills.

Expressive Vocabulary Test (EVT)

GENERAL INFORMATION

Author(s): Kathleen T. Williams
Publisher: American Guidance Service
Publication Date(s): 1997

Age Range: 2-6 to 90-11
Administration Time: 10 to 25 minutes

COMPOSITE MEASURE INFORMATION

SCORE INFORMATION

Standard scores	Percentiles	Stanines	Normal curve equivalents	Age equivalents	Grade equivalents

NORMING INFORMATION

Standardization Sample Size: 2,725

Sample Collection Date(s): 1995-96

Avg. Number per Age/Grade Interval:
  121 per year: 2-6 to 18-11
  138 per five years: 19-0 to 30-11
  117 per ten years: 31-0 to 60-11
  25 per ten years: 61-11 to 90-11

Demographic Variables:
  Gender   - male; female
  Geographic region - 4 regions; 46 states and The District of Columbia;
             172 communities
  Race/ethnicity - African-American; Hispanic; White; other
  SES   - parent/examinee education
  Other   - special education category (LD, SI, MR, HI, G/T)

Age Blocks in Norm Table:
  2 months: 2-6 to 6-11
  3 months: 7-0 to 18-11
  2 years: 19-0 to 24-11
  5 years: 25-0 to 40-11
  10 years: 41-0 to 90-11

VALIDITY

Types of Validity Evidence Reported in the Test Manual:

Content	Criterion	Construct

Validity Evidence Reported in Extant Literature: See Appendix C

CONTAINS AT LEAST ONE INDICATOR CONSISTENT WITH THE FOLLOWING LD ASSESSMENT AREA(S)

Oral Expression	Listening Comprehension	Written Expression	Basic Reading Skill	Reading Comprehension	Mathematics Calculation	Mathematics Reasoning

SPECIAL FEATURES

- Co-normed with the Peabody Picture Vocabulary Test-Third Edition (PPVT-III)
- Stimulus pictures are in full color and were balanced for gender and racial representations

Battery: EVT	Total Test	Age Range: 2-6 to 90-11

DESCRIPTION

The examinee is required to respond with a one-word answer that is a noun, verb, or adjective to questions asked by the examiner, and provide a synonym to a presented picture and stimulus card, within a carrier phrase.

RELIABILITY

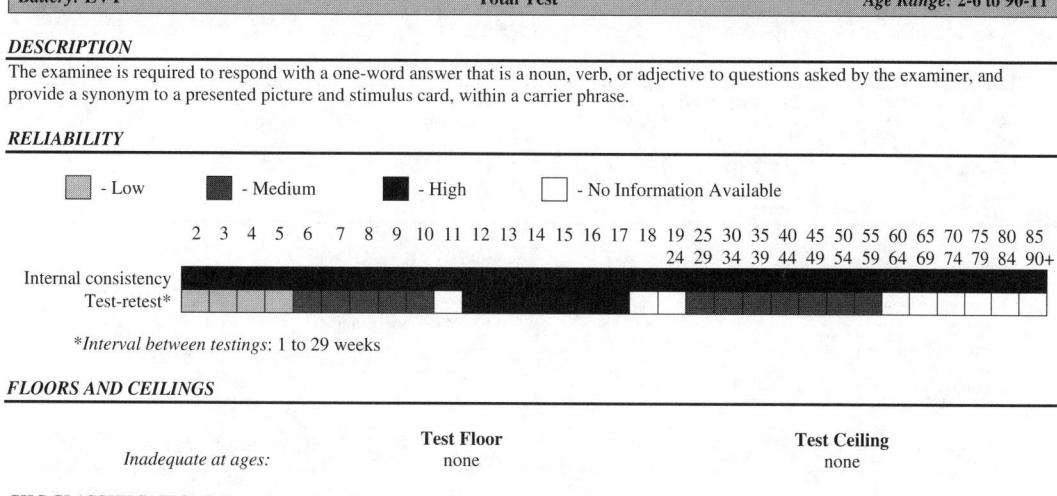

- Low   - Medium   - High   - No Information Available

	2	3	4	5	6	7	8	9	10	11	12	13	14	15	16	17	18	19 24	25 29	30 34	35 39	40 44	45 49	50 54	55 59	60 64	65 69	70 74	75 79	80 84	85 90+
Internal consistency																															
Test-retest*																															

*Interval between testings: 1 to 29 weeks

FLOORS AND CEILINGS

	Test Floor	Test Ceiling
Inadequate at ages:	none	none

CHC CLASSIFICATIONS (Broad: stratum II / Narrow: stratum I)

Crystallized Intelligence (Gc): *Lexical Knowledge[a] (VL)* - Extent of vocabulary that can be understood in terms of correct word meanings.

[a]The narrow CHC classification for this subset was determined by the authors because no agreement was reached through the group concensus process.

Illinois Test of Psycholinguistic Abilities-Third Edition (ITPA-3)

GENERAL INFORMATION

Author(s): Donald D. Hammill, Nancy Mather, and Rhia Roberts
Publisher: PRO-ED
Publication Date(s): 1961, 1968, 2001

Age Range: 5-0 to 12-11
Administration Time: 45 to 60 minutes

COMPOSITE MEASURE INFORMATION

General Language
Written Language
Grammar
Comprehension
Spelling
Sound-Symbol Processing

Spoken Language
Semantics
Phonology
Word Identification
Sight-Symbol Processing

SCORE INFORMATION

Standard scores	Percentiles	Stanines	Normal curve equivalents	Age equivalents	Grade equivalents

NORMING INFORMATION

Standardization Sample Size: 1,522

Avg. Number per Age/Grade Interval:
190 per year: 5-0 to 12-11

Age Blocks in Norm Table:
3 months: 5-0 to 10-11
1 year: 11-0 to 12-11

Sample Collection Date(s): 1999-2000

Demographic Variables:
Gender — *male; female*
Geographic region - *4 regions; 27 states*
Residence - *urban; rural*
Race/ethnicity - *White; Black; Native American; Hispanic; Asian; other*
SES - *parental education; family income*
Other - *disability status (none, LD, SLD, MR, other)*

VALIDITY

Types of Validity Evidence Reported in the Test Manual:

Content	Criterion	Construct

Test Review(s) and Validity Evidence Reported in Extant Literature: See Appendix C

CONTAINS AT LEAST ONE INDICATOR CONSISTENT WITH THE FOLLOWING LD ASSESSMENT AREA (S)

Oral Expression	Listening Comprehension	Written Expression	Basic Reading Skill	Reading Comprehension	Mathematics Reasoning	Mathematics Calculation

SPECIAL FEATURES

- Includes new subtests that are appropriate for school-age children
- Contains a description of the psycholinguistic model used in test construction to assist in test performance interpretation

DESCRIPTION

The examinee is required to state the correct word that best completes the analogy presented orally by the examiner.

RELIABILITY

■ - Low ■ - Medium ■ - High ☐ - No Information Available

	2	3	4	5	6	7	8	9	10	11	12	13	14	15	16	17	18	19-24	25-29	30-34	35-39	40-44	45-49	50-54	55-59	60-64	65-69	70-74	75-79	80-84	85-90+
Internal consistency																															
Test-retest*																															

*Interval between testings: 2 weeks

FLOORS AND CEILINGS

	Test Floor	Test Ceiling
Inadequate at ages:	5-0 to 6-5	7-9 to 12-11

CHC CLASSIFICATIONS (Broad: stratum II / Narrow: stratum I)

Crystallized Intelligence (Gc): *Lexical Knowledge[a] (VL)* - Extent of vocabulary that can be understood in terms of correct word meanings; *Language Development[a] (LD)* - General development, or the understanding of words, sentences, and paragraphs (not requiring reading), in spoken native language skills.

DESCRIPTION

The examinee is required to state a word that possesses an attribute associated with the word first stated by the examiner.

RELIABILITY

■ - Low ■ - Medium ■ - High ☐ - No Information Available

	2	3	4	5	6	7	8	9	10	11	12	13	14	15	16	17	18	19-24	25-29	30-34	35-39	40-44	45-49	50-54	55-59	60-64	65-69	70-74	75-79	80-84	85-90+
Test-retest*																															

*Interval between testings: 2 weeks

FLOORS AND CEILINGS

	Test Floor	Test Ceiling
Inadequate at ages:	5-0 to 6-5	9-0 to 12-11

CHC CLASSIFICATIONS (Broad: stratum II / Narrow: stratum I)

Crystallized Intelligence (Gc): *Language Development (LD)* - General development, or the understanding of words, sentences, and paragraphs (not requiring reading), in spoken native language skills

[a]The narrow CHC classifications for this test were determined by the authors because no agreement was reached through the group consensus process.

DESCRIPTION

The examinee is required to complete a phrase using the grammatically correct word after the phrase is presented orally by the examiner.

RELIABILITY

☐ - Low   ■ - Medium   ■ - High   ☐ - No Information Available

	2	3	4	5	6	7	8	9	10	11	12	13	14	15	16	17	18	19-24	25-29	30-34	35-39	40-44	45-49	50-54	55-59	60-64	65-69	70-74	75-79	80-84	85-90+
Internal consistency																															
Test-retest*																															

Interval between testings: 2 weeks

FLOORS AND CEILINGS

	Test Floor	Test Ceiling
Inadequate at ages:	5-0 to 11-11	7-6 to 12-11

CHC CLASSIFICATIONS (Broad: stratum II / Narrow: stratum I)

Crystallized Intelligence (Gc): *Grammatical Sensitivity (MY)* - Knowledge or awareness of the grammatical features of the native language.

DESCRIPTION

The examinee is required to repeat a series of syntactically and semantically correct nonsensical sentences as presented orally by the examiner.

RELIABILITY

☐ - Low   ■ - Medium   ■ - High   ☐ - No Information Available

	2	3	4	5	6	7	8	9	10	11	12	13	14	15	16	17	18	19-24	25-29	30-34	35-39	40-44	45-49	50-54	55-59	60-64	65-69	70-74	75-79	80-84	85-90+
Internal consistency																															
Test-retest*																															

Interval between testings: 2 weeks

FLOORS AND CEILINGS

	Test Floor	Test Ceiling
Inadequate at ages:	5-0 to 10-11	none

CHC CLASSIFICATIONS (Broad: stratum II / Narrow: stratum I)

Short-Term Memory (Gsm): *Memory Span (MS)* - Ability to attend to and immediately recall temporally ordered elements in the correct order after a single presentation.

DESCRIPTION

The examinee is required to delete word parts and phonemes from a word presented orally by the examiner.

RELIABILITY

☐ - Low   ■ - Medium   ■ - High   ☐ - No Information Available

	2	3	4	5	6	7	8	9	10	11	12	13	14	15	16	17	18	19 24	25 29	30 34	35 39	40 44	45 49	50 54	55 59	60 64	65 69	70 74	75 79	80 84	85 90+
Internal consistency																															
Test-retest*																															

Interval between testings: 2 weeks

FLOORS AND CEILINGS

	Test Floor	Test Ceiling
Inadequate at ages:	5-0 to 8-11	6-9 to 12-11

CHC CLASSIFICATIONS (Broad: stratum II / Narrow: stratum I)

Auditory Processing (Ga): *Phonetic Coding: Analysis (PC:A)* - Ability to segment larger units of speech sounds into smaller units of speech sounds.

DESCRIPTION

The examinee is required to repeat a string of words that increase in length as presented orally by the examiner.

RELIABILITY

☐ - Low   ■ - Medium   ■ - High   ☐ - No Information Available

	2	3	4	5	6	7	8	9	10	11	12	13	14	15	16	17	18	19 24	25 29	30 34	35 39	40 44	45 49	50 54	55 59	60 64	65 69	70 74	75 79	80 84	85 90+
Internal consistency																															
Test-retest*																															

Interval between testings: 2 weeks

FLOORS AND CEILINGS

	Test Floor	Test Ceiling
Inadequate at ages:	5-0 to 11-11	11-0 to 12-11

CHC CLASSIFICATIONS (Broad: stratum II / Narrow: stratum I)

Short-Term Memory (Gsm): *Memory Span (MS)* - Ability to attend to and immediately recall temporally ordered elements in the correct order after a single presentation.

DESCRIPTION

The examinee is required to read a series of sentences, then place them into a sequence to form a meaningful passage.

RELIABILITY

■ - Low   ■ - Medium   ■ - High   □ - No Information Available

	2	3	4	5	6	7	8	9	10	11	12	13	14	15	16	17	18	19 24	25 29	30 34	35 39	40 44	45 49	50 54	55 59	60 64	65 69	70 74	75 79	80 84	85 90+
Internal consistency					■	■	■	■	■	■	■																				
Test-retest*					■	■	■	■	■	■	■																				

Interval between testings: 2 weeks

FLOORS AND CEILINGS

	Test Floor	Test Ceiling
Inadequate at ages:	6-6 to 9-11	8-0 to 12-11

CHC CLASSIFICATIONS (Broad: stratum II / Narrow: stratum I)

Reading/Writing (*Grw*): *Reading Comprehension (RC)* - Ability to comprehend connected discourse during reading.

DESCRIPTION

The examinee is required to read an adjective silently and then write a noun that is appropriately associated with the adjective.

RELIABILITY

■ - Low   ■ - Medium   ■ - High   □ - No Information Available

	2	3	4	5	6	7	8	9	10	11	12	13	14	15	16	17	18	19 24	25 29	30 34	35 39	40 44	45 49	50 54	55 59	60 64	65 69	70 74	75 79	80 84	85 90+
Internal consistency					■	■	■	■	■	■	■																				
Test-retest*					■	■	■	■	■	■	■																				

Interval between testings: 2 weeks

FLOORS AND CEILINGS

	Test Floor	Test Ceiling
Inadequate at ages:	6-6 to 8-2	8-6 to 12-11

CHC CLASSIFICATIONS (Broad: stratum II / Narrow: stratum I)

Reading/Writing (*Grw*): *Verbal (printed) Language Comprehension[a] (V)* - General development, or the understanding of words, sentences, and paragraphs in native language, as measured by reading vocabulary and reading comprehension tests; *English Usage Knowledge[a] (EU)* - Knowledge of writing in the English language with respect to capitalization, punctuation, usage, and spelling.

[a]The narrow CHC classifications for this test were determined by the authors because no agreement was reached through the group consensus process.

DESCRIPTION

The examinee is required to pronounce a list of printed words that contain unusual orthographic elements or silent letters.

RELIABILITY

☐ - Low   ■ - Medium   ■ - High   ☐ - No Information Available

	2	3	4	5	6	7	8	9	10	11	12	13	14	15	16	17	18	19 24	25 29	30 34	35 39	40 44	45 49	50 54	55 59	60 64	65 69	70 74	75 79	80 84	85 90+
Internal consistency Test-retest*																															

Interval between testings: 2 weeks

FLOORS AND CEILINGS

	Test Floor	**Test Ceiling**
Inadequate at ages:	6-6 to 8-8	8-9 to 12-11

CHC CLASSIFICATIONS (**Broad: stratum II** / *Narrow: stratum I*)

Reading/Writing (*Grw*): *Reading Decoding (RD)* - Ability to recognize and decode words or pseudowords in reading.

DESCRIPTION

The examinee is required to pronounce a list of phonically regular names of make-believe creatures.

RELIABILITY

☐ - Low   ■ - Medium   ■ - High   ☐ - No Information Available

	2	3	4	5	6	7	8	9	10	11	12	13	14	15	16	17	18	19 24	25 29	30 34	35 39	40 44	45 49	50 54	55 59	60 64	65 69	70 74	75 79	80 84	85 90+
Internal consistency Test-retest*																															

Interval between testings: 2 weeks

FLOORS AND CEILINGS

	Test Floor	**Test Ceiling**
Inadequate at ages:	6-6 to 10-11	6-9 to 12-11

CHC CLASSIFICATIONS (**Broad: stratum II** / *Narrow: stratum I*)

Reading/Writing (*Grw*): *Reading Decoding (RD)* - Ability to recognize and decode words or pseudowords in reading.

DESCRIPTION

The examinee is required to fill in the missing letter(s) of words that are printed on a word list after the entire word is presented orally by the examiner.

RELIABILITY

■ - Low   ■ - Medium   ■ - High   ☐ - No Information Available

	2	3	4	5	6	7	8	9	10	11	12	13	14	15	16	17	18	19/24	25/29	30/34	35/39	40/44	45/49	50/54	55/59	60/64	65/69	70/74	75/79	80/84	85/90+
Internal consistency				■	■	■	■	■	■	■	■																				
Test-retest*				■	■	■	■	■	■	■	■																				

*Interval between testings: 2 weeks

FLOORS AND CEILINGS

	Test Floor	Test Ceiling
Inadequate at ages:	6-6 to 8-8	8-3 to 12-11

CHC CLASSIFICATIONS (Broad: stratum II / Narrow: stratum I)

Reading/Writing[a] (*Grw*): *Spelling Ability*[a] *(SG)* - Ability to spell.

DESCRIPTION

The examinee is required to write an entire nonsense word after it is presented orally by the examiner.

RELIABILITY

■ - Low   ■ - Medium   ■ - High   ☐ - No Information Available

	2	3	4	5	6	7	8	9	10	11	12	13	14	15	16	17	18	19/24	25/29	30/34	35/39	40/44	45/49	50/54	55/59	60/64	65/69	70/74	75/79	80/84	85/90+
Internal consistency				■	■	■	■	■	■	■	■																				
Test-retest*				■	■	■	■	■	■	■	■																				

*Interval between testings: 2 weeks

FLOORS AND CEILINGS

	Test Floor	Test Ceiling
Inadequate at ages:	6-6 to 9-11	7-0 to 12-11

CHC CLASSIFICATIONS (Broad: stratum II / Narrow: stratum I)

Reading/Writing (*Grw*): *Spelling Ability (SG)* - Ability to spell.

---

[a]The broad and narrow CHC classifications for this test were determined by the authors because no agreement was reached through the group consensus process.

Language Processing Test-Revised (LPT-R)

GENERAL INFORMATION

Author(s): Gail J. Richard and Mary Anne Hanner
Publisher: LinguiSystems
Publication Date(s): 1995

Age Range: 5-0 to 11-11
Administration Time: 35 minutes

COMPOSITE MEASURE INFORMATION

Total Test

SCORE INFORMATION

Standard scores	Percentiles	Stanines	Normal curve equivalents	Age equivalents	Grade equivalents

NORMING INFORMATION

Standardization Sample Size: 1,673

Sample Collection Date(s): 1994-95

Avg. Number per Age/Grade Interval:
239 per year: 5-0 to 11-11

Age Blocks in Norm Table:
6 months: 5-0 to 11-11

Demographic Variables:
Gender   - male; female
Geographic region - 5 states; 11 communities
Race/ethnicity   - Caucasians; African-Americans; Hispanic-
Americans; Asian-Americans and others

VALIDITY

Types of Validity Evidence Reported in the Test Manual:

Content	Criterion	Construct

Test Review(s) and Validity Evidence Reported in Extant Literature: See Appendix C

CONTAINS AT LEAST ONE INDICATOR CONSISTENT WITH THE FOLLOWING LD ASSESSMENT AREA(S)

Oral Expression	Listening Comprehension	Written Expression	Basic Reading Skill	Reading Comprehension	Mathematics Calculation	Mathematics Reasoning

SPECIAL FEATURES

DESCRIPTION

The examinee is required to name a series of pictures.

RELIABILITY (Not applicable)

☐ - Low   ■ - Medium   ■ - High   ☐ - No Information Available

	2	3	4	5	6	7	8	9	10	11	12	13	14	15	16	17	18	19 24	25 29	30 34	35 39	40 44	45 49	50 54	55 59	60 64	65 69	70 74	75 79	80 84	85 90+
Internal consistency																															
Test-retest*																															

   Interval between testings: not applicable

FLOORS AND CEILINGS

	Test Floor	**Test Ceiling**
Inadequate at ages:	none	none

CHC CLASSIFICATIONS (**Broad: stratum II** / *Narrow: stratum I*)

Crystallized Intelligence (*Gc*): *Lexical Knowledge[a] (VL)* - Extent of vocabulary that can be understood in terms of correct word meanings; *Language Development[a] (LD)* - General development, or the understanding of words, sentences, and paragraphs (not requiring reading), in spoken native language skills.

DESCRIPTION

The examinee is required to name the function of the specific noun presented.

RELIABILITY (Not applicable)

☐ - Low   ■ - Medium   ■ - High   ☐ - No Information Available

	2	3	4	5	6	7	8	9	10	11	12	13	14	15	16	17	18	19 24	25 29	30 34	35 39	40 44	45 49	50 54	55 59	60 64	65 69	70 74	75 79	80 84	85 90+
Internal consistency																															
Test-retest*																															

   Interval between testings: not applicable

FLOORS AND CEILINGS

	Test Floor	**Test Ceiling**
Inadequate at ages:	none	none

CHC CLASSIFICATIONS (**Broad: stratum II** / *Narrow: stratum I*)

Crystallized Intelligence (*Gc*): *Lexical Knowledge[a] (VL)* - Extent of vocabulary that can be understood in terms of correct word meanings; *Language Development[a] (LD)* - General development, or the understanding of words, sentences, and paragraphs (not requiring reading), in spoken native language skills.

[a]The narrow CHC classifications for this test were determined by the authors because no agreement was reached through the group consensus process.

Battery: LPT-R	Associations	Age Range: 5-0 to 11-11

DESCRIPTION

The examinee is required to name items that are typically associated with specific nouns presented.

RELIABILITY [1]

☐ - Low ■ - Medium ■ - High ☐ - No Information Available

	2	3	4	5	6	7	8	9	10	11	12	13	14	15	16	17	18	19/24	25/29	30/34	35/39	40/44	45/49	50/54	55/59	60/64	65/69	70/74	75/79	80/84	85/90+
Internal consistency																															
Test-retest*																															

*Interval between testings: unknown

FLOORS AND CEILINGS

	Test Floor	Test Ceiling
Inadequate at ages:	none	5-0 to 11-11

CHC CLASSIFICATIONS (Broad: stratum II / Narrow: stratum I)

Crystallized Intelligence (Gc): *Language Development (LD)* - General development, or the understanding of words, sentences, and paragraphs (not requiring reading), in spoken native language skills. **Long-Term Retrieval (Glr):** *Ideational Fluency[a] (FI)* - Ability to rapidly produce a series of ideas, words, or phrases related to a specific condition or object. Quantity not quality is emphasized. *Associational Fluency[a] (FA)* - Ability to produce rapidly words or phrases associated in meaning (semantically associated) with a given word or concept.

Battery: LPT-R	Categorization	Age Range: 5-0 to 11-11

DESCRIPTION

The examinee is required to name at least three items that belong to the specific categories presented.

RELIABILITY [1]

☐ - Low ■ - Medium ■ - High ☐ - No Information Available

	2	3	4	5	6	7	8	9	10	11	12	13	14	15	16	17	18	19/24	25/29	30/34	35/39	40/44	45/49	50/54	55/59	60/64	65/69	70/74	75/79	80/84	85/90+
Internal consistency																															
Test-retest*																															

*Interval between testings: unknown

FLOORS AND CEILINGS

	Test Floor	Test Ceiling
Inadequate at ages:	none	5-0 to 11-11

CHC CLASSIFICATIONS (Broad: stratum II / Narrow: stratum I)

Crystallized Intelligence[b] (Gc): *Language Development[b] (LD)* - General development, or the understanding of words, sentences, and paragraphs (not requiring reading), in spoken native language skills.

[1]Kuder-Richardson 20 coefficients were reported as estimates of internal consistency rather than coefficient alpha.
[a]The narrow ability CHC classifications for this test were determined by the authors because no agreement was reached through the group consensus process.
[b]The broad and narrow ability CHC classifications for this test were determined by the authors because no agreement was reached through the group consensus process.

DESCRIPTION

The examinee is required to state similar characteristics of the stimulus items.

RELIABILITY [1]

☐ - Low   ■ - Medium   ■ - High   ☐ - No Information Available

	2	3	4	5	6	7	8	9	10	11	12	13	14	15	16	17	18	19 24	25 29	30 34	35 39	40 44	45 49	50 54	55 59	60 64	65 69	70 74	75 79	80 84	85 90+
Internal consistency																															
Test-retest*																															

Interval between testings: unknown

FLOORS AND CEILINGS

	Test Floor	**Test Ceiling**
Inadequate at ages:	5-0 to 7-5	7-0 to 11-11

CHC CLASSIFICATIONS (**Broad: stratum II** / *Narrow: stratum I*)

Crystallized Intelligence (*Gc*): *Language Development (LD)* - General development, or the understanding of words, sentences, and paragraphs (<u>not</u> requiring reading), in spoken native language skills.

DESCRIPTION

The examinee is required to state the differences between the stimulus items.

RELIABILITY [1]

☐ - Low   ■ - Medium   ■ - High   ☐ - No Information Available

	2	3	4	5	6	7	8	9	10	11	12	13	14	15	16	17	18	19 24	25 29	30 34	35 39	40 44	45 49	50 54	55 59	60 64	65 69	70 74	75 79	80 84	85 90+
Internal consistency																															
Test-retest*																															

Interval between testings: unknown

FLOORS AND CEILINGS

	Test Floor	**Test Ceiling**
Inadequate at ages:	5-0 to 7-11	7-0 to 11-11

CHC CLASSIFICATIONS (**Broad: stratum II** / *Narrow: stratum I*)

Crystallized Intelligence (*Gc*): *Language Development (LD)* - General development, or the understanding of words, sentences, and paragraphs (<u>not</u> requiring reading), in spoken native language skills.

[1]Kuder-Richardson 20 coefficients were reported as estimates of internal consistency rather than coefficient alpha.

DESCRIPTION

The examinee is required to state three definitions for each stimulus word.

RELIABILITY [1]

☐ - Low   ■ - Medium   ■ - High   ☐ - No Information Available

	2	3	4	5	6	7	8	9	10	11	12	13	14	15	16	17	18	19/24	25/29	30/34	35/39	40/44	45/49	50/54	55/59	60/64	65/69	70/74	75/79	80/84	85/90+
Internal consistency					■	■	■	■	☐	☐																					
Test-retest*					■	■	■	■	■	☐																					

*Interval between testings: unknown

FLOORS AND CEILINGS

	Test Floor	Test Ceiling
Inadequate at ages:	6-0 to 8-5	7-0 to 11-11

CHC CLASSIFICATIONS (Broad: stratum II / Narrow: stratum I)

Crystallized Intelligence (Gc): *Lexical Knowledge (VL)* - Extent of vocabulary that can be understood in terms of correct word meanings.

DESCRIPTION

The examinee is required to generate specific attributes of words (e.g., function, components, color, accessory/necessity, size/shape, category, composition, location/origin).

RELIABILITY

☐ - Low   ■ - Medium   ■ - High   ☐ - No Information Available

	2	3	4	5	6	7	8	9	10	11	12	13	14	15	16	17	18	19/24	25/29	30/34	35/39	40/44	45/49	50/54	55/59	60/64	65/69	70/74	75/79	80/84	85/90+
Internal consistency																															
Test-retest*			☐	■	■	■	■	■	☐																						

*Interval between testings: unknown

FLOORS AND CEILINGS

	Test Floor	Test Ceiling
Inadequate at ages:	none	none

CHC CLASSIFICATIONS (Broad: stratum II / Narrow: stratum I)

Crystallized Intelligence (Gc): *Language Development (LD)* - General development, or the understanding of words, sentences, and paragraphs (<u>not</u> requiring reading), in spoken native language skills; *Lexical Knowledge (VL)* - Extent of vocabulary that can be understood in terms of correct word meanings.

---

[1] Kuder-Richardson 20 coefficients were reported as estimates of internal consistency rather than coefficient alpha.

Oral and Written Language Scales-List. Comp. /Oral Express. (OWLS: LC/OE)

GENERAL INFORMATION

Author(s): Elizabeth Carrow-Woolfolk
Publisher: American Guidance Service
Publication Date(s): 1995

Age Range: 3-0 to 21-11
Administration Time: 15 to 40 minutes

COMPOSITE MEASURE INFORMATION

SCORE INFORMATION

Standard scores	Percentiles	Stanines	Normal curve equivalents	Age equivalents	Grade equivalents

NORMING INFORMATION

Standardization Sample Size: 1,795

Sample Collection Date(s): 1992-1993

Avg. Number per Age/Grade Interval:
  94 per year: 3-0 to 21-11

Age Blocks in Norm Table:
  3 months: 3-0 to 8-11
  4 months: 9-0 to 13-11
  6 months: 14-0 to 18-11
  1 year: 19-0 to 21-11

Demographic Variables:
  Gender   - male; female
  Geographic region   - 4 regions; 36 states and The District of Columbia;
                112 communities
  Race/ethnicity   - Black; White; Hispanic; other
  SES   - mother's education

VALIDITY

Types of Validity Evidence Reported in the Test Manual:

Content	Criterion	Construct

Test Review(s) and Validity Evidence Reported in Extant Literature: See Appendix C

CONTAINS AT LEAST ONE INDICATOR CONSISTENT WITH THE FOLLOWING LD ASSESSMENT AREA(S)

Oral Expression	Listening Comprehension	Written Expression	Basic Reading Skill	Reading Comprehension	Mathematics Calculation	Mathematics Reasoning

SPECIAL FEATURES

- Can be administered individually or in a group
- Co-normed with the Written Expression Scale that together yield an overall Language Composite
- Contains a chapter in the manual that discusses a well-defined theory of language to assist in test performance interpretation
- Contains an appendix with grammar and usage guidelines

Battery: OWLS: LC/OE	Listening Comprehension Scale	Age Range: 3-0 to 21-11

DESCRIPTION

The examinee is required to listen to a verbal stimulus stated by the examiner and then point to one of four pictures (or state the number of the picture) that corresponds to the stimulus.

RELIABILITY [1]

☐ - Low ■ - Medium ■ - High ☐ - No Information Available

	2	3	4	5	6	7	8	9	10	11	12	13	14	15	16	17	18	19 24	25 29	30 34	35 39	40 44	45 49	50 54	55 59	60 64	65 69	70 74	75 79	80 84	85 90+
Internal consistency																															
Test-retest*																															

*Interval between testings: 3 to 24 weeks

FLOORS AND CEILINGS

	Test Floor	Test Ceiling
Inadequate at ages:	3-0 to 3-2	none

CHC CLASSIFICATIONS (Broad: stratum II / Narrow: stratum I)

Crystallized Intelligence (Gc): *Listening Ability[a] (LS)* - Ability to listen and comprehend oral communications; *Language Development[a] (LD)* - General development, or the understanding of words, sentences, and paragraphs (not requiring reading), in spoken native language skills.

Battery: OWLS: LC/OE	Oral Expression Scale	Age Range: 3-0 to 21-11

DESCRIPTION

The examinee is required to respond orally by answering a question, completing a sentence, or generating one or more sentences to a verbal stimulus and picture provided by the examiner.

RELIABILITY [1]

☐ - Low ■ - Medium ■ - High ☐ - No Information Available

	2	3	4	5	6	7	8	9	10	11	12	13	14	15	16	17	18	19 24	25 29	30 34	35 39	40 44	45 49	50 54	55 59	60 64	65 69	70 74	75 79	80 84	85 90+
Internal consistency																															
Test-retest*																															

*Interval between testings: 3 to 24 weeks

FLOORS AND CEILINGS

	Test Floor	Test Ceiling
Inadequate at ages:	none	none

CHC CLASSIFICATIONS (Broad: stratum II / Narrow: stratum I)

Crystallized Intelligence (Gc): *Communication Ability[a] (CM)* - Ability to speak in "real life" situations (e.g., lecture, group participation) in an adult-like manner; *Oral Production and Fluency[a] (OP)* - More specific or narrow oral communication skills than reflected by Communication Ability (CM); *Language Development[a] (LD)* - General development, or the understanding of words, sentences, and paragraphs (not requiring reading), in spoken native language skills.

[1]Item response theory coefficients were reported as estimates of internal consistency rather than coefficient alpha.
[a]The narrow ability CHC classifications for this test were determined by the authors because no agreement was reached through the group consensus process.

Peabody Picture Vocabulary Test III (PPVT III)

GENERAL INFORMATION

Author(s): Lloyd M. Dunn and Leota M. Dunn
Publisher: American Guidance Service
Publication Date(s): 1959, 1981, 1997

Age Range: 2-6 to 90-11
Administration Time: 8 to 16 minutes

COMPOSITE MEASURE INFORMATION

SCORE INFORMATION

Standard scores	Percentiles	Stanines	Normal curve equivalents	Age equivalents	Grade equivalents

NORMING INFORMATION

Standardization Sample Size: 2,725

Sample Collection Date(s): 1995-1996

Avg. Number per Age/Grade Interval:
121 per year: 2-6 to 18-11
115 per five years: 19-0 to 30-11
117 per ten years: 31-0 to 60-11
<100 per ten years: 61-0 to 90-11

Demographic Variables:
Gender   - male; female
Geographic region - 4 regions
Race/ethnicity   - African-American; Hispanic; White; other
SES   - parent/examinee education
Other   - special education category (LD, SI, MR, HI, G/T)

Age Blocks in Norm Table:
2 months: 2-6 to 6-11
3 months: 7-0 to 18-11
2 years: 19-0 to 24-11
5 years: 25-0 to 40-11
10 years: 41-0 to 90-11

VALIDITY

Types of Validity Evidence Reported in the Test Manual:

Content	Criterion	Construct

Test Review(s) and Validity Evidence Reported in Extant Literature: See Appendix C

CONTAINS AT LEAST ONE INDICATOR CONSISTENT WITH THE FOLLOWING LD ASSESSMENT AREA(S)

Oral Expression	Listening Comprehension	Written Expression	Basic Reading Skill	Reading Comprehension	Mathematics Calculation	Mathematics Reasoning

SPECIAL FEATURES

- Provides alternate test forms (A and B)
- Includes training items to ensure initial success
- Uses critical range testing by sets

| *Battery:* **PPVT III** | **Form IIIA** | *Age Range:* **2-6 to 90-11** |

DESCRIPTION

The examinee is required to select from four pictures the one that best represents the word stated by the examiner.

RELIABILITY

☐ - Low   ■ - Medium   ■ - High   ☐ - No Information Available

2 3 4 5 6 7 8 9 10 11 12 13 14 15 16 17 18 19 25 30 35 40 45 50 55 60 65 70 75 80 85
                                                    24 29 34 39 44 49 54 59 64 69 74 79 84 90+

Internal consistency
Test-retest*

*Interval between testings: 4 weeks

FLOORS AND CEILINGS

	Test Floor	**Test Ceiling**
Inadequate at ages:	none	none

CHC CLASSIFICATIONS (**Broad: stratum II** / *Narrow: stratum I*)

Crystallized Intelligence (*Gc*): *Lexical Knowledge (VL)* - Extent of vocabulary that can be understood in terms of correct word meanings.

| *Battery:* **PPVT III** | **Form IIIB** | *Age Range:* **2-6 to 90-11** |

DESCRIPTION

The examinee is required to select from four pictures the one that best represents the word stated by the examiner.

RELIABILITY

☐ - Low   ■ - Medium   ■ - High   ☐ - No Information Available

2 3 4 5 6 7 8 9 10 11 12 13 14 15 16 17 18 19 25 30 35 40 45 50 55 60 65 70 75 80 85
                                                    24 29 34 39 44 49 54 59 64 69 74 79 84 90+

Internal consistency
Test-retest*

*Interval between testings: 4 weeks

FLOORS AND CEILINGS

	Test Floor	**Test Ceiling**
Inadequate at ages:	none	none

CHC CLASSIFICATIONS (**Broad: stratum II** / *Narrow: stratum I*)

Crystallized Intelligence (*Gc*): *Lexical Knowledge (VL)* - Extent of vocabulary that can be understood in terms of correct word meanings.

Receptive One-Word Picture Vocabulary Test (RO-WPVT)

GENERAL INFORMATION

Author(s): Rick Brownell
Publisher: Academic Therapy Publications
Publication Date(s): 1985, 1987, 2000

Age Range: 2-0 to 18-11
Administration Time: 10 to 15 minutes

COMPOSITE MEASURE INFORMATION

SCORE INFORMATION

Standard scores	Percentiles	Stanines	Normal curve equivalents	Age equivalents	Grade equivalents

NORMING INFORMATION

Standardization Sample Size: 2,327

Sample Collection Date(s): 1999

Avg. Number per Age/Grade Interval:
137 per year: 2-0 to 18-11

Age Blocks in Norm Table:
1 month: 2-0 to 4-11
2 months: 5-0 to 10-11
3 months: 11-0 to 18-11

Demographic Variables:
Gender   *- male; female*
Geographic region   *- 4 regions; 32 states; 117 cities*
Residence   *- urban; rural*
Race/ethnicity   *- Asian; Black; Hispanic; White; other*
SES   *- parent education*
Other   *- disability status (none, LD, SLD, MR, other)*

VALIDITY

Types of Validity Evidence Reported in the Test Manual:

Content	Criterion	Construct

Test Review(s) and Validity Evidence Reported in Extant Literature: See Appendix C

CONTAINS AT LEAST ONE INDICATOR CONSISTENT WITH THE FOLLOWING LD ASSESSMENT AREA(S)

Oral Expression	Listening Comprehension	Written Expression	Basic Reading Skill	Reading Comprehension	Mathematics Calculation	Mathematics Reasoning

SPECIAL FEATURES

DESCRIPTION

The examinee is required to point to the pictures that correspond to the words stated by the examiner.

RELIABILITY

☐ - Low   ■ - Medium   ■ - High   ☐ - No Information Available

	2	3	4	5	6	7	8	9	10	11	12	13	14	15	16	17	18	19/24	25/29	30/34	35/39	40/44	45/49	50/54	55/59	60/64	65/69	70/74	75/79	80/84	85/90+
Internal consistency																															
Test-retest*																															

*Interval between testings: 3 weeks

FLOORS AND CEILINGS

	Test Floor	Test Ceiling
Inadequate at ages:	none	none

CHC CLASSIFICATIONS (Broad: stratum II / Narrow: stratum I)

Crystallized Intelligence (Gc): *Lexical Knowledge (VL)* - Extent of vocabulary that can be understood in terms of correct word meanings.

Test of Adolescent and Adult Language-Third Edition (TOAL-3)

GENERAL INFORMATION

Author(s): Donald D. Hammill, Virginia L. Brown, Stephen C. Larson, and J. Lee Wiederholt
Publisher: PRO-ED
Publication Date(s): 1980, 1987, 1994

Age Range: 12-0 to 24-11

Administration Time: 1 to 3 hours

COMPOSITE MEASURE INFORMATION

Listening
Reading
Spoken Language
Vocabulary
Receptive Language
General Language

Speaking
Writing
Written Language
Grammar
Expressive Language

SCORE INFORMATION

Standard scores	Percentiles	Stanines	Normal curve equivalents	Age equivalents	Grade equivalents

NORMING INFORMATION

Standardization Sample Size: 3,056

Avg. Number per Age/Grade Interval:
379 per year: 12-0 to 18-11
61 per five years: 19-0 to 24-11

Age Blocks in Norm Table:
6 months: 12-0 to 16-11
2 years: 17-0 to 18-11
6 years: 19-0 to 24-11

Sample Collection Date(s): 1980; 1986-1987; 1993

Demographic Variables:
Gender	*- male; female*
Geographic region	*- 4 regions; 26 states*
Residence	*- urban; rural*
Race/ethnicity	*- White; Black; Native American/Eskimo/Aleut; Hispanic; Oriental/Pacific Islander*
Other	*- post-secondary status (3 categories)*

VALIDITY

Types of Validity Evidence Reported in the Test Manual:

Content	Criterion	Construct

Test Review(s) and Validity Evidence Reported in Extant Literature: See Appendix C

CONTAINS AT LEAST ONE INDICATOR CONSISTENT WITH THE FOLLOWING LD ASSESSMENT AREA(S)

Oral Expression	Listening Comprehension	Written Expression	Basic Reading Skill	Reading Comprehension	Mathematics Calculation	Mathematics Reasoning

SPECIAL FEATURES

- Provides computer scoring and interpretive profiling report
- Includes lists of additional resources that focus specifically on language/learning disabilities
- Provides a checklist for reducing error variance attributable to examiners/scorers
- Six subtests can be administered individually or in a group

DESCRIPTION

The examinee is required to decide which two of four pictures best depict a stimulus word that is spoken by the examiner.

RELIABILITY

☐ - Low   ■ - Medium   ■ - High   ☐ - No Information Available

	2	3	4	5	6	7	8	9	10	11	12	13	14	15	16	17	18	19 24	25 29	30 34	35 39	40 44	45 49	50 54	55 59	60 64	65 69	70 74	75 79	80 84	85 90+
Internal consistency																															
Test-retest*																															

Interval between testings: 2 weeks

FLOORS AND CEILINGS

	Test Floor	**Test Ceiling**
Inadequate at ages:	none	19-0 to 24-11

CHC CLASSIFICATIONS (**Broad: stratum II** / *Narrow: stratum I*)

Crystallized Intelligence (Gc): *Lexical Knowledge (VL)* - Extent of vocabulary that can be understood in terms of correct word meanings.

DESCRIPTION

The examiner is required to indicate which two of three sentences read by the examiner have the same meaning.

RELIABILITY

☐ - Low   ■ - Medium   ■ - High   ☐ - No Information Available

	2	3	4	5	6	7	8	9	10	11	12	13	14	15	16	17	18	19 24	25 29	30 34	35 39	40 44	45 49	50 54	55 59	60 64	65 69	70 74	75 79	80 84	85 90+
Internal consistency																															
Test-retest*																															

Interval between testings: 2 weeks

FLOORS AND CEILINGS

	Test Floor	**Test Ceiling**
Inadequate at ages:	none	16-0 to 24-11

CHC CLASSIFICATIONS (**Broad: stratum II** / *Narrow: stratum I*)

Crystallized Intelligence (Gc): *Language Development (LD)* - General development, or the understanding of words, sentences, and paragraphs (not requiring reading), in spoken native language skills.

DESCRIPTION

The examinee is required to use a word stated by the examiner in a sentence.

RELIABILITY

☐ - Low   ■ - Medium   ■ - High   ☐ - No Information Available

	2	3	4	5	6	7	8	9	10	11	12	13	14	15	16	17	18	19/24	25/29	30/34	35/39	40/44	45/49	50/54	55/59	60/64	65/69	70/74	75/79	80/84	85/90+
Internal consistency																															
Test-retest*																															

Interval between testings: 2 weeks

FLOORS AND CEILINGS

	Test Floor	**Test Ceiling**
Inadequate at ages:	none	14-6 to 24-11

CHC CLASSIFICATIONS (Broad: stratum II / *Narrow: stratum I*)

Crystallized Intelligence (*Gc*): *Oral Production and Fluency (OP)* - More specific or narrow oral communication skills than reflected by Communication Ability (CM).

DESCRIPTION

The examinee is required to repeat verbatim a series of grammatically complex sentences stated by the examiner.

RELIABILITY

☐ - Low   ■ - Medium   ■ - High   ☐ - No Information Available

	2	3	4	5	6	7	8	9	10	11	12	13	14	15	16	17	18	19/24	25/29	30/34	35/39	40/44	45/49	50/54	55/59	60/64	65/69	70/74	75/79	80/84	85/90+
Internal consistency																															
Test-retest*																															

Interval between testings: 2 weeks

FLOORS AND CEILINGS

	Test Floor	**Test Ceiling**
Inadequate at ages:	none	none

CHC CLASSIFICATIONS (Broad: stratum II / *Narrow: stratum I*)

Short-Term Memory (*Gsm*): *Memory Span (MS)* - Ability to tend to and immediately recall temporally ordered elements in the correct order after a single presentation.

DESCRIPTION

The examinee is required to read silently three stimulus words that are related to a common concept and then select from four printed words the two words that are most closely related to the three stimulus words.

RELIABILITY

☐ - Low ■ - Medium ■ - High ☐ - No Information Available

	2	3	4	5	6	7	8	9	10	11	12	13	14	15	16	17	18	19 24	25 29	30 34	35 39	40 44	45 49	50 54	55 59	60 64	65 69	70 74	75 79	80 84	85 90+
Internal consistency Test-retest*											■	■	■	☐	☐	☐	☐	■													

*Interval between testings: 2 weeks

FLOORS AND CEILINGS

	Test Floor	**Test Ceiling**
Inadequate at ages:	none	15-6 to 24-11

CHC CLASSIFICATIONS (**Broad: stratum II** / *Narrow: stratum I*)

Reading/Writing (*Grw*): *Verbal (printed) Language Comprehension (V)* - General development or the understanding of words, sentences, and paragraphs in native language, as measured by reading vocabulary and reading comprehension tests.

DESCRIPTION

The examinee is required to read silently five sentences and then select the two sentences that are most similar in meaning.

RELIABILITY

☐ - Low ■ - Medium ■ - High ☐ - No Information Available

	2	3	4	5	6	7	8	9	10	11	12	13	14	15	16	17	18	19 24	25 29	30 34	35 39	40 44	45 49	50 54	55 59	60 64	65 69	70 74	75 79	80 84	85 90+
Internal consistency Test-retest*											■	■	☐	☐	■	■	■	☐													

*Interval between testings: 2 weeks

FLOORS AND CEILINGS

	Test Floor	**Test Ceiling**
Inadequate at ages:	none	12-0 to 24-11

CHC CLASSIFICATIONS (**Broad: stratum II** / *Narrow: stratum I*)

Reading/Writing (*Grw*): *Verbal (printed) Language Comprehension (V)* - General development or the understanding of words, sentences, and paragraphs in native language, as measured by reading vocabulary and reading comprehension tests.

DESCRIPTION

The examinee is required to read a word and then use the word properly in a written sentence.

RELIABILITY

☐ - Low   ■ - Medium   ■ - High   ☐ - No Information Available

	2	3	4	5	6	7	8	9	10	11	12	13	14	15	16	17	18	19 24	25 29	30 34	35 39	40 44	45 49	50 54	55 59	60 64	65 69	70 74	75 79	80 84	85 90+
Internal consistency																															
Test-retest*																															

*Interval between testings: 2 weeks

FLOORS AND CEILINGS

	Test Floor	Test Ceiling
Inadequate at ages:	none	15-6 to 24-11

CHC CLASSIFICATIONS (Broad: stratum II / Narrow: stratum I)

Reading/Writing (Grw): *Writing Ability (WA)* - Ability to write with the clarity of thought, organization, and good sentence structure; *Verbal (printed) Language Comprehension (V)* - General development or the understanding of words, sentences, and paragraphs in native language, as measured by reading vocabulary and reading comprehension tests.

DESCRIPTION

The examinee is required to read two or more sentences and combine them into a single grammatically and syntactically acceptable written sentence.

RELIABILITY

☐ - Low   ■ - Medium   ■ - High   ☐ - No Information Available

	2	3	4	5	6	7	8	9	10	11	12	13	14	15	16	17	18	19 24	25 29	30 34	35 39	40 44	45 49	50 54	55 59	60 64	65 69	70 74	75 79	80 84	85 90+
Internal consistency																															
Test-retest*																															

*Interval between testings: 2 weeks

FLOORS AND CEILINGS

	Test Floor	Test Ceiling
Inadequate at ages:	none	15-6 to 24-11

CHC CLASSIFICATIONS (Broad: stratum II / Narrow: stratum I)

Reading/Writing (Grw): *Writing Ability (WA)* - Ability to write with the clarity of thought, organization, and good sentence structure; *English Usage Knowledge (EU)* - Knowledge of writing in the English language with respect to capitalization, punctuation, usage, and spelling.

Test of Early Language Development-Third Edition (TELD-3)

GENERAL INFORMATION

Author(s): Wayne P. Hresko, D. Kim Reid, and Donald D. Hammill

Publisher: PRO-ED

Publication Date(s): 1981, 1991, 1999

Age Range: 2-0 to 7-11

Administration Time: 15 to 40 minutes

COMPOSITE MEASURE INFORMATION

Spoken Language Quotient

SCORE INFORMATION

Standard scores	Percentiles	Stanines	Normal curve equivalents	Age equivalents	Grade equivalents

NORMING INFORMATION

Standardization Sample Size: 2,217

Avg. Number per Age/Grade Interval:
370 per year: 2-0 to 7-11

Age Blocks in Norm Table:
3 months: 2-0 to 5-11
6 months: 6-0 to 7-11

Sample Collection Date(s): 1990-1991; 1996-1997

Demographic Variables:

Gender	- male; female
Geographic region	- 4 regions; 35 states
Residence	- urban; rural
Race/ethnicity	- White; Black; Native American/Eskimo/Aleut; Hispanic; Asian
SES	- parent education; family income
Other	- disability status (none, LD, SLD, MR, other)

VALIDITY

Types of Validity Evidence Reported in the Test Manual:

Content	Criterion	Construct

Test Review(s) and Validity Evidence Reported in Extant Literature: See Appendix C

CONTAINS AT LEAST ONE INDICATOR CONSISTENT WITH THE FOLLOWING LD ASSESSMENT AREA(S)

Oral Expression	Listening Comprehension	Written Expression	Basic Reading Skill	Reading Comprehension	Mathematics Calculation	Mathematics Reasoning

SPECIAL FEATURES

- Provides alternate forms (A and B)
- Addresses the reliability of parental reporting
- Pictures are in color to make them more appealing to children

DESCRIPTION

For younger children, parents or caregivers are required to provide information about their children's receptive language abilities (e.g., whether the child attends when his or her name is called). More advanced items require the examinee to point to different objects and to follow simple commands. Near the end of the test, the examinee is required to provide responses to more complex questions ("Does lamp go with light or dark?").

RELIABILITY

☐ - Low   ■ - Medium   ■ - High   ☐ - No Information Available

	2	3	4	5	6	7	8	9	10	11	12	13	14	15	16	17	18	19 24	25 29	30 34	35 39	40 44	45 49	50 54	55 59	60 64	65 69	70 74	75 79	80 84	85 90+
Internal consistency																															
Test-retest*																															

Interval between testings: 2 weeks

FLOORS AND CEILINGS

	Test Floor	**Test Ceiling**
Inadequate at ages:	2-0 to 2-11	5-9 to 7-11

CHC CLASSIFICATIONS (Broad: stratum II / *Narrow: stratum I*)

Crystallized Intelligence (*Gc*): *Listening Ability[a] (LS)* - Ability to listen and comprehend oral communications; *Language Development[a] (LD)* - General development, or the understanding of words, sentences, and paragraphs (not requiring reading), in spoken native language skills.

DESCRIPTION

For younger children, parents or caregivers are required to provide information about their children's expressive language abilities (e.g., size of their vocabulary). Other items require the examinee to repeat sentences and respond to various simple questions (e.g., How old are you?). Near the end of the test, the examinee is required to answer more complex questions ("What does the word paddle mean?").

RELIABILITY

☐ - Low   ■ - Medium   ■ - High   ☐ - No Information Available

	2	3	4	5	6	7	8	9	10	11	12	13	14	15	16	17	18	19 24	25 29	30 34	35 39	40 44	45 49	50 54	55 59	60 64	65 69	70 74	75 79	80 84	85 90+
Internal consistency																															
Test-retest*																															

Interval between testings: 2 weeks

FLOORS AND CEILINGS

	Test Floor	**Test Ceiling**
Inadequate at ages:	2-0 to 2-8	5-0 to 7-11

CHC CLASSIFICATIONS (Broad: stratum II / *Narrow: stratum I*)

Crystallized Intelligence (*Gc*): *Oral Production and Fluency[a] (OP)* - More specific or narrow oral communication skills than reflected by Communication Ability (CM); *Language Development[a] (LD)* - General development, or the understanding of words, sentences, and paragraphs (not requiring reading), in spoken native language skills.

[a]The narrow CHC classifications for this test were determined by the authors because no agreement was reached through the group consensus process.

DESCRIPTION

For younger children, parents or caregivers are required to provide information about their children's receptive language abilities (e.g., whether the child attends when his or her name is called). More advanced items require the examinee to point to different objects and to follow simple commands. Near the end of the test, the examinee is required to provide responses to more complex questions ("Does lamp go with light or dark?").

RELIABILITY

☐ - Low   ■ - Medium   ■ - High   ☐ - No Information Available

	2	3	4	5	6	7	8	9	10	11	12	13	14	15	16	17	18	19-24	25-29	30-34	35-39	40-44	45-49	50-54	55-59	60-64	65-69	70-74	75-79	80-84	85-90+
Internal consistency																															
Test-retest*																															

Interval between testings: 2 weeks

FLOORS AND CEILINGS

	Test Floor	Test Ceiling
Inadequate at ages:	2-0 to 2-11	5-9 to 7-11

CHC CLASSIFICATIONS (Broad: stratum II / *Narrow: stratum I*)

Crystallized Intelligence (Gc): *Listening Ability[a] (LS)* - Ability to listen and comprehend oral communications; *Language Development[a] (LD)* - General development, or the understanding of words, sentences, and paragraphs (not requiring reading), in spoken native language skills.

DESCRIPTION

For younger children, parents or caregivers are required to provide information about their children's expressive language abilities (e.g., size of their vocabulary). Other items require the examinee to repeat sentences and respond to various simple questions (e.g., How old are you?). Near the end of the test, the examinee is required to answer more complex questions ("What does the word paddle mean?").

RELIABILITY

☐ - Low   ■ - Medium   ■ - High   ☐ - No Information Available

	2	3	4	5	6	7	8	9	10	11	12	13	14	15	16	17	18	19-24	25-29	30-34	35-39	40-44	45-49	50-54	55-59	60-64	65-69	70-74	75-79	80-84	85-90+
Internal consistency																															
Test-retest*																															

Interval between testings: 2 weeks

FLOORS AND CEILINGS

	Test Floor	Test Ceiling
Inadequate at ages:	2-0 to 2-8	5-0 to 7-11

CHC CLASSIFICATIONS (Broad: stratum II / *Narrow: stratum I*)

Crystallized Intelligence (Gc): *Oral Production and Fluency[a] (OP)* - More specific or narrow oral communication skills than reflected by Communication Ability (CM); *Language Development[a] (LD)* - General development, or the understanding of words, sentences, and paragraphs (not requiring reading), in spoken native language skills.

[a]The narrow CHC classifications for this test were determined by the authors because no agreement was reached through the group consensus process.

Test of Language Development-Intermediate: Third Edition (TOLD-I:3)

GENERAL INFORMATION

Author(s): Donald D. Hammill and Phyllis L. Newcomer
Publisher: PRO-ED
Publication Date(s): 1977, 1982, 1988, 1997

Age Range: 8-0 to 12-11
Administration Time: 60 minutes

COMPOSITE MEASURE INFORMATION

Spoken Language
Speaking
Syntax

Listening
Semantics

SCORE INFORMATION

Standard scores	Percentiles	Stanines	Normal curve equivalents	Age equivalents	Grade equivalents

NORMING INFORMATION

Standardization Sample Size: 779

Sample Collection Date(s): 1996

Avg. Number per Age/Grade Interval:
  156 per year: 8-0 to 12-11

Age Blocks in Norm Table:
  6 months: 8-0 to 12-11

Demographic Variables:
  Gender - *male; female*
  Geographic region - *4 regions; 23 states*
  Residence - *urban; rural*
  Race/ethnicity - *White; Black; Native American; Hispanic; Asian; other*
  SES - *parent education*
  Other - *disability status (none, LD, SLD, MR, other)*

VALIDITY

Types of Validity Evidence Reported in the Test Manual:

Content	Criterion	Construct

Test Review(s) and Validity Evidence Reported in Extant Literature: See Appendix C

CONTAINS AT LEAST ONE INDICATOR CONSISTENT WITH THE FOLLOWING LD ASSESSMENT AREA(S)

Oral Expression	Listening Comprehension	Written Expression	Basic Reading Skill	Reading Comprehension	Mathematics Calculation	Mathematics Reasoning

SPECIAL FEATURES

DESCRIPTION

The examinee is required to form one compound or complex sentence from two or more simple sentences stated by the examiner.

RELIABILITY [1]

■ - Low   ■ - Medium   ■ - High   □ - No Information Available

	2	3	4	5	6	7	8	9	10	11	12	13	14	15	16	17	18	19 24	25 29	30 34	35 39	40 44	45 49	50 54	55 59	60 64	65 69	70 74	75 79	80 84	85 90+
Internal consistency																															
Test-retest*																															

Interval between testings: 1 week

FLOORS AND CEILINGS

	Test Floor	Test Ceiling
Inadequate at ages:	8-0 to 9-5	12-0 to 12-11

CHC CLASSIFICATIONS (Broad: stratum II / *Narrow: stratum I*)

Crystallized Intelligence (Gc): *Language Development[a] (LD)* - General development, or the understanding of words, sentences, and paragraphs (not requiring reading), in spoken native language skills.

DESCRIPTION

The examinee is required to point to the picture that best represents the stimulus phrase stated by the examiner.

RELIABILITY [1]

■ - Low   ■ - Medium   ■ - High   □ - No Information Available

	2	3	4	5	6	7	8	9	10	11	12	13	14	15	16	17	18	19 24	25 29	30 34	35 39	40 44	45 49	50 54	55 59	60 64	65 69	70 74	75 79	80 84	85 90+
Internal consistency																															
Test-retest*																															

Interval between testings: 1 week

FLOORS AND CEILINGS

	Test Floor	Test Ceiling
Inadequate at ages:	none	12-0 to 12-11

CHC CLASSIFICATIONS (Broad: stratum II / *Narrow: stratum I*)

Crystallized Intelligence (Gc): *Language Development (LD)* - General development, or the understanding of words, sentences, and paragraphs (not requiring reading), in spoken native language skills.

[1]Test-retest coefficients were reported by grade in the test manual. Therefore, corresponding ages were estimated by the authors.
[a]The narrow CHC classification for this test was determined by the authors because no agreement was reached through the group consensus process.

DESCRIPTION

The examinee is required to reorder a series of randomly ordered words stated by the examiner to form a complete, correct sentence.

RELIABILITY [1]

☐ - Low   ■ - Medium   ■ - High   ☐ - No Information Available

	2	3	4	5	6	7	8	9	10	11	12	13	14	15	16	17	18	19/24	25/29	30/34	35/39	40/44	45/49	50/54	55/59	60/64	65/69	70/74	75/79	80/84	85/90+
Internal consistency							■	■	■	■	■																				
Test-retest*									■	■	■																				

*Interval between testings: 1 week

FLOORS AND CEILINGS

	Test Floor	Test Ceiling
Inadequate at ages:	8-0 to 8-11	12-0 to 12-11

CHC CLASSIFICATIONS (Broad: stratum II / Narrow: stratum I)[2]

Crystallized Intelligence (Gc): *Listening Ability (LS)* - Ability to listen and comprehend oral communications. **Short-Term Memory (Gsm):** *Working Memory (MW)* - Ability to temporarily store and perform a set of cognitive operations on information that requires divided attention and the management of the limited capacity of short-term memory.

DESCRIPTION

The examinee is required to listen to three words stated by the examiner, then describe how the three words are "alike."

RELIABILITY [1]

☐ - Low   ■ - Medium   ■ - High   ☐ - No Information Available

	2	3	4	5	6	7	8	9	10	11	12	13	14	15	16	17	18	19/24	25/29	30/34	35/39	40/44	45/49	50/54	55/59	60/64	65/69	70/74	75/79	80/84	85/90+
Internal consistency							■	■	■	■	■																				
Test-retest*									■	■																					

*Interval between testings: 1 week

FLOORS AND CEILINGS

	Test Floor	Test Ceiling
Inadequate at ages:	8-0 to 10-5	12-0 to 12-11

CHC CLASSIFICATIONS (Broad: stratum II / Narrow: stratum I)

Crystallized Intelligence (Gc): *Language Development (LD)* - General development, or the understanding of words, sentences, and paragraphs (not requiring reading), in spoken native language skills.

[1]Test-retest coefficients were reported by grade in the test manual. Therefore, corresponding ages were estimated by the authors.
[2]This subtest was not included in the expert consensus process. Classifications were made by the authors.

DESCRIPTION

The examinee is required to listen to sentences stated by the examiner and identify which sentences are grammatically incorrect.

RELIABILITY [1]

☐ - Low   ■ - Medium   ■ - High   ☐ - No Information Available

	2	3	4	5	6	7	8	9	10	11	12	13	14	15	16	17	18	19 24	25 29	30 34	35 39	40 44	45 49	50 54	55 59	60 64	65 69	70 74	75 79	80 84	85 90+
Internal consistency																															
Test-retest*																															

Interval between testings: 1 week

FLOORS AND CEILINGS

	Test Floor	Test Ceiling
Inadequate at ages:	8-0 to 11-5	12-0 to 12-11

CHC CLASSIFICATIONS (Broad: stratum II / *Narrow: stratum I*)

Crystallized Intelligence (*Gc*): *Grammatical Sensitivity (MY)* - Knowledge or awareness of the grammatical features of the native language.

DESCRIPTION

The examinee is required to listen to sentences stated by the examiner, identify a malapropism, and provide an appropriate word in place of the malapropism.

RELIABILITY [1]

☐ - Low   ■ - Medium   ■ - High   ☐ - No Information Available

	2	3	4	5	6	7	8	9	10	11	12	13	14	15	16	17	18	19 24	25 29	30 34	35 39	40 44	45 49	50 54	55 59	60 64	65 69	70 74	75 79	80 84	85 90+
Internal consistency																															
Test-retest*																															

Interval between testings: 1 week

FLOORS AND CEILINGS

	Test Floor	Test Ceiling
Inadequate at ages:	8-0 to 8-5	11-6 to 12-11

CHC CLASSIFICATIONS (Broad: stratum II / *Narrow: stratum I*)

Crystallized Intelligence (*Gc*): *Grammatical Sensitivity[a] (MY)* - Knowledge or awareness of the grammatical features of the native language; *Lexical Knowledge[a] (VL)* - Extent of vocabulary that can be understood in terms of correct word meanings.

---

[1] Test-retest coefficients were reported by grade in the test manual. Therefore, corresponding ages were estimated by the authors.
[a] The narrow CHC classifications for this test were determined by the authors because no agreement was reached through the group consensus process.

Test of Language Development-Primary: Third Edition (TOLD-P:3)

GENERAL INFORMATION

Author(s): Phyllis L. Newcomer and Donald D. Hammill
Publisher: PRO-ED
Publication Date(s): 1977, 1982, 1988, 1997

Age Range: 4-0 to 8-11
Administration Time: 30 to 60 minutes

COMPOSITE MEASURE INFORMATION

Spoken Language
Organizing
Semantics

Listening
Speaking
Syntax

SCORE INFORMATION

Standard scores	Percentiles	Stanines	Normal curve equivalents	Age equivalents	Grade equivalents

NORMING INFORMATION

Standardization Sample Size: 1,000

Avg. Number per Age/Grade Interval:
  200 per year: 4-0 to 8-11

Age Blocks in Norm Table:
  6 months: 4-0 to 8-11

Sample Collection Date(s): 1996

Demographic Variables:
  Gender - *male; female*
  Geographic region - *4 regions; 28 states*
  Residence - *urban; rural*
  Race/ethnicity - *White; Black; Native American; Hispanic; Asian; other*
  SES - *parent education; family income*
  Other - *disability status (none, LD, SLD, MR, other)*

VALIDITY

Types of Validity Evidence Reported in the Test Manual:

Content	Criterion	Construct

Test Review(s) and Validity Evidence Reported in Extant Literature: See Appendix C

CONTAINS AT LEAST ONE INDICATOR CONSISTENT WITH THE FOLLOWING LD ASSESSMENT AREA(S)

Oral Expression	Listening Comprehension	Written Expression	Basic Reading Skill	Reading Comprehension	Mathematics Calculation	Mathematics Reasoning

SPECIAL FEATURES

- Provides computer scoring and interpretive profiling report
- Includes two new subtests (i.e., Phonemic Analysis and Relational Vocabulary) that measure important linguistic abilities not measured on previous editions
- Includes a new composite (i.e., Organizing) that represents linguistic abilities that mediate between receptive and expressive modes of communication
- Pictures are in color to present a more contemporary and appealing look to children

DESCRIPTION

The examinee is required to select from four pictures the one that best represents the meaning of a word stated by the examiner.

RELIABILITY [1]

■ - Low   ■ - Medium   ■ - High   ☐ - No Information Available

	2	3	4	5	6	7	8	9	10	11	12	13	14	15	16	17	18	19-24	25-29	30-34	35-39	40-44	45-49	50-54	55-59	60-64	65-69	70-74	75-79	80-84	85-90+
Internal consistency			M	M	M	M	L																								
Test-retest*				M	M	M																									

Interval between testings: 4 months

FLOORS AND CEILINGS

	Test Floor	Test Ceiling
Inadequate at ages:	4-0 to 5-5	none

CHC CLASSIFICATIONS (Broad: stratum II / *Narrow: stratum I*)

Crystallized Intelligence (*Gc*): *Lexical Knowledge (VL)* - Extent of vocabulary that can be understood in terms of correct word meanings.

DESCRIPTION

The examinee is required to express orally the relationship between two words stated by the examiner.

RELIABILITY [1]

■ - Low   ■ - Medium   ■ - High   ☐ - No Information Available

	2	3	4	5	6	7	8	9	10	11	12	13	14	15	16	17	18	19-24	25-29	30-34	35-39	40-44	45-49	50-54	55-59	60-64	65-69	70-74	75-79	80-84	85-90+
Internal consistency			M	M	M	M	M																								
Test-retest*				M	M	M																									

Interval between testings: 4 months

FLOORS AND CEILINGS

	Test Floor	Test Ceiling
Inadequate at ages:	4-0 to 5-5	none

CHC CLASSIFICATIONS (Broad: stratum II / *Narrow: stratum I*)

Crystallized Intelligence (*Gc*): *Language Development (LD)* - General development, or the understanding of words, sentences, and paragraphs (not requiring reading), in spoken native language skills.

[1]Test-retest coefficients were reported by grade in the test manual. Therefore, corresponding ages were estimated by the authors.

DESCRIPTION

The examinee is required to provide an oral definition for a common English word stated by the examiner.

RELIABILITY [1]

☐ - Low   ■ - Medium   ■ - High   ☐ - No Information Available

	2	3	4	5	6	7	8	9	10	11	12	13	14	15	16	17	18	19/24	25/29	30/34	35/39	40/44	45/49	50/54	55/59	60/64	65/69	70/74	75/79	80/84	85/90+
Internal consistency			■	■	■	■	■																								
Test-retest*		☐	■	■	■	■																									

Interval between testings: 4 months

FLOORS AND CEILINGS

	Test Floor	Test Ceiling
Inadequate at ages:	4-0 to 6-5	none

CHC CLASSIFICATIONS (Broad: stratum II / Narrow: stratum I)

Crystallized Intelligence (Gc): *Lexical Knowledge (VL)* - Extent of vocabulary that can be understood in terms of correct word meanings.

DESCRIPTION

The examinee is required to select from three pictures the one that most accurately represents the stimulus sentence supplied by the examiner.

RELIABILITY [1]

☐ - Low   ■ - Medium   ■ - High   ☐ - No Information Available

	2	3	4	5	6	7	8	9	10	11	12	13	14	15	16	17	18	19/24	25/29	30/34	35/39	40/44	45/49	50/54	55/59	60/64	65/69	70/74	75/79	80/84	85/90+
Internal consistency		■	■	■	■	■	☐																								
Test-retest*		☐	■	■	■	■																									

Interval between testings: 4 months

FLOORS AND CEILINGS

	Test Floor	Test Ceiling
Inadequate at ages:	4-0 to 4-11	6-6 to 8-11

CHC CLASSIFICATIONS (Broad: stratum II / Narrow: stratum I)

Crystallized Intelligence (Gc): *Language Development; (LD)* - General development, or the understanding of words, sentences, and paragraphs (not requiring reading), in spoken native language skills; *Listening Ability (LS)* - Ability to listen and comprehend oral communications.

---

[1]Test-retest coefficients were reported by grade in the test manual. Therefore, corresponding ages were estimated by the authors.

Battery: TOLD-P:3	Sentence Imitation	Age Range: 4-0 to 8-11

DESCRIPTION

The examinee is required to repeat sentences that are stated by the examiner.

RELIABILITY [1]

☐ - Low   ■ - Medium   ■ - High   ☐ - No Information Available

	2	3	4	5	6	7	8	9	10	11	12	13	14	15	16	17	18	19-24	25-29	30-34	35-39	40-44	45-49	50-54	55-59	60-64	65-69	70-74	75-79	80-84	85-90+
Internal consistency																															
Test-retest*																															

Interval between testings: 4 months

FLOORS AND CEILINGS

	Test Floor	Test Ceiling
Inadequate at ages:	4-0 to 5-5	7-6 to 8-11

CHC CLASSIFICATIONS (Broad: stratum II / *Narrow: stratum I*)

Short-Term Memory (*Gsm*): *Memory Span (MS)* - Ability to attend to and immediately recall temporally ordered elements in the correct order after a single presentation.

Battery: TOLD-P:3	Grammatic Completion	Age Range: 4-0 to 8-11

DESCRIPTION

The examinee is required to provide the missing morphological form to unfinished sentences stated by the examiner.

RELIABILITY [1]

☐ - Low   ■ - Medium   ■ - High   ☐ - No Information Available

	2	3	4	5	6	7	8	9	10	11	12	13	14	15	16	17	18	19-24	25-29	30-34	35-39	40-44	45-49	50-54	55-59	60-64	65-69	70-74	75-79	80-84	85-90+
Internal consistency																															
Test-retest*																															

Interval between testings: 4 months

FLOORS AND CEILINGS

	Test Floor	Test Ceiling
Inadequate at ages:	4-0 to 5-11	7-6 to 8-11

CHC CLASSIFICATIONS (Broad: stratum II / *Narrow: stratum I*)

Crystallized Intelligence (*Gc*): *Grammatical Sensitivity (MY)* - Knowledge or awareness of the grammatical features of the native language; *Listening Ability (LS)* - Ability to listen and comprehend oral communications.

[1]Test-retest coefficients were reported by grade in the test manual. Therefore, corresponding ages were estimated by the authors.

DESCRIPTION

The examinee is required to judge pairs of words, expressed orally by the examiner, as being either the same or different in sound.

RELIABILITY [1]

☐ - Low   ■ - Medium   ■ - High   ☐ - No Information Available

	2	3	4	5	6	7	8	9	10	11	12	13	14	15	16	17	18	19 24	25 29	30 34	35 39	40 44	45 49	50 54	55 59	60 64	65 69	70 74	75 79	80 84	85 90+
Internal consistency			■	■	■	■																									
Test-retest*			☐	☐	☐																										

Interval between testings: 4 months

FLOORS AND CEILINGS

	Test Floor	**Test Ceiling**
Inadequate at ages:	4-0 to 4-11	5-0 to 8-11

CHC CLASSIFICATIONS (Broad: stratum II / *Narrow: stratum I*)

Auditory Processing (*Ga*): *Speech/General Sound Discrimination (US/U3)* - Ability to detect differences in speech sounds under conditions of little distraction or distortion.

DESCRIPTION

The examinee is required to repeat a multi-syllabic word stated by the examiner without a certain part.

RELIABILITY [1]

☐ - Low   ■ - Medium   ■ - High   ☐ - No Information Available

	2	3	4	5	6	7	8	9	10	11	12	13	14	15	16	17	18	19 24	25 29	30 34	35 39	40 44	45 49	50 54	55 59	60 64	65 69	70 74	75 79	80 84	85 90+
Internal consistency			■	■	■	☐	■																								
Test-retest*			■	■	■																										

Interval between testings: 4 months

FLOORS AND CEILINGS

	Test Floor	**Test Ceiling**
Inadequate at ages:	4-0 to 6-5	4-6 to 8-11

CHC CLASSIFICATIONS (Broad: stratum II / *Narrow: stratum I*)

Auditory Processing (*Ga*): *Phonetic Coding: Analysis (PC:A)* - Ability to segment larger units of speech sounds into smaller units of speech sounds.

[1]Test-retest coefficients were reported by grade in the test manual. Therefore, corresponding ages were estimated by the authors.

DESCRIPTION

The examinee is required to articulate spontaneously various words that contain key speech sounds after being presented with a series of stimulus pictures and sentences.

RELIABILITY [1]

| | ☐ - Low | ■ - Medium | ■ - High | ☐ - No Information Available |

	2	3	4	5	6	7	8	9	10	11	12	13	14	15	16	17	18	19 24	25 29	30 34	35 39	40 44	45 49	50 54	55 59	60 64	65 69	70 74	75 79	80 84	85 90+
Internal consistency			■	■	■	■	■																									
Test-retest*			■	■	■	■																										

Interval between testings: 4 months

FLOORS AND CEILINGS

	Test Floor	**Test Ceiling**
Inadequate at ages:	none	4-0 to 8-11

CHC CLASSIFICATIONS (Broad: stratum II / *Narrow: stratum I*)

Not applicable

---

[1]Test-retest coefficients were reported by grade in the test manual. Therefore, corresponding ages were estimated by the authors.

ATDR *Summary Pages*

Specific Academic Skills— Phonological Processing Tests

Comprehensive Test of Phonological Processing (CTOPP)

GENERAL INFORMATION

Author(s): Richard K. Wagner, Joseph K. Torgesen, and Carol A. Rashotte
Publisher: PRO-ED
Publication Date(s): 1999

Age Range: 5-0 to 24-11

Administration Time: 30 minutes

COMPOSITE MEASURE INFORMATION

Phonological Awareness
Rapid Naming
Alternate Rapid Naming

Phonological Memory
Alternate Phonological Awareness

SCORE INFORMATION

Standard scores	Percentiles	Stanines	Normal curve equivalents	Age equivalents	Grade equivalents

NORMING INFORMATION

Standardization Sample Size: 1,656

Avg. Number per Age/Grade Interval:
119 per year: 5-0 to 17-11
80 per five years: 18-0 to 24-11

Age Blocks in Norm Table:
6 months: 5-0 to 7-11
1 year: 8-0 to 16-11
8 years: 17-0 to 24-11

Sample Collection Date(s): 1997-1998

Demographic Variables:
Gender - *male; female*
Geographic region - *4 regions; 30 states*
Residence - *urban; rural*
Race/ethnicity - *White; Black; Native American; Hispanic; Asian; other*
SES - *parent education; family income*
Other - *disability status (none, LD, SLD, MR, other)*

VALIDITY

Types of Validity Evidence Reported in the Test Manual:

Content	Criterion	Construct

Test Review(s) and Validity Evidence Reported in Extant Literature: None currently available

CONTAINS AT LEAST ONE INDICATOR CONSISTENT WITH THE FOLLOWING LD ASSESSMENT AREA(S)

Oral Expression	Listening Comprehension	Written Expression	Basic Reading Skill	Reading Comprehension	Mathematics Calculation	Mathematics Reasoning

SPECIAL FEATURES

- Each subtest contains practice items in order for the examinee to master the task and to receive feedback from the examiner regarding performance

DESCRIPTION

The examinee is required to repeat a compound word stated by the examiner and then say the word that remains after dropping (deleting) one of the compound words. Then the examinee is required to repeat a word spoken by the examiner, and then say the word that remains after dropping (deleting) a specific sound.

RELIABILITY

☐ - Low   ■ - Medium   ■ - High   ☐ - No Information Available

	2	3	4	5	6	7	8	9	10	11	12	13	14	15	16	17	18	19 24	25 29	30 34	35 39	40 44	45 49	50 54	55 59	60 64	65 69	70 74	75 79	80 84	85 90+
Internal consistency																															
Test-retest*																															

*Interval between testings: 2 weeks

FLOORS AND CEILINGS

	Test Floor	Test Ceiling
Inadequate at ages:	5-0 to 7-5	8-0 to 24-11

CHC CLASSIFICATIONS (Broad: stratum II / Narrow: stratum I)

Auditory Processing (Ga): *Phonetic Coding: Analysis (PC:A)* - Ability to segment larger units of speech sounds into smaller units of speech sounds.

DESCRIPTION

The examinee is required to combine separate sounds to make a whole word after listening to a series of tape-recorded separate sounds.

RELIABILITY

☐ - Low   ■ - Medium   ■ - High   ☐ - No Information Available

	2	3	4	5	6	7	8	9	10	11	12	13	14	15	16	17	18	19 24	25 29	30 34	35 39	40 44	45 49	50 54	55 59	60 64	65 69	70 74	75 79	80 84	85 90+
Internal consistency																															
Test-retest*																															

*Interval between testings: 2 weeks

FLOORS AND CEILINGS

	Test Floor	Test Ceiling
Inadequate at ages:	5-0 to 7-5	8-0 to 24-11

CHC CLASSIFICATIONS (Broad: stratum II / Narrow: stratum I)

Auditory Processing (Ga): *Phonetic Coding: Synthesis (PC:S)* - Ability to blend smaller units of speech together into larger units of speech.

Battery: CTOPP	Sound Matching	Age Range: 5-0 to 7-11

DESCRIPTION

For the first 10 items, the examinee is required to point to the picture that corresponds to the word that starts with the same sound as the first word the examiner says aloud. For the last 10 items, the same procedure is used, except the examinee is asked to point to the picture of the word that ends with the same last sound as the first word.

RELIABILITY

◻ - Low ◼ - Medium ◼ - High ☐ - No Information Available

	2	3	4	5	6	7	8	9	10	11	12	13	14	15	16	17	18	19/24	25/29	30/34	35/39	40/44	45/49	50/54	55/59	60/64	65/69	70/74	75/79	80/84	85/90+
Internal consistency				■	■	■																									
Test-retest*				■	■	■																									

*Interval between testings: 2 weeks

FLOORS AND CEILINGS

	Test Floor	Test Ceiling
Inadequate at ages:	5-0 to 6-11	5-0 to 7- 11

CHC CLASSIFICATIONS (Broad: stratum II / Narrow: stratum I)

Auditory Processing (Ga): *Phonetic Coding: Analysis (PC:A)* - Ability to segment larger units of speech sounds into smaller units of speech sounds.

Battery: CTOPP	Memory for Digits	Age Range: 5-0 to 24-11

DESCRIPTION

The examinee is required to listen to a series of tape-recorded numbers, presented at a rate of 2 per second, then sequentially repeat the numbers.

RELIABILITY

◻ - Low ◼ - Medium ◼ - High ☐ - No Information Available

	2	3	4	5	6	7	8	9	10	11	12	13	14	15	16	17	18	19/24	25/29	30/34	35/39	40/44	45/49	50/54	55/59	60/64	65/69	70/74	75/79	80/84	85/90+
Internal consistency				▨	▨	▨	■	■	■	■	■	■	■	■	■	■	■	■													
Test-retest*				▨	▨	■	■	■	■	■	■	■	■	■	■	■	■	■													

*Interval between testings: 2 weeks

FLOORS AND CEILINGS

	Test Floor	Test Ceiling
Inadequate at ages:	none	15-0 to 24-11

CHC CLASSIFICATIONS (Broad: stratum II / Narrow: stratum I)

Short-Term Memory (Gsm): *Memory Span (MS)* - Ability to attend to and immediately recall temporally ordered elements in the correct order after a single presentation.

Battery: CTOPP	Nonword Repetition	Age Range: 5-0 to 24-11

DESCRIPTION

The examinee is required to listen to a tape-recorded non-word then repeat it verbatim.

RELIABILITY

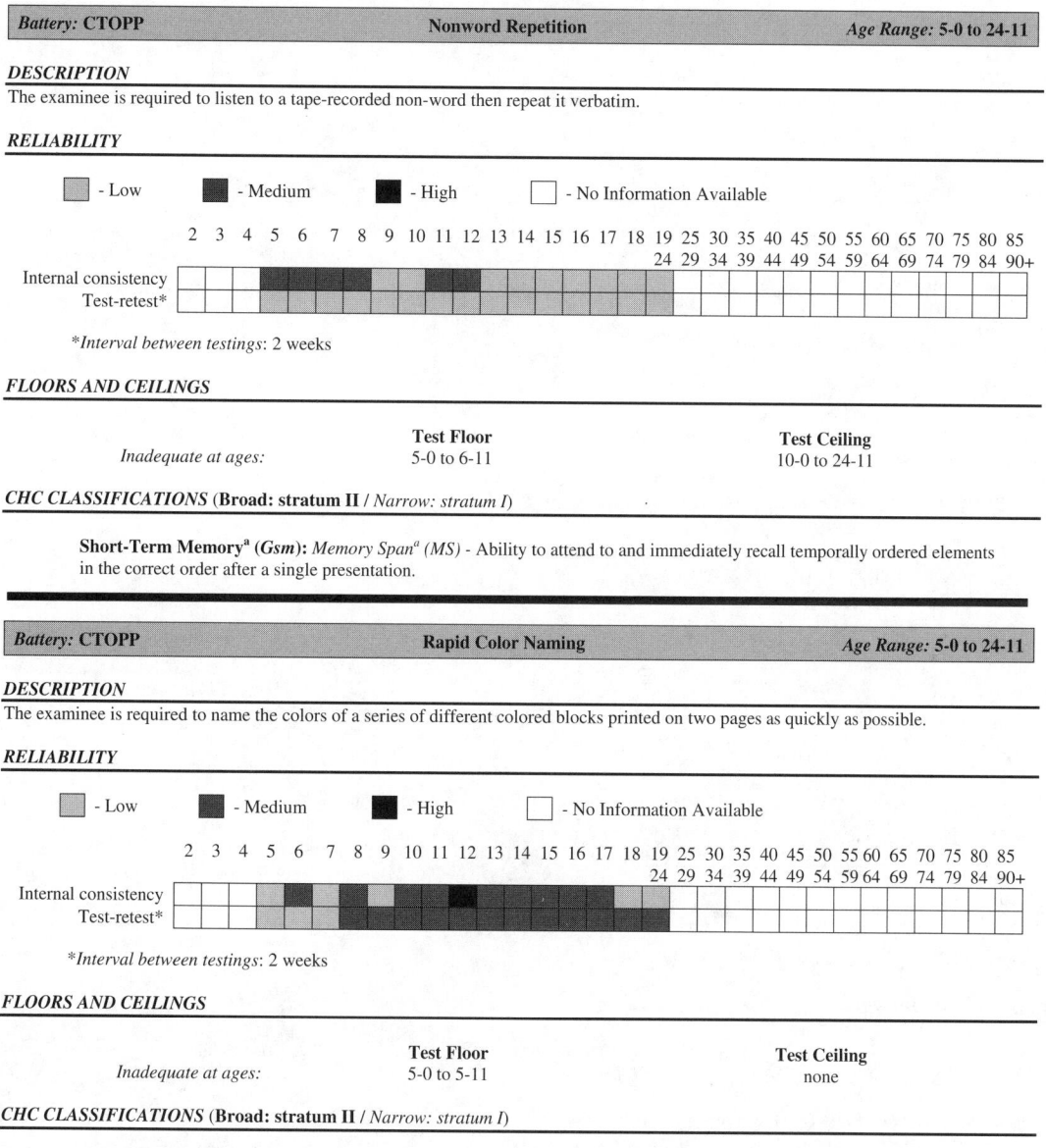

- Low   - Medium   - High   - No Information Available

| | 2 | 3 | 4 | 5 | 6 | 7 | 8 | 9 | 10 | 11 | 12 | 13 | 14 | 15 | 16 | 17 | 18 | 19 24 | 25 29 | 30 34 | 35 39 | 40 44 | 45 49 | 50 54 | 55 59 | 60 64 | 65 69 | 70 74 | 75 79 | 80 84 | 85 90+ |

Internal consistency
Test-retest*

Interval between testings: 2 weeks

FLOORS AND CEILINGS

	Test Floor	**Test Ceiling**
Inadequate at ages:	5-0 to 6-11	10-0 to 24-11

CHC CLASSIFICATIONS (Broad: stratum II / *Narrow: stratum I*)

Short-Term Memory[a] (***Gsm***): *Memory Span*[a] *(MS)* - Ability to attend to and immediately recall temporally ordered elements in the correct order after a single presentation.

Battery: CTOPP	Rapid Color Naming	Age Range: 5-0 to 24-11

DESCRIPTION

The examinee is required to name the colors of a series of different colored blocks printed on two pages as quickly as possible.

RELIABILITY

- Low   - Medium   - High   - No Information Available

| | 2 | 3 | 4 | 5 | 6 | 7 | 8 | 9 | 10 | 11 | 12 | 13 | 14 | 15 | 16 | 17 | 18 | 19 24 | 25 29 | 30 34 | 35 39 | 40 44 | 45 49 | 50 54 | 55 59 | 60 64 | 65 69 | 70 74 | 75 79 | 80 84 | 85 90+ |

Internal consistency
Test-retest*

Interval between testings: 2 weeks

FLOORS AND CEILINGS

	Test Floor	**Test Ceiling**
Inadequate at ages:	5-0 to 5-11	none

CHC CLASSIFICATIONS (Broad: stratum II / *Narrow: stratum I*)

Long Term Storage and Retrieval (*Glr*): *Naming Facility (NA)* - Ability to rapidly produce names for concepts when presented with a pictorial or verbal cue. **Processing Speed (*Gs*):** *Rate of Test Taking (R9)* - Ability to rapidly perform tests which are relatively easy or that require very simple decisions.

[a]The broad and narrow ability CHC classifications for this test were determined by the authors because no agreement was reached through the group consensus process.

DESCRIPTION

The examinee is required to name a series of objects printed on two pages as quickly as possible.

RELIABILITY

☐ - Low ■ - Medium ■ - High ☐ - No Information Available

	2	3	4	5	6	7	8	9	10	11	12	13	14	15	16	17	18	19 24	25 29	30 34	35 39	40 44	45 49	50 54	55 59	60 64	65 69	70 74	75 79	80 84	85 90+
Internal consistency																															
Test-retest*																															

Interval between testings: 2 weeks

FLOORS AND CEILINGS

	Test Floor	Test Ceiling
Inadequate at ages:	5-0 to 5-11	none

CHC CLASSIFICATIONS (Broad: stratum II / *Narrow: stratum I*)

Long Term Storage and Retrieval (*Glr*): *Naming Facility (NA)* - Ability to rapidly produce names for concepts when presented with a pictorial or verbal cue.

DESCRIPTION

The examinee is required to name the numbers printed on two pages as quickly as possible.

RELIABILITY

☐ - Low ■ - Medium ■ - High ☐ - No Information Available

	2	3	4	5	6	7	8	9	10	11	12	13	14	15	16	17	18	19 24	25 29	30 34	35 39	40 44	45 49	50 54	55 59	60 64	65 69	70 74	75 79	80 84	85 90+
Internal consistency																															
Test-retest*																															

Interval between testings: 2 weeks

FLOORS AND CEILINGS

	Test Floor	Test Ceiling
Inadequate at ages:	none	none

CHC CLASSIFICATIONS (Broad: stratum II / *Narrow: stratum I*)

Long Term Storage and Retrieval (*Glr*): *Naming Facility (NA)* - Ability to rapidly produce names for concepts when presented with a pictorial or verbal cue. **Processing Speed (*Gs*):** *Rate of Test Taking (R9)* - Ability to rapidly perform tests which are relatively easy or that require very simple decisions.

| Battery: CTOPP | Rapid Letter Naming | Age Range: 7-0 to 24-11 |

DESCRIPTION

The examinee is required to name the letters printed on two pages as quickly as possible.

RELIABILITY

▢ - Low   ◼ - Medium   ◼ - High   ☐ - No Information Available

	2	3	4	5	6	7	8	9	10	11	12	13	14	15	16	17	18	19-24	25-29	30-34	35-39	40-44	45-49	50-54	55-59	60-64	65-69	70-74	75-79	80-84	85-90+
Internal consistency																															
Test-retest*																															

*Interval between testings: 2 weeks

FLOORS AND CEILINGS

	Test Floor	Test Ceiling
Inadequate at ages:	none	none

CHC CLASSIFICATIONS (Broad: stratum II / Narrow: stratum I)

Long Term Storage and Retrieval[a] (Glr): *Naming Facility[a] (NA)* - Ability to rapidly produce names for concepts when presented with a pictorial or verbal cue. **Processing Speed[a] (Gs):** *Rate of Test Taking[a] (R9)* - Ability to rapidly perform tests which are relatively easy or that require very simple decisions.

| Battery: CTOPP | Blending Nonwords (Supplemental) | Age Range: 5-0 to 24-11 |

DESCRIPTION

The examinee is required to combine separate sounds together to form a non-word after listening to a series of tape-recorded separate sounds.

RELIABILITY

▢ - Low   ◼ - Medium   ◼ - High   ☐ - No Information Available

	2	3	4	5	6	7	8	9	10	11	12	13	14	15	16	17	18	19-24	25-29	30-34	35-39	40-44	45-49	50-54	55-59	60-64	65-69	70-74	75-79	80-84	85-90+
Internal consistency																															
Test-retest*																															

*Interval between testings: 2 weeks

FLOORS AND CEILINGS

	Test Floor	Test Ceiling
Inadequate at ages:	5-0 to 11-11	none

CHC CLASSIFICATIONS (Broad: stratum II / Narrow: stratum I)

Auditory Processing (Ga): *Phonetic Coding: Synthesis (PC:S)* - Ability to blend smaller units of speech together into larger units of speech.

[a]The broad and narrow ability CHC classifications for this test were determined by the authors because no agreement was reached through the group consensus process.

DESCRIPTION

The examinee is required to repeat each non-word, then say it backwards to form a real word after listening to a series of tape-recorded non-words.

RELIABILITY

☐ - Low   ◼ - Medium   ◼ - High   ☐ - No Information Available

	2	3	4	5	6	7	8	9	10	11	12	13	14	15	16	17	18	19/24	25/29	30/34	35/39	40/44	45/49	50/54	55/59	60/64	65/69	70/74	75/79	80/84	85/90+

Internal consistency / Test-retest* (shaded High and Medium across ages 7 through 19/24)

Interval between testings: 2 weeks

FLOORS AND CEILINGS

	Test Floor	Test Ceiling
Inadequate at ages:	7-0 to 14-11	15-0 to 24-11

CHC CLASSIFICATIONS (Broad: stratum II / *Narrow: stratum I*)

Short-Term Memory (*Gsm*): *Working Memory (MW)* - Ability to temporarily store and perform a set of cognitive operations on information that requires divided attention and the management of the limited capacity of short-term memory. **Auditory Processing (*Ga*):** *Phonetic Coding: Analysis[a] (PC:A)* - Ability to segment larger units of speech sounds into smaller units of speech sounds.

DESCRIPTION

The examinee is required to repeat a word then to say it one sound at a time.

RELIABILITY

☐ - Low   ◼ - Medium   ◼ - High   ☐ - No Information Available

	2	3	4	5	6	7	8	9	10	11	12	13	14	15	16	17	18	19/24	25/29	30/34	35/39	40/44	45/49	50/54	55/59	60/64	65/69	70/74	75/79	80/84	85/90+

Internal consistency / Test-retest* (shaded High and Medium across ages 7 through 19/24)

Interval between testings: 2 weeks

FLOORS AND CEILINGS

	Test Floor	Test Ceiling
Inadequate at ages:	7-0 to 24-11	10-0 to 24-11

CHC CLASSIFICATIONS (Broad: stratum II / *Narrow: stratum I*)

Auditory Processing (*Ga*): *Phonetic Coding: Analysis (PC:A)* - Ability to segment larger units of speech sounds into smaller units of speech sounds.

[a]The narrow Ga ability CHC classification was determined by the authors because no agreement was reached through the group consensus process.

DESCRIPTION

The examinee is required to repeat each non-word, then say it one sound at a time after listening to a tape-recorded series of non-words.

RELIABILITY

☐ - Low   ■ - Medium   ■ - High   ☐ - No Information Available

	2	3	4	5	6	7	8	9	10	11	12	13	14	15	16	17	18	19 / 24	25 / 29	30 / 34	35 / 39	40 / 44	45 / 49	50 / 54	55 / 59	60 / 64	65 / 69	70 / 74	75 / 79	80 / 84	85 / 90+
Internal consistency						■	■	■	■	■	■	■	■	■	■	■	■														
Test-retest*							■	■	■	■	■	■	■	■	■	■	■	☐													

*Interval between testings: 2 weeks

FLOORS AND CEILINGS

	Test Floor	Test Ceiling
Inadequate at ages:	7-0 to 9-11	8-0 to 24-11

CHC CLASSIFICATIONS (Broad: stratum II / Narrow: stratum I)

Auditory Processing (Ga): *Phonetic Coding: Analysis (PC:A)* - Ability to segment larger units of speech sounds into smaller units of speech sounds.

SCAN-C Test for Auditory Processing Disorders in Children-Revised (SCAN-C-R)

GENERAL INFORMATION

Author(s): Robert W. Keith
Publisher: The Psychological Corporation
Publication Date(s): 1986, 2000

Age Range: 5-0 to 11-11
Administration Time: 25 minutes

COMPOSITE MEASURE INFORMATION

Composite Standard Score

SCORE INFORMATION

Standard scores	Percentiles	Stanines	Normal curve equivalents	Age equivalents	Grade equivalents

NORMING INFORMATION

Standardization Sample Size: 650

Sample Collection Date(s): 1998-1999

Avg. Number per Age/Grade Interval:
108 per year: 5-0 to 11-11

Age Blocks in Norm Table:
1 year: 5-0 to 9-11
2 years: 10-0 to 11-11

Demographic Variables:
Gender - *male; female*
Geographic region - *4 regions*
Race/ethnicity - *African American; Hispanic; White; other*
SES - *parent education*

VALIDITY

Types of Validity Evidence Reported in the Test Manual:

Content	Criterion	Construct

Test Review(s) and Validity Evidence Reported in Extant Literature: None currently available

CONTAINS AT LEAST ONE INDICATOR CONSISTENT WITH THE FOLLOWING LD ASSESSMENT AREA(S)

Oral Expression	Listening Comprehension	Written Expression	Basic Reading Skill	Reading Comprehension	Mathematics Calculation	Mathematics Reasoning

SPECIAL FEATURES

- Includes a compact disc (CD) containing the pre-recorded test instructions, subtest practice items, and test items
- Includes recommendations for intervention for auditory processing disorders
- Provides guidelines for comparing Central Auditory Processing Disorder (CAPD) and Attention Deficit Hyperactivity Disorder (ADHD)

DESCRIPTION

The examinee is required to listen to and repeat words recorded on the CD. The stimulus words are filtered at 1000 Hz so that some of the acoustic spectrum is absent. This requires the child to "fill in" missing information to comprehend the whole word.

RELIABILITY

■ - Low   ■ - Medium   ■ - High   □ - No Information Available

	2	3	4	5	6	7	8	9	10	11	12	13	14	15	16	17	18	19 24	25 29	30 34	35 39	40 44	45 49	50 54	55 59	60 64	65 69	70 74	75 79	80 84	85 90+
Internal consistency																															
Test-retest*																															

*Interval between testings: 2 days to 6 weeks

FLOORS AND CEILINGS

	Test Floor	**Test Ceiling**
Inadequate at ages:	none	7-0 to 11-11

CHC CLASSIFICATIONS (**Broad: stratum II** / *Narrow: stratum I*)

Auditory Processing (*Ga*): *Resistance to Auditory Stimulus Distortion (UR)* - Ability to understand speech and language that has been distorted or masked in one or more ways.

DESCRIPTION

The examinee is required to listen for words spoken among background noise and then say those words.

RELIABILITY

■ - Low   ■ - Medium   ■ - High   □ - No Information Available

	2	3	4	5	6	7	8	9	10	11	12	13	14	15	16	17	18	19 24	25 29	30 34	35 39	40 44	45 49	50 54	55 59	60 64	65 69	70 74	75 79	80 84	85 90+
Internal consistency																															
Test-retest*																															

*Interval between testings: 2 days to 6 weeks

FLOORS AND CEILINGS

	Test Floor	**Test Ceiling**
Inadequate at ages:	none	10-0 to 11-11

CHC CLASSIFICATIONS (**Broad: stratum II** / *Narrow: stratum I*)

Auditory Processing (*Ga*): *Resistance to Auditory Stimulus Distortion (UR)* - Ability to understand speech and language that has been distorted or masked in one or more ways.

DESCRIPTION

The examinee is required to listen to two words presented at the same time: one in the right ear and one in the left ear. The examinee is then required to say the word spoken in the right ear first and say the word spoken in the left ear second.

RELIABILITY

☐ - Low ■ - Medium ■ - High ☐ - No Information Available

	2	3	4	5	6	7	8	9	10	11	12	13	14	15	16	17	18	19/24	25/29	30/34	35/39	40/44	45/49	50/54	55/59	60/64	65/69	70/74	75/79	80/84	85/90+
Internal consistency																															
Test-retest*																															

Interval between testings: 2 days to 6 weeks

FLOORS AND CEILINGS

	Test Floor	Test Ceiling
Inadequate at ages:	none	none

CHC CLASSIFICATIONS (Broad: stratum II / *Narrow: stratum I*)

Auditory Processing (*Ga*): *Sound Localization (UL)* - Ability to localize heard sounds in space.

DESCRIPTION

The examinee is required to listen to two sentences presented at the same time: one in the right ear and one in the left ear. The examinee is the required to say the sentence spoken in the left ear first and say the sentence spoken in the right ear second.

RELIABILITY

☐ - Low ■ - Medium ■ - High ☐ - No Information Available

	2	3	4	5	6	7	8	9	10	11	12	13	14	15	16	17	18	19/24	25/29	30/34	35/39	40/44	45/49	50/54	55/59	60/64	65/69	70/74	75/79	80/84	85/90+
Internal consistency																															
Test-retest*																															

Interval between testings: 2 days to 6 weeks

FLOORS AND CEILINGS

	Test Floor	Test Ceiling
Inadequate at ages:	5-0 to 6-11	9-0 to 11-11

CHC CLASSIFICATIONS (Broad: stratum II / *Narrow: stratum I*)

Auditory Processing (*Ga*): *Sound Localization (UL)* - Ability to localize heard sounds in space.

Test for Auditory Comprehension of Language-Third Edition (TACL-3)

GENERAL INFORMATION

Author(s): Elizabeth Carrow-Woolfolk
Publisher: PRO-ED
Publication Date(s): 1966, 1973, 1985, 1999

Age Range: 3-0 to 9-11
Administration Time: 20 to 30 minutes

COMPOSITE MEASURE INFORMATION

TACL-3 Quotient

SCORE INFORMATION

Standard scores	Percentiles	Stanines	Normal curve equivalents	Age equivalents	Grade equivalents

NORMING INFORMATION

Standardization Sample Size: 1,102

Sample Collection Date(s): 1997

Avg. Number per Age/Grade Interval:
  157 per year: 3-0 to 9-11

Age Blocks in Norm Table:
  3 months: 3-0 to 6-11
  6 months: 7-0 to 8-11
  1 year: 9-0 to 9-11

Demographic Variables:
  Gender - *male; female*
  Geographic region - *4 regions; 24 states*
  Residence - *urban; rural*
  Race/ethnicity - *White; Black; American Indian, Eskimo, Aleut; Hispanic; Asian, Pacific Islander; other*
  SES - *parent education*
  Other - *disability status (none LD, SLD, other)*

VALIDITY

Types of Validity Evidence Reported in the Test Manual:

Content	Criterion	Construct

Test Review(s) and Validity Evidence Reported in Extant Literature: See Appendix C

CONTAINS AT LEAST ONE INDICATOR CONSISTENT WITH THE FOLLOWING LD ASSESSMENT AREA(S)

Oral Expression	Listening Comprehension	Written Expression	Basic Reading Skill	Reading Comprehension	Mathematics Calculation	Mathematics Reasoning

SPECIAL FEATURES

- Pictures are drawn in color and reflect current styles of dress and sex roles, as well as ethnic diversity

DESCRIPTION

The examinee is required to select from four color pictures the one that best depicts the meaning of that word after listening to the examiner read aloud a stimulus word.

RELIABILITY [1]

■ - Low   ■ - Medium   ■ - High   ☐ - No Information Available

	2	3	4	5	6	7	8	9	10	11	12	13	14	15	16	17	18	19 24	25 29	30 34	35 39	40 44	45 49	50 54	55 59	60 64	65 69	70 74	75 79	80 84	85 90+
Internal consistency																															
Test-retest*																															

*Interval between testings: 2 weeks

FLOORS AND CEILINGS

	Test Floor	Test Ceiling
Inadequate at ages:	none	7-6 to 9-11

CHC CLASSIFICATIONS (Broad: stratum II / Narrow: stratum I)

Crystallized Intelligence (Gc): *Lexical Knowledge (VL)* - Extent of vocabulary that can be understood in terms of correct word meanings.

DESCRIPTION

The examinee is required to select from three color pictures the one that best depicts the meaning of that morpheme after the examiner reads aloud a stimulus morpheme.

RELIABILITY [1]

■ - Low   ■ - Medium   ■ - High   ☐ - No Information Available

	2	3	4	5	6	7	8	9	10	11	12	13	14	15	16	17	18	19 24	25 29	30 34	35 39	40 44	45 49	50 54	55 59	60 64	65 69	70 74	75 79	80 84	85 90+
Internal consistency																															
Test-retest*																															

*Interval between testings: 2 weeks

FLOORS AND CEILINGS

	Test Floor	Test Ceiling
Inadequate at ages:	3-0 to 5-8	7-0 to 9-11

CHC CLASSIFICATIONS (Broad: stratum II / Narrow: stratum I)

Crystallized Intelligence (Gc): *Lexical Knowledge (VL)* - Extent of vocabulary that can be understood in terms of correct word meanings.

---

[1]Test-retest coefficients were reported by grade in the test manual. Therefore, corresponding ages were estimated by the authors.

DESCRIPTION

The examinee is required to select from three color pictures the one that best depicts the meaning of the phrase or sentence after listening to the examiner read aloud a stimulus phrase or sentence.

RELIABILITY [1]

☐ - Low   ■ - Medium   ■ - High   ☐ - No Information Available

	2	3	4	5	6	7	8	9	10	11	12	13	14	15	16	17	18	19 24	25 29	30 34	35 39	40 44	45 49	50 54	55 59	60 64	65 69	70 74	75 79	80 84	85 90+
Internal consistency		■	■	■	■	■	■																								
Test-retest*				■		■	■																								

*Interval between testings: 2 weeks

FLOORS AND CEILINGS

	Test Floor	**Test Ceiling**
Inadequate at ages:	3-0 to 4-5	8-6 to 9-11

CHC CLASSIFICATIONS (Broad: stratum II / *Narrow: stratum I*)

Crystallized Intelligence (Gc): *Language Development (LD)* - General development, or the understanding of words, sentences, and paragraphs (<u>not</u> requiring reading), in spoken native language skills; *Listening Ability (LS)* - Ability to listen and comprehend oral communications.

---

[1]Test-retest coefficients were reported by grade in the test manual. Therefore, corresponding ages were estimated by the authors.

Test of Auditory-Perceptual Skills-Revised (TAPS-R)

GENERAL INFORMATION

Author(s): Morrison F. Gardner
Publisher: Psychological and Educational Publications, Inc.
Publication Date(s): 1985, 1996

Age Range: 4-1 to 13-0
Administration Time: 15 to 25 minutes

COMPOSITE MEASURE INFORMATION

Auditory Perceptual Quotient

SCORE INFORMATION

Standard scores	Percentiles	Stanines	Normal curve equivalents	Age equivalents	Grade equivalents

NORMING INFORMATION

Standardization Sample Size: 1,038

Avg. Number per Age/Grade Interval:
115 per year: 4-1 to 13-0

Age Blocks in Norm Table:
3 months: 4-1 to 13-0

Sample Collection Date(s): Unknown

Demographic Variables:
Gender   - male; female
Geographic region - various states
Race/ethnicity   - White; Black; Hispanic; Asian; other

VALIDITY

Types of Validity Evidence Reported in the Test Manual:

Content	Criterion	Construct

Test Review(s) and Validity Evidence Reported in Extant Literature: None currently available

CONTAINS AT LEAST ONE INDICATOR CONSISTENT WITH THE FOLLOWING LD ASSESSMENT AREA(S)

Oral Expression	Listening Comprehension	Written Expression	Basic Reading Skill	Reading Comprehension	Mathematics Calculation	Mathematics Reasoning

SPECIAL FEATURES

- Includes a questionnaire where parents can rate their children's hyperactive, social and emotional behavior-aspects of behavior that may affect test results
- Includes a pronunciation guide for the Auditory Word Memory and Auditory Word Discrimination subtests

DESCRIPTION

The examinee is required to listen as the examiner says a series of numbers then repeat back those numbers in the same order.

RELIABILITY

◻ - Low   ▩ - Medium   ■ - High   ☐ - No Information Available

	2	3	4	5	6	7	8	9	10	11	12	13	14	15	16	17	18	19–24	25–29	30–34	35–39	40–44	45–49	50–54	55–59	60–64	65–69	70–74	75–79	80–84	85–90+
Internal consistency Test-retest*			▩	▩	▩	▩	▩	▩	▩	▩	▩																				

Interval between testings: not applicable

FLOORS AND CEILINGS

	Test Floor	Test Ceiling
Inadequate at ages:	4-1 to 4-6	10-10 to 13-0

CHC CLASSIFICATIONS (Broad: stratum II / *Narrow: stratum I*)

Short-Term Memory (*Gsm*): *Memory Span (MS)* - Ability to attend to and immediately recall temporally ordered elements in the correct order after a single presentation.

DESCRIPTION

The examinee is required to listen as the examiner says a series of numbers then repeat back those numbers in the reverse order.

RELIABILITY

◻ - Low   ▩ - Medium   ■ - High   ☐ - No Information Available

	2	3	4	5	6	7	8	9	10	11	12	13	14	15	16	17	18	19–24	25–29	30–34	35–39	40–44	45–49	50–54	55–59	60–64	65–69	70–74	75–79	80–84	85–90+
Internal consistency Test-retest*		▩	▩	▩	▩	▩	▩	▩	▩	▩	▩																				

Interval between testings: not applicable

FLOORS AND CEILINGS

	Test Floor	Test Ceiling
Inadequate at ages:	4-1 to 13-0	none

CHC CLASSIFICATIONS (Broad: stratum II / *Narrow: stratum I*)

Short-Term Memory (*Gsm*): *Working Memory (MW)* - Ability to store temporarily and perform a set of cognitive operations on information that requires divided attention and the management of the limited capacity of short-term memory.

DESCRIPTION

The examinee is required to listen as the examiner says a sentence then repeat back that sentence exactly as it was spoken.

RELIABILITY

■ - Low   ■ - Medium   ■ - High   ☐ - No Information Available

	2	3	4	5	6	7	8	9	10	11	12	13	14	15	16	17	18	19 24	25 29	30 34	35 39	40 44	45 49	50 54	55 59	60 64	65 69	70 74	75 79	80 84	85 90+
Internal consistency																															
Test-retest*																															

Interval between testings: not applicable

FLOORS AND CEILINGS

	Test Floor	Test Ceiling
Inadequate at ages:	4-1 to 6-3	none

CHC CLASSIFICATIONS (Broad: stratum II / *Narrow: stratum I*)

Short-Term Memory (*Gsm*): *Memory Span (MS)* - Ability to attend to and immediately recall temporally ordered elements in the correct order after a single presentation.

DESCRIPTION

The examinee is required to listen as the examiner says a series of words then repeat these words in any order.

RELIABILITY

■ - Low   ■ - Medium   ■ - High   ☐ - No Information Available

	2	3	4	5	6	7	8	9	10	11	12	13	14	15	16	17	18	19 24	25 29	30 34	35 39	40 44	45 49	50 54	55 59	60 64	65 69	70 74	75 79	80 84	85 90+
Internal consistency																															
Test-retest*																															

Interval between testings: not applicable

FLOORS AND CEILINGS

	Test Floor	Test Ceiling
Inadequate at ages:	4-1 to 4-6	none

CHC CLASSIFICATIONS (Broad: stratum II / *Narrow: stratum I*)

Long-Term Retrieval (*Glr*): *Free Recall Memory (M6)* - Ability to recall as many unrelated items as possible, in any order, after a large collection of items is presented. **Short-Term Memory (*Gsm*):** *Working Memory (MW)* - Ability to store temporarily and perform a set of cognitive operations on information that requires divided attention and the management of the limited capacity of short-term memory.

DESCRIPTION

The examinee is required to comprehend, understand, and interpret a series of questions well enough to provide meaningful answers to them.

RELIABILITY

☐ - Low ■ - Medium ■ - High ☐ - No Information Available

	2	3	4	5	6	7	8	9	10	11	12	13	14	15	16	17	18	19/24	25/29	30/34	35/39	40/44	45/49	50/54	55/59	60/64	65/69	70/74	75/79	80/84	85/90+
Internal consistency																															
Test-retest*																															

*Interval between testings: not applicable

FLOORS AND CEILINGS

	Test Floor	Test Ceiling
Inadequate at ages:	4-1 to 9-6	none

CHC CLASSIFICATIONS (Broad: stratum II / Narrow: stratum I)

Crystallized Intelligence (Gc): *Language Development (LD)* - General development, or the understanding of words, sentences, and paragraphs (not requiring reading), in spoken native language skills; *Listening Ability (LS)* - Ability to listen and comprehend oral communications.

DESCRIPTION

The examinee is required to listen as the examiner says two words that sound alike then state whether those words are two different words that sound alike (homonyms) or if they are the same word spoken twice.

RELIABILITY

☐ - Low ■ - Medium ■ - High ☐ - No Information Available

	2	3	4	5	6	7	8	9	10	11	12	13	14	15	16	17	18	19/24	25/29	30/34	35/39	40/44	45/49	50/54	55/59	60/64	65/69	70/74	75/79	80/84	85/90+
Internal consistency																															
Test-retest*																															

*Interval between testings: not applicable

FLOORS AND CEILINGS

	Test Floor	Test Ceiling
Inadequate at ages:	none	4-1 to 13-0

CHC CLASSIFICATIONS (Broad: stratum II / Narrow: stratum I)

Auditory Processing (Ga): *Speech/General Sound Discrimination (US)* - Ability to detect differences in speech sounds under conditions of little distraction or distortion.

DESCRIPTION

The examinee is required to use common sense and ingenuity in solving common thought problems stated by the examiner.

RELIABILITY

☐ - Low   ■ - Medium   ■ - High   ☐ - No Information Available

	2	3	4	5	6	7	8	9	10	11	12	13	14	15	16	17	18	19/24	25/29	30/34	35/39	40/44	45/49	50/54	55/59	60/64	65/69	70/74	75/79	80/84	85/90+
Internal consistency			■	■	■	■	■	☐	☐	☐	■																				
Test-retest*																															

*Interval between testings: not applicable

FLOORS AND CEILINGS

	Test Floor	**Test Ceiling**
Inadequate at ages:	4-1 to 6-6	none

CHC CLASSIFICATIONS (**Broad: stratum II** / *Narrow: stratum I*)

Fluid Intelligence (*Gf*): *Induction (I)* - Ability to discover the underlying characteristic (e.g., rule, concept, process, trend, class membership) that governs a problem or set of materials; *General Sequential Reasoning (RG)* - Ability to start with stated rules, premises, or conditions, and to engage in one or more steps to reach a solution to a novel problem.

Test of Auditory-Perceptual Skills-Upper Level (TAPS-UL)

GENERAL INFORMATION

Author(s): Morrison F. Gardner
Publisher: Psychological and Educational Publications, Inc.
Publication Date(s): 1994

Age Range: 12-0 to 17-11
Administration Time: 15 to 25 minutes

COMPOSITE MEASURE INFORMATION

Auditory-Perceptual Quotient

SCORE INFORMATION

Standard scores	Percentiles	Stanines	Normal curve equivalents	Age equivalents	Grade equivalents

NORMING INFORMATION

Standardization Sample Size: 703

Sample Collection Date(s): 1993-1994

Avg. Number per Age/Grade Interval:
   117 per year: 12-0 to 17-11

Demographic Variables:
   Gender   - male; female
   Geographic region   - various states and one area of Canada

Age Blocks in Norm Table:
   6 months: 12-0 to 17-11

VALIDITY

Types of Validity Evidence Reported in the Test Manual:

Content	Criterion	Construct

Test Review(s) and Validity Evidence Reported in Extant Literature: None currently available

CONTAINS AT LEAST ONE INDICATOR CONSISTENT WITH THE FOLLOWING LD ASSESSMENT AREA(S)

Oral Expression	Listening Comprehension	Written Expression	Basic Reading Skill	Reading Comprehension	Mathematics Calculation	Mathematics Reasoning

SPECIAL FEATURES

- Includes a questionnaire where parents can rate their children's hyperactive, social and emotional behavior-aspects of behavior that may affect test results

DESCRIPTION

The examinee is required to listen as the examiner says a series of numbers then repeat back those numbers in the same order.

RELIABILITY

☐ - Low   ■ - Medium   ■ - High   ☐ - No Information Available

	2	3	4	5	6	7	8	9	10	11	12	13	14	15	16	17	18	19 24	25 29	30 34	35 39	40 44	45 49	50 54	55 59	60 64	65 69	70 74	75 79	80 84	85 90+
Internal consistency											▨	▨	▨	▨	▨	▨															
Test-retest*																															

*Interval between testings: not applicable

FLOORS AND CEILINGS

	Test Floor	Test Ceiling
Inadequate at ages:	none	none

CHC CLASSIFICATIONS (Broad: stratum II / Narrow: stratum I)

Short-Term Memory (Gsm): *Memory Span (MS)* - Ability to attend to and immediately recall temporally ordered elements in the correct order after a single presentation.

DESCRIPTION

The examinee is required to listen as the examiner says a series of numbers then repeat back those numbers in the reverse order.

RELIABILITY

☐ - Low   ■ - Medium   ■ - High   ☐ - No Information Available

	2	3	4	5	6	7	8	9	10	11	12	13	14	15	16	17	18	19 24	25 29	30 34	35 39	40 44	45 49	50 54	55 59	60 64	65 69	70 74	75 79	80 84	85 90+
Internal consistency											▨	▨	▨	▨	▨	▨															
Test-retest*																															

*Interval between testings: not applicable

FLOORS AND CEILINGS

	Test Floor	Test Ceiling
Inadequate at ages:	12-0 to 16-5	none

CHC CLASSIFICATIONS (Broad: stratum II / Narrow: stratum I)

Short-Term Memory (Gsm): *Working Memory (MW)* - Ability to store temporarily and perform a set of cognitive operations on information that requires divided attention and the management of the limited capacity of short-term memory.

DESCRIPTION

The examinee is required to listen as the examiner says a sentence then repeat back that sentence exactly as it was spoken.

RELIABILITY

☐ - Low   ■ - Medium   ■ - High   ☐ - No Information Available

	2	3	4	5	6	7	8	9	10	11	12	13	14	15	16	17	18	19–24	25–29	30–34	35–39	40–44	45–49	50–54	55–59	60–64	65–69	70–74	75–79	80–84	85 90+
Internal consistency																															
Test-retest*																															

Interval between testings: not applicable

FLOORS AND CEILINGS

	Test Floor	**Test Ceiling**
Inadequate at ages:	12-0 to 13-5	none

CHC CLASSIFICATIONS (Broad: stratum II / *Narrow: stratum I*)

Short-Term Memory (*Gsm*): *Memory Span (MS)* - Ability to attend to and immediately recall temporally ordered elements in the correct order after a single presentation.

DESCRIPTION

The examinee is required to listen as the examiner says a series of words then repeat these words in any order.

RELIABILITY

☐ - Low   ■ - Medium   ■ - High   ☐ - No Information Available

	2	3	4	5	6	7	8	9	10	11	12	13	14	15	16	17	18	19–24	25–29	30–34	35–39	40–44	45–49	50–54	55–59	60–64	65–69	70–74	75–79	80–84	85 90+
Internal consistency																															
Test-retest*																															

Interval between testings: not applicable

FLOORS AND CEILINGS

	Test Floor	**Test Ceiling**
Inadequate at ages:	12-0 to 14-11	none

CHC CLASSIFICATIONS (Broad: stratum II / *Narrow: stratum I*)

Long-Term Retrieval (*Glr*): *Free Recall Memory(M6)* - Ability to recall as many unrelated items as possible, in any order, after a large collection of items is presented. **Short-Term Memory (*Gsm*):** *Working Memory (MW)* - Ability to store temporarily and perform a set of cognitive operations on information that requires divided attention and the management of the limited capacity of short-term memory.

DESCRIPTION

The examinee is required to comprehend, understand, and interpret a series of questions well enough to provide meaningful answers to them.

RELIABILITY

☐ - Low   ■ - Medium   ■ - High   ☐ - No Information Available

	2	3	4	5	6	7	8	9	10	11	12	13	14	15	16	17	18	19 24	25 29	30 34	35 39	40 44	45 49	50 54	55 59	60 64	65 69	70 74	75 79	80 84	85 90+
Internal consistency Test-retest*											▨	▨	▨	▨	▨	▨															

*Interval between testings: not applicable

FLOORS AND CEILINGS

	Test Floor	**Test Ceiling**
Inadequate at ages:	12-0 to 17-11	none

CHC CLASSIFICATIONS (**Broad: stratum II** / *Narrow: stratum I*)

Crystallized Intelligence (Gc): *Language Development (LD)* - General development, or the understanding of words, sentences, and paragraphs (<u>not</u> requiring reading), in spoken native language skills; *Listening Ability (LS)* - Ability to listen and comprehend oral communications.

DESCRIPTION

The examinee is required to listen as the examiner says two words that sound alike then state whether those words are two different words that sound alike (homonyms) or if they are the same word spoken twice.

RELIABILITY

☐ - Low   ■ - Medium   ■ - High   ☐ - No Information Available

	2	3	4	5	6	7	8	9	10	11	12	13	14	15	16	17	18	19 24	25 29	30 34	35 39	40 44	45 49	50 54	55 59	60 64	65 69	70 74	75 79	80 84	85 90+
Internal consistency Test-retest*											▨	▨	▨	▨	▨	▨															

*Interval between testings: not applicable

FLOORS AND CEILINGS

	Test Floor	**Test Ceiling**
Inadequate at ages:	none	12-0 to 17-11

CHC CLASSIFICATIONS (**Broad: stratum II** / *Narrow: stratum I*)

Auditory Processing (Ga): *Speech/General Sound Discrimination (US)* - Ability to detect differences in speech sounds under conditions of little distraction or distortion.

DESCRIPTION

The examinee is required to use common sense and ingenuity in solving common thought problems stated by the examiner.

RELIABILITY

☐ - Low   ■ - Medium   ■ - High   ☐ - No Information Available

	2	3	4	5	6	7	8	9	10	11	12	13	14	15	16	17	18	19 24	25 29	30 34	35 39	40 44	45 49	50 54	55 59	60 64	65 69	70 74	75 79	80 84	85 90+
Internal consistency													▨	■	▨																	
Test-retest*																															

Interval between testings: not applicable

FLOORS AND CEILINGS

	Test Floor	Test Ceiling
Inadequate at ages:	none	none

CHC CLASSIFICATIONS (Broad: stratum II / *Narrow: stratum I*)

Fluid Intelligence (*Gf*): *Induction (I)* - Ability to discover the underlying characteristic (e.g., rule, concept, process, trend, class membership) that governs a problem or set of materials; *General Sequential Reasoning (RG)* - Ability to start with stated rules, premises, or conditions, and to engage in one or more steps to reach a solution to a novel problem.

Test of Phonological Awareness (TOPA)

GENERAL INFORMATION

Author(s): Joseph K. Torgesen and Brian R. Bryant
Publisher: PRO-ED
Publication Date(s): 1994

Age Range: 5-0 to 8-11
Administration Time: 15-20 minutes

COMPOSITE MEASURE INFORMATION

SCORE INFORMATION

Standard scores	Percentiles	Stanines	Normal curve equivalents	Age equivalents	Grade equivalents

NORMING INFORMATION

Standardization Sample Size: 4,327

Sample Collection Date(s): Unknown

Avg. Number per Age/Grade Interval:
1082 per year: 5-0 to 8-11

Demographic Variables:
Gender   *- male; female*
Geographic region   *- 4 regions; 10-38 states*

Age Blocks in Norm Table:
6 months: 5-0 to 6-11
1 year: 6-0 to 8-11

Residence   *- urban; rural*
Race/ethnicity   *- White; Black; Hispanic; Native American; Oriental;*
       other

VALIDITY

Types of Validity Evidence Reported in the Test Manual:

Content	Criterion	Construct

Test Review(s) and Validity Evidence Reported in Extant Literature: See Appendix C

CONTAINS AT LEAST ONE INDICATOR CONSISTENT WITH THE FOLLOWING LD ASSESSMENT AREA(S)

Oral Expression	Listening Comprehension	Written Expression	Basic Reading Skill	Reading Comprehension	Mathematics Calculation	Mathematics Reasoning

SPECIAL FEATURES

DESCRIPTION

The examinee is required to look at three pictures then point to the one that starts with the same letter as the stimulus picture and the one that starts with a different letter than the stimulus picture.

RELIABILITY

☐ - Low   ▨ - Medium   ■ - High   ☐ - No Information Available

	2	3	4	5	6	7	8	9	10	11	12	13	14	15	16	17	18	19 24	25 29	30 34	35 39	40 44	45 49	50 54	55 59	60 64	65 69	70 74	75 79	80 84	85 90+
Internal consistency Test-retest*				■	■																											

Interval between testings: 6 weeks

FLOORS AND CEILINGS

	Test Floor	**Test Ceiling**
Inadequate at ages:	5-0 to 5-5	5-0 to 6-11

CHC CLASSIFICATIONS (Broad: stratum II / Narrow: stratum I)

Auditory Processing[a] (**Ga**): *Phonetic Coding: Analysis*[a] *(PC:A)* - Ability to segment larger units of speech sounds into smaller units of speech sounds.

DESCRIPTION

The examinee is required to look at three pictures then point to the one that ends with the same letter as the stimulus picture and the one that ends with a different letter than the stimulus picture.

RELIABILITY [1]

☐ - Low   ▨ - Medium   ■ - High   ☐ - No Information Available

	2	3	4	5	6	7	8	9	10	11	12	13	14	15	16	17	18	19 24	25 29	30 34	35 39	40 44	45 49	50 54	55 59	60 64	65 69	70 74	75 79	80 84	85 90+
Internal consistency				▨	▨	▨																									
Test-retest*				▨																											

Interval between testings: 8 weeks

FLOORS AND CEILINGS

	Test Floor	**Test Ceiling**
Inadequate at ages:	none	6-0 to 8-11

CHC CLASSIFICATIONS (Broad: stratum II / Narrow: stratum I)

Auditory Processing[a] (**Ga**): *Phonetic Coding: Analysis*[a] *(PC:A)* - Ability to segment larger units of speech sounds into smaller units of speech sounds.

---

[1]Test-retest coefficients were reported by grade in the test manual. Therefore, corresponding ages were estimated by the authors.
[a]The broad and narrow ability CHC classifications for this test were determined by the authors because no agreement was reached through the group consensus process.

A Modern Operational Definition of Learning Disability

It is widely recognized that traditional models for determining learning disability (LD) are problematic. For example, they often fail to differentiate adequately students with learning disabilities from students without learning disabilities who are simply low achievers (e.g., Aaron, 1997; Brackett & McPherson, 1996; Kavale & Forness, 2000; Siegel, 1998, 1999; Stanovich, 1999). The literature suggests that the primary reasons why current models fail in this regard can be attributed to several common misconceptions—in particular the nature of IQ and intelligence, which remains a rather consistent and ubiquitous element in conceptualizations of LD. The misconceptions about IQ and intelligence include, but are not necessarily limited to, the following: (1) IQ is a highly accurate predictor of academic achievement; (2) IQ is synonymous with an individual's academic potential; (3) IQ tests assess specific cognitive dimensions that are important in reading as well as other academic areas; (4) all global ability scores (e.g., IQ) are interchangeable, regardless of the intelligence test used to derive such scores; (5) *aptitude* and ability are one and the same; (6) a significant discrepancy between IQ and achievement confirms the presence of a learning disability; (7) a significant discrepancy between any two scores is *clinically* significant; (8) all formulas for evaluating the statistical significance of an ability-achievement discrepancy are psychometrically valid and equivalent; and (9) *intra*-ability analysis and interpretation is independent of *inter*-ability analysis and interpretation (Flanagan & Ortiz, 2001; Kavale & Forness, 2000; Siegel, 1998, 1999; Stanovich, 1999).

If efforts to develop a more reliable and valid method of LD assessment are to succeed, it will be necessary to evaluate these misconceptions carefully and utilize methods that are based more on scientific evidence and theory than on clinical judgment and conjecture. Such is the central purpose and focus of this chapter. Each of the enumerated misconceptions will be critically evaluated in the following narrative against the backdrop of contemporary cognitive theory and with an eye toward the development of specific methods and approaches that may circumvent the perpetuation of such misunderstandings. This chapter concludes with a presentation of a theoretically based, operational definition of learning disability that incorporates the essential components necessary for advancing the reliability and validity of LD assessment. The proposed operational definition is intended to serve as a guide to best practices in the assessment of learning disabilities by integrating empirically supported, theoretical concepts and relationships with the core elements that define LD, and introducing important and defensible psychometric practices and innovations, such as integrated ability analyses of academic and cognitive performance.

We would also like to emphasize that the concepts and methods related to LD assessment, as will be discussed, revolve around decisions and judgments that are based primarily on data gathered from standardized tests. This is not to say that LD can be evaluated or identified only through the use of standardized test data, but rather that such data are the type most frequently collected in LD assessment and often form the bulk of the foundation for decisions regarding the presence or absence of LD. However, LD may be readily identified in any number of different ways without focusing solely on the use of standardized test data. Authentic measurement of performance across both cognitive and academic abilities may be gained through curriculum-based measures, collection of portfolios, criterion-referenced methods, work samples, dynamic assessment, task or error analysis, and other ways, and may provide sufficient and convincing evidence with which to identify LD. In fact, it would be poor practice to base any diagnosis of LD solely on the basis of standardized test scores in the absence of other corroborating data. Therefore, practitioners should regard the following discussion as applying mainly to interpretation of standardized test data, but should be aware that conclusions and final decisions regarding the presence or absence of LD must always be based on, and supported by, the whole of the collected data and not on any one type of data or single datum, no matter how compelling. Best practices in the assessment of LD, as with any other condition, rest on being able to support interpretation and subsequent conclusions on a preponderance of data that converge to form a clear and defensible position. We seek here to provide only more defensible interpretation of standardized test data in those cases where such data have been deemed useful and collected for the purposes of LD identification.

Common Misconceptions Found in the Application of Current Methods for Determining LD

Misconception 1: IQ Is a Highly Accurate Predictor of Academic Achievement

Current and traditional operational definitions of LD typically incorporate the use of a global ability score (derived from an intelligence battery) for use as an estimate or predictor of academic achievement, or more pointedly, as a measure of the individual's intellectual "potential." The most commonly used global ability scores are the Full Scale IQ (FSIQ), Verbal IQ (VIQ), and Performance IQ (PIQ) from the Wechsler Intelligence Scales (e.g., Wechsler Intelligence Scale for Children–Third Edition [WISC–III; Wechsler, 1991] and Wechsler Adult Intelligence Scale–Third Edition [WAIS–III; Wechsler, 1997]). Other examples of broad-ability scores include General Intellectual Ability (GIA) from the Woodcock-Johnson III (WJ III; Woodcock et al., 2001), Mental Processing Composite (MPC) from the Kaufman Assessment Battery for Children (K-ABC; Kaufman & Kaufman, 1983), General Conceptual Ability (GCA) from the Differential Ability Scales (DAS; Elliot, 1990), and so on. Although global ability scores in general, such as the FSIQ, are often cited as the "best" predictors of achievement, it is important to consider that they account only for approximately 25 to 35 percent of total achievement variance (Glutting, Youngstrom, Ward, Ward, & Hale, 1997; Niesser et al., 1996). This means that global ability measures cannot account for or explain about 65 to 75 percent of the variance in achievement (Vellutino, Scanlon, & Lyon, 2000). Of course, if IQ explained a very large portion of the variance in achievement, one might wonder whether there was in fact any real difference between the two. So the fact that IQ does not explain an enormous portion of variance in total achievement is not necessarily problematic, theoretically speaking, since it constitutes prima facie evidence that these two constructs are relatively independent, albeit related. Nevertheless, although IQ may well represent the best predictor of achievement in relation to other indices (Neisser et al., 1996), it simply leaves too much variance left unexplained relative to an individual's pattern of academic achievement to conclude that it is in any way a "highly accurate" predictor of academic success. Practitioners must recognize there are other significant factors that affect achievement and that global ability measures, such as IQ, although possessing some predictive power, are not infallible as predictors of academic achievement.

Misconception 2: IQ Is Synonymous with an Individual's Academic Potential

The misconception that IQ and intellectual potential are rather synonymous is closely related to the previous misconception. When it is assumed erroneously that IQ predicts achievement accurately, an equally erroneous assumption invariably follows—that is, that IQ represents an individual's capacity or potential for academic success. In other words, IQ becomes the marker or standard for what is expected from the individual. As Stanovich (1999) points out, "Psychometricians, developmental psychologists, and educational psychologists long ago gave up the belief that IQ test scores measured potential to any valid sense" (p. 354). He added, "At best, IQ test scores are gross measures of current cognitive functioning. In short, we have been basing systems of educational classification in the area of reading disabilities on special claims of unique potential that are neither conceptually nor psychometrically justifiable" (p. 354). The ramifications of these erroneous assumptions are especially pernicious because they foster the belief that LD exists only in individuals who have at least an average IQ or higher. There is no logical reason why individuals with low IQs could not also display learning disabilities of one kind or another.

However, as the number and severity of impairments in general cognitive and academic functioning decreases, it may be more accurate to attribute learning difficulties to something that is more pervasive and broader in terms of impact, such as mental retardation or other pervasive developmental disorders. Diagnosis of such conditions as mental retardation or pervasive developmental disorder generally supersede determination of LD since they may more accurately characterize the nature and extent of the individual's impairments. This line of reasoning is not entirely applicable to individuals at the opposite end of the IQ spectrum. Although individuals with high IQs are sometimes identified as being learning disabled, such practice is difficult to defend in cases where achievement, whether measured by tests or other means, remains within the average range compared to other individuals of the same age or grade in the general population. The label of LD—*disability* being the operative term—carries with it explicit connotations of functional learning impairment, and it would be rather inappropriate to apply the label of LD to anyone who displays average competency and proficiency in academic achievement. Given that not much is expected from those with low IQs, and that those with high IQs usually succeed quite well academically, the definition of LD has been applied mainly to those with average IQs, who are seen to be "tragically" unable to display their "true" academic potential as a result of some type of learning disability.

In a practical sense, the majority of individuals identified as being LD will very likely have average IQs, not so much because of any unrealized potential but more because of the fact that almost 70 percent of all individuals have IQs within normal limits (i.e., ±1SD from the mean). Moreover, the lowered expectations for individuals with low IQs and the relative academic success easily achieved by individuals with high IQs means that the pool of people with potential LD is further narrowed to those with average IQs. As such, identification of LD becomes largely a matter of numbers and often reflects a rather discriminatory selection process. Recognition of the restrictive nature in the definition of LD, along with an understanding of the distribution of IQ in the general population, and the meaning of scores at the extreme ends, is crucial to avoiding misconceptions about IQ as being synonymous with potential.

Misconception 3: IQ Tests Assess Cognitive Dimensions That Are Important in Reading and Other Academic Areas

Given the degree to which the Wechsler Intelligence Scales are entrenched in virtually every education and psychology training program in the United States, often to the exclusion of any other intelligence battery, the term *IQ* is almost always associated with a Wechsler Scale. For all intents and purposes, the phrase *IQ tests* has become rather synonymous with the Wechsler Scales. But what the Wechsler Scales actually measure has long been a very debated and relevant question in the field of psychometrics. According to the publisher of the Wechsler Scales (The Psychological Corporation) and many researchers (e.g., Horn, Carroll, Woodcock, to name a few), these scales measure mainly Visual Processing *(Gv)* abilities, such as spatial relations, and verbal abilities or Crystallized Intelligence *(Gc),* such as lexical knowledge and general information (Flanagan, McGrew, & Ortiz, 2000; Flanagan & Ortiz, 2001; McGrew & Flanagan, 1998). This is reflected clearly in the historical Verbal IQ and Performance IQ dichotomy that continues to underlie the structure of each Wechsler scale to the present day. However, the literature on the relations between specific cognitive abilities and reading achievement, for example, shows that although *Gc* contributes to the explanation of reading achievement, *Gv* presumably does not (see McGrew & Flanagan, 1998 and Chapter 2 of this text). Therefore, approximately 50 percent of a Wechsler FSIQ is comprised of abilities that are largely irrelevant to reading achievement. According to Vellutino and colleagues (2000):

> *IQ scores accounted for only 10% to 20%, at best, of the variance on the WRMT-R Word Identification and Word Attack subtests, which is hardly a basis for using IQ to predict achievement in beginning reading, to define reading disability, or to make determinations regarding access to instructional resources. Correlations between the IQ scores and the tests of reading comprehension were found to be somewhat higher, but only in the normal readers and only in the case of the comprehension test administered in third grade. (p. 233)*

Failure to measure abilities that are important in reading is not a criticism limited to the Wechsler Scales. Rather, this problem is endemic to most intelligence tests and thus creates a need for extreme caution when evaluating the results from such tests against observed patterns or data related to reading or other learning disabilities.

Misconception 4: All Global Ability Scores Are Interchangeable, Regardless of the Intelligence Test Used to Derive Such Scores

Although the failure to account for abilities relevant to reading is described as being quite common to IQ tests, this does not necessarily mean that all global or general ability scores are the same or readily interchangeable. There are, in fact, many intelligence batteries that measure specific cognitive abilities not assessed by the Wechslers, that *are relevant to* reading as well as other areas of academic achievement. In general, the total test scores of the major intelligence batteries consist of a combination of abilities that reflect either the underlying theoretical model of the instrument or the author's conception of intelligence. As a result, these combinations of abilities differ, sometimes substantially, across batteries.

   Table 11.1 shows the differences in the underlying abilities that contribute to the full scale or total test composites of the most prominent intelligence batteries. The description of broad abilities that contribute to total test scores in Table 11.1 are based largely on a series of theory-driven joint factor-analytic studies (narrow-ability classifications are based on expert consensus; Flanagan, McGrew, & Ortiz, 2000).

   As may be seen in Table 11.1, a significant amount of variation exists across intelligence batteries in terms of what abilities are included in their respective total test composites. For example, in addition to *Gv* and *Gc* abilities, the WJ III includes measures of *Ga* (mainly phonological processing), *Glr* (e.g., Associative Memory), *Gsm* (e.g., working memory), and *Gs* (speed of processing). Some of the abilities that are assessed by the WJ III and that comprise the WJ III General Intellectual Ability (GIA) score (i.e., the global ability score of the WJ III) show strong and consistent relations to reading achievement. Because the WJ III GIA encompasses more abilities that are related to reading as compared to the Wechsler FSIQ, it is a better predictor of reading (McGrew & Woodcock, 2001).

   Based on the content differences across total test composites of different intelligence batteries (see Table 11.1), it seems obvious that certain total test scores will predict certain academic achievement domains better than others will. That is to say, some intelligence tests measure abilities that are relevant to reading achievement as well as other achievement domains (e.g., mathematics) and others do not. Thus, the global test scores of the major intelligence batteries are not in fact created equally and may therefore differentially affect decisions that are made on their respective bases.

Misconception 5: Aptitude and Ability Are One and the Same

In short, aptitude and ability are not synonymous. According to Snow (1994), "The concept of aptitude includes any enduring personal characteristics that are propaedeutic to successful performance in some particular situation. This definition includes affective, conative,

TABLE 11.1 CHC Abilities Represented in Cognitive Battery Total Test Composites

CHC Ability	WPPSI-R FSIQ	WISC-III FSIQ	WAIS-III FSIQ	WASI FSIQ-4	DAS GCA (preschool)	DAS GCA (school age)	KAIT Composite IQ	K-ABC (MPC; ages 5:0 through 12:5)	WJ III GIA-Std.	CAS Full Scale
Gf										
RG							✓			
I			✓	✓	✓	✓	✓	✓	✓	✓
RQ			✓			✓				
Gq										
A3	✓	✓	✓		✓			✓		
KM					✓					
Gc										
LD	✓	✓	✓	✓	✓	✓	✓		✓	
VL	✓	✓	✓	✓	✓	✓	✓		✓	
LS						✓	✓			
KO	✓	✓	✓	✓						
Gsm										
MS			✓				✓	✓		✓
MW									✓	
MV (Gv)						✓	✓			
Gv										
Vz	✓	✓	✓	✓	✓	✓		✓	✓	
SR	✓	✓	✓	✓	✓	✓		✓	✓	
CS	✓	✓						✓		
CF	✓	✓	✓							
PI										✓
SS	✓									
Ga										
PC-S									✓	
UR										
Glr										
MA							✓		✓	
MM						✓				
NA										✓
Gs										
P									✓	
R9		✓	✓							✓
R4										
N										✓
Grw										
RD							✓			
V							✓			
SG							✓			

Note: Table includes primary and secondary abilities as well as "probable" and "possible" classifications (in a manner consistent with the *ITDR*) (McGrew & Flanagan, 1998).

and personality characteristics as well as cognitive and psychomotor abilities (Snow, 1992). However, cognitive abilities are a particularly important source of aptitude for learning and performance in many school and work situations" (p. 4). Thus, aptitude measures are validated for a particular purpose through demonstrating that they predict important criteria (e.g., specific academic skills).

One of the best examples of the distinction between global ability and aptitude, as defined by Snow (1994), may be seen through an examination of the clusters yielded by the WJ-R (Woodcock & Johnson, 1989). The WJ-R Scholastic Aptitude Clusters (e.g., the Reading, Math, Written Language, Oral Language, and Knowledge Aptitude Clusters) are based on an equally weighted combination of four separate tests drawn from the whole of the cognitive battery. The aptitude clusters were developed through a series of stepwise multiple regression analyses conducted over the entire age range of the WJ-R (McGrew et al., 1991). Consistent with the definition of aptitude, this statistical procedure identified "the optimal linear combination of variables that best predict[ed] a selected criterion variable" (p. 194). In the case of the WJ-R, these regression procedures identified the specific combinations of the four WJ-R Tests of Cognitive Ability that best predicted performance on the WJ-R Reading, Mathematics, Written Language, Oral Language, and Knowledge Achievement Clusters. Research on the differential prediction of the WJ-R Scholastic Aptitude clusters demonstrated that these clusters consistently predicted their respective outcome criterion *better than* both the 7-test and 14-test Broad Cognitive Ability (BCA or "IQ") scores of the WJ-R, explaining up to 50 to 70 percent of the variance in the outcome criterion. Clearly, "the differential predictive validity evidence, when combined with the superior prediction of achievement when compared to other intelligence batteries (i.e., Wechslers, K-ABC, SB:IV) (McGrew et al., 1991)" (McGrew, 1994, p. 211), highlights the basic but significant difference between aptitude and ability. Aptitude scores, unlike global ability scores, are comprised of specific measures of ability that are closely associated with their respective criterion measure. For example, the WJ-R Reading Aptitude Cluster is comprised of a test of lexical knowledge, a test of memory span, a test of phonological processing, and a test of speed of processing. Research has demonstrated consistently that these abilities predict reading achievement and are low in individuals with reading disabilities (see Chapter 2 for a review).

Misconception 6: A Significant Discrepancy between IQ and Achievement Confirms the Presence of a Learning Disability

By itself, a significant discrepancy between ability and achievement is neither synonymous with nor a necessary condition for identifying a learning disability. Contrary to popular belief in a wide variety of professions, discovery of a significant discrepancy does not carry the automatic diagnostic implication of learning disability. According to Siegel (1999), "Such a discrepancy is not a necessary part of the definition of a learning disability" (p. 311) and there may well be cases where learning disabilities are validly indicated in the absence of any such discrepancy. Yet, virtually every definition of learning disability continues to include the concept of discrepancy, in particular those emanating from legal mandates (Kavale & Forness, 2000). Even though the concept of discrepancy is incorporated into some legislative codes, mostly state regulations, it should not be construed as necessary to the process. IDEA allows for determination of learning disability through identification of a severe discrepancy, but it does not require that discrepancy analysis be used and it clearly specifies that no single score or procedure be used as the *sole* criterion for determining any type of disability (see Chapter 1). There exists in the literature an abundance of research that fully supports this stance and that argues unequivocally against the use of a significant ability-achievement discrepancy as the only criterion on which to base a learning disability.

Despite the growing number of learning disability definitions (see Chapter 1), there are some elements common among them that must be present in order to accurately identify LD that are better supported than the blind adherence to misguided notions of discrepancy. These elements generally include a verification of significant or substantial underachievement, identification of an underlying deficit in one or more basic psychological processes or cognitive ability functions, and exclusion of other factors that may account for the observed pattern of underachievement (Kavale & Forness, 2000). Given the general consensus reflected across the various extant definitions, reliable and valid evaluation of learning disabilities cannot rest on the basis of discrepancy alone, and, in fact, a severe discrepancy may not even be necessary.

Misconception 7: A Significant Discrepancy between Any Two Scores Is Clinically Significant

Evaluations of LD have not been confined to interpreting discrepancies between ability and achievement. Rather, many practitioners have long since adopted the notion that any type of discrepancy represents an unequivocal pathognomonic indicator of LD under the false and unsubstantiated assumption that "normal" individuals all possess relatively equal development across all abilities and that significant intra-ability deviation is "abnormal." This practice is perhaps best exemplified by the ipsative approach that seeks to uncover an individual's relative strengths and weaknesses, presumably to offer data that yield more relevant information that might better guide efforts at intervention and remediation (see Kaufman, 1979, 1994, for a discussion of the approach). As such, practitioners have searched relentlessly for discrepancies wherever they may exist, including among and between individual subtest scores, lower-level composite scores, and particularly global scores, whether on the same cognitive or achievement battery or across different cognitive and achievement batteries. Given that the most current Wechsler Scale (i.e., the WAIS-III) yields 3 IQs, 4 Index Scores, and up to 11 individual subtest scores, the sheer number of possible comparisons between scores just from within this battery alone are staggering.

Despite the fact that ipsative analysis has been roundly criticized in the literature (see McDermott, Fantuzzo, & Glutting, 1990; McDermott, Fantuzzo, Glutting, Watkins, & Baggaley, 1992; McDermott & Glutting, 1997), inappropriate and misguided comparisons persist, in particular between the readily available Wechsler VIQ and PIQ. For example, commenting on the LD evaluations submitted on behalf of the plaintiffs in *Guckenberger v. Boston University*, Siegel (1999) noted that "inferences about the learning disability were made on the basis of a discrepancy between the Verbal and Performance Scales of an IQ test (the WAIS-R). Many individuals have a learning disability but no significant discrepancy between verbal and performance IQ scores; conversely, many individuals with no evidence of a learning disability show a significant discrepancy between their scores on verbal and performance scales (Maller & McDermott, 1997). This verbal-performance discrepancy has been discredited" (p. 314). Whether this approach is useful or relevant to any given assessment is debatable, but what is certain is that a discrepancy between two scores of any kind, from within a single battery or across any two batteries, whether intelligence or achievement, is not, by itself, sufficient to establish the presence of a learning disability and, as indicated earlier, it may not even be necessary.

Misconception 8: All Formulas for Evaluating Statistical Significance of an Ability-Achievement Discrepancy Are Psychometrically Valid and Equivalent

Numerous formulas and methods for determining significant ability-achievement discrepancies exist, only a few of which are psychometrically valid. Among the most common are deviation from grade level, expectancy formulas, scatter analysis, standard score difference (simple-difference method), and predicted-achievement methods using regression formulas (Heath & Kush, 1991; McGrew, 1994). The first three methods are not recommended because they are technically limited and, therefore, interpretations that are drawn from the results of such methods are likely to be highly misleading (Flanagan & Alfonso, 1993a; McGrew, 1994). The simple-difference method, although more psychometrically sound than the first three approaches, does not take into account the imperfect correlation between the ability and achievement measures or regression toward the mean. As such, this method yields significantly more false positives among individuals with above average IQs and false negatives among individuals with below average IQs (for a comprehensive discussion of the uses, advantages, and limitations of these discrepancy methods, see Cone & Wilson, 1981; Gridley & Roid, 1998; Heath & Kush, 1991; McGrew, 1994; Reynolds, 1990).The practical implication of the simple-difference method is that it will overidentify individuals with high IQs as LD and underidentify individuals with low IQs as LD. Procedures that are based on the predicted-achievement and regression methods are among the most psychometrically defensible approaches to determining whether an ability-achievement discrepancy is significant (Hintze, 1996a, 1996b; Gridley & Roid, 1998; Flanagan & Alfonso, 1993a, 1993b). As will be discussed in the following section, formulas and methods for establishing the significance of any given discrepancy are not always valid and most assuredly are *not* equivalent.

Misconception 9: Intra-Ability Analysis and Interpretation Is Independent of Inter-Ability Analysis and Interpretation

Because it is commonly believed that a significant ability-achievement (or even a significant intra-achievement) discrepancy is synonymous with a learning disability, as noted in Misconception 7, little if any attention is paid to where actual individual performance falls relative to same-aged peers. Failure to evaluate performance from a normative, not merely relative, perspective is a common problem and frequently results in misdiagnosis. Consider the following scenario. Two students were referred for evaluation by their classroom teachers because they were achieving at a lower level than their classmates in reading. According to their teachers, these students appeared not to be performing up to their intellectual capabilities, as demonstrated through a variety of other academic performances. Student A demonstrated a significant discrepancy between her overall ability (Wechsler FSIQ of 120) and her measured reading achievement (standard score of 95). Student B obtained a Wechsler FSIQ of 110 and a reading achievement standard score of 95. The difference between Student B's ability and achievement scores was not significant. As a result of these evaluations, Student A was diagnosed with a learning disability and an educational plan was implemented in an attempt to improve her reading skills. Student B was not diagnosed with a learning disability and was described as being able to read at a level that was commensurate with his estimated intellectual potential. Yet, when compared to a representative sample of individuals of the same chronological age from the general population, their actual level of performance in reading is essentially equivalent and neither one could really be considered deficient in this respect. In the absence of other convincing data, it would be rather presumptuous to claim that any individual who reads as well as or better than almost 40 percent of his or her peers (SS = 95; 38th percentile) is a poor or disabled reader. Irrespective of the classification scheme used, both students clearly demonstrated that their reading ability, as measured on standardized tests, is average and completely within the range of *normal limits.*

When standardized tests are used, the range of *normal limits* is generally defined as the area under the normal probability curve where 68 percent of the general population is expected to fall. This area encompasses ±1 standard deviation from the normative mean (e.g., a standard score range of 85–115, inclusive). A standard score of 95, from the preceding illustration, falls squarely within normal limits (and in the average range of functioning compared to same-aged peers) and therefore cannot be construed as a normative weakness, deficit, disability, or impairment of any type. It is not only illogical but capricious to label Student A as reading *impaired* or reading *disabled* and Student B as an *average* reader simply because they performed marginally different on a measure of general intelligence (120 and 110, respectively). The fact is, they both obtained the very same standard score on a reading measure and they are both, unless otherwise suggested by other data, average readers relative to a representative sample of the general population, as measured by standardized tests. Thus, a standard score of 95, regardless of how discrepant it may be from any other single score or group of scores is average or normal, and should not be construed as deficient. *Intra*-ability (or person-relative) analysis and interpretation that is accomplished without consideration of *inter*-ability (or population-relative) analysis and interpretation often leads to significant errors in the evaluation of test scores of individuals suspected of having a learning disability.

Clarifying Misconceptions in the Application of Current Methods for Determining LD

The preceding section briefly outlined some of the major problems involved in the assessment and evaluation of individuals with suspected learning disabilities, particularly when data from standardized tests are used. To review, these misconceptions involved issues related to predicting achievement from IQ, equating IQ to academic "potential," the failure of IQ tests in measuring abilities specifically related to achievement, differences between global ability scores, differences between aptitude and ability, the meaning of significant ability-achievement discrepancies, the meaning of other significant discrepancies, differences in methods for evaluating the statistical significance of discrepancies, and the relationship between intra-and inter-ability analysis. In general, these problems can be placed into two broad categories related to LD assessment: (1) the relationship between cognitive and academic abilities and (2) defensible analysis of significant discrepancies. These issues are presented and discussed in the following section and provide the groundwork that is necessary to directly address the difficulties in the LD determination process, especially when using or interpreting test data, and assist in improving current practices in the assessment and evaluation of individuals suspected of having a learning disability.

Relationship between Cognitive and Academic Abilities

The de facto acceptance of IQ (and, by association, the Wechsler Scales) as a predictor of achievement and an infallible marker of potential within the LD field, combined with little if any consideration as to what it might actually measure, has done a great disservice to both the practice of learning disabilities assessment and the field of intellectual assessment. For example, there are some current researchers who believe that achievement tests alone are indeed sufficient to assess and diagnose learning disabilities properly and that intelligence tests (presumably because of the misconception about IQ) are irrelevant in this process (see Siegel, 1999; Stanovich, 1999). The controversy surrounding what kind of tests ought to be used in learning disability evaluations appears to have emerged, in part, because of (1) a lack of understanding of what intelligence or "IQ" tests and achievement tests measure (and, conversely, do not measure); (2) resistance in all assessment-related fields to broaden their understanding of intelligence beyond that which is measured by the Wechsler Scales; (3) the lack of a validated theory of the structure of abilities to guide test selection and interpretation; and (4) the overreliance on an invalid method of determining learning disability (i.e., ability-achievement discrepancy analysis). Taken together, these factors have had the effect of rendering intelligence tests "irrelevant" in the identification and diagnosis of learning disability according to prominent spokespersons in the LD literature (Siegel, 1998, 1999, p. 304; Stanovich, 1999).

As was evident from discussions in the initial chapters of this text, it is difficult to make a clear-cut distinction between cognitive ability and academic ability (or achievement). Likewise, it is difficult to make reliable distinctions between the meaning of broad-ability scores on these tests. Is the measurement of *Gq* on an intelligence test any more or less valid than the measurement of *Gq* on an achievement test? Are the WJ III (Cognitive Battery) Crystallized Intelligence (*Gc*) and Auditory Processing (*Ga*) clusters less useful in understanding learning disabilities than the WJ III (Achievement Battery) Basic Reading Skills Cluster merely because they fall within the context of an intelligence test rather than an achievement test? Moreover, the core processes that Siegel (1998) identified as being low or problematic in children with learning disability (e.g., auditory or phonological processing, short-term memory; see also Morris et al., 1998) are included in the CHC theory of abilities (see Chapter 2) and are measured by *both* intelligence and achievement tests (see McGrew & Flanagan, 1998; and Chapters 2 and 3 of this text). It stands to reason, therefore, that it is difficult to make a strong argument as to whether only achievement tests should be used to understand the source of specific academic problems because the distinction between cognitive ability and academic ability (or achievement) is primarily semantic. These two constructs overlap significantly (see Chapters 2 and 3). As such, a more reasonable argument may be that *both* intelligence and achievement tests yield useful information about learning and, by extension, learning disabilities.

By viewing cognitive and academic abilities as lying on a continuum (see Figure 2.4), assessment of learning disabilities becomes less a question regarding *what type of tests should be used (intelligence or achievement)* and more a question about *which test(s) will provide the most relevant information* about the various abilities and processes related to the reported academic difficulties. Once a battery of tests has been identified that are directly responsive to the purpose of assessment or referral concerns, whether it includes intelligence tests or achievement tests and whether it involves an existing battery or an individualized cross-battery, the benefit is obvious—time, effort, and other precious resources are saved and the collected data provide more relevant, valid, and reliable information that is specifically designed to answer the unique questions raised by the need for assessment. Moreover, when the assessment is conducted in accordance with the guiding principles of CHC Cross-Battery assessment (described in the next chapter), analysis and interpretation of individual performance is guided by contemporary theory and research, rather than popular misconception or pseudo-scientific procedures.

In short, as a result of the continuous rather than dichotomous nature of cognitive and academic abilities, coupled with an understanding of the utility of aptitude versus global ability measures in identifying specific sources of academic difficulty, it seems clear that advocating solely for *either* intelligence *or* achievement measures in the assessment and diagnosis of learning disability represents an inconsequential and largely semantic issue. Both types of measures, when used and interpreted appropriately, yield important information that can inform decisions regarding LD determination. The information yielded by intelligence tests is no more irrelevant to the process of LD determination (as some have asserted, e.g., Siegel, 1999) than the information yielded by achievement tests. Rather, it is more *the uninformed manner in which many practitioners use the scores* derived from intelligence tests (in particular the Wechsler IQs) that may be irrelevant to LD determination.

Intelligence tests (including carefully selected CHC-based cross-batteries) that are grounded firmly in contemporary psychometric theory clearly yield scores that are relevant to LD determination. For example, the WJ III provides scores related to phonological processing as well as specific memory processes—areas that are highly relevant to the investigation of factors that contribute to reading difficulties. The proper remedy regarding the use of intelligence tests, IQ scores, and aptitude scores does not appear to lie so much in their elimination from the LD assessment equation, as it does in correcting the manner in which they are used and understood. Excluding certain tests or test data from LD assessment because practitioners fail to use them properly is akin to blaming a perfectly tuned piano for producing discordant music rather than the amateur who is playing it. Tests do not diagnose; people do. Rather than attempting to restrict practitioners solely to the use of achievement tests in the evaluation of individuals suspected of having a learning disability, efforts might better be directed at educating practitioners in proper test selection and theory-based interpretation that are firmly grounded in and well supported by contemporary research.

Defensible Analysis of Significant Discrepancies

Any observed discrepancy between ability and achievement scores (or between ability scores only, or achievement scores only) may well be due to actual and normal differences in the makeup of an individual's ability repertoire. After all, an individual with uniformly developed abilities is the exception, not the rule. Yet, underlying the notion of discrepancy is an implicit assumption that an individual's abilities should be completely and relatively equally well developed. Such a notion is erroneous and untenable. The precise meaning underlying the identification of significant discrepancies should not be lost amid such seem-ingly intuitive, but unsupported views on the nature of human cognitive abilities. Abilities vary both within the individual and across individuals, sometimes greatly. Under the guise of objective statistical analysis, this fact is often lost in the pursuit of establishing the exist-ence of real and true discrepancies irrespective of how common they may actually be or whether they represent real performance deficits. At the very least, in order to improve the practice of discrepancy analysis and make it substantially more defensible, practitioners should (1) use proper methods for calculating discrepancies (e.g., accounting for imperfect correlation); (2) determine whether discrepancies are unusual or uncommon, not just real; (3) evaluate the impact of using different types of ability scores (e.g., aptitude or IQ); and (4) use normative-based analysis to establish deficient functioning (i.e., whether the lower of the two scores actually represents a real deficit).

Psychometrically Sound Methods for Calculating Discrepancies. Appropriate and defensible analysis of discrepancies must rest first on defensible and systematic mathematical methods that are used in their derivation. All too often, practitioners resort to taking the absolute arithmetic difference between standard scores. As Stanovich (1999) noted,

> *One of the most pernicious practices in our field that still persists is that many cli-nicians and diagnosticians (as well as many sate legislative guidelines) continue to define aptitude-achievement discrepancies in terms of differences in* standard scores *rather than in terms of regression calculations that appropriately adjust for the imperfect correlation between achievement and intelligence. (p. 355; emphasis in original)*

Such practice leads to problems with underidentification (in individuals with low IQs) and overidentification (in individuals with high IQs) of learning disabilities. Because there are readily available and more defensible methods (e.g., the predicted-achievement method), there is no reason for practitioners to use simple, arithmetic differences in the determination of discrepancies, let alone the diagnosis of LD.

The predicted-achievement method is superior to other methods of determining signif-icant ability-achievement discrepancies because it (1) accounts for the imperfect correlation between the ability measure and the achievement measure, (2) takes into consideration the standard error of measurement in decision making and (3) evaluates discrepancies relative to the frequency of occurrence of observed differences between the academic performance of the individual referred for evaluation and all other individuals that have the same level of global ability (e.g., the same IQ) (cited in Hintze, 1996b, p. 17). This method is quite defen-sible when used to evaluate discrepancies between a number of ability and achievement measures, including (1) Wechsler FSIQ and Wechsler Individual Achievement Test–Sec-ond Edition (WIAT-II; Psychological Corporation, 2001) subtests and composites, (2) WISC-III Verbal and Performance IQs and WIAT-II subtests and composites, (3) Cognitive Assessment System (CAS; Das & Naglieri, 1997) Full Scale score and WJ-R achievement tests and clusters; (4) Differential Ability Scales (Elliott, 1990) General Conceptual Ability score and Achievement clusters; and (5) WJ III GIA and achievement tests and clusters.

Although the predicted achievement method is technically valid, McGrew (1994) points out that among such methods for determining whether ability-achievement discrepancies are significant, some are better than others. McGrew demonstrates this in a hierarchical presentation of discrepancy procedures. Table 11.2 depicts McGrew's hierarchy and provides examples of ability-achievement analysis methods that correspond to qualitatively different levels of technical validity (and invalidity). An examination of Table 11.2 demonstrates that the features of *conorming* and use of *aptitude* measures demarcate the most superior method among technically valid ability-achievement discrepancy procedures.

TABLE 11.2 Hierarchy of Discrepancy Procedures by Technical Validity and Select Examples

Levels	Description	Example
Actual Discrepancy Norms[1]	(technically valid)	
Level 1	A differentiated scholastic aptitude measure and a measure of achievement	WJ III
Level 2	A broad (general) ability measure and a measure of achievement	WJ III DAS
Pseudo-Discrepancy Norms[2]	(technically valid)	
Level 3	A differentiated scholastic aptitude measure and a measure of achievement that are conormed	
Level 4	A broad (general) ability measure and a measure of achievement that are conormed	
Level 5	A differentiated scholastic aptitude measure and a measure of achievement that are *not* conormed	
Level 6	A broad (general) ability measure and a measure of achievement that are *not* conormed	WPPSI-R, WISC-III, WAIS-III/WIAT-II CAS/WJ-R ACH, WASI FSIQ-4/ WIAT
Absolute Score Difference	(technically invalid)	
Level 7	An absolute score difference between a differentiated scholastic aptitude measure and a measure of achievement that are conormed	
Level 8	An absolute score difference between a broad (general) ability measure and a measure of achievement that are conormed	
Level 9	An absolute score difference between a differentiated scholastic aptitude measure and a measure of achievement that are *not* conormed	
Level 10	An absolute score difference between a broad (general) ability measure and a measure of achievement that are *not* conormed	

[1] All measures must be conormed.
[2] Based only on a correction for regression.
Source: From D. P. Flanagan, K. S. McGrew, and S. O. Ortiz, *The Wechsler Intelligence Scales and Gf-Gc Theory: A Contemporary Approach to Interpretation.* Copyright © 2000 Allyn & Bacon. Adapted by permission.

Tests that are conormed are those that were administered to the same individuals during the standardization process. A common standardization sample allows normative information for both measures to be generated from the same representative group of subjects. The use of conormed tests removes the possibility that ability and achievement discrepancy scores may contain errors due to differences in the test norming samples. In the absence of conormed measures, practitioners need to evaluate whether the standardization sample from each measure is similar. According to McGrew (1994), "This is largely a judgment call that requires clinicians to devote significant time to studying the norming procedures used for each test. The most efficient and optimal solution is to use aptitude and achievement tests from within the same conormed battery" (p. 213). Another means of reducing error is to use ability and achievement measures that are statistically "linked" or "equated," meaning that although the tests do not have the same large and representative standardization sample, they share a common sample nonetheless. The common sample is then used to generate the data (e.g., pseudo-discrepancy norms; McGrew, 1994) necessary to determine significant ability-achievement discrepancies based on characteristics of the linking sample (see WIAT-II manual and CAS manual for details).

For discrepancy analysis to remain defensible, the derivation of a discrepancy between two scores cannot stray from methods that provide superior and more valid results. The predicted-achievement method (which corrects for regression) should be considered the method that provides the minimum level of technical validity necessary in such analysis. Moreover, when available, use of conormed batteries, linked or equated batteries, aptitude scores, and actual discrepancy norms can be used to enhance the psychometric rigor of the predicted-achievement method even further.

Determining Whether Discrepancies Are Unusual or Uncommon.   Appropriate and defensible analysis of discrepancies continues with an understanding of the difference between *statistically* significant discrepancies and *clinically* significant discrepancies. All too frequently, practitioners rely solely on analyses that examine whether one score differs significantly from another score on the basis of chance. When statistically significant discrepancies are uncovered, there appears to be a tendency to either misunderstand the meaning of the significance or ignore it altogether. Research confirms that not only are discrepancies derived from ipsative analysis insufficient to diagnosis a learning disability, but they are also not nearly as rare or unusual as they might seem. According to Reschly and Grimes (1995):

> On a Wechsler scale the Verbal-Performance Scale difference of about 10 points is statistically significant at the .01 level. Does this mean that only one percent of the standardization sample obtained Verbal and Performance scores at that magnitude of difference? No! In fact, nearly 25% of persons in the standardization sample obtained Verbal and Performance scores that were different by 15 points or more. The statistical significance indicates the likelihood that a difference of that magnitude would occur by chance. The .01 or .05 levels indicate that the difference is likely to be real, not whether the difference is unusual or unique. It is essential to keep in mind that real differences in profiles of scores do occur frequently. (pp. 766–767)

An observed discrepancy may well prove to be a reflection of a real difference between an individual's performance on two different ability measures. But, as eloquently pointed out by Reschly and Grimes (1995), the level of statistical significance that defines the difference as being true does not imply that it is automatically uncommon or clinically meaningful. Given the prevalence of such significant differences within the general population, failure to consider rarity as a factor in discrepancy analysis may well constitute an unpardonable sin.

Furthermore, it is important to understand that *statistical rarity* (which is associated with the term *unusual*) is not synonymous with *impairment*. Indeed, some deviations from normal or average are *valuable deviations* and not all rarities are unusual or abnormal in the negative sense. For example, although the difference between a WAIS-III Verbal IQ of 118 and Performance IQ of 139 (i.e., 21 points) is statistically significant and *rare* (i.e., a difference of this magnitude occurs in less than 10 percent of the standardization sample), it is not indicative of an impairment or disability. Performance at the lower end of this IQ comparison (i.e., the Verbal IQ) is ranked at the 87th percentile. Many practitioners interpret this difference as abnormal, stating that the individual who demonstrated such a discrepancy has a verbal information processing *impairment!* This interpretation is illogical. Even though various comparisons to the WAIS-III norming sample (i.e., a comparison to the number of individuals in the standardization sample with 21-point discrepancies between their Verbal and Performance IQs) may result in a statistically rare finding, the fact remains that when *actual* Verbal and Performance abilities, in this example, are evaluated relative to most people, it must be concluded that the individual is functioning in the high-average to very superior ranges, respectively.

Despite an unusually large (statistically rare) difference between the individual's Verbal and Performance IQs, in the preceding example, both scores are higher than most persons (of the same age) in the general population (as reflected by the WAIS-III norm group). Because Verbal IQ, the lower of the two IQs in this example, places the individual at a level of performance that exceeds 87 percent of individuals of the same age in the general population, this individual is high functioning in both verbal ability (Verbal IQ) and perceptual organization ability (Performance IQ). Thus, it is unreasonable to construe this individual as being impaired or disabled in this sense. Again, differences (even significant ones) in people's abilities are normal and expected. What is rare in this example is that the individual's Performance IQ is so high (i.e., 99th percentile). It would seem much more rational to say that, rather than having some type of "verbal information processing *impairment,*" this individual can be described more appropriately and accurately as demonstrating unusually high perceptual organization ability relative to most people. In short, differences between test scores may be statistically significant and rare but they are not always or necessarily clinically meaningful. Defensible analysis always seeks to establish meaningful clinical significance, not only statistical significance. "The major weakness of the statistical rarity approach is that it has *no* values; it lacks any system for differentiating between desirable and undesirable behaviors. Of course, most users of the statistical rarity approach acknowledge that not all rarities should be identified as abnormal" (Alloy, Acocella, & Bootzin, 1996, p. 6, emphasis in original). People are naturally better or worse in some things than they are in others.

Understanding the Impact of Different Types of Ability Scores.   Appropriate and defensible discrepancy analyses will also depend, in part, on the ability measure used. If, as described in the preceding section, global or general test scores do not consist of the same mix of particular cognitive abilities, then (assuming achievement remains constant) the magnitude of an ability-achievement discrepancy will differ primarily as a function of the particular ability measure. That is, differences in content across predictor variables will undoubtedly result in differing amounts of variance explained in the criterion variable. According to Stanovich (1999), "It has often been pointed out that changes in the characteristics of the IQ test used will result in different subgroups of children being identified as discrepant and alter the types of processing deficits that they will display" (p. 354; see also Stanovich, 1991). Apart from other criticisms, it would appear that this condition alone greatly undermines the utility and validity of the ability-achievement discrepancy procedure in learning disability diagnosis whenever there is a failure to adhere to defensible analytical principles as described in this section.

Confounding the issue related to differences in content across the total test scores of ability measures is the fact that different cognitive abilities have different relationships to academic skill areas. For example, phonological awareness, verbal short-term memory and rate (rapid automatic naming or naming facility) were found to be important in understanding reading acquisition and reading achievement (Morris et al., 1998). For a comprehensive review of the research on the differential effect of cognitive abilities on specific academic skills across the lifespan, refer to Flanagan, McGrew, and Ortiz (2000), Flanagan and Ortiz (2001), and McGrew and Flanagan (1998).

Consider for a moment the implications for diagnosis that emerge when a certain collection of measures of specific cognitive abilities taken together can explain up to 50 to 70 percent of the variance in specific academic abilities (such as Reading Decoding). Without question, knowledge of an individual's performance on these tests of cognitive abilities would appear to have substantial explanatory power in helping professionals and laypersons alike understand why an individual is performing poorly in the specific academic domain. For instance, if an individual was referred for reading difficulties and it was determined that standardized testing was warranted, then a comprehensive assessment of reading achievement would likely ensue. This assessment may include, at a minimum, tests of reading decoding, reading comprehension, and reading fluency. If, upon review of reading performance on these tests from the appropriate normative perspective, it is concluded that the individual is indeed deficient in reading, it seems important and even necessary to engage in continued assessment and evaluative procedures in an attempt to discern whether low reading achievement is the result of underlying cognitive ability or processing difficulties or perhaps some other factor(s) that is (are) external to the individual (e.g., poor instruction in reading or cultural/linguistic differences).

Because there are empirically established relationships between select cognitive abilities and reading achievement (e.g., *Ga, Gsm, Glr, Gs;* see Chapter 2—abilities that constitute an individual's aptitude for reading achievement), assessment of functioning in these areas seems reasonable if not indispensable. In other words, because it is known that phonological awareness, short-term memory processes, and long-term storage and retrieval processes (e.g., Naming Facility or Rapid Automatic Naming), for example, assist in explaining substantial variance in reading achievement, assessment of these functions may provide important clues about why an individual is experiencing difficulties in reading, if one or more of these areas are found to be deficient. These clues, in turn, may be particularly informative for the development of intervention plans. Conversely, if functioning in these areas is found to be within normal limits, then it is likely that other factors, perhaps factors that are noncognitive in nature, may be related to the individual's manifest reading difficulties. In this case, the nature of intervention and attempts at remediation will very likely take a different course of action.

Therefore, when an individual is referred for reading difficulties, it seems crucial to conduct a comprehensive evaluation of reading achievement as well as the specific cognitive abilities that constitute one's aptitude for reading. However, when aptitude scores are used in lieu of global ability scores in ability/aptitude-achievement discrepancy analysis, the result may be quite different for the individual who has specific cognitive deficits related to reading. Specifically, a reading aptitude score will predict reading achievement better than a global ability score *precisely because* it was designed for this purpose. As such, aptitude scores are actually *less* likely to result in significant aptitude-achievement discrepancies (as compared to global ability scores) for individuals whose difficulties in reading are *intrinsic* in nature (e.g., related to one or more underlying cognitive processing or ability deficits, as measured by one or more tests that comprise the aptitude score). In such cases one might more appropriately expect to find an aptitude-achievement *consistency.*[1]

Consider the following example. A fifth-grader has both relative- and normative-based weaknesses in specific *Ga, Glr,* and *Gs* abilities, in an otherwise average profile of broad cognitive abilities, and concomitant reading deficits. This individual most likely will *not* demonstrate a severe ability-reading achievement discrepancy when her ability score is based on an aggregate of mainly *Ga, Glr,* and *Gs* ability scores, because these abilities have been shown to be significantly predictive of reading achievement in the elementary school years. Rather, as suggested previously, this individual would likely demonstrate an ability-achievement *consistency,* rather than discrepancy. This is because the ability score in this case no longer represents a measure of *general* ability but rather a measure of abilities *specific* to the development of reading and is, in essence, an *aptitude* score. A low score on this "global" measure would predict a low score on reading achievement, and the finding of this type of consistency may provide evidence for an underlying learning disability. Conversely, this same individual would tend to show a significant ability-reading achievement discrepancy when, for example, her ability score was based on an aggregate of mainly *Gf* and *Gv* ability scores—abilities that do not demonstrate a significant relation to reading achievement in the elementary school years. Note that, in this second scenario, such a discrepancy would be used by many practitioners as evidence for a learning disability, even when no underlying deficits intrinsic to the individual have been identified as factors that would logically contribute to manifest reading difficulties.

Such practice is at best questionable, and this example represents only one of many erroneous assumptions that result from sole reliance or overreliance on the discrepancy model and from misconceptions surrounding the difference between global ability and aptitude scores. In the former situation (no ability-achievement discrepancy), many practitioners would conclude that the individual *is not* learning disabled. In the latter situation (significant ability-achievement discrepancy), many practitioners would conclude that the individual *is* learning disabled. Neither conclusion is justified because neither conclusion accounts for the differential impact resulting from the deliberate or unintentional inclusion or exclusion of abilities specifically related to the academic skill of interest. This type of careful and logic-driven evaluation is critical to the process of defensible discrepancy analysis.

Use of Normative Analysis to Establish Deficient Functioning.   In a previous example, a comparison was drawn between Student A, who had a FSIQ of 120 and a reading standard score of 95, and Student B, who had a FSIQ of 110 and a reading standard score of 95. Very often the presence of a significant discrepancy alone, as in the case of Student A, is used as justification for establishing a learning disability. It was pointed out, however, that the presence of a discrepancy in Student A's case could not be used in isolation to suggest or identify the presence of a learning disability. This is because Student A's reading score (and Student B's as well) falls well within the average range of normal functioning in comparison to other individuals of the same age or grade (38th percentile). In essence, the discrepancy is irrelevant in both cases, precisely because there is nothing to establish that either student is a poor reader relative to a representative sample of same age peers from the general population. To establish this fact would require data and information above and beyond or contrary to that provided by the test data.

Now suppose all the scores in this example were shifted 13 standard score points (nearly one entire SD) downward. Student A would still demonstrate a significant discrepancy between her overall ability (Wechsler FSIQ of 107) and her measured reading achievement (standard score of 82). Student B would have a Wechsler FSIQ of 97, and a reading achievement standard score of 82. Like the previous example, suppose that the difference between student B's ability and achievement is not significant. In the previous example, Student A was diagnosed as LD on the basis of the significant discrepancy, whereas Student B was not (because it was believed that he was performing commensurate with his ability or potential). Even with a shift of nearly one standard deviation below prior levels, interpretation without consideration of normative standing would result in the same faulty conclusion as before. Student A would be seen as learning disabled and Student B as merely performing within his range of capability. Student A would probably receive special education services or accommodations and Student B would not, in spite of equivalent reading performance as indicated by these data.

When compared to a representative sample of individuals of the same chronological age or grade within the general population, it is clear that both students actually demonstrate low-average reading ability as measured by standardized tests and both demonstrate a *normative weakness* in reading ability (i.e., a standard score less than 85 or below the 16th percentile). The current pattern of scores seen in Student A's case may now well represent the presence of a learning disability, not so much because of the discrepancy, but because the achievement score in this example does indeed fall below normal limits. More data and information, of course, would be necessary to make a determination of LD. This contrasts with the previous example, where Student A's achievement score was within normal limits. Thus, the presence of a discrepancy alone is not sufficient to establish the presence of a learning disability. Rather, when standardized, norm-referenced tests are used, the achievement score (or the lower score in other types of discrepancies) should fall below normal limits in order to provide evidence that is necessary, but not necessarily sufficient, for LD determination.

Similarly, the absence of a discrepancy in Student B's case does not effectively rule out the possibility of a learning disability. In both the initial and current examples, Student B does not demonstrate a discrepancy between ability and achievement. But whereas achievement was formerly within normal limits, in the present case it is now outside and below normal limits. Given that the manifest reading performance, as measured by a standardized, norm-referenced test of achievement, is essentially equivalent in both cases, what justification exists to say that Student A is disabled, but not Student B? What justification exists for providing remedial services to Student A but not to Student B? Would not both students benefit from intervention? According to Stanovich (1999), this latter situation "would be the direct cause of discriminatory treatment that would be indefensible [in a court of law] from any standpoint" (p. 353).

Thus, failure to integrate normative analysis with relative analysis can have potentially serious consequences in the use and interpretation of the test data. It creates a system that arbitrarily identifies individuals as disabled, and therefore entitled to services, based on factors that have only marginal relevancy in differentiating LD from non-LD groups. Clearly, this example illustrates that illogical conclusions often result when test data, particularly the findings of ability-achievement discrepancy analysis, are interpreted without consideration of where performance falls relative to a normative standard or norm group, often to the exclusion of other data that may help support or refute identification of LD.

Conclusions regarding the meaningfulness of discrepancies in standardized test data must be based on careful consideration of the implications of normative analysis rather than remain locked into the narrow and highly misleading perspective offered by person-relative analysis. Failure to assess where performance (in particular performance as reflected by the lower score used in the discrepancy determination) lies with respect to the general population can lead to conclusions that average or high-average functioning is somehow deficient merely because it is discrepant (and lower) than some single outlier score or the average of all of the individuals' other scores. Discrepancy identification alone provides no substantive basis for any such conclusions related to actual deficits in ability or functioning. With respect to test data, only normative analysis reveals credible evidence that may or may not support actual deficits in functioning.

To summarize, the practice of discrepancy analysis is fraught with peril and remains one of the most difficult aspects of LD determination. Ironically, it may be largely irrelevant to the process because evaluation of underachievement may be accomplished through analysis of consistency. Discrepancy analysis requires that practitioners and clinicians utilize more sophisticated and reasoned methods and procedures than have been typically applied in assessment in order to avoid the many pitfalls and illogical conclusions that can result. Although the methods and illustrations presented in this section are rather simple and lack appropriate context (e.g., case history information, appropriate evaluation of exclusionary factors, etc.), they nevertheless demonstrate the most common error in the decision process whereby "nonsignificant discrepancy = *no learning disability* and significant discrepancy = *learning disability*" to which practitioners routinely and blindly adhere often under pressures related to existing federal and state special education eligibility criteria. Regardless of the various extrinsic influences or intrinsic motivational factors, decisions regarding the meaningfulness of observed discrepancies that are made without use of technically valid methods for calculating discrepancies, without knowledge of the construction and composition of ability and aptitude scores, without consideration of the relationships between specific cognitive abilities and academic skills, and without appropriate normative comparisons, are and will remain subject to being easily discredited in the literature and quite indefensible in practice.

Essential Elements of an Operational Definition of Learning Disabilities

Perhaps the greatest obstacle to reliable LD assessment has been the lack of a useful or even commonly accepted operational definition of the very construct. Not surprisingly, the lack of a guiding theory, practical operational definition, and dependable assessment framework has caused the practice of LD assessment to stumble badly, at times leaving practitioners to search blindly through a wide array of conditions, specifications, and test results in the hope that some sort of data might emerge that could presumably establish the presence of LD. The first issue regarding a guiding theory was addressed directly in Chapter 2, where CHC theory was presented as a modern and useful guiding paradigm within which LD can be well understood and operationalized. The third issue will be addressed in Chapter 14, which proposes a systematic, comprehensive framework for LD determination that is defensible and provides a practical method that is easily followed. The focus of this chapter is therefore primarily in response to the second issue—the establishment of a viable, practical operational definition of LD that is in keeping with currunt theory and that can be evaluated within the proposed framework.

Kavale and Forness (2000) reviewed critically the available definitions of LD and methods for their operationalization and found them to be largely inadequate. They then proposed a modest, hierarchical definition that contained the most salient and crucial aspects of the literature with regard to achieving a definition that reflected current research on the nature of this condition. This definition is illustrated in Figure 11.1. The operational definition offered by Kavale and Forness (2000) attempted to incorporate the complex and multivariate nature of LD. In their schematic operational definition, LD is determined through evaluation of several levels that specify particular diagnostic conditions. Each level of their evaluation hierarchy represented a necessary but not sufficient condition for determination of LD. The authors contend that it is only when the specified criteria are met at all five levels that LD can be established as a "discrete and independent condition" (p. 251). Clearly, in their attempt to resolve the LD definition problem, Kavale and Forness provided much more rational and defensible guidance than what had been offered by their predecessors. Their operationalization of LD, which uses "foundation principles in guiding the selection of elements that explicate the nature of LD" (p. 251), represents both a departure from and an important new direction for current practice.

There were in our opinion, however, some difficulties with the operational definition put forth by Kavale and Forness (2000). Although we essentially agree with their basic operational definition, particularly as it applies to the complex and multivariate nature of LD, their model did not directly incorporate a well-validated theoretical paradigm and there was no specific guidance given on what methods might be used to accomplish effective measurement of LD. In addition, the hierarchical structure seems to imply somewhat of a linear approach to assessment, whereas we tend to view the process as more recursive and iterative. Consequently, the major differences between their operational definition and the one

FIGURE 11.1   Example of an Operational Definition of Learning Disability by Kavale and Forness (2000)

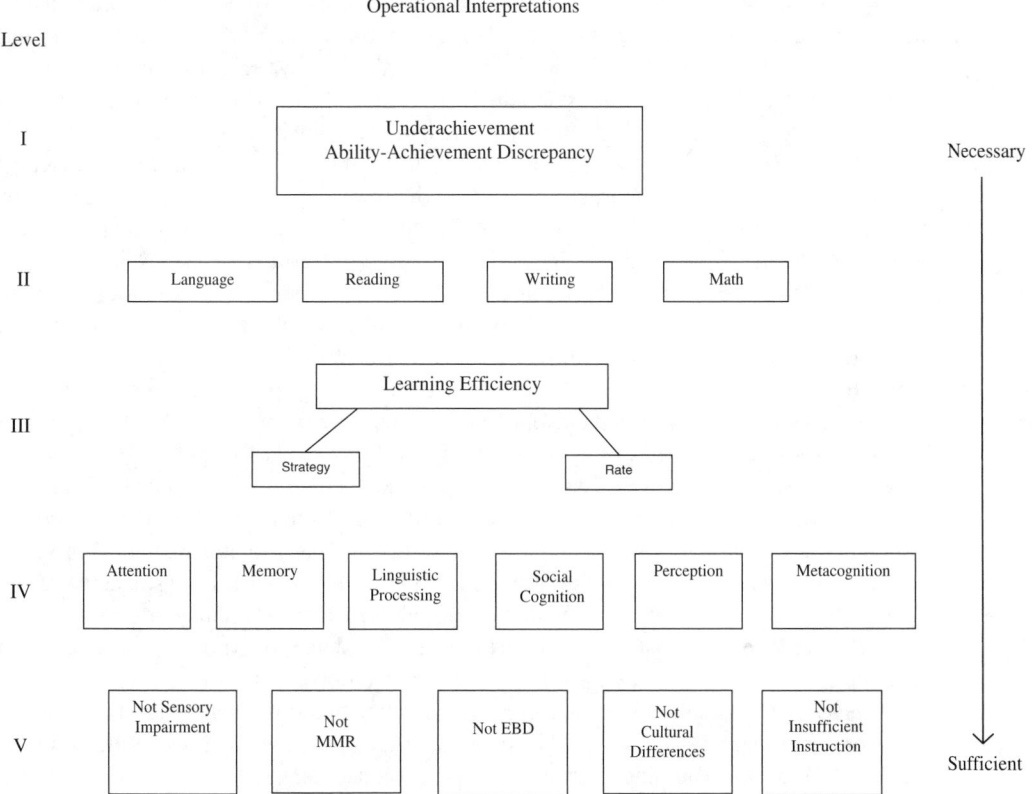

Source: K. A. Kavale and S. R. Forness, "What Definitions of Learning Disability Say and Don't Say: A Critical Analysis," *Journal of Learning Disabilities, 33,* 3 (2000): 239–256. Reprinted by permission of Sage Publications Ltd.

we propose here is related primarily to the inclusion and integration of CHC theory as well as other considerations we felt to be crucial to the creation of an accurate definition. A detailed discussion of the content and manner in which Kavale and Forness's scheme was modified in order to create the current operational definition follows.

Our current proposal for an operational definition of LD is presented in Figure 11.2. The essential elements in defining LD as illustrated in the figure include (1) inter-academic ability analysis and evaluation of mitigating and exclusionary factors, (2) inter-cognitive ability analysis and evaluation of mitigating and exclusionary factors, (3) integrated ability analysis, and (4) evaluation of interference with learning. These elements are depicted as distinct levels in Figure 11.2 and together form the complete operational definition of LD that we believe provides a means for accomplishing reliable and valid assessment. The levels illustrated in Figure 11.2 represent an adaptation and extension of the recommendations offered by Kavale and Forness (2000) but also include concepts from a variety of other researchers (e.g., Flanagan, McGrew, & Ortiz, 2000; Flanagan & Ortiz, 2001; McGrew & Flanagan, 1998; Siegel, 1999; Stanovich, 1999; Vellutino et al., 2000).

In general, the various levels of the operational definition of LD presented in Figure 11.2 differ significantly from the ones presented in Kavale and Forness (2000) in four important ways. First, the current levels are firmly grounded in an established contemporary theory on the structure of abilities (i.e., CHC theory), a component that is absent from Kavale and Forness's model. Second, Kavale and Forness seem to suggest that a significant ability-achievement discrepancy must be established at the initial phase, prior to proceeding through the next four levels of their model. In other words, in their view, an ability-achievement discrepancy is a necessary but not sufficient condition for LD. In contrast, this type of discrepancy analysis occurs much later, at Level III, in the framework presented here. Moreover, much as has been suggested by Siegel (1999) and Stanovich (1999), among others, the proposed framework accommodates the notion that a significant discrepancy *need not be present* to establish LD primarily because the finding of a significant ability-achievement discrepancy is dependent on the ability measure used in the discrepancy formula (Flanagan, McGrew, & Ortiz, 2000). That is, different ability measures will result in different discrepancies (either significant or nonsignificant) for different reasons. Third, the final level of Kavale and Forness's model is the exclusionary clause that is found in most definitions of LD. This clause is depicted in the present framework at Levels I-B and II-B because we believe that evaluation of exclusionary criteria should occur early in the process of assessment and evaluation of LD in order to prevent individuals from having to undergo needless and potentially invasive testing. And fourth, although there is a somewhat logical progression from one level to the next, we seek to reinforce the notion that LD assessment is a recursive process and that information generated and evaluated at one level may inform decisions made at other levels and that a return to prior levels could well be warranted depending on the unique circumstances of the case. The recursive or iterative nature of LD assessment was not included in the Kavale and Forness conceptualization but forms an important component in the present model. Readers should be aware that the operational definition illustrated in Figure 11.2 is by no means linear in nature and is best conceptualized as cyclical or recursive. This notion becomes particularly evident in Chapter 14, where this operational definition is embedded within the presentation and discussion of a comprehensive framework for LD assessment. The recursive process of LD assessment that we advocate is clearly identifiable within this structure (see Figure 14.1) and practitioners should guard against engaging in activities that utilize linear logic or flow. Readers may wish to refer often to Figure 11.2 for clarification of the descriptions of the essential elements of our proposed operational definition of LD that follow.

Because this discussion focuses on the essential components of an operational definition of LD within the context of the school setting, it is assumed that the levels of evaluation represented in Figure 11.2 begin after some form of prereferral assessment activity has been carefully conducted and only when a focused evaluation of specific abilities through standardized testing has been deemed necessary. Evaluation of the presence of a learning disability beginning with Level I is based on the presumption that an individual has been specifically referred for testing due to observed learning difficulties and that these difficulties have undergone some sort of ameliorative prereferral intervention or instructional accommodation process with little or no apparent success. Moreover, prior to beginning LD assessment through the use of standardized tests, other important and significant data sources should have already been uncovered within the context of these intervention activities, including such things as results from informal testing, direct observation of behaviors,

Level I-A: Measurement of Specific Academic Skills and Acquired Knowledge — Inter-Academic Ability Analysis

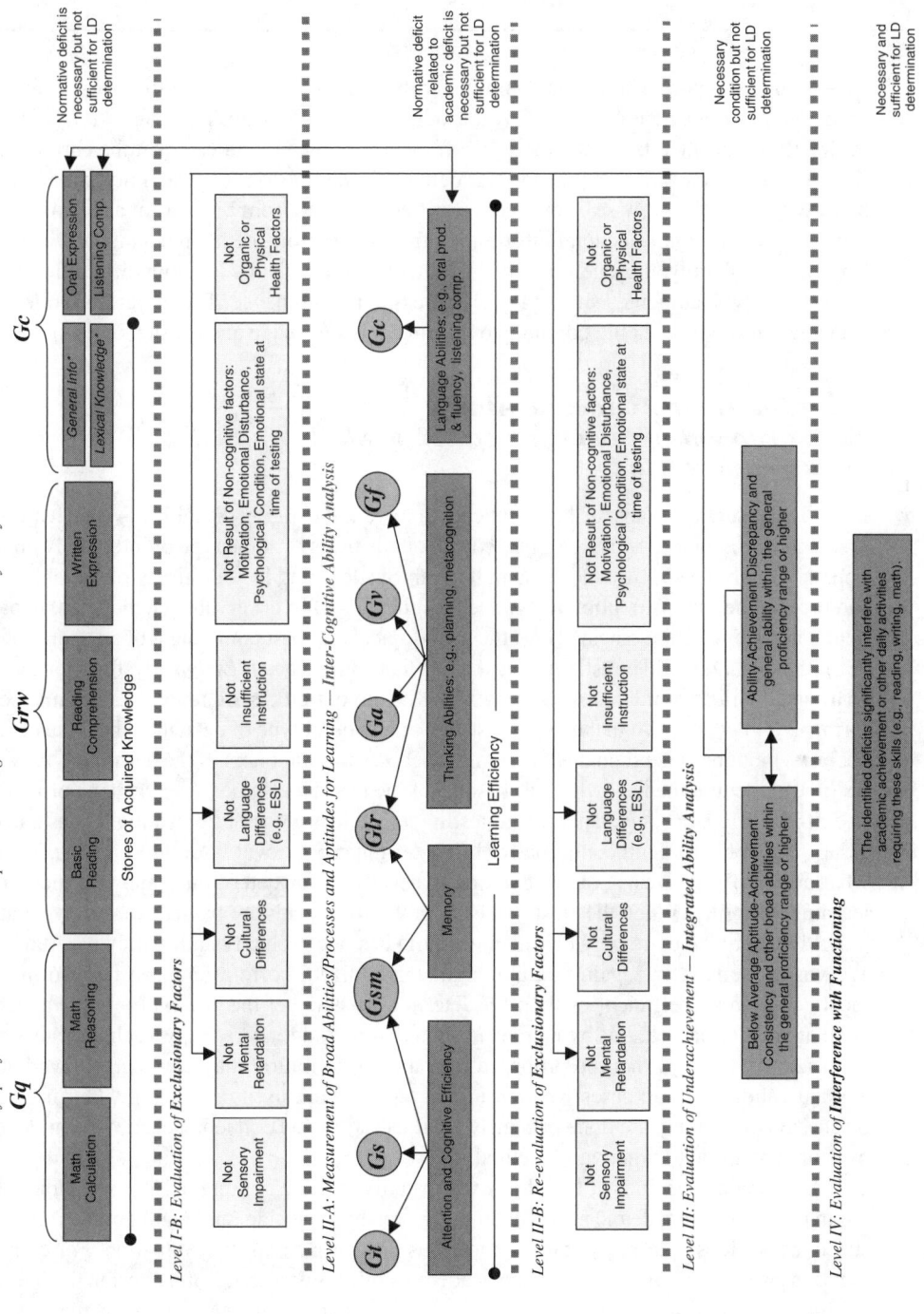

Level I-B: Evaluation of Exclusionary Factors

Level II-A: Measurement of Broad Abilities/Processes and Aptitudes for Learning — Inter-Cognitive Ability Analysis

Level II-B: Re-evaluation of Exclusionary Factors

Level III: Evaluation of Underachievement — Integrated Ability Analysis

Level IV: Evaluation of Interference with Functioning

*These areas of Gc are not specifically included in the wording contained in IDEA.

FIGURE 11.2   Essential Elements of an Operational Definition of Learning Disability

work samples, reports from people familiar with the individual's difficulties such as teachers or parents, information provided by the individual, and so forth. The diagnosis of LD can be bolstered considerably when there is sufficient evidence to indicate that the current difficulties have been well documented through a recorded history of academic achievement below what might otherwise be expected as reflected in and from a review of academic transcripts, grade reports, anecdotal information from instructors, developmental data, and the like. In general, only after the scope and nature of an individual's learning difficulties have been carefully documented should Level I assessment commence. Thereafter, the collected data and information should continue to inform decisions made at each step in the process.

Level I-A: Inter-Academic Ability Analysis— Measurement of Specific Academic Skills and Acquired Knowledge

Level I represents perhaps the basic concept involved in learning disabilities—that learning is somehow disrupted from its normal course on the basis of some type of internal dysfunction. Although the specific mechanism that inhibits learning is not directly observable, we can proceed on the assumption that it does manifest itself in observable phenomena, in particular academic achievement. Thus, the most logical and first component of an operational definition of LD should be establishing the fact that some type of *learning* dysfunction exists apart and distinct from just low reading ability. If no deficit can be found in academic performance, whether through the use of test data or any other type of data, then the issue of LD becomes moot because such dysfunction is a necessary component of the definition. As will become evident in the following discussions of the next levels, the presence of a normative deficit identified through standardized testing is one method for establishing this as a necessary, but not sufficient, condition for LD determination. Level I-A represents the first of what are, in effect, "tests" of the conditions necessary for determining the presence of a learning disability. When the "tests" at each of the four levels are passed, we believe that a practitioner can be extremely confident that LD has been reliably and validly ascertained. We wish to emphasize again that although standardized, norm-referenced tests form the most common and efficient method for determining whether the criteria (or tests) at each level are met or passed, it is by no means the only method for arriving at such conclusions. Rather, we recognize that the proposed operational definition may well be followed and applied validly even in cases where minimal test data are used or available. Our use and discussion of test data are done primarily for illustration and convenience, not to endorse it over or in addition to other valid methods.

Assessment activities at Level I-A will usually involve comprehensive assessment of the major areas of academic achievement (e.g., reading, writing, and math abilities) or any subset of abilities that may comprise the focus and purpose of the evaluation. For convenience as well as practical reasons, the academic abilities depicted at this level in the hierarchy are organized according to the seven areas of achievement specified in the federal definition of LD as outlined in the Individuals with Disabilities Education Act (IDEA; P.L. 105-17)—namely, math calculation, math reasoning, basic reading, reading comprehension, and so on. The rationale for using the areas from IDEA is based primarily on the fact that these learning domains are included in nearly all prevailing definitions of LD. We have noted already that these definitions, however, remain rather inadequate because they are not based on any particular theoretical formulation and thus remain quite vague and nonspecific. Therefore, for theoretical and psychometric reasons, the academic abilities depicted at this level have also been organized according to the broad CHC abilities that encompass these achievement domains (i.e., *Gq, Grw,* and *Gc*). Consistent with the discussion of CHC theory in earlier chapters, generally speaking, Level I abilities tend to represent an individual's *stores of acquired knowledge* (Carroll, 1993; Woodcock, 1993). These specific knowledge bases (i.e., *Gq, Grw,* and *Gc*) develop almost exclusively as a function of formal instruction, schooling, and educationally related experiences. It was also noted in Chapter 2 that *Gc* tends to be somewhat of an exception to this rule. The abilities found under *Gc* include not only examples of repositories of learned material (e.g., lexical knowledge, general information, etc.) but also abilities that reflect the processing of information, such as oral production and fluency and listening comprehension. Consequently, we have chosen to make a slight distinction between these narrow abilities as represented under *Gc* in Level II-A (see Figure 11.2) and at Level I-A. It seems reasonable that the *Gc* abilities representing the stores of acquired knowledge will be those that are of main interest at Level I-A, whereas any assessment that progresses to Level II-A will likely focus more on the process-oriented abilities. The dual nature of *Gc* in this respect is illustrated by the two-way arrows that link *Gc* (and its narrow abilities) at Level I-A and Level II-A, respectively.

Evaluation of LD, irrespective of the particular level of activity, should also be driven by presumptions of normal functioning rather than preconceptions of dysfunction. That is, it is important to assume that an individual is not learning disabled prior to evaluating any data in order to prevent confirmatory bias (Sandoval, 1998). *Confirmatory bias* is the tendency to look only for data that support a preconception and to ignore data that tend to refute it. Beginning with the presumption of "deficit" increases the chances that one will be found. We believe that adoption of the view that establishes normal functioning as the prevailing assumption is more appropriate and equitable for the examinee. Furthermore, the assumption of normal functioning must remain true unless and until the data clearly demonstrate otherwise. With respect to standardized test data, this means that in the absence of any gross physiological trauma or developmental dysfunction, and given a history of appropriate and sufficient instruction and opportunity to learn, it is expected that an individual undergoing LD assessment will perform within normal limits on tests of academic achievement (i.e., standard scores of 85 to 115, inclusive). This remains true for any and all areas depicted at Level I-A in Figure 11.2 that may have been evaluated.

Determination as to whether or not the null hypothesis is supportable may be determined by analyzing performance of the individual against that of the test's norm sample. This is the first test: Is performance relative to individuals of the same age in the general population within normal limits? Note that the comparison is not based on performance within the individual, but rather performance of the individual against other individuals. Thus, person-relative deficits, no matter how large, are largely meaningless as indicators of dysfunction unless one of the individual's scores on a reliable and valid test falls below and outside the normative deficit range (i.e., standard score of less than 85). Unless test data clearly point to a normative deficit in one or more areas of academic functioning, advancement to Level I-B analysis is largely unwarranted. When no scores exist to support the presence of a true normative weaknesses (i.e., standard scores greater than 1 standard deviation *below* the normative mean), the first test of LD determination is failed and a necessary condition for LD diagnosis is not met. At this point, the evaluator should seek either to evaluate the sufficiency of the academic evaluation or to reexamine the referral questions and concerns. For example, it is entirely possible that the test selected for initial evaluation simply failed to adequately assess the specific area of dysfunction. In addition, any identified academic deficits should be in the area in which the individual was reported to have difficulties. That is, the documented deficit must be consistent with referral concerns, academic history, teacher reports, and so forth. Unexpected or spurious findings of academic deficits unrelated to the referral concerns should be reconciled with prereferral data before contemplating further assessment. It would be rather capricious to move forward in assessment if either no deficiencies in performance or if some deficiency in an unexpected area were found.

Level I-B: Evaluation of Exclusionary Factors

The test at Level I-B involves evaluation as to whether the documented academic skill or knowledge deficit found through Level I-A analysis is *primarily* the result of factors that are largely external to the individual or noncognitive in nature. Because the reasons for deficit performance are many and do not always reflect an actual manifestation of LD, clinicians must be careful not to ascribe causal links to LD prematurely and should develop reasonable hypotheses related to other potential causes. For example, cultural or language differences are two common factors that can adversely affect test performance and result in data that appear to suggest LD. In addition, lack of motivation, emotional disturbance, performance anxiety, psychiatric disorders, sensory impairments and medical conditions (e.g., hearing or vision problems), and so on, need to be ruled out as potential explanatory correlates to any deficiencies identified at Level I-A. The crux of the test rests on the extent to which any external or noncognitive factor can be determined as being the primary reason for the deficit in academic performance uncovered in Level I-A. If any such reason is found that meets this criterion, then the second test of LD is failed and the operational definition of LD is not met.

Note, however, that external factors may well be present and may even negatively affect results to a certain degree. Certainly, individuals who may have vision problems, chronic illnesses, limited-English proficiency, and so forth, can also be learning disabled. The test is not failed when such external factors are simply present or even when they may be contributing to the poor performance. The test is failed only when those factors are determined to be *primarily* responsible for the performance. In cases where they are believed to represent only *contributory* causes and the deficit performance is believed to be a valid reflection of true performance and functioning, the test is not failed and the condition for evaluating exclusionary variables may well be met. It is possible that LD may coexist with or be exacerbated by the presence of other performance-inhibiting variables but LD is not the focus of evaluation at this level. Rather, it is the direct examination of exclusionary variables that remains the focus here in order to ensure fair and equitable evaluation of the extant data. Evaluation at this level is not intended to rule in LD but rather to specifically rule out other possible explanations apart from LD. Recall that the determination of LD is made only after all five tests are passed. Assessment should not proceed to the next level until there is sufficient evidence and data to conclude confidently that the observed pattern of learning difficulties is not due primarily to these exclusionary factors, even if they are contributory.

One of the major reasons for placing evaluation of exclusionary factors at this point in the assessment process is to provide a mechanism that is efficient in both time and effort and that may prevent the unnecessary administration of tests or imposition of any further invasive and unnecessary evaluative procedures. Use of standardized tests, especially IQ tests, cannot be considered a benign process. The implications and ramifications that can result from their use demands that they be carefully and selectively applied only when absolutely necessary. We recognize, of course, that it may not be possible to completely and convincingly rule out all the numerous potential factors at this stage in the assessment process. Consider, for example, that "lack of motivation" appears to be a rather tangible and circumscribed construct but is in fact a manifest variable that may emerge from an almost endless number of possibilities (e.g., drug use, poor nutrition, family dysfunction, etc.). The actual number of possibilities that may explain poor performance on any given test of achievement are indeed infinite. Proper assessment must therefore seek to uncover and evaluate as many possibilities as is practical or necessary.

It is also recognized that some relevant and important factors may not be uncovered until much later in the assessment process. This is because evaluation of exclusionary factors tends to be a recursive activity, occurring throughout the entire process of evaluation. In other words, as the evaluation of learning difficulties unfolds, the practitioner continually tests and retests hypotheses that the primary correlates to the manifest academic deficiencies are, for example, external to the individual, rather than the result of intrinsic deficits (e.g., cognitive processing deficits). New data often lead to new hypotheses. Also, it may not be possible to rule out certain conditions at this level, such as mental retardation, which may well necessitate Level II-A assessment. Thus, the process of ruling out exclusionary factors that contribute significantly to poor academic achievement—including psychological conditions, pervasive low ability (e.g., mental retardation), and so forth—is perhaps best conceptualized as beginning early in the evaluation process but continuing through the final level of analysis as may be necessary and appropriate. When the conditions listed at Level I-B have been assessed, at least those that can be reliably evaluated and determined not to be the primary reason for the observed academic deficits, assessment may advance confidently to examination of Level II-A criteria.

Level II-A: Inter-Cognitive Ability Analysis— Measurement of Broad Abilities/Processes and Aptitudes for Learning

The test at Level II-A is similar to the one at Level I-A except that it is conducted with data from the assessment of cognitive abilities and processes. In general, the process of assessment at Level II-A, when using standardized tests, as with the measurement of abilities at Level I-A, proceeds with the expectation that an individual will perform within normal limits (i.e., standard scores of 85 to 115, inclusive) in each of the areas represented in Level II-A (see Figure 11.2). The essence of the test at this level is the question: Is performance on tests of cognitive ability or processes within normal limits relative to people of the same age in the general population? Of the more salient aspects involved in creating an operational definition of LD, none is more central than the need to establish the presence of a normative deficit in a particular cognitive ability that is logically related to and the presumptive cause of the observed academic deficits (e.g., from Level I-A analysis and other data). This condition has historically been rather poorly defined and remains rather vague. The reason may well be due primarily to the lack of a guiding theory. Clinicians have long understood the need to identify some sort of psychological dysfunction as an explanatory mechanism for deficient academic performance—yet there has been little if any theoretical specification to guide or support the myriad illogical assumptions that were often made. Thus, in order to arrive at an effective operational definition of LD, theory must once again come to the forefront and play a significant role in the evaluation process.

The cognitive abilities depicted at this level in the evaluation hierarchy are organized according to the broad abilities specified by CHC theory (i.e., *Gs, Gsm, Glr, Ga, Gv, Gf,* and *Gc*). These CHC abilities are organized further according to the processes they represent primarily within an information processing perspective, including attention and cognitive efficiency, memory, "thinking abilities," and language abilities (e.g., Dean & Woodcock, 1999; Woodcock, 1993). The latter category represents the collection of *Gc* narrow abilities that more accurately reflect processing skills as opposed to the abilities that represent stores of acquired knowledge that were evaluated at Level I-A. Generally speaking, the abilities depicted at Level II-A provide valuable information about an individual's *learning efficiency*. Development of the cognitive abilities represented at this level tend to be less dependent on formal classroom instruction and schooling as compared to the "academic" abilities presented at Level I-A. Furthermore, specific or narrow abilities within many of the CHC areas listed in Level II-A may be combined to yield specific aptitudes for learning in different areas (e.g., reading, math, writing). These aptitudes would be expected to be logically related (as specified by theory) and, in terms of performance, consistent with their respective academic criterion measured at Level I-A. When standardized tests are used, clinicians are encouraged to use the CHC worksheets included in Appendix A to assist them in selecting tests to ensure that the specific cognitive areas to be assessed are evaluated directly and thoroughly from a contemporary and well-validated theory of human cognitive abilities. In addition, detailed guidelines for selecting tests for Level II-A analysis as well as the specific broad and narrow abilities to be assessed vis-à-vis referral information will be presented in detail in Chapter 12.

Data generated at this level of analysis, in similar fashion to data generated at Level I-A, also provide input for Level III analyses, should the process advance to the third level. Very often, aside from data on specific cognitive abilities and processes, a global ability score or one or more aptitude scores are derived for later use in ability-achievement discrepancy or aptitude-achievement consistency analysis, as appropriate. Other uses of data notwithstanding, the test at Level II-A is passed only when two specific criteria are met: (1) identification of a population-relative normative deficit in at least one area of cognitive ability or processing and (2) identification of empirical or logical and theoretically specified causal links between deficit functioning in at least one area of cognitive ability or processing and a corresponding deficit in academic performance (as identified in Level I-A analysis). The first criterion is necessary in order to establish the presence of a psychological processing disorder or dysfunction as defined by the literature pertaining to LD. Poor achievement performance, in the absence of any cognitive impairment, does not meet the operational definition proposed here or in most other definitions for that matter. In addition, the cognitive impairment must be normatively based, not person based, and so-called weaknesses derived from ipsative analysis are irrelevant, no matter how significant, until and unless the "relative weakness" also falls within the normative weakness range. The second criterion is necessary in order to establish a valid basis for linking the cognitive dysfunction with the academic dysfunction. For example, when an individual is referred for reading difficulties, one would expect to find manifest reading difficulties (i.e., *Grw*) and to find difficulties with the cognitive processes that underlie reading difficulties—for example, *Ga, Gc, Glr, Gs,* and so on, as specified by theory and supported by empirical research. One would not expect to find difficulties in say, *Gv*, given that it plays a rather nonsignificant role in the development of reading. As such, in the case of a referral for reading difficulties, identification of *Gv* as the presumed cause of the reading problems is illogical and unsupportable according to theory and research and thus fails to meet the second criterion of the test. Such a pattern of results does not form the necessary conditions with which to proceed in the determination of LD.

Level II-B: Reevaluation of Exclusionary Factors

Determining the presence of a normative-based cognitive deficit that is empirically or logically connected to the deficit area(s) identified at Level I-A is the core of the test at Level II-A but it is not the only consideration. Although the absence of a defensible relationship between Level I-A and Level II-A deficits effectively eliminates the need to advance to the next stage of assessment, the process can also be halted or redirected through reevaluation of mitigating or exclusionary factors as accomplished previously in Level I-B. The presence of verifiable cognitive deficits directly related to academic performance difficulties is fundamental to the operational definition of LD proposed herein, but these deficits must not be primarily the result of exclusionary factors. Hypotheses regarding any reasonable explanations for any observed cognitive deficit(s) must be entertained in order to establish confidence that the data represent an accurate and valid reflection of true ability. Rather than representing a new or unique level in the operational definition of LD, reevaluation of these mitigating and exclusionary factors illustrate the recursive and iterative nature of the process as defined by the essential components of LD here at Level II-B. The exclusion of attenuating variables on performance is an important consideration that occurs prior to the use of standardized tests as well as following each administration of standardized tests. Reliable and valid measurement of LD depends heavily on being able to exclude the many factors that could play a part in negatively affecting performance particularly on standardized tests. When such factors have been carefully evaluated and excluded as the primary reason for the observed cognitive deficits, and when the two necessary criteria for the test at this level have been met, the process may appropriately advance to the third level.

Level III: Integrated Ability Analysis—
Evaluation of Underachievement

Integrated ability analysis, as defined and explained here, specifically revolves around theory-guided examination of individual performance across all data (cognitive and academic) in order to establish logical, research-based conditions that are necessary in the operational definition of LD. We seek to be clear that integrated ability analysis in this sense bears no relationship or similarity to ipsative analysis whatsoever. Evaluation at this point does not seek to find statistically significant, person-relative or "intra-individual" discrepancies within the context of an individual's own pattern of cognitive or academic abilities. In fact, ipsative analysis, the search for statistically significant "strengths and weaknesses," does not provide any information beyond that which can already be obtained through normative analysis. The nature of the integrated ability analysis that we describe here in Level III is related to evaluation of differences between broad patterns of cognitive and academic abilities that establishes a clear picture of academic underachievement. The criteria for evaluation stems from application of theory and research that provides a scientific basis for deriving meaning from the patterns found in the collected data.

Advancement to this level automatically implies that three necessary conditions for determination of LD have already been met: (1) one or more academic ability deficits have been identified, (2) one or more logically related normative-based deficits in cognitive abilities or processes have been identified, and (3) the academic and cognitive deficits have been determined not to be the result of exclusionary factors. What has not yet been determined, however, is whether the pattern of results supports the notion of underachievement in the manner that might be expected in cases of suspected LD or whether the pattern of results may be better explained via alternative causes such as mild mental retardation or other factors known to have an adverse impact on both academic and cognitive performance (e.g., sensory-motor handicaps, lack of English language proficiency, etc.). Thus, the test at Level III involves a demonstration that not only does an individual possess specific, circumscribed, and related academic and cognitive deficits but also that these deficits exist within an otherwise *normal ability* profile and thus suggest underachievement. When standardized tests are used, determining whether the criteria are met for this particular Level III test can take one of two forms—analysis of aptitude-achievement consistency or ability-achievement discrepancy.

When accomplished within the scope of CHC theory as outlined in Chapter 2, test data generated from Level II-A assessment will produce broad-ability cluster scores (e.g., *Gf*, *Gc*, *Gv*, etc.) and either specific aptitude scores (e.g., reading aptitude) or global/general ability scores (e.g., FSIQ, VIQ, PIQ, etc.). When broad CHC ability clusters and *specific aptitude clusters* are generated at Level II-A, it is most appropriate to conduct an *aptitude-achievement consistency analysis* at Level III to determine a pattern of underachievement suggestive of LD. Given the historical predominance of the discrepancy model, evaluation of consistency may appear rather strange at first. As noted previously an aptitude score is comprised specifically of tests that are most directly relevant to the development and acquisition of specific academic skills and thus form the best predictor of the corresponding achievement area. For example, an individual with low reading ability and isolated cognitive deficits in one or more areas related to reading achievement (e.g., phonological awareness, processing speed, short-term memory) will most likely demonstrate consistency between scores of reading aptitude and reading achievement. Likewise, a high reading aptitude score would predict high reading achievement—the two scores are more likely to be *consistent* with each other, not discrepant.

Because consistency in scores that are within normal limits or even above it would have already failed to demonstrate normative-based deficits, LD determination at this level is more concerned with scores that fall below the average range. A low aptitude score coupled with a low academic achievement score is insufficient, however, in order to pass the current test unless it occurs within the context of otherwise average or better functioning. Meeting the requirement involves evaluation of consistency between low aptitude and low achievement scores as well as a pattern of results that demonstrates average or better functioning in other cognitive abilities. Low aptitude scores across the board or multiple low aptitude scores with corresponding low achievement scores may be more suggestive of mild mental retardation—a condition that would preclude determination of LD in this definition. In the case of the individual with reading difficulties, it would be necessary to determine the level of performance or functioning in areas largely unrelated to the manifest academic deficit—for example, broad *Gf* and *Gv* abilities. If the majority of these abilities are within normal limits relative to same-aged people in the general population, then the practitioner can be reasonably confident that underachievement represented by the consistency between aptitude and achievement is most likely the primary result of the observed cognitive deficits, effectively ruling out other potential explanatory causes, such as low cognitive ability or lack of English language proficiency.

When the assessment activities at Level II-A are designed in a manner that generates broad CHC ability clusters and a global or general ability score (as opposed to specific aptitude clusters), it is possible to engage in *ability-achievement discrepancy analysis*—its technical problems notwithstanding. If it is found that the academic and cognitive normative deficits identified at Levels I-A and II-A, respectively, are logically related to one another and are circumscribed (i.e., most *broad* CHC ability clusters are within normal limits), and if the measures of the specific ability deficit(s) identified at Level II-A are *not included* in the global ability score, it would then be logical to expect that global ability will be within normal limits and significantly discrepant from the identified deficits in academic area(s). Discrepancy occurs in this case primarily because the global ability score contains no tests on which the individual has any difficulties, and therefore expectation of consistency is unwarranted. If, on the other hand, the global ability score was derived using one or more measures in which the individual did demonstrate a deficit, the global ability estimate becomes attenuated (and begins to resemble an aptitude score) and would not likely be significantly discrepant from the academic area of deficiency. In this situation, evaluation of consistency becomes salient again and it is imperative that practitioners examine functioning across the broad CHC clusters to determine if most, but not necessarily all, broad abilities fall within normal limits. This would be especially true in cases where the global ability score falls below and outside normal limits (i.e., a standard score less than 85).

Although consistency analysis represents a reasonable and theoretically defensible method for evaluating underachievement, the same cannot be said for discrepancy analysis. Discrepancy analysis has persisted despite its inherent logical flaws and technical inadequacy primarily because of its apparent intuitive appeal. Nevertheless, it has been roundly criticized and discredited in the literature (Badian, 1999; Finlan, 1992; Fletcher, Francis, Rourke, Shaywitz, & Shaywitz, 1992; Fletcher, Francis, Shaywitz, Lyon, Foorman, Stuebing, & Shaywitz, 1998; Gaskill & Brantley, 1996; Heath & Kush, 1991; Meyer, 2000; Reynolds, 1990; Ross, 1992; Siegel, 1999; Stanovich, 1991) to the point that clinicians ought to consider abandoning the concept altogether. In the operational definition of LD proposed here, identification of an ability-achievement discrepancy is accommodated but it may well be irrelevant and it is neither a necessary nor sufficient condition for reliable and valid determination of LD. Consistency analysis by itself can be used reliably to determine LD and represents a far superior method that is both psychometrically and theoretically defensible and should be considered over discrepancy analysis in any LD evaluation.

Level IV: Evaluation of Interference with Functioning

When LD determination reaches this point, analysis at the previous three levels has presumably passed each test and met every necessary condition required to support the presence of a learning disability. A fourth test seems hardly necessary but an operational definition of

LD based only on the previous criteria would still remain relatively incomplete. One of the basic eligibility requirements contained in both the legal and clinical prescriptions for establishing learning disability refers to whether the suspected learning disorder actually results in significant or substantial academic failure or other restriction/limitation in daily life functioning. Of course, *learning disorder* is a rather broad term and is not necessarily limited simply to classroom work, although that is one environment in which the disorder should be most evident in children, given the specific focus on learning activities and development. Functioning can extend beyond traditional academic subjects and may include an individual's ability to partake in other education-related activities such as physical education, art, music, and so on. Accordingly, in the matter of determining LD, the test of this final analysis boils down to evaluation of the extent to which functioning, whether in the classroom or in other major life activities that require the skill, has been significantly and negatively affected.

The legal and diagnostic specifications of LD, indispensable parts of operationalizing LD into everyday practice, necessitate that practitioners review the whole of the collected data and make a professional judgment about the extent of the negative impact that any measured disorder has had on an individual's performance in one or more areas of functioning or academic achievement. Essentially, Level IV analysis serves as a kind of "quality control" test that is designed to prevent the application of LD diagnosis in cases where real-world functioning is not in fact substantially impaired as compared to others in the general population, irrespective of the patterns seen in the data.

The notion of interference with learning is not unique to the specification of LD contained in IDEA. The *Diagnostic and Statistical Manual of Mental Disorders, Fourth Edition* (*DSM-IV;* American Psychiatric Association, 1994) provides a very similar criterion with respect to the diagnosis of academically related disorders. According to *DSM-IV,* "The learning problems significantly interfere with academic achievement or activities of daily living that require reading, mathematical, or writing skills" (p. 46).

The deficit or impairment in ability identified across Levels I, II, and III, respectively, must significantly interfere with academic performance (in one or more of the seven areas of achievement specified under IDEA) or any other area involved in daily life functioning or activity that requires the use or application of said ability according to *DSM-IV.* Unfortunately, there is no accepted operational standard by which the conditions of "significant interference" or "adverse effects" can be readily evaluated. Perhaps the most reasonable standard comes from evaluation used already to establish the preceding normative deficits—general learning performance that falls outside the average range and is significantly below that of the average person in the general population. In children, this may be best evaluated by a review of an individual's record of achievement, including grades, report cards, transcripts, prior evaluations, group achievement test scores, educational attainment, and so on. Clearly, some type of developmental data and history of academic difficulties as related specifically to the identified learning problems from the process of LD determination would be minimally necessary in order to pass this fourth and final test. A determination of LD in an individual who does not demonstrate a history of substantial impairment in learning is unlikely to be defensible. When the fourth test is passed, in combination with the three previous tests, LD may now be ascertained. When this test is failed, the case may need to be reviewed and reconceptualized and other hypotheses developed and tested with additional data.

Ultimately, this final criterion reflects the need to take a very broad survey of not only the entire array of data collected on an individual during the course of assessment but also the real-world manifestations and practical implications of any presumed disability. In general, if the principles specified in Levels I through III have been followed and the criteria adhered to, it is very likely that in the vast majority of cases, Level IV analysis serves only to confirm conclusions that have already been drawn up to this point. However, in cases where data may be equivocal, Level IV analysis becomes an important safety valve, ensuring that any representations of LD suggested by the data are indeed manifest in observable impairments in one or more areas of functioning in real-life settings. Level IV analysis helps to guard against the tendency to identify LD on the basis of insufficient data or inappropriate criteria (e.g., presence of a discrepancy in the absence of normative deficits or statistically significant but largely irrelevant relative deficits).

Summary of the Proposed Operational Definition of LD

When each test is met at each of the four levels necessary for LD determination (as depicted in Figure 11.2), it may be concluded that the data gathered are sufficient to support a diagnosis of LD. As such, much like the one offered by Kavale and Forness (2000), the operational definition presented in this chapter represents an initial proposal toward a more complete and defensible operational definition as well as a guide to the process of evaluation. Although the specifications and procedures implied by this definition are grounded in current theory and research as well as in recent literature on LD assessment, no assertions can be made at this time regarding the actual validity of this operational definition. As with any new development, only future empirical research can provide a more substantive basis for claims of validity. Nevertheless, it is our contention that when the levels of LD determination and the corresponding evaluative activities are followed in accordance with the guidelines and conditions described, the psychometric and theoretical defensibility of LD determination is significantly increased. It is our hope that this type of operational definition might lead to a potential increase in the agreement among professionals with respect to who does and does not have a learning disability.

Conclusions

This chapter began with a discussion of the problems that exist with traditional operational definitions and models for determining learning disabilities. It was noted that such models have fared poorly in practice and research and have failed to differentiate students with learning disabilities from students without learning disabilities who are more or less underachievers (e.g., Aaron, 1997; Brackett & McPherson, 1996; Kavale & Forness, 2000; Siegel, 1998, 1999; Stanovich, 1999). The reasons why traditional models are inadequate were discussed and include three major problems: (1) lack of an empirically supportable guiding theory, (2) vague and nonspecific operational definitions of LD, and (3) lack of a systematic, comprehensive framework for LD assessment. This chapter focused primarily on the issue of providing a modern, practical operationalization of LD that corrects many of the errors and misconceptions about achievement and cognitive ability that appear to plague tradi-

tional definitions. The definition presented here is an initial attempt to integrate modern theory on the structure of human cognitive abilities with accepted and supported notions of LD.
This operational definition consists of four essential levels that effectively constitute *tests*
along the way to LD determination. Passing all four tests and conducting the entire assessment within the context of a systematic, comprehensive assessment framework is necessary
for making a definitive diagnosis of LD. The operational definition presented here is
intended to provide a best practices approach to the assessment of learning difficulties. In
sum, the resulting four-level operational definition provides practitioners and researchers
with an inherently practical method for LD assessment that clearly specifies relationships
between and among both cognitive and academic abilities, definitions of aptitude and global
ability scores, and a recursive process that accommodates essential elements necessary for
high-quality evaluation of learning difficulties.

Endnote

1. The term *consistency,* as it is used here and within
the operational definition of LD, refers to actual
standard score performances in both aptitudes and
achievements that are less than 85. It is only when
aptitude and achievement are consistently low
within the context of an otherwise normal-ability
profile that such domain-specific weaknesses
(related aptitudes and achievements) may be indicative of an underlying LD.

CHC Cross-Battery Assessment with Academic Ability Tests

There are few prominent spokespersons in any assessment-related field who would argue that theory is *unimportant* in the measurement and interpretation of cognitive and academic functioning. Rather, most would agree that the validity of interpretations about performance on any ability test, intelligence or achievement, is related directly to the extent to which they reflect current theory and research. Notwithstanding, academic abilities, in particular, have seldom been associated with or linked to a theoretical model of the structure of abilities, let alone *cognitive* abilities. However, it is clear from the discussion in the early part of this text that the abilities measured by individually administered achievement tests are indeed cognitive in nature.

Chapter 2 presented an ability continuum that ranged from those abilities that develop largely as a result of education and formal instruction at the far right to those processes that develop largely independent of formal education and schooling experiences at the far left. The adjectives *academic* and *cognitive* were used to describe the abilities that fell closest to the right and left ends of this continuum, respectively (see Figure 2.4 and related discussion). Regardless of where abilities fall along this continuum, they are all part of the structure of human cognitive abilities represented by the Cattell-Horn-Carroll theory of cognitive abilities (CHC theory). Because this theory encompasses a great breadth of abilities, it can be used to guide the selection and interpretation of both intelligence and achievement tests. In addition, its solid research base can be used to inform interpretations within and between ability domains. A method for assessing and interpreting CHC abilities using intelligence tests has been developed. This method is known as the *CHC Cross-Battery approach* (Flanagan, McGrew, & Ortiz, 2000; Flanagan & Ortiz, 2001, McGrew & Flanagan, 1998). To date, the CHC Cross-Battery approach to assessment and interpretation has not been fully extended for use with achievement tests. In order to draw more valid and useful conclusions from academic ability tests alone or in combination with cognitive ability tests, organization and interpretation of such measures should be grounded in contemporary theory and research. The CHC Cross-Battery method provides practitioners with a means to organize assessments according to the well-validated CHC theory and make interpretations that follow directly from the research base that supports this theory.

The purpose of this chapter is to describe the CHC Cross-Battery approach and demonstrate, step by step, how this method of assessment can be applied to the organization and interpretation of achievement tests. Worksheets and data summary sheets will be introduced to facilitate organization and interpretation of cross-battery data. The steps and guidelines for assessment of academic abilities within the context of the CHC Cross-Battery approach presented here will provide practitioners with the skills necessary to organize more comprehensive and valid assessments of important academic abilities, particularly those inherent in IDEA.

The CHC Cross-Battery Approach

The CHC Cross-Battery approach was designed to spell out how practitioners can conduct assessments that approximate the total range of broad cognitive abilities more adequately than is typically accomplished through a single battery of tests (intelligence or achievement). According to Carroll (1998), this approach "can be used to develop the most appropriate information about an individual in a given testing situation" (p. xi). Furthermore, the approach serves to "elevate [test] interpretation to a higher level, to add theory to psychometrics and thereby to improve the quality of... psychometric assessment" (Kaufman, 2000, p. xv).

According to its developers, the CHC Cross-Battery approach is a time-efficient method of assessment that is grounded in contemporary psychometric theory and research on the structure of human cognitive abilities (McGrew & Flanagan, 1998). It allows practitioners to measure validly a wide *comprehensive* range or an in-depth but *selective* range of abilities. In many instances, the breadth and depth of measurement achieved through use of the CHC Cross-Battery method is greater than that typically represented by a single battery.

In general terms, Comprehensive Cross-Battery assessment (C-CB) is typically implemented when one is interested in measuring a comprehensive or broad range of cognitive and academic abilities. C-CB assessment involves selecting a minimum of two qualitatively different indicators (or subtests) of the broad stratum II abilities that comprise CHC theory (e.g., *Gf, Gc, Gv, Gsm, Glr, Gs, Ga, Gq, Grw*) and that are of interest. Thus, in C-CB assessment the goal is typically to gather baseline information about cognitive and academic functioning within most of the broad-ability domains that define stratum II of the CHC theory. C-CB assessment is appropriate, for example, when little information is available on an individual's current level of functioning and when referral concerns are not well defined. Selective Cross-Battery assessment (S-CB), in contrast, is generally pursued when one is interested in measuring select broad abilities comprehensively (e.g., only *Gc* and *Grw*). In the case of S-CB, the selection of tests is based on the practitioner's decisions regarding those broad-ability domains that are most important to assess given the specific referral concerns. Thus, C-CB assessment is concerned with *breadth* of measurement, whereas S-CB assessment is concerned with *depth* of measurement.

The CHC Cross-Battery approach, including C-CB and S-CB methods, is based on three foundational sources or pillars of information (Flanagan & McGrew, 1997; Flanagan, McGrew, & Ortiz, 2000; McGrew & Flanagan, 1998). Together, the three pillars provide the knowledge base necessary to organize C-CB and S-CB assessments. The pillars of the CHC Cross-Battery approach are described briefly here as they apply to tests of academic ability, in particular.

Pillar #1: A Well-Validated Theoretical Foundation

The first pillar of the CHC Cross-Battery approach is a comprehensive taxonomic framework for describing the structure and nature of abilities, both cognitive and academic. This taxonomy is reflected in CHC theory. This theory was described in detail in Chapter 2 and therefore will not be defined again here. Because the approach is grounded firmly in CHC theory and research, the nature and quality of its empirical foundation are noteworthy.

Overall, the CHC structure of abilities is supported extensively by factor-analytic (i.e., structural) evidence as well as developmental, neurocognitive, and heritability evidence (see Horn & Noll, 1997, for a summary; Messick, 1992). In addition, there is a mounting body of research available on the relationships between specific CHC cognitive and academic abilities within the model (see Chapter 2 for a review of this literature). Studies have shown also that the CHC structural model is invariant across the lifespan (e.g., Bickley, Keith, & Wolfe, 1995) and across gender and ethnic groups (e.g., Carroll, 1993; Gustafsson & Balke, 1993; Keith, 1997, 1999). In general, the CHC theory is based on a more thorough network of validity evidence than other contemporary multidimensional ability models (see Kranzler & Keith, 1999; McGrew & Flanagan, 1998; Messick, 1992; Sternberg & Kaufman, 1998). Succinctly stated, "Never before has a psychometric ability model been so firmly grounded in data" (Daniel, 1997, p. 1043).

CHC theory is the foundation for the CHC Cross-Battery approach because it is currently the most researched, empirically supported, and comprehensive descriptive hierarchical psychometric framework from which to organize thinking about ability test interpretation. Although "the empirical evidence in favor of [this] hierarchical arrangement of abilities is overwhelming" (Gustafsson & Undheim, 1996, p. 204), much of this (structural) research focused on the cognitive rather than the academic abilities inherent in the CHC model. Nevertheless, the impressive research base for CHC theory makes it among the most promising models currently available for understanding, measuring, and interpreting both cognitive and academic functioning. As such, the CHC theory is the taxonomic framework around which cross-battery assessment and interpretation is organized in this text (see also Carroll, 1997, 1998; Flanagan, Genshaft, & Harrison, 1997; McGrew, 1997; McGrew & Flanagan, 1998; Woodcock, 1990; Ysseldyke, 1990).

Pillar #2: Broad-Ability Classifications

The second pillar of the CHC Cross-Battery approach is the CHC *broad (stratum II) classifications* of cognitive and academic ability tests. As described in Chapter 3, CHC broad-ability classifications are typically based on the results of theory-driven cross-battery (or joint) confirmatory factor-analysis (CFA) studies. For example, Flanagan and colleagues classified all the subtests of the major intelligence batteries according to the particular CHC broad cognitive abilities they measure using the results of a series of CFA studies (Flanagan, McGrew, & Ortiz, 2000; Flanagan & Ortiz, 2001; McGrew & Flanagan, 1998). To date, however, few academic achievement batteries have been included in theory-driven CFA studies to allow for empirically based classifications of individual achievement tests at the CHC broad-ability level. Therefore, with some exceptions, these classifications were based on an expert consensus process (see Chapter 3 for details).

As reported in Chapter 3, the expert consensus process resulted in 96 percent agreement with respect to the CHC *broad*-ability classifications. That is, most experts were in agreement with regard to which tests of the achievement batteries included in this *Desk Reference* measured one or more aspects of the broad CHC abilities. Perhaps because the overwhelming majority of academic achievement tests appear to measure one or more aspects of only four distinct broad CHC abilities, including *Grw, Gq, Ga,* and *Gc,* agreement at the broad-ability level was quite high.

Classification of all tests at the broad-ability level was necessary to improve on the validity of academic ability assessment and interpretation. Specifically, broad- ability classifications are necessary because they ensure that the CHC constructs that underlie such assessments are minimally affected by construct irrelevant variance (Messick, 1989, 1995). In other words, knowing what tests measure what abilities enables practitioners to organize tests into clusters that contain only measures that are *relevant* to the construct or ability of interest. Clusters that contain one or more measures that are *irrelevant* to the construct of interest (i.e., the construct presumed to underlie the cluster) are difficult to interpret. It should be noted that 4 percent (12 of 323) of the tests were classified as measuring two constructs (mixed measures) at the broad-ability level.

To clarify further, *construct-irrelevant variance* is present when an "assessment is too broad, containing excess reliable variance associated with other distinct constructs . . . that affects responses in a manner irrelevant to the interpreted constructs" (Messick, 1995, p. 742). Construct irrelevant variance can operate at the cluster or subtest level. Most academic achievement batteries (see McGrew & Flanagan, 1998) yield *construct-relevant* clusters (or composites). That is, the subtests that comprise academic ability clusters, such as the Broad Reading Cluster on the WJ III, typically measure aspects of only the broad ability intended to be measured (e.g., *Grw*). Because achievements tests rarely focus on measurement of specific narrow abilities, construct-irrelevant variance occurs more frequently in academic achievement batteries at the subtest level rather than the cluster level.

For example, according to its authors, the Writing Fluency test of the WJ III (Woodcock et al., 2001) measures both *Grw* and *Gs* (McGrew & Woodcock, 2001). Likewise, according to expert consensus, the Writing Fluency test measures a narrow ability (Writing Ability; WA) associated with *Grw* and a narrow ability (Rate of Test Taking; R9) associated with *Gs*. Therefore, this test is considered a *mixed* measure of abilities. Use of mixed measures of abilities in assessment complicates interpretation of performance on those measures (e.g., is poor performance due to difficulty writing [*Grw*] or processing information quickly [*Gs*] or both?).

In short, interpretation is less complicated when clusters include subtests that measure aspects of one broad ability only (e.g., *Grw* or *Gs,* but not both). In other words, the clusters should include only subtests that are relevant to the ability intended to underlie the cluster, and these subtests should be considered *relatively pure* measures of the underlying broad-ability construct, rather than mixed measures of two broad constructs. "Any test [or cluster] that measures more than one common factor to a substantial degree yields scores that are psychologically ambiguous and very difficult to interpret" (Guilford, 1954, p. 356; cited in Briggs & Cheek, 1986). Therefore, CHC Cross-Battery assessments should be designed using only those tests and subtests that were classified as relatively pure measures of a CHC broad ability, rather than mixed measures of two or more broad CHC abilities, following the information presented on the CHC worksheets in Appendix A (discussed later in this chapter).

There is an exception to the guidelines for organizing construct-relevant CHC clusters with relatively pure (not mixed) measures of ability. For example, *Gq* consists of two narrow abilities: Math Achievement (A3) and Math Knowledge (KM). These narrow abilities are typically measured by math calculation and math knowledge (or math concepts) tests on academic achievement batteries. Despite the fact that *Gq* is a broad stratum II ability in the CHC model, it is rather narrowly defined. This is evidenced by the fact that most achievement batteries that purport to measure mathematics ability comprehensively usually include a *math reasoning* test in addition to one or more measures of A3 and KM (e.g., WJ III Applied Problems, WIAT-II Mathematics Reasoning). Tasks that involve the ability to reason inductively and deductively with numbers, however, appear to measure a narrow ability associated with *Gf*, not *Gq*, in the CHC model—namely, Quantitative Reasoning (RQ). Therefore, by their very nature, math reasoning tests are very likely mixed measures of two distinct abilities within the context of CHC theory (i.e., *Gq* and *Gf*).

Because *Gq* represents an individual's store of acquired mathematical knowledge (see Woodcock, 1993), it is defined by narrow math achievement and math knowledge abilities, which are typically measured by math calculation and math knowledge tests, respectively. RQ, a narrow ability subsumed by *Gf*, represents the ability to *reason* inductively and deductively when solving *quantitative* problems and is measured typically by math reasoning tests. However, because RQ is a "thinking ability" rather than a "store of acquired knowledge" per se (Woodcock, 1993), it is more appropriately grouped with other *Gf* or reasoning abilities. Furthermore, the placement of RQ with other *Gf* abilities, such as Induction (I) and General Sequential Reasoning (RG), in the CHC model is supported by factor-analytic research (see McGrew, 1997; McGrew & Flanagan, 1998; McGrew & Woodcock, 2001). Notwithstanding, when a comprehensive assessment of mathematics is warranted, it seems necessary to evaluate the extent to which basic math skills and math knowledge have been acquired (i.e., *Gq*) as well as how efficiently an individual reasons with this quantitative information (RQ). In essence, RQ is an important ability to assess when information about either general reasoning ability or general mathematics ability is sought. Therefore, both the *Gq* and *Gf* worksheets in Appendix A include tests that have been classified as RQ. The decision to place tests of RQ from academic achievement batteries on the *Gq* worksheet in Appendix A was made primarily because this text focuses on the comprehensive assessment of academic abilities and *the ability to reason with numbers* (i.e., RQ) is part of a comprehensive assessment of mathematics ability. Moreover, of the two math achievement areas listed in IDEA's definition of learning disability, one (i.e., math reasoning) appears to be entirely consistent with RQ, thereby providing further support for including RQ on the *Gq* worksheet with other math abilities.

Because measures of RQ are included on both the *Gq* and *Gf* worksheets, practitioners who conduct cross-battery assessments must make a decision as to whether to group math reasoning tests with other *Gq* tests or other *Gf* tests. If the *ability to reason* is a major focus of an assessment, math reasoning tests may be more appropriately grouped with other measures of *Gf*, rather than with measures of A3 and KM (i.e., *Gq* tests). Conversely, when comprehensive assessment of mathematics ability is the goal, it seems logical to group RQ tests with other tests of *Gq*. The worksheets in Appendix A allow for RQ tests to be included with other measures of *Gf* or *Gq* depending on the nature of the referral. However, when RQ tests are grouped with tests of A3 and KM, they must be interpreted carefully. For example, when performance on RQ measures is significantly lower than performance on A3 and KM measures, it is necessary to examine closely the extent to which general problem solving and reasoning (i.e., *Gf*) difficulties may have attenuated performance. As this situation demonstrates, although it is preferable to avoid using mixed measures of abilities to construct CHC clusters (e.g., tests that measure both *Gq* and *Gf*), there are times when this situation cannot be avoided.

As a general rule of thumb, if constructs are broad and multifaceted, like those represented at stratum II in the CHC model, then each component (i.e., CHC broad ability) "should be specified and measured as *cleanly* as possible" (Briggs & Cheek, 1986, p. 130, emphasis added). Because the CHC Cross-Battery approach emphasizes the use of relatively pure (rather than mixed) measures of CHC abilities (whenever possible) in the construction of appropriate (i.e., construct relevant) clusters, it offers a valid means of measuring the broad CHC constructs (see McGrew & Flanagan, 1998).

Approximately 300 CHC broad-ability academic classifications have been made based on the results of expert consensus and extant CFA studies (e.g., WJ III), with an approximately 15 additional classifications made on a logical basis by the authors. These classifications are included in the *Desk Reference* section of this text (i.e., Chapters 4 through 10) and on the worksheets in Appendix A. These classifications of academic ability tests assist practitioners in identifying measures that assess various aspects of the broad abilities (such as *Grw* and *Gq*) represented in CHC theory.

Pillar #3: Narrow-Ability Classifications

The third pillar of the CHC Cross-Battery approach is the CHC *narrow (stratum I) classifications* of cognitive and academic ability tests. Narrow-ability classifications of academic achievement tests, like the broad-ability classifications, are located in the *Desk Reference* section of this book as well as on the worksheets in Appendix A. Classification of cognitive ability tests according to CHC theory are presented elsewhere (e.g., McGrew & Flanagan, 1998) but many are also included on the worksheets in Appendix A. Whereas the process of classifying academic achievement tests at the broad-ability level was relatively straightforward, classifying tests at the narrow-ability level was slightly more arduous, particularly because of the often subtle and nebulous distinctions that exist between narrow-ability definitions. Nevertheless, substantial agreement among experts (i.e., 87 percent) was achieved at the narrow-ability level (see Chapter 3 and Appendix H for details).

Classifications of academic ability tests according to content, format, and task demand at the narrow-ability level were conducted via an expert consensus process to improve further on the validity of academic ability assessment and interpretation (see Messick, 1989). Specifically, these narrow-ability classifications were necessary to ensure that the CHC constructs that underlie assessments are well represented, as opposed to underrepresented. According to Messick (1995), *construct underrepresentation* is present when an "assessment is too narrow and fails to include important dimensions or facets of the construct" (p. 742).

Interpreting the Wide Range Achievement Test–Third Edition (WRAT 3; Wilkinson, 1993) Reading subtest as a measure of broad reading ability is an example of construct underrepresentation. This is because this reading test measures only *one* narrow aspect of reading or *Grw* (i.e., Reading Decoding [RD]). At least one other *Grw* measure of reading that is *qualitatively different* from Reading Decoding is minimally necessary to include in an assessment to ensure adequate representation of the Reading construct as reflected in *Grw*. That is, *two or more qualitatively different indicators* (i.e., measures of two or more narrow abilities subsumed by the broad ability) are needed for adequate construct representation (see Comrey, 1988; Messick, 1989, 1995). The aggregate of WRAT 3 Reading (a measure of Reading Decoding at the narrow-ability level) and a test of Reading Comprehension, for example, would provide a better understanding of overall reading ability as well as a better estimate of the broad *Grw* ability because both tests represent qualitatively different aspects of Reading and of *Grw*.

Adequate representation of broad *Grw* poses a unique circumstance when compared to all other broad abilities in the CHC model and therefore deserves further discussion here. Specifically, this broad ability appears to be a mixed measure in and of itself, consisting of narrow abilities that measure aspects of both reading and writing. That is, *Grw* consists of reading decoding (RD), reading comprehension (RC), cloze ability (CZ), verbal (printed) language comprehension (V) and reading speed (RS), all of which measure different aspects of reading ability. In addition, *Grw* consists of spelling ability (SG), writing ability (WA), and English Usage Knowledge (EU), which measure different aspects of writing ability. It seems odd, therefore, that the CHC model includes a *combined* Reading and Writing stratum II ability (*Grw*) rather than separate reading and writing broad abilities. The primary reason for a combined reading/writing or broad *Grw* ability construct, however, stems from the results of a factor-analysis study conducted by Woodcock (1998) using the standardization data of the WJ-R, which supported a combined reading and writing factor. Clearly, reading and writing are closely related abilities. Although Woodcock chose the label *Grw* for his combined reading and writing factor, it may be more accurately labeled "literacy" or "symbolic language" (see Chapter 2 for a discussion).

Because of the strong empirical association between reading and writing abilities, they comprise one broad factor in the CHC model. Notwithstanding, practitioners are accustomed to measuring and interpreting these academic ability constructs separately. Therefore, when an adequate assessment of reading ability is warranted, practitioners should ensure that *at least* two qualitatively different narrow reading abilities subsumed by *Grw* are included. Likewise, at least two qualitatively different narrow writing abilities should be included in an assessment of writing ability. Under these circumstances, and within the context of CHC Cross-Battery assessment, separate reading and writing clusters may be calculated and interpreted independently. To facilitate this process, two *Grw* worksheets were constructed, one for reading (*Grw*-R) and one for writing (*Grw*-W). When assessment of a wide range of academic abilities is necessary and examination within and between various academic domains (reading, writing, math) is warranted, separate reading (*Grw*-R), writing (*Grw*-W), and Math (*Gq*) ability clusters are desirable. Notwithstanding the unidimensional nature of reading and writing skills as possibly representing a broad literacy factor, *Grw*-R and *Grw*-W worksheets are provided in Appendix A and Appendix D1 to allow for the calculation of reading and writing ability clusters that are consistent with the separate but related conception of these ability domains in the academic achievement literature.

When adequate representation of a broad academic ability is necessary for the purpose of ensuring that a particular academic ability reflects a broad stratum II construct (e.g., *Grw* [*Grw*-R, *Grw*-W], *Gq, Ga, Gc,* etc.), practitioners should ensure that *at least two qualitatively different measures* of the broad ability are included in the assessment. Table 12.1 provides information about the breadth of narrow abilities assessed by the various comprehensive, brief/screening, and specific academic skills tests included in this text. As may be seen in this table, some instruments measure *Grw*-R, *Grw*-W, and *Gq* (i.e., math) more comprehensively than others. For example, of the comprehensive achievement batteries listed in Table 12.1, the WJ III provides more qualitatively different measures of reading, writing, and math than all other comprehensive batteries. This table shows that in the area

Table with columns (left to right): PPVT-3, OWLS, LPT-R, ITPA-3, EVT, EO-WPVT, CREVT-A, CREVT, CASL, CELF-3, [Language], YCAT, WRAT-3, TOCL, TAAS-R, MBA, K-SEALS, K-FAST, HAMAT, [Brief/Screeners], WJ III, WIAT-II, PIAT-R/NU, KTEA/NU, DATA-2, DAB-3, [Comprehensive], Ability.

PPVT-3	OWLS	LPT-R	ITPA-3	EVT	EO-WPVT	CREVT-A	CREVT	CASL	CELF-3		YCAT	WRAT-3	TOCL	TAAS-R	MBA	K-SEALS	K-FAST	HAMAT		WJ III	WIAT-II	PIAT-R/NU	KTEA/NU	DATA-2	DAB-3		Ability
																											Grw-R – Reading
																											BASIC READING
			✓								✓	✓	✓	✓	✓					✓	✓	✓	✓	✓	✓		Reading Decoding
																				✓							Verbal Language Comprehension
																											READING COMPREHENSION
			✓											✓	✓		✓			✓	✓	✓	✓	✓	✓		Reading Comprehension
																	✓			✓							Cloze Ability
																											READING OTHER
																				✓							Reading Speed
			✓											✓						✓					✓		Phonetic Coding (Ga)
																											Grw-W – Writing
																											BASIC WRITING
			✓								✓	✓	✓	✓						✓	✓	✓	✓	✓	✓		Spelling Ability
													✓		✓			✓		✓					✓		English Usage Knowledge
																											WRITTEN EXPRESSION
													✓							✓	✓	✓		✓	✓		Writing Ability
																											WRITING OTHER
			✓					✓	✓											✓				✓	✓		Grammatical Sensitivity (Gc)
																											Gq – Quantitative Knowledge
																											MATH CALCULATION
											✓	✓		✓	✓	✓	✓	✓		✓	✓		✓	✓	✓		Math Achievement
													✓	✓						✓		✓			✓		Math Knowledge
																											MATH REASONING
															✓					✓	✓						Quantitative Reasoning
																											MATH OTHER
																				✓							Number Facility
																											Gc – Crystallized Intelligence
																											LISTENING COMPREHENSION
	✓							✓	✓				✓							✓	✓				✓		Listening Ability
																											LISTENING COMPREHENSION - OTHER
								✓	✓															✓			Language Development – Receptive
✓						✓	✓	✓												✓							Lexical Knowledge – Receptive
																											ORAL EXPRESSION
	✓								✓																		Oral Production & Fluency
																											ORAL EXPRESSION - OTHER
		✓	✓					✓	✓		✓										✓						Language Development – Expressive
		✓		✓	✓	✓	✓	✓			✓		✓		✓									✓	✓		Lexical Knowledge – Expressive

TABLE 12.1 Narrow CHC Abilities Measured by Achievement Batteries

TEWL-2	OWLS	Writing	WRMT-R/NU	WDRB	TOWRE	TORC-3	TERA-3	SRI-2	GSRT	GORT-4	Reading	TOPA	TAPS-R	TACL-3	SCAN-C:R	CTOPP	Phonological	TOMA-2	S-DMS	KeyMath	Math	TOLD-P:3	TOLD-I:3	TELD-3	TOAL-3	RO-WPVT	Language	
																												Grw-R – Reading
																												BASIC READING
			✓	✓	✓		✓	✓		✓																		Reading Decoding
				✓	✓	✓	✓																			✓		Verbal Language Comprehension
																												READING COMPREHENSION
					✓	✓	✓	✓	✓						✓													Reading Comprehension
			✓	✓																								Cloze Ability
																												READING OTHER
					✓					✓																		Reading Speed
				✓								✓				✓						✓						Phonetic Coding (*Ga*)
																												Grw-W – Writing
																												BASIC WRITING
																												Spelling Ability
✓						✓																			✓			English Usage Knowledge
																												WRITTEN EXPRESSION
✓	✓																								✓			Writing Ability
																												WRITING OTHER
					✓																	✓	✓					Grammatical Sensitivity (*Gc*)
																												Gq – Quantitative Knowledge
																												MATH CALCULATION
																		✓	✓	✓								Math Achievement
																		✓	✓	✓								Math Knowledge
																												MATH REASONING
																		✓		✓								Quantitative Reasoning
																												MATH OTHER
																												Number Facility
																												Gc – Crystallized Intelligence
																												LISTENING COMPREHENSION
			✓										✓	✓								✓		✓				Listening Ability
																												LISTENING COMPREHENSION - OTHER
	✓												✓	✓											✓			Language Development – Receptive
														✓								✓	✓		✓	✓		Lexical Knowledge – Receptive
																												ORAL EXPRESSION
																								✓	✓			Oral Production & Fluency
																												ORAL EXPRESSION - OTHER
				✓																		✓						Language Development – Expressive
			✓	✓																		✓	✓					Lexical Knowledge – Expressive

Continued

TWS-4	TOWL-3	TOWE	Writing	
				Grw-R – Reading
				BASIC READING
				Reading Decoding
				Verbal Language Comprehension
				READING COMPREHENSION
				Reading Comprehension
				Cloze Ability
				READING OTHER
				Reading Speed
				Phonetic Coding (*Ga*)
				Grw-W – Writing
				BASIC WRITING
✓	✓			Spelling Ability
	✓	✓		English Usage Knowledge
				WRITTEN EXPRESSION
	✓	✓		Writing Ability
				WRITING OTHER
				Grammatical Sensitivity (*Gc*)
				Gq – Quantitative Knowledge
				MATH CALCULATION
				Math Achievement
				Math Knowledge
				MATH REASONING
				Quantitative Reasoning
				MATH OTHER
				Number Facility
				Gc – Crystallized Intelligence
				LISTENING COMPREHENSION
				Listening Ability
				LISTENING COMPREHENSION - OTHER
				Language Development – Receptive
				Lexical Knowledge – Receptive
				ORAL EXPRESSION
				Oral Production & Fluency
				ORAL EXPRESSION - OTHER
				Language Development – Expression
				Lexical Knowledge – Expression

TABLE 12.1   *Continued*

of reading, the WJ III includes tests of reading decoding (RD), verbal (printed) language comprehension (V), reading comprehension (RC), reading speed (RS), and phonetic coding (PC). Most other comprehensive batteries include measures of reading decoding and reading comprehension only. Although most comprehensive achievement batteries contain two qualitatively different measures of *Grw*-R and therefore adequately assess the construct of reading, the more qualitatively different measures used to assess a construct (such as reading), the better the representation of that construct. Thus, the WJ III provides good representation of the reading construct, whereas the other comprehensive achievement batteries in Table 12.1 provide adequate representation of this construct.

Table 12.1 can be used to identify academic ability batteries that include two or more qualitatively different measures of Reading (*Grw*-R), Writing (*Grw*-W), and Math (*Gq*) ability. In addition, Table 12.1 identifies those batteries that include measures of listening comprehension and oral expression (i.e., *Gc* abilities)—two abilities, in addition to those previously mentioned, that are included in the federal definition of learning disability (i.e., IDEA).

Similar to the *Grw* situation just described, although oral expression and listening comprehension constitute different academic ability clusters on achievement batteries (e.g., Test of Language Development–Primary: Third Edition; TOLD–P:3 Speaking and Listening Composites), both abilities are considered narrow abilities that, in combination with other abilities, give rise to the broad *Gc* ability. That is, oral expression and listening comprehension tests typically measure oral production and fluency (OP) and listening ability (LS), respectively, two narrow abilities subsumed by *Gc* in CHC theory. In order to examine functioning in the areas of oral expression and listening comprehension adequately, a minimum of two measures of each ability should be administered. This would allow for the calculation of either a narrow OP cluster or Oral Expression cluster and either a narrow LS cluster or Listening Comprehension cluster (see Chapter 13 for details).

It is important to understand that although one measure of Oral Expression (e.g., either a measure of OP or a measure of Communication Ability [CM]) and one measure of Listening Comprehension (e.g., a measure of LS) can be combined under certain circumstances to yield a broad *Gc* cluster, adequate measurement of the Oral Expression and Listening Comprehension domains within the context of IDEA's definition of LD probably necessitates a more in-depth assessment. Specifically, with few exceptions, measurement of any one of the seven academic areas of LD listed in the federal definition should involve more than the administration of a single subtest within each domain. Thus, broad CHC abilities should be represented by two or more qualitatively different indicators (i.e., subtests) and narrow abilities, when constituting the focus of evaluation (e.g., measuring Listening Comprehension) should be represented by at least two indicators (e.g., two tests of Listening Comprehension that contain slightly different task demands and test stimuli). Appendix F contains information regarding task characteristics and may prove to be particularly useful to practitioners when selecting tests to represent *narrow* abilities.

In general, "a scale [or broad CHC ability cluster] will yield far more information—and, hence, be a more valid measure of a construct—if it contains more differentiated items [or tests]" (Clarke & Watson, 1995). CHC Cross-Battery assessment circumvents the misinterpretations that can result from underrepresented constructs by specifying the use of two or more qualitatively different indicators to represent each *broad* CHC ability. In order to ensure that qualitatively different aspects of broad abilities are represented in assessment, classification of academic ability tests at the narrow (stratum I) ability level was necessary (see Appendix A and *Desk Reference*). These classifications aid in the selection of qualitatively different test indicators for each of the broad abilities represented in CHC Cross-Battery assessments as well as each of the seven areas of academic ability listed in the federal definition of LD. Through adequate representation of abilities, construct validity is maximized rather than compromised (McGrew & Flanagan, 1998; Messick, 1995).

In summary, the broad and narrow classifications of cognitive and academic ability tests guard against two ubiquitous sources of invalidity in assessment: construct-irrelevant variance and construct underrepresentation. Taken together, the three pillars underlying the CHC Cross-Battery approach provide the necessary foundation from which to organize assessments of cognitive and academic abilities that are theory driven, comprehensive, and valid.

Rationale for CHC Cross-Battery Assessment with Academic Ability Tests

As stated earlier, evaluation of academic abilities is seldom grounded in contemporary theory. Linking academic ability assessment to a well-validated theory through cross-battery principles and procedures allows for the interpretation of academic functioning to be based firmly in the research base for the theory. Interpretations that are based on current theory and research are more defensible and have more accountability than those based solely on clinical judgment. As such, the general practice of assessing and interpreting academic performance will benefit from cross-battery procedures.

The practice of "crossing" batteries is carried out routinely by astute practitioners (e.g., Brackett & McPherson, 1996; Wilson, 1992) for a number of reasons, including (1) to test hypotheses about aberrant test performance within a given cognitive or achievement battery, (2) to conduct more in-depth assessment in any given cognitive or academic ability area of interest, (3) to acquire information about performance in a particular domain not assessed by a given cognitive or achievement battery, and (4) to examine the relationship between potential (or general cognitive ability) and level of academic performance (e.g., ability-achievement discrepancy analysis). The method of crossing batteries, then, is not new. This practice is commonplace in just about all assessment-related fields, particularly as it applies to the ubiquitous practice of ability-achievement discrepancy analysis. Indeed, one of the most prominent spokespersons in assessment-related fields, Alan S. Kaufman, has been advocating for and instructing practitioners in supplemental testing methods for more than a decade (see Kaufman, 1994, 2000; Kaufman, Lichtenberger, & Naglieri, 1999). Notwithstanding, a time-efficient, theory-based, method for crossing batteries was not formally operationalized until recently (Flanagan, McGrew, & Ortiz, 2000; Flanagan & Ortiz, 2001; McGrew & Flanagan, 1998). Flanagan and colleagues initially operationalized a cross-battery approach for use with intelligence tests only and now this method of assessment and interpretation is extended here to include academic ability tests. The rationale for extending the cross-battery methods and procedures to academic ability tests is twofold.

First, measurement and interpretation of academic abilities are seldom grounded in contemporary theory. Because CHC theory includes academic ability constructs in its structure, linking academic ability assessment to this theory and its research base through the CHC Cross-Battery approach will allow for more informed and empirically supported representation and interpretation of academic ability constructs. The CHC Cross-Battery approach to test selection is grounded in content validity (i.e., the substantive empirical and logical CHC classifications of individual tests) and measurement of abilities within the context of this approach follows the principles of measurement theory and construct validation research (e.g., Messick, 1995). Therefore, constructs in assessment are well represented and performance on measures of specific ability constructs are interpreted from a solid research base. For example, many practitioners assess reading ability with either a single subtest, usually a reading decoding test (e.g., WRAT 3 Reading), or through the use of both a reading decoding and reading comprehension test. Examination of the narrow abilities subsumed by *Grw*-R shows that, in addition to Reading Decoding and Reading Comprehension, abilities such as Verbal (printed) Language Comprehension, Cloze Ability, and Reading Speed are important in understanding broad reading ability (see Table 2.4 for definitions). Therefore, knowledge of the breadth of narrow abilities that define *Grw*-R as well as the classifications of reading tests according to the narrow reading abilities they measure will lead to more appropriate representation of the reading construct in assessment and clearly defined interpretations of performance on individual measures of reading.

Second, information derived from tests of cognitive ability and tests of academic ability are seldom integrated and interpreted systematically. The most common example of the unsystematic use of cognitive and academic ability scores is reflected in the random, unjustified, and unsupported manner in which these scores are often used in ability-achievement discrepancy analyses (see Chapter 11). Because the CHC Cross-Battery approach systematically guides test selection and interpretation, misuse of tests, test data, and discrepancy analysis procedures is reduced substantially. For example, because interpretation is guided by the mounting research base on the relationship between cognitive abilities and specific academic skills (see Chapter 2), cross-battery procedures can be used to evaluate the cognitive processes involved in the acquisition and efficient use of acquired reading, writing, and math knowledge. This information is important in discerning the underlying source(s) of manifest academic skill deficits. Thus, the CHC Cross-Battery approach has been extended to academic ability tests to provide a systematic means for practitioners to make valid, *up-to-date* interpretations of current achievement batteries, to augment them in a way that is consistent with the empirically supported CHC theory, and to use them with tests of cognitive abilities to obtain a comprehensive understanding of overall functioning.

Application of the CHC Cross-Battery Approach

In order to ensure that CHC Cross-Battery assessment procedures are psychometrically and theoretically defensible, practitioners should adhere to three guiding principles. It is important to note that the CHC Cross-Battery worksheets in Appendix A incorporate these principles in order to facilitate the application of this method of assessment.

Guiding Principle 1

When constructing broad (stratum II) ability clusters (e.g., *Grw* [*Grw*-R, *Grw*-W], *Gq, Gc, Ga,* etc.), one should include only tests that have been classified as *relatively pure* measures of CHC abilities, rather than mixed measures. In addition, it is preferable to select tests that were classified *empirically* as relatively pure measures of their respective broad CHC factor, over those that were classified *logically*. However, as discussed in Chapter 3, few academic ability tests, to date, have been included in the type of analyses that would allow for empirical classifications (i.e., CHC driven, *cross-battery* confirmatory factor analyses). Therefore, with the exception of the WJ III Tests of Achievement, nearly all other academic ability tests were classified logically through an expert consensus process. Despite the lack of empirical classifications of academic ability tests at the broad CHC ability level, consensus resulted in 96 percent agreement between experts with respect to the broad abilities measured by the 323 academic ability tests included in the *Desk Reference*. Thus, construction of broad academic ability clusters (*Grw* [*Grw*-R, *Grw*-W], *Gq, Gc,* and *Ga*) can be carried out confidently using the expert classifications. All other CHC broad-ability clusters (*Gf, Ga, Gv, Gs, Glr*) can be constructed using predominately empirical classifications (see Flanagan, McGrew, & Ortiz, 2000; Flanagan & Ortiz, 2001; McGrew & Flanagan, 1998). Use of the broad-ability classifications, mainly *empirical* in the case of cognitive ability tests and mainly *logical* in the case of academic ability tests, will ensure that only *construct-relevant* tests are included in cross-battery assessments. (Empirically and logically classified tests are clearly marked on the CHC Cross-Battery worksheets presented in Appendix A.)

Guiding Principle 2

When constructing broad (stratum II) ability clusters, include *two or more qualitatively different* narrow (stratum I) ability indicators for each CHC broad-ability domain to ensure appropriate construct representation. Without sufficient empirically or logically classified tests available to represent constructs adequately, inferences about an individual's broad (stratum II) ability cannot be made. For example, when a composite is derived from two measures of Reading Decoding (RD) (e.g., WJ III Letter-Word Identification and Word Attack), it is inappropriate to generalize about an individual's *broad Grw*-R ability because the *Grw*-R construct is underrepresented. In this case, the aggregate of Letter-Word Identification and Word Attack is best interpreted as a measure of Reading Decoding (a narrow stratum I ability) rather than *Grw*-R (a broad stratum II ability). Alternatively, inferences can be made about an individual's broad *Grw*-R ability based on a composite that is derived from one measure of Reading Decoding and one measure of Reading Comprehension (i.e., two qualitatively different indicators of *Grw*-R). Of course, as stated earlier, the more broadly an ability is represented (i.e., through the derivation of composites based on *multiple* qualitatively different narrow-ability indicators), the more confidence one has in drawing inferences about that broad ability based on the composite score. A minimum of two qualitatively different indicators per CHC broad-ability domain is recommended for practical reasons (i.e., time efficient assessment) (McGrew & Flanagan, 1998).

Guiding Principle 3

When conducting CHC Cross-Battery assessments, it is important to select tests from the *smallest number* of batteries (preferably only two) to minimize the effect of spurious differences between test scores that may be attributable to differences in the characteristics of independent norm samples (McGrew, 1994). For example, the "Flynn effect" (Flynn, 1984) indicates that there is, on average, a difference of three standard score points between the test scores of tests that were standardized 10 years apart. To minimize the effects of spurious differences between scores derived from two separate batteries, the tests included on the worksheets in Appendix A were limited to those published between 1993 and 2001, inclusive. Selecting supplemental tests that are reliable and valid and that were normed relatively close to the time frame in which the core battery was normed will facilitate an appropriate and comprehensive assessment of most CHC broad abilities (Flanagan, 2000; McGrew & Flanagan, 1998). Very often, publishers will issue periodic normative updates that greatly facilitate adherence to this guiding principle; where such updates are available, they should be used. When selecting core and supplemental batteries, practitioners are well advised to examine carefully the test characteristic information (e.g., reliability, floors and ceilings, etc.) reported in the *Desk Reference* for each achievement battery to determine the adequacy of any given test for use in assessment. The steps that follow later in this chapter will describe the circumstances under which it may be necessary to cross batteries and demonstrate the manner in which supplemental batteries should be selected.

In summary, the pillars and guiding principles underlying the CHC Cross-Battery approach provide the necessary foundation from which to conduct comprehensive assessments of the broad CHC constructs that define the structure of abilities (cognitive and academic) in current psychometric theory and research (Flanagan, McGrew, & Ortiz, 2000; Flanagan & Ortiz, 2001; McGrew & Flanagan, 1998). Preliminary studies using tests of cognitive abilities have shown that assessments organized around CHC theory, following cross-battery principles and procedures, explain certain academic skills (e.g., reading decoding, reading comprehension) better than assessments organized around traditional theoretical models. These studies are summarized briefly next (see Flanagan, 2000; Flanagan, McGrew, & Ortiz, 2000, for a more in-depth review).

Research Foundation of CHC Cross-Battery Assessment

The entire CHC Cross-Battery approach was built on research. Kaufman (2000) comments that this new approach to assessment and interpretation "is based on an impressive compilation and integration of research investigations" (p. xv). Specifically, the approach ensures that assessments are organized and interpreted according to the well-researched CHC theory. In addition, the classifications necessary to organize assessments according to CHC theory are either empirically based or the result of an expert consensus process. Thus, the CHC Cross-Battery approach rests on a strong research foundation. These strengths notwithstanding, the validity of the assessment *method* was not evaluated until recently.

Because the CHC Cross-Battery approach was formally introduced to the field recently (McGrew & Flanagan, 1998) and, to date, has been used only with cognitive ability tests, little research on its utility is available. The few investigations that have been conducted using cognitive ability cross-battery datasets, however, are promising. In general, these studies found that use of the CHC classifications and procedures of the CHC Cross-Battery approach resulted in valid measurement of seven CHC constructs (i.e., *Gf, Gc, Gv, Ga, Glr, Gsm,* and *Gs*). For example, confirmatory factor analysis with a WISC-R/WJ-R cross-battery dataset demonstrated that these data fit a 7-factor CHC model well and better than a popular competing atheoretical Wechsler model (see Flanagan, 2000, for details). In a similar investigation of the cross-battery principles and procedures for organizing tests in assessment, Mascolo (2001) demonstrated through confirmatory factor analysis that an independent WISC-III-based cross-battery dataset fit a 7-factor CHC model better than a traditional competing Wechsler model. Likewise, Flanagan (2001) showed that a CAS/WJ III cross-battery dataset fit a 7-factor CHC model better than a competing PASS model (see Keith, Kranzler, & Flanagan, 2001). Thus, when the WISC-R, WISC-III, and CAS were supplemented with select tests from the WJ-R/WJ III (and in some instances, other batteries [see Mascolo, 2001]) in a systematic manner, following the steps of the CHC Cross-Battery approach, the resultant CHC structural model underlying these datasets was supported and, indeed, consistent with the extant factor-analytic cognitive abilities research. To fully demonstrate the utility of the CHC Cross-Battery approach, it is necessary to cross-validate these findings and conduct similar research with intelligence batteries other than the WJ-R/WJ III following cross-battery principles and procedures. In addition, it is necessary to examine the validity of the CHC Cross-Battery procedures using tests of academic ability.

In short, these initial validity studies demonstrated that when the CHC Cross-Battery procedures were used to augment tests from the WISC-R, WISC-III, and CAS with tests from other batteries, a structurally valid CHC model emerged as the best-fitting model in all respective cross-battery datasets. Additional validity support for the resultant cross-battery CHC broad-ability constructs was demonstrated through their significant (and expected) relations to external measures (general and specific reading abilities) (see Flanagan, 2000, for details). Thus, the results of this growing body of research provide preliminary validity support for the construction of CHC broad-ability clusters (i.e., *Gf, Gc, Gv, Gsm, Glr, Gs, Ga*) following the CHC Cross-Battery approach. Additional research in this area should include measures of *Grw* and *Gq* in order to evaluate the validity of these constructs specifically as it applies to their representation in C-CB assessment via cross-battery procedures.

CHC Cross-Battery Worksheets

In order to facilitate the decision-making process as well as streamline the calculations necessary in CHC Cross-Battery assessment, worksheets have been created for practitioner use (see Appendix A). As stated earlier, these worksheets are organized in a manner consistent with the CHC Cross-Battery guiding principles. The worksheets are especially helpful when decisions regarding which constructs are of interest have already been made, because the practitioner is able to refer directly to a set of tests that have been classified jointly along this dimension. These worksheets, together with the step-by-step approach to CHC Cross-Battery assessment that follows, provide a bridge between CHC theory and practice. Although many of the calculations necessary to complete the worksheets can be completed easily by hand, the use of a calculator is recommended in order to ensure accuracy and expedite the process. Alternatively, practitioners may choose to utilize one of the many existing computer-based spreadsheets developed by a number of researchers that automate and greatly facilitate the calculation process. Although there are some differences between these automated spreadsheets, virtually all of them will at least automatically convert all test standard scores to a common metric, calculate the broad- and narrow-ability averages, and plot the score bands on a normal probability curve. Caution, of course, must be used when attempting to interpret broad-ability clusters, particularly in cases when they are derived from underlying scores where there is no overlap in confidence bands. The fact that cluster scores are calculated routinely in cases where it may have been inappropriate only serves to highlight the fact that responsibility for proper interpretation of results always rests with the practitioner, not the scoring program. Many of these spreadsheets are available via the Internet and can be downloaded freely from the following websites:

CHC Cross-Battery Online: http://facpub.stjohns.edu/~ortizs/cross-battery/

The WWW School Psychology Homepage: http://facpub.stjohns.edu/~ortizs/

Ron Dumont and John Willis's webpages: http://alpha.fdu.edu/~dumont/

The Institute for Applied Psychometrics: http://www.iapsych.com/

The worksheets in Appendix A are an adaptation of those presented in Flanagan and Ortiz (2001). Practitioners are encouraged to photocopy these worksheets and utilize them to facilitate the cross-battery assessment method presented here. There are 10 cross-battery worksheets in all, one for each of the broad abilities that comprise stratum II of CHC theory (with *Grw* constituting two worksheets, one for reading and one for writing). A *Gt* worksheet (which would represent the final stratum II ability in CHC theory) was not included because none of the ability tests included in the *Desk Reference* of this book or in current cognitive ability batteries measures *Gt*. The worksheets include subtests from 50 academic ability instruments as well as several cognitive ability batteries. Tests of academic ability are listed first on the worksheets followed by tests of cognitive ability. Each worksheet follows the same convention of listing tests as that found on previously presented cross-battery worksheets (Flanagan, McGrew, & Ortiz, 2000; Flanagan & Ortiz, 2001; McGrew & Flanagan, 1998): (1) tests that were classified empirically as either strong or moderate measures of their respective broad CHC factor are printed in bold capital and bold lowercase letters, respectively; and (2) tests that were classified logically as measures of the respective broad CHC abilities are printed in regular lowercase letters.[1] Each worksheet groups the subtests according to the narrow ability that they measure. For example, the *Grw*-R worksheet groups subtests according to those that measure either Reading Decoding (RD), Reading Comprehension (RC), Verbal (printed) Language Comprehension (V), Cloze Ability (CZ) or Reading Speed (RS)-five narrow abilities subsumed by *Grw*-R.

It should be noted that when a test was classified as a measure of two different narrow abilities (subsumed by the same broad ability), it was grouped with measures of one narrow ability, and the other narrow ability was reported in parentheses next to the subtest. For example, a review of the *Grw*-W worksheet (see Figure 12.1) shows that the WJ III Spelling of Sounds is a measure of Spelling Ability (SG), because it is grouped with other measures

FIGURE 12.1   Writing Ability (*Grw*-W) CHC Cross-Battery Worksheet

Grw–W–WRITING ABILITY
CHC CROSS-BATTERY WORKSHEET

Battery or Test	Age	*Grw–W*–Writing Ability Narrow Ability Tests	LD Area	SS*	SS (100 ± 15)
Spelling Ability (SG)					
Tests of Achievement					
DAB-3	6-14	Spelling	WE		
DATA-2	12-18	Spelling	WE		
ITPA-3	5-12	Sight Spelling	WE		
ITPA-3	5-12	Sound Spelling	WE		
K-TEA/NU	6-22	Spelling	WE		
PIAT-R/NU	5-7	Written Expression (Level I) (EU)	WE		
PIAT-R/NU	5-22	Spelling	WE		
TAAS-R	5-14	Spelling	WE		
TOCL	5-8	Writing Skills (EU)	WE		
TOWL-3	7-17	Spelling	WE		
TWS-4	6-18	Test of Written Spelling – 4th Ed.	WE		
WIAT-II	5-19	Spelling	WE		
WJ III	2-90	**SPELLING**	WE		
WJ III	6-90	**SPELL. OF SOUNDS (*Ga*-PC:S)**	WE		
WRAT-3	5-74	Spelling	WE		
YCAT	4-7	Writing	WE		
Other					
Tests of Cognitive Ability					
Other					
		1. Sum of column			
		2. Divide by number of tests			
		3. **Spelling Ability** average			

		Writing Ability (WA)			
Tests of Achievement					
DAB-3	6-14	Contextual Language	WE		
DAB-3	6-14	Story Construction	WE		
DATA-2	12-18	Writing Composition	WE		
OWLS	5-21	Written Expression Scale	WE		
PIAT-R/NU	7-18	Written Expression (Level II)	WE		
TEWL-2	5-10	Contextual Writing	WE		
TOCL	5-8	Original Writing	WE		
TOWE	8-14	Essay	WE		
TOWL-3	7-17	Contextual Conventions (EU)	WE		
TOWL-3	7-17	Contextual Language	WE		
TOWL-3	7-17	Story Construction	WE		
TOWL-3	7-17	Vocabulary	WE		
WIAT-II	8-19	Written Language	WE		
WJ III	7-90	**WRITING FLUENCY (*Gs*-R9)**	WE		
WJ III	5-90	**WRITING SAMPLES**	WE		
Other					
Tests of Cognitive Ability					
Other					
		1. Sum of column			
		2. Divide by number of tests			
		3. **Writing Ability** average			

Name:_____
Age: _____
Grade:_____
Examiner:_____
Date of Evaluation: _____

WRITING ABILITY *is an acquired store of knowledge that includes basic writing skills required for the expression of language via writing. It includes the following narrow abilities:*

Spelling Ability (SG): Ability to spell words correctly, in particular words that are spelled nonphonetically or are irregular.

Writing Ability (WA): Ability to write with clarity of thought, organization, and good sentence structure.

English Usage Knowledge (EU): Knowledge of writing in the English language with respect to capitalization, punctuation, usage, and spelling.

FIGURE 12.1 *Continued*

English Usage Knowledge (EU)

Tests of Achievement					
DAB-3	6-14	Capitalization	WE		
DAB-3	6-14	Punctuation	WE		
HAMAT	7-17	Writing	WE		
MBA	4-95	Writing	WE		
TERA-3	5-8	Conventions			
TEWL-2	3-10	Basic Writing	WE		
TOAL-3	12-24	Writing/Grammar (WA)	WE		
TOWE	6:6-14	Items	WE		
TOWL-3	7-17	Logical Sentences	WE		
TOWL-3	7-17	Sentence Combining (WA)	WE		
TOWL-3	7-17	Style	WE		
WJ III	6-90	**PUNCT. & CAPIT. (*Gc*-MY)**	WE		
Other					

Tests of Cognitive Ability					
Other					
		1. Sum of column			
		2. Divide by number of tests			
		3. **English Usage Knowledge** average			

Sum/No. of Narrow-Ability Averages

Cluster Average**
__ Broad (__)
__ Narrow (__)

of SG on the worksheet. However, because the Spelling of Sounds subtest was classified also as a measure of Phonetic Coding: Synthesis (*Ga*-PC:S), the code "*Ga*-PC:S" is printed in parentheses next to this subtest. The right side of each worksheet provides the definitions of the respective broad and narrow CHC abilities. Although brief, these definitions provide a quick reference and may facilitate test selection, test interpretation, and report writing.

In addition to broad and narrow CHC classifications, most academic ability tests were classified as a measure of one or more of the seven areas of achievement included in the federal definition of LD (IDEA). For example, Figure 12.1 shows that the KTEA/NU Spelling subtest has an "LD Area" code of "WE," which stands for Written Expression. In addition to WE, the remaining LD areas include Basic Reading Skills (BR), Reading Comprehension (RC), Math Calculation (MC), Math Reasoning (MR), Listening Comprehension (LC), and Oral Expression (OE). Academic ability tests were classified by LD area in order to assist practitioners in quickly identifying those tests that are most relevant to the assessment of individuals suspected of having a learning disability in one or more specific achievement areas listed in the federal definition.

Unlike the broad and narrow abilities specified by CHC theory, the seven areas of LD are not theoretical constructs nor were they derived through any empirical method. Rather, they tend to represent descriptions of particular areas of academic functioning relevant to the educational setting. In our opinion, they more closely resemble "clinical clusters" or composites formed by an aggregate of relatively distinct abilities that are necessary in combination for successful performance or acquisition of some skill or behavior. From the CHC perspective, such composites are often "messy" in that they are usually represented by abilities that reflect more than one broad ability. Much like other clinical clusters, academic composites that correspond to the academic descriptors delineated by IDEA may provide useful information regarding specific areas of dysfunction responsible for breakdowns in performance that may not be readily identified through separate analysis of individual abilities. In order to distinguish the seven LD-related achievement areas specified in IDEA from the theoretically and empirically derived CHC broad- and narrow-ability clusters, we will refer to our operationalization of them as Academic Clinical Composites (ACC).

In order to document that an individual has a deficit in Basic Reading Skills, for example, it would likely be necessary to assess more than just Reading Decoding ability. There are several other narrow CHC abilities that appear to contribute to an understanding of Basic Reading Skills, including Verbal (printed) Language Comprehension (*Gc*-V), Phonetic Coding: Analysis (*Ga*-PC:A), Phonetic Coding: Synthesis (*Ga*-PC:S), and Reading Speed (*Grw*-R-RS). Note that these abilities represent aspects of three different CHC broad abilities. When documentation of an individual's Basic Reading Skills is warranted, a test of RD may be augmented with one or more qualitatively different tests of other basic reading skills to derive a Basic Reading Skills Clinical Composite and to achieve a comprehensive evaluation of this academic domain.

In addition to Basic Reading Skills, the remaining six Academic Clinical Composites that correspond to the academic descriptors listed in the federal definition of LD (i.e., Reading Comprehension, Math Calculation, Math Reasoning, Written Expression, Listening Comprehension, and Oral Expression) can be assessed by two or more CHC narrow abilities. The specific correspondence between the seven areas of LD and CHC narrow abilities is shown in Table 12.2. This table should be used to identify the CHC abilities that contribute to an understanding of the seven academic achievement areas that are assessed routinely in individuals suspected of having a learning disability. For example, Table 12.2 shows that SG, WA, EU, and MY are qualitatively different aspects of Written Expression. Tests that measure two or more of these abilities can be combined to yield an Academic Clinical Compose—in this case, a *Written Expression Clinical Composite.* Prior to concluding that an individual has a deficit in Written Expression, practitioners should ensure that this academic area was assessed comprehensively. In general, at least two CHC narrow abilities that correspond to the LD assessment areas listed in Table 12.2 should be included to derive an Academic Clinical Composite.

The specific purpose(s) for using standardized instruments in the assessment of academic performance will determine whether practitioners should organize their batteries in accordance with either the broad CHC academic abilities (e.g., *Grw*-R, *Grw*-W, *Gq*, etc.) or one or more of the seven areas of academic ability listed in the federal definition (i.e., the Academic Clinical Composites). Specifically, practitioners should decide whether a given assessment initially warrants a sampling of functioning in a given domain or whether a more in-depth assessment of a particular academic skill area is warranted. This decision will affect how an initial cross-battery assessment is organized. Suppose a practitioner was interested in obtaining an adequate sampling of functioning in *Grw*-R, *Grw*-W, and *Gq*. The first step to ensuring adequate representation of these abilities would involve examining Table 12.1 (or Appendix A) to identify a battery that contains two or more qualitatively different abilities within each of these three domains. The WJ III battery, for example, could be used to achieve this goal.

However, it may not always be possible to begin an assessment of *Grw*-R, *Grw*-W, and *Gq* with a battery that adequately measures each broad ability through the inclusion of two qualitatively different indicators. For example, a practitioner may not have access to certain comprehensive batteries or may not be trained in the administration, scoring, and interpretation of these batteries. In such instances, it may be necessary to supplement a core battery of

TABLE 12.2 Correspondence between LD Assessment Areas in the Federal Definition (IDEA) and CHC Narrow Abilities

Learning Disability Assessment Area	Corresponding CHC Abilities[1]
Basic Reading Skills	Reading Decoding (RD) Verbal (printed) Language Comprehension (V) Reading Speed (RS) Phonetic Coding: Analysis (PC:A) Phonetic Coding: Synthesis (PC:S)
Reading Comprehension	Reading Comprehension (RC) Cloze Ability (CZ)
Written Expression	Spelling Ability (SG) Writing Ability (WA) English Usage Knowledge (EU) Grammatical Sensitivity (MY)[2] —LC/OE
Math Calculation	Math Knowledge (KM) Math Achievement (A3) Number Facility (N)
Math Reasoning	Math Knowledge (KM) Math Achievement (A3) Quantitative Reasoning (RQ)
Listening Comprehension	Listening Ability (LS) Language Development (LD)—Receptive Lexical Knowledge (VL)—Receptive
Oral Expression	Oral Production and Fluency (OP) Language Development (LD)—Expressive Lexical Knowledge (VL)—Expressive Communication Ability (CM)

Note: A detailed listing of subtests and their corresponding CHC narrow-ability/LD area domains is provided in Appendix A. Narrow-ability definitions are located in Chapter 2 and Appendix A.
[1]Test indicators corresponding to two or more qualitatively different indicators of the Learning Disability Assessment Areas are combined to yield *Academic Clinical Composites (ACC).*
[2]Depending on the nature of the task, Grammatical Sensitivity (MY) measures may involve either Listening Comprehension (LC) or Oral Expression (OE).

choice (or availability) to ensure sufficient measurement of the targeted academic abilities. For example, the Peabody Individual Achievement Test–Revised (PIAT-R/NU; Markwardt, 1997) does not include a measure of mathematics reasoning and the Kaufman-Test of Educational Achievement/Normative Update (K-TEA/NU; Kaufman & Kaufman, 1997) does not provide adequate coverage of *Grw*-W. When adequate representation of *Grw*-R, *Grw*-W, and *Gq* abilities is the goal and the core battery of choice (e.g., PIAT-R/NU) does not include sufficient indicators of one or more of these abilities, practitioners should use a psychometrically sound instrument to augment the core battery, in accordance with the guiding principles outlined earlier, thereby ensuring the inclusion of two qualitatively different indicators for each broad-ability domain of interest.

Although representation of CHC broad abilities through the use of two qualitatively different indicators of each ability provides an adequate sampling of functioning within broad CHC ability domains, it is possible to measure broad CHC abilities more comprehensively through the inclusion of multiple narrow-ability indicators of each broad ability by crossing batteries. Table 12.3 shows that the K-TEA/NU includes two qualitatively different indicators of *Grw*-R (i.e., Reading Decoding [RD] and Reading Comprehension [RC]) and *Gq* (i.e., Math Computation [A3] and Math Applications [KM, A3]). Therefore, the KTEA/NU samples functioning in the broad *Grw*-R and *Gq* domains adequately. *Grw*-W, however, is underrepresented on the K-TEA/NU. That is, this battery contains only one indicator of *Grw*-W (i.e., Spelling [SG]). As seen in Table 12.3, the K-TEA/NU battery can be supplemented in this area via the inclusion of a subtest of writing ability from another battery, such as the PIAT-R/NU. Table 12.3 shows that when the K-TEA/NU battery is crossed with a writing ability subtest from another battery, adequate representation of *Grw*-R, *Grw*-W, and *Gq* is achieved. Furthermore, crossing the K-TEA/NU with the PIAT-R/NU eliminates concerns related to comparing test results from batteries that have different normative samples (see Flanagan & Ortiz, 2001, for a discussion) because they were conormed.

Table 12.3 also shows that additional tests from the WJ III, for example, can be used to broaden measurement of K-TEA/NU-based *Grw*-R, *Grw*-W, and *Gq* abilities further in the event that a more in-depth assessment in any one of these areas was warranted. For example, in addition to measures of RD and RC in the area of *Grw*-R, tests of Verbal (printed) Language Comprehension (V) and Reading Speed (RS) could be administered to gain a more comprehensive understanding of reading ability. In general, most comprehensive achievement batteries provide adequate representation of at least two of the three major academic ability domains: Reading (*Grw*-R), Writing (*Grw*-W), and Math (*Gq*). In-depth assessment of these academic ability domains, however, will require crossing batteries in most cases.

It is likely that assessment of broad academic ability domains will remain focused on ensuring adequate or in-depth representation of CHC abilities for practitioners who are either familiar with CHC Cross-Battery assessment as it applies to tests of cognitive ability (e.g., Flanagan, McGrew, & Ortiz, 2000; Flanagan & Ortiz, 2001; McGrew & Flanagan, 1998) or who are interested in directly comparing broad CHC academic abilities with broad CHC cognitive abilities. For example, the operational definition of learning disability presented in Chapter 11 requires an evaluation of the relationship between functioning in specific academic skills and underlying cognitive processes and abilities. Organizing assessments according to broad CHC academic and cognitive ability domains would facilitate this process (see Chapter 14 for a case example). Practitioners who engage in the assessment of both academic and cognitive abilities would therefore benefit from organizing assessment batteries in accordance with the broad CHC domains.

Not all practitioners are involved in assessment of both academic and cognitive abilities, however. Many practitioners focus exclusively on either one or the other. For those practitioners who focus mainly on the assessment of academic abilities under the provisions of IDEA, it is likely that a focus on the seven Academic Clinical Composites, as opposed to the CHC domains, would be desirable. For example, learning disability specialists, educational evaluators, reading specialists, and similar personnel involved in academic assessment-related activities may work as part of a multidisciplinary team wherein their contribution focuses on assessment and evaluation of one or more academic ability

Table 12.3   Example of K-TEA/NU-Based Cross-Battery Assessment

Assessment Goals	Basic Reading and Reading Comprehension (Grw—R)	Writing (Grw—W)	Math Calculation and Math Reasoning (Gq)
Adequate Representation of CHC Broad Academic Abilities	K-TEA/NU Reading Decoding (RD) K-TEA/NU Reading Comprehension (RC)	K-TEA/NU Spelling (SG) *PIAT-R/NU Written Expression Level 1 (SG); Level II (WA)*	K-TEA/NU Math Computation (A3) K-TEA/NU Math Applications (KM, A3)
In-Depth Assessment of CHC Broad Academic Abilities—Includes augmenting the K-TEA/NU core battery with one or more of the following: *Grw*—R (V, RS, CZ) *Grw*—W (EU) *Gq* (N) *Gc* (LD, VL, MY, CM) *Ga* (PC:A, PC:S)	K-TEA/NU Reading Decoding (RD) K-TEA/NU Reading Comprehension (RC) *WJ III Reading Vocabulary (V, Gc-VL)* *WJ III Reading Fluency (RS)*	K-TEA/NU Spelling (SG) *WJ III Writing Samples (WA)* *WJ III Punct. and Cap. (EU)* *WJ III Editing (Eu;Gc-MY)*	K-TEA/NU Math Computation (A3) K-TEA/NU Math Applications (KM, A3) K-TEA/NU Math Computation (A3) K-TEA/NU Mathmatics Applications (KM, A3) *WJ III Quantitative Concepts (KM, Gf-RQ)* *WJ III Math Fluency (A3, Gs-N)*

Note: Tests printed in italics represent possible supplements to the K-TEA/NU for the purpose of adequate or in-depth measures of constructs. The abilities listed for Basic Reading and Reading Comprehension, Writing, and Math Calculation and Math Reasoning can be measured using tests that vary in task demands and task stimuli. Appendices F1–F7 can be used to select tests that meet the specific requirements of the assessment (e.g., selection of tests that closely match curriculum). Appendices F1–F7 can also be used to evaluate potential factors that may have resulted in differences in performance on two tests that measure the same underlying CHC ability (e.g., difference in test format, test stimuli, etc.).

A3 = Mathematics Achievement; CZ = Cloze Ability; EU = English Usage Knowledge; *Ga* = Auditory Processing; *Gc* = Crystallized Intelligence; *Gq* = Quantitative Knowledge; *Grw*—R = Reading and Writing—Reading Factor; *Grw*—W = Reading and Writing—Writing Factor; *Gs* = Processing Speed; KM = Mathematical Knowledge; LD = Language Development; MY = Grammatical Sensitivity; N = Number Facility; PC:A = Phonetic Coding: Analysis; PC:S = Phonetic Coding: Synthesis; R9 = Rate-of-Test-Taking; RC = Reading Comprehension; RD = Reading Decoding; RQ = Quantitative Reasoning; RS = Reading Speed; SG = Spelling Ability; V = Verbal (printed) Language Comprehension; VL = Lexical Knowledge; WA = Writing Ability.

Definitions of broad and narrow CHC abilities are found in Chapter 2 and Appendix A.

[1]When adequate assessment of *Grw*—W is necessary and the K-TEA/NU is selected as the core battery, the PIAT-R/NU represents an ideal supplement because these two measures were conormed.

domains, particularly in special education referrals of individuals with learning difficulties. When the focus of assessment is related primarily to academic abilities under these conditions, organization of tests according to the seven Academic Clinical Composites, as described and operationalized earlier, seems most appropriate.

Table 12.4 shows the tests of five comprehensive achievement batteries that correspond to the seven academic areas of the federal definition and, by extension, the given Academic Clinical Composites delineated thus far. The WIAT-II, WJ III, and DATA-2 include at least one measure for each of the seven composites. However, not all comprehensive achievement batteries include measures of certain academic ability areas, such as listening comprehension and oral expression that are listed in the federal definition. Table 12.4 shows that neither the K-TEA/NU nor the PIAT-R/NU includes measures of these abilities. Therefore, when these batteries are used and assessment of Listening Comprehension (LC) and Oral Expression (OE) is desirable in addition to the abilities measured by these instruments, practitioners may choose tests from another battery as supplements (e.g., Oral and Written Language Scales [OWLS]; Carrow-Woolfolk, 1995). For example, Table 12.4 shows that the OWLS' Oral Expression Scale can be used to obtain adequate representation of Oral Expression in assessment. Similarly, the OWLS' Listening Comprehension Scale allows for adequate assessment of Listening Comprehension. Supplementing the K-TEA/NU battery in a manner consistent with the aforementioned example allows for a broader representation of academic ability areas and thus more reliable and valid measurement of the various Academic Clinical Composites.

Despite a battery's inclusion of at least one subtest per ACC, as stated earlier, adequate assessment of each of the seven composites necessitates a minimum of two qualitatively different indicators of each ability. According to Messick (1989), failure to represent constructs by more than one measure (or subtest) leads to *nomological noise*. That is, "because no single test is a pure exemplar of the construct but contains variance due to other constructs and method contaminants, there is no solid basis for concluding that an observed score relationship stems from that part of the test variance reflective of the construct. By using two or more tests to represent the construct . . . one can disentangle shared variance from unshared variance and discern which aspects of construct meaning, if any, derive from the shared and unshared parts" (p. 48). Therefore, practitioners should consult Table 12.2 to determine the types of abilities that may be represented in an assessment of one or more of the seven achievement areas. The steps that follow in the next section will demonstrate how to select tests and organize assessments to ensure adequate coverage of each academic ability domain as reflected by the respective Academic Clinical Composites.

Besides having knowledge of the narrow CHC abilities that correspond to the seven academic achievement areas (Table 12.2), it is important to understand that not all tests of specific academic abilities (e.g., reading comprehension tests) have the same task demands and requirements. For example, some measures of reading comprehension may not be consistent with the reading comprehension demands of an examinee's core curriculum (e.g., some reading comprehension tests require drawing inferences and responding to multiple-choice questions, whereas others do not). Depending on the reading test used, the examinee's performance may or may not reflect his or her performance in the classroom. It may therefore be necessary to evaluate reading comprehension in different ways in order to understand the specific area of difficulty. Appendices F1 through F7 provide information

Table 12.4 Representation of Academic Clinical Composites on Select Comprehensive Achievement Batteries

	Grw - R		Gq		Gc		Grw - W
	Basic Reading Skills	Reading Comprehension	Math Calculation	Math Reasoning	Oral Expression	Listening Comprehension	Written Expression
K-TEA /NU	Reading Decoding (RD)	Reading Comprehension (RC)	Mathematics Computation (A3)	Mathematics Applications (A3, KM)	*OWLS Oral Expression Scale (OP, CM, LD)*	*OWLS Listening Comprehension Scale (LS, LD)*	Spelling (SG)
WIAT-II	Word Reading (RD) Pseudoword Decoding (RD)	Reading Comprehension (RC)	Numerical Operations (A3)	Mathematics Reasoning (RQ)	Oral Expression (CM)	Listening Comprehension (LS)	Spelling (SG) Written Expression (WA)
WJ III	Letter-Word Identification (RD) Word Attack (RD; *Ga*-PC:A) Reading Fluency (RS)	Passage Comprehension (RC, CZ) Reading Vocabulary (V: *Gc*-VL)	Quantitative Concepts (KM; *Gf*-RQ) Calculation (A3)	Applied Problems (A3, KM; *Gf*-RQ)	Picture Vocabulary (VL, LD)	Understanding Directions (LS; *Gsm*-MW) Oral Comprehension (LS)	Spelling (SG) Spelling of Sounds (SG; *Ga*-PC:A) Writing Fluency (WA; *Gs*-R9) Writing Samples (WA) Punctuation & Capitaliz. (EU) Editing (Eu; *Gc*-MY)
DATA-2	Word Identification (RD)	Reading Comprehension (RC)	Math Calculation (A3)	Math Problem Solving (A3; *Gf*-RQ)	Expressive Vocabulary (OP)	Receptive Vocabulary (VL, LD) Receptive Grammar (MY)	Spelling (SG) Writing Composition (WA)
PIAT-R/NU	Reading Recognition (RD)	Reading Comprehension (RC)	Mathematics (A3)	*K-TEA-R/NU Mathematics Applications (A3, KM)*	*OWLS Oral Expression Scale (OP, CM, LD)*	*OWLS Listening Comprehension Scale (LS, LD)*	Spelling (SG: *Ga*-PC:A) Written Expression Level I (SG) Written Expression (Level II) (WA)

Note.: Tests in italics are examples of measures that may be used to supplement core batteries in areas that are not measured by the core battery. K-TEA/NU = Kaufman Test of Educational Achievement–Revised/Normative Update; WIAT–II = Wechsler Individual Achievement Test–Second Edition; WJ III = Woodcock-Johnson Tests of Achievement–Third Edition; DATA-2 = Diagnostic Achievement Test for Adolescents–Second Edition; PIAT-R/NU = Peabody Individual Achievement Test–Revised/Normative Update.

with regard to the variation in task characteristics among tests that purport to measure the same academic ability (e.g., reading decoding, reading comprehension, spelling, etc.). For example, some tests assess reading comprehension using a cloze format, whereas others may use open-ended questions or a multiple-choice format. In order to gain information from standardized tests that may or may not corroborate teacher reports and work samples, practitioners should use the information in Appendices F1 through F7 to ensure that they are assessing the targeted academic skill in the desired manner. Moreover, examination of performance on two tasks that measure the same academic skill (Reading Comprehension) in qualitatively different ways (multiple choice, cloze) may provide valuable information regarding the nature of an individual's difficulties in that area.

The preceding examples demonstrate common instances in which it may be necessary to supplement a comprehensive achievement battery (e.g., WJ III, WIAT-II, K-TEA/NU, PIAT-R/NU, DATA-2) to achieve the desired level of breadth and depth of measurement of one or more academic abilities included in IDEA's definition of learning disability and subsumed by several broad CHC domains (e.g., *Grw* and *Gq*) as specified in our operationalization of the corresponding Academic Clinical Composites. Thus, depending on the core battery selected, when a comprehensive assessment of multiple academic abilities is desired, C-CB procedures may be necessary to ensure adequate and appropriate coverage of the targeted academic domains.

Comprehensive assessment of a broad range of academic abilities is not necessarily the goal of every evaluation of achievement. At times, practitioners may be interested only in assessing a specific academic ability domain in depth, such as reading ability. This situation would constitute an assessment that is more selective in nature. When a selective assessment of a particular academic ability domain is the goal, practitioners should examine the depth of coverage of the specific academic domain on the batteries that they use routinely. Most comprehensive batteries, for example, include a measure of reading decoding and reading comprehension. However, these two specific reading skills may not represent fully the depth of measurement of overall reading ability that may be desired or warranted by the referral. Therefore, it may be necessary to either augment the reading tests of a particular comprehensive core battery with tests from another battery or to use a test that was developed to assess reading ability comprehensively (e.g., WDRB). Again, the information contained in Appendix A and Tables 12.1 and 12.2 will aid practitioners in the selection of the appropriate battery or combination of tests that are necessary to assess reading ability (or any other academic ability) comprehensively.

There are of course times when a practitioner desires neither a comprehensive assessment of academic abilities (e.g., one that adequately measures *Grw*-R, *Grw*-W, *Gq,* and perhaps other abilities) nor a selective, in-depth assessment of a particular academic ability domain (e.g., *Grw*-R). Rather, a practitioner may be interested in simply administering a brief measure of academic achievement that provides a cursory assessment of functioning in one or more academic abilities for screening purposes.

Brief or screening measures of academic ability are used primarily to determine whether a problem might exist in one or more academic ability areas (e.g., reading, math, written language). When brief/screening measures are used in this way, and a potential difficulty is detected, then additional assessment at a more in-depth level is necessary to test the hypothesis that performance in the targeted area(s) is within normal limits. In order to test this hypothesis, it is necessary to select tests that measure two or more qualitatively different aspects of the targeted ability domain using psychometrically sound instruments.

In summary, practitioners may find it necessary to engage in C-CB and S-CB assessment for a number of reasons. When either cross-battery method is deemed necessary, practitioners should use Appendix A and Tables 12.1 and 12.2 to identify the most appropriate measures to use to assess academic functioning. The following steps provide guidelines for crossing batteries when it is deemed necessary to do so, in a psychometrically and theoretically defensible manner.

Implementing CHC Cross-Battery Assessment Step by Step

Step 1: Conduct a Comprehensive, Brief/Screening or Selective Assessment

The first step in the assessment of academic abilities is to determine the type of assessment that is required based on referral information. A *comprehensive* assessment of academic abilities would require either (1) adequate representation of *Grw*-R, *Grw*-W, *Gq,* and *Gc,* particularly as it applies to Oral Production and Fluency (OP; Oral Expression) and Listening Ability (LS; Listening Comprehension); or (2) adequate representation of the Academic Clinical Composites corresponding to the seven areas of academic ability listed in the federal definition of LD. A *brief/screening* assessment of academic abilities would require identifying the range of academic abilities of interest (e.g., reading and math only, reading, math, and written language, etc.). A *selective* assessment of academic abilities would require identifying the depth of measurement necessary to achieve a comprehensive assessment of one or more targeted areas. Regardless of whether it is determined that assessment will be comprehensive, brief, or selective, a "core" battery must be chosen that is appropriate and responsive to several factors, including age and developmental level of the examinee, availability of test batteries, examiner's familiarity and expertise with certain batteries, and so forth. The examiner should choose the battery that comes closest to measuring the abilities of interest. Moreover, at this point in the test selection process, practitioners should decide if their assessments will be organized around broad CHC abilities (e.g., *Grw*-R) or one or more of the seven Academic Clinical Composites (e.g., Basic Reading Skills). The next steps will determine whether a core battery of choice needs to be augmented with tests from another battery to achieve the desired goal and, if so, to describe how to augment a battery systematically.

With respect to comprehensive assessment, the practitioner will first need to review the worksheets (in Appendix A) or Tables 12.1 and 12.2 to determine which CHC abilities are and are not adequately represented on the chosen core battery. Again, adequate representation of a broad CHC ability or an Academic Clinical Composite necessitates the administration of at least two qualitatively different measures of that ability. If a battery includes more than two qualitatively different measures of a broad ability, then the practitioner should decide whether all or only two measures are necessary to administer vis-à-vis referral information and purpose of assessment.

The decision as to which two (or more) tests are to be selected and administered for each broad academic ability area in a comprehensive assessment is based on joint consideration of several factors. First, the two tests should represent qualitatively different aspects of the same broad ability (e.g., *Grw*-R) or academic area (e.g., Basic Reading Skills). For example, in deciding how to measure *Grw*-R, two tests whose narrow-ability (stratum I) classifications are the same (e.g., Reading Decoding [RD]) are not qualitatively different, despite the fact that they may differ with respect to task characteristics (see Appendices F1 through F7). Therefore, only one of these tests should be used and it should be coupled with a test that measures a qualitatively different aspect of *Grw*-R, such as Reading Comprehension (RC). Second, tests should be selected to be as responsive to the referral concerns as possible. For instance, if the referral is related to the quality and clarity of an individual's thoughts when writing, then tests assessing the narrow ability of writing ability (*Grw*-W-WA) may be more appropriate than a test that primarily assesses spelling ability (*Grw*-W-SG). Third, attention to the issues mentioned previously, in particular age and developmental level of the child, should play a part in making final decisions regarding the suitability of any particular test or combination of tests. Fourth, the variation in task characteristics (see Appendices F1 through F7) should be reviewed to determine if task stimuli and demands are appropriate to the unique requirements of the assessment. Fifth, practitioners should consider the standardization sample characteristics, as well as the reliability and validity of the tests included in assessments, and select tests with the best psychometric qualities in situations where more than one test could be used to represent an ability. The *Desk Reference* section of this book includes information about the psychometric characteristics of nearly all commonly used comprehensive, brief/screening, and specific academic ability tests published since 1993.

In the case of brief/screening assessment, the practitioner will need to review the information in Table 12.1 to determine which academic abilities are measured by the chosen instrument. For example, some brief/screening tests measure reading decoding (e.g., MBA, WRAT 3, YCAT), wherease others measure reading comprehension (K-FAST, HAMAT). Also, some screening batteries assess narrow aspects of reading, math, and written language (MBA, WRAT 3, HAMAT), whereas others assess basic skills in only two of these three broad academic ability domains (e.g., K-FAST). Finally, none of the brief/screening tests listed in Table 12.1 assess listening comprehension and oral expression *directly*. Therefore, when a brief/screening assessment of these latter two areas is desirable—over and above reading, math, and writing—selective assessment procedures will be necessary.

In the case of selective assessment, the practitioner will need to review the specific academic skill tests listed in Table 12.1 to determine which ones approximate the desired depth of assessment in any given CHC broad-ability or academic area. For example, if the goal was in-depth assessment of *Grw*-R, Table 12.1 shows that the WDRB contains three tests that measure qualitatively different aspects of this domain (i.e., Reading Decoding, Cloze Ability, and Phonetic Coding). Likewise, if the goal of assessment was in-depth assessment of the Basic Reading Skills ACC, Table 12.1 shows that the WDRB includes measures of three narrow CHC abilities that correspond to this academic composite (see Table 12.2)—namely, Reading Decoding, Phonetic Coding: Analysis, and Phonetic Coding: Synthesis. Alternatively, the practitioner may refer to the specific Cross-Battery worksheet(s) in Appendix A that correspond(s) to the ability (abilities) that will form the focus of the evaluation. These worksheets allow practitioners to review the relevant information that is needed in order to begin assembling the most appropriate measures for the academic ability or abilities of interest. When an in-depth evaluation of a particular ability is the focus of assessment, then the practitioner should keep in mind that the more qualitatively different indicators that are included to represent a given ability, the better the estimate of that ability.

Step 2: Identify Absence or Underrepresentation of CHC Abilities on the Core Battery

Once the purpose of assessment is established (comprehensive, brief/screening, selective) and a core battery has been selected, identification of the relevant CHC abilities that are either not represented or that are underrepresented on a given core battery can be achieved by reviewing either the CHC Cross-Battery worksheets in Appendix A or Tables 12.1 and 12.2. At this time, the only comprehensive achievement batteries that provide adequate representation of *Grw*-R, *Grw*-W, and *Gq* are the WIAT-II, WJ III, DATA-2, and DAB-3. There are no published tests of academic abilities that provide adequate representation of all seven Academic Clinical Composites when the guideline of two qualitatively different indicators of each area is used. However, the WIAT-II, WJ III, and DATA-2 do include measures of all seven academic ability domains. Most comprehensive batteries of academic ability include only one test each of the seven academic areas listed in the federal definition that correspond to the Academic Clinical Composites. The areas of listening comprehension and oral expression are not measured at all by two of the six comprehensive achievement batteries (i.e., K-TEA/NU and PIAT-R/NU). It is unlikely that valid conclusions regarding functioning in any one of the seven academic areas can be drawn from a single subtest. Therefore, the practitioner will need to identify those abilities that will require supplementation through the use of tests from other batteries in order to form valid composites. Even if batteries were available that provided adequate coverage and representation of all academic abilities, crossing batteries may still prove useful in light of other considerations, such as task requirements, developmental appropriateness, cultural and linguistic implications, and so on. Once again, in selecting tests that will be used to supplement the core battery, the practitioner should make every effort to accommodate the unique and idiosyncratic factors that may be involved so that assessment is tailored in a highly individualized manner.

Table 12.1 provides a quick reference for the purpose of identifying abilities that are either not represented (i.e., absent) or not represented adequately (i.e., underrepresented) on comprehensive, brief/screening, and specific academic skills tests. By using this table, practitioners can quickly identify the area(s) in which their core battery may need to be supplemented.

Step 3: Select Tests Needed to Supplement the Core Battery

In determining which subtests are necessary in order to approximate or ensure adequate representation of absent or underrepresented abilities, one of the most important factors is the need to keep the number of batteries that will be used to a minimum (preferably two). If practitioners have a diverse range of academic ability instruments at their disposal, it will rarely be necessary to cross more than two batteries.

Table 12.3 provided one of several possibilities for ensuring either adequate representation or in-depth assessment of the broad *Grw*-R, *Grw*-W, and *Gq* abilities when the K-TEA/NU was selected as the core battery in assessment. Table 12.5 provides an example of the WJ III tests that may be used to supplement the WIAT-II core battery when adequate representation of the seven academic areas is necessary. The WJ III was used in this example to augment the WIAT-II for two main reasons. First, it is the most comprehensive achievement battery currently available. Therefore, if the WJ III is not selected as the battery of choice, practitioners should consider using select tests from this battery to supplement other, less comprehensive, instruments. Second, the WJ III was normed at approximately the same time as the WIAT-II, suggesting that they both reflect the most current U.S. census data.

Step 4: Administer and Score Core Battery and Supplemental Tests

Because CHC Cross-Battery assessment is not an individual test in and of itself, but rather a battery of tests individualized, organized, and constructed according to particular referral concerns and based on a contemporary theoretical perspective, there are no unique administration instructions to be followed. Nevertheless, the practitioner must incorporate both general testing considerations applicable to the use of standardized tests as well as the specific guidelines provided by test publishers in the manuals of any tests that may be used.

First, practitioners should attend to issues such as the creation of an appropriate testing environment, proper use of testing materials and equipment, establishing and maintaining rapport with the examinee, and so forth (see Kaufman, Lichtenberger, & Naglieri, 1999, pp. 15–19). Because CHC Cross-Battery assessment is accomplished through the use of standardized tests, it is imperative that these guidelines be followed just as they would be with any other standardized test battery in order to ensure optimum performance by the examinee. Second, the particular instructions provided by the publishers of any tests that are being administered within the context of CHC Cross-Battery assessment should also be followed verbatim. There is no reason for any variance from specified procedures, and modification of these principles will reduce the confidence that can be placed in the validity and reliability of obtained results every bit as much as when using a single battery. Likewise, the scoring specifications and calculation instructions provided by the publishers of tests must be fol-

TABLE 12.5 Example of WIAT-II-Based Cross-Battery When Adequate Representation of the Seven Academic Clinical Composites Is Necessary

Basic Reading Skills	Reading Comprehension	Math Calculation	Math Reasoning
WIAT-II Word Reading (RD) *WJ III Reading Fluency (RS)*	WIAT-II Reading Comprehension (RC) *WJ III Reading Vocabulary (V; Gc-Vl)*	WIAT-II Numerical Operations (A3) *WJ III Quantitative Concepts (KM; Gf-RQ)*	WIAT-II Math Reasoning (RQ) *WJ III Applied Problems (RQ, A3; KM)*

Note: Tests printed in italics represent possible supplements to the WIAT-II for the purpose of adequate measurement of the seven academic ability areas listed in the federal definition of LD. Adequate representation requires a minimum of two qualitatively different measures of an ability or construct.

lowed rigorously. In order to complete CHC Cross-Battery assessment, standard scores (or scaled scores) must be calculated for each test that is administered in a manner consistent with the test publisher and author(s) of the respective tests.

One concern raised in CHC Cross-Battery assessment relates to the issue of giving tests outside the comprehensive sequential framework of standardization. The concern is one of whether in cases where a test battery was standardized using a particular order of subtest administration, does using only selected tests necessarily violate standardization? In other words, in the absence of explicit instructions from the publisher that allows for the administration of only specific subtests, are test administrators legally required to administer the entire test, even if they may be interested in only a particular set of tests or composite score? We believe the answer is *no* and it is our contention that in a wide variety of cases, individuals have routinely been given only a portion of certain batteries because other portions were deemed inappropriate or unnecessary for that individual. For example, giving only the subtests that comprise the Broad Reading Cluster of the WJ-R to individuals referred for reading difficulties was a common practice and will no doubt continue unabated with the WJ III.

Similar "selective" administrations are often done with individuals referred for specific written language, oral language, and math problems, and selective test administration using only a subset of tests from comprehensive achievement batteries has been the foundation of many past and current procedures used in the field of psychoeducational assessment. Therefore, unless a test's manual specifically states that the reliability and validity of the test is maintained *only when every single subtest is given,* we see no reason why CHC Cross-Battery methods should violate standardization any more or less than the other "selective" procedures that are in common practice today. In fact, in its standardization, the tests of the WJ III (Woodcock et al., 2001) utilized a varied administration sequence, presumably to eliminate concerns regarding selective testing procedures and perhaps even to encourage individualized assessment. Moreover, not only do test publishers routinely *omit* prescriptions against using selected subtests or portions of the test but they also do not state that the use of the battery and interpretation of resulting scores is valid only if all subtests are administered. Therefore, it would seem that any alternative use of a test (whether with particular populations or through different theoretical foundations) is left up to the professional judgment of the examiner and that the examiner, in such cases, is wholly liable for providing a suitable (i.e., defensible) rationale for whatever decisions were made and actions taken.

TABLE 12.5 *Continued*

Written Expression	Listening Comprehension[1]	Oral Expression
WIAT-II Spelling (SG) *WIAT-II Written Expression (WA)*	WIAT-II Listening Comprehension (LS) *WJ III Oral Comprehension (LS)*	WIAT-II Oral Expression (CM) *WJ III Picture Vocabulary (VL, LD)*

[1]Within the CHC framework, Listening Ability (LS) appears to be the only ability that corresponds directly with Listening Comprehension. However, LS tests vary greatly in task demands. Therefore, practitioners should consult Appendix F6 to ensure that the measures they select are significantly different to allow for task analysis.

Clearly, the emphasis on both *systematic evaluation* and *empirically and theoretically based decision making* inherent in the CHC Cross-Battery approach make it a method that is highly defensible.

Step 5: Complete the CHC Cross-Battery Worksheets

Once the selected tests have been administered and scored, the data can be recorded on the appropriate worksheets in the column marked "SS*." The adjacent column, marked "SS (100 ± 15)" is used for recording the converted standard score in cases where tests utilize a metric that does not have a mean of 100 and a standard deviation of 15 (e.g., Test of Reading Comprehension–Third Edition [TORC–3; Brown, Hammill, & Wiederholt, 1995]). In such cases, the score must be converted to one that is consistent with this particular metric. A Percentile Rank and Standard Score Conversion Table is included in Appendix B for just this purpose. Tests that use this metric (e.g., WIAT-II, WJ III, PIAT-R/NU, etc.) may be entered directly in this second column, since no conversion is necessary. Note also that all academic achievement batteries included in the *Desk Reference* section of this book provide *age-based* norms; however, some tests (e.g., WJ III) have both age- and grade-based norms. Therefore, when such tests are utilized, standard scores from the age-based norms should be used in order to derive appropriate comparisons with other batteries. It is also important to note that some tests (e.g., the WJ III) yield *extended standard scores* (i.e., <40 and >160; Woodcock et al., 2001). As such, this can be problematic when it comes to combining or comparing such standard scores with standard scores from other tests used in the assessment.

The standard scores for most academic achievement batteries and specific academic skills tests represent *normalized standard scores* that are based on an area (plus linear) transformation of the raw score distribution. Very low or high normalized standard scores are typically calculated via extrapolation. As a result, low and high extrapolated scores are not based on "real" subjects (Woodcock, 1989). This problem is addressed typically by specifying a cutoff score at both the top and bottom of the standard score scale. For example, the WIAT-II norm tables include composite scores that range from 40 to 160 (Psychological Corporation, 2001). In contrast, the WJ III standard scores are not extrapolated. They are based on the *linear transformation of W (Rasch) scores* that utilize two unique standard deviations to produce the observed 10th and 90th percentiles in the distribution. As a result, the WJ III standard scores can range from 1 to 200 (Woodcock et al., 2001). Thus, combining extreme WJ III standard scores (i.e., < 40 and > 160) with standard scores from other tests (e.g., WIAT-II) that are constrained within a certain range (e.g., 40 to 160 inclusive) could potentially result in misleading cluster averages. Therefore, it is necessary to employ a method for reporting WJ III standard scores that "emulate" those computed via more traditional methods. Following the logic of Woodcock (1989), whenever a standard score from any test that produces extended standard scores falls below 40, a value of 40 should be recorded on the appropriate CHC worksheet. Likewise, whenever a standard score (or a score from any test) exceeds 160, a score of 160 should be recorded.

Within each section of the worksheets related to a specific narrow ability, there is a simple three-step set of directions for calculating the average standard score for that narrow ability (see Figure 12.1). Although derivation of averages is very simple, from this point on use of an electronic calculator or an automated scoring program (spreadsheet) is highly recommended in order to ensure accuracy and provide efficiency in double-checking calculations. Step 1 is simply to sum the scores in the *converted* SS column and place the total in the corresponding box. In Step 2, the number of tests that comprise the total sum is entered in the next box just underneath the box containing the total sum. Step 3 involves dividing the sum total of standard scores by the number of tests which comprise it and putting the result in the final box within that section. This final score represents the respective *narrow-ability average.* This three-step process is repeated for all narrow-ability sections in which data exist.

Once all the narrow-ability averages are calculated, the shaded lines leading from the rows in which the narrow-ability averages are recorded can be followed down to a box labeled "Sum of Narrow-Ability Averages." This box is used to record the total *sum* of the narrow-ability averages followed by the *number* of narrow-ability averages reported on the worksheet. The resulting ratio is calculated (i.e., total sum/number of averages) and entered in the final box at the far bottom, right-hand side of the worksheet and denotes the *cluster average.* Averages that result in fractions of one-half or more are rounded up to the nearest whole number.

The final step in completing the worksheets involves specifying whether the cluster average should be interpreted as a broad or narrow estimate of the ability. This determination is indicated by circling the appropriate description found immediately above the cluster average box. A cluster score (or average) would be considered a *broad* estimate of ability if it were derived by summing the standard scores or standard score averages that include at least two tests of qualitatively *different* narrow abilities subsumed by the broad ability in accordance with Guiding Principle 2. When this is the case, the word *Broad* is circled on the worksheet and the respective broad (stratum II) code (e.g., *Grw-R, Grw-W, Gq, Gc,* etc.) is written in the parentheses adjacent to the word *Broad.* Stated more simply, if the total cluster average includes tests from more than one narrow ability box on the worksheet, then the average is a broad estimate of the ability. Conversely, if the cluster average was derived by summing the standard scores of two or more tests of the same narrow ability, then this average would be interpreted most appropriately as representing a narrow (stratum I) ability rather than a broad (stratum II) ability. In other words, if the total cluster average includes tests from a single narrow-ability box on the worksheet, then the average is a narrow estimate of the ability. In this case, the word *Narrow* should be circled and the narrow (stratum I) code (e.g., *Grw*-R-RD) should be written in the parentheses adjacent to the word *Narrow.* Practitioners should be aware that in cases where there is a significant difference between the two scores that are being combined to form the broad- or narrow-ability clusters, a cluster average should not be computed or graphed. The particular reasons for doing so will be discussed further in Chapter 13.

The process of entering standard scores, converting standard scores (if necessary), computing narrow-ability averages, computing cluster averages, and specifying measurement of narrow or broad abilities is completed for each of the measured CHC constructs. In the case of S-CB, this may represent only one or two such constructs (requiring use of only one or two worksheets), whereas in the case of C-CB, it is possible that multiple worksheets will need to be completed. However, even when there is a need for comprehensive assessment of abilities, the amount of time necessary to complete the worksheets is not inordinately increased since the calculations are quite simple and automated scoring programs (spreadsheets) are available.

Step 6: Transfer Scores and Averages to LD Area or CHC Data Summary Sheet and Normative Analysis Graph

Summary sheets for recoding, plotting, and analyzing academic ability test standard scores and broad and narrow academic ability cluster averages from cross-battery assessments can be found in Appendices D1, D2, D3, and E. These appendices also correspond directly to the various levels of the operational definition of LD presented earlier in Chapter 11. Appendix D1 allows for academic ability data to be organized according to the broad and narrow abilities specified by CHC theory consistent with Level I-A of the operational definition. Appendix D2 allows for the organization of data from the worksheets according to CHC cognitive ability domains and is consistent with Level II-A of the operational definition. Appendix D3 allows for the organization of all data (both academic and cognitive) for the purpose of examining ability differences and consistencies in performance within and between cognitive and academic domains from an integrated perspective. It is consistent with Level III of the operational definition of LD. Appendix E allows for the organization of data from the worksheets according to the specific Academic Clinical Composites defined herein that correspond to the seven areas of academic ability listed in the federal definition of LD. Much like Appendix D1, it is consistent with Level I-A of the operational definition of LD. Appendix D1 is probably most useful to practitioners who wish to compare cognitive and academic abilities within the context of CHC theory. Appendix E, however, would be very helpful to practitioners who primarily conduct academic ability assessments and who prefer to maintain the language inherent in the federal definition of LD.

Use of these forms is extremely helpful in being able to organize cross-battery data in a manner that greatly facilitates interpretation, particularly within the context of LD evaluation. Therefore, completion of these forms should be considered a standard part of the assessment and interpretation process. Appendices D1, D2, D3, and E are divided into two parts. The first part provides a *Data Summary* form for recording subtest names and CHC ability codes, Academic Clinical Composites (Appendix E), and CHC broad- and narrow-ability averages (Appendices D1, D2, and D3) as well as other important descriptive information (e.g., confidence intervals, percentile ranks, and ability classifications). The second part provides a *Normative Analysis Graph* that includes a place for plotting the Academic Clinical Composite averages that correspond to each of the seven LD areas of academic ability (Appendix E) or for the broad CHC abilities (Appendices D1, D2, and D3). In addition, space is provided on the normative analysis graph for plotting the standard scores (based on a mean of 100 and standard deviation of 15) for several narrow-ability test indicators. The cluster (ACC or CHC Area) averages are plotted on the *thick bars* and the standard scores for the narrow-ability test indicators are plotted on the *thin bars,* allowing for a visual representation of cross-battery data. A set of standard scores runs across the outside top of each thick bar on the summary sheet. In summary, practitioners can carry out Level I analysis (inter-academic) using the forms in either Appendix D1 or E, Level II analysis (inter-cognitive) using the forms in Appendix D2, and Level III analysis (integrated ability) using the forms in Appendix D3 within the context of the operational definition of LD presented in the previous chapter.

Data Transfer from Worksheets to Data Summary Form. The process of completing the data summary forms begins with the transfer of data from the CHC Cross-Battery worksheets (Appendix A). By transferring the data collected and standard score ranges calculated and listed on the worksheets, data from the entire assessment can be condensed efficiently on a single summary sheet. The Data Summary sheet contains space for entering data on an ability cluster or composite (as appropriate) as well as the standard score ranges for the narrow-ability indicators for each of the broad-ability domains or Academic Clinical Composites that may have been measured. The names of the tests used, and the names of the batteries from which they were drawn, as well as the CHC narrow-ability code, are entered in the spaces provided to the left. To the right of this information, the standard score, standard score confidence interval, percentile rank, and performance or normative classification for the narrow-ability indicators and any broad- or narrow-ability clusters can be entered. Although the summary sheets are entirely numerical, it is an extremely efficient format for reporting the full breadth of the data that have been generated. The summary sheet in Appendix D3 is most useful for this purpose because it allows for data to be recorded from the assessment of both cognitive and academic abilities.

Data Transfer from Worksheets to Normative Analysis Graph. The first step in completing the Normative Analysis Graph is to transfer the appropriate data (cluster averages and individual test standard scores) from the Data Summary sheet to the correct location on the graph. This is accomplished by placing a vertical hash mark on the thick bars corresponding to the standard score cluster or composite averages. On the CHC Normative Analysis Graphs (Appendices D1, D2, and D3), practitioners should make sure to indicate whether the average represents a broad- or narrow-ability cluster (by circling one or the other), as this is a critical component for test interpretation (see Chapter 13). This information should have been transferred from the bottom of the CHC Cross-Battery worksheets to the Data Summary sheet. Thus, this information is available in two locations. Next, the standard scores of the tests that comprise each cluster or composite average should be recorded directly below their respective ACC or CHC area cluster averages. The CHC codes corresponding to the narrow-ability classifications of these tests may also be recorded in the parentheses located just to the right of the subtest names. (A case example and corresponding worksheets, data summary sheets, and normative analysis graphs will be presented in Chapter 14.)

Specifying Confidence Bands on the Normative Analysis Graph. The next step in completing the Normative Analysis Graph is to specify and mark the appropriate *confidence band* for each academic or cognitive ability score that is recorded on the Data Summary sheet or transferred from the worksheets. Confidence bands for cluster and composite averages and narrow-ability test indicator standard scores correspond to ± 1 standard error of measurement (SEM). Confidence bands represent the region in which an individual's true test score most likely will fall and extends from 1 SEM below the obtained score to 1 SEM above the obtained score. The SEM estimates for *all* cross-battery cluster or composite averages is ± 5 and the SEM for individual test standard scores is ± 7. The confidence bands that were constructed for the cross-battery academic ability scores (based on ±1 SEM) are also called *68 percent confidence bands* because they represent the standard score range in which an individual's true score falls two out of three times. The purpose of reporting confidence bands is to demonstrate the degree of precision (or imprecision) that is present in the cross-battery scores. Examining a test score on a profile as a confidence band (as opposed to a single or exact score) is usually preferred (Woodcock & Mather, 1989). We recommend using 68 percent confidence bands because they are considered appropriate and sufficient for the type of clinical decision making that is characteristic of most comprehensive assessment approaches, including the hypothesis-generation CHC Cross-Battery approach described in the next chapter.

It should be noted that given the large number of individual academic achievement tests that can be used in CHC Cross-Battery assessment, it is not practical to calculate and report the composite reliability and SEM estimates for every possible combination of tests. Because the WJ III broad-ability clusters are based on CHC theory (the foundation of CHC Cross-Battery assessment) and are derived from two-test combinations (like the clusters in CHC Cross-Battery assessment), the broad-ability cluster SEMs reported in the *WJ III Technical Manual* (McGrew & Woodcock, 2001) were used to estimate a SEM value for the broad CHC Cross-Battery clusters. For similar reasons, it is impractical to report all published SEMs for all individual tests that might be interpreted in CHC Cross-Battery assessments. Therefore, the SEMs reported across the 22 WJ III academic ability tests across all age ranges were reviewed to identify a reasonable SEM estimate that could be used as a general rule-of-thumb for all individual tests used in CHC Cross-Battery assessments. Furthermore, the respective subtest and composite SEMs reported for other achievement batteries (e.g., WIAT-II) were reviewed to ensure that these SEM rules-of-thumb values were reasonable approximate values across a variety of instruments. Thus, the respective values presented here (±5 and ±7) represent the average (median) CHC cluster and subtest SEM across all age ranges in the WJ III norm sample, respectively.

When completed properly, the Normative Analysis Graphs visually display the data obtained from the administration of the various academic and/or cognitive ability tests chosen for the assessment. As such, these graphs are easy to understand and provide a meaningful basis for making CHC-based ability comparisons that may be necessary in evaluating functioning (e.g., inter-academic–inter-cognitive, and integrated ability-based strengths and weaknesses).

Conclusions

Through application and integration of the various guiding principles and methods described in this book, practitioners can effectively organize, select, and administer tests, as well as interpret the results of their cross-battery assessments. By carefully augmenting a preferred core battery, measurement of a wider range or a more in-depth but selective range of abilities according to contemporary CHC theory and research can be accomplished—a result that cannot be achieved readily through the administration of most single achievement batteries in publication to date. The foundational sources of information upon which the CHC Cross-Battery approach was built (e.g., the classification of cognitive and academic ability tests according to CHC theory) provide a means to systematically construct a more theoretically driven, comprehensive, and valid measure of abilities. When the CHC Cross-Battery approach is applied, it is possible to measure important abilities that might otherwise go unassessed or that may be poorly assessed—abilities that are important in understanding learning disability as well as educational, vocational, and occupational outcomes.

The CHC Cross-Battery approach allows for the effective measurement of the broad academic and cognitive areas specified in the CHC theoretical framework with emphasis on those considered most critical on the basis of history, observation, and available test data. The CHC classifications of a multitude of academic and cognitive ability tests (presented here and in Flanagan, McGrew, & Ortiz, 2000; Flanagan & Ortiz, 2001; and McGrew & Flanagan, 1998) bring stronger content and construct validity evidence to the evaluation and interpretation process. With a strong research base and a multiplicity of CHC measures available, CHC Cross-Battery procedures can aid practitioners not only in the comprehensive measurement of cognitive abilities but also in the selective measurement of both academic and cognitive abilities that are deemed important with respect to the examinee's presenting problem(s). Adherence to the guiding principles, careful attention to key decision points, and integration of specific referral concerns can result in the creation of highly individualized batteries that are ideally suited for whatever the intended purpose of assessment may be. The next chapter provides a comprehensive set of guidelines for interpreting cross-battery data.

Endnote

1. Empirical classifications of academic achievement tests as strong, moderate, or mixed measures of CHC abilities were based on the following criteria. A classification of *strong* was given to a test that had a substantial factor loading ($\geq .50$) on a primary factor and a secondary factor loading (if present) that was equal to or less than one-half of its loading on the primary factor. A classification of *moderate* was given to a test that had a primary factor loading of $< .50$ and a secondary factor loading (if present) that was less than one-half of the primary loading, or any primary factor loading and secondary loading between one-half and seven-tenths of the primary loading. A classification of *mixed* was given to a test that had a factor loading on a secondary factor that was greater than seven-tenths of its loading on the primary factor. These criteria were derived from Woodcock (1990).

CHC Cross-Battery Interpretation of Academic and Cognitive Ability Data

The previous chapter provided a step-by-step approach to the selection and organization of academic ability tests according to CHC broad abilities and seven Academic Clinical Composites corresponding to the areas of achievement listed in the federal definition of learning disability (IDEA). The CHC Cross-Battery approach was offered as the method for test selection and organization of assessment batteries because it is theory and research based as well as psychometrically sound. The purpose of this chapter is to provide a set of guidelines for interpreting cross-battery data. These guidelines are particularly relevant for interpreting test data within the context of the operational definition of learning disability (LD) presented in Chapter 11. Specifically, practitioners will be provided with interpretive guidelines that will allow them to conduct systematic inter-academic, inter-cognitive, and integrated ability analyses. When standardized tests are used, adherence to these guidelines within the context of an operational definition of LD determination will result in more defensible eligibility and placement decisions than those currently in use.

Overview of Data Analysis

Following the collection of cross-battery data in accordance with the steps outlined in Chapter 12, the examiner is able to accomplish several different levels of analysis. These types of analyses include evaluation of (1) inter-academic and inter-cognitive performance (i.e., normative comparison against same age peers); (2) differences between broad, stratum II ability clusters; (3) differences between Academic Clinical Composites in accordance with the areas listed in the federal definition of LD; (4) differences between narrow, stratum I ability clusters; and (5) integrated ability analysis (e.g., comparison between cognitive and academic abilities). As discussed in the previous chapter, CHC Cross-Battery assessment places emphasis on the derivation and use of empirically based and statistically defensible ability clusters. Such clusters are created through the careful selection and organization of tests that provide adequate construct representation. Although the interpretive levels themselves are rather straightforward, explanation of the decision-making steps that guide the interpretive process is a little more complex.

From a broad perspective, interpretation of cross-battery data comprises two major activities, including comparison of data to a normative standard and evaluation of the relationships between cognitive and academic abilities. Initially, the practitioner must evaluate the numerical data collected within a CHC Cross-Battery assessment and evaluate those data in accordance with some normative standard. CHC Cross-Battery assessment uses the properties of the normal probability curve for making such evaluative judgments and decisions. The normal probability curve was selected because it represents the most useful statistically based comparative standard and because it is able to accommodate the practice of crossing batteries (and in effect norm groups) in order to conduct more comprehensive and theoretically meaningful assessments. The utility of the normal probability curve is evident because it "has very practical applications for comparing and evaluating psychological data in that the position of any test score on a standard deviation unit scale, in itself, defines the proportion of people taking the test who will obtain scores above or below a given score" (Lezak, 1976, p. 123). In addition, if practitioners adhere to the practice of selecting tests that have been normed within a few years of one another (e.g., WIAT-II and WJ III) or using normative updates, the potential for measurement error that may result from "crossing" batteries is reduced significantly.

The practice of evaluating cross-battery data in accordance with a normative standard includes both inter-academic and inter-cognitive ability analyses. The term *inter-ability* analysis will be used hereafter to refer to both inter-academic and inter-cognitive analyses. In general, *inter*-ability analysis is accomplished through comparison of normative scores and provides *population-relative* information and reveals *between*-individual differences. As such, normative scores yield information concerning an individual's performance, functioning, or ability with respect to individuals of the same age or "norm group" (Anastasi & Urbina, 1997; Woodcock, 1994). Moreover, normative scores for one ability are not artificially altered by the individual's scores on other abilities as they are with ipsative or intra-individual scores.[1] Inter-ability analysis is used mainly to evaluate scale (or cluster) performance and to assist in formulating diagnostic impressions and classification. This type of analysis is necessary at Levels I, II, and III of the operational definition of LD (see Chapter 11). Inter-academic and inter-cognitive ability analysis should not be confused with *intra*-ability analysis. Intra-ability analysis differs from inter-ability analysis in that the information is *person relative* and reveals *within*-individual differences as determined by ipsative score comparisons.

In summary, use of the normal probability curve provides practitioners with a basis for accomplishing comparative evaluations of performance on any tests that may have been administered within the context of cross-battery assessment. Additional details and guidelines for making judgments and decisions about academic and cognitive ability performance follow in subsequent sections of this chapter.

When conducting inter-ability analysis, practitioners should test the null hypothesis (Flanagan & Ortiz, 2001). The null hypothesis specifies that the individual's measured performance on any test or tests of ability will fall within the normal limits of functioning (i.e., standard scores of 85 to 115, inclusive) as compared to other individuals of the same age. Thus, when comparing performance to a normative standard, practitioners must decide whether the data suggest that the null hypothesis with regard to functioning is "correct" (i.e., supported) and should therefore be retained, or whether the data suggest that the null hypothesis is not supported and should be rejected in favor of an alternative hypothesis.

Guidelines for Conducting Inter-Academic and Inter-Cognitive Analysis with CHC Cross-Battery Data

When only a single battery is used in assessment, the data derived from the scoring process tend to remain on the same scale and are based on a norming sample that has the same mean and standard deviation. This, of course, provides for straightforward and direct comparison of scores and facilitates the interpretive process. In the case of CHC Cross-Battery assessment, the test scores come from at least two and possibly more different sources or tests. Consequently, it is possible that each data source uses a different metric, making direct comparisons inappropriate (e.g., WIAT-II subtests have a mean of 100 and an SD of 15, whereas the TOLD-P:3 subtests have a mean of 10 and an SD of 3). In addition, CHC Cross-Battery assessment may be carried out with a collection of tests that were developed at different times, in different places, on different samples, with different scoring procedures, and for different purposes (Lezak, 1976, 1995).

In CHC Cross-Battery assessment, these obstacles are overcome through the process of converting all test scores to a common metric and identifying a normative standard by which such scores may be appropriately compared. This process provides a basis for making inter-ability comparisons and interpretation of CHC Cross-Battery data psychometrically defensible. Step 5 of the guidelines for administering and scoring CHC Cross-Battery assessments (see Chapter 12) specified the need to convert all standard scores collected in cross-battery assessments to a common metric having a mean of 100 and standard deviation of 15. A Percentile Rank and Standard Score Conversion Table is provided for just this purpose in Appendix B. By converting all scores to this metric, concerns regarding the feasibility of drawing useful and valid conclusions from tests with different means and standard deviations are addressed directly. Practitioners can thus administer tests with different metrics and through the process of conversion are able to combine performance data from separate sources into reliable, construct-relevant clusters[2] or composites. Once this is accomplished, the practitioner then evaluates and compares these scores to a *normative standard*. Use of such a normative standard is necessary because cross-battery assessment has no internal "norm" group, and therefore some control must be made for potential differences across normative samples.

As discussed previously, use of the normal probability curve provides the means for achieving normative-based comparisons of CHC Cross-Battery data. Table 13.1 provides a listing of the possible range of ability scores that can be generated from CHC Cross-Battery data as well as a description of such scores with respect to the normal probability curve (i.e., percent of cases that fall under various portions of the normal curve). Table 13.1 also provides practitioners with a taxonomy of ability classifications or categories that correspond to different standard score and percentile rank ranges. Three categories for classifying performance are listed, including a descriptive (e.g., average, high average, superior, etc.), a normative (e.g., normative weakness, within normal limits, normative strength, etc.), and a proficiency taxonomy (e.g., limited, general, advanced, etc.). Each taxonomy has advantages for particular applications where performance needs to be described, and practitioners may select whichever is most appropriate for a specific purpose.

In general, the classifications provided in Table 13.1 closely approximate the classification schemata in common use and are not significantly different from what practitioners are accustomed to using. The "Result" column and its corresponding standard score ranges,

TABLE 13.1   Standard Score, Percentile Ranks, and Corresponding Performance Classifications

Result		Classification of Performance		
Standard Score Range	Percentile Rank Range	Descriptive	Normative	Proficiency
≥131	98 to 99+	Very Superior	Normative Strength 16% of population (> +1 standard deviation)	Very Advanced
121 to 130	92 to 97	Superior		Advanced
116 to 120	86 to 91	Above Average		
111 to 115	76 to 84	High Average	Normal Limits 68% of population (≤ ±1 standard deviation)	General
90 to 110	25 to 75	Average		
85 to 89	16 to 24	Low Average		
80 to 84	9 to 15	Below Average	Normative Weakness 16% of Population (> -1 standard deviation)	Limited
70 to 79	3 to 8	Deficient		
≤ 69	≤ 2	Very Deficient		Very Limited

Note: Some of these classifications are based in part on those described in Flanagan and Ortiz (2001) and were originally adapted from Woodcock and Mather (1989).

percentile rank ranges, and performance classifications, are provided as a means for establishing the criteria necessary to test the *a priori* and *a posteriori* hypotheses that guide the interpretive process (see Chapter 14 for an in-depth discussion and case example). In CHC Cross-Battery assessment, the basic criterion for rejecting the null hypothesis is set at the level of > ±1 SD from the mean. Note that by adopting such a range, performance can be considered to be exceptional when it falls either significantly above or below the mean, indicating both normative strengths and weaknesses in functioning, respectively.[3] As discussed in Chapter 11, a great deal of assessment is conducted with respect to the investigation of potential or suspected deficits in performance; therefore, most attention will likely be paid to performance that is significantly *below* the mean.

The null hypothesis in inter-ability analysis with CHC Cross-Battery data was described earlier as the assumption that measured performance on any test of ability will fall within the normal limits of functioning as compared to individuals of the same age. Therefore, in order to reject the null hypothesis in favor of the alternative (i.e., that an individual's performance is in fact significantly different from that of other individuals of the same age), the entire standard score range (including the uppermost and lowermost points of that range) must be greater than ±1SD (15 points) from the normative mean (i.e., 100). When this is the case, practitioners may confidently interpret such findings as indications that performance cannot be considered normal or average but only if other data sources are available to support this conclusion.

Examples of how confidence bands are to be interpreted with respect to being significantly different from the average range or not (both above and below the mean) are illustrated in Figure 13.1. Example A in this figure demonstrates a case where the entire standard score range falls within normal limits. Two black bands are shown, each representing a typical standard score range and each illustrating that ranges can fall entirely within normal limits (i.e., between 85 and 115 inclusive). Example B in Figure 13.1, like Example A, represents nonsignificant deviation from the mean (i.e., 100) even though the midpoints of the standard score ranges fall right at the cutoff points of 85 and 115. Note that constraining the deviation to the extreme points within the confidence bands, as opposed to the midpoint or average of the range, represents a conservative approach to defining significant deviation. Because the confidence bands represent the range in which practitioners can have 68 percent confidence that the individual's true score falls somewhere inside, using the midpoint would halve the confidence level as indicated in Example B. Likewise, Example C in Figure 13.1 is still nonsignificant because the possibility remains that the individual's true score (which can fall anywhere within the range with equal probability) might actually be right on the cutoff point and therefore still be within normal limits. Example D in Figure 13.1 is the only illustration of a significant deviation because the entire standard score range falls either below the lower cutoff point (normative weakness) or above the higher cutoff point (normative strength). Application of this hypothesis testing and evaluation framework can be used whenever performance on any measure of ability is evaluated, including narrow- and broad-ability clusters as well as Academic Clinical Composites.

Additional Considerations in Inter-Ability Analysis

From a normative standpoint, practitioners will find in some cases that the initial CHC Cross-Battery data fully support the null hypotheses regarding expected normal functioning as compared to peers in the general population. On the basis of such findings, it may well be appropriate to conclude that the individual's functioning is entirely within the normal range and therefore no further testing is necessary. Practitioners should recall, however, the guiding principles in CHC Cross-Battery assessment that specify the identification of convergence among indicators of ability (i.e., similar measures should produce similar results) and the need to interpret cluster scores only on the basis of two or more distinct, nondiscrepant

FIGURE 13.1   Interpretation of Confidence Bands

Example A: Within Normal Limits = Nonsignificant deviation

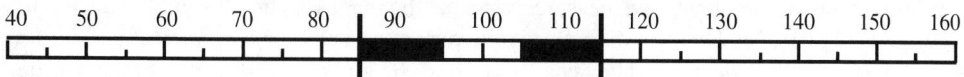

Example B: Within Normal Limits = Nonsignificant deviation

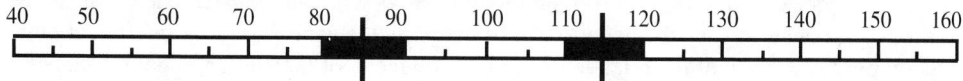

Example C: Within Normal Limits = Nonsignificant deviation

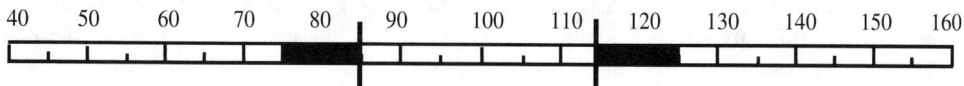

Example D: Outside Normal Limits = Significant deviation

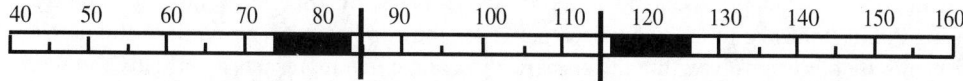

Normative Weakness	Normal Limits	Normative Strength
Greater than 1 SD below mean	± 1 SD from mean	Greater than 1 SD above mean

■■■■■ = ± 1SEM or confidence band of 68%.

Note: SEM for clusters = ± 5 and SEM for subtests = ± 7; examples shown above use cluster SEM.

measures. Therefore, additional interpretive guidelines are necessary when evaluating two or more confidence bands simultaneously.

Before inter-ability analysis is carried out with cluster scores (i.e., comparing cluster scores to a normative standard), practitioners should examine the data in order to ensure that convergence among indicators is present. For the purpose of CHC Cross-Battery interpretation, *convergence* is defined as the touching or overlapping of two or more standard score ranges within broad-ability domains, a condition predicted by the construct validation literature. Specifically, convergence is predicted to occur among the qualitatively different narrow abilities that subsume the same broad domain (e.g., K-TEA/NU Spelling as a measure of Spelling Ability [*Grw*-W] and WJ III Writing Samples as a measure of Writing Ability

[*Grw*-W] as well as among qualitatively similar narrow abilities (e.g., K-TEA/NU Reading Comprehension and WIAT-II Reading Comprehension). These measures are expected to correlate highly; and thus, performance on one measure is expected to be consistent with performance on another related measure. Note that the ranges for broad abilities can overlap (e.g., the confidence band for *Grw*-R might overlap the band for *Gq*), indicating uniform ability across these domains. However, because CHC theory specifies that broad abilities are relatively distinct entities from one another, and therefore only moderately intercorrelated, high performance on one broad ability does not necessarily suggest that performance should be high on any or all other broad abilities. When the standard score bands for measures that are expected to converge (narrow-ability indicators within the same broad-ability area) do, in fact, converge (i.e., the bands touch or overlap), the general rule for interpretation is accomplished via use of the relative position of the mean of the cluster's confidence band along the normal curve presented in Table 13.1. The manner in which a mean and confidence band for any given cluster is calculated was described in the previous chapter and it is important to remember that such means and bands are used only when an ability has been measured validly (i.e., through two or more reliable and qualitatively different narrow-ability indicators [for broad-ability clusters] and two or more reliable and qualitatively similar narrow-ability indicators [for narrow-ability clusters]).

There is an exception, however, to the definition of convergence. On occasion, the standard score bands for two measures that are expected to converge may not actually touch or overlap as predicted, but may still fall completely within the same normative classification category. For example, the standard score bands for *Grw*-SG (Spelling) and *Grw*-WA (Writing Ability) may be found to be discrepant (i.e., they do not touch or overlap) although the bands are both entirely within the classification range that represents a normative strength, (i.e., >1 SD above the mean). In such cases, functioning in the broad domain (i.e., *Grw*-W) can be effectively interpreted as a normative strength, since both narrow-ability measures do in essence converge within the same normative range. Because it is unlikely (statistically speaking) that true performance on this broad ability would fall outside this range, interpretation in this manner represents a reasonable inference. This type of exception (i.e., interpreting broad-ability performance using normative classification descriptions, such as *normative strength* or *normative weakness*) is referred to as a *nonconvergent ability description* and can occur whenever two measures that are expected to converge do not (e.g., one measure of *Grw*-SG and one measure of *Grw* -WA), although they still fall completely within the same normative range (strength, weakness, or within normal limits). This exception also applies to the interpretation of qualitatively similar narrow abilities that do not converge as expected but still fall completely within the same normative range. In this case, normative classifications can be used to describe narrow-ability performance. Figure 13.2 illustrates these scenarios.

The first three examples show bands that do not overlap but that fall completely within the normative weakness, normal limits, and normative strength ranges, respectively. Although both bands in the fourth example are not within the same normative range, it is included in Figure 13.2 primarily because evaluations are generally concerned with whether performance falls outside and *below* normal limits as opposed to within and *above* normal limits. This fourth example illustrates bands that do not overlap but where one band falls entirely within normal limits and the other band either spans between the normal limits and normative strength ranges or falls entirely within the normative strength range. The gray-

FIGURE 13.2 Examples of Interpretable Nonconvergent-Ability Descriptions

Example 1: Nonconvergent ability description: *Grw*–R (Reading) is a normative weakness

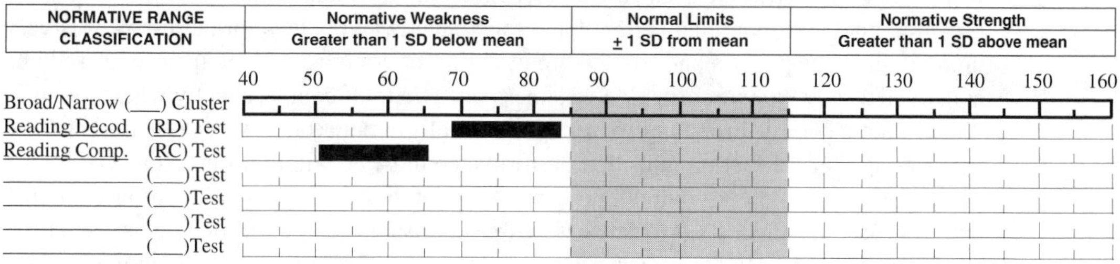

NORMATIVE RANGE	Normative Weakness	Normal Limits	Normative Strength
CLASSIFICATION	Greater than 1 SD below mean	± 1 SD from mean	Greater than 1 SD above mean

| | 40 | 50 | 60 | 70 | 80 | 90 | 100 | 110 | 120 | 130 | 140 | 150 | 160 |

Broad/Narrow (___) Cluster
Reading Decod. (RD) Test
Reading Comp.   (RC) Test
_____ (___)Test
_____ (___)Test
_____ (___)Test
_____ (___)Test

Example 2: Nonconvergent ability description: *Grw*–R (Reading) is within normal limits

NORMATIVE RANGE	Normative Weakness	Normal Limits	Normative Strength
CLASSIFICATION	Greater than 1 SD below mean	± 1 SD from mean	Greater than 1 SD above mean

| | 40 | 50 | 60 | 70 | 80 | 90 | 100 | 110 | 120 | 130 | 140 | 150 | 160 |

Broad/Narrow (___) Cluster
Reading Decod. (RD) Test
Reading Comp.   (RC) Test
_____ (___)Test
_____ (___)Test
_____ (___)Test
_____ (___)Test

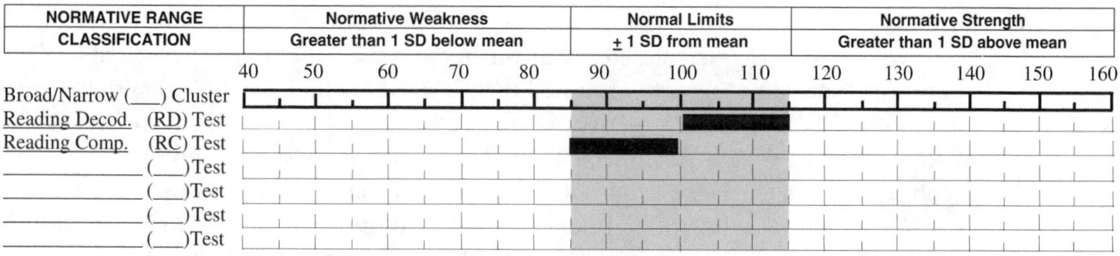

Example 3: Nonconvergent ability description: *Grw*–R (Reading) is a normative strength

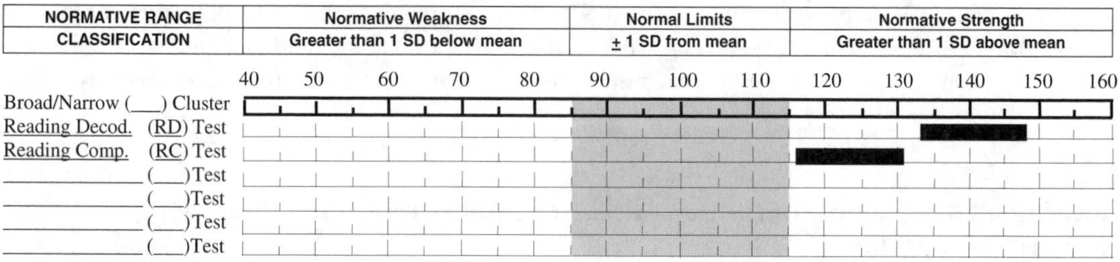

NORMATIVE RANGE	Normative Weakness	Normal Limits	Normative Strength
CLASSIFICATION	Greater than 1 SD below mean	± 1 SD from mean	Greater than 1 SD above mean

| | 40 | 50 | 60 | 70 | 80 | 90 | 100 | 110 | 120 | 130 | 140 | 150 | 160 |

Broad/Narrow (___) Cluster
Reading Decod. (RD) Test
Reading Comp.   (RC) Test
_____ (___)Test
_____ (___)Test
_____ (___)Test
_____ (___)Test

Example 4: Nonconvergent ability description: *Grw*–R (Reading) is within normal limits or higher

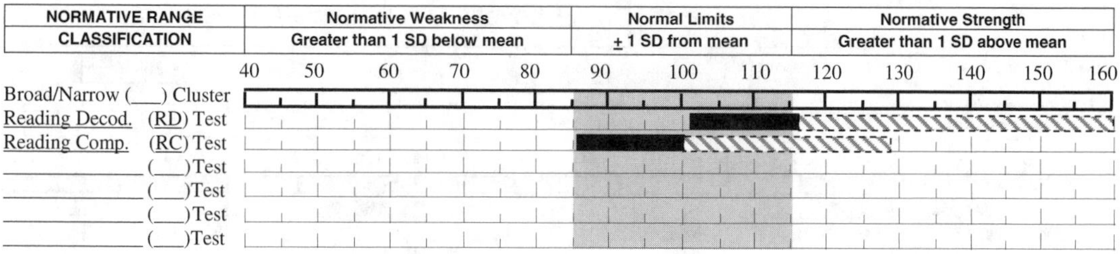

NORMATIVE RANGE	Normative Weakness	Normal Limits	Normative Strength
CLASSIFICATION	Greater than 1 SD below mean	± 1 SD from mean	Greater than 1 SD above mean

| | 40 | 50 | 60 | 70 | 80 | 90 | 100 | 110 | 120 | 130 | 140 | 150 | 160 |

Broad/Narrow (___) Cluster
Reading Decod. (RD) Test
Reading Comp.   (RC) Test
_____ (___)Test
_____ (___)Test
_____ (___)Test
_____ (___)Test

Note: In examples 1-4, only *ability descriptions* are reported. In these examples, a *Grw*–R cluster is not calculated because the narrow reading ability performances are significantly discrepant.

and-white diagonal stripes to the right of the bands represent the areas in which the standard score ranges for each indicator could fall. If the bands fall somewhere along the gray-and-white diagonal striped areas and are discrepant from one another, then the following interpretation applies. Given that neither band falls outside and below normal limits, it is very unlikely that true performance on the broad-ability or composite being measured could be construed as any type of normative weakness or deficit. Of course, exactly where the individual's actual or true broad-ability performance falls remains unclear because the bands do not overlap, but the fact remains that performance must be within normal limits or higher and therefore can be considered a nonconvergent ability description. Practitioners should therefore assume that test performances that meet this ability description indicate functioning in the broad-ability domain that is within normal limits or higher. Note, however, that means and confidence bands for this type of ability description are not calculated, first because it remains statistically inappropriate, and second because there is no practical reason to do so.

An example was given previously in which the construct of interest centered on *Grw* and two measures of *Grw* were identified (K-TEA/NU Spelling and WJ III Writing Samples). Both of these tests have been classified as measures of *Grw*-W, and therefore administration of these two tests to the same individual should produce relatively similar results. Suppose for a moment, however, that the converted standard score range obtained on the K-TEA/NU Spelling was 103 to 117, and for the WJ III Writing Samples, 63 to 77. The resulting average score calculated according to CHC Cross-Battery methods would be 90, with a range of 85 to 95, giving an impression that this individual's functioning along the *Grw*-W ability domain is within the normal range. However, when these data are plotted on the CHC Cross-Battery Normative Analysis Graph (see Appendix D), it is readily apparent that the confidence bands for each measure do not overlap each other and they fall in different normative ranges. This situation is illustrated in Figure 13.3 using these scores as they would appear when graphed.

FIGURE 13.3　Example of Discrepant Narrow-Ability Indicators Underlying Broad *Grw*-W Ability

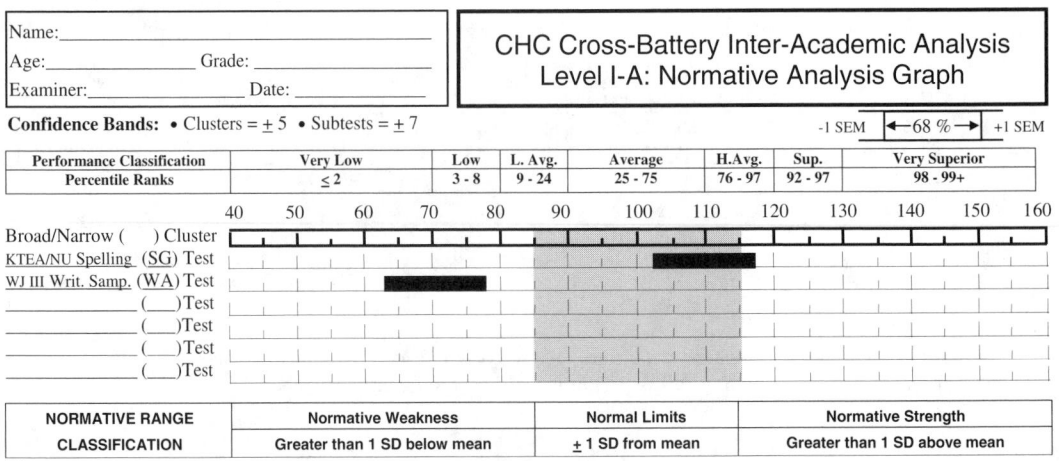

There are two basic guidelines to follow in interpreting differences between standard score confidence bands as used in CHC Cross-Battery assessment. First, if the confidence bands for any two test scores or clusters "touch" or overlap, practitioners can assume that the difference between ability scores being compared is not significant. Second, if the confidence bands for any two test scores or clusters do not touch or overlap, practitioners can assume that the difference between ability scores being compared for any given individual is significant. These guidelines are consistent with research that demonstrates that when the "nonoverlapping" guideline is used, practitioners can be 84 percent confident that there exists a true difference in scores (McGrew et al., 1991). Given the clinical nature of the types of comparisons that are likely to be made in CHC Cross-Battery assessments, this level of confidence should prove to be appropriate and acceptable in the majority of cases.

Returning for a moment to the example presented in Figure 13.3, it is clear that the confidence bands for the K-TEA/NU Spelling and WJ III Writing Samples subtests do not overlap. In accordance with the guidelines specified earlier, the discrepancy between these two measures is significant and therefore precludes valid interpretation of the broad *Grw*-W ability cluster. The average of the two scores attenuates the fact that one narrow ability related to *Grw*-W (Spelling Ability-SG) falls within the average range, whereas the other narrow ability related to *Grw*-W (Writing Ability—WA) is well below average. Thus, the true nature of the individual's functioning along the broad-ability domain of *Grw*-W cannot be reliably determined on the basis of these data alone.

It is important to remember that CHC Cross-Battery assessment operates under the assumption that similar measures will converge. This means that there is an expectation that whenever a battery of tests are administered to any given individual, measures of the same narrow abilities and aspects of the same broad abilities should produce similar results. In other words, "persons high on the construct should score high on a variety of indicators of that construct" (Messick, 1989, p. 51). When scores on similar measures do not converge as expected in accordance with the construct validation literature, practitioners may not be able to immediately determine exactly why one score is unusually different from the other. There are numerous reasons why this situation might occur, including inherent differences in an individual's narrow abilities, differences in the demands required by one task versus another, anomalous or extraneous influences that affect administration or performance, cultural or linguistic factors, chance, error, and so on. Nevertheless, CHC Cross-Battery assessment allows practitioners the opportunity to investigate such discrepant findings in order to establish a basis for defensible interpretation as may be necessary or relevant to the purpose of assessment.

Irrespective of the logic and rationale behind the guidelines for interpretation presented here (particularly those that deal with significant differences), practitioners are reminded that such rules are meant to assist in making decisions about performance within the context of other data sources. There will be times when scores or score bands fall right at or close to the stated cutoff points, thereby complicating the interpretation and decision-making process. In such cases, decision making should be exercised vis-à-vis an examination of other data sources. In other words, additional sources of objective data may support (or fail to support) an interpretation of a score band that falls at the cutoff point between normative deficit and normal limits as representing deficiency (and vice versa). Test data and the accompanying rules for analysis are intended to assist practitioners in evaluating performance and drawing inferences.

In the previous example presented in Figure 13.3, it was noted that although the Spelling and Writing Samples subtests are measures of the same broad-ability (*Grw*-W), convergence did not occur and a significant discrepancy was found between the two. When significantly disparate scores are found within broad-ability domains, the meaning of the discrepancy is unlikely to be easily determined. Careful and selective additional assessment can, however, assist in clarifying the discrepancy and help determine whether this difference is simply an anomalous or irrelevant finding (Kamphaus, 1993). In CHC Cross-Battery assessment, interpretations and diagnostic conclusions should never be made on the basis of a single outlying test score, irrespective of the extent of deviation from the mean or from other scores (Atkinson, 1991; Lezak, 1995). Rather, CHC Cross-Battery assessment provides an iterative process that helps shed additional light on any results that appear unusual or ambiguous.

To investigate functioning in areas that, for whatever reason, cannot be reliably interpreted after the initial round of testing, practitioners have the option of administering an additional measure. Although two additional measures could be given, one for each of the corresponding narrow abilities measured in the initial assessment, in many cases it is not necessary or practical. This is because the focus of assessment is more often concerned with performance that is below the average or low-average ranges, not above them, as in the identification and diagnosis of disabilities or impairments (e.g., special education and disability evaluation). Therefore, the focus on clarifying discrepant findings will ordinarily be on determining whether the lower standard score range, not the higher standard score range, is or is not anomalous.

For practical reasons, most evaluators should thus select an additional narrow-ability measure that corresponds to the narrow ability with the lowest standard score range. Continuing with the example already presented in Figure 13.3, Writing Samples had the lower standard score range (63–77) compared to Spelling (103–117). A review of the CHC Cross-Battery worksheets (see Appendix A) provides practitioners with several options for supplemental investigation of the narrow ability reflected by Writing Samples (i.e., Writing Ability—*Grw*-WA). Because the example has so far only supplemented the core K-TEA/NU battery with the WJ III, it would make most sense to select another subtest from the WJ III as the second measure of Writing Ability because it would mean not having to cross a third battery. This is in accordance with the first guiding principle of CHC Cross-Battery assessment that specifies the use of the fewest number of batteries possible. The WJ III, like all comprehensive achievement batteries that include measures of *Grw*-W, includes only one measure of WA. Therefore, a third battery must be crossed. Practitioners are encouraged to use the task-characteristic information in Appendices F1–F7 when selecting additional measures. A review of the task-characteristic information in Appendix F3 shows that the WIAT-II Written Expression test represents an appropriate choice because although both tests are similar in terms of the narrow-ability area measured (i.e., WA), they differ in terms of the task characteristics. Specifically, whereas both tests use real words written in the context of connected writing (e.g., sentences, paragraphs), the WIAT-II Written Expression test also utilizes a standardized written prompt (e.g., story starter) and imposes a time constraint (e.g., 15 minutes). Much like before, an *a posteriori* hypothesis would be generated (i.e., performance on this new test will be within normal limits as compared to same age peers in the general population) and then the test would be administered and scored.

At this point in the assessment and interpretive process, there are five basic outcome scenarios. These outcomes are illustrated consecutively in Figures 13.4 to 13.8, using the CHC Cross-Battery Normative Analysis Graph with the data from the initial assessment on *Grw*-W as presented previously. Outcome A, as depicted in Figure 13.4, shows the first possible scenario that could result whenever an additional test is given (in this case, WIAT-II Written Expression). In this scenario, the resulting standard score range for Written Expression (*Grw*-WA) is lower than the standard score range originally obtained on the initial measure of Writing Ability (i.e., WJ III Writing Samples). The range for the additional *Grw*-W measure is indicated by the dark gray confidence band, with the gray and white striped extension representing the area in which the band could fit and remain consistent with the interpretations offered for this scenario. Note that the bands for Writing Samples and Written Expression do not touch or overlap as expected, indicating there is a significant difference between the two Writing Ability scores. However, although there is no convergence (as defined by overlap) among the two indicators, there is convergence with respect to the normative classification since both are completely and entirely in the normative weakness range. This is an example in which a *nonconvergent ability description* (i.e., normative weakness), as discussed previously, can be used to interpret performance in the area of Writing Ability. However, a Writing Ability cluster (i.e., the average of the two narrow-ability Writing Ability scores) is not represented on the graph because calculation of a confidence band for this type of cluster is inappropriate. Note also that, as in the prior round of testing, the confidence band for the second measure of *Grw*-WA (i.e., WIAT-II Written Expression) does not overlap with the measure of *Grw*-SG. Thus, the lack of convergence and difference

FIGURE 13.4   Outcome A: Nonconvergent Narrow-Ability Bands

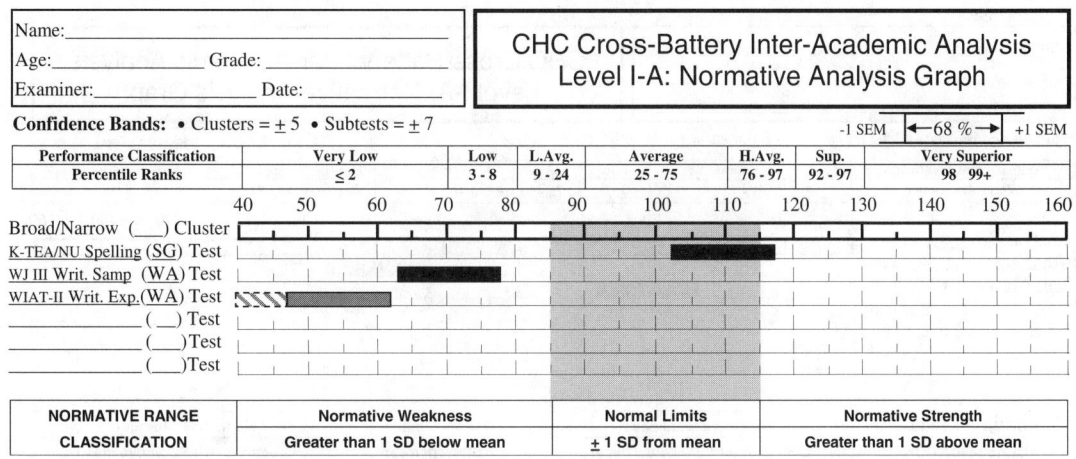

Interpretation of Outcome A:

a) Broad-ability *Grw*–W cannot be interpreted;

b) Narrow-ability *Grw*–WA can be interpreted as a Normative Weakness (nonconvergent ability description).

in normative ranges here precludes interpretation of a broad-ability *Grw*-W cluster. Interpretation of Outcome A would be as follows: (1) Broad-ability (*Grw*-W) cannot be interpreted because there is no convergence between any two qualitatively different narrow-ability indicators (i.e., the standard score band for *Grw*-SG and any one of the bands for *Grw*-WA do not touch or overlap, *and* no two different narrow-ability bands are completely within the same normative range) and (2) Narrow-ability *Grw*-WA can be interpreted as a normative weakness because although the standard score ranges for both indicators do not touch or overlap each other, they both fall completely within the same range, allowing for a *nonconvergent ability description.*

Outcome B, as depicted in Figure 13.5, shows the next possible scenario in this example. This illustration depicts a result in which the standard score range for the second measure of *Grw*-WA is convergent with the standard score range originally obtained on the initial measure of *Grw*-WA (i.e., Writing Samples). In this figure, a dark gray confidence band for Written Expression that corresponds closely to the existing band for Writing Samples is shown. The new band is flanked by gray-and-white diagonal hash marks that, again, represent the potential degree to which the standard score range for Written Expression could vary (depending on the obtained score) and still be considered convergent (nondiscrepant) with the results obtained previously with Writing Samples as well as consistent with the following interpretations. Because there is convergence among the two *Grw*-WA narrow-ability indicators, it is appropriate to calculate a confidence band for this cluster in order to guide interpretation. The dark gray band along the top of the graph flanked by gray-and-white diagonal hash marks represents the area in which this band could fall (again,

FIGURE 13.5   Outcome B: Convergent Narrow-Ability Bands

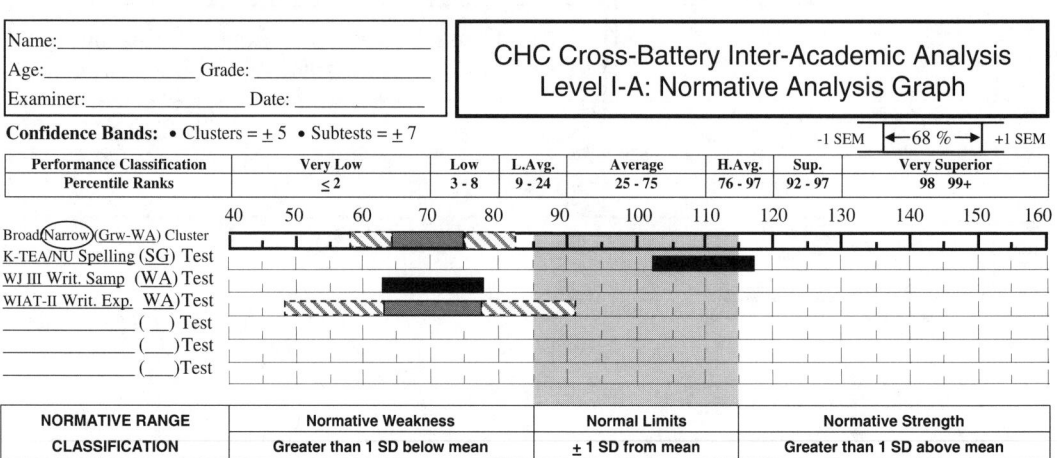

Interpretation of Outcome B:

a) Broad-ability *Grw*–W cannot be interpreted;

b) Narrow-ability *Grw*–WA can be interpreted as a Normative Weakness (convergent cluster).

depending on the obtained score on Written Expression). Interpretation of Outcome B would be as follows: (1) Broad-ability *Grw*-W cannot be interpreted because there is no convergence between any two qualitatively different narrow-ability indicators (i.e., the standard score band for *Grw*-SG and any one of the bands for *Grw*-WA do not touch or overlap, *and* no two different narrow ability bands are completely within the same normative range) and (2) Narrow-ability *Grw*-WA can be interpreted as a normative weakness because the standard score ranges for both indicators touch or overlap, forming a convergent cluster.

Outcome C is depicted in Figure 13.6 and shows the third variation of the possible scenarios for the current example. This case is similar to the initial one depicted in Figure 13.4, because the standard score range for Written Expression *Grw*-WA does not converge with the initial measure of Writing Ability (i.e., Writing Samples). However, in this example, the standard score range for Written Expression is higher instead of lower. The dark gray confidence band and surrounding gray-and-white striped area show the range in which results would be subject to the interpretations that follow. Note that although the standard score range for Written Expression is higher and discrepant from the standard score range for Writing Samples, it still does not touch or overlap the confidence band for Spelling. Therefore, no convergence is seen for the broad-ability *Grw*-W, and no cluster confidence bands are calculated or graphed. Accordingly, interpretation of Outcome C would be as follows: (1) Broad-ability *Grw*-W cannot be interpreted because the standard score ranges for all of the narrow-ability indicators (including *Grw*-WA and *Grw*-SG) are all significantly discrepant from each other and no two indicators fall completely within the same normative range and (2) Narrow-ability *Grw*-WA cannot be interpreted because the standard score ranges for both *Grw*-WA indicators do not converge (i.e., touch or overlap each other). Although

FIGURE 13.6   Outcome C: Nonconvergent Narrow-Ability Bands

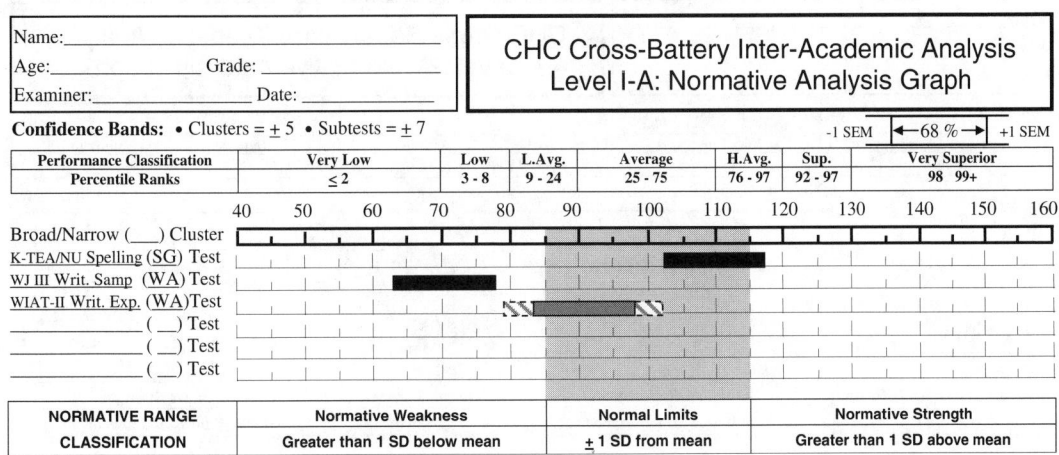

Interpretation of Outcome C:

a) Broad-ability *Grw*–W cannot be interpreted;

b) Narrow-ability *Grw*–WA cannot be interpreted.

improbable, this scenario depicts the need to explore alternative hypotheses for the lack of expected convergence within the area of *Grw*-W (e.g., differences in task demands on the writing ability tests, noncognitive factors, and so forth).

Outcome D is depicted in Figure 13.7 and illustrates the fourth variation of the possible scenarios in this example. This case is identical to the previous outcome depicted in Figure 13.6 with the exception that the standard score range for Written Expression (*Grw*-WA) now touches or overlaps the confidence band for Spelling (*Grw*-SG). This overlap is indicated by the dark gray confidence band depicted directly under the black band originally obtained for *Grw*-SG. As before, the bands on either end of the new standard score range (shown by gray-and-white diagonal stripes) represent the area in which the standard score range for Written Expression could vary and still maintain convergence with the confidence band for Spelling, and thus remain subject to the interpretations for this scenario. As in the previous case, the standard score range for Written Expression is higher and discrepant from the standard score range for Writing Samples, and they do not both fall within the same normative range. This lack of convergence precludes interpretation of *Grw*-WA as a narrow-ability cluster. However, the convergence between Written Expression (*Grw*-WA) and Spelling (*Grw*-SG) now represents a convergent broad-ability cluster as a function of the overlap of two qualitatively different narrow-ability indicators. Accordingly, the confidence band for this broad-ability cluster is calculated and depicted at the top of the graph. This band is flanked by gray-and-white stripes, which represent the area in which the band could fall, depending on the score range for Written Expression. Interpretation of Outcome D would be as follows: (1) Broad-ability cluster *Grw*-W can be interpreted as being within

FIGURE 13.7   Outcome D: Convergent Narrow-Ability Bands

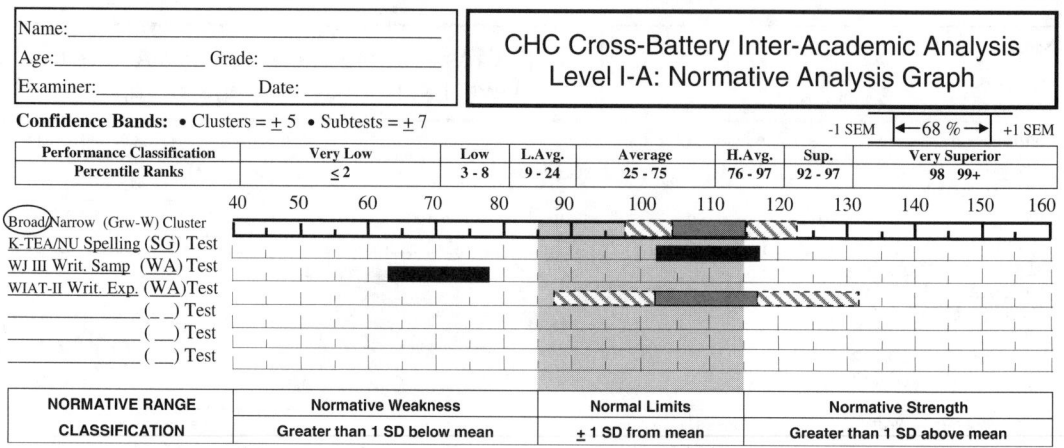

Interpretation of Outcome D:

a) Broad-ability *Grw*–W can be interpreted as Average to High Average or Within Normal Limits;

b) Narrow-ability *Grw*–WA cannot be interpreted.

normal limits because the average standard score ranges for two *different* narrow-ability indicators (one *Grw*-WA test and the *Grw*-SG test) converge and (2) Narrow-ability *Grw*-WA cannot be interpreted because the standard score ranges for both *Grw*-WA indicators do not converge (i.e., touch or overlap each other).

The final scenario in this example is portrayed as Outcome E in Figure 13.8. This case is a variation on the previous outcome, with the exception that the standard score range for Written Expression (*Grw*-WA) no longer converges (i.e., its band does not touch or overlap) with the standard score range for Spelling (*Grw*-SG), but actually exceeds it. As can be seen in Figure 13.8, the standard score range for Written Expression (represented by the dark gray confidence band) is completely above the standard score range for Writing Samples. The gray-and-white diagonal stripes to the right of this band represent the area in which the standard score range for Written Expression could fall, remain above and discrepant from the standard score range for Writing Samples, and still be consistent with the following interpretations. The lack of actual statistical (i.e., both bands overlap) or normative range convergence precludes the formation of any valid cluster, and therefore no cluster-level confidence bands are calculated or graphed. However, although there is no convergence (as defined by overlap) among the two indicators, one band ranges from within normal limits to normative strength and the other is entirely within the normative strength range. This configuration corresponds to the fourth example of a nonconvergent ability description presented earlier in Figure 13.2 and indicates that performance at the broad-ability level (i.e., *Grw*-W) is likely within normal limits or higher. This inference, however, should be supported by additional data, given the fact that one measure of *Grw*-WA is within the normative weakness range and

FIGURE 13.8   Outcome E: Nonconvergent Narrow-Ability Bands

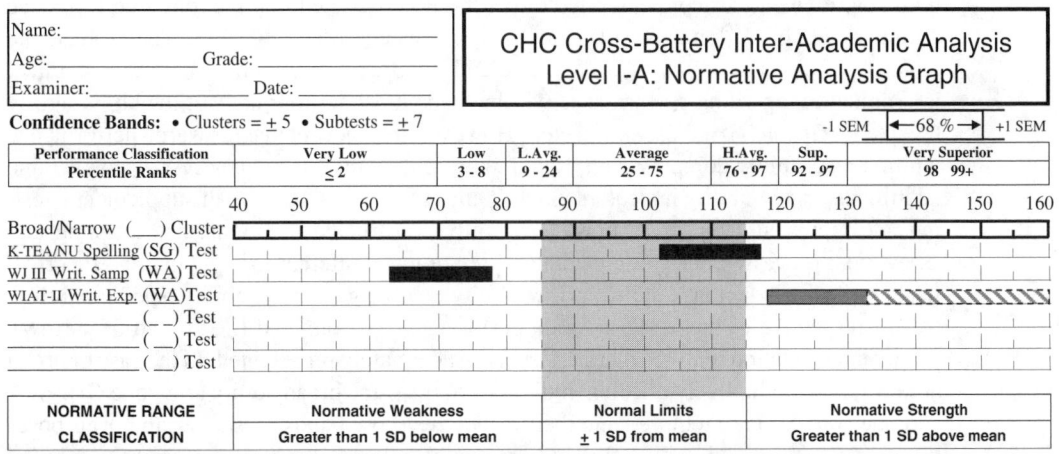

Interpretation of Outcome E:

a) Broad-ability *Grw*–W can be interpreted as Within Normal Limits or higher (nonconvergent ability description);

b) Narrow-ability *Grw*–WA cannot be interpreted.

one is within the normative strength range. Interpretation of Outcome E would be as follows: (1) Broad-ability *Grw*-W can be interpreted as within normal limits or higher because although the standard score ranges for both indicators do not touch or overlap each other, one spans from normal limits to normative strength and the other is entirely within the normative strength range, allowing for a *nonconvergent ability description* and (2) Narrow-ability *Grw*-WA cannot be interpreted because the standard score ranges for both *Grw*-WA indicators do not converge (i.e., their bands do not touch or overlap each other).

The examples illustrated (in Figures 13.4 through 13.8) relate primarily to cases in which two qualitatively different narrow abilities (from the same broad domain) are measured in the initial round of assessment, and the resulting discrepancy (lack of convergence) between the bands necessitates an additional iteration in the testing process. The same need for an additional iteration in testing can occur in some instances in which the initial measurement of abilities might deliberately include only two qualitatively similar narrow-ability measures (from the same broad domain), such as in investigations of specific areas of functioning or ability. Such focus on narrow-ability indicators, however, obviously precludes the measurement and interpretation of broad abilities. Nevertheless, if a practitioner is interested only in narrow abilities, there may well be occasions in which results from initial measurement of two similar narrow abilities are discrepant (do not converge), and thus another iteration in testing is also warranted. The second iteration of testing may be accomplished with either a third qualitatively similar narrow-ability indicator or with one that is qualitatively different, depending on the specific referral needs. Irrespective of the type of third narrow-ability measure selected, the interpretive rules described previously remain unaltered in any way and should be followed as specified.

In summary, because the underlying CHC classification system of the CHC Cross-Battery approach allows for reasonably accurate selection of multiple and varied indicators of both cognitive and academic ability constructs, it is expected that measured performance within broad-ability domains will be relatively consistent (Messick, 1995). Therefore, in the majority of cases in which inter-cognitive and inter-academic ability analysis is applied, interpretation regarding performance will be made most appropriately at the broad-ability level (e.g., *Grw*-R, *Grw*-W, *Gq*, *Gc*, etc.). However, in the event that measured performance within broad-ability domains is not found to be consistent, it may be necessary to examine additional narrow-ability indicators. Such examination takes the form of supplemental testing and represents the application of carefully constructed iterations in the testing and assessment process. Once completed, interpretation and inferences about measured performance will likely be made at the narrow-ability level (e.g., writing ability, spelling ability, etc.). Irrespective of the level at which performance is examined (i.e., broad or narrow), proper interpretation requires that constructs be adequately represented. In the case of broad abilities, two qualitatively different indicators of the same broad ability (e.g., one *Grw*-WA and one *Grw*-SG) are required and their respective score bands must overlap for purposes of calculating a broad-ability cluster from which inferences about performance may be drawn (except in the case of nonconvergent ability descriptions presented earlier). In the case of narrow abilities, two indicators of the same narrow ability (e.g., two measures of *Grw*-WA) would be needed and their respective score bands must also overlap to allow for the calculation of a narrow-ability cluster from which inferences may be drawn (again, with the exception already noted). Adherence to these guidelines in constructing and interpreting clusters produces adequate reliability and construct validity that is seldom attainable through the interpretation of subtests in isolation.

Cautions in the Interpretation of Cluster Scores

The main purpose of CHC Cross-Battery assessment is to identify inter-cognitive and inter-academic strengths and weaknesses (or some combination thereof) among the multiple broad (stratum II) abilities that essentially comprise the structure of cognitive and academic abilities as it is understood and explained by present-day theory. Because it is based on a well-validated theory and because it incorporates many advances in cognitive psychology, CHC Cross-Battery assessment allows practitioners to measure a much broader range of skills and abilities specifically related to learning and processing of information than that which can be measured through the use of most single cognitive and achievement batteries (Flanagan, McGrew, & Ortiz, 2000; Flanagan & Ortiz, 2001; McGrew & Flanagan, 1998). The comprehensive method of CHC Cross-Battery assessment (C-CB) can generate up to 10 broad-ability cluster scores that can be interpreted for the purpose of identifying specific academic ability and cognitive processing strengths or weaknesses—an important consideration in documenting learning disabilities. However, because some of the scores that may be used for such purposes may represent the aggregate average of tests from two or more different test batteries, there are some cautions that should be noted.

Although CHC Cross-Battery assessment is a psychometrically and theoretically defensible procedure for identifying academic ability and cognitive processing strengths and weaknesses, broad clusters derived in the process are not recommended for use in discrepancy formulas (e.g., ability-achievement). This is primarily because many of the assumptions carried by "discrepancy models" are not truly valid for the purpose of documenting learning disabilities. Nevertheless, CHC Cross-Battery assessment remains flexible enough to accommodate practitioners whose situations may require the identification of a cognitive processing deficit (or deficits) as well as an ability-achievement discrepancy. Methods for accomplishing this type of assessment are discussed in detail later in this chapter and in Chapter 14 (see also Flanagan & Ortiz, 2001).

Another caution in the use of broad-cluster scores derived from application of CHC Cross-Battery methods relates to the fact that actual normed cluster scores are not always equal to the average of the individual standard scores they comprise (McGrew, 1994). The basis for this statement is related to the magnitude of the intercorrelations and number of tests in the cluster (Paik & Nebenzahl, 1987). In general, the lower the intercorrelations between tests that contribute to a cluster score, the more extreme the difference will be between a cluster score that is "normed" and a cluster score that is based on the arithmetic average of tests. The only time a cluster standard score will equal the average of the individual tests that comprise it is when all the tests of the cluster are correlated perfectly, an obviously undesirable condition in test construction (Paik & Nebenzahl, 1987). As such, use of the simple averaging method for deriving cluster scores in CHC Cross-Battery assessment suggests that such scores will deviate slightly from what the "normed" cluster scores would have been. However, given the rigor with which the clusters have been constructed (e.g., based on the results of theory-driven, cross-battery factor analyses and expert consensus), it is highly probable that they would, in fact, not differ significantly from corresponding normed clusters based on a theoretical "cross-battery norm group." Furthermore, when CHC Cross-Battery cluster scores are reported and interpreted with their corresponding confidence bands, deviation from normed aggregates is negligible and comparisons of performance relative to a normative standard (i.e., the normal probability curve), or relative to individual average performance, can be considered reliable. Practitioners are advised to view CHC Cross-Battery data as only one component in a multifaceted assessment approach that focuses interpretation not only on a convergence of indicators within various academic and cognitive ability domains but also on convergence among various types and sources of data that support the overall conclusions that may be offered.

Guidelines for Conducting Ability-Achievement Discrepancy and Aptitude-Achievement Consistency Analysis with CHC Cross-Battery Data

Level III integrated ability analysis of our operational definition of LD encompasses either Ability-Achievement Discrepancy or Aptitude-Achievement Consistency analysis. In order to have progressed to Level III, practitioners would have had to have met the necessary criteria specified in Levels I and II of the definition. For instance, one or more manifest academic skill deficits were documented at Level I-A; it was determined, at Level I-B, that none of the exclusionary factors was the primary cause of the deficit(s) at Level I-A; and one or more cognitive ability deficits were documented at Level II following the criteria for identifying "deficit" presented earlier. At this point in the evaluation process (Level III), what is clear is that the individual has deficits in academic and cognitive abilities that cannot be attributed to any of the exclusionary factors that were evaluated at Levels I-B and II-B. What may not be readily apparent prior to Level III analysis is whether the individual's academic and cognitive deficits are related either empirically or logically and whether they are among a subset of circumscribed deficits within an otherwise normal ability profile. Therefore, the goal of Level III integrated ability analysis is twofold. First, following an examination of the academic and cognitive ability clusters that fell in the deficit range of functioning (data from Levels I-A and II-A analyses, recorded on the Normative Analysis Graph in Appendix D3), practitioners must determine whether there is in fact an empirical or logical relation between them. A review of the relations between cognitive and academic abilities that was reported in Chapter 2 (see Table 2.14), for example, would be useful in making this determination. Second, practitioners need to determine whether the individual has, in spite of related cognitive and academic deficits, other abilities that are within normal limits or better (i.e., intact functioning). This is determined by examining whether cognitive and academic ability clusters fall within normal limits (i.e., the shaded region of the Normative Analysis Graph in Appendix D3) or above. This latter criterion has to do with documenting underachievement or demonstrating that the individual has one or more deficits in specific academic abilities, despite intact abilities in other cognitive domains or in overall global functioning (e.g., FSIQ). In addition, examination and identification of intact functioning at this level may also be necessary to rule out other conditions as the primary cause of documented deficits at Levels I-A and II-A, such as cultural and linguistic factors or MR. Level III analysis can be carried out in one of two ways—namely, through ability-achievement discrepancy analysis or aptitude-achievement consistency analysis.

Interestingly, when the plotted score bands that fall in the deficit range on the Normative Analysis Graph in Appendix D3 are examined and the relation between the academic and cognitive abilities associated with these score bands has been documented (e.g., empirically, following the research literature), then, in essence, an aptitude-achievement *consistency* has already been established (e.g., deficits in *Ga* and *Gc* correspond to deficits in reading). If this individual also has abilities that fall within normal limits or better, then the most critical elements of the operational definition of LD have been met, suggesting no need to engage in ability-achievement discrepancy analysis. In fact, to do so, either at this point or in lieu of aptitude-achievement consistency analysis flies in the face of current research, logic, and best practices in measurement and interpretation of academic and cognitive abilities.

The inherent flaws in ability-achievement discrepancy analysis were discussed in Chapter 11 and have been discussed in numerous articles, books, and journals in assessment-related fields for over a decade. Suffice it to say that in spite of the abundance of well-reasoned and empirically supported arguments *against* using ability-achievement discrepancy criteria to diagnose learning disability, "the fact remains that many clinicians are obligated by law and regulations to determine such discrepancies on a daily basis" (Gridley & Roid, 1998, p. 252). Therefore, it is likely that practitioners will continue to obtain IQ scores for the purpose, and perhaps the sole purpose, of conducting ability-achievement discrepancy analysis. However, by relegating this type of analysis to Level III in the operational definition, the practice of relying solely on a discrepancy between ability and achievement as the defining characteristic of LD, in the absence of any documented intrinsic cause (e.g., underlying cognitive processing deficit) for the discrepancy, is avoided.

In instances where practitioners are obligated to derive IQ scores for the purpose of ability-achievement discrepancy analysis, they may do so at Level III but should realize the implications. Suppose an obtained IQ was within normal limits and documented as such for the purpose of Level III analysis. Remember that at this level, one purpose is to determine intact functioning, defined by cognitive abilities or an overall global ability within normal limits or better. Thus, an individual's IQ could be used at Level III to determine whether overall cognitive functioning is intact. What then would be the purpose of an ability-achievement discrepancy analysis? All essential criteria of the operational definition of LD have been met: academic skill deficit at Level I-A; cognitive ability or processing deficit at Level II-A; neither Level I nor Level II deficits are the primary result of exclusionary factors (Levels I-B, II-B); a relation exists between the abilities that were identified as deficient at Levels I and II; and overall global ability is within normal limits. For all intents and purposes, these data are sufficient to warrant a diagnosis of LD under IDEA and engaging in an ability-achievement discrepancy analysis at this point is an exercise in futility. The reason is because the primary cause of the deficit at Level I-A was determined to be *primarily* due to an underlying cognitive ability or processing deficit identified at Level II-A, which was established following a systematic approach to test selection, organization, and interpretation within a psychometrically and theoretically defensible framework. Knowing that there is a discrepancy between IQ and some manifest academic skill deficit does not provide any insight regarding *why the discrepancy exists*. Also, if the ability measure was confounded by measures of abilities that are deficient and that are related to the manifest academic skill deficit, then an ability-achievement discrepancy may not emerge, which is not to say, based on this finding alone, that there is no evidence of LD. In short, if a defensible explanation cannot be offered with regard to why a significant ability-achievement discrepancy exists for one or more pairs of scores for a given individual, then any conclusions that are drawn from such a finding are invalid.

Conclusions

This chapter provided specific guidelines to assist practitioners in properly evaluating CHC Cross-Battery data and for drawing appropriate inferences and making accurate interpretations on the basis of the patterns evident in the data. The process of interpretation within the context of CHC Cross-Battery assessments is both systematic and integrated and represents a method of test interpretation that is psychometrically defensible and grounded in contemporary theory and research.

The guideline for interpreting an individual's performance across the various academic and cognitive CHC clusters presented in this chapter may provide greater diagnostic and prescriptive information than that which is ordinarily obtained with traditional methods of individual subtest analysis. Overall, the interpretive process presented here represents a balance between the practitioner's need for clinically meaningful data and the need to make decisions that are objective, defensible, and have accountability.

Because CHC Cross-Battery assessment is supported by a growing body of research on the relationships between cognitive and academic abilities (as specified by CHC theory), the process can ensure that assessments and interpretations reflect current research findings. In addition, when applied in a selective manner (S-CB), such assessment provides a means for significantly reducing or eliminating the evaluation of abilities that are unrelated to the academic ability(s) in question and is particularly useful in all types of special education evaluations.

Investigations regarding the predictive utility of CHC Cross-Battery assessment over traditional assessment were discussed; however, the diagnostic and treatment validity of the approach, just as with any new and innovative assessment approach, is not yet well developed. Traditional assessment approaches have not fared well in this respect. This is most evident in research involving the Wechsler Intelligence Scales, which have for decades demonstrated convincingly that "it is impossible to predict specific disabilities and areas of cognitive competency or dysfunction from the averaged ability test scores" (i.e., IQs; Lezak, 1995). Because CHC Cross-Battery data reflect the various broad and narrow cognitive and academic abilities that comprise CHC theory, this approach may eventually prove to yield more clinically meaningful and diagnostically relevant information than has historically been obtained via the ubiquitous global IQ and ability-achievement discrepancy approach.

The next chapter will present a comprehensive framework for assessment that incorporates the CHC Cross-Battery approach and demonstrates how adherence to this framework serves to reduce the possibility of interpretive error and confirmatory bias. Guidelines will be offered for specifying both *a priori* and *a posteriori* hypotheses and data will be presented that demonstrate the entire assessment and interpretation process in accordance with the operational definition of LD presented in this book.

Endnotes

1. Because cognitive ability tests show non-zero positive intercorrelations, the scores yielded by a given battery of tests will reflect these intercorrelations. That is, the higher the correlation between two cognitive ability measures, the greater the likelihood that the traits underlying these measures will vary consistently. This is because "average intercorrelations of normative attributes is determined mainly by the relationships among the contents of attribute scales and the psychological characteristics of the respondent population" (McDermott et al., 1992, p. 509). Conversely, ipsative scores have near zero (and often negative) intercorrelations. "The discovery of . . . near zero average relationships among ability attributes runs contrary to the theoretical expectation for constructs that might reflect some meaningful aspect of Spearman's *g*" (McDermott et al., 1992, p. 510). Thus, as opposed to normative scores, ipsative scores have "personological" ability dimensions (Brouerman, 1961). That is, through factor analysis of ipsative measures, Brouerman observed that the "consequent dimensions retained a certain reciprocally exclusive character whereby, as an individual exhibited greater ability in one area, commensurate inability was apparent in another area" (cited in McDermott et al., 1992, p. 518).

2. Clusters derived from two tests that have reliability coefficients of $\leq .85$ and that correlate $\geq .45$ will result in a cluster score having a reliability of $\geq .90$.

3. Typically, a score that is ≥ 1 SD above or below the mean is considered a normative strength or weakness, respectively (Lezak, 1976, 1995).

Comprehensive Framework for LD Determination and CHC Cross-Battery Assessment

A Case Study

In the discussion presented in Chapter 11 regarding a modern, theoretically based operational definition of LD, it was noted that one of the other major reasons for the problems that have followed LD assessment has been the lack of a comprehensive and practical guiding framework. Indeed, attempts to evaluate LD, irrespective of an operational definition, can be hampered solely on the basis of problems inherent in the specific approach used in the course of the assessment. Adherence to all best practices in assessment is crucial to the reliable and valid identification of LD. To that end, the purpose of this chapter is to present a comprehensive framework for assessment that follows established principles for valid assessment using CHC Cross-Battery methods and incorporates the operational definition detailed in Chapter 11. The format for this discussion will be based on a case study example that illustrates, primarily through the use of standardized tests, the various components of the assessment process, and the decisions that must be made at each step in order to provide a solid basis for the determination of LD. The case study will highlight the manner in which practitioners are expected to make decisions relevant to the identification of LD, in particular those decisions related to the sufficiency of any evaluation that was conducted, normative versus deficit functioning, attributions of performance, evaluation of potential mitigating factors, evaluation of underachievement, and interference with learning. In addition, a discussion related to the importance and use of an hypothesis testing approach will be presented as well as how this approach may be integrated within the whole of the proposed assessment framework. It is hoped that the case study in this chapter can serve as one model for practitioners in learning how to blend the crucial elements of the assessment process in a manner that is consistent with the theoretical principles and practical procedures for LD determination that have been presented.

A Comprehensive Framework for LD Determination

Assessment of LD is perhaps best thought of as an exercise in decision making. Relevant and pertinent data are collected at various stages of assessment and evaluated carefully to determine the next step and direction of the process. The decisions must be guided by convergence of the best available evidence that fully support the actions taken and conclusions reached by the evaluator. The whole process may therefore be characterized as a course that is charted and unfolds on the basis of what the collected data and data patterns reveal. The process of LD assessment that we propose is in keeping with these principles and is illustrated as a decision-based flowchart found in Figure 14.1. The flowchart is easily navigated via the specification of particular assessment activities and evaluation procedures that proceed on the basis of answers to "yes" or "no" questions. We wish again to reiterate an earlier point related to the manner in which this framework will be described. As with the operational definition outlined in Chapter 11, the comprehensive framework for assessment depicted in Figure 14.1 may well be carried out through the collection of a wide variety and types of data. We do not mean to imply or suggest that the integrated operational definition of LD or the entire framework itself applies only or exclusively to the use of data garnered from the administration of standardized tests. Because standardized tests are perhaps the most common and efficient methods of gathering data for the purpose of LD determination, we will use this particular type of data to illustrate and describe the framework as was done with the operational definition.

Perceived Academic Difficulties

Although the process of assessment as depicted in Figure 14.1 starts with the perception of academic difficulties, this does not imply that the process of assessment has not already begun. There is a tendency to view assessment and evaluation as beginning at the point where "testing" becomes central to the process (i.e., when the individual is referred for such testing). However, it is more appropriate to view assessment and evaluation as having begun the moment an individual's behavior, performance, and so on, became suspect and was examined with greater scrutiny than ordinary. In the educational setting, for example, this may occur where there is some sort of "prereferral" system in place—the function of which is to address observed learning problems prior to making any formal referrals for psychoeducational evaluation (i.e., special education evaluations conducted under the provisions of IDEA). Thus, the activities that comprise the process of assessment and evaluation should be viewed as including both pre- and postreferral activities.

Admittedly, academically related prereferral activities are conducted for slightly different reasons than postreferral activities. In the former case, the goal is to identify areas of need and provide appropriate modifications and interventions that may assist in improving the individual's learning process. The same can be said for the latter case, but in many instances, there is an additional goal that revolves around issues related to identification of intrinsic learning difficulties. When so identified, assessment goals in the latter may also encompass a need for establishing a specific diagnosis, determining classification, and evaluating eligibility. As such, the relationship between assessment and intervention is central to both pre- and postreferral activities. In the case of prereferral activities, the need to evaluate the success of current interventions forms an important component that affects the decision regarding whether to proceed with formal referral. Reschly (1990) comments on the nature of this relationship by recommending that "cognitive assessment should be pursued only after interventions have been attempted systematically and evaluated rigorously, and then only when learning problems appear to be pervasive and persistent" (p. 262). It is clear

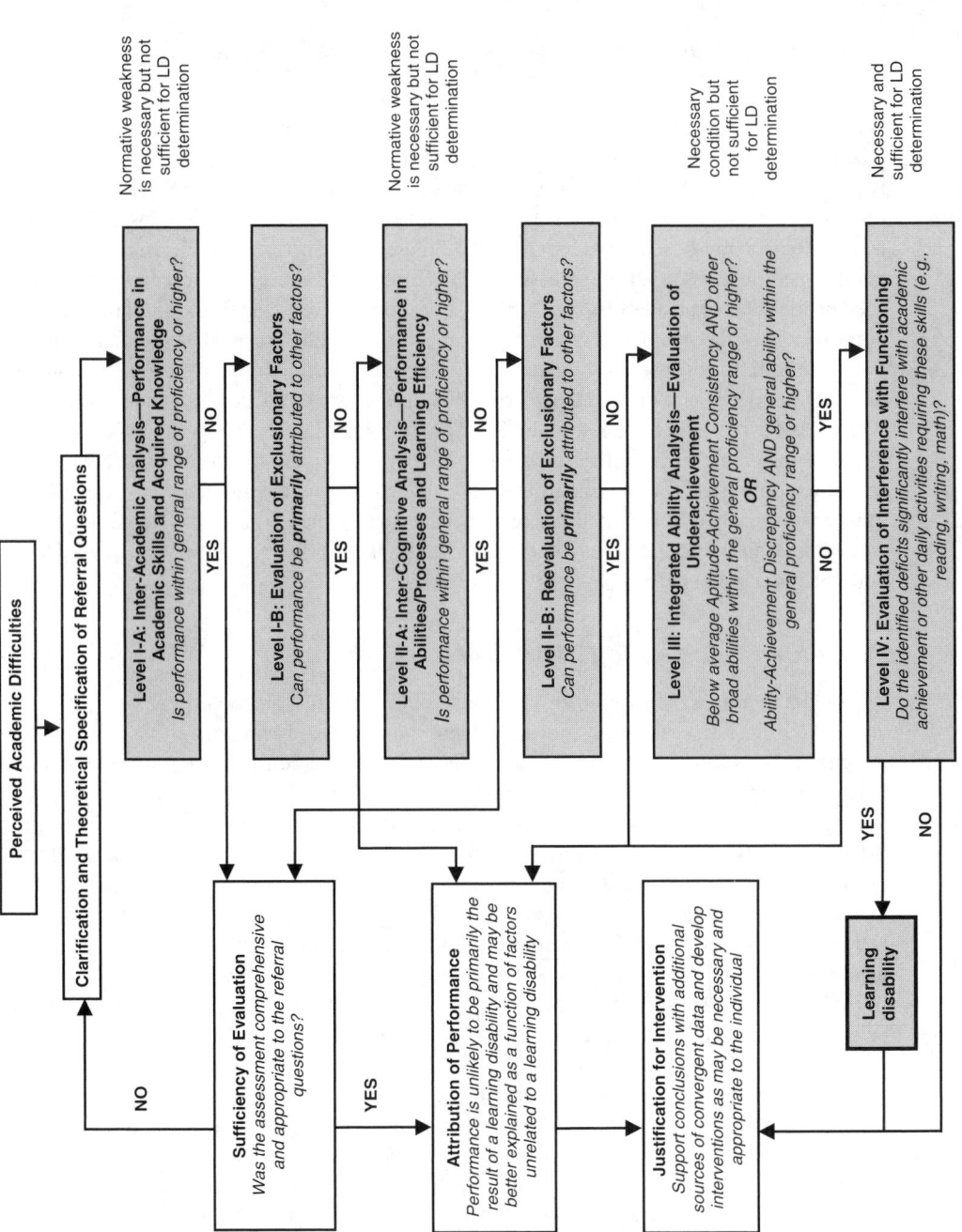

FIGURE 14.1 Decision Flowchart and Framework for Comprehensive Assessment and Determination of Learning Disability

that postreferral evaluations that focus primarily or exclusively on diagnosis do not retain links to intervention even when prior interventions have been unsuccessful. Practitioners should recognize that the process of measuring an individual's functioning is not, in and of itself, an intervention but rather only an attempt to sample the individual's behavior in such a way that it might improve understanding of the individual's learning needs. Practitioners should also remain aware that implications for intervention exist irrespective of the success or failure of attempts to identify suspected cognitive or academic functioning deficits.

Clarification and Theoretical Specification of Referral Questions

Perception of academic difficulties that are not responsive to systematic and carefully planned intervention and remediation attempts will most often serve as the trigger for additional evaluation, in particular the use of standardized tests. The second box in Figure 14.1 represents this stage in the process and reflects the need to operationalize the referral issues and questions so that they may be answered by additional data. When standardized tests are used, consistent with the CHC Cross-Battery guiding principles outlined in Chapters 12 and 13, evaluators should strive to measure the relevant abilities in a manner that is both theoretically and empirically supportable so that the sufficiency of the evaluation is ensured. For example, this includes the use of relatively "pure" measures of ability, use of two qualitatively different narrow-ability indicators, and use of the smallest number of test batteries possible. The CHC Cross-Battery approach to assessment establishes a scientifically and psychometrically defensible process for identifying cognitive and academic deficits that is based on sound theory and research to a degree not attainable by current methods. Without clarification and specification of constructs based on theory and proper representation, it may be difficult if not impossible to determine whether the tests given were sufficiently comprehensive and reliable to produce data that can assist in addressing the specific referral questions. The same can be said for other types of data collection—whatever the method, the specific referral questions must be operationalized in a defensible and systematic manner.

Hypothesis-Driven Assessment

The boxes on the right side of Figure 14.1 represent the four levels (I–IV) that comprise the operational definition of LD that was discussed in detail in Chapter 11. It is not necessary to present these levels again here, except to point out the decision-making process is based on a hypothesis-driven approach. The comprehensive framework for LD determination, and the CHC Cross-Battery methods that underlie it, both emphasize the need and value in conducting assessments using an hypothesis-testing approach. Although this approach can be applied to the collection of data apart from that generated by standardized tests, it is perhaps most important for practitioners to adhere to guidelines based on a philosophy of hypothesis generation and testing precisely when tests are used. Psychometric data often appear to be objective but are no less subject to interpretive mistakes as any other type of data. Reduction of incorrect or unsupportable inferences about data can be achieved by utilization of hypothesis generation and testing throughout the assessment.

The main benefit of using hypotheses in the assessment process is the decrease in confirmatory bias that often accompanies the use of standardized, norm-referenced tests. In general, confirmatory bias occurs primarily when an examiner possesses preconceived notions about an individual's expected performance on a given task or test. Naturally, once the data have been collected, the reviewing examiner will tend to look for patterns and results that support, not refute, the preconception. In essence, on the basis of the preconception, the examiner has been predisposed to see only those patterns in the data that tend to support these initial assumptions while at the same time minimizing, ignoring, or completely rejecting any data that may run against it (Sandoval, 1998). Thus, if the tendency to "see" patterns of disabilities or dysfunction in data where in fact none exist is to be prevented, diagnostic interpretation of data must not be contaminated by presumptions regarding preexisting deficits. Collection and interpretation of test data must be guided by the assumption that an individual undergoing assessment is normal, or unimpaired. This notion provides the basis for expectations regarding performance (global functioning as well as functioning across individual tasks or tests) that suggest that the individual will perform within the range of normal limits or general proficiency. Such expectations can be operationalized into the form of the null hypothesis, which is then evaluated to determine whether it must be retained (because performance is indeed generally proficient) or rejected in favor of the alternative hypothesis (i.e., that performance is outside this range). With respect to standardized test data, the specific criteria for making these decisions were presented in the previous chapters and involve basically the identification of population-relative performance that falls more than one standard deviation *below* average. Note that the criteria do not suggest rejection of the null hypothesis in cases where performance falls more than one standard deviation *above* average, because this reflects superior, not deficient, functioning. Only when the null hypothesis is rejected in favor of the alternative hypothesis under these conditions can the data be considered to be supportive of any notions regarding disability or deficient functioning.

Adoption of the stance that expected performance for a given individual will be generally proficient until and unless contraindicated convincingly by the data significantly reduces the chance that data will be inadvertently evaluated and interpreted in a manner that supports preexisting beliefs about dysfunction. The null hypothesis that specifies adequate or proficient performance should never be dismissed summarily or discarded out of hand in assessment, even in cases where an individual's functional deficits may seem rather obvious. Practitioners involved in assessment, particularly those engaged in conducting evaluations related to identifying LD, should remain faithful to the fundamental hypothesis that favors the individual and that presumes that performance will prove to be unremarkable. It is, of course, rather difficult not to entertain suspicions of dysfunction in the process of evaluation, especially because individuals undergoing evaluation have very likely already undergone either a screening process or have failed to respond to remedial efforts and pre-referral intervention strategies. But personal suspicions must remain distinct from the specific hypotheses that are to be evaluated in the course of assessment. Opinions, conjecture, or suppositions on the part of the practitioner may well be unavoidable, but they cannot be allowed to enter into the equation that seeks to ascribe meaning to collected data. Rather, the process of assessment is based solely on evaluation and testing of hypotheses that are specified *a priori*. Personal suspicions are not subject to evaluation or testing and therefore they cannot be appropriately examined within the full context of the data. Once again, confirmatory bias is reduced only when the null hypothesis that performance will be adequate or generally proficient is adopted and evaluated, and is not rejected until and unless the data suggest convincingly otherwise, irrespective of the examiner's belief or suspicion to the contrary. Note also that whenever the null hypothesis is indeed rejected in favor of the alternative hypothesis, the most reasonable conclusion that can be drawn is that the data do not support the notion that performance is proficient but rather suggest that performance is in all likelihood outside of this range. Even when the data point toward the alternative hypothesis, this does not provide de facto support for the presence of a disability as much as it simply indicates that functioning cannot be considered unremarkable.

The hypothesis-driven approach is intended only to be a broad stroke that guides the interpretive process in assessment with respect to the use of standardized tests. As was described previously, data collected at one level of the framework (e.g., Level I-A) is often reconsidered and reevaluated in the context of additional data collected at another level (e.g., Level III—refer to Figure 11.3). Thus, the process of assessment as related to LD determination comprises a sequence of activities that are iterative and recursive in nature. The cyclic nature of this approach to assessment is also evident in the decision points found in CHC Cross-Battery assessment where evaluation of *a priori* hypotheses may well lead to additional testing and the specification and testing of additional *(a posteriori)* hypotheses. Thus, determination of LD through the use of CHC Cross-Battery assessment represents an integrative process as well as movement from the evaluation of data from an individual battery or test to the evaluation of multiple data sources.

Sufficiency of Evaluation

There are many different ways that any particular referral question or concern might be operationalized and the nature and manner of data collection can vary widely. As noted previously, utilization of CHC Cross-Battery assessment is one method that is very helpful in this respect, particularly when standardized tests are deemed appropriate in the assessment and evaluation of LD. However, even careful and deliberate selection of standardized tests according to this approach may not always result in direct or sufficient measurement of the exact areas of dysfunction that may be the underlying cause of an individual's difficulties. As such, it may be difficult, if not impossible, to properly evaluate *a priori* hypotheses. In some cases, performance on standardized tests may reveal functioning on both academic and cognitive ability tests that is otherwise unremarkable and generally within the proficient range. If there are other extant data that appear to contradict this scenario, evaluators may need to consider whether the scope of their evaluation, as conducted, was sufficient in breadth or depth to adequately measure the dysfunction. If it is determined that the evaluation either failed to evaluate the specific area of concern, or failed to evaluate it sufficiently, additional evaluation based on the construction of a new set of tests or cross-battery is certainly one option. Alternatively, if it is determined that the evaluation did indeed provide sufficient and specific data to adequately evaluate the area of concern, and performance was found to be generally proficient, practitioners may need to review the referral information and case history, and reexamine current functioning more carefully in order to determine the precise nature of the individual's difficulties. It may well be that in some cases, data other than that from standardized tests will be necessary in order to reveal the pattern of dysfunction that has been observed.

Attribution of Performance

When an evaluation of academic skills or cognitive abilities has passed the test of sufficiency and has resulted in data that support a normative deficit, the next step in the process is to evaluate the particular reasons why an individual's performance has been found to be significantly deviant from the general proficiency range. Most often, this will entail investigation of mitigating or inhibitory factors external to the individual being assessed. Information gathered from a wide variety of sources should be brought to light and evaluated within the context of the individual's complete learning environment. The essential question of this step in the process is the gathering of data that allow determination of whether deficit performance can be *primarily* attributed to other factors. If the answer is "yes," then attribution of performance will revolve around other factors unrelated to a learning disability. Non-cognitive factors can include motivation, anxiety, psychological disturbances, cultural and linguistic differences, pervasive developmental dysfunction, mental retardation, and so on. If the answer is "no," then the process of identifying LD may reasonably continue.

Evaluation of Underachievement

As has been discussed repeatedly, the vast majority of evaluations carried out in attempts to identify LD are generally not guided by theory, research, or established practice but largely by a diverse set of legal and procedural guidelines that vary widely from state to state and even from school district to school district. The impetus for unreliable practice often rests squarely with the need for legal compliance. The imprecision of existing diagnostic taxonomies (e.g., *DSM-IV*) and the vague and nebulous definitions of LD found in legal statutes (e.g., IDEA) with their concomitant arcane and illogical procedural specifications serve only to compound the problem. There is no reason why any assessment of LD, conducted under the provisions of IDEA or otherwise, cannot be easily accomplished using the CHC classifications and definitions that form the basis of this book. However, in cases where practitioners are compelled to adhere to the rather arbitrary language contained in federal and state regulations, the flexibility of the Cross-Battery approach can accommodate a variety of assessment requirements and needs.

The need to deviate from sound theory and principles occurs most often in cases where practitioners may be required to derive a global ability score or use a discrepancy method of analysis in order to support the determination of LD. Although we have argued that it is more logical to examine the relationship of "consistency" between aptitude and achievement than the "discrepancy" between global ability and achievement, the purpose of each is still the same—to establish some basis of underachievement. The evaluation of underachievement is an important component in LD determination and is incorporated within the operational definition that has already been proposed, albeit with recommendations for moving toward consistency analysis over discrepancy analysis due to the flaws in logic that characterize the latter.

Related to the concept of underachievement is the requirement that some demonstration of interference with learning be present in order to determine the presence of LD that is contained in *DSM-IV* and IDEA. The question becomes evaluation of whether the suspected learning disability has resulted in academic failure or other restriction or limitation in daily life functioning. It is possible that an individual may well have learning problems but that the problem has not significantly impaired the individual's functioning to the point that it could legally or medically be construed as a learning disability.

Justification for Intervention

Irrespective of the decisions that are made and the conclusions that are reached in any assessment, determination of a finding of LD must be corroborated by additional supporting evidence and data (e.g., from review of school records, work samples, observations, diagnostic interviews, etc.) that converge on the notion of disability. Reliable and valid determination of LD is only accomplished via the collection of a broad range of data, as specified in the comprehensive framework, and collection of standardized test data forms only one procedure within the entire scope of assessment-related activities. In the absence of sufficient and convincing corroborating data, a diagnosis of learning disability made solely on the basis of a single standardized test is both poor practice and wholly indefensible. The comprehensive framework for LD determination described herein, as well as the CHC Cross-Battery assessment and interpretive process, continue to require careful evaluation of case history information (e.g., educational records, medical records, prereferral meeting notes, etc.), the inclusion of data from relevant sources (e.g., parents, siblings, teachers, friends, employers), and the framing of an individual's difficulties within the context of CHC theory and research. No matter how compelling, no single procedure or test should be used to make definitive interpretations or clinical decisions regarding the identification of LD in the absence of other sources of corroborating data.

Corroborating and convergent evidence is crucial irrespective of whether LD is identified or not identified because in either case, it forms the basis from which the development of necessary and appropriate interventions will proceed. The mere act of evaluating an individual suspected of having a learning disability does not resolve his or her academic difficulties. Although those individuals identified as having LD may be entitled to particular programs and services (i.e., special education), those not identified as having LD are equally entitled to some appropriate form of intervention to resolve their particular issues. Interventions must therefore be justified on the basis of the collected data and decisions regarding their format, schedule, or intensity are also guided by the whole of the data generated and applied within the most appropriate context.

A Case Study in LD Determination

Overview

The comprehensive framework for LD determination presented in the previous section is intended to serve as one example, out of many other possibilities, for conducting an evaluation of learning disability that is systematic, practical, theory based, and defensible, and that represents an approach founded on established principles of best practices in assessment. Given the current development and extension of traditional notions of LD, some of the particular elements within the framework are new and may not be familiar to practitioners. Thus, we believe it may be helpful to further clarify the various aspects of this approach to the assessment of learning disabilities through the use of an illustrative case study. Although the flowchart by itself is reasonably easy to follow, a narrative case study with explanations and concrete examples often helps to highlight the nature and scope of the process. In addition, the results and conclusions of the case study to be presented have been distilled into a psychological report that is available for review in Appendix G. This sample psychological report provides another model for practitioners who may have questions regarding the exact format for organization and presentation of results generated from assessment conducted using the comprehensive framework for LD determination and CHC Cross-Battery methods. There is no single correct way that results from any assessment must be presented, and the report that stems from the following case study merely represents a suggestion for only one of the many ways in which this task can be accomplished. Practitioners are encouraged to utilize whatever report format is most comfortable and appropriate and to adapt the various elements critical to establishing LD from the sample report into any preferred format or report style.

The Case of Carsam

Examiner A has been asked to attend a prereferral intervention meeting where the case of Carsam, a 10-year-old student who is currently in the fifth grade at a local elementary school, is to be discussed. At the meeting, Examiner A learns that Carsam has displayed significant difficulty developing grade-appropriate reading and writing skills. Even when compared to his same-age peers who have comparable cultural and linguistic histories (Carsam is Caucasian and a native English speaker from a middle-class background with family roots in the United States that go back several generations), he does not appear to be acquiring grade-level literacy skills to any degree that could be considered average or comparable to his peers. At the meeting, the participants conduct a careful review of Carsam's existing educational records, examine work samples provided by his present and previous teachers, evaluate information offered by the parents, compare various aspects of performance with other children of similar experiential and educational backgrounds, and analyze the interventions and modifications already attempted in directed efforts to ameliorate his learning difficulties. Ultimately, the members in attendance (including the parents) decide that Carsam's observed learning difficulties cannot be adequately or fully explained by environmental, systemic, or ecological factors at this time, and so the primary cause of his observed learning difficulties remains unknown.

The absence of evidence pointing toward extrinsic causes (e.g., lack of opportunity to learn) for Carsam's learning problems leads the members at the meeting to believe that an evaluation is necessary in order to rule out the possibility of a learning disability or other type of cognitive dysfunction. Examiner A is asked to conduct an evaluation of cognitive and academic functioning in order to gather information that might shed light on the nature of Carsam's difficulties and assist in the development of appropriate curricular and teaching modifications and interventions. With permission from Carsam's parents, Examiner A began the process of evaluation utilizing the comprehensive framework for LD determination (see Figure 14.1).

Clarification and Theoretical Specification of Referral Questions

Methods.   Because the concerns regarding Carsam's academic difficulties are rather well circumscribed, centering on reading and writing only, Examiner A chose to focus specifically on these areas as defined in IDEA (e.g., basic reading skills, reading comprehension, and written expression). Had there been concerns in other areas of academic functioning (e.g., listening comprehension, mathematics reasoning, etc.), a comprehensive approach might have been more appropriate. There are in fact instances where, despite the lack of concern, it may be necessary to evaluate functioning along a broad spectrum in order to gather data that might assist in establishing whether an individual's ability to master material actually being taught in the classroom is impaired or not. An example of this need often arises when there is a suspicion of mental retardation that necessitates documentation of significantly subaverage functioning in a variety of domains. Functioning that is found to be generally proficient or average in one or more areas may well assist in differentiating severe learning disability from mental retardation or other related impairments.

In the case of Carsam, Examiner A chose to utilize the WIAT-II, since this was the achievement test with which he was most familiar. In addition, assessment at this level is being couched within the LD area classifications specified by IDEA, which represent descriptions only, not actual theoretically specified constructs. Accordingly, Examiner A will focus on evaluating the relevant Academic Clinical Composites. The second guiding principle of CHC Cross-Battery assessment that requires that constructs be adequately represented by two qualitatively different constructs does not strictly apply to the Academic Clinical Composites as it would if the constructs were actually theoretically based (e.g., *Grw*-R, *Grw*-W, *Gc*, etc.). Nevertheless, Examiner A recognizes the basic underlying precept that a single measure of anything may not be a reliable estimate of performance. According to the guidelines mentioned in the previous chapter, when assessment uses the LD area definitions instead of the CHC broad-ability constructs, then measurement of that area should still be supported by either an additional standardized test in the same area or some other source of reliable data. As presented in Table 14.1, the WIAT-II does contain tests that parallel the LD categories contained in IDEA, but provides only one measure of basic reading and one measure of reading comprehension. It does, however, provide two measures of written expression. Therefore, Examiner A decided to supplement his assessment by selecting and administering additional standardized tests of basic reading and reading comprehension.

Examiner A did not act hastily in selecting additional tests. Rather, although there was no necessary requirement to try to represent constructs with qualitatively different indicators, Examiner A did take this into consideration because it would provide a broader base to the assessment of the abilities central to the referral. Examiner A recalled that Carsam's teacher had observed more difficulties in reading comprehension when he was forced to select a word that would best complete a sentence. Examiner A hypothesized that a reading

TABLE 14.1   Measurement of LD Areas Specified by IDEA from WIAT-II

IDEA LD CATEGORIES	TESTS FROM WIAT-II	
	Measure 1	Measure 2
Oral Expression	*Oral Expression*	
Listening Comprehension	*Listening Comprehension*	
Written Expression	*Written Expression*	*Spelling*
Basic Reading Skills	*Word Reading*	
Reading Comprehension	*Reading Comprehension*	
Mathematics Calculation	*Numerical Operations*	
Mathematics Reasoning	*Math Reasoning*	

comprehension task that utilized a cloze method in administration would be an excellent way to further evaluate the teacher's observations. In similar fashion, Examiner A noted that the Word Reading test of the WIAT-II was essentially a measure of decoding ability, but information raised at the prereferral meeting suggested that Carsam's difficulties appeared related more to vocabulary development as opposed to purely phonetic difficulties. Examiner A carefully reviewed the CHC Cross-Battery worksheet for *Grw*-R (see Appendix A) and noted that two tests from the WJ III would meet his goals for assessment of Carsam's academic abilities quite well. He selected Passage Comprehension from the WJ III to augment Reading Comprehension from the WIAT-II, because it not only measured reading comprehension but it did so utilizing a cloze-type procedure.

Examiner A then selected the WJ III Reading Vocabulary test because it was directly related to the referral concerns. It represents a qualitatively different aspect of basic reading skills related to verbal language comprehension that is not measured by the Word Reading test from the WIAT-II. In this way, Examiner A was able to assemble a cross-battery that was responsive not only to the basic principles of the CHC Cross-Battery approach but well in line with the questions that initially prompted the referral. Note also that the WIAT-II did provide two measures of written expression, and so no additional tests were needed in that area. In this manner, Examiner A was able to develop an assessment that was both appropriate and sufficient to operationalize the referral questions and concerns. The complete cross-battery set of tests selected by Examiner A (six in all) and their relationship to the LD categories contained in IDEA and the respective Academic Clinical Composites is illustrated in Table 14.2.

Level I-A: Inter-Academic Analysis—Performance in Academic Skills and Acquired Knowledge

Methods. Although Examiner A is focusing on the evaluation of LD through the use of the Academic Clinical Composites corresponding to the achievement areas specified in IDEA, initial results from the administration of the cross-battery designed by Examiner A are first entered into the appropriate CHC Cross-Battery worksheets—in this case *Grw*-R and *Grw*-W (see Appendix A). Despite the fact that Examiner A was not specifically concerned about adequate CHC broad-ability representation of academic abilities *at this point,* use of these worksheets was done for two reasons. First, these worksheets facilitate conversion of standard scores and provide spaces for raw data entry as may be necessary before conversion. Second, the worksheets organize the data according to CHC broad- and narrow-ability constructs, which is necessary for later integrated ability analysis should the assessment proceed to Level III. Examiner A thus entered the data from testing on these worksheets in accordance with the instructions provided in Chapter 12, which included conversion of any score in a metric different from that specified by the CHC Cross-Battery approach (e.g., mean = 100, SD = 15). All subsequent test data collected by Examiner A in the assessment of Carsam (e.g., from tests of cognitive ability) were also first entered on the appropriate CHC Cross-Battery worksheets (see Appendix A) and converted to this common metric prior to being included on the level-specific data summary sheets and normative analysis graphs.

Because the current assessment involves LD determination under the provisions of state and federal special education statutes, it is most appropriate for Examiner A to use the data summary and normative analysis graph for Academic Clinical Composites (see Appendix E) for analyzing and interpreting data because they are specifically organized according to LD area rather than CHC broad-ability constructs. Use of the correct sheets is important in establishing a systematic approach to the assessment and keeping the data arranged in a way that facilitates interpretation of results. Thus, Examiner A transferred the data from the CHC Cross-Battery worksheets to the data summary and normative analysis graph for Academic Clinical Composites to begin his analysis of the results.

Analysis. In keeping with attempts to avoid confirmatory bias, Examiner A hypothesized that Carsam's measured performance would be in the general proficiency range in each area measured. In the absence of any previously diagnosed cognitive processing impairment, and with a history of appropriate and sufficient instruction and opportunity to learn, it is expected that Carsam will perform within normal limits (i.e., standard scores of 85 to 115, inclusive) in any areas evaluated as depicted in Level I-A of the comprehensive framework

TABLE 14.2 WIAT-II/WJ III Cross-Battery Academic Assessment for Carsam

IDEA LD CATEGORIES	WIAT-II/WJ III ACHIEVEMENT CROSS-BATTERY			ACADEMIC CLINICAL COMPOSITES
	WIAT-II - TEST 1	WIAT-II - TEST 2	WJ III TESTS	
Oral Expression				
Listening Comprehension				
Written Expression	Written Expression			ACC – Written Expression
Basic Reading Skills	Word Reading	Spelling		ACC – Basic Reading Skills
Reading Comprehension	Reading Comprehension		Reading Vocabulary / Passage Comprehension	ACC – Reading Comprehension
Mathematics Calculation				
Mathematics Reasoning				

(see Figure 14.1). Because the fundamental requirement for establishing LD rests on the premise of significant or substantial deficiencies in one or more areas of academic achievement, advancement of the assessment process is contingent on analysis of data at Level I-A where one or more specific academic skills or knowledge *deficits* must be documented. In the case of standardized test data, the individual must demonstrate one or more normative weaknesses (i.e., standard scores greater than 1 standard deviation *below* the normative mean; that is, standard scores < 85), relative to a representative sample of individuals of the same chronological age from the general population. Additionally, any observed weaknesses should be in those areas that were specifically observed *a priori* to be problematic. That is, the weakness should be consistent with referral concerns, academic history, teacher reports, and so forth. Apparent deficiencies in areas that were not the main focus of evaluation may necessitate a return to the prereferral level where the manifest difficulties are reexamined and clarified with more specificity.

In this case, Examiner A utilized a selective approach and focused specifically on the areas of suspected disability and deliberately avoided an "exploratory" approach to assessment. Using the criteria for classification specified in Table 13.1, Examiner A reviewed the data contained in the Data Summary for Level I-A (see Figure 14.2) and concluded that Carsam's performance in all of the Academic Clinical Composites (i.e., Written Expression [ACC/WE], Basic Reading Skills [ACC/BR], and Reading Comprehension [ACC/RC]) were outside and below the average or normal limits range. In the case of ACC/BR and ACC/RC, the bands for each of the two indicators comprising the respective composites overlapped, indicating the formation of an interpretable score. In keeping with basic CHC Cross-Battery assessment principles, the bands for the two indicators comprising ACC/WE did not overlap and therefore no composite score was calculated. However, the configuration of the indicators was consistent with a nonconvergent ability description because both bands fell entirely within the normative weakness range.

The value of using standard score ranges, as opposed to the mean standard score, and of plotting the ranges on a graph is readily apparent in Figure 14.3. Although this figure contains the exact same information as that presented in the data summary illustrated in Figure 14.2, the normative analysis graph provides a much easier basis from which to evaluate data and draw appropriate interpretations. For example, it is clearly evident that five of the six standard score bands for the tests administered to Carsam fall completely within the normative weakness range (greater than 1 SD below the mean) and are thus counter to the general proficiency range hypothesis. In addition, performance within the two tests that comprise ACC/WE is discrepant; that is, the bands do not touch or overlap and, in accordance with cross-battery guiding principles, no composite is calculated or graphed. Because both bands are within the same normative range (Normative Weakness), this condition represents an example of what was referred to as a nonconvergent ability description in Chapter 13 and is easily determined by noting that the bands fall entirely to the left of the middle shaded portion of the graph that represents the range of normal limits.

Interpretation. The proper interpretation for the results generated at this level of analysis are relatively straightforward and suggest that the null hypothesis (that Carsam's performance in each academic area would be within the general proficiency range) is not tenable. First, with respect to the area of Written Expression (ACC/WE), performance can

FIGURE 14.2   Level I-A Data Summary for Inter-Academic Analysis

Name: Carsam Age: 10 Grade: 5	CHC Cross-Battery Academic Clinical Composites
Examiner: A Date: 10/24	Level I-A: Data Summary

LD AREA	Test Battery	Subtest Name		CHC Ability Measured	Standard Score	Confidence Interval	%ile Rank	Classification
OE – Oral Expression			*OE Area Average =*					
LC – Listening Comprehension			*LC Area average =*					
WE – Written Expression			*WE Area Average =*					
	WIAT-II	Spelling		*Grw*-SG	77	70-84	6	Low
	WIAT-II	Written Expression		*Grw*-WA	61	54-68	1	V. Low
BR – Basic Reading Skills			*BR Area Average =*		75	70-80	5	Low
	WIAT-II	Word Reading		*Grw*-RD	78	71-85	8	Low
	WJ III	Reading Vocabulary		*Grw*-V	72	65-79	3	Low
RC – Reading Comprehension			*RC Area Average =*		79	74-84	8	Low
	WIAT-II	Reading Comprehension		*Grw*-RC	85	78-92	16	L. Average
	WJ III	Passage Comprehension		*Grw*-CZ	73	66-80	3	Low
MC – Mathematics Calculation			*MC Area Average =*					
MR – Mathematics Reasoning			*MR Area Average =*					
GK – General Knowledge[1]			*GK Area Average =*					

[1]*GK*, which includes general information and lexical knowledge, is not an "official" academic area listed in IDEA's definition of learning disability but represents another store of acquired knowledge consistent with the other stores of acquired knowledge that are listed (e.g., reading, math, writing).

Note: All standard scores are based on age norms   **Confidence Bands:** • Clusters = ± 5   • Subtests = ± 7

FIGURE 14.3   Level I-A: Normative Analysis Graph for Inter-Academic Analysis

Name: ___Carsam___ Age: _10_ Grade: _5_
Examiner: __A__ Date: __10/24__

**CHC Cross-Battery Academic Clinical Composites
Level I-A: Normative Analysis Graph**

Confidence Bands: • Clusters = $\pm$ 5 • Subtests = $\pm$ 7

-1 SEM   ←—68 %—→   +1 SEM

Performance Classification	Very Low	Low	L Avg.	Average	H.Avg.	Sup.	Very Superior
Percentile Ranks	≤ 2	3 - 8	9 - 24	25 - 75	76-97	92 - 97	98 - 99+

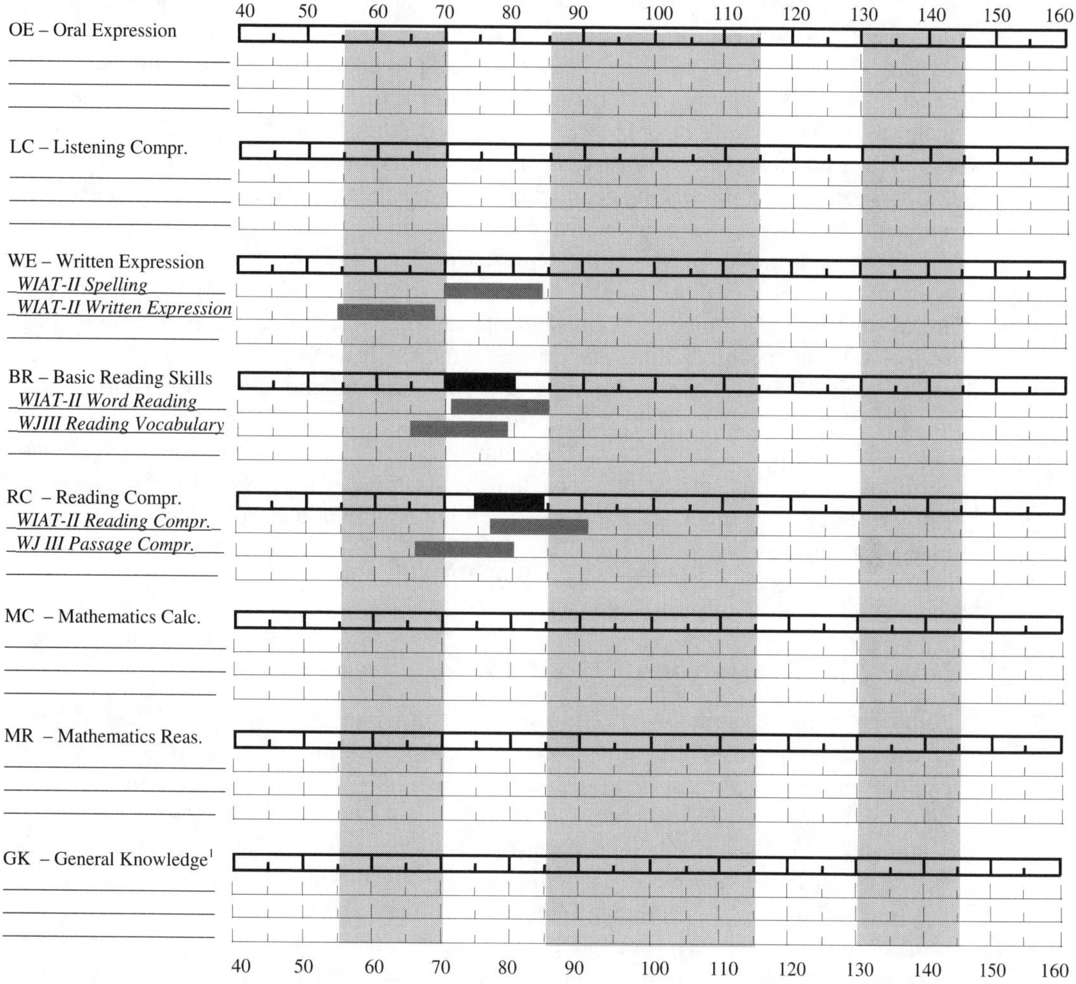

40   50   60   70   80   90   100   110   120   130   140   150   160

OE – Oral Expression

LC – Listening Compr.

WE – Written Expression
WIAT-II Spelling
WIAT-II Written Expression

BR – Basic Reading Skills
WIAT-II Word Reading
WJIII Reading Vocabulary

RC – Reading Compr.
WIAT-II Reading Compr.
WJ III Passage Compr.

MC – Mathematics Calc.

MR – Mathematics Reas.

GK – General Knowledge[1]

40   50   60   70   80   90   100   110   120   130   140   150   160

NORMATIVE RANGE CLASSIFICATION	Normative Weakness Greater than 1 SD below mean	Normal Limits ± 1 SD from mean	Normative Strength Greater than 1 SD above mean

[1]*GK*, which includes general information and lexical knowledge, is not an "official" academic area listed in IDEA's definition of learning disability but represents another store of acquired knowledge consistent with the other stores of acquired knowledge that are listed (e.g., reading, math, writing).

be described as a normative weakness reflected by a nonconvergent ability description with written language ability significantly less well developed than that of spelling. Second, performance in the area of Basic Reading Skills (ACC/BR) also reflects a normative weakness given that both SS ranges are within the normative weakness range and overlap to form the composite. And third, with respect to Reading Comprehension (ACC/RC), performance at the composite level is within the normative weakness range, however, reading comprehension ability seems to vary considerably despite the overlap in bands that forms this composite. Examiner A concluded (with the assistance of information provided in Appendix F on test characteristics) that the nature of the task demands on the WJ III Passage Comprehension test, which uses a cloze procedure to evaluate comprehension, caused Carsam's measured performance to be lower than when his comprehension was measured by a task requiring only recall of facts and information as on the WIAT-II Reading Comprehension test. This finding was consistent with other data available to Examiner A that suggested Carsam's reading comprehension was adversely affected as a function of the manner in which comprehension was to be demonstrated.

In sum, Carsam displays normative-based weaknesses in each of the three academic areas that were evaluated. Although the specific reasons for his relatively poor performance are, as yet, unknown, Examiner A is confident that there were no extraneous or confounding variables during testing that may have affected the validity of Carsam's test performance. Thus, because the null hypothesis that Carsam's academic functioning is within normal limits cannot be maintained in light of the collected evidence, it may be reasonably rejected in favor of the alternative. Given that the essential test for LD at this level is whether academic performance is within normal limits, and that the data suggest the answer to this question is "no," Examiner A concluded that it was appropriate to continue to the next level in the assessment process.

Level I-B: Evaluation of Exclusionary Factors

Although many possibilities related to Carsam's observed learning difficulties had been raised and investigated during the prereferral process, Examiner A recognized the value in carefully reviewing the collected data and evaluating it within the context of Carsam's unique experiences, present circumstances, and overall situation. Examiner A knew that in accordance with IDEA regulations, it was necessary to make sure that any problems identified in the course of the assessment could not be ascribed primarily to factors such as sensory-motor impairment, cultural or linguistic differences, environmental or economic disadvantage, or other such attenuating variables. In general, Examiner A needed to evaluate whether the observed normative deficits found in Level I-A were the result of factors *external* to Carsam or if they were *noncognitive* in nature. Through interviews and review of available school records and documents, Examiner A learned that Carsam was a native English speaker and that both of his parents were high school graduates whose language was advanced enough to support school learning in the home. Carsam and his family were very well acculturated into the mainstream and could trace their roots back several generations. Carsam's parents were both employed and neither parent had reported any economic difficulties or problems in being able to provide suitable maintenance for him. According to the nurse, Carsam's hearing and vision were well within normal limits and he was of average height and weight for his age and appeared well nourished and healthy.

In reviewing prior information, including interview information and observational data, Examiner A concluded that factors such as lack of motivation, poor attitude, disinterest, or emotional disturbance were not present and could not serve as reasonable explanatory correlates to the deficiencies identified at Level I-A. In addition, according to his parents and his teacher, Carsam displayed normal progress in mathematics, age-appropriate skill in gross and fine motor abilities, typical language development and ability, and solid interpersonal friendships. These observations made it clear that Carsam was unlikely to have any type of severe or pervasive developmental problem, such as mental retardation. Ultimately, the only factor that seemed somewhat plausible with respect to Carsam's learning difficulties revolved around his attendance record. In his third-grade year, he had missed approximately 20 days of school due to a chronic respiratory problem. However, his attendance before and after third grade was relatively good, with only an average of about 6 to 10 absences in any given year. Examiner A concluded that although his absences were probably somewhat of a *contributory* factor in his learning problems, they could not be reasonably considered as the *primary* cause of his difficulties. The absences may have affected his learning to some degree, but they were deemed not to be excessive and therefore insufficient to account for the significant problems that had been observed in his academic performance. Having considered and rejected reasonable hypotheses related to potential external causes of Carsam's academic difficulties, Examiner A felt confident that advancement to Level II-A in the assessment process was warranted and appropriate.

Level II-A: Inter-Cognitive Analysis—Performance in Abilities/Processes and Learning Efficiency

Methods.   The main focus of Level II-A assessment is measurement and evaluation of broad cognitive abilities, particularly those that underlie development and acquisition of academic skills. Assessment at this level reflects one of the criterion in IDEA related to the identification of learning disabilities that specifies the presence of a cognitive processing deficit presumed to be responsible for the manifest learning difficulties. IDEA is rather vague regarding the exact meaning of "basic psychological processes" (§300.7) and most states leave the definition rather ambiguous. In any event, more rigor is provided by specification of psychological processes (basic, advanced, or otherwise) within the context of a modern, empirically supported theoretical framework. Evaluation of the stratum II, broad abilities, as specified in CHC theory and described previously, is wholly consistent with both the spirit and intent of the regulation in IDEA. Additional measurement and specification rigor is generated through the use of CHC Cross-Battery guiding principles, in particular the requirement for adequately representing a construct by using two or more qualitatively different indicators. Although there was some adherence to this principle at Level I-A, it was not strictly necessary because the vague and mostly descriptive LD definitions found in IDEA (and the corresponding Academic Clinical Composites we have operationalized) do not represent actual theoretical constructs. Without theory to predict the existence of and define meaningful constructs, little can be done to improve their measurement, and such are the concessions to best practices resulting from arbitrary and imprecise definitions that lack any theoretical foundation. In contrast, evaluation of cognitive abilities within the CHC theoretical framework, combined with CHC Cross-Battery assessment principles, represents a highly sophisticated method for reliably and validly measuring abilities specifically defined by theory.

Examiner A's current assessment is a selective one, focused on particular areas of functioning in an attempt to evaluate specific causes of Carsam's observed learning difficulties. Naturally, since assessment at Level I-A was limited to the areas of concern as dictated by the referral information, selection of broad cognitive abilities to be evaluated at Level II-A should also be equally focused and *related* to academic abilities measured at Level I-A. Fortunately, there is some correspondence between the legal and theoretical specifications of LD constructs such that both suggest the presence of a logical link between cognitive processes and academic functioning. Thus, Examiner A began Level II-A assessment by reviewing the extant research and knowledge base that links development or acquisition of particular academic skills with specific cognitive abilities. Examiner A noted that according to the literature, one of the most robust findings is that reading difficulties are very often associated with difficulties in phonological processing (the sound patterns of language) and phonemic awareness (the sounds of language). Based on this information (see Chapter 2), Examiner A concluded that assessment of auditory processing abilities (*Ga*) was perhaps most warranted. In a further review of the literature, Examiner A also learned that reading and writing ability seem to depend in large part on an acquired store of knowledge, including lexical knowledge, vocabulary, and general information. These abilities are subsumed under *Gc* or crystallized intelligence, and Examiner A decided to include it as another important ability to be evaluated. And finally, because there appears to be a moderate link with reading and writing, and because there had been reports of problems with simple copying from the board, Examiner A felt that investigation of short-term memory functioning (*Gsm*) was also appropriate.

Examiner A had an additional issue to consider at this level. Because he worked in a state that mandated the use of a global ability score for calculating an ability-achievement discrepancy (even though discrepancy analysis is allowed but not specifically required under the provisions of IDEA) as part of the criteria for establishing the presence of a specific learning disability, Examiner A wanted to assemble a cross-battery that could provide all of the necessary data but that remained efficient in terms of time and effort. Upon reviewing the CHC Cross-Battery worksheets for *Ga*, *Gc*, and *Gsm* (see Appendix A), Examiner A realized that a Selective Cross-Battery (S-CB) consisting of four tests from the WJ III Tests of Cognitive Ability and all four tests from the Wechsler Abbreviated Scales of Intelligence (WASI) would provide the best combination of tests to suit his needs.

Discrepancy analysis, as has been discussed in prior chapters, is often an illogical and technically invalid method of determining the presence of LD, and use of an abbreviated global ability score for this purpose does not make it any less illogical. By definition, a brief global ability score tends to be rather narrow and limited in capturing performance that spans the full range of intellectual abilities. An ability composite that is based only on a few tests, none of which the individual has any deficits, will very likely lead to the identification of significant discrepancies. On the other hand, use of a global ability score that is quite comprehensive may prove inadequate and inappropriate for discrepancy analysis precisely because it can be attenuated by very low scores on tests that tap actual cognitive deficits leading to a failure to find a significant discrepancy. Thus, the chances of finding a significant discrepancy would seem to be a function of both the particular deficits that a given individual may have and the specific composition of tests that comprise the brief global ability score. Therefore, whenever a brief ability score is contemplated for use in calculating discrepancies with regression-based or other mathematical formulas, it is imperative that these issues be closely examined. Moreover, discrepancy analysis is only one small part of the much larger process of LD identification and cannot stand alone as irrefutable evidence of LD. In the final analysis, professional judgment will dictate the manner in and extent to which a brief global ability score (e.g., the WASI FSIQ-4, WJ III BIA) is appropriate for use in the evaluation process. Brief measures of intelligence and global ability, however, are unsuitable and should not be used for diagnostic purposes (e.g., identification of mental retardation or giftedness).

In addition to generating a reliable global ability score, another benefit of Examiner A's selection of the WASI is that it also provides adequate representation of *Gc*. Use of the WJ III adds only four additional tests but offers information about certain broad abilities not available from any other cognitive battery—namely, *Ga* or auditory processing ability—while at the same time providing adequate representation for measuring *Gsm*. Again, the selective nature of the assessment leads to a significant reduction in test-related activities and keeps the number of tests to be administered to a minimum. As is evident in this example, Examiner A's eight-subtest WASI/WJ III cross-battery adequately measures the three main broad areas of concern (*Ga*, *Gc*, *Gsm*) related to reading and writing plus it provides an estimate of overall ability using only four subtests—less than what would be required from the administration of the WISC-III or the WJ III in their entirety. The final WASI/WJ III cross-battery assembled by examiner A is presented in Table 14.3.

Analysis.   Examiner A began inter-cognitive analysis by completing the CHC Cross-Battery Data Summary and Normative Analysis Graph designed specifically for Level II-A analysis (see Appendix D2). As before, the Data Summary (Figure 14.4) simply provides a numerically based table that organizes the collected data. However, whereas the data collected at Level I-A were arranged by LD area, at this level they are organized in accordance with the stratum II, broad abilities specified by CHC theory. Likewise, the Normative Analysis Graph (Figure 14.5) is arranged in similar fashion but provides a more visual representation of results and is generally easier to interpret. Although there are suspicions of dysfunction, particularly because the process of assessment has advanced this far and there has already been documentation of some normative deficits in academic functioning, interpretation remains hypothesis driven in the sense that the expectation is that Carsam will perform within normal limits (i.e., standard scores of 85 to 115, inclusive) in each of the broad-ability areas being measured.

A review of the data obtained following administration of the WASI/WJ III cross-battery developed by Examiner A revealed the formation of three valid, broad-ability clusters (*Gc*, *Gsm*, *Ga*), and the measurement of two individual narrow abilities, *Gf*—Induction and *Gv*—Spatial Relations. All three broad-ability clusters are interpretable because their validity is assured through the use of two qualitatively different narrow-ability indicators and because the resultant SS bands for each narrow-ability pair overlap (within each broad-ability domain). If the cross-battery developed by Examiner A had used two narrow-ability indi-

TABLE 14.3   WASI/WJ III Cross-Battery Cognitive Assessment for Carsam

| WASI/WJ III COGNITIVE CROSS-BATTERY | | | | CHC BROAD-ABILITY CLUSTERS |
| WASI | | WJ III | | |
TEST 1	TEST 2	TEST 1	TEST 2	
Similarities (LD)	Vocabulary (VL)			Gc – Crystallized Intelligence
Matrix Reasoning (I)				Gf – Fluid Reasoning
Block Design (SR, Vz)				Gv – Visual Processing
		Memory for Words (MS)	Auditory Working Memory (MW)	Gsm – Short-term Memory
				Glr – Long-term Retrieval
		Sound Blending (PC:S)	Auditory Attention (US/U3)	Ga – Auditory Processing
				Gs – Processing Speed

Note: Shading indicates adequate representation of CHC ability.

FIGURE 14.4 Level II-A: Data Summary for Inter-Cognitive Analysis

Name: Carsam	Age: 10 Grade: 5	CHC Cross-Battery Inter-Cognitive Analysis
Examiner: A	Date: 10/24	Level II-A: Data Summary

Cluster	Test Battery	Subtest Name + (CHC ability code)	Standard Score	Standard Score Confidence Interval	Percentile Rank	Classification
Gc (Crystallized Intelligence)		**Gc Cluster Average =**	83	78-88	13	L. Average
	WASI	Similarities (LD)	80	73-87	9	L. Average
	WASI	Vocabulary (VL)	85	78-92	16	L. Average
Gf (Fluid Reasoning)		**Gf Cluster Average =**				
	WASI	Matrix Reasoning (I)	90	83-97	25	Average
Gv (Visual Processing)		**Gv Cluster Average =**				
	WASI	Block Design (SR,Vz)	95	88-102	38	Average
Gsm (Short-term Memory)		**Gsm Cluster Average =**	92	87-97	29	Average
	WJ III	Memory for Words (MS)	95	88-102	38	Average
	WJ III	Auditory Working Memory (MW)	88	81-95	21	L. Average
Glr (Long-term Retrieval)		**Glr Cluster Average =**				
Ga (Auditory Processing)		**Ga Cluster Average =**	72	67-77	3	Low
	WJ III	Auditory Attention (US/U3)	68	61-75	2	V. Low
	WJ III	Sound Blending (PC:S)	75	68-82	5	Low
Gs (Processing Speed)		**Gs Cluster Average =**				

Note: All standard scores are based on age norms **Confidence Bands:** • Clusters = ± 5 • Subtests = ± 7

FIGURE 14.5   Level II-A: Normative Analysis Graph for Inter-Cognitive Analysis

Name: Carsam   Age: 10 Grade: 5

Examiner: A   Date: 10/24

CHC Cross-Battery Inter-Cognitive Analysis
Level II-A: Normative Analysis Graph

Confidence Bands: • Clusters = ± 5 • Subtests = ± 7

-1 SEM |← 68 % →| +1 SEM

Performance Classification	Very Low	Low	L Avg.	Average	H.Avg.	Sup.	Very Superior
Percentile Ranks	≤ 2	3 - 8	9 - 24	25 - 75	76-97	92 - 97	98 - 99+

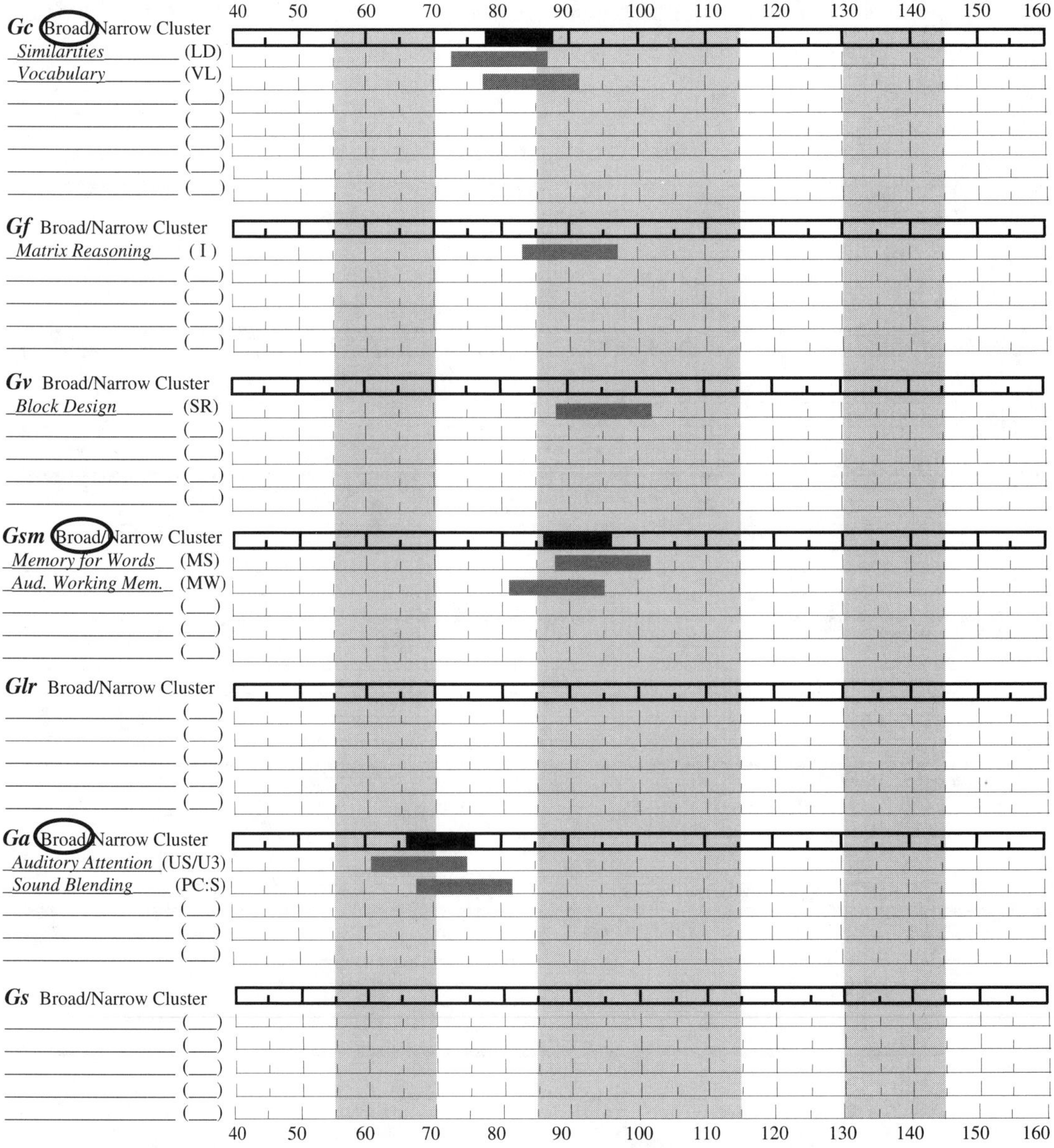

Gc Broad/Narrow Cluster
 Similarities (LD)
 Vocabulary (VL)
 (___)
 (___)
 (___)
 (___)
 (___)

Gf Broad/Narrow Cluster
 Matrix Reasoning (I)
 (___)
 (___)
 (___)
 (___)

Gv Broad/Narrow Cluster
 Block Design (SR)
 (___)
 (___)
 (___)
 (___)

Gsm Broad/Narrow Cluster
 Memory for Words (MS)
 Aud. Working Mem. (MW)
 (___)
 (___)
 (___)

Glr Broad/Narrow Cluster
 (___)
 (___)
 (___)
 (___)
 (___)

Ga Broad/Narrow Cluster
 Auditory Attention (US/U3)
 Sound Blending (PC:S)
 (___)
 (___)
 (___)

Gs Broad/Narrow Cluster
 (___)
 (___)
 (___)
 (___)
 (___)

40   50   60   70   80   90   100   110   120   130   140   150   160

NORMATIVE RANGE CLASSIFICATION	Normative Weakness	Normal Limits	Normative Strength
	Greater than 1 SD below mean	± 1 SD from mean	Greater than 1 SD above mean

cators of the same type (e.g., two measures of *Gf*—Induction) for any given broad construct, or if the SS bands for two different narrow-ability indicators did not overlap, interpretation of performance in the broad-ability domains would not have been appropriate. Although the WASI included measures of *Gf* and *Gv*, use of a single narrow-ability indicator precludes interpretation of either the broad-ability cluster or any narrow-ability cluster (i.e., a cluster formed by two qualitatively similar narrow ability indicators such as two measures of *Gf*-I). Single tests provide only an estimate of functioning relative to the narrow ability being measured.

Interpretation. Carsam's performance with respect to *Gc*, Crystallized Intelligence, can be interpreted as being within the Low to Low-Average range (SS = 78–88). His performance on Similarities, a measure of language development (LD) is slightly lower (SS range = 73–87) but not significantly different from his performance on Vocabulary (SS range = 78–92), a measure of lexical knowledge (VL), because both SS bands overlap considerably. Because the SS band for the *Gc* cluster and the individual bands for *Gc*-LD and *Gc*-VL (Similarities and Vocabulary, respectively) all span into the range of normal limits (i.e., 85 to 115 inclusive), *Gc* cannot be construed definitively as a Normative Weakness. Nevertheless, because performance falls almost entirely within the Low to Low-Average classifications, it is clear that *Gc* is an area in which Carsam has not fully attained proficiency in acquiring knowledge and that he is still somewhat limited in this area of functioning.

Carsam's overall short-term memory ability can be interpreted as being within the Low-Average to Average range (SS range = 87–97). His performance on Memory for Words (SS range = 88–102), a measure of memory span (MS), is slightly higher but not significantly different from his performance on Auditory Working Memory (SS range = 81–95), which is a measure of working memory (MW), because both SS bands overlap considerably. Additionally, because the SS band for the *Gsm* cluster and the individual bands for *Gsm*-MS and *Gsm*-MW either fall entirely within or span well into the range of normal limits (i.e., 85 to 115 inclusive), *Gsm* can be reliably interpreted as being within normal limits. Again, the logic behind this conclusion is perhaps most evident in the graphic representation in Figure 14.5, which clearly illustrates that two of three SS bands fall entirely within normal limits and the third falls much more in the normal limit than weakness range. This pattern of results differs qualitatively from that of *Gc* primarily because performance never drops below the Low-Average range in contrast to the SS bands for *Gc* where all three SS bands overlapped the Low classification range. Therefore, in *Gsm,* Carsam does appear to have attained a general level of proficiency.

A review of Carsam's performance with respect to *Ga* reveals that his overall auditory processing ability can be interpreted as being Very Low to Low (SS range = 67–77). His performance on Auditory Attention (SS range = 61–75), a measure of speech and general sound discrimination (US/U3), is slightly lower but not significantly different from his performance on Sound Blending (SS range = 68–82), a measure of phonetic coding–synthesis (PC:S), because the SS bands overlap each other. Moreover, because the SS band for the *Ga* cluster and the individual bands for *Ga*-US/U3 and *Ga*-PC:S all fall completely outside the range of normal limits (i.e., 85 to 115 inclusive), *Ga* can be reliably interpreted as a Normative Weakness. Figure 14.5 provides an illustration of these conclusions where it is evident that performance along *Ga* never reaches the range of Normal Limits and only one SS band (*Ga*-PC:S) extends very slightly into the Low-Average classification. In comparison to performance on *Gc* and *Gsm*, *Ga* demonstrates a relatively unambiguous pattern of perfor-mance that cannot be considered normal or average to any degree. Carsam's ability or proficiency in processing and working with auditory information and stimuli is quite lim-ited.

In sum, the *a priori* hypothesis that Carsam's performance in each area would be within normal limits is not supported in the case of *Ga*, is more equivocal in the case of *Gc*, and is fully supported in the case of *Gsm*. The data gathered at this level of assessment suggest that the answer to the question, "Is cognitive performance within normal limits?" is most likely "no." The identification of normative-based weaknesses in performance along the various broad abilities that comprise the focus of assessment at this level represents the essential test for continuing the assessment process. This requirement is consistent with the regulations provided in IDEA that specify the existence of impairment in basic psychological processes necessary as the presumed underlying cause of manifest learning problems. Given that the available evidence provides a sufficient basis for concluding that at least one cognitive impairment exists, Examiner A concluded that it was appropriate to proceed to Level II-B assessment.

Level II-B: Reevaluation of Exclusionary Factors

Methods.   Inclusion of this step in assessment is primarily adherence to best practices but also reflects the iterative and recursive nature of LD determination. Whenever standardized tests are used in the course of an assessment, it is both necessary and prudent to ascertain whether performance, as measured through testing, is a reliable and valid estimate of true functioning or whether the results may be better explained via alternative factors apart from true ability. Accordingly, the very same process of evaluation of mitigating or exclusionary hypotheses described in Level I-B should be conducted once again. This is not to say that every potential hypothesis should be evaluated once more, but rather that care is taken to ensure that the observed deficits in performance reflected in the results of the standardized tests that were administered cannot be reasonably explained by any other factors external to the individual.

Although many external or environmentally related factors have probably already been ruled out prior to arriving at this level in the assessment process, there are noncognitive fac-tors that may yet operate to influence or attenuate test results. For example, lack of motiva-tion, poor attitude, disinterest, or emotional disturbance can represent transient influences that may not necessarily have been present or previously identified at earlier stages in the process but could well operate during this particular phase of testing. Examiner A thus con-sidered and rejected any reasonable, current hypotheses that could potentially have been related to the normative deficits identified in Carsam's cognitive abilities, and having found none, he proceeded to Level III.

Level III: Integrated Ability Analysis—Evaluation of Underachievement

Methods.   Examiner A's main goal at this level of the assessment process is to evaluate all of the collected test data in an integrated manner that seeks to uncover evidence that establishes the presence of underachievement. Underachievement is a component in the current operational definition as well as state and federal legislation (i.e., IDEA) and relates primarily to being able to substantiate that if not for a learning disability, academic performance would very likely be within normal limits. The manner in which this condition is evaluated rests primarily on the collection of evidence that suggests general or overall functioning, apart from specific areas of deficit, is intact and relatively unimpaired. Integrated ability analysis in this sense does not refer to the ipsatization of scores in search of relative-based strengths and weaknesses but rather the conjoint evaluation of data across the respective domains of cognitive and academic functioning. Integrated ability analysis within the context of LD determination involves no ipsatized scores whatsoever and centers only on evaluation of cognitive, academic, and other available data within the context of what is known about the individual in order to determine whether an actual pattern of underachievement exists.

Consistency Analysis.   Examiner A recognized that there must exist a logical or empirical relationship between any cognitive deficits identified at Level II-A and academic deficits identified at Level I-A. When either no deficits are found or spurious deficits are uncovered that are unrelated to specific referral concerns, the examiner may need to evaluate the sufficiency of the evaluation at this level and perhaps even return to previous levels to reexamine the manifest difficulties with greater specificity and better measurement. Because Examiner A had deliberately and intentionally selected which broad cognitive areas should be assessed as a function of their empirical relationship to the development and acquisition of reading and writing skills, and because the assessment was selectively focused only on these broad abilities, the nature of the evaluative decision at hand proved relatively straightforward. The observed Level II-A cognitive deficits found by Examiner A (*Ga*, and to an extent *Gc* as well) are indeed logically and empirically related to Carsam's academic difficulties as determined by Level I-A assessment (i.e., reading and writing).

This is an example of the relative efficiency of the selective approach to assessment versus those that may be unnecessarily complex or exploratory in nature. For example, had Examiner A adopted a more comprehensive approach, the construction of a cross-battery for Level II-A assessment may have resulted in measurement of constructs that were not of central interest or that bore uncertain relationships with the academic problems initially specified in the referral. Even in the present case where the approach was selective, Examiner A was left with measures of *Gf*-I and *Gv*-SR as a result of the need to use the WASI to obtain an estimate of global ability functioning. Comprehensive assessment of broad cognitive abilities at Level II-A, in the absence of established *a priori* links to suspected academic dysfunction, will yield data that require extremely careful and deliberate analysis, may fail to adequately assess the suspected area of dysfunction, and that may ultimately prove to be uninterpretable. In addition, selection of a different test or combination of tests, constraints from different regulations, unique or unusual referral demands, special measurement needs, and many other factors that affect prior assessment decisions may result in the creation of one or more unintended or irrelevant broad-ability constructs. An identified cognitive deficit (e.g., *Gs*) with no logical or empirical relationship to observed academic problems (e.g., oral language) provides no suitable or defensible basis for conclusions regarding the presence of a learning disability. The findings may be no more than anomalous and should not be construed as evidence of LD.

Had any deficient areas of cognitive functioning been found at Level II-A that could not be logically or empirically linked to the identified academic deficits found at Level I-A, it would have been most appropriate for Examiner A to evaluate the sufficiency of the cognitive assessment and perhaps would have necessitated a critical reevaluation of prereferral data and possibly the construction of a more specific and appropriate cognitive battery or the collection of different forms of data. In Carsam's case, Examiner A noted that deficits in reading and writing corresponded to identified deficits in auditory processing (*Ga*) and crystallized intelligence (*Gc*). In other words, there was *consistency* between performance on academic skills measures and performance on 9 measures of ability that underlie development of those skills.

The notion of consistency between cognitive and academic abilities is crucial because logic and theory specify not only which deficits should correspond to which but also, by implication, which should not. Because evaluations of suspected learning or other disabilities are generally concerned with performance that is dysfunctional in some way, examination of consistency refers only to related abilities that fall below and outside the general proficiency range (i.e., normative weakness). Consistencies among academic and cognitive abilities that fall within normal limits or higher do not inform the process of LD determination and are not evaluated. That is, if there is no logical or empirical relationship between a particular cognitive ability (e.g., *Gv*) and a particular academic skill (e.g., Oral Expression), then development of the latter is not specified as being significantly related to development of the former and it reveals nothing regarding LD. This does not mean, however, that cognitive abilities with little or no relationship to any identified academic deficits will automatically be within normal limits or that in the absence of any academic deficits that such abilities should be low or high. They are simply uncorrelated.

Because the notion of underachievement implies achievement that is below one's actual or true capacity, some evidence is necessary in order to demonstrate that global ability or general intellectual functioning remains otherwise intact. This requirement stems primarily from the need to differentiate learning disability from mental retardation or low general ability that results in low achievement. This is not to suggest that individuals who are mentally retarded or low functioning cannot be learning disabled, but rather that there is often a need to identify what may be the most salient and primary cause of any observed performance deficits. Should inter-cognitive (Level II-A) analysis suggest that all cognitive abilities are within the deficient range, then hypotheses regarding LD may need to yield to other hypotheses, including those related to variables likely to have a more pervasive impact on cognitive functioning and that offer a more accurate explanation regarding patterns of ability and disability. Evaluation of cognitive abilities unrelated to the specific academic deficits identified in Level I-A analysis thus represents a second and important component in analysis of consistency.

Examiner A reviewed the collected test data in Carsam's case and entered it into the CHC Cross-Battery Data Summary and Normative Analysis Graph designed specifically for Level III (see Appendix D3). Although the data summary sheet for this level of analysis is similar to the ones used in Levels I-A and II-A (see Figures 14.2 and 14.4 or Appendices E and D2), it is different in that it integrates all the broad cognitive and academic ability domains, thus providing a means for reviewing all data concurrently. In addition, the data from Level I-A analysis is now framed within CHC theoretical constructs as opposed to the Academic Clinical Composites used previously. The data, as entered by Examiner A on the data summary sheet, are illustrated in Figure 14.6. The Normative Analysis Graph provides graphical depiction of the full range of collected test data and, as before, tends to simplify analysis of the patterns. Examiner A completed this sheet and the results are shown in Figure 14.7.

At this point in the assessment, Examiner A has already established four important conditions for documenting LD, including (1) identification of one or more academic ability deficits, (2) identification of one or more cognitive ability deficits, (3) elimination of non-cognitive and external factors as the primary cause of the identified academic and cognitive deficits, and (4) consistency in deficit performance between cognitive and academic abilities that are empirically or logically related to each other. These conditions provide considerable support for the presence of a learning disability in Carsam's case, as related to reading and written language. However, Examiner A recognized that underachievement still needed to be determined by establishing support for intact general or global ability and functioning as derived from evaluation of data pertaining to cognitive abilities less related to the identified academic deficits.

After carefully reviewing the results as charted on the Normative Analysis Graph (see Figure 14.7), Examiner A concluded that there was sufficient evidence to support the notion of normal functioning in areas largely unrelated to the development or acquisition of reading and writing skills. This evidence included the fact that the broad cluster representing short-term memory (*Gsm*) was within normal limits and that the single narrow-ability measures for both *Gf* and *Gv* fell well within the average range. In addition, Examiner A knew from prereferral information that Carsam was not having any difficulties in other core subject areas such as math, had achieved his early childhood developmental milestones without delay, and had never displayed any type of adaptive behavior problem. Thus, without using any measure of global ability, Examiner A was able to defend his opinion and conclude confidently that Carsam's general or overall intellectual functioning was relatively normal or average and was not pervasively or extensively impaired to any degree. Nevertheless, because Examiner A was required by his state's law to derive a global ability score, this information was available to him and calculation of the WASI FSIQ-4 revealed that it was also within the average range (SS = 91). Thus, Carsam's cognitive deficits in *Ga* and *Gc* appear to be rather circumscribed and are evident in what is an otherwise unremarkable or normal ability profile, effectively eliminating the possibility that performance might be due to any substantial, broad-based impairment.

Discrepancy Analysis.   The pattern of results up to this point in Carsam's case provide clear and convincing evidence to support the notion that the essential test for Level III analysis (establishing underachievement) has been met. As such, Examiner A could very well have proceeded confidently to the next phase in assessment. However, Examiner A recognized that his state education statutes contained specific requirements for establishing underachievement (and by definition, LD) not through consistency analysis, but through discrepancy analysis. Although IDEA allows its use in determining LD, it does not specifically require or mandate identification of any significant discrepancy for establishing eligibility under the category of specific learning disability (SLD). Interpretations of IDEA notwithstanding, the state education code and district policy influenced Examiner A's decisions

FIGURE 14.6 Level III: Data Summary for Intregrated Ability Analysis

Name: Carsam Age: 10 Grade: 5
Examiner: A Date: 10/24

CHC Cross-Battery Integrated Ability Analysis
Level III – Data Summary

Cluster	Test Battery	Subtest Name + (CHC ability code)	Standard Score	Standard Score Confidence Interval	Percentile Rank	Classification
Grw (Reading/Writing Ability)		*Grw Cluster Average =*	74	69-79	4	Low
	WIAT-II	Spelling	77	70-84	3	Low
	WIAT-II	Written Expression	61	54-68	1	V. Low
	WIAT-II	Word Reading	78	71-85	8	Low
	WJ III	Reading Vocabulary	72	65-79	3	Low
	WIAT-II	Reading Comprehension	85	78-92	16	L. Average
	WJ III	Passage Comprehension	73	66-80	3	Low
Gc (Crystallized Intelligence)		*Gc Cluster Average =*	83	78-88	13	L. Average
	WASI	Similarities (LD)	80	73-87	9	L. Average
	WASI	Vocabulary (VL)	85	78-92	16	L. Average
Gq (Quantitative Knowledge)		*Gq Cluster Average =*				
Gf (Fluid Reasoning)		*Gf Cluster Average =*				
	WASI	Matrix Reasoning (I)	90	83-17	25	Average
Gv (Visual Processing)		*Gv Cluster Average =*				
	WASI	Block Design (SR,Vz)	95	88-102	50	Average
Gsm (Short-term Memory)		*Gsm Cluster Average =*	92	87-97	29	Average
	WJ III	Memory for Words (MS)	95	88-102	38	Average
	WJ III	Auditory Working Memory (MW)	88	81-95	21	Average
Glr (Long-term Retrieval)		*Glr Cluster Average =*				
Ga (Auditory Processing)		*Ga Cluster Average =*	72	67-77	3	Low
	WJ III	Auditory Attention (US/U3)	68	61-75	2	V. Low
	WJ III	Sound Blending (PC:S)	75	68-82	5	Low
Gs (Processing Speed)		*Gs Cluster Average =*				

Note: All standard scores are based on age norms   **Confidence Bands:** • Clusters = ± 5 • Subtests = ± 7

FIGURE 14.7   Level III: Normative Analysis Graph for Integrated Ability Analysis

Name: __Carsam__   Age: _10_ Grade: _5_

Examiner: __A__   Date: __10/24__

CHC Cross-Battery Integrated Ability Analysis
Level III - Normative Analysis Graph

Confidence Bands: • Clusters = ± 5 • Subtests = ± 7

-1 SEM ←—68 %—→ +1 SEM

Performance Classification	Very Low	Low	L Avg.	Average	H.Avg.	Sup.	Very Superior
Percentile Ranks	≤ 2	3 - 8	9 - 24	25 - 75	76-97	92 - 97	98 - 99+

Grw Broad/Narrow Cluster
- _Spelling_ (SG)
- _Written Expression_ (WA)
- _Word Reading_ (RD)
- _Reading Vocabulary_ (V)
- _Reading Compr._ (RC)
- _Passage Compr._ (CZ)

Gc Broad/Narrow Cluster
- _Similarities_ (LD)
- _Vocabulary_ (VL)
- (_)
- (_)
- (_)
- (_)

Gq Broad/Narrow Cluster
- (_)
- (_)
- (_)
- (_)

Gf Broad/Narrow Cluster
- _Matrix Reasoning_ (I)
- (_)
- (_)
- (_)

Gv Broad/Narrow Cluster
- _Block Design_ (SR)
- (_)
- (_)
- (_)

Gsm Broad/Narrow Cluster
- _Memory for Words_ (MS)
- _Aud. Working Mem._ (MW)
- (_)
- (_)

Glr Broad/Narrow Cluster
- (_)
- (_)
- (_)
- (_)

Ga Broad/Narrow Cluster
- _Auditory Attention_ (US/U3)
- _Sound Blending_ (PC:S)
- (_)
- (_)

Gs Broad/Narrow Cluster
- (_)
- (_)
- (_)
- (_)

NORMATIVE RANGE CLASSIFICATION	Normative Weakness Greater than 1 SD below mean	Normal Limits ± 1 SD from mean	Normative Strength Greater than 1 SD above mean

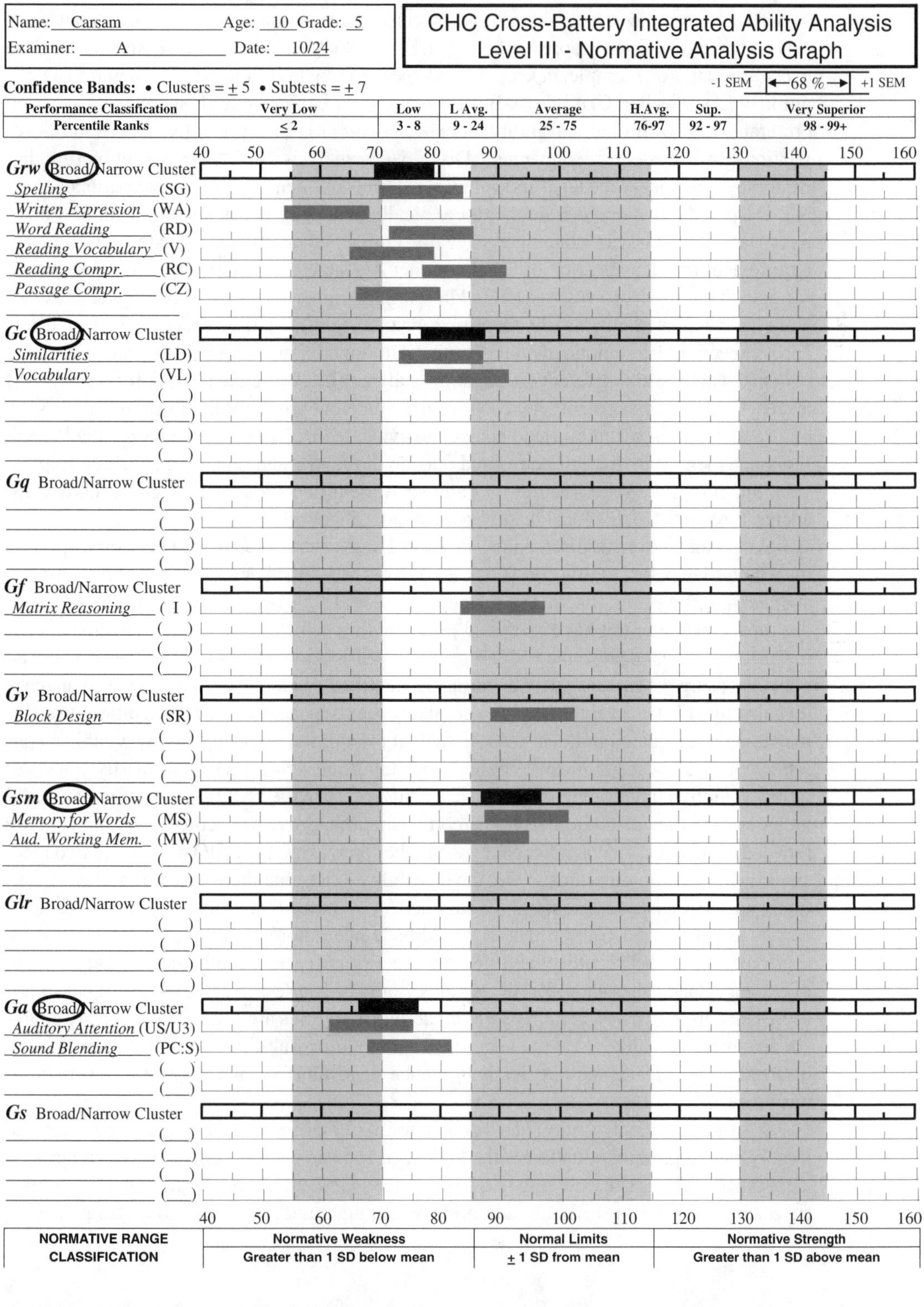

early on in the assessment process because of the eventual need for a global ability score to use in discrepancy analysis (hence his selection of the WASI over other instruments). It is important to recognize that if there was no specific requirement to conduct discrepancy analysis or if no global ability score were needed, Examiner A's choices for assessment may have been different. For example, in keeping with the components of the present operational definition of LD as well as CHC Cross-Battery methods, use of an aptitude score may have been preferable to an overall global ability score because of its greater predictive power and closer relationship to academic achievement. Discrepancy analysis too often represents yet another example of the misguided legal and policy constraints frequently placed on practitioners.

Despite the fact that it is neither theoretically necessary nor in keeping with best practices, Examiner A was nonetheless legally compelled to meet his state's discrepancy requirement for identification of LD. Examiner A's state regulations called for the use of a formula that corrects for regression, addressing the imperfect correlation between tests of ability and achievement, and the identification of a significant discrepancy based on differences exceeding 1.5 standard deviation units. Although Examiner A could conceivably have conducted at least six different discrepancy analyses (i.e., using the FSIQ-4 from the WASI and each test of achievement), he recognized the inherent problems involved in making such multiple comparisons and instead decided to evaluate discrepancies using only the WIAT-II achievement tests that fell below and outside of the average range (i.e., Written Expression, Spelling, and Word Reading). Examiner A identified statistically significant discrepancies as required by his local district policy and state regulations.

After conducting his discrepancy analysis, Examiner A noted that had Carsam's performance on Matrix Reasoning and Block Design of the WASI been lower but still within the average range, it is possible that no discrepancy would have been found or that the observed discrepancies might not have exceeded the standard set forth by state law. This may occur in Carsam's case, because the FSIQ-4 of the WASI is attenuated—having been comprised of two measures of *Gc* that partly underlie his identified academic deficits. Level III analysis revealed that *Gc* (in addition to *Ga*) were likely the root causes of the difficulties observed in reading as evaluated in Level I-A. As such, it is natural to expect that they would be *consistent*; that is, low academic performance in reading and writing occurs primarily as a result of low cognitive functioning in *Gc* and *Ga*. Thus, because the FSIQ-4 score from the WASI includes measures of *Gc* to derive the composite, this drove the score down and actually reduced the chances that a discrepancy would be found. Had the FSIQ-4 included two measures of *Gc* and two measures of *Ga*, the possibility exists that there would have been absolutely no discrepancy. Interestingly, Examiner A also noted that if the FSIQ-4 were actually comprised of *Gc* and *Ga* abilities, it would have been more akin to an aptitude score—a score comprised specifically of abilities most necessary for the development and acquisition of reading. Hence, the search for discrepancy would be fruitless in cases where global ability scores that are based to a certain extent on deficient abilities are used in discrepancy analysis. Examiner A realized that the very selection of a broad-ability score for the purposes of discrepancy analysis alone can greatly influence the results from what is already a very dubious process.

In summary, identification of a discrepancy in Carsam's case was legally necessary but largely meaningless. Evaluation of the logical and consistent relationship between his deficient broad abilities (i.e., *Ga* and, to a lesser extent, *Gc*) and his deficient academic abilities (in reading and writing) had already provided enough evidence to demonstrate plausible, even theoretically predicted, explanations and support for circumscribed underachievement within an otherwise average ability profile. Identification of an ability-achievement discrepancy was an exercise in legal compliance only, and provided no additional diagnostic information upon which determination of LD was logically or theoretically necessary. By evaluating patterns in the data within the context of the operational definition contained in the comprehensive assessment framework, Examiner A was readily able to determine that Carsam met the essential test at this level concerning evaluation of underachievement. Consistency analysis alone is clearly capable of providing sufficient evidence to warrant continuation of the assessment process in efforts to definitively establish the presence of a learning disability irrespective of the presence or absence of any type of discrepancy.

Level IV: Evaluation of Interference with Functioning

Because Examiner A had designed the assessment of Carsam's abilities in a careful, systematic way using the comprehensive framework for LD assessment and CHC Cross-Battery assessment methods, evaluation as to whether Carsam's measured deficits actually interfere with his learning has already been substantially verified. Beginning with Level I-A analysis, continuation of the assessment process is contingent on the identification of normative weaknesses in academic performance. If no normative deficits are identified in the measured academic abilities in Level I-A, then school-based learning with respect to skill development can hardly be construed as problematic or dysfunctional. Moreover, Levels I-B and II-B analyses ensure that any deficits that are observed are indeed related to actual performance and not to any extrinsic variables or confounding influences. When coupled with CHC Cross-Battery methods, by the time assessment has reached Level IV analysis, the comprehensive framework for LD determination has almost fully established that any identified learning disabilities probably do adversely affect educational performance. Examiner A recognized that this level of analysis represents somewhat of a safety valve that can prevent the misidentification of learning disabilities in cases where the comprehensive framework for LD determination has not been followed, where CHC Cross-Battery assessment has not been utilized or the guiding principles severely compromised, where little if any attention has been paid to exclusionary variables, where dysfunctional classroom performance has not been demonstrated, and where the search for discrepancies has clouded the fact that functioning must be normatively, not relatively, deficient.

Analysis of the data obtained in Carsam's case clearly shows deficits in reading and writing at Level I-A, corresponding cognitive ability deficits at Level II-A, and a pattern of underachievement in the context of a relatively normal ability profile at Level III. Carsam's cognitive deficits are seen to be strongly related to the reported classroom learning difficulties. Although there is no set or standard criteria by which to make such an evaluation, a good rule of thumb is to base conclusions on data that show achievement to be substantially below that of the average person in the general population (i.e., normative comparison). Examiner A took a very broad survey of the entire range of data collected in the course of assessing Carsam (not just test data) and concluded that ample evidence existed to support his professional opinion that Carsam's everyday "real-world" classroom performance was directly and adversely affected by the presence of the identified learning difficulties in reading and writing. Consequently, Examiner A felt comfortable in offering an opinion that Carsam was indeed learning disabled.

Had Examiner A believed that Carsam's academic and cognitive difficulties did not result in any significant academic failure or substantial restriction and limitation in his daily life that required these particular skills (reading and writing), he may have concluded rightly that Carsam possessed learning *problems* but was not learning *disabled*. The distinction here is more than just semantic. It reflects the very purpose of this level of evaluation, which is to underscore the fact that disabling conditions require some type of significant, manifest impairment. For example, even under the auspices of IDEA, individuals may not be determined to be eligible for special education services for any disabling condition or category unless there is evidence that the disability adversely affects educational performance (which includes nonacademic activities, such as physical education, etc.). In the case of such profound disabilities as severe mental retardation, deafness or blindness, or major orthopedic impairments, the adverse effect requirement is clearly met. In the case of milder forms of disabilities (e.g., attention deficit disorder), adverse effects on educational performance are not always so evident. Such is the case with learning disabilities.

Justification for Intervention

Although Examiner A has established all five of the essential components for LD determination, it is important to remember that any conclusions emanating from assessment must be supportable by additional sources of data and that appropriate interventions should be developed. In general, if the process of assessment has been followed in a manner similar to the framework outlined in this chapter, it is very likely that considerable evidence will be available that provides convergent validity for whatever conclusions have been made. In the case of Carsam, Examiner A already has considerable evidence from a wide variety of sources that provide additional support for the diagnosis of LD that has been made. For example, data from review of Carsam's school records, collection of authentic work samples, direct behavioral and interactive observations during reading and written language instruction, and informational interviews with his teachers and parents, all reveal patterns of academic dysfunction in reading and writing that are unexplainable by any other factors. Moreover, the deficits uncovered in Carsam's case by Examiner A are fully consistent with the information and documentation generated from the prereferral process and every attempt has been made to consider mitigating and exclusionary hypotheses. Examiner A's assessment has been thorough, systematic, theoretically based, hypothesis driven, and consistent with best practices in assessment and statistical analysis. Examiner A feels confident that the results of this assessment, as documented in the report in Appendix G, are reliable and valid and represent a wholly defensible approach in the assessment of learning disability. Examiner A also recognized that assessment must always be linked to intervention and that the data collected in the course of Carsam's assessment should serve as the basis for the development of appropriate remedial programs and services, irrespective of whether Carsam is or is not learning disabled. Learning problems are not resolved merely because an individual is assessed. Assessment is simply a necessary step toward enhancing the learning process and improving academic functioning. No matter what the results of assessment reveal, it is important to use all available data as a guide for developing and justifying specific instructional interventions that address the unique learning needs of the individual.

Conclusions

Current legal mandates at both the federal and state levels continue to influence the practice of LD assessment in ways that remain atheoretical, illogical, and ambiguous. In the case of Carsam, the examiner was legally required to engage in certain practices that provided more confusion, led to unnecessary expenditures of time and effort, and in the end did nothing to enhance or contribute to the process of determining LD. For example, Examiner A's state regulations (as is common in many states) required that he engage in the process of ability-achievement discrepancy in order to establish LD. To do so, Examiner A needed to generate a full-scale IQ score, which he did rather efficiently by use of the WASI. But these efforts were superfluous because Examiner A had sufficient data with which to examine the consistency between cognitive abilities or processes and related academic achievement skills in order to establish the presence of LD. Given the current state of LD assessment and today's prevailing legal environment, the case of Carsam represents a compromise effort in that it was forced to retain one foot mired in antiquated definitions and practices while the other foot sought to step forward toward theory, better definitions, and modern assessment procedures.

The case of Carsam illustrates the various aspects involved in the assessment of learning disability as defined and operationalized throughout the chapters of this book. The rationale and need to couch the assessment of academic skills, and by implication LD, within the context of modern cognitive theory was discussed in Chapter 2. The *Desk Reference* component of this volume (Chapters 4–10) accomplishes this task by providing practitioners the information necessary to evaluate the suitability of any given test of achievement for any given purpose in assessment. In particular, information is provided on the broad and narrow abilities measured by each test within the context of CHC theory. Application of theory to the assessment of learning disabilities is perhaps one of the most significant advances necessary if LD assessment is to move out of the dark ages. Chapter 11 provided a detailed operational definition that is practical, logical, and driven mainly by the specifications of modern cognitive theory. Development of useful operational models of LD have been notoriously poor in the utilization and application of theory and the result has been the perpetuation of vague, nebulous, and ill-defined constructs that have been virtually impossible to measure reliably.

Chapters 12 and 13 presented the CHC Cross-Battery approach, including methods and procedures for measurement and interpretation that provide a modern and psychometrically defensible basis from which reliable and valid inferences can be drawn. This final chapter provided yet another crucial component to the LD determination process—a comprehensive assessment framework that adheres to best practices in cognitive and academic evaluation while incorporating the proposed operational definition and the CHC Cross-Battery methods that serve as the foundation for technical adequacy and statistical rigor. We believe that assessment of learning disability will remain elusive and misguided until these components—theory, definition, and assessment—are fully integrated in clinical practice. What we have proposed here is but one example of how such integration can be readily accomplished, and it is our hope that it can guide practitioners everywhere toward a more cohesive and common frame of reference with respect to their own efforts at evaluating LD.

CHC Cross-Battery Worksheets

The following information pertains to all CHC Cross-Battery worksheets included in this Appendix. These worksheets were adapted from McGrew and Flanagan (1998), Flanagan, McGrew, and Ortiz (2000), and Flanagan and Ortiz (2001).

Tests printed in bold, uppercase letters are strong measures as defined empirically; tests printed in bold, lowercase letters are moderate measures as defined empirically; tests printed in regular-face, lowercase letters were classified logically through expert consensus.

Tests printed in regular-face, lowercase letters annotated by a superscripted letter "a" (i.e., [a]) indicate that the broad and narrow abilities were both classified logically by the authors.

Tests printed in regular-face, lowercase letters annotated by a superscripted letter "b" (i.e., [b]) indicate that the broad ability was classified by expert consensus but the narrow abilities were classified logically by the authors.

In the case of tests with two narrow-ability classifications, the second classification is reported in parentheses. This classification system was described in Chapter 3 of this book; a description of how to use these worksheets appears in Chapter 12.

> * If a test score is on a standard score scale with a mean and standard deviation other than 100 and 15 respectively, record the score in the column marked by an asterisk. Refer to the *Percentile Rank and Standard Score Conversion Table* (Appendix B) to convert the score to the scale used in CHC Cross-Battery assessment (i.e., mean of 100, SD of 15). Record the new score in the next column.

> **If the cluster includes two or more qualitatively different broad CHC indicators, then place a (✓) next to the word *Broad* and record the appropriate CHC code in the parentheses. If the cluster includes indicators from only one narrow ability subsumed by the broad CHC ability, then place a (✓) next to the word *Narrow* and record the respective narrow ability code in the parentheses.

For a more complete description of the tests included on these worksheets, see the *Desk Reference* section of this book (Chapters 4–10).

Grw–R–READING ABILITY
CHC CROSS-BATTERY WORKSHEET

Battery or Test	Age	*Grw–R*–Reading Ability Narrow Ability Tests	LD Area	SS*	SS (100 ± 15)
		Reading Decoding (RD)			
Tests of Achievement					
DAB-3	6-14	Alphabet/Word Knowledge	BR		
DATA-2	12-18	Word Identification	BR		
GORT-4	6-18	Accuracy	BR		
ITPA-3	6-12	Sight Decoding	BR		
ITPA-3	6-12	Sound Decoding	BR		
K-TEA/NU	6-22	Reading Decoding	BR		
MBA[b]	4-95	Reading (RC, V)	BR		
PIAT-R/NU	5-22	Reading Recognition	BR		
SRI-2	6-14	Word Recognition Accuracy	BR		
TAAS-R	5-14	Letter-Word Reading	BR		
TAAS-R	5-14	Oral Reading Accuracy	BR		
TERA-3	3:6-8:6	Alphabet	BR		
TOCL	5-8	Word Recognition (RC)	BR		
TOWRE	6-24	Sight Word Efficiency (RS)	BR		
TOWRE	6-24	Phonemic Decoding Efficiency	BR		
WDRB	2-95	Letter-Word Identification	BR		
WDRB	4-95	Word Attack	BR		
WIAT-II	4-19	Pseudoword Decoding	BR		
WIAT-II	4-19	Word Reading	BR		
WJ III	2-90	**LETTER-WORD IDENT.**	BR		
WJ III	4-90	**WORD ATTACK (*Ga*-PC:A)**	BR		
WRAT-3	5-74	Reading	BR		
WRMT-R/NU[a]	5-75	Letter Identification	BR		
WRMT-R/NU	5-75	Supplementary Letter Checklist	BR		
WRMT-R/NU	5-75	Word Identification	BR		
WRMT-R/NU	5-75	Word Attack	BR		
YCAT[b]	4-7	Reading	BR		
Other					
Tests of Cognitive Ability					
Other					
		1. Sum of column			
		2. Divide by number of tests			
		3. **Reading Decoding** average			

READING ABILITY *is an acquired store of knowledge that includes basic reading skills required for the comprehension of written language. It includes the following narrow abilities:*

Reading Decoding (RD): Ability to recognize and decode words or pseudo-words in reading.

Reading Comprehension (RC): Ability to comprehend connected discourse during reading.

Verbal (printed) Language Comprehension (V): General development, or the understanding of words, sentences, and paragraphs in native language, as measured by *reading* vocabulary and *reading* comprehension tests.

Cloze Ability (CZ): Ability to supply words deleted from prose passages that must be read.

Reading Speed (RS): Time required to silently read a passage or series of sentences as quickly as possible.

Name:_____
Age: _____
Grade:_____
Examiner:_____
Date of Evaluation: _____

Reading Comprehension (RC)

Battery or Test	Age	Narrow Ability Tests	LD Area	SS*	SS
Tests of Achievement					
DAB-3	6-14	Reading Comprehension	RC		
DATA-2	12-18	Reading Comprehension	RC		
GORT-4	6-18	Comprehension	RC		
GSRT	7-25	Silent Reading Comp.	RC		
ITPA-3	6-12	Sentence Sequencing	RC		
K-FAST[b]	15-85	Reading (*Gc*-K2)	RC		
K-TEA/NU	6-22	Reading Comprehension	RC		
PIAT-R/NU	5-22	Reading Comprehension	RC		
SRI-2	6-14	Passage Comprehension	RC		
TAAS-R	5-14	Story Comprehension	RC		
TOCL	5-8	Reading Comprehension	RC		
TORC-3	7-17	Paragraph Reading	RC		
TORC-3[a]	7-17	Sentence Sequencing	RC		
TORC-3	7-12	Rdng the Directions of Schoolwork	RC		
WIAT-II	4-19	Reading Comprehension	RC		

WRMT-R/NU	5-75	Passage Comprehension	RC		
Other					

Tests of Cognitive Ability

Other					
		1. Sum of column			
		2. Divide by number of tests			
		3. **Reading Comprehension** average			

Verbal (printed) Language Comprehension (V)

Tests of Achievement

ITPA-3[b]	6-12	Written Vocabulary (EU)	BR		
SRI-2	6-14	Vocabulary in Context	RC		
TERA-3	3:6-8:6	Meaning (RC)	RC		
TOAL-3	12-24	Reading/Grammar	RC		
TOAL-3	12-24	Reading/Vocabulary	BR		
TOAL-3	12-24	Writing/Vocabulary (WA)	WE		
TORC-3	7-17	Syntactic Similarities	LC		
WJ III	5-90	**READING VOCAB. (*Gc*-VL)**	BR		
Other					

Tests of Cognitive Ability

Other					
		1. Sum of column			
		2. Divide by number of tests			
		3. **Verbal Language Comprehension** average			

Cloze Ability (CZ)

Tests of Achievement

HAMAT	7-17	Reading	RC		
WDRB	4-95	Passage Comprehension	RC		
WJ III	2-90	**PASSAGE COMP. (RC)**	RC		
Other					

Tests of Cognitive Ability

Other					
		1. Sum of column			
		2. Divide by number of tests			
		3. **Cloze Ability** average			

Reading Speed (RS)

Tests of Achievement

GORT-4	6-18	Rate	BR		
GORT-4	6-18	Fluency (RD)	BR		
WJ III	6-90	**READING FLUENCY**	BR		
Other					

Tests of Cognitive Ability

Other					
		1. Sum of column			
		2. Divide by number of tests			
		3. **Reading Speed** average			

Sum/No. of
Narrow-
Ability
Averages

**Cluster
Average**
__ Broad (__)
__ Narrow (__)

Grw–W–WRITING ABILITY

CHC CROSS-BATTERY WORKSHEET

Battery or Test	Age	*Grw–W*–Writing Ability Narrow Ability Tests	LD Area	SS*	SS (100 ± 15)
Spelling Ability (SG)					
Tests of Achievement					
DAB-3	6-14	Spelling	WE		
DATA-2	12-18	Spelling	WE		
ITPA-3[a]	6-12	Sight Spelling	WE		
ITPA-3	6-12	Sound Spelling	WE		
K-TEA/NU	6-22	Spelling	WE		
PIAT-R/NU	5-7	Written Expression (Level I)	WE		
PIAT-R/NU	5-22	Spelling (*Ga*-PC:A)	WE		
TAAS-R	5-14	Spelling	WE		
TOCL	5-8	Writing Skills (EU)	WE		
TOWL-3	7-17	Spelling	WE		
TWS-4	6-18	Test of Written Spelling – 4th Ed.	WE		
WIAT-II	5-19	Spelling	WE		
WJ III	2-90	**SPELLING**	WE		
WJ III	6-90	**SPELL. OF SOUNDS (*Ga*-PC:A)**	WE		
WRAT-3	5-74	Spelling	WE		
YCAT	4-7	Writing	WE		
Other					
Tests of Cognitive Ability					
Other					
		1. Sum of column			
		2. Divide by number of tests			
		3. **Spelling Ability** average			

WRITING ABILITY *is an acquired store of knowledge that includes basic writing skills required for the expression of language via writing. It includes the following narrow abilities:*

Spelling Ability (SG): Ability to spell words correctly, in particular words that are spelled nonphonetically or are irregular.

Writing Ability (WA): Ability to write with clarity of thought, organization, and good sentence structure.

English Usage Knowledge (EU): Knowledge of writing in the English language with respect to capitalization, punctuation, usage, and spelling.

Name:_____

Age: _____

Grade:_____

Examiner:_____

Date of Evaluation: _____

Writing Ability (WA)

Battery or Test	Age	Narrow Ability Tests	LD Area	SS*	SS
Tests of Achievement					
DAB-3	7-14	Contextual Language	WE		
DAB-3	6-14	Story Construction	WE		
DATA-2	12-18	Writing Composition	WE		
OWLS	5-21	Written Expression Scale	WE		
PIAT-R/NU	7-18	Written Expression (Level II)	WE		
TEWL-2	5-10	Contextual Writing	WE		
TOCL	5-8	Original Writing	WE		
TOWE	8-14	Essay	WE		
TOWL-3	7-17	Contextual Conventions (EU)	WE		
TOWL-3	7-17	Contextual Language	WE		
TOWL-3	7-17	Story Construction	WE		
TOWL-3	7-17	Vocabulary	WE		
WIAT-II	4-19	Written Expression	WE		
WJ III	7-90	**WRITING FLUENCY (*Gs*-R9)**	WE		
WJ III	5-90	**WRITING SAMPLES**	WE		
Other					
Tests of Cognitive Ability					
Other					
		1. Sum of column			
		2. Divide by number of tests			
		3. **Writing Ability** average			

English Usage Knowledge (EU)

Tests of Achievement					
DAB-3	6-14	Capitalization	WE		
DAB-3	6-14	Punctuation	WE		
HAMAT[b]	7-17	Writing A/B	WE		
MBA	4-95	Writing	WE		
TERA-3	5-8	Conventions			
TEWL-2[a]	3-10	Basic Writing A/B	WE		
TOAL-3	12-24	Writing/Grammar (WA)	WE		
TOWE	6:6-14	Items	WE		
TOWL-3	7-17	Logical Sentences	WE		
TOWL-3[b]	7-17	Sentence Combining A/B (WA)	WE		
TOWL-3	7-17	Style	WE		
WJ III	6-90	**PUNCT. & CAPITLN.**	WE		
Other					
Tests of Cognitive Ability					
Other					
		1. Sum of column			
		2. Divide by number of tests			
		3. **English Usage Knowledge** average			

Sum/No.of Narrow-Ability Averages

Cluster Average**
__ Broad (___)
__ Narrow (___)

Gq– QUANTITATIVE KNOWLEDGE
CHC CROSS-BATTERY WORKSHEET

Battery or Test	Age	*Gq* – Quantitative Knowledge Narrow Ability Tests	LD Area	SS*	SS (100 ± 15)
Mathematical Knowledge (KM)					
Tests of Achievement					
DAB-3	6-14	Math Reasoning	MR/MC		
KeyMath	5:6-22	Measurement (A3)	MC		
KeyMath	6:6-22	Time and Money	MC		
KeyMath[b]	7:6-22	Interpreting Data (A3)	MR		
K-SEALS	3-6	Numbers, Letters, Words	MC		
MBA	4-95	Mathematics (A3)	MC		
PIAT-R/NU	5-22	Mathematics	MC		
S-DMS	6-13	Math Concepts	MC		
TAAS-R	5-16	Arithmetic (Oral)	MC		
TOMA-2	8-18	General Information (A3)	MC		
TOMA-2[a]	8-18	Vocabulary (*Gc*-VL)			
TORC-3	7-17	Mathematics Vocabulary			
WJ III	2-90	**QUANT. CONCEPTS (*Gf*-RQ)**	MC		
Other					
Tests of Cognitive Ability					
Other					
		1. Sum of column			
		2. Divide by number of tests			
		3. **Mathematical Knowledge** average			

		Mathematical Achievement (A3)			
Tests of Achievement					
DAB-3	6-14	Math Calculation	MC		
DATA-2	12-18	Math Calculation	MC		
DATA-2	12-18	Math Problem Solving	MR		
HAMAT	7-17	Arithmetic	MC		
KeyMath	6:9-22	Estimation	MC		
KeyMath	5-22	Numeration (KM)	MC		
KeyMath	8:9-22	Rational Numbers	MC		
KeyMath	6:3-22	Subtraction	MC		
KeyMath	8-22	Multiplication	MC		
KeyMath	8-22	Division	MC		
KeyMath	8:3-22	Mental Computation	MC		
KeyMath	7:6-22	Problem Solving (*Gf*-RQ)	MR		
KeyMath	5:6-22	Addition	MC		
K-FAST[a]	15-85	Arithmetic (KM)	MC		
KTEA-NU	6-22	Math Applications (KM)	MR		
KTEA-NU	6-22	Mathematics Computation	MC		
S-DMS	6-13	Math Calculation	MC		
S-DMS	6-13	Math Problem Solving	MR		
TAAS-R	5-14	Arithmetic (Written)	MC		
TOMA-2	8-18	Computation	MC		
TOMA-2	8-18	Story Problems (KM; *Gf*-RQ)	MR		
WIAT-II	5-19	Numerical Operations	MC		
WJ III	5-90	**CALCULATION**	MC		
WRAT-3	5-74	Arithmetic	MC		
YCAT	4-7	Mathematics	MC		
Other					
Tests of Cognitive Ability					
WECH	3-74	Arithmetic	MC		
Other					

Name:_____
Age: _____
Grade:_____
Examiner:_____
Date of Evaluation: _____

QUANTITATIVE KNOWLEDGE
represents an individual's store of acquired quantitative declarative and procedural knowledge. It involves the ability to use quantitative information and manipulate numeric symbols. It includes the following narrow abilities:

Mathematical Knowledge (KM):
Range of general knowledge about mathematics.

Mathematical Achievement (A3):
Measured mathematics achievement.

		1. Sum of column			
		2. Divide by number of tests			
		3. **Mathematical Achievement** average			

Quantitative Reasoning (RQ)

Tests of Achievement					
WIAT-II	4-19	Mathematics Reasoning	MR		
WJ III	2-90	**APPLIED PROBLEMS (A3, KM)**	MR		
Other					
		1. Sum of column			
		2. Divide by number of tests			
		3. **Quantitative Reasoning** average			

Sum/No. of
Narrow-
Ability
Averages

**Cluster
Average****
__ Broad (__)
__ Narrow (__)

[1] RQ is a narrow *Gf* ability. It is included on this worksheet because it is assessed often in a comprehensive evaluation of mathematics ability.

Gc – CRYSTALLIZED INTELLIGENCE
CHC CROSS-BATTERY WORKSHEET

Battery or Test	Age	Gc – Crystallized Intelligence Narrow Ability Tests	LD Area	SS*	SS (100 ± 15)
		**Language Development (LD)**			
Tests of Achievement					
CASL[b]	7-21	Nonliteral Language (K2)	OE		
CASL	11-21	Sent. Comp. of Syntax	LC		
CELF-3	6-21	Word Classes	LC		
CELF-3[b]	9-21	Sentence Assembly (MY)	OE		
DATA-2	12-18	Receptive Vocabulary	LC		
ITPA-3	5-12	Spoken Vocabulary	OE		
LPT-R[b]	5-11	Associations (*Glr*-FA, FI)	OE		
LPT-R	5-11	Attributes (VL)	OE		
LPT-R[a]	5-11	Categorization	OE		
LPT-R	5-11	Differences	OE		
LPT-R	5-11	Similarities	OE		
TAPS-R	4:1-13	Aud. Interpretation of Directions (LS)	LC		
TOAL-3	12-24	Listening/Grammar	LC		
TOLD I:3	8-12	Generals	OE		
TOLD-I:3	8-12	Picture Vocabulary	LC		
TOLD-P:3	4-8	Relational Vocabulary	OE		
TORC-3	7-17	Social Studies Vocabulary (VL)			
Other					
Tests of Cognitive Ability					
DTLA-4	6-17	Word Opposites			
DTLA-4	6-17	Story Construction			
WECH	3-74	**COMPREHENSION (K0)**			
WECH	3-74	**SIMILARITIES (VL)**			
Other					
		1. Sum of column			
		2. Divide by number of tests			
		3. **Language Development** average			

Battery or Test	Age	Narrow Ability Tests	LD Area	SS*	SS
		**Lexical Knowledge (VL)**			
Tests of Achievement					
CASL	11-21	Ambiguous Sentences	OE		
CASL[b]	3-6	Comp. of Basic Concepts (LD)	LC		
CASL	7-21	Synonyms	LC		
CASL	5-21	Antonyms	OE		
CREVT	4-17	Receptive Vocabulary	LC		
CREVT	5-17	Expressive Vocabulary	OE		
CREVT-A	18-89	Receptive Vocabulary	LC		
CREVT-A	18-89	Expressive Vocabulary	OE		
DAB-3	6-14	Synonyms	OE		
EOWPVT	2-18	Expressive Vocabulary (LD)	OE		
EVT[b]	2-90	Expressive Vocabulary Test	OE		
ITPA-3[b]	5-12	Spoken Analogies (LD)	OE		
K-SEALS[b]	3-6	Vocabulary (LD)	OE		
LPT-R[b]	5-11	Pretest 1 (LD)	OE		
LPT-R[b]	5-11	Pretest 2 (LD)	OE		
LPT-R	6-11	Multiple Meanings	OE		
PPVT-3	2:6-90	Peabody Picture Voc. Test- 3rd Ed.	LC		
ROWPVT	2-18	Receptive Vocabulary	LC		
TACL-3	3-9	Grammatical Morphemes	LC		
TACL-3	3-9	Vocabulary	LC		
TOAL-3	12-24	Listening/Vocabulary	LC		
TOLD-P:3	4-8	Picture Vocabulary	LC		

Name:_____
Age: _____
Grade:_____
Examiner:_____
Date of Evaluation: _____

CRYSTALLIZED INTELLIGENCE
is the breadth and depth of a person's acquired knowledge of a culture and the effective application of this knowledge. It includes the following narrow abilities:

Language Development (LD):
General development, or the understanding of words, sentences, and paragraphs (not requiring reading) in spoken native language skills.

Lexical Knowledge (VL): Extent of vocabulary that can be understood in terms of correct word meanings.

Listening Ability (LS): Ability to listen and comprehend oral communications.

General Information (K0): Range of general knowledge.

Information About Culture (K2): Range of cultural knowledge (e.g., music, art).

General Science Information (K1): Range of scientific knowledge (e.g., biology, physics, engineering, mechanics, electronics, chemistry).

Geography Achievement (A5): Range of geographic knowledge.

Communication Ability (CM): Ability to speak in "real life" situations (e.g., lecture, group participation) in an adult-like manner.

Oral Production and Fluency (OP): More specific or narrow oral communication skills than reflected by communication ability.

Grammatical Sensitivity (MY): Knowledge or awareness of the grammatical features of the native language.

TOLD-P:3	4-8	Oral Vocabulary	OE		
TORC-3[a]	7-17	General Vocabulary (LD; *Grw*-V)	BR		
WDRB	4-95	Reading Vocabulary	BR		
WDRB	4-95	Oral Vocabulary (LD)	OE		
WJ III	2-90	**PICTURE VOCAB. (LD)**	BR		
WRMT-R/NU	5-75	Word Comprehension	BR		
YCAT	4-7	Spoken Language (LD)	LC/OE		
Other					
Tests of Cognitive Ability					
NEPSY	3-4	Body Part Naming (K0)			
WECH	3-74	**VOCABULARY (LD)**			
WJ III	2-85	**VERBAL COMP. (LD)**			
Other					
		1. Sum of column			
		2. Divide by number of tests			
		3. **Lexical Knowledge** average			

Listening Ability (LS)

Tests of Achievement					
CASL	11-21	Idiomatic Language (LD)	LC		
CASL	3-21	Sentence Completion	LC/WE		
CASL	5-12	Paragraph Comp. of Syntax (LD)	LC		
CASL[b]	11-21	Meaning from Context (LD)	OE		
CELF-3	6-21	Listening to Paragraphs	LC		
CELF-3	6-8	Sentence Structure	LC		
CELF-3	9-21	Semantic Relationships	LC		
CELF-3	6-8	Word Structure	LC/WE		
DAB-3	6-14	Characteristics	LC		
DAB-3	6-14	Story Comprehension	LC		
OWLS[b]	3-21	Listening Comprehension (LD)	LC		
TAAS-R	5-14	Listening Comprehension	LC		
TACL-3	3-9	Elaborated Phrases & Sent. (LD)	LC		
TELD-3[b]	2-7	Receptive Language A/B (LD)	LC		
TOLD-I:3	8-12	Word Ordering (*Gsm*-MW)	LC		
TOLD-P:3	4-8	Grammatic Understanding (LD)	LC		
WDRB	4-95	Listening Comprehension	LC		
WIAT-II	4-19	Listening Comprehension	LC		
WJ III	2-90	**UNDSTDG. DIR. (*Gsm*-MW)**	LC		
WJ III	2-90	**ORAL COMPREHENSION**	LC		
Other					
Tests of Cognitive Ability					
NEPSY	3-12	Comp of Instructions (LD)			
Other					
		1. Sum of column			
		2. Divide by number of tests			
		3. **Listening Ability** average			

General Information (K0)

Tests of Achievement					
CASL	3-21	Pragmatic Judgment (LD)			
CASL	7-17	Inference	LC		
DATA-2	12-18	Social Studies			
DATA-2	12-18	Reference Skills			
HAMAT	7-17	Facts			
MBA	4-95	Factual Knowledge			
PIAT-R/NU	5-22	General Information			
WJ III	2-90	**ACADEMIC KNWLDG. (K2)**			
YCAT	4-7	General Information			
Other					

Tests of Cognitive Ability					
DTLA-4	6-17	Basic Information			
WECH	3-74	**INFORMATION**			
WJ III	2-85	**GENERAL INFORMATION**			
Other					
		1. Sum of column			
		2. Divide by number of tests			
		3. **General Information** average			

Information About Culture (K2)

Tests of Achievement					
Other					
Tests of Cognitive Ability					
KAIT	11-85	**FAMOUS FACES**			
Other					
		1. Sum of column			
		2. Divide by number of tests			
		3. **Information About Culture** average			

General Science Information (K1)

Tests of Achievement					
DATA-2	12-18	Science			
TORC-3[b]	7-17	Science Vocabulary			
Other					
Tests of Cognitive Ability					
Other					
		1. Sum of column			
		2. Divide by number of tests			
		3. **General Science Inf.** average			

Geography Achievement (A5)

Tests of Achievement					
Other					
Tests of Cognitive Ability					
Other					
		1. Sum of column			
		2. Divide by number of tests			
		3. **Geography Achievement** average			

Communication Ability (CM)

Tests of Achievement					
WIAT-II	4-19	Oral Expression	OE		
OWLS[b]	3-21	Oral Expression (OP, LD)	OE		
Other					
Tests of Cognitive Ability					
Other					
		1. Sum of column			
		2. Divide by number of tests			
		3. **Communication Ability** average			

Oral Production and Fluency (OP)

Tests of Achievement					
CELF-3	6-21	Formulated Sentences	OE		

DATA-2[b]	12-18	Expressive Vocabulary	OE		
TELD-3[b]	2-7	Expressive Language (LD)	OE		
TOAL-3	12-24	Speaking/Vocabulary	OE		
Other					
Tests of Cognitive Ability					
Other					
		1. Sum of column			
		2. Divide by number of tests			
		3. **Oral Prod. & Fluency** average			

Grammatical Sensitivity (MY)

Tests of Achievement					
CASL[b]	3-21	Syntax Construction (OP)	OE/WE		
CASL	7-21	Grammatical Morphemes	OE/WE		
CASL	7-21	Grammaticality Judgment	LC/WE		
DAB-3	6-14	Grammatic Completion	OE		
DATA-2	12-18	Receptive Grammar	LC		
ITPA-3	5-12	Morphological Closure	OE		
TOCL	5-8	Spoken Language (*Grw*-EU)	LC		
TOLD-I:3[b]	8-12	Malapropisms (VL)	LC		
TOLD-I:3	8-12	Grammatic Comprehension	LC		
TOLD-I:3[b]	8-12	Sentence Combining (LD)	WE		
TOLD-P:3	4-8	Grammatic Completion (LS)	LC/WE		
WJ III	6-90	**EDITING (*Grw*-EU)**	WE		
Other					
Tests of Cognitive Ability					
Other					
		1. Sum of column			
		2. Divide by number of tests			
		3. **Grammatical Sensitivity** average			

Sum/No. of Narrow-Ability Averages

Cluster Average**
___Broad (__)
___Narrow (__)

Ga – AUDITORY PROCESSING
CHC CROSS-BATTERY WORKSHEET

Battery or Test	Age	*Ga* – Auditory Processing Narrow Ability Tests	LD Area	SS*	SS (100 ± 15)

Phonetic Coding: Analysis (PC:A)

Tests of Achievement					
CTOPP	5-24	Elision	BR		
CTOPP	5-7	Sound Matching	BR		
CTOPP	7-24	Segmenting Words	BR		
CTOPP	7-24	Segmenting Nonwords	BR		
DAB-3	6-14	Phonemic Analysis	BR		
ITPA-3	5-12	Sound Deletion	BR		
TOCL	5-8	Knowledge of Print	BR		
TOLD-P:3	4-8	Phonemic Analysis	BR		
TOPA[a]	5-6	Initial Sounds	BR		
TOPA[a]	6-8	Ending Sounds	BR		
WJ III	4–90	**SOUND AWARENESS (PC:S)**	BR		
Other					

Tests of Cognitive Ability					
NEPSY	3-12	Phonological Processing (PC:S)			
TPAT	5-9	Segmentation			
TPAT	5-9	Isolation			
TPAT	5-9	Deletion			
TPAT	5-9	Rhyming			
WJ III	2-85	**INCOMPLETE WORDS (PC:S)**			
Other					
		1. Sum of column			
		2. Divide by number of tests			
		3. **Phonetic Coding: Analysis** average			

Phonetic Coding: Synthesis (PC:S)

Tests of Achievement					
CTOPP	5-24	Blending Nonwords	BR		
CTOPP	5-24	Blending Words	BR		
WDRB	2-95	Incomplete Words (PC:A)	BR		
WDRB	4-95	Sound Blending	BR		
TOLD-P:3[a]	4-8	Word Articulation (*Gc*-LD)	BR		
Other					

Tests of Cognitive Ability					
TPAT	5-9	Substitution			
TPAT	5-9	Blending			
WJ III	4-85	**SOUND BLENDING**			
Other					
		1. Sum of column			
		2. Divide by number of tests			
		3. **Phonetic Coding: Synthesis** average			

Speech/General Sound Discrimination (US/U3)

Tests of Achievement					
TAPS-R	4:1-13	Auditory Word Discrimination			
TOLD-P:3	4-8	Word Discrimination			
Other					

Tests of Cognitive Ability					
WJ III	4-85	**AUDITORY ATTENTION (UR)**			
Other					
		1. Sum of column			
		2. Divide by number of tests			

Name:_____
Age: _____
Grade:_____
Examiner:_____
Date of Evaluation: _____

AUDITORY PROCESSING *is the ability to perceive, analyze, and synthesize patterns among auditory stimuli. It includes the following narrow abilities:*

Phonetic Coding (Analysis) (PC:A): Ability to process speech sounds, as in identifying, isolating, and analyzing sounds.

Phonetic Coding (Synthesis) (PC:S): Ability to process speech sounds, as in identifying, isolating, and blending or synthesizing sounds.

Speech/General Sound Discrimination (US/U3): Ability to detect differences in speech sounds under conditions of little distraction or distortion.

Sound Localization (UL) Ability to localize sounds heard in space.

Resistance to Auditory Stimulus Distortion (UR): Ability to understand speech and language that has been distorted or masked in one or more ways.

3. **Speech/General Sound Discrimination** average		

Sound Localization (UL)

Tests of Achievement				
SCAN-C-R	5-11	Competing Words		
SCAN-C-R	5-11	Competing Sentences		
Other				

Tests of Cognitive Ability			
Other			
1. Sum of column		
2. Divide by number of tests		
3. **Sound Localization** average		

Resistance to Auditory Stimulus Distortion (UR)

Tests of Achievement				
SCAN-C-R	5-11	Auditory Figure-Ground		
SCAN-C-R	5-11	Filtered Words		
Other				

Tests of Cognitive Ability			
Other			
1. Sum of column		
2. Divide by number of tests		
3. **Resistance to Auditory Stimulus Distortion** avg.		

Sum/No. of
Narrow-
Ability
Averages

**Cluster
Average****
__ Broad (___)
__ Narrow (___)

Gf – FLUID INTELLIGENCE
CHC CROSS-BATTERY WORKSHEET

Battery or Test	Age	*Gf* – Fluid Intelligence Narrow Ability Tests	LD Area	SS*	SS (100 ± 15)
Induction (I)					
Tests of Cognitive Ability					
CAS	5-17	Nonverbal Matrices			
CTONI	6-18	Geometric Sequences (RG)			
DTLA-4	6-17	**SYMBOLIC RELATIONS**			
KAIT	11-85	**MYSTERY CODES**			
KSNAP	11-85	Four-Letter Words			
Leiter-R	2-6	Classification			
Leiter-R	5-18	Design Analogies			
Leiter-R	2-18	Repeated Patterns			
Leiter-R	2-18	Sequential Order			
TONI-3	5-85	Test of Nonverbal Intelligence-3rdEd.			
UNIT	5-17	**ANALOGIC REASONING**			
WAIS-III	16-89	**MATRIX REASONING**			
WASI	4-89	**MATRIX REASONING**			
WJ III	2-85	**CONCEPT FORMATION**			
Other					
Tests of Achievement					
TAPS-R	4:1-13	Auditory Processing (RG)			
Other					
		1. Sum of column			
		2. Divide by number of tests			
		3. **Induction** average			

General Sequential Reasoning (RG)					
Tests of Cognitive Ability					
KAIT	11-85	**LOGICAL STEPS**			
Leiter-R	2-10	Picture Context			
Leiter-R	6-18	Visual Coding			
UNIT	5-17	**CUBE DESIGN**			
WJ III	4-85	**ANALYSIS-SYNTHESIS**			
Other					
Tests of Achievement					
Other					
		1. Sum of column			
		2. Divide by number of tests			
		3. **General Sequential Reasoning** average			

Quantitative Reasoning (RQ)					
Tests of Achievement					
WIAT-II	4-19	Mathematics Reasoning	MR		
WJ III	2-90	**APP. PROBLEMS (*Gq*-A3, KM)**	MR		
Other					
		1. Sum of column			
		2. Divide by number of tests			
		3. **Quantitative Reasoning** average			

Name:_____
Age: _____
Grade:_____
Examiner:_____
Date of Evaluation: _____

FLUID INTELLIGENCE *is the ability to use and engage in various mental operations when faced with a relatively novel task that cannot be performed automatically. It includes the following narrow abilities:*

Induction (I): Ability to discover the underlying characteristic that governs a problem or set of materials.

General Sequential Reasoning (RG): Ability to start with stated rules, premises or conditions and to engage in one or more steps to reach a solution to a problem.

Quantitative Reasoning (RQ): Ability to inductively and deductively reason with concepts involving mathematical relations and properties.

Sum/No. of Narrow-Ability Averages

Cluster Average**
__ Broad (__)
__ Narrow (__)

Gv – VISUAL PROCESSING
CHC CROSS-BATTERY WORKSHEET

Battery or Test	Age	*Gv* – Visual Processing Narrow Ability Tests	LD Area	SS*	SS (100 ± 15)
		Spatial Relations (SR)			
Tests of Cognitive Ability					
Leiter-R	11-18	Figure Rotation (Vz)			
UNIT	5-17	Cube Design (Vz)			
WECH	3-74	**BLOCK DESIGN (Vz)**			
Other					
Tests of Achievement					
KeyMath[a]	5-22	Geometry (Vz)	MC		
Other					
		1. Sum of column			
		2. Divide by number of tests			
		3. **Spatial Relations** average			

		Visualization (Vz)			
Tests of Cognitive Ability					
Leiter-R	2-10	Matching			
Leiter-R	2-18	Form Completion (SR)			
Leiter-R	11-18	Paper Folding			
NEPSY	3-12	Block Construction			
WJ III	4-85	**SPATIAL RELATIONS (SR)**			
Other					
Tests of Achievement					
Other					
		1. Sum of column			
		2. Divide by number of tests			
		3. **Visualization** average			

		Visual Memory (MV)			
Tests of Cognitive Ability					
CMS	5-16	Dot Locations			
CMS	5-16	Dot Locations 2			
CMS	5-16	Picture Locations			
DTLA-4	6-17	Design Sequences			
DTLA-4	6-17	Design Reproduction			
KAIT	11-85	**MEM. FOR BLOCK DESIGNS**			
LAMB	20-60	Simple Figure			
LAMB	20-60	Complex Figure			
Leiter-R	4-10	Immediate Recognition			
Leiter-R	2-18	Forward Memory			
NEPSY	3-12	Imitating Hand Positions			
TOMAL	5-19	Facial Memory			
TOMAL	5-19	Abstract Visual Memory			
TOMAL	5-19	Manual Imitation			
TOMAL	5-19	Del Rec: Visual Sel. Reminding			
UNIT	5-17	**OBJECT MEMORY**			
UNIT	5-17	**SPATIAL MEMORY**			
UNIT	5-17	**SYMBOLIC MEMORY**			
WJ III	4-85	**PICTURE RECOGNITION**			
WMS-III	16-89	Visual Reproduction I			
WRAML	5-17	Picture Memory			
WRAML	5-17	Design Memory			
Other					

Name:_____
Age: _____
Grade:_____
Examiner:_____
Date of Evaluation: _____

VISUAL PROCESSING *is the ability to generate, perceive, analyze, synthesize, manipulate, transform, and think with visual patterns and stimuli. It includes the following narrow abilities:*

Spatial Relations (SR): Ability to perceive and manipulate visual patterns rapidly or to maintain orientation with respect to objects in space.

Visualization (Vz): Ability to manipulate objects or visual patterns mentally and to "see" how they would appear under altered conditions.

Visual Memory (MV): Ability to form and store a mental representation or image of a visual stimulus and then recognize or recall it later.

Closure Speed (CS): Ability to combine disconnected, vague, or partially obscured visual stimuli or patterns quickly into a meaningful whole, without knowing in advance what the pattern is.

Spatial Scanning (SS): Ability to survey a spatial field or pattern accurately and quickly and identify a path through the visual field or pattern.

Flexibility of Closure (CF): Ability to identify a visual figure or pattern embedded in a complex visual array, when knowing in advance what the pattern is.

Serial Perceptual Integration (PI): Ability to identify a pictorial or visual pattern when parts of the pattern are presented rapidly in order.

Tests of Achievement					
Other					
	1. Sum of column				
	2. Divide by number of tests				
	3. **Visual Memory** average				

Closure Speed (CS)

Tests of Cognitive Ability					
KSNAP	11-85	Gestalt Closure			
WECH	3-74	**OBJECT ASSEMBLY (SR)**			
Other					
Tests of Achievement					
Other					
	1. Sum of column				
	2. Divide by number of tests				
	3. **Closure Speed** average				

Spatial Scanning (SS)

Tests of Cognitive Ability					
NEPSY	5-12	Route Finding			
UNIT	5-17	**Mazes**			
WISC-III	6-16	**Mazes**			
Tests of Achievement					
Other					
	1. Sum of column				
	2. Divide by number of tests				
	3. **Spatial Scanning** average				

Flexibility of Closure (CF)

Tests of Cognitive Ability					
CAS	5-17	**FIGURE MEMORY (MV)**			
Leiter-R	2-18	Figure Ground			
Other					
Tests of Achievement					
Other					
	1. Sum of column				
	2. Divide by number of tests				
	3. **Flexibility of Closure** average				

Serial Perceptual Integration (PI)

Tests of Cognitive Ability					
CAS	5-17	**VERBAL SPATIAL RELATIONS**			
Other					
Tests of Achievement					
Other					
	1. Sum of column				
	2. Divide by number of tests				
	3. **Serial Perceptual Integration** average				

Sum/No. of
Narrow-
Ability
Averages

**Cluster
Averages****
__ Broad (__)
__ Narrow (__)

Gsm – SHORT-TERM MEMORY
CHC CROSS-BATTERY WORKSHEET

Battery or Test	Age	*Gsm* – Short-term Memory Narrow Ability Tests	LD Area	SS*	SS (100 ± 15)
Memory Span (MS)					
Tests of Cognitive Ability					
CAS	5-17	**WORD SERIES**			
CAS	5-17	**SENTENCE REPETITION**			
CAS	5-17	**SENTENCE QUESTIONS**			
CMS	5-16	Numbers (MW)			
CMS	5-16	Stories*** (*Gc*-LS)			
KSNAP	11-85	Number Recall			
LAMB	20-60	Digit Span			
LAMB	20-60	Supraspan Digit			
NEPSY	5-12	Repetition of Nonsense Words			
NEPSY	3-12	Sentence Repetition			
TOMAL	519	Digits Forward			
TOMAL	5-19	Letters Forward			
WAIS-III	6-89	**DIGIT SPAN (MW)**			
WISC-III	6-16	**DIGIT SPAN (MW)**			
WJ III	4-85	**MEMORY FOR WORDS**			
WMS-III	16-89	Logical Memory I*** (*Gc*-LS)			
WMS-III	16-89	Digit Span (MW)			
WRAML	5-17	Number/Letter Memory			
Other					
Tests of Achievement					
CELF-3	6-21	Concepts and Directions	LC		
CELF-3	6-21	Recalling Sentences	LC		
CTOPP	5-24	Memory for Digits	LC		
CTOPP[a]	5-24	Nonword Repetition	LC		
DATA-2	12-18	Expressive Grammar	LC		
ITPA-3	5-12	Rhyming Sequences			
ITPA-3	5-12	Syntactic Sentences			
TAPS-R	4:1-13	Auditory Number Memory-Forward	LC		
TAPS-R	4:1-13	Auditory Sent. Memory	LC		
TOAL-3	12-24	Speaking/Grammar	LC		
TOLD-P:3	4-8	Sentence Imitation	LC		
WDRB	4-95	Memory for Sentences	LC		
Other					
		1. Sum of column			
		2. Divide by number of tests			
		3. **Memory Span** average			

Working Memory (MW)

Battery or Test	Age	Narrow Ability Tests	LD Area	SS*	SS
Tests of Cognitive Ability					
CMS	5-16	Sequences			
NEPSY	5-12	Knock and Tap			
WAIS-III	16-89	**LETTER-NUMBER SEQ.**			
WJ III	4-85	**AUDITORY WORKING MEM**			
WJ III	4-85	**NUMBERS REVERSED**			
WMS-III	16-89	Letter-Number Sequencing			
WMS-III	16-89	Mental Control			
Other					
Tests of Achievement					
CTOPP	7-24	Phoneme Reversal (*Ga*-PC:A)	BR		
TAPS-R	4:1-13	Auditory Number Memory-Reversed	LC		

Name:_____
Age: _____
Grade:_____
Examiner:_____
Date of Evaluation: _____

SHORT-TERM MEMORY *is the ability to apprehend and hold information in immediate awareness and then use it within a few seconds. It includes the following narrow abilities:*

Memory Span (MS): Ability to attend to and immediately recall temporally ordered elements in the correct order after a single presentation.

Working Memory (MW): Ability to store temporarily and perform a set of cognitive operations on information that requires divided attention and the management of the limited capacity of short-term memory.

Other			
1. Sum of column			
2. Divide by number of tests			
3. **Working Memory** average			

Sum/No. of Narrow-Ability Averages

Cluster Average**
__ Broad (__)
__ Narrow (__)

*** Although these tests are mixed measures of two CHC abilities (i.e., they also involve Listening ability in addition to Memory Span), they are included on this worksheet because they are necessary to administer prior to administering Stories 2 and Logical Memory II, respectively (measures of *Glr*- MM).

Glr – LONG-TERM RETRIEVAL
CHC CROSS-BATTERY WORKSHEET

Battery or Test	Age	*Glr* – Long-term Retrieval Narrow Ability Tests	LD Area	SS*	SS (100 ± 15)
Associative Memory (MA)					
Tests of Cognitive Ability					
CMS	5-16	Word Pairs			
CMS	5-16	Word Pairs 2			
KAIT	11-85	**REBUS LEARNING**			
KAIT	11-85	**REBUS DELAYED RECALL**			
LAMB	20-60	Word Pairs (FI)			
Leiter-R	4-10	Delayed Recognition			
Leiter-R	2-18	Associated Pairs (MM)			
Leiter-R	6-18	Delayed Pairs (MM)			
NEPSY	5-12	Memory for Names			
TOMAL	5-19	Paired Recall			
WJ III	2-85	**VISUAL-AUD LEARNING (MM)**			
WJ III	4-85	**DEL REC: VIS-AUD LRNG (MM)**			
WMS-III	16-89	Verbal Paired Associates I			
WMS-III	16-89	Verbal Paired Associates II			
WRAML	5-17	Sound Symbol			
Other					
Tests of Achievement					
WRMT-R/NU	5-75	Visual-Auditory Learning			
Other					
		1. Sum of column			
		2. Divide by number of tests			
		3. **Associative Memory** average			

Ideational Fluency (FI)

Tests of Cognitive Ability					
WJ III	4-85	**RETRIEVAL FLUENCY (FA)**			
Other					
Tests of Achievement					
CELF-3	6-21	Word Associations	OE		
Other					
		1. Sum of column			
		2. Divide by number of tests			
		3. **Ideational Fluency** average			

Figural Fluency (FF)

Tests of Cognitive Ability					
NEPSY	5-12	Design Fluency			
Other					
Tests of Achievement					
Other					
		1. Sum of column			
		2. Divide by number of tests			
		3. **Figural Fluency** average			

Naming Facility (NA)

Tests of Cognitive Ability					
CAS	5-17	Expressive Attention			
NEPSY	5-12	Speeded Naming			
WJ III	4-85	**RAPID PICTURE NAMING**			
Other					

Name:_____
Age:_____
Grade:_____
Examiner:_____
Date of Evaluation: _____

LONG-TERM RETRIEVAL *is the ability to store information (e.g., concepts, ideas, items, or names) in long-term memory and to retrieve it later fluently through association. It includes the following narrow abilities:*

Associative Memory (MA): Ability to recall one part of a previously learned but unrelated pair of items when the other part is presented (i.e., paired-associative learning).

Ideational Fluency (FI): Ability to produce rapidly a series of ideas, words, or phrases related to a specific condition or object.

Figural Fluency (FF): Ability to draw or sketch several examples or elaborations rapidly when given a starting visual stimulus.

Naming Facility (NA): Ability to produce names for concepts rapidly.

Free Recall Memory (M6): Ability to recall as many unrelated items as possible, in any order, after a large collection of items is presented.

Meaningful Memory (MM): Ability to recall a set of items where there is a meaningful relation between items or the items create a meaningful story or connected discourse.

Tests of Achievement					
CELF-3	6-21	Rapid Automatic Naming (FI)			
CTOPP	5-24	Rapid Color Naming (*Gs*-R9)			
CTOPP	5-24	Rapid Object Naming			
CTOPP[a]	7-24	Rapid Letter Naming (*Gs*-R9)			
CTOPP	7-24	Rapid Digit Naming (*Gs*-R9)			
Other					
		1. Sum of column			
		2. Divide by number of tests			
		3. **Naming Facility** average			

Free Recall Memory (M6)

Tests of Cognitive Ability					
CMS	5-16	Word Lists			
CMS	5-16	Word Lists 2 (MA)			
LAMB	20-60	Wordlist (MA)			
NEPSY	7-12	List Learning			
TOMAL	5-19	Word Selective Reminding			
TOMAL	5-19	Del Rec: Word Selective Reminding			
WMS-III	16-89	Word Lists I			
WMS-III	16-89	Word Lists II (MA)			
WRAML	5-17	Verbal Learning			
Other					
Tests of Achievement					
TAPS-R	4:1-13:0	Auditory Word Memory (*Gsm*-MW)	LC		
Other					
		1. Sum of column			
		2. Divide by number of tests			
		3. **Free Recall Memory** average			

Meaningful Memory (MM)

Tests of Cognitive Ability					
CMS	5-16	Stories 2			
WMS-III	16-74	Logical Memory II			
Other					
Tests of Achievement					
TOCL	5-8	Writing from Memory	WE		
WJ III	2-90	**STORY RECALL (*Gc*-LS)**	LC		
WJ III	3-90	**STORY RECALL – DELAYED**	LC		
Other					
		1. Sum of column			
		2. Divide by number of tests			
		3. **Meaningful Memory** average			

Sum/No. of Narrow-Ability Averages

Cluster Average**
___ Broad (___)
___ Narrow (___)

Gs – PROCESSING SPEED
CHC CROSS-BATTERY WORKSHEET

Battery or Test	Age	*Gs* – Processing Speed Narrow Ability Tests	LD Area	SS*	SS (100 ± 15)
Perceptual Speed (P)					
Tests of Cognitive Ability					
CAS	5-17	**RECEPTIVE ATTENTION (R4)**			
CAS	5-17	**PLANNED CONNECTIONS (R9)**			
Leiter-R	2-18	Attention Sustained (R9)			
WAIS-III	16-74	**SYMBOL SEARCH (R9)**			
WISC-III	6-16	**SYMBOL SEARCH (R9)**			
WJ III	2-85	**VISUAL MATCHING (R9)**			
Other					
Tests of Achievement					
WDRB	4-95	Visual Matching			
Other					
		1. Sum of column			
		2. Divide by number of tests			
		3. **Perceptual Speed** Average			

Battery or Test	Age	Narrow Ability Tests	LD Area	SS*	SS
Rate-of-test-taking (R9)					
Tests of Cognitive Ability					
CAS	5-17	**PLANNED CODES**			
WAIS-III	16-74	**DIGIT SYMBOL-CODING**			
WISC-III	6-16	**CODING**			
WJ III	4-84	**DECISION SPEED (R4)**			
Other					
Tests of Achievement					
Other					
		1. Sum of column			
		2. Divide by number of tests			
		3. **Rate-of-test-taking** average			

Battery or Test	Age	Narrow Ability Tests	LD Area	SS*	SS
Number Facility (N)					
Tests of Cognitive Ability					
CAS	5-17	**NUMBER DETECTION (R9)**			
CAS	5-17	**MATCHING NUMBERS (R9)**			
Other					
Tests of Achievement					
WJ III	7-90	**MATH FLUENCY (*Gq*-A3)**	MC		
Other					
		1. Sum of column			
		2. Divide by number of tests			
		3. **Mental Comparison Speed** average			

Name:_____
Age: _____
Grade:_____
Examiner:_____
Date of Evaluation: _____

PROCESSING SPEED *is the ability to perform cognitive tasks fluently and automatically, especially when under pressure to maintain focused attention and concentration. It includes the following narrow abilities:*

Perceptual Speed (P): Ability to search for and compare visual symbols rapidly when presented side-by-side or separated in a visual field.

Rate-of-test-taking (R9): Ability to perform tests that are relatively easy or that require very simple decisions rapidly.

Number Facility (N): Ability to manipulate and deal with numbers rapidly and accurately.

Semantic Processing Speed (R4): Reaction time when the decision requires some encoding and mental manipulation of stimulus content.

Sum/No. of Narrow-Ability Averages

Cluster Average**
__ Broad (___)
__ Narrow (___)

Percentile Rank and Standard Score Conversion Table

Percentile Rank	Standard Score		
	Tests with a Mean of 100 and Standard Deviation of 15	Tests with a Mean of 50 and Standard Deviation of 10	Tests with a Mean of 10 and Standard Deviation of 3
99.99	160	90	
99.99	159	89	
99.99	158	89	
99.99	157	88	
99.99	156	87	
99.99	155	87	
99.99	154	86	
99.98	153	85	
99.98	153	85	
99.97	152	85	
99.96	151	84	
99.95	150	83	
99.94	149	83	
99.93	148	82	
99.93	147	81	
99.89	146	81	
99.87	145	80	19
99.84	144	79	
99.80	143	79	
99.75	142	78	
99.70	141	77	
99.64	140	77	18
99.57	139	76	
99	138	75	
99	138	75	
99	137	75	
99	136	74	
99	135	73	17
99	134	73	
99	133	72	

Percentile Rank	Standard Score		
	Tests with a Mean of 100 and Standard Deviation of 15	Tests with a Mean of 50 and Standard Deviation of 10	Tests with a Mean of 10 and Standard Deviation of 3
98	132	71	
98	131	71	
98	130	70	16
97	129	69	
97	128	69	
97	127	68	
96	126	67	
95	125	67	15
95	124	66	
94	123	65	
93	123	65	
92	122	65	
92	121	64	
91	120	63	14
89	119	63	
88	118	62	
87	117	61	
86	116	61	
84	115	60	13
83	114	59	
81	113	59	
79	112	58	
77	111	57	
75	110	57	12
73	109	56	
71	108	55	
69	108	55	
67	107	55	
65	106	54	
65	105	53	11
62	104	53	
57	103	52	
55	102	51	
52	101	51	
50	100	50	10
48	99	49	
45	98	49	
43	97	48	
40	96	47	
38	95	47	9
35	94	46	
33	93	45	
31	93	45	
29	92	45	
27	91	44	
25	90	43	8
23	89	43	
21	88	42	
19	87	41	
17	86	41	
16	85	40	7

Continued

Percentile Rank	Standard Score		
	Tests with a Mean of 100 and Standard Deviation of 15	Tests with a Mean of 50 and Standard Deviation of 10	Tests with a Mean of 10 and Standard Deviation of 3
14	84	39	
13	83	39	
12	82	38	
11	81	37	
9	80	37	6
8	79	36	
8	78	35	
7	78	35	
6	77	35	
5	76	34	
5	75	33	5
4	74	33	
3	73	32	
3	72	31	
3	71	31	
2	70	30	4
2	69	29	
2	68	29	
1	67	28	
1	66	27	
1	65	27	3
1	64	26	
1	63	25	
1	63	25	
1	62	25	
.49	61	24	
.36	60	23	2
.30	59	23	
.25	58	22	
.20	57	21	
.16	56	21	
.16	55	20	1
.11	54	19	
.09	53	19	
.07	52	18	
.06	51	17	
.05	50	17	
.04	49	16	
.03	48	15	
.02	48	15	
.02	47	15	
.01	46	14	
.01	44	13	
.01	43	12	
.01	42	11	
.01	41	11	
.01	40	10	

Test Reviews and Validity Evidence Reported in the Extant Literature

I. COMPREHENSIVE TEST BATTERIES

1. Diagnostic Achievement Battery–Third Edition (DAB–3)

Test Reviews

Brown, L., & Bryant, B. R. (1984). Critical reviews of three individually administered achievement tests: Peabody Individual Achievement Test, Wide Range Achievement Test, and Diagnostic Achievement Battery. *Remedial and Special Education, 5,* 53–60.

Keyser, D., & Sweetland, R. (1985). *Critique of the Diagnostic Achievement Battery* (Test critiques: Vol. 2). Austin, TX: PRO-ED.

Lesiak, J. (1984). Test review: Diagnostic Achievement Battery. *Journal of Psychoeducational Assessment, 2,* 353–358.

Lewandowski, L. J. (1985). Test review: Diagnostic Achievement Battery. *Reading Teacher, 39,* 306–309.

Prasse, D. P. (1984). Test review: Diagnostic Achievement Battery. *Journal of Psychoeducational Assessment, 2,* 359–361.

Webster, W. J. (1985). Review of the Diagnostic Achievement Battery. In J. V. Mitchell (Ed.), *The ninth mental measurements yearbook* (pp. 474–475). Lincoln: University of Nebraska.

Validity Evidence

Arcangelo, K., & Lewandowski, L. J. (1989). Evidence of validity for the Diagnostic Achievement Battery. *Journal of Psychoeducational Assessment, 7,* 46–55.

Daub, D., & Colarusso, R. P. (1996). The validity of the WJ-R, PIAT-R, and DAB-2 reading subtests with students with learning disabilities. *Learning Disabilities Research and Practice, 11,* 90–95.

2. Diagnostic Achievement Test for Adolescents–Second Edition (DATA–2)

Test Review

Schumm, J. (1987). Test review: Diagnostic Achievement Test for Adolescents. *Journal of Reading, 31,* 186–189.

3. Kaufman Test of Educational Achievement/Normative Update (K-TEA/NU)

Test Reviews

Doll, E. S. (1985). Review of the Kaufman Test of Educational Achievement. In J. C. Conoley & R. Sweetland (Eds.), *The tenth mental measurements yearbook* (pp. 410–412). Lincoln: University of Nebraska.

Keyser, D., & Sweetland, R. (1985). *Critique of the Kaufman Test of Educational Achievement* (Test critiques: Vol. 4). Austin, TX: PRO-ED.

Lewandowski, L. (1986). Test review: Kaufman Test of Educational Achievement. *Journal of Reading, 30,* 258–261.

Sattler, J. M. (1985). Review of the Kaufman Test of Educational Achievement. In J. C. Conoley & R. Sweetland (Eds.), *The tenth mental measurements yearbook* (pp. 412–413). Lincoln: University of Nebraska.

Worthington, C. (1987). Kaufman Test of Educational Achievement, Comprehensive Form and Brief Form. *Journal of Counseling and Development, 65,* 325–327.

Validity Evidence

Bookman, J., & Peach, W. (1988). A comparison of the standard scores obtained by special education students on the Diagnostic Achievement Battery, Kaufman Test of Educational Achievement, and the Peabody Individual Achievement Test. *Journal of Instructional Psychology, 15,* 37–39.

Gentry, N., Sapp, G. L., & Daw, J. L. (1995). Scores on the Wechsler Individual Achievement Test and the Kaufman Test of Educational Achievement Comprehensive Form for emotionally conflicted adolescents. *Psychological Reports, 76,* 607–610.

Kamphaus, R., Schmitt, C., & Mings, D. (1986). Three studies of the validity of the Kaufman Test of Educational Achievement. *Journal of Psychoeducational Assessment, 4,* 299–305.

Posey, W., Snapp, G., & Gladding, S. (1989). Validating the Kaufman Test of Educational Achievement, Brief Form with educable mentally retarded students. *Psychological Reports, 65,* 1225–1226.

Prewett, P., & Farhney, M. (1994). The concurrent validity of the Matrix Analogies Test–Short Form with the Stanford-Binet: Fourth Edition and K-TEA-BF. *Psychology in the Schools, 31,* 20–25.

Prewett, P., Lilis, W., & Bardos, A. (1991). Relationship between the Kaufman Test of Educational Achievement-Brief Form and the Wide Range Achievement Test- Revised level 2 with incarcerated juvenile delinquents. *Psychological Reports, 68,* 147–150.

Prewett, P., & McCaffery, L. K. (1993). A comparison of the Kaufman Brief Intelligence Test, the Stanford-Binet Intelligence Scale Fourth Edition, and the Kaufman Test of Educational Achievement. *Psychology in the Schools, 30,* 299–304.

Webster, R., Hewett, J., & Crumbacker, H. (1989). Criterion-related validity of the WRAT-R and K-TEA with teacher's estimates of actual classroom academic performance. *Psychology in the Schools, 26,* 243–248.

4. Peabody Individual Achievement Test–Revised/Normative Update (PIAT–R/NU)

Test Reviews

Benes, K. M. (1992). Review of the Peabody Individual Achievement Test, Revised. In J. J. Kramer & J. C. Conoley (Eds.), *The eleventh mental measurements yearbook* (pp. 649–652). Lincoln: University of Nebraska

Costenbader, V. K., & Adams, J. W. (1991). A review of the psychometric and administrative features of the PIAT-R: Implications for the practitioner. *Journal of School Psychology, 29,* 219–228.

Keyser, D., & Sweetland, R. (1985). *Critique of the Peabody Individual Achievement Test Revised* (Test critiques: Vol. 3). Austin, TX: PRO-ED.

Lazarus, B. (1997). Peabody Individual Achievement Test Revised. *Diagnostique, 15,* 135–148.

Luther, J. B. (1992). Review of the Peabody Individual Achievement Test. *Journal of School Psychology, 30,* 31–39.

Rogers, B. G. (1992). Review of the Peabody Individual Achievement Test, Revised. In J. J. Kramer & J. C. Conoley (Eds.), *The eleventh mental measurements yearbook* (pp. 652–654). Lincoln: University of Nebraska.

Validity Evidence

Altrows, I. (1986). Employing teachers' ratings in selection of achievement tests in reading and mathematics with a behaviorally disturbed population. *Psychology in the Schools, 23,* 316–319.

Bookman, J., & Peach, W. (1988). A comparison of the standard scores obtained by special education students on the Diagnostic Achievement Battery, Kaufman Test of Educational Achievement, and the Peabody Individual Achievement Test. *Journal of Instructional Psychology, 15,* 37–39.

Brown, L., & Bryant, B. R. (1984). Critical reviews of three individually administered achievement tests: Peabody Individual Achievement Test, Wide Range Achievement Test, and Diagnostic Achievement Battery. *Remedial and Special Education, 5,* 53–60.

Campbell, J. (1991). Construct validity of the computerized continuous performance test with measures of intelligence, achievement, and behavior. *Journal of School Psychology, 29,* 143–150.

Caskey, W. E. (1985). The use of the Peabody Individual Achievement Test and the Woodcock Reading Mastery Tests in the diagnosis of a learning disability in reading: A caveat. *Diagnostique, 11,* 14–20.

Curry, J. F., Anderson, D. R., Zitlin, M., & Guise, G. (1987). Validity of academic achievement measures with emotionally handicapped children. *Journal of Clinical Child Psychology, 16,* 51–56.

Daub, D., & Colarusso, R. (1996). The validity of the WJ-R, PIAT-R, and DAB-2 reading subtests with students with learning disabilities. *Learning Disabilities Research and Practice, 11,* 90–95.

Eaves, R., & Cutchen, M. (1990). The construct validity of the Cognitive Levels Test and the Academic Levels Test when compared with the WISC-R and PIAT for a group of adjudicated delinquents. *Journal of Psychoeducational Assessment, 8,* 61–73.

Eaves, R., Darch, C., & Haynes, M. (1989). The concurrent validity of the Peabody Individual Achievement Test and Woodcock Reading Mastery Tests among students with mild learning problems. *Psychology in the Schools, 26,* 261–266.

Eaves, R. C., & Simpson, R. G. (1984). The concurrent validity of the Peabody Individual Achievement Test relative to the Key Math Diagnostic Arithmetic Test among adolescents. *Psychology in the Schools, 21,* 165–167.

Good, R., & Salvia, J. (1988). Curriculum bias in published, norm-referenced reading tests: Demonstrable effects. *School Psychology Review, 17,* 51–60.

Gresham, F. (1987). Teachers as "tests": Classification accuracy and concurrent validation in the identification of learning disabled children. *School Psychology Review, 16,* 543–553.

Muenz, T., Ouchi, B., & Cole, J. (1999). Item analysis of written expression scoring systems from the PIAT-R and WIAT. *Psychology in the Schools, 36,* 31–40.

Riccio, C., Boan, C., Staniszewski, D., & Hynd, G. (1997). Concurrent validity of standardized measures of written expression. *Diagnostique, 23,* 203–211.

Slate, J. R. (1996). Interrelations of frequently administered achievement measures in the determination of specific learning disabilities. *Learning Disabilities Research and Practice, 11,* 86–89.

Slate, J. R. (1997). Achievement test score differences for students with specific learning disabilities: A replication. *Journal of Special Education, 21,* 16–30.

5. Wechsler Individual Achievement Test

Test Reviews

Ackerman, T. (1998). Review of the Wechsler Individual Achievement Test. In J. C. Impara & B. S. Plake (Eds.), *The thirteenth mental measurements yearbook* (pp. 1125–1128). Lincoln: University of Nebraska.

Cohen, L. (1993). Wechsler Individual Achievement Test. *Diagnostique, 18,* 255–268.

Ferrara, S. (1998). Review of the Wechsler Individual Achievement Test. In J. C. Impara & B. S. Plake (Eds.), *The thirteenth mental measurements yearbook* (pp. 1128–1132). Lincoln: University of Nebraska.

Validity Evidence

Curry, J. F., Anderson, D. R., Zitlin, M., & Guise, G. (1987). Validity of academic achievement measures with emotionally handicapped children. *Journal of Clinical Child Psychology, 16,* 51–56.

Gentry, N., Sapp, G. L., & Daw, J. L. (1995). Scores on the Wechsler Individual Achievement Test and the Kaufman Test of Educational Achievement Comprehensive Form for emotionally conflicted adolescents. *Psychological Reports, 76,* 607–610.

Konold, T. R. (1999). Evaluating discrepancy analyses with the WISC III and WIAT. *Journal of Psychoeducational Assessment, 17,* 24–35.

Muenz, T., Ouchi, B., & Cole, J. (1999). Item analysis of written expression scoring systems from the PIAT-R and WIAT. *Psychology in the Schools, 36,* 31–40.

Riccio, C., Boan, C., Staniszewski, D., & Hynd, G. (1997). Concurrent validity of standardized measures of written expression. *Diagnostique, 23,* 203–211.

Slate, J. R. (1996). Interrelations of frequently administered achievement measures in the determination of specific learning disabilities. *Learning Disabilities Research and Practice, 11,* 86–89.

Slate, J. R. (1997). Achievement test score differences for students with specific learning disabilities: A replication. *Journal of Special Education, 21,* 16–30.

6. Woodcock-Johnson Tests of Achievement

Test Reviews

Cuenin, L. H. (1990). Use of the Woodcock-Johnson Psycho-Educational Battery with learning disabled adults. *Learning Disabilities Focus, 5,* 110–123.

Cummings, J. A. (1995). Review of the Woodcock-Johnson Psycho-Educational Battery, Revised. In J. C. Conoley & J. C. Impara (Eds.), *The twelfth mental measurements yearbook* (pp. 1111–1117). Lincoln: University of Nebraska.

Keyser, D., & Sweetland, R. (1994). *Critique of the Woodcock-Johnson Tests of Achievement* (Test critiques: Vol. 10). Austin, TX: PRO-ED.

Taylor, R. (1990). Woodcock-Johnson Psycho-Educational Battery Revised. *Diagnostique, 15,* 264–276.

Validity Evidence

Beden, I., Rohr, L., & Ellsworth, R. (1987). A public school validation study of the achievement sections of the Woodcock-Johnson Psycho-Educational Battery with learning disabled students. *Educational and Psychological Measurement, 47,* 711–717.

Daub, D., & Colarusso, R. (1996). The validity of the WJ-R, PIAT-R, and DAB-2 reading subtests with students with learning disabilities. *Learning Disabilities Research and Practice, 11,* 90–95.

Mather, N. (1989) Comparison of the new and existing Woodcock-Johnson Writing Tests to other writing measures. *Learning Disabilities Focus, 4,* 84–94.

Phelps, L., & Rosso, M. (1985). Validity assessment of the Woodcock-Johnson Broad Cognitive Ability and Scholastic Aptitude Cluster scores for behavior disordered adolescents. *Psychology in the Schools, 22,* 398–403.

Reilly, T., Drudge, O. W., Rosen, J. C., Loew, D. E., & Fischer, M. (1985). Concurrent and predictive validity of the WISC-R, McCarthy Scales, Woodcock-Johnson, and academic achievement. *Psychology in the Schools, 22,* 380–382.

II. BRIEF ACHIEVEMENT TESTS/SCREENERS

1. Kaufman Functional Academic Skills Test (K-FAST)

Test Reviews

Shaw S. R. (1998). Review of the Kaufman Functional Academic Skills Test. In J. C. Impara & B. S. Plake (Eds.), *The thirteenth mental measurements yearbook* (pp. 568–570). Lincoln: University of Nebraska.

Williams, R. T. (1998). Review of the Kaufman Functional Academic Skills Test. In J. C. Impara & B. S. Plake (Eds.), *The thirteenth mental measurements yearbook* (pp. 570–572). Lincoln: University of Nebraska.

Validity Evidence

Flanagan, D. P., McGrew, K. S., Abramowitz, E., Untiedt, S., & Armstrong, H. (1997). Improvement in academic screening instruments? A concurrent validity investigation of the K-FAST, MBA, and WRAT-3. *Journal of Psychoeducational Assessment, 15,* 99–112.

2. Kaufman Survey of Early Academic and Language Skills (K-SEALS)

Test Reviews

Ackerman, P. L. (1995). Review of the Kaufman Survey of Early Academic and Language Skills. In J. C. Conoley & J. C. Impara (Eds.), *The twelfth mental measurements yearbook* (pp. 536–537). Lincoln: University of Nebraska.

Ford, L. & Turk, K. (1995). Review of the Kaufman Survey of Early Academic and Language Skills. In J. C. Conoley & J. C. Impara (Eds.), *The twelfth mental measurements yearbook* (pp. 537–538). Lincoln: University of Nebraska.

3. Mini-Battery of Achievement (MBA)

Test Reviews

Michael, W. B. (1998). Review of the Woodcock-McGrew-Werder Mini-Battery of Achievement. In J. C. Impara & B. S. Plake (Eds.), *The thirteenth mental measurements yearbook* (pp. 1140–1142). Lincoln: University of Nebraska.

Stanford, E. E. (1998). Review of the Woodcock-McGrew-Werder Mini-Battery of Achievement. In J. C. Impara & B. S. Plake (Eds.), *The thirteenth mental measurements yearbook* (pp. 1142–1143). Lincoln: University of Nebraska.

Validity Evidence

Flanagan, D., McGrew, K., Abramowitz, E., & Untiedt, S., & Armstrong, H. (1997). Improvement in academic screening instruments? A concurrent validity investigation of the K-FAST, MBA, and WRAT-3. *Journal of Psychoeducational Assessment, 15,* 99–112.

4. Wide Range Achievement Test 3 (WRAT3)

Test Reviews

Keyser, D., & Sweetland, R. (1984). *Critique of the Wide Range Achievement Test* (Test critiques: Vol. 1). Austin, TX: PRO-ED.

Marby, L. (1995). Review of the Wide Range Achievement Test, Third Edition. In J. C. Conoley & J. C. Impara (Eds.), *The twelfth mental measurements yearbook* (pp. 1108–1110). Lincoln: University of Nebraska.

Ward, A. W. (1995). Review of the Wide Range Achievement Test, Third Edition. In J. C. Conoley & J. C. Impara (Eds.), *The twelfth mental measurements yearbook* (pp. 1110–1111). Lincoln: University of Nebraska.

Validity Evidence

Brown, L., & Bryant, B. R. (1984). Critical reviews of three individually administered achievement tests: Peabody Individual Achievement Test, Wide Range Achievement Test, and Diagnostic Achievement Battery. *Remedial and Special Education, 5,* 53–60.

Campbell, J. (1991). Construct validity of the computerized continuous performance test with measures of intelligence, achievement, and behavior. *Journal of School Psychology, 29,* 143–150.

Estes, R., Hallock, J. E., & Bray, N. M. (1985). Comparison of arithmetic measures with learning disabled students. *Perceptual and Motor Skills, 61,* 711–716.

Flanagan, D., McGrew, K., Abramowitz, E., Untiedt, S., & Armstrong, H. (1997). Improvement in academic screening instruments? A concurrent validity investigation of the K-FAST, MBA, and WRAT-3. *Journal of Psychoeducational Assessment, 15,* 99–112.

Good, R., & Salvia, J. (1988). Curriculum bias in published, norm-referenced reading tests: Demonstrable effects. *School Psychology Review, 17,* 51–60.

Johnson, M. E., Fisher, D. G., Rhodes, F., & Booth, R. (1996). Test re-test stability and concurrent validity of two reading tests with a drug-abusing population. *Assessment, 3,* 111–114.

Morton, L. (1985). Educational psychometric implications of preinstructional spelling proficiency at the grade three level. *Canadian Journal for Special Education, 1,* 92–97.

Mpofu, E. (1996). The differential validity of standardized achievement tests for special educational placement purposes: Results and implications of a Zimbabwean study. *School Psychology International, 17,* 81–92.

Slate, J. R., Jones, C. H., Graham, L. S., & Bower, J. (1994). Correlations of WISC- III, WRAT-R, KM-R, and PPVT-R scores in students with specific learning disabilities. *Learning Disabilities Research and Practice, 9,* 104–107.

Smith, T., Smith, B. L., & Smithson, M. M. (1995). The relationship between the WISC-III and the WRAT3 in a sample of rural referred children. *Psychology in the Schools, 32,* 291–295.

Vance, B., Kitson, D., & Singer, M. G. (1985). Relationship between the standard scores of Peabody Picture Vocabulary Test-Revised and Wide Range Achievement Test. *Journal of Clinical Psychology, 41,* 691–693.

Webster, R., Hewett, J., & Crumbacker, H. (1989). Criterion-related validity of the WRAT-R and K-TEA with teacher's estimates of actual classroom academic performance. *Psychology in the Schools, 26,* 243–248.

III. SPECIFIC ACADEMIC SKILLS—READING TESTS

1. Gray Oral Reading Tests–Fourth Edition (GORT–4)

Test Reviews

Hickman, J. A. (1989). Review of the Gray Oral Reading Tests, Revised. In J. C. Conoley & J. C. Impara (Eds.), *The tenth mental measurements yearbook* (pp. 334–337). Lincoln: University of Nebraska.

Keyser D., & Sweetland, R. (1986). *Critique of the Gray Oral Reading Tests-Revised* (Test critiques: Vol. 5). Austin, TX: PRO-ED.

King, J. D. (1995). Review of the Gray Oral Reading Tests, Third Edition. In J. C. Conoley & J. J. Kramer (Eds.), *The twelfth mental measurements yearbook* (pp. 422). Lincoln: University of Nebraska.

Kundert, D. (1995). Review of the Gray Oral Reading Tests, Third Edition. In J. C. Conoley & J. J. Kramer (Eds.), *The twelfth mental measurements yearbook* (pp. 423–425). Lincoln: University of Nebraska.

Tierney, R. J. (1989). Review of the Gray Oral Reading Tests, Revised. In J. C. Conoley & J. C. Impara (Eds.), *The tenth mental measurements yearbook* (pp. 337–338). Lincoln: University of Nebraska.

Radencich, M. C. (1986). Test review: Gray Oral Reading Tests–Revised. *Journal of Reading, 30,* 136–139.

2. Standardized Reading Inventory-Second Edition (SRI-2)

Test Reviews

Howell, K. W. (1989). Review of the Standardized Reading Inventory. In J. C. Conoley & J. J. Kramer (Eds.), *The tenth mental measurements yearbook* (pp. 763–764). Lincoln: University of Nebraska.

Mathewson, G. (1988). Test review: Standardized Reading Inventory. *Reading Teacher, 41,* 462–465.

Maddux, C. D. (1989). Review of the Standardized Reading Inventory. In J. C. Conoley & J. J. Kramer (Eds.), *The tenth mental measurements yearbook* (pp. 764–765). Lincoln: University of Nebraska.

3. Test of Early Reading Ability–Third Edition (TERA–3)

Test Reviews

Keyser D., & Sweetland, R. (1986). *Critique of the Test of Early Reading Ability* (Test critiques: Vol. 5). Austin, TX: PRO-ED.

Rothlisberg, B. A. (1995). Review of the Test of Early Reading Ability. In J. C. Coloney & J. C. Impara (Eds.), *The twelfth mental measurements yearbook* (pp. 1049–1051). Lincoln: University of Nebraska.

Toubanos, E. S. (1995). Review of the Test of Early Reading Ability. In J. C. Coloney & J. C. Impara (Eds.), *The twelfth mental measurements yearbook* (pp. 1051–1053). Lincoln: University of Nebraska.

Wisxon, S. E. (1985). Test review: The Test of Early Reading Ability (TERA). *Reading Teacher, 38,* 544–547.

Validity Evidence

Day, K. C., & Day, H. D. (1991). The concurrent validity of four tests of metalinguistic awareness. *Reading-Psychology, 12,* 1–11.

4. Test of Reading Comprehension–Third Edition (TORC–3)

Test Reviews

Green, F. S. (1998). Review of the Test of Reading Comprehension, Third Edition. In J. C. Impara & B. S. Plake (Eds.), *The thirteenth mental measurements yearbook* (pp. 1052–1053). Lincoln: University of Nebraska.

Misulis, K. (1989). Test of Reading Comprehension (TORC), revised edition. *Journal of Reading, 33,* 228–229.

Perlman, C. (1998). Review of the Test of Reading Comprehension Third Edition. In J. C. Impara & B. S. Plake (Eds.), *The thirteenth mental measurements yearbook* (pp. 1053–1055). Lincoln: University of Nebraska.

5. Woodcock Reading Mastery Tests–Revised/Normative Update (WRMT–R/NU)

Test Reviews

Cooter, R. B. (1989). Review of the Woodcock Reading Mastery Tests, Revised. In J. C. Conoley & J. J. Kramer (Eds.), *The tenth mental measurements yearbook* (pp. 910–913). Lincoln: University of Nebraska.

Eaves, R. (1990). Woodcock Reading Mastery Tests-Revised. *Diagnostique, 15,* 277–297.

Jaeger, R. M. (1989). Review of the Woodcock Reading Mastery Tests, Revised. In J. C. Conoley & J. J. Kramer (Eds.), *The tenth mental measurements yearbook* (pp. 913–916). Lincoln: University of Nebraska.

Keyser D., & Sweetland, R. (1985). *Critique of the Woodcock Reading Mastery Test Revised* (Test critiques, Vol. 4). Austin, TX: PRO-ED.

Lewandowski, L. J., & Martens, B. K. (1990). Selecting and evaluating standardized reading tests (test review). *Journal of Reading, 33,* 384–388.

Validity Evidence

Caskey, W. E. (1985). The use of the Peabody Individual Achievement Test and the Woodcock Reading Mastery Tests in the diagnosis of a learning disability in reading: A caveat. *Diagnostique, 11,* 14–20.

Eaves, R. (1992). Diagnostic accuracy of the Cognitive Levels Test, the Key Math Revised, and the Woodcock Reading Mastery Tests-Revised. *Diagnostique, 17,* 163–175.

Eaves, R., Darch, C., & Haynes, M. (1989). The concurrent validity of the Peabody Individual Achievement Test and Woodcock Reading Mastery Tests among students with mild learning problems. *Psychology in the Schools, 26,* 261–266.

Johnson, M. E., Fisher, D. G., Rhodes, F., & Booth, R. (1996). Test-retest stability and concurrent validity of two reading tests with a drug-abusing population. *Assessment, 3,* 111–114.

Salstone, R., Taylor, S. M., & Fraboni, M. (1989). A note on the Word Identification subtest of the Woodcock Reading Mastery Tests- Revised: Different classification consequences of Forms G and H. *Journal of Psychoeducational Assessment, 7,* 343–345.

Simpson, R. G., & Halpin, G. (1987). The effects of altering the ceiling criterion on the passage comprehension test of the Woodcock Reading Mastery Tests. *Educational and Psychological Measurement, 47,* 215–221.

Slate, J. R. (1996). Interrelations of frequently administered achievement measures in the determination of specific learning disabilities. *Learning Disabilities Research and Practice, 11,* 86–89.

Slate, J. R. (1997). Achievement test score differences for students with specific learning disabilities: A replication. *Journal of Special Education, 21,* 16–30.

IV. MATH TESTS

1. Key Math-Revised/ Normative Update (KM-R/NU)

Test Reviews

Beck, M. D. (1992). Review of the Key Math, Revised. In J. J. Kramer & J. C. Conoley (Eds.), *The eleventh mental measurements yearbook* (pp. 437–438). Lincoln: University of Nebraska.

Finley, C. J. (1992). Review of the Key Math, Revised. In J. J. Kramer & J. C. Conoley (Eds.), *The eleventh mental measurements yearbook* (pp. 438–439). Lincoln: University of Nebraska.

Keyser, D., & Sweetland, R. (1994). *Critique of the Key Math Revised* (Test critiques: Vol. 10). Austin, TX: PRO-ED.

Validity Evidence

Eaves, R. (1992). Diagnostic accuracy of the Cognitive Levels Test, the Key Math Revised, and the Woodcock Reading Mastery Tests-Revised. *Diagnostique, 17,* 163–175.

Eaves, R. C., & Simpson, R. G. (1984). The concurrent validity of the Peabody Individual Achievement Test relative to the Key Math Diagnostic Arithmetic Test among adolescents. *Psychology in the Schools, 21,* 165–167.

Estes, R., Hallock, J., & Bray, N. (1985). Comparison of arithmetic measures with learning disabled students. *Perceptual and Motor Skills, 61,* 711–716.

Hippisley, J., & Douglas, F. (1998). The reliability and validity of an interactive arithmetic test. *British Journal of Educational Technology, 29,* 303–320.

Slate, J. R. (1996). Interrelations of frequently administered achievement measures in the determination of specific learning disabilities. *Learning Disabilities Research and Practice, 11,* 86–89.

Slate, J. R. (1997). Achievement test score differences for students with specific learning disabilities: A replication. *Journal of Special Education, 21,* 16–30.

Slate, J. R., Jones, C. H., Graham, L. S., & Bower, J. (1994). Correlations of WISC- III, WRAT-R, KM-R, and PPVT-R scores in students with specific learning disabilities. *Learning Disabilities Research and Practice, 9,* 104–107.

2. Test of Mathematical Abilities–Second Edition (TOMA–2)

Test Reviews

Griffin, H. (1997). Review of the Test of Mathematical Abilities. *Measurement and Evaluation in Counseling and Development, 29,* 242–247.

Howell, K. (1990). Test of Mathematical Abilities. *Diagnostique, 15,* 210–217.

V. SPECIFIC ACADEMIC SKILLS–WRITTEN LANGUAGE TESTS

1. Test of Early Written Language–Second Edition (TEWL–2)

Test Reviews

Hurford, D. P. (1998). Review of the Test of Early Written Language Second Edition. In J. C. Impara & B. S. Plake (Eds.), *The thirteenth mental measurements yearbook* (pp. 1027–1030). Lincoln: University of Nebraska.

Isaacson, S. L. (1992). Early screening of written language skill: The Test of Early Written Language. *Learning Disabilities Research and Practice, 7,* 231–234.

Trevisan, M. S. (1998). Review of the Test of Early Written Language Second Edition. In J. C. Impara & B. S. Plake (Eds.), *The thirteenth mental measurements yearbook* (pp. 1030–1031). Lincoln: University of Nebraska.

Validity Evidence

Isaacson, S. (1992). Early screening of written language skill: The Test of Early Written Language. *Learning Disabilities Research and Practice, 7,* 231–234.

2. Test of Written Expression (TOWE)

Test Reviews

Ehrler, D. (1996). Test of Written Expression: A critical review. *Journal of School Psychology, 34,* 387–391.

Murray-Ward, M. (1998). Review of the Test of Written Expression. In J. C. Impara & B. S. Plake (Eds.), *The thirteenth mental measurements yearbook* (pp. 1067–1068). Lincoln: University of Nebraska.

Perlman, C. (1998). Review of the Test of Written Expression. In J. C. Impara & B. S. Plake (Eds.), *The thirteenth mental measurements yearbook* (pp. 1068–1069). Lincoln: University of Nebraska.

3. Test of Written Language–Third Edition (TOWL–3)

Test Reviews

Bucy, J. E., & Swerdlik, M. E. (1998). Review of the Test of Written Language, Third Edition. In J. C. Impara & B. S. Plake (Eds.), *The thirteenth mental measurements yearbook* (pp. 1072–1074). Lincoln: University of Nebraska.

Graham, S. (1989). Is new necessarily better? A review of the TOWL-2. *Learning Disabilities Focus, 5,* 47–49.

Hansen, J. B. (1998). Review of the Test of Written Language Third Edition. In J. C. Impara & B. S. Plake (Eds.), *The thirteenth mental measurements yearbook* (pp. 1060–1072). Lincoln: University of Nebraska.

Jacobson, J. (1991). Test of Written Language-2: Test review. *Journal of Reading, 34,* 663–665.

Keyser, D., & Sweetland, R. (1984). *Critique of the Test of Written Language* (Test critiques: Vol. 1). Austin, TX: PRO-ED.

Poteet, J. A. (1990). Test of Written Language Second Edition. *Diagnostique, 15,* 228–242.

Yarger, C. (1996). An examination of the Test of Written Language-3. *Volta Review, 98,* 211–215.

Validity Evidence

Day, K., & Day, H. (1991). The concurrent validity of four tests of metalinguistic awareness. *Reading Psychology, 12,* 1–11.

Riccio, C., Boan, C., Staniszewski, D., & Hynd, G. (1997). Concurrent validity of standardized measures of written expression. *Diagnostique, 23,* 203–211.

4. Test of Written Spelling–Fourth Edition (TWS–4)

Test Reviews

Keyser, D., & Sweetland, R. (1986). *Critique of the Test of Written Spelling* (Test critiques: Vol. 5). Austin, TX: PRO-ED.

Longo, A. P. (1998). Review of the Test of Written Spelling, Fourth Edition. In J. C. Impara & B. S. Plake (Eds.), *The thirteenth mental measurements yearbook* (pp. 1074–1075). Lincoln: University of Nebraska.

Suen, H. K. (1998). Review of the Test of Written Spelling, Fourth Edition. In J. C. Impara & B. S. Plake (Eds.), *The thirteenth mental measurements yearbook* (pp. 1076–1077). Lincoln: University of Nebraska.

Validity Evidence

Morton, L. (1985). Educational psychometric implications of preinstructional spelling proficiency at the grade three level. *Canadian Journal for Special Education, 1,* 92–97.

VI. SPECIFIC ACADEMIC SKILLS—ORAL LANGUAGE TESTS

1. Clinical Evaluation of Language Fundamentals–Third Edition (CELF–3)

Test Reviews

Gillam, R. B. (1998). Review of Clinical Evaluation of Language Fundamentals Third Edition. In J. C. Impara & B. S. Plake (Eds.), *The thirteenth mental measurements yearbook* (pp. 261–262). Lincoln: University of Nebraska.

MacDonald, J. (1998). Review of Clinical Evaluation of Language Fundamentals Third Edition. In J. C. Impara & B. S. Plake (Eds.), *The thirteenth mental measurements yearbook* (pp. 262–263). Lincoln: University of Nebraska.

Validity Evidence

Powell, T. W. (1993). Critical values for evaluating CELF-R receptive and expressive language score discrepancies. *Perceptual and Motor Skills, 76,* 367–370.

Summers, P. (1996). Test-retest comparisons using the CELF-RST and BLT-2S with kindergartners. *Language, Speech, and Hearing Services in the Schools, 27,* 324–329.

Turkstra, L. (1999). Language testing in adolescents with brain injury: A consideration of the CELF-3. *Language, Speech, and Hearing Services in Schools, 30,* 132–140.

2. Comprehensive Receptive and Expressive Vocabulary Test (CREVT)

Test Reviews

Kaufman, A. S., & Kaufman, N. L. (1998). Review of the Comprehensive Receptive and Expressive Vocabulary Test. In J. C. Impara & B.S. Plake (Eds.), *The thirteenth mental measurements yearbook* (pp. 301–303). Lincoln: University of Nebraska.

McLellan, M. J. (1998). Review of the Comprehensive Receptive and Expressive Vocabulary Test. In J. C. Impara & B.S. Plake (Eds.), *The thirteenth mental measurements yearbook* (pp. 304–305). Lincoln: University of Nebraska.

3. Expressive One-Word Picture Vocabulary Test (EO-WPVT)

Validity Evidence

Channell, R., & Peek, M. (1989). Four measures of vocabulary ability compared in older preschool children. *Language, Speech, and Hearing Services in the Schools, 20,* 407–419.

Furlong, M., & Teuber, J. (1984). Validity of the Expressive One Word Picture Vocabulary Test for learning disabled children. *Journal of Psychoeducational Assessment, 2,* 29–36.

Kutsick, K., Vance, B., Schwarting, F. G., & West, R. (1988). A comparison of three different measures of intelligence with preschool children identified at-risk. *Psychology in the Schools, 25,* 270–275.

Teuber, J., & Furlong, M. (1985). The concurrent validity of the Expressive One-Word Picture Vocabulary Test for Mexican-American children. *Psychology in the Schools, 22,* 269–273.

Vance, B. (1986). Concurrent validity of the Peabody Picture Vocabulary Test-R and the Expressive One-Word Picture Vocabulary Test for language-delayed and non-language-delayed young children. *Diagnostique, 13,* 3–9.

4. Illinois Test of Psycholinguistic Abilities–Third Edition (ITPA–3)

Test Review

Keyser, D., & Sweetland, R. (1984). *Critique of the Illinois Test of Psycholinguistic Abilities-Revised* (Test critiques, Vol. 1). Austin, TX: PRO-ED.

Validity Evidence

Channell, R. W., & Ford, C. T. (1991). Four grammatic measures of language ability. *Language , Speech, and Hearing Services in Schools*, 22, 211–218.

Kuusinen, J., & Leskinen, E. (1988). Latent structure analysis of longitudinal data on relations between intellectual abilities and school achievement. *Multivariate Behavioral Research, 23*, 103–118.

5. Language Processing Test–Revised (LPT–R)

Test Reviews

Haber L. (1989). Review of the Language Processing Test. In J. C. Conoley & J. J. Kramer (Eds.), *The tenth mental measurements yearbook* (pp. 432–434). Lincoln: University of Nebraska.

Keyser, D., & Sweetland, R. (1988). *Critique of the Language Processing Test* (Test critiques: Vol. 7). Austin, TX: PRO-ED.

6. Peabody Picture Vocabulary Test III (PPVT-III)

Test Reviews

Keyser, D., & Sweetland, R. (1985). *Critique of the Peabody Picture Vocabulary Test* (Test critiques: Vol. 3). Austin, TX: PRO-ED.

McCallum, R. S. (1985). Review of the Peabody Picture Vocabulary Test. In J. V. Mitchell, Jr. (Ed.), *The ninth mental measurements yearbook* (pp. 1126–1127). Lincoln: University of Nebraska.

Vance, R., & Stone, J. (1990). Peabody Picture Vocabulary Test, Revised. *Diagnostique, 15*, 149–160.

Wiig, E. H.(1985). Review of the Peabody Picture Vocabulary Test. In J. V. Mitchell, Jr. (Ed.), *The ninth mental measurements yearbook* (pp. 1127–1128). Lincoln: University of Nebraska.

Validity Evidence

Beck, F. (1985). The concurrent validity of the Peabody Picture Vocabulary Test-Revised relative to the Comprehensive Tests of Basic Skills. *Educational and Psychological Measurement, 45*, 705–710.

Childers, J. S., Durham, T. W., & Wilson, S. (1994). Relation of performance on the Kaufman Brief Intelligence Test with the Peabody Picture Vocabulary Test- Revised among preschool children. *Perceptual and Motor Skills, 79*, 1195–1199.

Davis, S., & Kramer, J. (1985). Comparison of the PPVT-R and WISC-R: A validation study with second-grade students. *Psychology in the Schools, 22*, 265–268.

Flipsen, P. (1998). Assessing receptive vocabulary in small-town Canadian kindergarten children: Findings for the PPVT-R. *Journal of Speech Language Pathology and Audiology, 22*, 88–93.

Friend, T., & Channell, R. (1987). A comparison of two measures of receptive vocabulary. *Language, Speech, and Hearing in the Schools, 18*, 231–237.

Hadapp, A. F., & Gerken, K. C. (1999). Correlations between scores for Peabody Picture Vocabulary Test-III and the Wechsler Intelligence Scale for Children-III. *Psychological Reports, 84*, 1139–1142.

Hadapp, A. F., & Hass, J. K. (1997). Correlations between the Wechsler Intelligence Scale for Children-III and Form M of the Peabody Picture Vocabulary Test-Revised. *Psychological Reports, 80,* 491–495.

Hunter, M., Ballash, J. B., & Chen, A. N. (1992). Comparison of the Peabody Picture Vocabulary Test-Revised and the Stanford-Binet Intelligence Scale 4th Edition with elementary students referred for learning problems. *Diagnostique, 17,* 108–114.

Ingram, F., Caroselli, J., Robinson, H., Hetzel, R., Reed, K., & Masel, B. (1998). The PPVT-R: Validity as a quick screen of intelligence in a post-acute rehabilitation setting for brain-injured adults. *Journal of Clinical Psychology, 54,* 877–884.

Kutsick, K., Vance, B., Schwarting, F. G., & West, R. (1988). A comparison of three different measures of intelligence with preschool children identified at-risk. *Psychology in the Schools, 25,* 270–275.

Miller, L. T., & Lee, C. J. (1993). Construct validation of the Peabody Picture Vocabulary Test-Revised: A structural equation model of the acquisition order of words. *Psychological Assessment, 5,* 438–441.

Morrison, M. W. (1994). The use of psychological tests to detect malingered intellectual impairment. *American Journal of Forensic Psychology, 12,* 47–64.

Slate, J. R., Jones, C. H., Graham, L. S., & Bower, J. (1994). Correlations of WISC- III, WRAT-R, KM-R, and PPVT-R scores in students with specific learning disabilities. *Learning Disabilities Research and Practice, 9,* 104–107.

Stevenson, J. (1986). Alternate form reliability and concurrent validity of the PPVT-R for referred rehabilitation agency adults. *Journal of Clinical Psychology, 42,* 650–653.

Teuber, J., & Furlong, M. (1985). The concurrent validity of the Expressive One-Word Picture Vocabulary Test for Mexican-American children. *Psychology in the Schools, 22,* 269–273.

Vance, B. (1985). Relationship between the standard scores of Peabody Picture Vocabulary Test-Revised and Wide Range Achievement Test. *Journal of Clinical Psychology, 41,* 691–693.

Vance, B. (1986). Concurrent validity of the Peabody Picture Vocabulary Test-R and the Expressive One-Word Picture Vocabulary Test for language-delayed and non-language-delayed young children. *Diagnostique, 13,* 3–9.

7. Receptive One-Word Picture Vocabulary Test (RO-WPVT)

Test Review

Amster, J. (1987). Test review: Receptive One-Word Picture Vocabulary Test. *Reading Teacher, 40,* 452–455.

Validity Evidence

Channell, R., & Peek, M. (1989). Four measures of vocabulary ability compared in older preschool children. *Language, Speech, and Hearing Services in the Schools, 20,* 407–419.

8. Test of Adolescent and Adult Language–Third Edition (TOAL–3)

Test Reviews

MacDonald, J. (1998). Review of the Test of Adolescent and Adult Language, Third Edition. In J. C. Impara & B. S. Plake (Eds.), *The thirteenth mental measurements yearbook* (pp. 1018–1019). Lincoln: University of Nebraska.

Richards, R. A. (1998). Review of the Test of Adolescent and Adult Language Third Edition. In J. C. Impara & B. S. Plake (Eds.), *The thirteenth mental measurements yearbook* (pp. 1019–1021). Lincoln: University of Nebraska.

Roberts, R., & Mather, N. (1998). Test review: Test of Adolescent and Adult Language, Third Edition. *Journal of Psychoeducational Assessment, 16,* 75–83.

Validity Evidence

Johnson, C., Taback, N., Escobar, M., Wilson, B., & Beitchman, J. (1999). Local norming of the Test of Adolescent and Adult Language-3 in the Ottawa Speech and Language Study. *Journal of Speech, Language, and Hearing Research, 42,* 761–766.

9. Test of Early Language Development–Third Edition (TELD–3)

Test Reviews

Bartlett, A., Slade, D., & Bellerose, P. (1987). Test review: The Test of Early Language Development. *Reading Teacher, 40,* 546–548.

Crawford, A. (1985). Test review: Test of Early Language Development. *Reading Teacher, 38,* 428–431.

Kaiser, J. (1995). Review of the Test of Early Language Development. In J. C. Conoley & J. C. Impara (Eds.), *The twelfth mental measurements yearbook* (pp. 1045–1046). Lincoln: University of Nebraska.

Keyser, D., & Sweetland, R. (1986). *Critique of the Test of Early Language Development* (Test critiques: Vol. 5). Austin, TX: PRO-ED.

Shapiro, D. A. (1995). Review of the Test of Early Language Development. In J. C. Conoley & J. C. Impara (Eds.), *The twelfth mental measurements yearbook* (pp. 1046–1048). Lincoln: University of Nebraska.

Validity Evidence

Dale, P., & Henderson, V. (1987). An evaluation of the Test of Early Language Development as a measure of receptive and expressive language. *Language,Speech, and Hearing in the Schools, 18,* 179–187.

10. Test of Language Development–Intermediate: Third Edition (TOLD–I:3)

Test Reviews

Channell, R., & Ford, C. (1991). Four grammatical completion measures of language ability. *Language, Speech, and Hearing Services in the Schools, 22,* 211–218.

Cole, K. (1984). Test of Language Development: Primary. *Journal of Psychoeducational Assessment, 2,* 169–172.

Richmond, B. (1984). Test review: Test of Language Development: Intermediate. *Journal of Psychoeducational Assessment, 2,* 363–366.

Shipley, K. G. (1992). Review of the Test of Language Development Intermediate. In J. J. Kramer & J. C. Conoley (Eds.), *The eleventh mental measurements yearbook* (pp. 963–966). Lincoln: University of Nebraska.

Validity Evidence

Illerbrun, D. (1985). Language identification screening test for kindergarten: A comparison with four screening and three diagnostic language tests. *Language, Speech, and Hearing Services in the Schools, 16,* 280–292.

Lieberman, R., & Michael, A. (1986). Content relevance and content coverage in tests of grammatical ability. *Journal of Speech and Hearing Disorders, 51,* 71–81.

11. Test of Language Development–Primary: Third Edition (TOLD–P:3)

Test Reviews

Crocker, L. (1992). Review of the Test of Language Development Primary. In J. J. Kramer & J. C. Conoley (Eds.), *The eleventh mental measurements yearbook* (pp. 964–965). Lincoln: University of Nebraska.

Fodness, R., McNeilly, J., & Bradley, J. (1991). Test-retest reliability of the Test of Language Development-2: Primary and Test of Language Development-2: Intermediate. *Journal of School Psychology, 29,* 1612–1665.

Keyser, D., & Sweetland, R. (1994). *Critique of the Test of Language Development Primary, Third Edition* (Test critiques: Vol. 10). Austin, TX: PRO-ED.

Westby, C. E. (1992). Review of the Test of Language Development Primary. In J. J. Kramer & J. C. Conoley (Eds.), *The eleventh mental measurements yearbook* (pp. 965–966). Lincoln: University of Nebraska.

Validity Evidence

Channell, R., & Ford, C. (1991). Four grammatical completion measures of language ability. *Language, Speech, and Hearing in Schools, 22,* 211–218.

Friend, T., & Channell, R. (1987). A comparison of two measures of receptive vocabulary. *Language, Speech, and Hearing in the Schools, 18,* 231–237.

Grossman, F. M. (1986). Statistical interpretation variability on the Test of Language Development-Primary. *Perceptual and Motor Skills, 63,* 329–330.

VII. SPECIFIC ACADEMIC SKILLS—PHONOLOGICAL PROCESSING TESTS

1. Test of Auditory Comprehension of Language–Third Edition (TACL–3)

Test Reviews

Haynes, M. (1990). Test of Auditory Comprehension of Language-Revised. *Diagnostique, 15,* 197–209.

Wnuk, L. (1987). A review of the Bzoch League Receptive Expressive Emergent Language Scale and the Test for Auditory Comprehension of Language. *Canadian Journal for Exceptional Children, 3,* 95–98.

Validity Evidence

Beisler, J. M., Tsai, L. Y., & Vonk, D. (1987). Comparisons between autistic and nonautistic children on the Test for Auditory Comprehension of Language. *Journal of Autism and Developmental Disorders, 17,* 95–102.

Brown, J. R. (1985). The relation of chronological age of normal children in kindergarten and Grade 1 to their performance on the Test for Auditory Comprehension of Language. *Journal of Auditory Research, 25,* 129–132.

Illerbrun, D. (1985). Language identification screening test for kindergarten: A comparison with four screening and three diagnostic language tests. *Language, Speech, and Hearing Services in the Schools, 16,* 280–292.

Robinson, D. (1988). Auditory only and auditory-visual presentations of the Test of Auditory Comprehension to hearing impaired children. *Language, Speech, and Hearing Services in the Schools, 19,* 349–351.

Tsai, L., & Beisler, J. (1984). Research in infantile autism: A methodological problem in using language comprehension as the basis for selecting matched controls. *Journal of the American Academy of Child Psychiatry, 23,* 700–703.

2. Test of Phonological Awareness (TOPA)

Test Reviews

Dohan, M. (1996). The Test of Phonological Awareness: A critical review. *Journal of Speech Language Pathology and Audiology, 20,* 22–26.

Long, S. H. (1998). Review of the Test of Phonological Awareness. In J. C. Impara & B. S. Plake (Eds.), *The thirteenth mental measurements yearbook* (pp. 1049–1050). Lincoln: University of Nebraska.

McCauley, R. (1998). Review of the Test of Phonological Awareness. In J. C. Impara & B. S. Plake (Eds.), *The thirteenth mental measurements yearbook* (pp. 1050–1051). Lincoln: University of Nebraska.

Validity Evidence

Badian, N. (1998). A validation of the role of preschool phonological and orthographic skills in the prediction of reading. *Journal of Learning Disabilities, 31,* 472–481.

CHC Cross-Battery Level I-A: Data Summary and Normative Analysis Graph for Inter-Academic Analysis

| Name:_____ Age: ____ Grade: ____ | CHC Cross-Battery Inter-Academic Analysis |
| Examiner:_____ Date: _____ | Level I-A: Data Summary |

Cluster	Test Battery	Subtest Name + (CHC ability code)	Standard Score	Standard Score Confidence Interval	Percentile Rank	Classification
Grw-R (Reading Ability)		*Grw-R Cluster Average =*				
Grw-W (Writing Ability)		*Grw-W Cluster Average =*				
Gc (Crystallized Intelligence)		*Gc Cluster Average =*				
Gq (Quantitative Knowledge)		*Gq Cluster Average =*				

Note: All standard scores are based on age norms.   **Confidence Bands:** • Clusters = ± 5 • Subtests = ± 7

Name:_____ Age: ____ Grade: ____	**CHC Cross-Battery Inter-Academic Analysis**
Examiner:_____ Date: _____	**Level I-A: Normative Analysis Graph**

Confidence Bands: • Clusters = ± 5 • Subtests = ± 7

-1 SEM ←—68 %—→ +1 SEM

Performance Classification	Very Low	Low	L Avg.	Average	H.Avg.	Sup.	Very Superior
Percentile Ranks	≤ 2	3 - 8	9 - 24	25 - 75	76-97	92 - 97	98 - 99+

40   50   60   70   80   90   100   110   120   130   140   150   160

***Grw*–R** Broad/Narrow Cl.
_____ (__)
_____ (__)
_____ (__)
_____ (__)
_____ (__)
_____ (__)
_____ (__)
_____ (__)

***Grw*–W** Broad/Narrow Cl.
_____ (__)
_____ (__)
_____ (__)
_____ (__)
_____ (__)
_____ (__)
_____ (__)
_____ (__)

Gc Broad/Narrow Cluster
_____ (__)
_____ (__)
_____ (__)
_____ (__)
_____ (__)
_____ (__)
_____ (__)
_____ (__)
_____ (__)

Gq Broad/Narrow Cluster
_____ (__)
_____ (__)
_____ (__)
_____ (__)
_____ (__)
_____ (__)
_____ (__)
_____ (__)

40   50   60   70   80   90   100   110   120   130   140   150   160

NORMATIVE RANGE CLASSIFICATION	Normative Deficit Greater than 1 SD below mean	Normal Limits ± 1 SD from mean	Normative Strength Greater than 1 SD above mean

CHC Cross-Battery Level II-A: Data Summary and Normative Analysis Graph for Inter-Cognitive Analysis

| Name:_____ Age: ____ Grade: ____ |
| Examiner:_____ Date: _____ |

CHC Cross-Battery Inter-Cognitive Analysis
Level II-A: Data Summary

Cluster	Test Battery	Subtest Name + (CHC ability code)	Standard Score	Standard Score Confidence Interval	Percentile Rank	Classification
Gc (Crystallized Intelligence)		*Gc Cluster Average =*				
Gf (Fluid Reasoning)		*Gf Cluster Average =*				
Gv (Visual Processing)		*Gv Cluster Average =*				
Gsm (Short-term Memory)		*Gsm Cluster Average =*				
Glr (Long-term Retrieval)		*Glr Cluster Average =*				
Ga (Auditory Processing)		*Ga Cluster Average =*				
Gs (Processing Speed)		*Gs Cluster Average =*				

Note: All standard scores are based on age norms.   **Confidence Bands:** • Clusters = ± 5 • Subtests = ± 7

Name:	Age: ____ Grade: ____
Examiner:	Date: ____

CHC Cross-Battery Inter-Cognitive Analysis
Level II-A: Normative Analysis Graph

Confidence Bands: • Clusters = ± 5 • Subtests = ± 7

-1 SEM ←—68 %—→ +1 SEM

Performance Classification	Very Low	Low	L Avg.	Average	H.Avg.	Sup.	Very Superior
Percentile Ranks	≤ 2	3 - 8	9 - 24	25 - 75	76-97	92 - 97	98 - 99+

40 50 60 70 80 90 100 110 120 130 140 150 160

Gc Broad/Narrow Cluster
_____ (__)
_____ (__)
_____ (__)
_____ (__)
_____ (__)
_____ (__)
_____ (__)

Gf Broad/Narrow Cluster
_____ (__)
_____ (__)
_____ (__)
_____ (__)
_____ (__)
_____ (__)

Gv Broad/Narrow Cluster
_____ (__)
_____ (__)
_____ (__)
_____ (__)
_____ (__)

Gsm Broad/Narrow Cluster
_____ (__)
_____ (__)
_____ (__)
_____ (__)
_____ (__)

Glr Broad/Narrow Cluster
_____ (__)
_____ (__)
_____ (__)
_____ (__)
_____ (__)

Ga Broad/Narrow Cluster
_____ (__)
_____ (__)
_____ (__)
_____ (__)
_____ (__)

Gs Broad/Narrow Cluster
_____ (__)
_____ (__)
_____ (__)
_____ (__)
_____ (__)

40 50 60 70 80 90 100 110 120 130 140 150 160

NORMATIVE RANGE	Normative Deficit	Normal Limits	Normative Strength
CLASSIFICATION	Greater than 1 SD below mean	$\pm$ 1 SD from mean	Greater than 1 SD above mean

CHC Cross-Battery Level III: Data Summary and Normative Analysis Graph for Integrated Ability Analysis

				CHC Cross-Battery Integrated Ability Analysis Level III – Data Summary		

Name:_____ Age: ____ Grade: ____
Examiner:_____ Date: _____

Cluster	Test Battery	Subtest Name + (CHC ability code)	Standard Score	Standard Score Confidence Interval	Percentile Rank	Classification
Grw (Reading/Writing)		*Grw Cluster Average =*				
Gc (Crystallized Intelligence)		*Gc Cluster Average =*				
Gq (Quantitative Knowledge)		*Gq Cluster Average =*				
Gf (Fluid Reasoning)		*Gf Cluster Average =*				
Gv (Visual Processing)		*Gv Cluster Average =*				
Gsm (Short-term Memory)		*Gsm Cluster Average =*				
Glr (Long-term Retrieval)		*Glr Cluster Average =*				
Ga (Auditory Processing)		*Ga Cluster Average =*				
Gs (Processing Speed)		*Gs Cluster Average =*				

Note: All standard scores are based on age norms. **Confidence Bands:** • Clusters = ± 5 • Subtests = ± 7

Name:_____ Age:____ Grade:____
Examiner:_____ Date:_____

CHC Cross-Battery Integrated Ability Analysis
Level III - Normative Analysis Graph

Confidence Bands: • Clusters = ± 5 • Subtests = ± 7

-1 SEM ←—68 %—→ +1 SEM

Performance Classification	Very Low	Low	L Avg.	Average	H.Avg.	Sup.	Very Superior
Percentile Ranks	≤ 2	3 - 8	9 - 24	25 - 75	76-97	92 - 97	98 - 99+

40 50 60 70 80 90 100 110 120 130 140 150 160

Grw Broad/Narrow Cluster
_____ (__)
_____ (__)
_____ (__)
_____ (__)
_____ (__)
_____ (__)
_____ (__)

Gc Broad/Narrow Cluster
_____ (__)
_____ (__)
_____ (__)
_____ (__)
_____ (__)
_____ (__)
_____ (__)

Gq Broad/Narrow Cluster
_____ (__)
_____ (__)
_____ (__)
_____ (__)

Gf Broad/Narrow Cluster
_____ (__)
_____ (__)
_____ (__)
_____ (__)

Gv Broad/Narrow Cluster
_____ (__)
_____ (__)
_____ (__)
_____ (__)

Gsm Broad/Narrow Cluster
_____ (__)
_____ (__)
_____ (__)
_____ (__)

Glr Broad/Narrow Cluster
_____ (__)
_____ (__)
_____ (__)
_____ (__)

Ga Broad/Narrow Cluster
_____ (__)
_____ (__)
_____ (__)
_____ (__)

Gs Broad/Narrow Cluster
_____ (__)
_____ (__)
_____ (__)
_____ (__)

40 50 60 70 80 90 100 110 120 130 140 150 160

NORMATIVE RANGE CLASSIFICATION	Normative Weakness Greater than 1 SD below mean	Normal Limits ± 1 SD from mean	Normative Strength Greater than 1 SD above mean

CHC Cross-Battery Level I-A: Data Summary and Normative Analysis Graph for Academic Clinical Composites[1]

[1]This form allows for in-depth assessment of the Academic Clinical Composites that correspond to the seven LD areas specified in IDEA and may be used in lieu of the forms in Appendix D1, as appropriate.

Name:
Age:_____ Grade:_____
Examiner:_____ Date:_____

CHC Cross-Battery Academic Clinical Composites
Level I-A: Data Summary

LD AREA	Test Battery	Subtest Name	CHC Ability Measured	Standard Score	Confidence Interval	%ile Rank	Classification
OE – Oral Expression		OE Area Average =					
LC – Listening Comprehension		LC Area average =					
WE – Written Expression		WE Area Average =					
BR – Basic Reading Skills		BR Area Average =					
RC – Reading Comprehension		RC Area Average =					
MC – Mathematics Calculation		MC Area Average =					
MR – Mathematics Reasoning		MR Area Average =					
GK – General Knowledge[1]		GK Area Average =					

[1]*GK*, which includes general information and lexical knowledge, is not an "official" academic area listed in IDEA's definition of learning disability but represents another store of acquired knowledge consistent with the other stores of acquired knowledge that are listed (e.g., reading, math, writing, etc.).

Note: All standard scores are based on age norms.   **Confidence Bands:** • Clusters = ± 5 • Subtests = ± 7

Name:_____

Age:_____ Grade: _____

Examiner:_____ Date: _____

CHC Cross-Battery Academic Clinical Composites
Level I-A: Normative Analysis Graph

Confidence Bands: • Clusters = ± 5 • Subtests = ± 7

-1 SEM ←—68 %—→ +1 SEM

Performance Classification	Very Low	Low	L Avg.	Average	H.Avg.	Sup.	Very Superior
Percentile Ranks	≤ 2	3 - 8	9 - 24	25 - 75	76-97	92 - 97	98 - 99+

40 50 60 70 80 90 100 110 120 130 140 150 160

OE – Oral Expression
_____ (__)
_____ (__)
_____ (__)
_____ (__)
_____ (__)

LC – Listening Compr.
_____ (__)
_____ (__)
_____ (__)
_____ (__)
_____ (__)

WE – Written Expression
_____ (__)
_____ (__)
_____ (__)
_____ (__)
_____ (__)

BR – Basic Writing Skills
_____ (__)
_____ (__)
_____ (__)
_____ (__)
_____ (__)

RC – Reading Compr.
_____ (__)
_____ (__)
_____ (__)
_____ (__)
_____ (__)

MC – Mathematics Calc.
_____ (__)
_____ (__)
_____ (__)
_____ (__)
_____ (__)

MR – Mathematics Reas.
_____ (__)
_____ (__)
_____ (__)
_____ (__)
_____ (__)

GK – General Knowledge[1]
_____ (__)
_____ (__)
_____ (__)
_____ (__)
_____ (__)

40 50 60 70 80 90 100 110 120 130 140 150 160

NORMATIVE RANGE	Normative Deficit	Normal Limits	Normative Strength
CLASSIFICATION	Greater than 1 SD below mean	± 1 SD from mean	Greater than 1 SD above mean

[1]*GK*, which includes general information and lexical knowledge, is not an "official" academic area listed in IDEA's definition of learning disability but represents another store of acquired knowledge consistent with the other stores of acquired knowledge that are listed (e.g., reading, math, writing).

Variations in Task Characteristics of Basic Reading Skills Tests

BATTERY Subtest	Regular Words	Pseudowords	Isolated Stimuli (letters, words)	Connected Text	Time Limit
DAB-3					
Alphabet/Word Knowledge	✓		✓		
Phonemic Analysis	✓		✓		
DATA-2					
Word Identification	✓		✓		
K-TEA/NU					
Reading Decoding	✓		✓		
PIAT-R/NU					
Reading Recognition	✓		✓		
WIAT-II					
Word Reading	✓		✓		
Pseudoword Decoding		✓	✓		
WJ III					
Letter-Word Identification	✓		✓		
Reading Fluency	✓			✓	✓
Word Attack	✓	✓	✓		
Reading Vocabulary	✓		✓		
Sound Awareness	✓				
K-SEALS					
Numbers, Letters, Words	✓		✓		
MBA					
Reading	✓		✓	✓	
TAAS-R					
Letter-Word Reading	✓		✓		
Oral Reading Accuracy	✓			✓	
TOCL					
Knowledge of Print	✓			✓	
Word Recognition	✓			✓	
WRAT-3					
Reading	✓		✓		
YCAT					
Reading	✓		✓	✓	
GORT-4					
Rate, Accuracy, Fluency	✓			✓	✓
SRI-2					
Word Recognition Accuracy	✓		✓	✓	
TERA-3					
Alphabet	✓		✓		
Conventions	✓		✓	✓	
TOWRE					
Sight Word Efficiency	✓		✓		✓
Phonemic Decoding Efficiency		✓	✓		✓
WDRB					
Letter-Word Identification	✓		✓		
Word Attack		✓	✓		

BATTERY Subtest	Regular Words	Pseudowords	Isolated Stimuli (letters, words)	Connected Text	Time Limit
WDRB (cont'd)					
Reading Vocabulary	✓		✓		
Incomplete Words	✓		✓		
Sound Blending	✓		✓		
WRMT-R/NU					
Letter Identification	✓		✓		
Supplementary Letter Checklist	✓		✓		
Word Identification	✓		✓		
Word Attack		✓	✓		
Word Comprehension	✓		✓		
ITPA-3					
Sight Decoding	✓		✓		
Sound Decoding		✓	✓		
Sound Deletion	✓		✓		
Written Vocabulary	✓		✓		
TOAL-3					
Reading/Vocabulary	✓		✓		
TOLD-P:3					
Phonemic Analysis	✓		✓		
CTOPP					
Elision	✓		✓		
Blending Words	✓		✓		
Sound Matching	✓		✓		
Blending Nonwords		✓	✓		
Phoneme Reversal	✓		✓		
Segmenting Words	✓		✓		
Segmenting Nonwords		✓	✓		
TOPA					
Initial Sound	✓		✓		

Variations in Task Characteristics of Reading Comprehension Tests

BATTERY Subtest	Cloze Format	Open-Ended Questions	Multiple Choice	Literal Questions	Inferential Questions	Silent Reading	Oral Reading	Examiner Reads	Examinee Reads	Examiner/ Examinee Read	Time Limit	Examinee Can Refer Back To Text
DAB-3												
Reading Comp.		✓		✓	✓	✓				✓		
DATA-2												
Reading Comp.		✓		✓	✓	✓			✓			
K-TEA/NU												
Reading Comp.		✓		✓	✓	✓			✓			✓
PIAT-R/NU												
Reading Comp.			✓			✓			✓			
WIAT-II												
Reading Comp.		✓		✓	✓	✓				✓		✓
WJ III												
Passage Comp.	✓					✓			✓			✓
HAMAT												
Reading	✓		✓			✓			✓			✓
K-FAST												
Reading	✓	✓		✓		✓			✓			
TAAS-R												
Reading Comp.		✓		✓			✓		✓			
TOCL												
Reading Comp.		✓				✓				✓		
GORT-4												
Comprehension			✓	✓	✓		✓			✓		
GSRT												
Silent Reading Comp.			✓	✓	✓	✓			✓			✓
SRI-2												
Vocabulary in Context			✓			✓			✓			✓
Passage Comp.		✓	✓	✓	✓	✓	✓			✓		
TERA-3												
Meaning	✓	✓	✓	✓	✓		✓			✓		
TORC-3												
Paragraph Reading			✓	✓	✓	✓			✓			✓
Sentence Sequencing			✓			✓			✓			
Reading Dir. Schoolwork						✓			✓			
General Vocabulary			✓			✓		✓				
Syntactic Similarities			✓			✓			✓			
WDRB												
Passage Comp.	✓		✓			✓			✓			✓
WRMT-R/NU												
Passage Comp.	✓					✓			✓			✓
ITPA-3												
Sentence Sequencing			✓			✓		✓				✓
TOAL-3												
Reading/Grammar			✓			✓			✓			

Variations in Task Characteristics of Written Expression Tests

BATTERY Subtest	Dictated Spelling (Isolation)	Dictated Spelling (Context)	Multiple Choice	Real Words	Nonsense Words	Isolated Response (e.g., single words)	Connected Response (e.g., sentences, phrases)	Writing Mechanics Assessed (punct., capitlzn., usage)	Proofing/Editing Required	Time Limit	Picture Prompt	Oral Prompt	Written Prompt
DAB-3													
Capitalization				✓		✓		✓	✓				✓
Punctuation				✓		✓		✓	✓				✓
Spelling		✓		✓		✓						✓	
Contextual Language				✓			✓	✓		✓	✓	✓	
Story Construction				✓			✓			✓	✓	✓	
DATA-2													
Spelling	✓	✓		✓		✓		✓				✓	
Writing Composition				✓			✓				✓		
K-TEA/NU													
Spelling	✓			✓		✓						✓	
PIAT-R/NU													
Spelling		✓	✓	✓		✓		✓				✓	
Writ. Exp. (Level I)				✓		✓	✓	✓				✓	
Writ. Exp. (Level II)				✓			✓	✓			✓		
WIAT-II													
Spelling	✓			✓		✓		✓				✓	
Written Expression				✓			✓			✓			✓
WJ III													
Spelling	✓			✓		✓		✓				✓	
Writing Fluency				✓			✓			✓	✓		✓
Writing Samples				✓			✓	✓			✓		✓
Editing				✓			✓	✓	✓				✓
Spelling of Sounds	✓			✓	✓	✓						✓	
Punct. and Cap.				✓		✓		✓	✓				
HAMAT													
Writing				✓			✓	✓				✓	
MBA													
Writing		✓		✓		✓		✓	✓				✓
TAAS-R													
Spelling		✓		✓		✓						✓	
TOCL													
Writing Skills				✓		✓	✓	✓				✓	✓
Writing from Mem.				✓			✓				✓		
Original Writing				✓			✓	✓				✓	✓
WRAT-3													
Spelling		✓		✓		✓						✓	
YCAT													
Writing		✓		✓		✓	✓	✓			✓	✓	✓

BATTERY / Subtest	Dictated Spelling (Isolation)	Dictated Spelling (Context)	Multiple Choice	Real Words	Nonsense Words	Isolated Response (e.g., single words)	Connected Response (e.g., sentences, phrases)	Writing Mechanics Assessed (punct., capitlzn., usage)	Proofing/Editing Required	Time Limit	Picture Prompt	Oral Prompt	Written Prompt
OWLS													
Written Exp. Scale				✓		✓	✓					✓	
TEWL-2													
Basic Writing		✓	✓	✓		✓	✓	✓	✓		✓	✓	✓
Contextual Writing				✓			✓	✓			✓		
TOWE													
Items		✓		✓		✓	✓	✓			✓	✓	✓
Essay				✓			✓			✓		✓	✓
TOWL-3													
Vocabulary				✓			✓						✓
Spelling		✓		✓			✓	✓				✓	
Style				✓			✓	✓				✓	
Logical Sentences				✓		✓	✓		✓				✓
Sentence Combining				✓			✓	✓					✓
Contextual Convent.				✓			✓	✓			✓		
Contextual Language				✓			✓	✓			✓		
Story Construction				✓			✓	✓			✓		
TWS-4													
Test of Writ. Spelling		✓		✓		✓						✓	
CELF-3													
Word Structure													
CASL													
Sentence Completion				✓		✓						✓	
Syntax Construction				✓		✓	✓				✓		
Gram. Morphemes				✓		✓					✓	✓	
Gram. Judgment				✓		✓						✓	
ITPA-3													
Sight Spelling	✓			✓		✓						✓	✓
Sound Spelling	✓				✓	✓						✓	✓
Sentence Sequencing				✓			✓						✓
TOAL-3													
Listening/Grammar			✓	✓								✓	
Writing/Vocabulary				✓			✓						✓
Writing/Grammar				✓			✓						✓
TOLD I:3													
Sentence Combining				✓			✓					✓	
TOLD-P:3													
Gram. Understanding			✓	✓							✓	✓	
Gram. Completion				✓		✓						✓	
TACL-3													
Gram. Morphemes			✓	✓							✓	✓	
Written Vocabulary				✓		✓		✓					✓

Variations in Task Characteristics of Math Calculation Tests

BATTERY Subtest	Uses Worksheet	Easel Format	Time Limit	Mental Computations	Paper/Pencil Computations	Scrap Paper Allowed	Multiple Choice	Examiner Reads	Examinee Reads	Examiner and/or Examinee Reads
DAB-3										
Math Calculation	✓				✓	✓			✓	
DATA-2										
Math Calculations	✓				✓	✓			✓	
K-TEA/NU										
Math. Computation	✓				✓				✓	
PIAT-R/NU										
Mathematics		✓		✓			✓			✓
WIAT-II										
Num. Operations	✓				✓	✓				✓
WJ III										
Calculation	✓				✓					
Math Fluency	✓		✓		✓					
Quant. Concepts		✓						✓		
HAMAT										
Arithmetic	✓				✓	✓			✓	
K-FAST										
Arithmetic		✓		✓		✓		✓		
K-SEALS										
Num., Ltrs., & Words		✓		✓				✓		
TAAS-R										
Arithmetic (Written)	✓				✓	✓			✓	
WRAT-3										
Arithmetic	✓		✓	✓	✓					✓
YCAT										
Mathematics	✓	✓		✓	✓			✓		
KeyMath-R/NU										
Numeration		✓		✓						✓
Rational Numbers		✓		✓						✓
Geometry		✓		✓						✓
Addition	✓				✓					
Subtraction	✓				✓					
Multiplication	✓				✓					
Division	✓				✓					
Mental Computation		✓		✓						✓
Measurement		✓								✓
Time and Money		✓								✓
Estimation		✓								✓
SDMS										
Math Concepts	✓				✓	✓		✓		
Math Calculation	✓			✓	✓	✓		✓		
TOMA-2										
Computation	✓				✓	✓			✓	
General Information	✓			✓	✓			✓		

Variations in Task Characteristics of Math Reasoning Tests

BATTERY Subtest	Uses Worksheet	Easel Format	Time Limit	Mental Computations	Paper/Pencil Computations	Scrap Paper Allowed	Uses Visual Stimuli	Word Problems	Multiple Choice	Examiner Reads	Examinee Reads	Examiner and/or Examinee Reads
DAB-3												
Math Reasoning	✓			✓			✓	✓		✓		
DATA-2												
Math Prob. Solving	✓							✓		✓		
K-TEA/NU												
Math. Applications		✓		✓			✓			✓		
WIAT-II												
Math. Reasoning		✓		✓		✓	✓	✓		✓		
WJ III												
Applied Problems		✓		✓		✓	✓	✓		✓		
MBA												
Mathematics	✓			✓	✓	✓		✓				✓
TAAS-R												
Arithmetic (Oral)	✓			✓				✓		✓		
KeyMath-R/NU												
Interpreting Data		✓		✓			✓			✓		
Problem Solving		✓		✓			✓			✓		
SDMS												
Math Prob. Solving	✓				✓	✓		✓				✓
TOMA-2												
Story Problems	✓				✓	✓		✓			✓	

Variations in Task Characteristics of Listening Comprehension Tests

BATTERY / Subtest	Use of Tape Recorder/CD	Examiner Reads	Requires Verbatim Repetition	Multiple Choice	Requires Examinee to Perform Action Based on What They Hear	Use of Pictures	Pointing Response Required/Allowed	Oral Response Required	Single-Word Response	Multi-Word Response	Isolated Stimuli (e.g., single words)	Connected Stimuli (phrase, sentences)
DAB-3												
Story Comp.	✓		✓					✓	✓	✓		✓
Characteristics		✓						✓	✓			✓
DATA-2												
Receptive Vocabulary		✓						✓	✓		✓	
Receptive Grammar		✓						✓	✓			✓
Expressive Grammar		✓	✓					✓		✓		✓
WIAT-II												
Listening Comp.		✓				✓	✓	✓		✓	✓	✓
WJ III												
Story Recall	✓	✓						✓		✓		✓
Understanding Directions	✓				✓	✓	✓					✓
Story Recall-Delayed		✓						✓		✓		✓
Oral Comprehension	✓							✓	✓			✓
TAAS-R												
Listening Comp.		✓						✓	✓	✓		✓
TOCL												
Spoken Language		✓						✓		✓		✓
YCAT												
Spoken Language		✓	✓			✓	✓	✓	✓	✓	✓	✓
TORC-3												
Syntactic Similarities		✓						✓	✓			✓
WDRB												
Memory for Sentences	✓		✓					✓		✓		✓
Listening Comp.	✓							✓	✓			✓
CELF-3												
Sentence Structure		✓		✓		✓	✓					✓
Word Structure		✓				✓		✓	✓	✓		✓
Concepts and Direct.		✓				✓	✓				✓	
Word Classes		✓						✓	✓		✓	
Recalling Sentences		✓	✓					✓		✓		✓
Semantic Relations.		✓		✓				✓		✓		✓
List. to Paragraphs		✓						✓		✓		✓
CASL												
Comp. of Basic Concepts		✓		✓		✓	✓				✓	
Synonyms		✓		✓				✓	✓		✓	
Sentence Completion		✓						✓	✓			✓
Idiomatic Language		✓						✓	✓			✓
Par. Comp of Syntax		✓		✓					✓			✓
Sent. Comp of Syntax		✓						✓	✓			✓
Gram. Judgment		✓						✓	✓			✓
Inference		✓						✓		✓		✓

BATTERY / Subtest	Use of Tape Recorder/CD	Examiner Reads	Requires Verbatim Repetition	Multiple Choice	Requires Examinee to Perform Action Based on What They Hear	Use of Pictures	Pointing Response Required/Allowed	Oral Response Required	Single-Word Response	Multi-Word Response	Isolated Stimuli (e.g., single words)	Connected Stimuli (phrase, sentences)
CREVT												
Receptive Vocabulary		✓		✓		✓	✓				✓	
CREVT-A												
Receptive Vocabulary		✓		✓		✓	✓				✓	
OWLS												
List. Comp. Scale		✓		✓		✓	✓	✓			✓	✓
PPVT III												
Form III		✓		✓		✓	✓				✓	
R-OWPVT												
Receptive Vocabulary		✓		✓		✓	✓				✓	
TOAL-3												
Listening/Vocabulary		✓		✓		✓	✓				✓	
Listening/Grammar		✓		✓				✓	✓			✓
Speaking/Grammar		✓	✓					✓		✓		✓
TELD-3												
Receptive Language		✓		✓	✓	✓	✓	✓	✓		✓	✓
TOLD-I:3												
Picture Vocabulary		✓		✓		✓	✓					✓
Gram. Comp.		✓						✓	✓			✓
Malapropisms		✓						✓	✓			✓
TOLD-P:3												
Picture Vocabulary		✓		✓		✓	✓				✓	
Gram. Understanding		✓		✓		✓	✓					✓
Sentence Imitation		✓	✓					✓		✓		✓
Gram. Completion		✓						✓	✓			✓
Listening Comprehension		✓						✓	✓		✓	
CTOPP												
Memory for Digits	✓		✓					✓		✓		✓
Nonword Repetition	✓		✓					✓	✓		✓	
TACL-3												
Vocabulary		✓		✓		✓	✓				✓	
Gram. Morphemes		✓		✓		✓	✓				✓	
Elaboration of Phrases/Sent.		✓		✓		✓	✓					✓
TAPS-R												
Auditory Num. Memory (f)		✓	✓					✓				✓
Auditory Num. Memory (r)		✓	✓					✓				✓
Auditory Sent. Memory		✓	✓					✓		✓		✓
Auditory Word Memory		✓	✓					✓	✓		✓	
Auditory Interp. Directions		✓						✓		✓		

Variations in Task Characteristics of Oral Expression Tests

BATTERY Subtest	Multiword Response	Single Word Response	Time Limit	Visual Stimuli	Examiner Reads	Examinee Reads	Examiner and/or Examinee Reads
DAB-3							
Synonyms		✓			✓		
Grammatic Comp.		✓			✓		
DATA-2							
Expressive Vocabulary	✓				✓		
WIAT-II							
Oral Expression	✓			✓	✓		
YCAT							
Spoken Language	✓	✓		✓			✓
WDRB							
Oral Vocabulary		✓			✓		
CELF-3							
Formulated Sent.	✓			✓			
Sentence Assembly	✓				✓		
Word Associations		✓	✓		✓		
CASL							
Antonyms		✓			✓		
Syntax Construction	✓	✓		✓			✓
Gram. Morphemes		✓		✓	✓		
Nonliteral Language	✓				✓		
Meaning from Context	✓				✓		
Ambiguous Sent.	✓				✓		
Pragmatic Judgment	✓			✓	✓		
CREVT							
Expressive Vocabulary	✓				✓		
CREVT-A							
Expressive Vocabulary	✓				✓		
CTOPP							
Rapid Digit Naming		✓	✓	✓		✓	
Rapid Letter Naming		✓	✓	✓		✓	
Rapid Color Naming		✓	✓	✓		✓	
Rapid Object Naming		✓	✓	✓		✓	
E-OWPVT							
Expressive Vocabulary		✓		✓			
EVT							
Exp. Vocabulary Test		✓		✓	✓		

BATTERY Subtest	Multiword Response	Single Word Response	Time Limit	Visual Stimuli	Examiner Reads	Examinee Reads	Examiner and/or Examinee Reads
ITPA-3							
Spoken Vocabulary		✓			✓		
Spoken Analogies		✓			✓		
Morph. Closure		✓			✓		
Syntactic Sentences	✓				✓		
Rhyming Sequences		✓			✓		
LPT-R							
Pretest 2	✓				✓		
Associations		✓			✓		
Categorization	✓				✓		
Similarities	✓				✓		
Differences	✓				✓		
Multiple Meanings	✓				✓		
Attributes	✓				✓		
Labeling		✓		✓	✓		
OWLS							
Oral Express. Scale	✓			✓	✓		
TOAL-3							
Speaking/Vocabulary	✓				✓		
TELD-3							
Expressive Language	✓	✓		✓	✓		
TOLD-I:3							
Word Ordering	✓				✓		
Generals	✓	✓			✓		
TOLD-P:3							
Relational Vocabulary	✓				✓		
Oral Vocabulary	✓				✓		
Word Articulation		✓		✓	✓		

Case Report

Report of Psychoeducational Evaluation

NAME: Carsam

EVALUATED BY: Examiner A
SCHOOL: Everytown Elementary
TEACHER: Jones
BIRTHDATE: August 13
ETHNICITY: Anglo-American
FIRST LANGUAGE: English

REPORT DATE: October 18

EVALUATION DATES: Oct. 10–Oct. 17
DISTRICT: Everytown Union School District
GRADE: 5
CHRONOLOGICAL AGE: 10-2
INSTRUCTIONAL LANGUAGE: English
SECOND LANGUAGE: None

Primary Referral Concerns

According to information contained in his school records and from interviews with his teacher and parents, Carsam has had difficulty in learning to read and write since entering school. Initially, the problems were only slight and it was believed that he might be slow in his maturation and that with time, his skills might improve. However, as he progressed through the grades, Carsam's development of literacy skills has steadily fallen further and further behind that of his age and grade-level peers. Consequently, Carsam was brought to the prereferral assistance team at the beginning of his fifth-grade year by his teacher, who was concerned about his apparent lack of appropriate academic progress, in particular language arts. At that time, the team developed and implemented a range of interventions and modification strategies designed to help Carsam perform better. The strategies included extra peer and adult tutoring, remedial reading assistance before and after school, modification of assignments, a change of seat closer to the teacher, increased one-to-one attention, and more involvement with small group instruction. Carsam's progress was carefully monitored for about two months, but he displayed only minor improvement in his ability to acquire better reading and writing skills. Consequently, the prereferral team referred Carsam for special education evaluation in order to assess the possibility of the presence of a learning disability.

Background Information

Educational and Family History

Carsam was born in Everytown, United States, where his family has resided for several generations. Carsam's ethnic heritage is Anglo-American and he and his family reside in a home located in an older, well-established local community. The socioeconomic status of Carsam's family was noted to be average and there were no indications of economic hardship being significant factors in his educational development. Carsam attended a local preschool at ages 3 and 4 prior to beginning his education at Everytown Elementary at the age of 5, where he remains enrolled. Carsam's parents indicate that the only language spoken in the home is English and that he has had no exposure to a second language in the home or the community. A review of his records also indicates that there was some consideration of retention in third grade, primarily due to his reported difficulties in language arts development and an extended absence of about 20 days from a chronic respiratory infection that required hospitalization and subsequent rest at home. Despite the concerns, he was promoted to the fourth grade and his attendance, apart from his third-grade year, has been consistent, with absences ranging from only about 6 to 10 days in any given year. Carsam's father is a local real estate agent and his mother teaches junior high classes at a neighboring school district. He has two older siblings, a brother in seventh grade and a sister in tenth grade, both of whom are reported to be doing well and not experiencing any significant academic problems.

Health and Developmental History

According to the information provided by Carsam's mother, as well as the nurse's screening results, Carsam's vision and hearing are within normal limits. Carsam was a full-term birth. His mother reports that she did not experience any complications during pregnancy and that labor and delivery were normal. Carsam's mother reports that he met all of his developmental milestones (walking, talking, toilet training, etc.) normally. However, she did comment that Carsam had a significant history of otitis media and underwent repeated courses of antibiotic treatment between the ages of 2 and 4. Just prior to kindergarten, Carsam's physician had considered surgical implantation of eustachian tubes but the frequency of infection dropped off markedly and the procedure was never carried out. Apart from this particular finding, there appear to be no other physical factors present that might be related to Carsam's observed educational difficulties.

Procedures of Evaluation

Procedures: Informative

10-10	Review of school records
10-12	Interview: Current teacher
	Interview: Parent(s)
10-12	Observation: Classroom
	Observation: Playground
10-15	Interview: Last year's teacher
	Interview: Student
10-15	Observation: Home
10-16	Review of student's Health and Developmental History Report

Procedures: Evaluative

10-16   Wechsler Individual Achievement Test–Second Edition (reading and writing tests only*)
Woodcock-Johnson III: Tests of Achievement (selected tests)*

10-17   Wechsler Abbreviated Scale of Intelligence
Woodcock-Johnson III: Tests of Cognitive Abilities (selected tests*)

Observations

Natural Settings

Carsam was observed in a variety of settings and during a variety of different classroom tasks, with particular attention paid to reading and writing. On the playground and during recess he was observed to engage in many activities and had little difficulty relating to his peers. In classroom situations, although he displayed adequate focus and effort in completing his work, Carsam was clearly not as successful as many of his classmates. The mechanical quality of his written work (e.g., legibility) was not problematic but he did display problems with spelling and being able to express his thoughts on paper. Carsam tended to use simple, familiar words and often resorted to invented spelling or just guessing when trying to formulate sentences and paragraphs. Carsam had obvious difficulties when reading aloud, particularly with regard to proper tone, rhythm, and fluency, but seemed to have less difficulty with comprehension. In addition, there were problems evident in his ability to successfully decode grade-level words. Despite his desire to complete his assigned tasks, Carsam would occasionally display signs of frustration, especially on those involving significant amounts of reading and writing. Naturally, Carsam displayed a tendency to withdraw from activities that he appeared to find difficult and was much more enthusiastic in other activities that did not rely as much on language arts skills. Carsam seems well aware of the fact that he is unable to keep up with his classmates in most subjects and it appears as if it is beginning to undermine his self-confidence and self-esteem. Compared to other students in the class, the quality and level of Carsam's work is not up to the level as that seen in the vast majority of his classroom peers. Without some of the current modifications being made by his teacher, Carsam would very likely have even greater difficulty meeting the expectations of his current curriculum. Overall, his motivation to succeed appears good and, despite his problems, he has a positive and enthusiastic attitude toward learning and school.

Evaluation Settings

Carsam was very cooperative in his interactions with this evaluator; during testing he appeared to put forth his best effort on all tasks. Rapport was easily established and main-

---

*Because the focus of this evaluation is solely on functioning related to reading and writing difficulties and any corresponding underlying cognitive deficits, only those tests from each battery relevant to the these concerns were administered in accordance with the principles that guide CHC Selective Cross-Battery (S-CB) assessment.

tained throughout the testing session. Although Carsam indicated that some items were "hard to do," he persisted in his attempts to resolve the more difficult items and was very focused while completing the requested tasks. Carsam seemed to have no trouble comprehending the test instructions, even when they tended to be lengthy. On reading comprehension items, Carsam often paused during the course of reading the passages, and seemed to take extra time before responding with a fair amount of confidence. It was evident, again, that tests that required some aspect of language arts ability were clearly the most problematic for him. Overall, the current test results appear to represent a reliable and valid estimate of Carsam's cognitive and academic abilities.

Inter-Academic Analysis

Written Expression

Carsam's overall performance in the area of Written Expression (WE), as reflected by the combination of spelling and written expression tasks, cannot be appropriately classified because of the significant difference between the scores that comprise this Academic Clinical Composite (ACC). The fact that this difference exists in these two measures precludes the formation of a reliable cluster, and calculation of an average score (i.e., between the Spelling and Written Expression subtests of the WIAT-II) could be a misleading estimate of Carsam's true performance. As such, performance is more appropriately interpreted through individual tests. Carsam's performance on the Spelling subtest ranged from Low to Low Average (SS = 77; 6th percentile; range = 70–84), whereas his performance on the Written Expression subtest fell within the Very Low range (SS = 61; 1st percentile; range = 54–68). This indicates better functioning in spelling skills versus written expression skills. Normative analysis, however, does provide an estimate of overall performance in the Written Expression domain because both SS ranges for spelling and written expression actually fall entirely within the Normative Weakness range. This type of pattern is called a nonconvergent ability description; therefore, despite the discrepancy between the two SS bands, Carsam's performance with regard to the Written Expression can be reliably interpreted as falling below and outside normal limits (i.e, normative deficit).

Basic Reading Skills

Carsam's overall performance in the area of Basic Reading Skills (ACC/BR), as reflected by the combination of basic reading and reading vocabulary tasks, can be classified as Low (SS = 75; 5th percentile; range = 70–80). In this case, there is no significant difference between the scores obtained on the basic reading and reading vocabulary tasks. Hence, the ACC/BR composite reported previously represents a reliable and valid estimate of his functioning in this domain. With respect to normative analysis, comparison of Carsam's performance to other individuals of the same age and grade indicates that his functioning in this area falls greater than 1 SD below the mean, indicating a normative deficit.

Reading Comprehension

Finally, Carsam's performance in the area of Reading Comprehension (ACC/RC), as reflected by the combination of reading and passage comprehension tasks that were administered, can be classified as being Low to Low Average (SS = 79; 8th percentile; range = 74–84). As in the previous case, there is no significant difference between the scores obtained on the reading and passage comprehension tasks given to Carsam. Therefore, the ACC/RC composite reported previously also represents a reliable and valid estimate of his functioning in this domain. However, although the difference in performance on these two measures is not statistically significant, it is likely that the nature of the task demands on the WJ III Passage Comprehension test (which uses a cloze-type procedure to evaluate comprehension) may have resulted in a lower score than when comprehension was measured by a task requiring only recall of facts and information, as is the case in the WIAT-II Reading Comprehension test. This finding is supported by observational and interview data that confirm the observation that reading comprehension is more adversely affected depending on the manner in which it is measured. With respect to normative analysis, comparison of Carsam's overall performance to other individuals of the same age and grade indicates that his functioning in this area also falls greater than 1 SD below the mean, suggesting a normative deficit.

In sum, Carsam displays normative-based weakness in each of the three academic areas that were evaluated. Five of the six standard score bands for the tests administered to Carsam fall below and outside normal limits (i.e., greater than 1 SD below the mean) with the sixth extending only slightly into the average range. It is believed that these deficits cannot be attributed to extraneous or confounding variables that may have occurred during testing and that the results provide a reliable and valid estimate of Carsam's current academic functioning.

Inter-Cognitive Analysis

Gc—Crystallized Intelligence

Carsam's overall performance with respect to Gc, Crystallized Intelligence, as reflected by the combination of the two WASI tests (Similarities and Vocabulary), can be classified as falling within the Low to Low-Average range (SS = 83; 13th percentile; range = 78–88). The SS bands for the two tests overlap considerably, indicating no significant difference between his language development and lexical knowledge skills. Accordingly, the Gc composite score reported previously represents a reliable and valid estimate of his functioning in this domain. With respect to normative analysis, however, Gc should be construed as only a *probable* deficit because the SS band for the Gc cluster and the individual bands for Gc-LD and Gc-VL (Similarities and Vocabulary, respectively) all extend slightly into the range of normal limits (i.e., between 85 and 115 inclusive). Although it is conceivable that Carsam's true performance relative to Gc could fall within the normal range, the fact that his measured performance in both narrow abilities falls predominantly outside of normal limits and entirely within the Low to Low-Average classifications suggest that Gc is indeed an area in which Carsam has difficulty. Marginal functioning in this area is seen to be consistent with the academic deficits identified earlier, suggesting that this is not a spurious or anomalous finding.

Gsm—Short-Term Memory

Carsam's overall performance with respect to *Gsm*, Short-Term Memory, as reflected by the combination of the two WJ III tests (Memory for Words and Auditory Working Memory), is classified as falling within the Low-Average to Average range (SS = 92; 29th percentile; range = 87–97). His performance on Memory for Words, a measure of memory span (MS), is slightly higher but not significantly different from his performance on Auditory Working Memory, a measure of working memory (MW). The *Gsm* composite is therefore believed to represent a reliable and valid estimate of his functioning in this domain. With respect to normative analysis, *Gsm* functioning is within normal limits. The SS band for MS falls entirely within this normative range and the band for MW dips only slightly into the normative deficit range. Overall, given the existing pattern of scores, the most prudent interpretation remains that of functioning within normal limits.

Ga—Auditory Processing

Carsam's overall performance with respect to *Ga*, Auditory Processing, as reflected by the combination of the two WJ III tests (Auditory Attention and Sound Blending), can be classified as falling within the Very Low to Low range (SS = 72; 3rd percentile; range = 67–77). His performance on Auditory Attention, a measure of speech and general sound discrimination (US/U3), is slightly lower but not significantly different from his performance on sound blending, a measure of phonetic coding–synthesis (PC:S). The composite *Ga* score is therefore believed to represent a reliable and valid estimate of his functioning in this domain. With respect to normative analysis, *Ga* is seen as a clear deficit because the SS band for the *Ga* cluster and the individual bands for *Ga*-US/U3 and *Ga*-PC:S are all greater than 1 SD below the mean and do not extend into the normal limits range. The well-established connection between phonological processing abilities and language arts development provides evidence that Carsam's difficulties in developing grade-appropriate reading and writing skills may well be due to impairments in this domain.

Other Abilities

Results from the administration of the WASI revealed a FSIQ-4 of 91 (27th percentile, range = 85–97). Descriptive classification of Carsam's performance on the WASI can thus be characterized as ranging from the Low-Average to Average range and evaluated normatively as being within normal limits. In addition, because the WASI is constructed from two tests that form the core of one of Carsam's observed cognitive deficits (i.e., in *Gc*), his broad ability is likely to be underestimated by the attenuating effect of the inclusion of tests of *Gc*. Nevertheless, Carsam's measured global ability is still within the average range.

Use of the WASI also produced two additional scores, one a measure of *Gf* (Fluid Reasoning) and the other a measure of *Gv* (Visual Processing), both by-products of the need to derive a global ability score. The most substantive statement that can be made based on these individual subtests is that Carsam's functioning in the area of *Gf*-I (Induction) and *Gv*-SR (Spatial Relations) is *likely* within normal limits. This conclusion is supported by the fact that the SS bands for each narrow ability (102–112 and 95–109, respectively) span the Average to High-Average ranges.

Integrated Ability Analysis

Evaluation of Exclusionary Factors

The results of inter-academic and inter-cognitive analysis have thus far established the presence of both academic and cognitive impairments in Carsam's functioning. The validity of these impairments is supported by convergence with other data that assist in ruling out other reasonable causes for Carsam's poor performance. These data include the fact that Carsam's cultural heritage is entirely mainstream, he and his parents are native English speakers, the school nurse has found his vision and hearing to be within normal limits, he has received sufficient school instruction and opportunity to learn, he is properly motivated, and he has no apparent organic condition or psychological disturbance. Taken together, these data point strongly toward intrinsic factors as the primary cause of Carsam's reading and writing problems.

Consistency Analysis

The presence of LD is also supported via examination of consistency among empirically related tests in an integrated fashion. For example, if the cause of Carsam's reading and writing difficulties is truly intrinsic, then the data should reveal a pattern that provides evidence of consistent dysfunction in those cognitive abilities most logically and empirically related to the development and acquisition of literacy skills (i.e., *Ga* and *Gc*). A review of the obtained results demonstrates just such a pattern in that *Ga* has been identified as a clear deficit and *Gc* has been identified as a probable deficit. Additionally, mental retardation has been excluded as the primary cause of Carsam's learning difficulties because performance in the area of *Gsm* was identified as being within normal limits, performance on narrow-ability measures of *Gf*-I and *Gv*-SR were identified as being within normal limits, performance in other school subjects is adequate, and development in other adaptive areas (e.g., communication, self-care skills, fine and gross motor abilities) have never been observed as anything other than normal. Overall, Carsam's academic and cognitive deficits are circumscribed within an otherwise normal ability profile, thereby appropriately supporting the presence of LD.

Discrepancy Analysis

With respect to the state requirement of an ability-achievement discrepancy, the calculation of the discrepancy between Carsam's global ability (SS = 91) as measured by the WASI and his written expression (ACC/WE SS = 69), and basic reading skills (ACC/BR SS = 75) yielded a significant difference of at least 1.5 standard deviations. The difference between Carsam's global ability and performance in reading comprehension (ACC/RC SS = 79) did not meet this state requirement.

Summary

Conclusions

When all the data collected in the course of Carsam's assessment are examined and evaluated together and within the context of his educational, physical, social, and cultural histories and experiences, there appear to be sufficient data to conclude that Carsam is indeed learning disabled in the areas of Written Expression, Basic Reading Skills, and Reading Comprehension. Moreover, the patterns seen in the data support the conclusion that his difficulties in these areas are likely the direct result of deficiencies in his basic psychological processes, including *Gc*–crystallized intelligence and *Ga*–auditory processing. It is the opinion of this evaluator that there are no significant external factors or other types of dysfunction present in Carsam's case to which his educational difficulties could be primarily attributed. In addition, the data provide support in accordance with state regulations for the identification of learning disability. The data also support the conclusion that Carsam is currently unable to meet the demands of the curriculum even with existing support strategies in place. It seems clear that without some type of substantial instructional intervention, Carsam will likely continue to have significant problems in developing grade-level reading and writing skills and will fall further and further behind the level of his peers.

Recommendations

Inasmuch as the purpose of psychoeducational assessment is to diagnose, it is also necessary to generate data that may be used to develop effective interventions. Although there are many options available for providing Carsam with the level of intervention services he requires, the following recommendations are presented as suggestions and starting points of discussion in the development of an appropriate instructional program. Irrespective of the type of interventions that are developed, ongoing evaluation of their effectiveness should continue in order to monitor their success or failure in ameliorating Carsam's academic difficulties. The integration of collaborative information from records review, direct observation, teacher and parent interviews, analysis of actual work samples, standardized tests, and prereferral data all provided the basis for the following recommendations:

1. Because Carsam's auditory processing deficit causes his difficulty in decoding unfamiliar words, it is recommended that he receive training in phoneme segmentation and sound blending. Examples of these activities include identifying words beginning with the same sound (word matching), isolating individual sounds (e.g., recognizing the first sound in a word), identifying the numbers of phonemes in a word (phoneme counting), and identifying how the removal of a sound would change a given word (phoneme deletion). Teaching Carsam how to organize sounds in order to assemble or put a word together (i.e., sound blending) and instruction that focuses on development of a greater sight word vocabulary is also recommended.

2. Carsam's deficit in crystallized intelligence seems more attributable to poor language development and lack of grade-level lexical knowledge. Thus, it may be helpful to focus on advancing Carsam's semantic and grammatical language ability. This can be accomplished by reviewing the basic rules of correct grammatical structure and reinforcing

Carsam's learning of them and his ability to apply them in written assignments. It may also be helpful to set "limits" on his expressive writing vocabulary so that he is forced to seek out and use words that will expand his repertoire beyond those he commonly uses (e.g., not allowing use of adjectives such as *cool, good, great,* etc.). Carsam should also be encouraged and guided in his oral expressive language as a way of enhancing the related ability to express himself on paper. Instruction that emphasizes oral language (such as debates, impromptu speaking, guided discussion, etc.) would both advance his vocabulary and oral language abilities while at the same time providing a framework for development of specific lexical knowledge useful in writing.

Respectfully submitted,

_____

Examiner A
School Psychologist

| Name: Carsam | Age: 10 Grade: 5 |
| Examiner: Examiner A | Date: 10/18 |

**CHC Cross-Battery Academic Clinical Composites
Level I-A: Data Summary**

LD AREA	Test Battery	Subtest Name	CHC Ability Measured	Standard Score	Confidence Interval	%ile Rank	Classification
OE – Oral Expression			OE Area Average =				
LC – Listening Comprehension			LC Area average =				
WE – Written Expression			WE Area Average =				
	WIAT-II	Spelling	Grw-SG	77	70-84	6	Low
	WIAT-II	Written Expression	Grw-WA	61	54-68	1	V. Low
BR – Basic Reading Skills			BR Area Average =	75	70-80	5	Low
	WIAT-II	Word Reading	Grw-RD	78	71-85	8	Low
	WJ III	Reading Vocabulary	Grw-V	72	65-79	3	Low
RC – Reading Comprehension			RC Area Average =	79	74-84	8	Low
	WIAT-II	Reading Comprehension	Grw-RC	85	78-92	16	L. Average
	WJ III	Passage Comprehension	Grw-CZ	73	66-80	3	Low
MC – Mathematics Calculation			MC Area Average =				
MR – Mathematics Reasoning			MR Area Average =				
GK – General Knowledge[1]			GK Area Average =				

[1]*GK* , which includes general information and lexical knowledge, is not an "official" academic area listed in IDEA's definition of learning disability but represents another store of acquired knowledge consistent with the other stores of acquired knowledge that are listed (e.g., reading, math, writing).

Note: All standard scores are based on age norms.   Confidence Bands: • Clusters = ± 5   • Subtests = ± 7

Name: Carsam Age: 10 Grade: 5	**CHC Cross-Battery Academic Clinical Composites**
Examiner: Examiner A Date: 10/18	**Level I-A: Normative Analysis Graph**

Confidence Bands: • Clusters = ± 5 • Subtests = ± 7

-1 SEM ← 68 % → +1 SEM

Performance Classification	Very Low	Low	L Avg.	Average	H.Avg.	Sup.	Very Superior
Percentile Ranks	≤ 2	3 - 8	9 - 24	25 - 75	76-97	92 - 97	98 - 99+

40 50 60 70 80 90 100 110 120 130 140 150 160

OE – Oral Expression

LC – Listening Compr.

WE – Written Expression
WIAT-II Spelling
WIAT-II Written Expression

BR – Basic Reading Skills
WIAT-II Word Reading
WJIII Reading Vocabulary

RC – Reading Compr.
WIAT-II Reading Compr.
WJ III Passage Compr.

MC – Mathematics Calc.

MR – Mathematics Reas.

GK – General Knowledge[1]

40 50 60 70 80 90 100 110 120 130 140 150 160

NORMATIVE RANGE CLASSIFICATION	Normative Weakness Greater than 1 SD below mean	Normal Limits ± 1 SD from mean	Normative Strength Greater than 1 SD above mean

[1]*GK*, which includes general information and lexical knowledge, is not an "official" academic area listed in IDEA's definition of learning disability but represents another store of acquired knowledge consistent with the other stores of acquired knowledge that are listed (e.g., reading, math, writing).

| Name: Carsam   Age: 10 Grade: 5 | | CHC Cross-Battery Inter-Cognitive Analysis |
| Examiner: Examiner A   Date: 10/18 | | Level II-A: Data Summary |

Cluster	Test Battery	Subtest Name + (CHC ability code)	Standard Score	Standard Score Confidence Interval	Percentile Rank	Classification
Gc (Crystallized Intelligence)		*Gc Cluster Average =*	83	78-88	13	L. Average
	WASI	Similarities (LD)	80	73-87	9	L. Average
	WASI	Vocabulary (VL)	85	78-92	16	L. Average
Gf (Fluid Reasoning)		*Gf Cluster Average =*				
	WASI	Matrix Reasoning (I)	90	83-97	25	Average
Gv (Visual Processing)		*Gv Cluster Average =*				
	WASI	Block Design (SR,Vz)	95	88-102	38	Average
Gsm (Short-term Memory)		*Gsm Cluster Average =*	92	87-97	29	Average
	WJ III	Memory for Words (MS)	95	88-102	38	Average
	WJ III	Auditory Working Memory (MW)	88	81-95	21	L. Average
Glr (Long-term Retrieval)		*Glr Cluster Average =*				
Ga (Auditory Processing)		*Ga Cluster Average =*	72	67-77	3	Low
	WJ III	Auditory Attention (US/U3)	68	61-75	2	V. Low
	WJ III	Sound Blending (PC:S)	75	68-82	5	Low
Gs (Processing Speed)		*Gs Cluster Average =*				

Note: All standard scores are based on age norms.   Confidence Bands: • Clusters = $\pm\,5$ • Subtests = $\pm\,7$

Name: Carsam	Age: 10 Grade: 5	CHC Cross-Battery Inter-Cognitive Analysis
Examiner: Examiner A	Date: 10/18	Level II-A: Normative Analysis Graph

Confidence Bands: • Clusters = ± 5 • Subtests = ± 7

-1 SEM ← 68 % → +1 SEM

Performance Classification	Very Low	Low	L Avg.	Average	H.Avg.	Sup.	Very Superior
Percentile Ranks	≤ 2	3 - 8	9 - 24	25 - 75	76-97	92 - 97	98 - 99+

40   50   60   70   80   90   100   110   120   130   140   150   160

Gc Broad/Narrow Cluster
Similarities (LD)
Vocabulary (VL)
_____ (__)
_____ (__)
_____ (__)
_____ (__)
_____ (__)

Gf Broad/Narrow Cluster
Matrix Reasoning (I)
_____ (__)
_____ (__)
_____ (__)
_____ (__)

Gv Broad/Narrow Cluster
Block Design (SR)
_____ (__)
_____ (__)
_____ (__)
_____ (__)

Gsm Broad/Narrow Cluster
Memory for Words (MS)
Aud. Working Mem. (MW)
_____ (__)
_____ (__)
_____ (__)

Glr Broad/Narrow Cluster
_____ (__)
_____ (__)
_____ (__)
_____ (__)
_____ (__)

Ga Broad/Narrow Cluster
Auditory Attention (US/U3)
Sound Blending (PC:S)
_____ (__)
_____ (__)
_____ (__)

Gs Broad/Narrow Cluster
_____ (__)
_____ (__)
_____ (__)
_____ (__)
_____ (__)

40   50   60   70   80   90   100   110   120   130   140   150   160

NORMATIVE RANGE CLASSIFICATION	Normative Weakness Greater than 1 SD below mean	Normal Limits ± 1 SD from mean	Normative Strength Greater than 1 SD above mean

| Name: Carsam | Age: 10 Grade: 5 | CHC Cross-Battery Integrated Ability Analysis |
| Examiner: Examiner A | Date: 10/18 | Level III – Data Summary |

Cluster	Test Battery	Subtest Name + (CHC ability code)	Standard Score	Standard Score Confidence Interval	Percentile Rank	Classification
Grw (Reading/Writing Ability)		*Grw Cluster Average =*	74	69-79	4	Low
	WIAT-II	Spelling	77	70-84	3	Low
	WIAT-II	Written Expression	61	54-68	1	V. Low
	WIAT-II	Word Reading	78	71-85	8	Low
	WJ III	Reading Vocabulary	72	65-79	3	Low
	WIAT-II	Reading Comprehension	85	78-92	16	L. Average
	WJ III	Passage Comprehension	73	66-80	3	Low
Gc (Crystallized Intelligence)		*Gc Cluster Average =*	83	78-88	13	L. Average
	WASI	Similarities (LD)	80	73-87	9	L. Average
	WASI	Vocabulary (VL)	85	78-92	16	L. Average
Gq (Quantitative Knowledge)		*Gq Cluster Average =*				
Gf (Fluid Reasoning)		*Gf Cluster Average =*				
	WASI	Matrix Reasoning (I)	90	83-17	25	Average
Gv (Visual Processing)		*Gv Cluster Average =*				
	WASI	Block Design (SR,Vz)	95	88-102	50	Average
Gsm (Short-term Memory)		*Gsm Cluster Average =*	92	87-97	29	Average
	WJ III	Memory for Words (MS)	95	88-102	38	Average
	WJ III	Auditory Working Memory (MW)	88	81-95	21	Average
Glr (Long-term Retrieval)		*Glr Cluster Average =*				
Ga (Auditory Processing)		*Ga Cluster Average =*	72	67-77	3	Low
	WJ III	Auditory Attention (US/U3)	68	61-75	2	V. Low
	WJ III	Sound Blending (PC:S)	75	68-82	5	Low
Gs (Processing Speed)		*Gs Cluster Average =*				

Note: All standard scores are based on age norms.   Confidence Bands: • Clusters = ± 5   • Subtests = ± 7

Name: Carsam   Age: _10_ Grade: _5_
Examiner: _Examiner A_   Date: _10/18_

CHC Cross-Battery Integrated Ability Analysis
Level III - Normative Analysis Graph

Confidence Bands: • Clusters = ± 5 • Subtests = ± 7

-1 SEM ◄—68 %—► +1 SEM

Performance Classification	Very Low	Low	L Avg.	Average	H.Avg.	Sup.	Very Superior
Percentile Ranks	≤ 2	3 - 8	9 - 24	25 - 75	76-97	92 - 97	98 - 99+

40   50   60   70   80   90   100   110   120   130   140   150   160

Grw Broad/Narrow Cluster
 Spelling   (SG)
 Written Expression (WA)
 Word Reading   (RD)
 Reading Vocabulary (V)
 Reading Compr.   (RC)
 Passage Compr.   (CZ)

Gc Broad/Narrow Cluster
 Similarities   (LD)
 Vocabulary   (VL)
 _____   (__)
 _____   (__)
 _____   (__)
 _____   (__)

Gq Broad/Narrow Cluster
 _____   (__)
 _____   (__)
 _____   (__)
 _____   (__)

Gf Broad/Narrow Cluster
 Matrix Reasoning   (I)
 _____   (__)
 _____   (__)
 _____   (__)

Gv Broad/Narrow Cluster
 Block Design   (SR)
 _____   (__)
 _____   (__)
 _____   (__)

Gsm Broad/Narrow Cluster
 Memory for Words   (MS)
 Aud. Working Mem. (MW)
 _____   (__)
 _____   (__)

Glr Broad/Narrow Cluster
 _____   (__)
 _____   (__)
 _____   (__)
 _____   (__)

Ga Broad/Narrow Cluster
 Auditory Attention (US/U3)
 Sound Blending   (PC:S)
 _____   (__)
 _____   (__)

Gs Broad/Narrow Cluster
 _____   (__)
 _____   (__)
 _____   (__)
 _____   (__)

40   50   60   70   80   90   100   110   120   130   140   150   160

NORMATIVE RANGE CLASSIFICATION	Normative Weakness	Normal Limits	Normative Strength
	Greater than 1 SD below mean	± 1 SD from mean	Greater than 1 SD above mean

Expert Consensus Study Data

Expert Consensus Study Data

Comprehensive Tests	Primary Broad		Secondary Broad		Primary Narrow		Secondary Narrow	
Test Name	Code	% Agmt	Code	% Agmt	Code	% Agmt	Code	% Agmt
DAB-3: Story Comprehension	Gc	73	-	-	LS	88	-	-
DAB-3: Characteristics	Gc	82	-	-	LS	88	-	-
DAB-3: Synonyms	Gc	100	-	-	VL	91	-	-
DAB-3: Grammatic Completion	Gc	100	-	-	MY	60	-	-
DAB-3: Alphabet/Word Knowledge	Grw	91	-	-	RD	100	-	-
DAB-3: Reading Comprehension	Grw	91	-	-	RC	100	-	-
DAB-3: Capitalization	Grw	100	-	-	EU	100	-	-
DAB-3: Punctuation	Grw	100	-	-	EU	100	-	-
DAB-3: Spelling	Grw	100	-	-	SG	100	-	-
DAB-3: Contextual Language	Grw	100	-	-	WA	100	-	-
DAB-3: Story Construction	Grw	100	-	-	WA	100	-	-
DAB-3: Math Reasoning	Gq	100	-	-	KM	91	-	-
DAB-3: Math Calculation	Gq	100	-	-	A3	100	-	-
DAB-3: Phonemic Analysis	Ga	100	-	-	PC:A	100	-	-
DATA-2: Receptive Vocabulary	Gc	100	-	-	LD	67	-	-
DATA-2: Receptive Grammar	Gc	93	-	-	MY	80	-	-
DATA-2: Expressive Vocabulary[b]	Gc	87	-	-	OP	-	-	-
DATA-2: Expressive Grammar	Gsm	93	-	-	MS	100	-	-
DATA-2: Word Identification	Grw	100	-	-	RD	100	-	-
DATA-2: Reading Comprehension	Grw	100	-	-	RC	100	-	-
DATA-2: Math Calculations	Gq	100	-	-	A3	86	-	-
DATA-2: Math Problem Solving	Gq	80	-	-	A3	64	-	-
DATA-2: Spelling	Grw	100	-	-	SG	100	-	-
DATA-2: Writing Composition	Grw	100	-	-	WA	100	-	-
DATA-2: Science	Gc	100	-	-	K1	71	-	-
DATA-2: Social Studies	Gc	100	-	-	K0	80	-	-
DATA-2: Reference Skills	Gc	93	-	-	K0	75	-	-
K-TEA/NU: Math Applications	Gq	80	-	-	A3	58	KM	42
K-TEA/NU: Reading Decoding	Grw	100	-	-	RD	100	-	-
K-TEA/NU: Spelling	Grw	100	-	-	SG	93	-	-
K-TEA/NU: Reading Comp	Grw	100	-	-	RC	87	-	-
K-TEA/NU: Math Computation	Gq	87	-	-	A3	100	-	-
PIAT-R/NU: General Information	Gc	100	-	-	K0	100	-	-
PIAT-R/NU: Reading Recognition	Grw	100	-	-	RD	100	-	-
PIAT-R/NU: Reading Comp	Grw	87	-	-	RC	70	-	-
PIAT-R/NU: Mathematics	Gq	73	-	-	KM	73	-	-
PIAT-R/NU: Spelling	Grw	60	Ga	40	SG	67	PC:A	100
PIAT-R/NU: Written Expression I	Grw	86	-	-	SG	60	-	-
PIAT-R/NU: Written Expression II A	Grw	100	-	-	WA	100	-	-
PIAT-R/NU: Written Expression II B	Grw	100	-	-	WA	100	-	-
WIAT-II: Word Reading	Grw	100	-	-	RD	100	-	-
WIAT-II: Pseudoword Decoding	Grw	94	-	-	RD	100	-	-
WIAT-II: Mathematics Reasoning	Gf	93	-	-	RQ	100	-	-
WIAT-II: Spelling	Grw	100	-	-	SG	100	-	-
WIAT-II: Reading Comprehension	Grw	100	-	-	RC	87	-	-
WIAT-II: Numerical Operations	Gq	100	-	-	A3	73	-	-

Test Name	Code	% Agmt	Code	% Agmt	Code	% Agmt	Code	% Agmt
WIAT-II: Listening Comprehension	Gc	93	-	-	LS	70	-	-
WIAT-II: Oral Expression	Gc	93	-	-	CM	67	-	-
WIAT-II: Written Expression	Grw	100	-	-	WA	93	-	-
WJ III: Letter-word Identification	Grw	93	-	-	RD	93	-	-
WJ III: Reading Fluency	Grw	93	-	-	RS	93	-	-
WJ III: Story Recall	Glr	50	Gsm	43	MM	100	MS	100
WJ III: Understanding Directions	Gc	64	Gsm	36	LS	100	MW	81
WJ III: Calculation	Gq	100	-	-	A3	91	-	-
WJ III: Math Fluency	Gs	64	-	-	N	88	-	-
WJ III: Spelling	Grw	93	-	-	SG	92	-	-
WJ III: Writing Fluency	Grw	94	-	-	WA	81	-	-
WJ III: Passage Comprehension	Grw	71	-	-	CZ	75	-	-
WJ III: Applied Problems	Gq	71	-	-	KM	58	A3	42
WJ III: Writing Samples	Grw	100	-	-	WA	100	-	-
WJ III: Story Recall-Delayed	Glr	94	-	-	MM	82	-	-
WJ III: Word Attack	Grw	94	-	-	RD	100	-	-
WJ III: Picture Vocabulary	Gc	82	-	-	VL	64	-	-
WJ III: Oral Comprehension	Gc	89	-	-	LS	94	-	-
WJ III: Editing	Grw	100	-	-	EU	100	-	-
WJ III: Reading Vocabulary	Gc	83	-	-	LD	47	VL	47
WJ III: Quantitative Concepts	Gq	89	-	-	KM	100	-	-
WJ III: Academic Knowledge	Gc	100	-	-	K0	94	-	-
WJ III: Spelling Sounds	Grw	65	-	-	SG	100	-	-
WJ III: Sound Awareness	Ga	89	-	-	PC:A	75	-	-
WJ III: Punctuation & Capital	Grw	100	-	-	EU	100	-	-
Brief/Screening Tests	**Primary Broad**		**Secondary Broad**		**Primary Narrow**		**Secondary Narrow**	
HAMAT: Reading A	Grw	100	-	-	CZ	87	-	-
HAMAT: Writing A[b]	Grw	100	-	-	EU	-	-	-
HAMAT: Arithmetic A	Gq	100	-	-	A3	87	-	-
HAMAT: Facts A	Gc	100	-	-	K0	100	-	-
HAMAT: Reading B	Grw	100	-	-	CZ	87	-	-
HAMAT: Writing B[b]	Grw	100	-	-	EU	-	-	-
HAMAT: Arithmetic B	Gq	100	-	-	A3	87	-	-
HAMAT: Facts B	Gc	100	-	-	K0	100	-	-
K-FAST: Arithmetic[a]	Gq	-	-	-	A3	-	KM	-
K-FAST: Reading[b]	Grw	47	Gc	40	RC	71	K2	-
K-SEALS: Vocabulary[b]	Gc	87	-	-	VL	-	LD	-
K-SEALS: #'s, Letters, & Words	Gq	100	-	-	KM	93	-	-
MBA: Reading[b]	Grw	87	-	-	RD	-	RC,V	-
MBA: Writing	Grw	100	-	-	EU	93	-	-
MBA: Mathematics	Gq	73	-	-	A3	50	KM	50
MBA: Factual Knowledge	Gc	100	-	-	K0	87	-	-
TAAS-R: Spelling	Grw	93	-	-	SG	79	-	-
TAAS-R: Letter-Word Reading	Grw	100	-	-	RD	100	-	-
TAAS-R: Listening Comp	Gc	93	-	-	LS	93	-	-
TAAS-R: Arithmetic (Oral)	Gq	100	-	-	KM	87	-	-
TAAS-R: Arithmetic (Written)	Gq	100	-	-	A3	87	-	-
TAAS-R: Oral Reading Accuracy	Grw	100	-	-	RD	94	-	-

Test Name	Code	% Agmt	Code	% Agmt	Code	% Agmt	Code	% Agmt
TAAS-R: Story Comprehension	*Grw*	75	-	-	RC	92	-	-
TOCL: Spoken Language[b]	*Gc*	50	*Grw*	50	MY	83	EU	-
TOCL: Knowledge of Print	*Ga*	69	-	-	PC:A	82	-	-
TOCL: Word Recognition	*Grw*	100	-	-	RD	50	RC	50
TOCL: Reading Comprehension	*Grw*	100	-	-	RC	100	-	-
TOCL: Writing Skills	*Grw*	94	-	-	SG	40	EU	40
TOCL: Writing from Memory	*Glr*	93	-	-	MM	85	-	-
TOCL: Original Writing	*Grw*	100	-	-	WA	100	-	-
WRAT-3: Reading A	*Grw*	100	-	-	RD	94	-	-
WRAT-3: Spelling A	*Grw*	94	-	-	SG	80	-	-
WRAT-3: Arithmetic A	*Gq*	100	-	-	A3	70	-	-
WRAT-3: Reading B	*Grw*	100	-	-	RD	94	-	-
WRAT-3: Spelling B	*Grw*	94	-	-	SG	80	-	-
WRAT-3: Arithmetic B	*Gq*	100	-	-	A3	70	-	-
YCAT: General Information	*Gc*	100	-	-	K0	100	-	-
YCAT: Reading[b]	*Grw*	94	-	-	RD	-	-	-
YCAT: Mathematics	*Gq*	100	-	-	A3	87	-	-
YCAT: Writing	*Grw*	94	-	-	SG	67	-	-
YCAT: Spoken Language	*Gc*	80	-	-	VL	55	LD	45

Specific Academic Skills Reading Tests	**Primary Broad**		**Secondary Broad**		**Primary Narrow**		**Secondary Narrow**	
GORT-4: Rate	*Grw*	91	-	-	RS	90	-	-
GORT-4: Accuracy	*Grw*	100	-	-	RD	73	-	-
GORT-4: Fluency	*Grw*	91	-	-	RS	60	RD	40
GORT-4: Comprehension	*Grw*	100	-	-	RC	100	-	-
GSRT: Silent Reading Comp A	*Grw*	100	-	-	RC	94	-	-
GSRT: Silent Reading Comp B	*Grw*	100	-	-	RC	94	-	-
SRI-2: Vocabulary in Context A	*Grw*	63	-	-	V	90	-	-
SRI-2: Word Rec Accuracy A	*Grw*	100	-	-	RD	100	-	-
SRI-2: Passage Comprehension A	*Grw*	100	-	-	RC	94	-	-
SRI-2: Vocabulary in Context B	*Grw*	63	-	-	V	90	-	-
SRI-2: Word Rec Accuracy B	*Grw*	100	-	-	RD	100	-	-
SRI-2: Passage Comprehension B	*Grw*	100	-	-	RC	94	-	-
TERA-3: Alphabet	*Grw*	82	-	-	RD	100	-	-
TERA-3: Conventions	*Grw*	93	-	-	EU	100	-	-
TERA-3: Meaning	*Grw*	82	-	-	V	56	RC	44
TORC-3: General Vocabulary[a]	*Gc*	-	*Grw*	-	VL, LD	-	V	-
TORC-3: Syntactic Similarities	*Grw*	63	-	-	V	70	-	-
TORC-3: Paragraph Reading	*Grw*	100	-	-	RC	100	-	-
TORC-3: Sentence Sequencing[a]	*Grw*	-	-	-	RC	-	-	-
TORC-3: Mathematics Vocabulary	*Gq*	75	-	-	KM	100	-	-
TORC-3: Social Studies Vocab	*Gc*	84	-	-	LD	50	VL	42
TORC-3: Science Vocabulary[b]	*Gc*	100	-	-	K1	-	-	-
TORC-3: Reading Directions	*Grw*	100	-	-	RC	80	-	-
TOWRE: Sight Word Efficiency	*Grw*	88	-	-	RD	57	RS	43

Test Name	Code	% Agmt	Code	% Agmt	Code	% Agmt	Code	% Agmt
TOWRE: Phonemic Decoding Eff	*Grw*	75	-	-	RD	83	-	-
WDRB: Letter-Word Identification	*Grw*	94	-	-	RD	93	-	-
WDRB: Word Attack	*Grw*	94	-	-	RD	100	-	-
WDRB: Reading Vocabulary	*Gc*	81	-	-	VL	62	-	-
WDRB: Passage Comprehension	*Grw*	100	-	-	CZ	80	-	-
WDRB: Memory for Sentences	*Gsm*	100	-	-	MS	93	-	-
WDRB: Visual Matching	*Gs*	88	-	-	P	100	-	-
WDRB: Incomplete Words	*Ga*	100	-	-	PC:S	64	-	-
WDRB: Sound Blending	*Ga*	100	-	-	PC:S	100	-	-
WDRB: Oral Vocabulary	*Gc*	86	-	-	VL	58	LD	42
WDRB: Listening Comprehension	*Gc*	80	-	-	LS	100	-	-
WRMT-R/NU: Vis-Aud Learning	*Glr*	64	-	-	MA	100	-	-
WRMT-R/NU: Letter ID[a]	*Grw*	-	-	-	RD	-	-	-
WRMT-R/NU: Letter Checklist	*Grw*	64	-	-	RD	89	-	-
WRMT-R/NU: Word ID	*Grw*	100	-	-	RD	100	-	-
WRMT-R/NU: Word Attack	*Grw*	79	-	-	RD	100	-	-
WRMT-R/NU: Word Comp	*Gc*	88	-	-	VL	93	-	-
WRMT-R/NU: Passage Comp	*Grw*	94	-	-	RC	94	-	-
Specific Academic Skills Math Tests	**Primary Broad**		**Secondary Broad**		**Primary Narrow**		**Secondary Narrow**	
KM-R/NU: Numeration	*Gq*	71	-	-	A3	50	KM	50
KM-R/NU: Rational Numbers	*Gq*	100	-	-	A3	80	-	-
KM-R/NU: Geometry[a]	*Gv*	-	-	-	SR	-	Vz	-
KM-R/NU: Addition	*Gq*	79	-	-	A3	73	-	-
KM-R/NU: Subtraction	*Gq*	93	-	-	A3	62	-	-
KM-R/NU: Multiplication	*Gq*	86	-	-	A3	83	-	-
KM-R/NU: Division	*Gq*	100	-	-	A3	94	-	-
KM-R/NU: Mental Computation	*Gq*	88	-	-	A3	67	-	-
KM-R/NU: Measurement	*Gq*	71	-	-	KM	58	A3	42
KM-R/NU: Time and Money	*Gq*	79	-	-	KM	72	-	-
KM-R/NU: Estimation	*Gq*	94	-	-	A3	75	-	-
KM-R/NU: Interpreting Data[b]	*Gq*	71	-	-	KM	-	A3	-
KM-R/NU: Problem Solving	*Gq*	53	*Gf*	47	A3	67	RQ	100
S-DMS: Math Concepts	*Gq*	100	-	-	KM	94	-	-
S-DMS: Math Problem-Solving	*Gq*	100	-	-	A3	82	-	-
S-DMS: Math Calculation	*Gq*	100	-	-	A3	94	-	-
TOMA-2: Vocabulary[a]	*Gq*	-	*Gc*	-	KM	-	VL	-
TOMA-2: Computation	*Gq*	100	-	-	A3	76	-	-
TOMA-2: General Information	*Gq*	76	-	-	KM	54	A3	46
TOMA-2: Story Problems	*Gq*	50	*Gf*	50	KM, A3	60, 40	RQ	86
Specific Academic Skills Written Language Tests	**Primary Broad**		**Secondary Broad**		**Primary Narrow**		**Secondary Narrow**	
OWLS: WE: Written Expression	*Grw*	94	-	-	WA	69	-	-
TEWL-2: Basic Writing A[a]	*Grw*	-	-	-	EU	-	-	-
TEWL-2: Contextual Writing A	*Grw*	100	-	-	WA	100	-	-
TEWL-2: Basic Writing B[a]	*Grw*	-	-	-	EU	-	-	-

Written Language Tests (Cont'd)

Test Name	Code	% Agmt	Code	% Agmt	Code	% Agmt	Code	% Agmt
TEWL-2: Contextual Writing B	*Grw*	100	-	-	WA	100	-	-
TOWE: Items	*Grw*	82	-	-	EU	100	-	-
TOWE: Essay	*Grw*	100	-	-	WA	100	-	-
TOWL-3: Vocabulary A	*Grw*	88	-	-	WA	93	-	-
TOWL-3: Spelling A	*Grw*	94	-	-	SG	93	-	-
TOWL-3: Style A	*Grw*	94	-	-	EU	100	-	-
TOWL-3: Logical Sentences A	*Grw*	88	-	-	EU	67	-	-
TOWL-3: Sentence Combining A[b]	*Grw*	93	-	-	EU	-	WA	-
TOWL-3: Contextual Conventions A	*Grw*	100	-	-	WA	53	EU	47
TOWL-3: Contextual Language A	*Grw*	94	-	-	WA	75	-	-
TOWL-3: Story Construction A	*Grw*	100	-	-	WA	100	-	-
TOWL-3: Vocabulary B	*Grw*	88	-	-	WA	93	-	-
TOWL-3: Spelling B	*Grw*	94	-	-	SG	93	-	-
TOWL-3: Style B	*Grw*	94	-	-	EU	100	-	-
TOWL-3: Logical Sentences B	*Grw*	88	-	-	EU	67	-	-
TOWL-3: Sentence Combining B[b]	*Grw*	93	-	-	EU	-	WA	-
TOWL-3: Contextual Conventions B	*Grw*	100	-	-	WA	53	EU	47
TOWL-3: Contextual Language B	*Grw*	94	-	-	WA	75	-	-
TOWL-3: Story Construction B	*Grw*	100	-	-	WA	100	-	-
TWS-4: Forms A	*Grw*	94	-	-	SG	80	-	-
TWS-4: Forms B	*Grw*	94	-	-	SG	80	-	-
Specific Academic Skills Oral Language Tests	**Primary Broad**		**Secondary Broad**		**Primary Narrow**		**Secondary Narrow**	
CELF-3: Sentence Structure	*Gc*	82	-	-	LS	64	-	-
CELF-3: Word Structure	*Gc*	71	-	-	LS	92	-	-
CELF-3: Concepts and Directions	*Gsm*	82	-	-	MS	93	-	-
CELF-3: Formulated Sentences	*Gc*	94	-	-	OP	71	-	-
CELF-3: Word Classes	*Gc*	89	-	-	LD	70	-	-
CELF-3: Recalling Sentences	*Gsm*	100	-	-	MS	100	-	-
CELF-3: Sentence Assembly[b]	*Gc*	78	-	-	LD	-	MY	-
CELF-3: Semantic Relationships	*Gc*	78	-	-	LS	71	-	-
CELF-3: Word Associations	*Glr*	81	-	-	FI	100	-	-
CELF-3: Listening to Paragraphs	*Gc*	100	-	-	LS	81	-	-
CELF-3: Rapid Automatic Naming	*Glr*	60	-	-	NA	55	FI	45
CASL: Comp of Basic Concepts[b]	*Gc*	78	-	-	VL	-	LD	-
CASL: Antonyms	*Gc*	100	-	-	VL	78	-	-
CASL: Synonyms	*Gc*	83	-	-	VL	67	-	-
CASL: Sentence Completions	*Gc*	78	-	-	LS	100	-	-
CASL: Idiomatic Language	*Gc*	83	-	-	LS	47	LD	40
CASL: Syntax Construction[b]	*Gc*	94	-	-	MY	-	OP	-
CASL: Paragraph Comp of Syntax	*Gc*	94	-	-	LS	60	LD	40
CASL: Grammatical Morphemes	*Gc*	100	-	-	MY	63	-	-
CASL: Sentence Comp of Syntax	*Gc*	100	-	-	LD	81	-	-
CASL: Grammaticality Judgment	*Gc*	93	-	-	MY	100	-	-
CASL: Non-literal Language[b]	*Gc*	100	-	-	LD	-	K2	-
CASL: Meaning from Context[b]	*Gc*	88	-	-	LS	-	LD	-
CASL: Inference	*Gc*	100	-	-	K0	63	-	-
CASL: Ambiguous Sentences	*Gc*	94	-	-	VL	67	-	-
CASL: Pragmatic Judgment	*Gc*	63	-	-	K0	40	LD	40

Test Name	Code	% Agmt	Code	% Agmt	Code	% Agmt	Code	% Agmt
CREVT: Receptive Vocabulary A	Gc	90	-	-	VL	69	-	-
CREVT: Expressive Vocabulary A	Gc	100	-	-	VL	90	-	-
CREVT: Receptive Vocabulary B	Gc	90	-	-	VL	69	-	-
CREVT: Expressive Vocabulary B	Gc	100	-	-	VL	90	-	-
CREVT-A: Receptive Vocabulary A	Gc	89	-	-	VL	69	-	-
CREVT-A: Expressive Vocab A	Gc	100	-	-	VL	90	-	-
CREVT-A: Receptive Vocabulary B	Gc	89	-	-	VL	69	-	-
CREVT-A: Expressive Vocab B	Gc	100	-	-	VL	90	-	-
EO-WPVT: Expressive Vocabulary	Gc	78	-	-	VL	57	LD	40
EVT: Total Test[b]	Gc	94	-	-	VL	-	-	-
ITPA 3: Spoken Analogies[b]	Gc	64	-	-	VL	-	LD	-
ITPA 3: Spoken Vocabulary	Gc	100	-	-	LD	82	-	-
ITPA 3: Morphological Closure	Gc	100	-	-	MY	64	-	-
ITPA 3: Syntactic Sentences	Gsm	91	-	-	MS	100	-	-
ITPA 3: Sound Deletion	Ga	100	-	-	PC:A	100	-	-
ITPA 3: Rhyming Sequences	Gsm	100	-	-	MS	100	-	-
ITPA 3: Sentence Sequencing	Grw	100	-	-	RC	73	-	-
ITPA 3: Written Vocabulary[b]	Grw	100	-	-	V	-	EU	-
ITPA 3: Sight Decoding	Grw	91	-	-	RD	100	-	-
ITPA 3: Sound Decoding	Grw	100	-	-	RD	100	-	-
ITPA 3: Sight Spelling[a]	Grw	-	-	-	SG	-	-	-
ITPA 3: Sound Spelling	Grw	82	-	-	SG	100	-	-
LPT-R: Pretest 1[b]	Gc	72	-	-	VL	-	LD	-
LPT-R: Pretest 2[b]	Gc	94	-	-	VL	-	LD	-
LPT-R: Associations[b]	Gc	55	Glr	44	LD	60	FA, FI	-
LPT-R: Categorization[a]	Gc	-	-	-	LD	-	-	-
LPT-R: Similarities	Gc	83	-	-	LD	64	-	-
LPT-R: Differences	Gc	83	-	-	LD	80	-	-
LPT-R: Multiple Meanings	Gc	100	-	-	VL	94	-	-
LPT-R: Attributes	Gc	81	-	-	LD	53	VL	47
PPVT III: Form III A	Gc	94	-	-	VL	73	-	-
PPVT III: Form III B	Gc	94	-	-	VL	73	-	-
OWLS: Listening Comprehension[b]	Gc	94	-	-	LS	-	LD	-
OWLS: Oral Expression[b]	Gc	100	-	-	CM	-	OP, LD	-
RO-WPVT: Receptive Vocabulary	Gc	94	-	-	VL	67	-	-
TOAL-3: Listening/Vocabulary	Gc	94	-	-	VL	60	-	-
TOAL-3: Listening/Grammar	Gc	100	-	-	LD	63	-	-
TOAL-3: Speaking/Vocabulary	Gc	100	-	-	OP	81	-	-
TOAL-3: Speaking/Grammar	Gsm	93	-	-	MS	100	-	-
TOAL-3: Reading/Vocabulary	Grw	93	-	-	V	86	-	-
TOAL-3: Reading/Grammar	Grw	100	-	-	V	73	-	-
TOAL-3: Writing/Vocabulary	Grw	81	-	-	V	53	WA	47
TOAL-3: Writing/Grammar	Grw	92	-	-	EU	57	WA	43
TELD-3: Receptive Language A[b]	Gc	100	-	-	LS	-	LD	-
TELD-3: Expressive Language A[b]	Gc	100	-	-	OP	-	LD	-
TELD-3: Receptive Language B[b]	Gc	100	-	-	LS	-	LD	-
TELD-3: Expressive Language B[b]	Gc	100	-	-	OP	-	LD	-
TOLD-I:3: Sentence Combining[b]	Gc	100	-	-	LD	-	-	-
TOLD-I:3: Picture Vocabulary	Gc	94	-	-	LD	60	-	-

Test Name	Code	% Agmt	Code	% Agmt	Code	% Agmt	Code	% Agmt
TOLD-I:3: Word Ordering[a]	Gc	-	Gsm	-	LS	-	MW	-
TOLD-I:3: Generals	Gc	100	-	-	LD	88	-	-
TOLD-I:3: Grammatic Comp	Gc	100	-	-	MY	100	-	-
TOLD-I:3: Malapropisms[b]	Gc	88	-	-	MY	-	VL	-
TOLD-P:3: Picture Vocabulary	Gc	100	-	-	VL	88	-	-
TOLD-P:3: Relational Vocabulary	Gc	94	-	-	LD	93	-	-
TOLD-P:3: Oral Vocabulary	Gc	100	-	-	VL	100	-	-
TOLD-P:3: Gramm Understanding	Gc	81	-	-	LD	44	LS	44
TOLD-P:3: Sentence Imitation	Gsm	94	-	-	MS	100	-	-
TOLD-P:3: Grammatic Completion	Gc	75	-	-	MY	50	LS	50
TOLD-P:3: Phonemic Analysis	Ga	80	-	-	PC:A	91	-	-
TOLD-P:3: Word Articulation	-	-	-	-	-	-	-	-
TOLD-P:3: Word Discrimination	Ga	75	-	-	US/U3	60	-	-

Specific Academic Skills Phonological Processing Tests	Primary Broad		Secondary Broad		Primary Narrow		Secondary Narrow	
CTOPP: Elision	Ga	92	-	-	PC:A	100	-	-
CTOPP: Blending Words	Ga	100	-	-	PC:S	100	-	-
CTOPP: Sound Matching	Ga	92	-	-	PC:A	91	-	-
CTOPP: Memory for Digits	Gsm	100	-	-	MS	100	-	-
CTOPP: Non-word Repetition[a]	Gsm	-	-	-	MS	-	-	-
CTOPP: Rapid Color Naming	Glr	50	Gs	44	NA	100	R9	75
CTOPP: Rapid Object Naming	Glr	65	-	-	NA	100	-	-
CTOPP: Rapid Digit Naming	Gs	60	Glr	40	R9	100	NA	100
CTOPP: Rapid Letter Naming[a]	Glr	-	Gs	-	NA	-	R9	-
CTOPP: Blending Non-words	Ga	100	-	-	PC:S	90	-	-
CTOPP: Phoneme Reversal	Gsm	56	Ga	44	MW	100	PC:A	-
CTOPP: Segmenting Words	Ga	100	-	-	PC:A	100	-	-
CTOPP: Segmenting Non-words	Ga	83	-	-	PC:A	93	-	-
SCAN-C-R: Filtered Words	Ga	94	-	-	UR	88	-	-
SCAN-C-R: Aud Figure-Ground	Ga	100	-	-	UR	100	-	-
SCAN-C-R: Competing Words	Ga	100	-	-	UL	100	-	-
SCAN-C-R: Competing Sentences	Ga	75	-	-	UL	83	-	-
TACL-3: Vocabulary	Gc	100	-	-	VL	80	-	-
TACL-3: Grammatical Morphemes	Gc	93	-	-	VL	65	-	-
TACL-3: Elab Phrases & Sent	Gc	81	-	-	LS	50	LD	50
TAPS-R: Number Mem Forward	Gsm	100	-	-	MS	81	-	-
TAPS-R: Number Mem Reversed	Gsm	100	-	-	MW	80	-	-
TAPS-R: Aud Sentences Memory	Gsm	100	-	-	MS	100	-	-
TAPS-R: Auditory Word Memory	Glr	53	Gsm	47	M6	100	MW	100
TAPS-R: Aud Interp of Directions	Gc	88	-	-	LD	50	LS	50
TAPS-R: Auditory Word Discrim.	Ga	78	-	-	US	100	-	-
TAPS-R: Auditory Processing	Gf	83	-	-	I	44	RG	44
TOPA: Initial Sound[a]	Ga	-	-	-	PC:A	-	-	-
TOPA: Ending Sound[a]	Ga	-	-	-	PC:A	-	-	-

[a]For these tests, consensus according to the established classification criteria was not reached at the broad- or narrow-ability level. Therefore both the broad- and narrow-ability classifications in these cases were determined logically by the authors.

(continued)

[b]For these tests, consensus according to the established classification criteria was reached at the broad ability level but not at the narrow ability level. Therefore the narrow-ability classifications in these cases were determined logically by the authors.

Note: The following evaluative criteria were used for broad-ability classifications: (1) agreement of 80% or higher on a single broad-ability received a single broad-ability classification; (2) agreement of ≥ 60% on a single broad-ability and no agreement of ≥ 40% on any other broad ability received a single broad-ability classification; and (3) agreement of ≥ 40% on two different broad abilities received a mixed broad-ability classification. Any other pattern of agreement was believed to indicate that no consensus was achieved and thus classifications for such cases were made logically by the authors. The same criteria were followed for narrow-ability classifications and were dependent on the corresponding broad ability classifications as follows. When any of the above criteria were met at the broad-ability level, then classification decisions were made based only on the narrow abilities corresponding to the broad ability (or abilities) for which agreement was reached. Figures reported in this table were based on the total classifications made by the 57 participants in the expert consensus study. Each test listed in the table was classified by an average of 15 experts (range = 11–18) and an average of 31 ratings per test (range = 22–36) were made. Refer to Chapter 3 for more detailed information regarding the expert consensus process and to Figure 3.1 for a summary of the findings.

List of Participants in the Expert Consensus Study

Vincent Alfonso
Dorrie Berstein
Julie Esparza Brown
Lenny F. Caltabiano
Rhonda Johnson Cash
Renee A. Chituk
Susanna S. Christie
Denise Conti
James M. Creed
Amy Drost
Ron Dumont
Catherine A. Fiorello
Linda M. Fishman
Dawn Flanagan
Randy G. Floyd
Jeffrey J. Froh
Richard A. Frohwirth
Charles Granger
Yuvelin Gutierrez
Ron Hockman
John Horn
V. Curtis Hunter
Matthew Jacofsky
Samantha W. Kohn
Roger Ladouceur
Melissa B. Tarnofsky
Jennifer Turetzky
Jeanne Marie Villani
John O. Willis

Ana Landron
Mary M. Lang
Sharon A. Leis
Roni N. Loud
Jennifer Mascolo
Nancy Mather
Kevin McGrew
Michelle Meskin
David G. Mirich
Robert W. Misak
Craig Montagne
Susan Morbey
Samuel O. Ortiz
Patrick Owen
Kristen M. Peters
Helene Reveliotis
Cara M. Riebe
Nancee G. Santandreu
Susan M. Schermerhorn
Matthew Schleider
Fredrick A. Schrank
Shawn Seybert
Lisa Solazzo
Anna Lee Speer
Jennifer Sutherland
Richard Woodcock
Stephen Zimmermann
Amy Zgodny

References

Aaron, P. G. (1995). Differential diagnosis of reading disabilities. *School Psychology Review, 24 (3)*, 345–360.

Aaron, P. G. (1997). The impending demise of the discrepancy formula. *Review of Educational Research, 67 (4)*, 461–502.

Abbott, R. D., & Berninger, V. W. (1993). Structural equation modeling of relationships among developmental skills and writing skills in primary- and intermediate-grade writers. *Journal of Educational Psychology, 85 (3)*, 478–508.

Abbott, S. P., & Berninger, V. W. (1999). It's never too late to remediate: Teaching word recognition to students with reading disabilities in grades 4–7. *Annals of Dyslexia, 49*, 223–250.

Ackerman, P. L., & Heggestad, E. D. (1997). Intelligence, personality, and interests: Evidence for overlapping traits. *Psychological Bulletin, 121 (2)*, 219–245.

Ackerman, P. T., Anhalt, J. M., & Dykman, R. A. (1986). Arithmetic automatization failure in children with attention and reading disorders: Association and sequelae. *Journal of Learning Disabilities, 19*, 222–232.

Adams, A., Bourke, L., & Willis, C. (1999). Working memory and spoken language comprehension in young children. *International Journal of Psychology, 34 (5–6)*, 364–373.

Aiken, L. R. (2000). *Psychological testing and assessment* (10th ed.). Allyn and Bacon: Boston.

Alloy, L. B., Acocella, J., & Bootzin, R. R. (1996). *Abnormal psychology: Current perspectives* (7th ed.) New York: McGraw-Hill.

American Educational Research Association, American Psychological Association, American Council on Measurement. (1985). *Standards for educational and psychological tests*. Washington, DC: American Psychological Association.

American Educational Research Association, American Psychological Association, American Council on Measurement. (1999). *Standards for educational and psychological testing*. Washington, DC: American Educational Research Association.

American Psychiatric Association. (1994). *Diagnostic and statistical manual of mental disorders* (4th ed.). Washington, DC: Author.

American Psychiatric Association. (2000). *Diagnostic and statistical manual of mental disorders* (4th ed., text revision). Washington, DC: Author.

American Psychological Association Ethics Committee. (1992). Ethical principles of psychologists and code of conduct. *American Psychologist, 47 (12)*, 1597–1611.

Anastasi, A., & Urbina, S. (1997). *Psychological testing* (7th ed.). Upper Saddle River, NJ: Prentice-Hall.

Atkinson, L. (1991). On WAIS-R difference scores in the standardization sample. *Psychological Assessment, 3*, 292–294.

Baddeley, A. (1986). *Working memory*. Oxford: Oxford University Press.

Baddeley, A. (1992). Is working memory working? The fifteenth Bartlett Lecture. *Quarterly Journal of Experimental Psychology, 44A*, 1–31.

Badian, N. A. (1988). A prediction of good and poor reading before kindergarten entry: A nine-year follow-up. *Journal of Learning Disabilities, 21 (2)*, 98–103, 123.

Badian, N. A. (1999). Reading disability defined as a discrepancy between listening and reading comprehension: A longitudinal study of stability, gender differences, and prevalence. *Journal of Learning Disabilities, 32 (2)*, 138–148.

Badian, N. A., Duffy, F. H., Als, H., & McAnulty, G. B. (1991). Linguistic profiles of dyslexic and good readers. *Annals of Dyslexia, 41*, 221–245.

Baker, L. A., Decker, S. N., & DeFries, J. C. (1984). Cognitive abilities in reading-disabled children: A longitudinal study. *Journal of Child Psychology & Psychiatry & Allied Disciplines, 25 (1)*, 111–117.

Ball, E. W. (1993). Phonological awareness: What's important and to whom? *Reading & Writing, 5 (2)*, 141–159.

Ball, E. W., & Blachman, B. A. (1991). Does phoneme awareness training in kindergarten make a difference in early word recognition & developmental spelling? *Reading Research Quarterly, 25*, 49–66.

Barenbaum, E., & Newcomer, P. (1996). *Test of children's Language*. Austin, TX: PRO-ED.

Bateman, B. (1965). Learning disabilities: An overview. *Journal of School Psychology, 3 (3)*, 1–12.

Bear, D. R., & Barone, D. (1991). The relationship between rapid automatized naming and orthographic knowledge. *National Reading Conference Yearbook, 40*, 179–184.

Benbow, C. P. (1992). Academic achievement in mathematics and science of students between ages 13 and 23: Are there differences among students in the top one percent of mathematical ability? *Journal of Educational Psychology, 84 (1)*, 51–61.

Benbow, C. P., & Arjmand, O. (1990). Predictors of high academic achievement in mathematics and science by mathematically talented students: A longitudinal study. *Journal of Educational Psychology, 82 (3)*, 430–441.

Bensen, J. (1998). Developing a strong program of construct validation: A test anxiety example. *Educational Measurement: Issues and Practice*, 10–22.

Berninger, V. W. (1990). Multiple orthographic codes: Key to alternative instructional methodologies for developing the orthographic phonological connections underlying word identification. *School Psychology Review, 19 (4)*, 518–533.

Berninger, V. W. (1997). Introduction to interventions for students with learning problems: Myths and realities. *School Psychology Review, 26 (3)*, 326–332.

Berninger, V. W., Abbott, R. D., & Alsdorf, B. J. (1997). Lexical- and sentence-level processes in comprehension of written sentences. *Reading & Writing, 9 (2)*, 135–162.

Berninger, V. W., Abbott, R. D., Zook, D., Ogier, S., Lemos-Britton, Z., & Brooksher, R. (1999). Early intervention for reading disabilities: Teaching the alphabet principle in a connectionist framework. *Journal of Learning Disabilities, 32 (6)*, 491–503.

Berninger, V. W., Cartwright, A. C., Yates, C. M., Swanson, H. L., et al. (1994). Developmental skills related to writing and reading acquisition in the intermediate grades: Shared and unique functional systems. *Reading & Writing, 6 (2)*, 161–196.

Bickley, P. G., Keith, T. Z., & Wolfe, L. M. (1995). The three-stratum theory of cognitive abilities: Test of the structure of intelligence across the life span. *Intelligence, 20*, 309–328.

Bishop, A. J. (1980). Spatial abilities and mathematical education: A review. *Educational Studies in Mathematics, 11*, 257–269.

Booth, J. R., & Hall, W. S. (1994). Role of the cognitive internal state lexicon in reading comprehension. *Journal of Educational Psychology, 86 (3)*, 413–422.

Bowers, P. G., Sunseth, K., & Golden, J. (1999). The route between rapid naming and reading progress. *Scientific Studies of Reading, 3 (1)*, 31–53.

Bowey, J. A. (1995). Socioeconomic status differences in preschool phonological sensitivity and first-grade reading achievement. *Journal of Educational Psychology, 87 (3)*, 476–487.

Bowey, J. A., Cain, M. T., & Ryan, S. M. (1992). A reading-level design study of phonological skills underlying fourth-grade children's word reading difficulties. *Child Development, 63*, 999–1011.

Bowey, J. A., & Patel, R. K. (1988). Metalinguistic ability and early reading achievement. *Applied Psycholinguistics*, 367–383.

Bracken, B. A. (1987). Limitations of preschool instruments and standards for minimal levels of technical adequacy. *Journal of Psychoeducational Assessment, 4*, 313–326.

Brackett, J., & McPherson, A. (1996). Learning disabilities diagnosis in postsecondary students: A comparison of discrepancy-based diagnostic models. In N. Gregg, C. Hoy, & A. F. Gay (Eds.), *Adults with learning disabilities: Theoretical and practical perspectives* (pp. 68–84). New York: Guilford.

Brady, S., Shankweiler, D., & Mann, V. (1983). Speech perception and memory coding in relation to reading ability. *Journal of Experimental Child Psychology, 35*, 345–367.

Briggs, S. R., & Cheek, J. M. (1986). The role of factor analysis in the development and evaluation of personality scales. Special issue: Methodological developments in personality research. *Journal of Personality, 54 (1)*, 106–148.

Brinckerhoff, L. C., Shaw, S. F., & McGuire, J. M. (1992). Promoting access, accommodations, and independence for college students with learning disabilities. *Journal of Learning Disabilities, 25 (7)*, 417–429.

Brouerman, D. M. (1961). Effects of score transformations in the Q and R factor analysis techniques. *Psychological Review, 68*, 68–80.

Brown, V. L., Cronin, M. E., & McEntire, E. (1994). *Test of Mathematical Abilities* (3rd ed.). Austin, TX: PRO-ED.

Brown, V. L., Hammill, D. D., & Wiederholt, J. L. (1995). *Test of Reading Comprehension* (3rd ed.). Austin, TX: PRO-ED.

Bryant, P. E., Bradley, L., Maclean, M., & Crossland, J. (1989). Nursery rhymes, phonological skills and reading. *Child Language, 16,* 407–428.

Byrne, B., & Fielding-Barnsley, R. (1995). Evaluation of a program to teach phonemic awareness to young children: A 2- and 3-year follow-up and a new preschool trial. *Journal of Educational Psychology, 87 (3),* 488–503.

Caltabiano, L., Flanagan, D. P., Ortiz, S. O., & Alfonso, V. C. (2002). *Linking academic achievement tests to contemporary theory: Content validation through expert consensus.* Manuscript in preparation.

Carnine, L., Carnine, D., & Gersten, R. M. (1984). Analysis of oral reading errors made by economically disadvantaged students taught with a synthetic-phonics approach. *Reading Research Quarterly, 19 (3),* 343–356.

Carroll, J. B. (1993). *Human cognitive abilities: A survey of factor-analytic studies.* Cambridge: Cambridge University Press.

Carroll, J. B. (1997). The three-stratum theory of cognitive abilities. In D. P. Flanagan, J. L. Genshaft, & P. L. Harrison (Eds.), *Contemporary intellectual assessment: Theories, tests, and issues* (pp. 122–130). New York: Guilford.

Carroll, J. B. (1998). Foreword. In K. S. McGrew & D. P. Flanagan, *The intelligence test desk reference (ITDR): Gf-Gc cross-battery assessment* (pp. xi–xii). Boston: Allyn and Bacon.

Carroll, J. B., & Maxwell, S. E. (1979). Individual differences in cognitive abilities. *Annual Review of Psychology, 30,* 603–640.

Carrow-Woolfolk, E. (1995). *Oral and Written Language Scales–Listening Comprehension/Oral Expression.* Circle Pines, MN: American Guidance Service.

Carrow-Woolfolk, E. (1999). *Test for Auditory Comprehension of Language—Third Edition (TACL-3).* Austin, TX: PRO-ED.

Casey, M. B., Nuttall, R. L., & Pezaris, E. (1997). Mediators of gender differences in mathematics college entrance test scores: A comparison of spatial skills with internalized beliefs and anxieties. *Developmental Psychology, 33 (4),* 669–680.

Cattell, R. B. (1957). *Personality and motivation structure and measurement.* New York: World Book.

Catts, H. W. (1993). The relationship between speech-language impairments and reading disabilities. *Journal of Speech & Hearing Research, 36 (5),* 948–958.

Chen, J-Q., & Gardner, H. (1997). Alternative assessment from a multiple intelligences theoretical perspective. In D. P. Flanagan, J. L. Genshaft, & P. L. Harrison (Eds.), *Contemporary intellectual assessment: Theories, tests, and issues* (pp. 105–121). New York: Guilford.

Clarke, L. A., & Watson, D. (1995). Constructing validity: Basic issues in objective scale development. *Psychological Assessment, 7,* 309–319.

Clemens, S. D. (1966). *Minimal brain dysfunction in children: Terminology and identification* (NINDS Monograph No. 3, U.S. Public Health Service Publication No. 1415). Washington, DC: Dept. of Health, Education and Welfare, p. 241.

Collier, V. P. (1992). A synthesis of studies examining long-term language minority student data on academic achievement. *Bilingual Research Journal, 16,* 187–212.

Comrey, A. L. (1988). Factor-analytic methods of scale development in personality and clinical psychology. *Journal of Consulting and Clinical Psychology, 56 (5),* 754–761.

Cone, T. E., & Wilson, L. R. (1981). Quantifying a severe discrepancy: A critical analysis. *Learning Disability Quarterly, 4,* 359–371.

Connolly, A. J. (1998). *KeyMath–Revised: A Diagnostic Inventory of Essential Mathematics.* Circle Pines, MN: American Guidance Service.

Connolly, A. J. (1998). *KeyMath–Revised/Normative Update.* Circle Pines, MN: American Guidance Service.

Cooney, J. B., & Swanson, L. H. (1990). Individual differences in memory for mathematical story problems: Memory span and problem perception. *Journal of Educational Psychology, 82 (3),* 570–577.

Cormier, P., & Dea, S. (1997). Distinctive patterns of relationship of phonological awareness and working memory with reading development. *Reading & Writing, 9 (3),* 193–206.

Council for Learning Disabilities. (1986). Inclusion of non-handicapped low achievers and underachievers in learning disability programs: A position statement by the board of trustees of the Council for Learning Disabilities. *Learning Disability Quarterly, 9,* 245–246.

Crocker, L., & Algina, J. (1986). *Introduction to classical and modern test theory.* New York: Holt, Rinehart, and Winston.

Cronin, V., & Carver, P. (1998). Phonological sensitivity, rapid naming, and beginning reading. *Applied Psycholinguistics, 19 (3),* 447–461.

Daneman, M., & Carpenter, P. A. (1980). Individual differences in working memory and reading. *Journal of Verbal Learning and Verbal Behavior, 19,* 450–466.

Daneman, M., & Merikle, P. M. (1996). Working memory and language comprehension: A meta-analysis. *Psychonomic Bulletin & Review, 3 (4),* 422–433.

Daneman, M., Nemeth, S., Stainton, M., & Huelsmann, K. (1995). Working memory as a predictor of reading achievement in orally educated hearing-impaired children. *Volta Review, 97 (4),* 225–241.

Daniel, M. H. (1997). Intelligence testing: Status and trends. *American Psychologist, 52 (10),* 1038–1045.

Das, J. P., & Naglieri, J. A. (1997). *Cognitive Assessment System.* Itasca, IL: Riverside.

Das, J. P., & Siu, I. (1982). Good and poor readers' word naming time, memory span, and story recall. *Journal of Experimental Education, 57 (2),* 101–114.

Dean, R., & Woodcock, R. (1999). *The WJ-R and Bateria-R in neuropsychological assessment: Woodcock psychological and educational assessment research report no. 3.* Itasca, IL: Riverside.

Decker, S. N., & DeFries, J. C. (1980). Cognitive abilities in families with reading disabled children. *Journal of Learning Disabilities, 13 (9),* 517–522.

de Jong, P. F., & van der Leij, A. (1999). Specific contributions of phonological abilities to early reading acquisition: Results from a Dutch latent variable longitudinal study. *Journal of Educational Psychology, 91 (3),* 450–476.

Denckla, M. B., & Cutting, L. E. (1999). History and significance of rapid automatized naming. *Annals of Dyslexia, 49,* 29–42.

Dunn, L. M., & Dunn, L. M. (1997). *Peabody Picture Vocabulary Test III.* Circle Pines, MN: American Guidance Service.

Eden, G. F., Stein, J. F., Wood, H. M., & Wood, F. B. (1996). Differences in visuospatial judgment in reading-disability and normal children. *Perceptual and Motor Skills, 82,* 155–177.

Education of the Handicapped Law Report: Statutes, regulations, indices and highlights. (1992). Horsham, PA: LRP Publications.

Elliott, C. D. (1990). *Differential Ability Scales: Introductory and technical handbook.* San Antonio, TX: The Psychological Corporation.

Engle, R. W., Cantor, J., & Carullo, J. J. (1992). Individual differences in working memory and comprehension: Test of four hypotheses. *Journal of Experimental Psychology, 18 (5),* 972–992.

Engle, R. W., Nations, J. K., & Cantor, J. (1990). Is "working memory capacity" just another name for word knowledge? *Journal of Educational Psychology, 82 (4),* 799–804.

Epps, S., Ysseldyke, J., & Algozzine, B. (1982). *Public-policy implications of different definitions of learning disabilities.* University of Minnesota Institute for Research on Learning Disabilities.

Farmer, M. F., & Klein, R. M. (1995). The evidence for a temporal processing deficit linked to dyslexia: A review. *Psychonomic Bulletin and Review, 2 (4),* 460–493.

Felton, R. H., & Pepper, P. P. (1995). Early identification and intervention of phonological deficits in kindergarten and early elementary children at risk for reading disability. *School Psychology Review, 24,* 405–414.

Finlan, T. G. (1992). Do state methods of quantifying a severe discrepancy result in fewer students with learning disabilities? *Learning Disability Quarterly, 15 (2),* 129–134.

Flanagan, D. P. (2000). Wechsler-based CHC cross-battery assessment and reading achievement: Strengthening the validity of interpretations drawn from Wechsler test scores. *School Psychology Quarterly, 15 (3),* 295–329.

Flanagan, D. P., & Alfonso, V. C. (1993a). Differences required for significance between Wechsler verbal and performance IQs and the WIAT subtests and composites: The predicted-achievement method. *Psychology in the Schools, 30,* 125–132.

Flanagan, D. P., & Alfonso, V. C. (1993b). WIAT subtest and composite predicted-achievement values based on WISC-III verbal and performance IQs. *Psychology in the Schools, 30,* 310–320.

Flanagan, D. P., & Alfonso, V. C. (1995). A critical review of the technical characteristics of new and recently revised intelligence tests for preschool children. *Journal of Psychoeducational Assessment, 13,* 66–90.

Flanagan, D. P., Andrews, T. J., & Genshaft, J. L. (1997). The functional utility of intelligence tests with special education populations. In D. P. Flanagan, J. L. Genshaft, & P. L. Harrison (Eds.), *Contemporary intellectual assessment: Theories, tests, and issues* (pp. 457–483). New York: Guilford.

Flanagan, D. P., Genshaft, J. L., & Harrison, P. L. (Eds.). (1997). *Contemporary intellectual assessment: Theories, tests, and issues.* New York: Guilford.

Flanagan, D. P., Mascolo, J. & Genshaft, J. L. (2000). A conceptual framework for interpreting preschool intelligence tests. In B. A. Bracken (Ed.), *The psychoeducational assessment of preschool children* (3rd ed.). Boston: Allyn and Bacon.

Flanagan, D. P., & McGrew, K. S. (1997). A cross-battery approach to assessing and interpreting cognitive abilities: Narrowing the gap between practice and cognitive science. In D. P. Flanagan, J. L. Genshaft, & P. L. Harrison (Eds.), *Contemporary intellectual assessment: Theories, tests, and issues* (pp. 314–325). New York: Guilford.

Flanagan, D. P., & McGrew, K. S. (1998). *The intelligence test desk reference (ITDR): Gf-Gc cross-battery assessment.* Boston: Allyn and Bacon.

Flanagan, D. P., McGrew, K. S., & Ortiz, S. O. (2000). *The Wechsler intelligence scales and Gf-Gc theory: A contemporary approach to interpretation.* Boston: Allyn and Bacon.

Flanagan, D. P., & Ortiz, S. O. (2001). *Essentials of cross-battery assessment.* New York: Wiley.

Fletcher, J., & Clayton, I. (1994). Measuring listening comprehension in adolescents with intellectual disability. *Australia & New Zealand Journal of Developmental Disabilities, 19 (1),* 53–59.

Fletcher, J. M., Francis, D. J., Rourke, B. P., Shaywitz, S. E., et al. (1992). The validity of discrepancy-based definitions of reading disabilities. *Journal of Learning Disabilities, 25 (9),* 555–561, 573.

Fletcher, J. M., Francis, D. J., Shaywitz, S. E., Lyon, G. R., Foorman, B. R., Stuebing, K. K., & Shaywitz, B. A. (1998). Intelligent testing and the discrepancy model for children with learning disabilities. *Learning Disabilities Research & Practice, 13 (4),* 186–203.

Flynn, J. R. (1984). The mean IQ of Americans: Massive gains 1932 to 1978. *Psychological Bulletin, 95,* 29–51.

Friedman, L. (1995). The space factor in mathematics: Gender differences. *Review of Educational Research, 65 (1),* 22–50.

Gagne, E. D. (1985). *The cognitive psychology of school learning.* Boston: Little, Brown.

Garcia, G. M., & Stafford, M. E. (2000). Prediction of reading by *Ga* and *Gc* specific cognitive abilities for low-SES White and Hispanic English-speaking children. *Psychology in the Schools, 37 (3),* 227–235.

Gardner, H. (1987a). Beyond the IQ: Education and human development. *Harvard Educational Review, 57,* 187–193.

Gardner, H. (1987b). The theory of multiple intelligences. *Annals of Dyslexia, 37,* 19–35.

Gaskill, F. W., & Brantley, J. C. (1996). Changes in ability and achievement scores over time: Implications for children classified as learning disabled. *Journal of Psychoeducational Assessment, 14 (3),* 220–228.

Geary, D. C. (1993). Mathematical disabilities: Cognitive, neuropsychological, and genetic components. *Psychological Bulletin, 114 (2),* 345–362.

Glass, G. G. (1973). *Teaching decoding as separate from reading.* New York: Adelphi University.

Glutting, J. J., McDermott, P. A., & Konold, T. R. (1997). Ontology, structure, and diagnostic benefits of a normative subtest taxonomy from the WISC-III standardization sample. In D. P. Flanagan, J. L. Genshaft, & P. L. Harrison (Eds.), *Contemporary intellectual assessment: Theories, tests, and issues* (pp. 349–372). New York: Guilford.

Glutting, J. J., McDermott, P. A., Watkins, M. M., Kush, J. C., & Konold, T. R. (1997). The base rate problem and its consequences for interpreting children's ability profiles. *School Psychology Review, 26 (2),* 176–188.

Glutting, J. J., Youngstrom, E. A., Hale, R. L., Ward, T., & Ward, S. (1997). Incremental efficacy of WISC-III factor scores in predicting achievement: What do they tell us? *Psychological Assessment, 9 (3),* 295–301.

Gould, S. J. (1981). *The mismeasure of man.* New York: W. W. Norton.

Greene, B. A., & Royer, J. M. (1994). A developmental review of response time data that support a cognitive components model of reading. *Educational Psychology Review, 6 (2),* 141–172.

Greenspan, S. (1991). A universal approach to measuring disability severity: Implications of a model of general competence. In F. Hafferty, S. C. Hey, G. Kiger, & D. Pfeiffer (Eds.), *Translating disability: At the individual, institutional and societal levels* (pp. 127–132). Portland, OR: Society for Disability Studies.

Greenspan, S., & Driscoll, J. (1997). The role of intelligence in a broad model of personal competence. In D. P. Flanagan, J. L. Genshaft, & P. L. Harrison (Eds.), *Contemporary intellectual assessment: Theories, tests, and issues* (pp. 131–150). New York: Guilford.

Gregory, R. J. (2000). *Psychological testing: History, principles, and applications* (3rd ed.). Boston: Allyn and Bacon.

Gridley, B. E., & Roid, G. H. (1998). The use of the WISC-III with achievement tests. In A. Prifitera & D. Saklofske (Eds.), *WISC-III clinical use and interpretation: Scientist-practitioner perspectives* (pp. 249–288). San Diego, CA: Academic Press.

Griswold, P. C., Gelzheiser, L. M., & Shepherd, M. J. (1987). Does a production deficiency hypothesis account for vocabulary learning among adolescents with learning disabilities? *Journal of Learning Disabilities, 20 (10),* 620–626.

Gupta, A., & Garg, A. (1996). Visuo-perceptual and phonological processing in dyslexic children. *Journal of Personality & Clinical Studies, 12 (1–2),* 67–73.

Gustafsson, J. E. (1994). General intelligence. In R. J. Sternberg (Ed.), *Encyclopedia of human intelligence* (pp. 469–475). New York: Macmillan.

Gustafsson, J. E., & Balke, G. (1993). General and specific abilities as predictors of school achievement. *Multivariate Behavioral Research, 28* (4), 407–434.

Gustafsson, J. E., & Undheim, J. O. (1996). Individual differences in cognitive functions. In D. C. Berliner & R. C. Calfee (Eds.), *Handbook of educational psychology* (pp. 186–242). New York: Macmillan.

Hakistan, A. R., & Bennet, R. W. (1977). Validity studies using the Comprehensive Ability Scale (CAB): I. Academic achievement criteria. *Educational and Psychological Measurement, 37,* 425–437.

Hale, R. L. (1981). Concurrent validity of the WISC-R factor scores. *Journal of School Psychology, 19 (3),* 274–278.

Hammill, D. D. (1990). On defining learning disabilities: An emerging consensus. *Journal of Learning Disabilities, 23 (2),* 74–84.

Hammill, D. D., Brown, V. L., & Bryant, B. R. (1992). *A consumer's guide to tests in print.* Austin, TX: PRO-ED.

Hammill, D. D., Brown, V. L., Larsen, S. C., & Wiederholt, J. L. (1994). *Test of Adolescent and Adult Language* (3rd ed.). Austin, TX: PRO-ED.

Hammill, D. D., Hresko, W. P., Ammer, J. J., Cronin, M. E., & Quinby, S. S. (1998). *Hammill Multiability Achievement Test.* Austin, TX: PRO-ED.

Hammill, D. D., & Larsen, S. C. (1996). *Test of Written Language–3.* Austin, TX: PRO-ED.

Hammill, D. D., & Newcomer, P. L. (1997). *Test of Language Development—Intermediate* (3rd ed.). Austin, TX: PRO-ED.

Heath, C. P., & Kush, J. C. (1991). Use of discrepancy formulas in the assessment of learning disabilities. In J. E. Orzut & G. W. Hynd (Eds.), *Neuropsychological foundations of learning disabilities: A handbook of issues, methods, and practice.* New York: Academic Press.

Hegarty, M., & Kozhevnikov, M. (1999). Types of visual-spatial representations and mathematical problem solving. *Journal of Educational Psychology, 91 (4),* 684–689.

Henry, M., Ganshow, L., & Miles, T. R. (2000). The issue of definition: Some problems. *Perspectives, 26 (1).*

Hessler, G. L. (1993). *Use and interpretation of the Woodcock-Johnson psycho-educational battery—revised.* Chicago: Riverside.

Hinshelwood, J. (1917). *Congenital word blindness.* London: HK Lewis.

Hintze, J. M. (1996a). Discrepancy analysis. *The Connecticut School Psychologist, 3 (2),* 20–25.

Hintze, J. M. (1996b). A statistically justifiable approach to comparing multiple IQ and achievement test scores: Issues regarding multiple comparisons. *The Connecticut School Psychologist, 3 (3),* 17–23.

Hishinuma, E. S., & Tadaki, S. (1997). The problem with grade and age equivalents: WIAT as a case in point. *Journal of Psychoeducational Assessment, 15 (3),* 214–225.

Hitch, G. J. (1978). The role of short-term working memory in mental arithmetic. *Cognitive Psychology, 10,* 302–323.

Horn, J. L. (1965). *Fluid and crystallized intelligence: A factor analytic and developmental study of the structure among primary mental abilities.* Unpublished doctoral dissertation, University of Illinois, Champaign.

Horn, J. L. (1985). Remodeling old theories of intelligence: *Gf-Gc* theory. In B. B. Wolman (Ed.), *Handbook of intelligence* (pp. 267–300). New York: Wiley.

Horn, J. L. (1988). Thinking about human abilities. In J. R. Nesselroade & R. B. Cattell (Eds.), *Handbook of multivariate psychology* (rev. ed., pp. 645–685). New York: Academic Press.

Horn, J. L. (1991). Measurement of intellectual capabilities: A review of theory. In K. S. McGrew, J. K. Werder, & R. W. Woodcock (Eds.), *Woodcock-Johnson Technical Manual* (pp. 197–232). Chicago: Riverside.

Horn, J. L. (1994). Theory of fluid and crystallized intelligence. In R. J. Sternberg (Ed.), *Encyclopedia of human intelligence* (pp. 443–451). New York: Macmillan.

Horn, J. L., & Noll, J. (1997). Human cognitive capabilities: *Gf-Gc* theory. In D. P. Flanagan, J. L. Genshaft, & P. L. Harrison (Eds.), *Contemporary intellectual assessment: Theories, tests, and issues* (pp. 53–91). New York: Guilford.

Hoskyn, M., & Swanson, H. L. (2000). Cognitive processing of low achievers and children with reading disabilities: A selective meta-analytic review of the published literature. *School Psychology Review, 29 (1),* 102–119.

Hresko, W. P., Herron, S. R., & Peak, P. K. (1998). *Test of Early Written Language* (2nd ed.). Austin, TX: PRO-ED.

Iversen, S., & Tunmer, W. E. (1993). Phonological processing skills and the Reading Recovery Program. *Journal of Educational Psychology, 85 (1),* 112–126.

Jackson, N. E., Donaldson, G. W., & Cleland, L. N. (1988). The structure of precocious reading ability. *Journal of Educational Psychology, 80 (2),* 234–243.

Jensen, A. R. (1997, July). *What we know and don't know about the g factor.* Keynote address delivered at the bi-annual convention of the International Society for the Study of Individual Differences, Aarhus, Denmark.

Jensen, A. R. (1998). *The g factor: The science of mental ability.* Westport, CT: Praeger.

John, K. (1998). Selected short-term memory tests as predictors of reading readiness. *Psychology in the Schools, 35 (2),* 137–144.

John, K. R., & Rattan, G. (1991). A comparison of short-term memory tests as predictors of reading achievement for learning-disabled and educable mentally retarded students. *Journal of School Psychology, 29 (4),* 309–318.

Johnson, D. J. (1993). Relationship between oral and written language. *School Psychology Review, 22 (4),* 595–609.

Joshi, R. M. (1995). Assessing reading and spelling skills. *School Psychology Review, 24 (3),* 361–375.

Joshi, R. M., & Aaron, P. G. (2000). The component model of reading: Simple view of reading made a little more complex. *Reading Psychology, 21 (2),* 85–97.

Just, M. A., & Carpenter, P. A. (1992). A capacity theory of comprehension: Individual differences in working memory. *Psychological Review, 99 (1),* 122–149.

Kail, R. (1991). Developmental changes in speed of processing during childhood and adolescence. *Psychological Bulletin, 109,* 490–501.

Kail, R., & Hall, L. K. (1999). Sources of developmental change in children's word-problem performance. *Journal of Educational Psychology, 91 (4),* 660–668.

Kamphaus, R. W. (1993). *Clinical assessment of children's intelligence.* Boston: Allyn and Bacon.

Kamphaus, R. W. (1998). Intelligence test interpretation: Acting in the absence of evidence. In A. Prifitera & D. Saklofske (Eds.), *WISC-III clinical use and interpretation.* San Diego: Academic Press.

Kamphaus, R. W., Petoskey, M. D., & Morgan, A. W. (1997). A history of intelligence test interpretation. In D. P. Flanagan, J. L. Genshaft, & P. L. Harrison (Eds.), *Contemporary intellectual assessment: Theories, tests, and issues* (pp. 32–51). New York: Guilford.

Kass, C. E., & Myklebust, H. R. (1969). Learning disability: An educational definition. *Journal of Learning Disabilities, 2 (7),* 377–379.

Kaufman, A. S. (1979). *Intelligent testing with the WISC-R.* New York: Wiley & Sons.

Kaufman, A. S. (1994). *Intelligent testing with the WISC-III.* New York: Wiley.

Kaufman, A. S. (2000). Foreword. In D. P. Flanagan, K. S. McGrew, & S. O. Ortiz, *The Wechsler intelligence scales and Gf-Gc theory: A contemporary approach to interpretation.* Boston: Allyn and Bacon.

Kaufman, A. S., & Kaufman, N. L. (1983). *Kaufman Assessment Battery for Children.* Circle Pines, MN: American Guidance Service.

Kaufman, A. S., & Kaufman, N. L. (1997). The Kaufman Adolescent and Adult Intelligence Test. In D. P. Flanagan, J. L. Genshaft, & P. L. Harrison (Eds.), *Contemporary intellectual assessment: Theories, tests, and issues* (pp. 209–229). New York: Guilford.

Kaufman, A. S., Lichtenberger, E. O., & Naglieri, J. A. (1999). Intelligence testing in the schools. In C. R. Reynolds & T. B. Gutkin (Eds.), *The handbook of school psychology* (pp. 307–349). New York: Wiley.

Kavale, K. A. (1982). Meta-analysis of the relationship between visual perceptual skills and reading achievement. *Journal of Learning Disabilities, 15 (1),* 42–51.

Kavale, K. A., & Forness, S. R. (1995). *The nature of learning disabilities: Critical elements of diagnosis and classification.* Hillsdale, NJ: Erlbaum.

Kavale, K. A., & Forness, S. R. (2000). What definitions of learning disability say and don't say: A critical analysis. *Journal of Learning Disabilities, 33 (3),* 239–256.

Keith, T. (1988). Research methods in school psychology: An overview. *School Psychology Review, 17,* 502–520.

Keith, T. Z. (1997). Using confirmatory factor analysis to aid in understanding the constructs measured by intelligence tests. In D. P. Flanagan, J. L. Genshaft, & P. L. Harrison, *Contemporary intellectual assessment: Theories, tests, and issues* (pp. 373–402). New York: Guilford.

Keith, T. Z., & Kranzler, J. H. (1999). The absence of structural fidelity precludes construct validity: Rejoinder to Naglieri on what the Cognitive Assessment System does and does not measure. *School Psychology Review, 28 (2),* 303–321.

Keith, T. Z., Kranzler, J., & Flanagan, D. P. (2001). What does the Cognitive Assessment System (CAS) measure? Joint confirmatory factor analysis of the CAS and the Woodcock-Johnson Tests of Cognitive Ability (Third Edition). *School Psychology Review, 30,* 89–119.

Keith, T. Z., & Witta, E. L. (1997). Hierarchical and cross-age confirmatory factor analysis of the WISC-III: What does it measure? *School Psychology Quarterly, 12,* 89–107.

Kintsch, W. (1988). The role of knowledge in discourse comprehension: A construction-integration model. *Psychological Review, 95 (2),* 163–182.

Kirby, J. R., & Becker, L. D. (1988). Cognitive components of learning problems in arithmetic. *RASE: Remedial & Special Education, 9 (5),* 7–15, 27.

Kirk, S. A., & Bateman, B. (1962). *Educating exceptional children.* Boston: Houghton Mifflin.

Kranzler, J. H., & Keith, T. Z. (1999). Independent confirmatory factor analysis of the Cognitive Assessment System (CAS): What does the CAS measure? *School Psychology Review, 28,* 117–144.

Kranzler, J. H., Keith, T. Z., & Flanagan, D. P. (2000). Independent examination of the factor structure of the Cognitive Assessment System (CAS): Further evidence challenging the construct validity of the CAS. *Journal of Psychoeducational Assessment, 18 (2),* 143–159.

Kreiner, D. S., & Gough, P. B. (1990). Two ideas about spelling: Rules and word-specific memory. *Journal of Memory & Language, 29 (1),* 103–118.

LaBuda, M. C., & DeFries, J. C. (1988). Cognitive abilities in children with reading disabilities and controls: A follow-up study. *Journal of Learning Disabilities, 21 (9),* 562–566.

Leather, C. V., & Henry, L. A. (1994). Working memory span and phonological awareness tasks as predictors of early reading ability. *Journal of Experimental Child Psychology, 58,* 88–111.

Lehto, J. (1995). Working memory and school achievement in the Ninth Form. *Educational Psychology, 15 (3),* 271–281.

Lehto, J. (1996). Working memory capacity and summarizing skills in ninth-graders. *Scandinavian Journal of Psychology, 37 (1),* 84–92.

Lemaire, P., Abdi, H., & Fayol, M. (1996). The role of working memory resources in simple cognitive arithmetic. *European Journal of Cognitive Psychology, 8 (1)*, 73–103.

Lennon, J. E., & Slesinski, C. (1999). Early intervention in reading: Results of a screening and intervention program for kindergarten students. *School Psychology Review, 28 (3)*, 353–364.

Leong, C. K. (1999). Phonological coding and children's spelling. *Annals of Dyslexia, 49*, 195–220.

Levy, B. A., Bourassa, D. C., & Horn, C. (1999). Fast and slow namers: Benefits of segmentation and whole word training. *Journal of Experimental Child Psychology, 73 (2)*, 115–138.

Lezak, M. D. (1976). *Neuropsychological assessment.* New York: Oxford University Press.

Lezak, M. D. (1995). *Neuropsychological assessment* (3rd ed.). New York: Oxford University Press.

Liberman, I. Y., Shankweiler, D., Fischer, F. W., & Carter, B. (1974). Explicit syllable and phoneme segmentation in the young child. *Journal of Experimental Child Psychology, 18 (2)*, 201–212.

Logie, R. (1996). The seven ages of working memory. In J. Richardson, R. Engle, L. Hasher, R. Logie, E. Stoltzfus, & R. Zacks (Eds.), *Working memory and human cognition* (pp. 31–65). New York: Oxford.

Lohman, D. F. (1989). Human intelligence: An introduction to advances in theory and research. *Review of Educational Research, 59 (4)*, 333–373.

Lohman, D. F. (1994). Spatial ability. In R. J. Sternberg (Ed.), *Encyclopedia of human intelligence* (pp. 1000–1007). New York: Macmillan.

Lord, F., & Novick, M. (1968). *Statistical theories of mental test scores.* Reading, MA: Addison Wesley.

Lyon, G. R. (1995). Toward a definition of dyslexia. *Annals of Dyslexia, 45*, 3–27.

MacDonald, G. W., & Cornwall, A. (1995). The relationship between phonological awareness and reading and spelling achievement eleven years later. *Journal of Learning Disabilities, 28 (8)*, 523–527.

MacMillan, D. L., Gresham, F. M., & Bocian, K. M. (1998). Discrepancy between definitions of learning disabilities and school practices: An empirical investigation. *Journal of Learning Disabilities, 31 (4)*, 314–326.

MacMillan, D., Gresham, F., Siperstein, G., & Bocian, K. (1996). The labyrinth of I.D.E.A.: School decisions on referred students with subaverage general intelligence. *American Journal on Mental Retardation, 101.*

Maller, S. J., & McDermott, P. A. (1997). WAIS-R profile analysis for college students with learning disabilities. *School Psychology Review, 26 (4)*, 575–585.

Manger, T., & Eikeland, O. J. (1996). Relationship between boys' and girls' nonverbal ability and mathematical achievement. *School Psychology International, 17*, 71–80.

Manis, F. R., Seidenberg, M. S., Stallings, L., Joanisse, M., Bailey, C., Freedman, L., Curtin, S., & Keating, P. (1999). Development of dyslexic subgroups: A one-year follow up. *Annals of Dyslexia, 49*, 105–134.

Mann, V. A., & Liberman, I. Y. (1984). Phonological awareness and verbal short-term memory. *Journal of Learning Disabilities, 10*, 592–599.

Markwardt, F. C., Jr. (1997). *Peabody Individual Achievement Test-Revised/Normative Update.* Circle Pines, MN: American Guidance Service.

Margolese, S. K., & Kline, R. B. (1999). Prediction of basic reading skills among young children with diverse linguistic backgrounds. *Canadian Journal of Behavioral Science, 31 (4)*, 209–216.

Marjoribanks, K. (1976). Academic achievement, intelligence and creativity: A regression surface analysis. *Multivariate Behavioral Research, 11 (1)*, 105–118.

Mascolo, J. (2001). *Interpreting cross-battery data from contemporary theory: Cross-validation of the CHC model in a referred sample.* Unpublished doctoral dissertation, St. John's University.

Mather, N. (1991). *An instructional guide to the Woodcock-Johnson psycho-educational battery—Revised.* Brandon, VT: Clinical Psychology Publishing.

Mather, N., & Roberts, R. (1994). Learning disabilities: A field in danger of extinction? *Learning Disabilities Research & Practice, 9 (1)*, 49–58.

Mather, N., & Woodcock, R. W. (2001). *Woodcock-Johnson III tests of achievement.* Itasca, IL: Riverside Publishing.

McBride-Chang, C. (1995). Phonological processing, speech perception, and reading disability: An integrative review. *Educational Psychologist, 30 (3)*, 109–121.

McCutchen, D., Covill, A., Hoyne, S. H., & Mildes, K. (1994). Individual differences in writing: Implications of translating fluency *Journal of Educational Psychology, 86 (2)*, 256–266.

McDermott, P. A., Fantuzzo, J. W., & Glutting, J. J. (1990). Just say no to subtest analysis: A critique on Wechsler theory and practice. *Journal of Psychoeducational Assessment, 8,* 290–302.

McDermott, P. A., Fantuzzo, J. W., & Glutting, J. J., Watkins, M. W., & Baggaley, R. A. (1992). Illusions of meaning in the ipsative assessment of children's ability. *Journal of Special Education, 25,* 504–526.

McDermott, P. A., & Glutting, J. J. (1997). Informing stylistic leaning behavior, disposition, and achievement through ability subtests—Or, more illusions of meaning? *School Psychology Review, 26,* 163–175.

McGhee, R., Bryant, B. R., Larsen, S. C., & Rivera, D. M. (1995). *Test of Written Expression.* Austin, TX: PRO-ED.

McGrew, K. S. (1993). The relationship between the WJ-R *Gf-Gc* cognitive clusters and reading achievement across the lifespan. *Journal of Psychoeducational Assessment* [Monograph Series: WJ-R Monograph], 39–53.

McGrew, K. S. (1994). *Clinical interpretation of the Woodcock-Johnson Tests of Cognitive Ability—Revised.* Boston: Allyn and Bacon.

McGrew, K. S. (1997). Analysis of the major intelligence batteries according to a proposed comprehensive *Gf-Gc* framework. In D. P. Flanagan, J. L. Genshaft, & P. L. Harrison (Eds.), *Contemporary intellectual assessment: Theories, tests, and issues* (pp. 151–180). New York: Guilford.

McGrew, K. S., & Flanagan, D. P. (1998). *The intelligence test desk reference (ITDR): Gf-Gc cross-battery assessment.* Boston: Allyn and Bacon.

McGrew, K. S., Flanagan, D. P., Keith, T. Z., & Vanderwood, M. (1997). Beyond g: The impact of *Gf-Gc* specific cognitive abilities research on the future use and interpretation of intelligence tests in the schools. *School Psychology Review, 26,* 177–189.

McGrew, K. S., & Hessler, G. L. (1995). The relationship between the WJ-R *Gf-Gc* cognitive clusters and mathematics achievement across the life-span. *Journal of Psychoeducational Assessment, 13 (1),* 21–38.

McGrew, K. S., & Knopik, S. N. (1993). The relationship between the WJ-R *Gf-Gc* cognitive clusters and writing achievement across the life-span. *School Psychology Review, 22 (4),* 687–695.

McGrew, K. S., & Knopik, S. N. (1996). The relationship between intra-cognitive scatter on the Woodcock-Johnson Psychoeducational Battery and the WISC-R. *Journal of School Psychology, 26,* 275–281.

McGrew, K. S., & Pehl, J. (1988). Prediction of future achievement by the Woodcock-Johnson Psycho-Educational Battery and the WISC-R. *Journal of School Psychology, 26,* 275–281.

McGrew, K. S., Werder, J. K., & Woodcock, R. W. (1991). *Woodcock-Johnson Psycho-Educational Battery—Revised technical manual.* Chicago: Riverside.

McGrew, K. S., & Woodcock, R. W. (2001). Technical manual. *Woodcock-Johnson III.* Itasca, IL: Riverside.

McGuinness, D., McGuiness, C., & Donohue, J. (1995). Phonological training and the alphabet principle: Evidence for reciprocal causality. *Reading Research Quarterly, 30 (4),* 830–852.

Mercer, C. D. (1997). *Students with learning disabilities* (5th ed.). Upper Saddle River, NJ: Prentice-Hall.

Mercer, C. D., Forgnone, C., & Wolking, W. D. (1976). Definitions of learning disabilities used in the United States. *Journal of Learning Disabilities, 9 (6),* 376–386.

Mercer, C. D., Hughes, C. A., & Mercer, A. R. (1985). Learning disabilities definitions used by state education departments. *Learning Disability Quarterly, 8 (1),* 45–55.

Mercer, C., King-Sears, P., & Mercer, A. (1990). Learning disabilities definitions and criteria used by state education departments. *Learning Disability Quarterly, 13,* 141–152.

Messick, S. (1989). Validity. In R. Linn (Ed.), *Educational measurement* (3rd ed.) (pp. 104–131). Washington, DC: American Council on Education.

Messick, S. (1992). Multiple intelligences or multilevel intelligence? Selective emphasis on distinctive properties of hierarchy: On Gardner's *Frames of Mind* and Sternberg's *Beyond IQ* in the context of theory and research on the structure of human abilities. *Psychological Inquiry, 3 (4),* 365–384.

Messick, S. (1995). Validity of psychological assessment: Validation of inferences from persons' responses and performances as scientific inquiry into score meaning. In A. E. Kazdin (Ed.), *Methodological issues and strategies in clinical research*

(2nd ed., pp. 241–261). Washington, DC: American Psychological Association.

Metsala, J. L. (1997). Spoken word recognition in reading disabled children. *Journal of Educational Psychology, 89 (1)*, 159–169.

Meyer, M. S. (2000). The ability-achievement discrepancy: Does it contribute to an understanding of learning disabilities? *Educational Psychology Review, 12 (3)*, 315–337.

Meyer, M. S., Wood, F. B., Hart, L. A., & Felton, R. H. (1998). Selective predictive value of rapid automatized naming in poor readers. *Journal of Learning Disabilities, 31 (2)*, 106–117.

Mills, J. R., & Jackson, N. E. (1990). Predictive significance of early giftedness: The case of precocious reading. *Journal of Educational Psychology, 82 (3)*, 410–419.

Moats, L. C., & Lyon, G. R. (1993). Learning disabilities in the United States: Advocacy, science, and the future of the field. *Journal of Learning Disabilities, 26 (5)*, 282–294.

Montgomery, J. W. (1995). Sentence comprehension in children with specific language impairment: The role of phonological working memory. *Journal of Speech and Hearing Research, 38 (1)*, 187–199.

Morgan, W. (1896). A case of congenital word blindness. *British Medical Journal, 2*, 178.

Morris, R. D., Stuebing, K. K., Fletcher, J. M., Shaywitz, S. E., Lyon, G. R., Shankweiler, D. P., Katz, L., Francis, D. J., & Shaywitz, B. A. (1998). Subtypes of reading disability: Variability around a phonological core. *Journal of Educational Psychology, 90 (3)*, 347–373.

Neisser, U., Boodoo, G., Bouchard, T. J., Boykin, A. W., Brody, N., Ceci, S. J., Halpern, D. F., Loehlin, J. C., Perloff, R., Sternberg, R. J., & Urbina, S. (1996). Intelligence: Knowns and unknowns. *American Psychologist, 51*, 77–101.

Nettelbeck, T. (1994). Speediness. In R. J. Sternberg (Ed.), *Encyclopedia of human intelligence* (pp. 1014–1019). New York: Macmillan.

Newcomer, P. L., & Bryant, B. R. (1993). *Diagnostic Achievement Test for Adolescents* (2nd ed.). Austin, TX: PRO-ED.

Newcomer, P. L., & Hammill, D. D. (1997). *Test of Language Development–3: Primary.* Austin, TX: PRO-ED.

Nunnally, J. S. (1978). *Psychometric theories.* New York: McGraw-Hill.

O'Connor, R. E., Jenkins, J. R., & Slocum, T. A. (1995). Transfer among phonological tasks in kindergarten: Essential instructional content. *Journal of Educational Psychology, 87 (2)*, 202–217.

Orton, S. (1925). "Word blindness" in school children. *Archives of Neurology and Psychiatry, 14*, 581–613.

Orton, S. (1937). *Reading, writing, and speech problems in children and selected papers.* Austin, TX: PRO-ED.

Owens, R. E., Jr. (1994). Development of communication, language, and speech. In C. D. Mercer (Ed.), *Students with learning disabilities* (5th ed.). Upper Saddle River, NJ: Prentice-Hall.

Paik, M., & Nebenzahl, E. (1987). The overall percentile rank versus the individual percentile ranks. *The American Statistician, 41*, 136–138.

Palinscar, A. S., & Perry, N. E. (1995). Developmental, cognitive, and sociocultural perspectives on assessing and instructing reading. *School Psychology Review, 24 (3)*, 331–344.

Popham, W. J. (2000). *Modern educational measurement: Practical guidelines for educational leaders* (3rd ed.). Boston: Allyn and Bacon.

Psychological Corporation. (1992). *Wechsler Individual Achievement Test Manual.* San Antonio, TX: Author.

Psychological Corporation. (1999). *Wechsler Abbreviated Scale of Intelligence.* San Antonio, TX: Author.

Psychological Corporation. (2001). *Wechsler Individual Achievement Test* (2nd ed.). San Antonio, TX: Author.

Rasanen, P., & Ahonen, T. (1995). Arithmetic disabilities with and without reading difficulties: A comparison of arithmetic errors. *Developmental Neuropsychology, 11 (3)*, 275–295.

Reschly, D. J., & Grimes, J. P. (1995). Intellectual assessment. In A. Thomas and J. Grimes (Eds.), *Best practices in school psychology–III.* Washington, DC: National Association of School Psychologists.

Reynolds, C. R. (1990). Conceptual and technical problems in learning disability diagnosis. In C. R. Reynolds & R. W. Kamphaus (Eds.), *Handbook of psychological and educational assessment of children: Intelligence and achievement* (pp. 571–592). New York: Guilford.

Reynolds, C. R., & Kaufman, A. S. (1990). Assessment of children's intelligence with the Wechsler Intelligence Scale for Children–Revised (WISC–R). In C. R. Reynolds & R. W. Kamphaus (Eds.), *Handbook of psychological and educational assessment of children: Intelligence and achievement* (pp. 127–165). New York: Guilford.

Richardson, J. (1996). Evolving concepts of working memory. In J. Richardson, R. Engle, L. Hasher, R. Logie, E. Stoltzfus, & R. Zacks (Eds.), *Working memory and human cognition* (pp. 3–30). New York: Oxford.

Ross, R. P. (1992). Accuracy in analysis of discrepancy scores: A nationwide study of school psychologists. *School Psychology Review, 21 (3),* 480–493.

Salvia, J., & Ysseldyke, J. (1991). *Assessment in special and remedial education* (5th ed.) Boston: Houghton Mifflin.

Sandoval, J. (1998). Critical thinking in test interpretation. In J. Sandoval, C. L. Frisby, K. F. Geisinger, J. D. Scheuneman, & J. R. Grenier (Eds.), *Test interpretation and diversity: Achieving equity in assessment* (pp. 31–50). Washington, DC: American Psychological Association.

Santos, O. B. (1989). Language skills and cognitive processes related to poor reading comprehension performance. *Journal of Learning Disabilities, 22,* 131–133.

Sattler, J. (1992). *Assessment of children* (rev. and updated 3rd ed.). San Diego, CA: Sattler.

Sattler, J. M. (2001). *Assessment of children: Cognitive applications* (4th ed.). La Mesa, CA: Jerome M. Sattler, Publisher.

Scarborough, H. S. (1998). Predicting the future achievement of second graders with reading disabilities: Contributions of phonemic awareness, verbal memory, rapid naming, and IQ. *Annals of Dyslexia, 48,* 115–136.

Sears, S., & Keogh, B. (1993). Predicting reading performance using the Slingerland procedures. *Annals of Dyslexia, 43,* 78–89.

Semel, E., Wiig, E. H., & Secord, W. A. (1995). *Clinical Evaluation of Language Fundamentals* (3rd ed.). San Antonio, TX: Psychological Corporation.

Shankweiler, D., Liberman, I. Y., Mark, L. S., Fowler, C. A., & Fischer, F. W. (1979). Human learning and memory. *Journal of Experimental Psychology, 5 (6),* 531–545.

Shaw, S. F., Cullen, J. P., McGuire, J. M., & Brinckerhoff, L. C. (1995). Operationalizing a definition of learning disabilities. *Journal of Learning Disabilities, 28 (9),* 586–597.

Siegel, L. S. (1989). IQ is irrelevant to the definition of learning disabilities. *Journal of Learning Disabilities, 22 (8),* 469–478, 486.

Siegel, L. S. (1998). The discrepancy formula: Its use and abuse. In B. K. Shapiro, P. J. Accardo, & A. J. Capute (Eds.), *Specific reading disability: A view of the spectrum* (pp. 123–136). Timonium, MD: York Press.

Siegel, L. S. (1999). Issues in the definition and diagnosis of learning disabilities: A perspective on *Guckenberger* v. *Boston University. Journal of Learning Disabilities, 32 (4),* 304–319.

Sinatra, G. M., & Royer, J. M. (1993). *Journal of Educational Psychology, 85 (3),* 509–519.

Snider, V. E. (1989). Reading comprehension performance of adolescents with learning disabilities. *Learning Disability Quarterly, 12 (2),* 87–96.

Snider, V. E., & Tarver, S. G. (1987). The effect of early reading failure on acquisition of knowledge among students with learning disabilities. *Journal of Learning Disabilities, 20 (6),* 351–356, 373.

Snow R. E. (1992). Aptitude theory: Yesterday, today and tomorrow. *Educational Psychologist, 27 (1),* 5–32.

Snow, R. E. (1994). Abilities and aptitudes. In R. J. Sternberg (Ed.), *Encyclopedia of human intelligence* (pp. 3–5). New York: Macmillan.

Snow, R. E., & Swanson, J. (1992). Instructional psychology: Aptitude, adaptation, and assessment. *Annual Review of Psychology, 43,* 583–626.

Snyder, L. S., & Downey, D. M. (1997). Developmental differences in the relationship between oral language deficits and reading. *Topics in Language Disorders, 17 (3),* 27–40.

Spector, J. E. (1992). Predicting progress in beginning reading: Dynamic assessment of phonemic awareness. *Journal of Educational Psychology, 84 (3),* 353–363.

Stahl, S. A., & Murray, B. A. (1994). Defining phonological awareness and its relationship to early reading. *Journal of Educational Psychology, 86 (2),* 221–234.

Stankov, L. (1994). Auditory abilities. In R. J. Sternberg (Ed.), *Encyclopedia of human intelligence* (pp. 157–162). New York: Macmillan.

Stankov, L., & Horn, J. L. (1980). Human abilities revealed through auditory tests. *Journal of Educational Psychology, 72 (1),* 21–44.

Stanovich, K. E. (1991). Discrepancy definitions of reading disability: Has intelligence led us astray? *Reading Research Quarterly, 26 (1),* 7–29.

Stanovich, K. E. (1999). The sociopsychometrics of learning disabilities. *Journal of Learning Disabilities, 32 (4),* 350–361.

Stanovich, K. E., Cunningham, A. E., & Feeman, D. J. (1984). Intelligence, cognitive skills, and early reading progress. *Reading Research Quarterly, 19,* 278–303.

Stanovich, K. E., & Siegel, L. S. (1994). Phenotypic performance profile of children with reading disabilities: A regression-based test of the phonological-core variable-difference model. *Journal of Educational Psychology, 86 (1),* 24–53.

Steffler, D. J., Varnhagen, C. K., Friesen, C. K., & Treiman, R. (1998). There's more to children's spelling than the errors they make: Strategic and automatic processes for one-syllable words. *Journal of Educational Psychology, 90 (3),* 492–505.

Sternberg, R. J. (1985). *Beyond IQ: A triarchic theory of human intelligence.* New York: Cambridge University Press.

Sternberg, R. J. (1997). The triarchic theory of intelligence. In D. P. Flanagan, J. L. Genshaft, & P. L. Harrison (Eds.), *Contemporary intellectual assessment: Theories, tests, and issues* (pp. 92–104). New York: Guilford.

Sternberg, R. J., & Kaufman, J. C. (1998). Human abilities. *Annual Review of Psychology, 49,* 479–502.

Stevenson, H. W., Parker, T., Wilkinson, A., Hegion, A., & Fish, E. (1976). Longitudinal study of individual differences in cognitive development and scholastic achievement. *Journal of Educational Psychology, 68 (4),* 377–400.

Strauss, A., & Lehtinen, L. (1947). *Psychopathology and education of the brain-injured child.* New York: Grune & Stratton.

Swanson, H. L. (1982). Verbal short-term memory encoding of learning disabled, deaf, and normal readers. *Learning Disabilities Quarterly, 5,* 21–28.

Swanson, H. L. (1986). Learning disabled readers' verbal coding difficulties: A problem of storage or retrieval? *Learning Disabilities Research, 1,* 73–82.

Swanson, H. L. (1992). Generality and modifiability of working memory among skilled and less skilled readers. *Journal of Educational Psychology, 84 (4),* 473–488.

Swanson, H. L. (1994). Short-term memory and working memory: Do both contribute to our understanding of academic achievement in children and adults with learning disabilities? *Journal of Learning Disabilities, 27 (1),* 34–50.

Swanson, H. L. (1996). Individual and age-related differences in children's working memory. *Memory and Cognition, 24 (1),* 70–82.

Swanson, H. L., & Berninger, V. W. (1995). The role of working memory in skilled and less skilled readers' comprehension. *Intelligence, 21,* 83–108.

Swanson, H. L., & Berninger, V. W. (1996). Individual differences in children's working memory and writing skill. *Journal of Experimental Child Psychology, 63 (2),* 358–385.

Swanson, H. L., Mink, J., & Bocian, K. M. (1999). Cognitive processing deficits in poor readers with symptoms of reading disabilities and ADHD: More alike than different? *Journal of Educational Psychology, 91 (2),* 321–333.

Taylor, L. C., Brown, F. G., & Michael, W. B. (1976). The validity of cognitive, affective, and demographic variables in the prediction of achievement in high school algebra and geometry: Implications for the definition of mathematical aptitude. *Educational and Psychological Measurement, 36,* 971–982.

Taylor, T. R. (1994). A review of three approaches to cognitive assessment, and a proposed integrated approach based on a unifying theoretical framework. *South African Journal of Psychology, 24 (4),* 183–193.

Thomas, W. P., & Collier, V. P. (1997). *School effectiveness for language minority students.* Washington, DC: National Clearinghouse on Bilingual Education.

Thorndike, R. L., & Hagen, E. (1969). *Measurement and evaluation in psychology and education* (3rd ed.). New York: Wiley.

Torgesen, J. K. (1988). Studies of children with learning disabilities who perform poorly on memory-span tasks. *Journal of Learning Disabilities, 21 (10),* 605–612.

Torgesen, J. K., & Wagner, R. K. (1998). Alternative diagnostic approaches for specific developmental reading disabilities. *Learning Disabilities Research & Practice, 13 (4),* 220–232.

Torgesen, J. K., Wagner, R. K., & Rashotte, C. A. (1994). Longitudinal studies of phonological processing and reading. *Journal of Learning Disabilities, 27 (5),* 276–286.

Torgesen, J. K., Wagner, R. K., Rashotte, C. A., Burgess, S., & Hecht, S. (1997). Contributions of phonological awareness and rapid automatic naming ability to the growth of word-reading skills in second- to fifth-grade children. *Scientific Studies of Reading, 1 (2),* 161–185.

Torgesen, J. K., Wagner, R. K., Rashotte, C. A., Rose, E., Lindamood, P., Conway, T., & Garvan, C. (1999). Preventing reading failure in young children with phonological processing disabilities: Group and individual responses to instruction. *Journal of Educational Psychology, 91 (4),* 579–593.

Treiman, R., Berch, D., Tincoff, R., & Weatherson, S. (1993). Phonology and spelling: The case of syllabic consonants. *Journal of Experimental Child Psychology, 56 (3),* 267–290.

Turner, M. L., & Engle, R. W. (1989). Is working memory capacity task dependent? *Journal of Memory and Language, 28,* 127–154.

Uhry, J. K. (1993). Predicting low reading from phonological awareness and classroom print. *Educational Assessment, 1 (4),* 349–368.

U.S. Department of Education. (1995). IDEA amendments Public Law 105–17, 11 stat. 37 [20 USC 1401 (26)], June 4, 1997.

van Daal, V., & van der Leij, A. (1999). Developmental dyslexia: Related to specific or general deficits? *Annals of Dyslexia, 49,* 71–104.

Vanderwood, M. L., McGrew, K. S., Flanagan, D. P., & Keith, T. Z. (1999). *Examination of the contribution of general and specific cognitive abilities to reading achievement.* Manuscript submitted for publication.

Vellutino, F. R., Scanlon, D. M., & Lyon, G. R. (2000). Differentiating between difficult-to-remediate and readily remediated poor readers: More evidence against the IQ-achievement discrepancy definition of reading disability. *Journal of Learning Disabilities, 33 (3),* 223–238.

Vellutino, F. R., Scanlon, D. M., Sipay, E. R., Small, S. G., Pratt, A., Chen, R., & Denckla, M. B. (1996). Cognitive profiles of difficult-to-remediate and readily remediated poor readers: Early intervention as a vehicle for distinguishing between cognitive and experiential deficits as basic causes of specific reading disability. *Journal of Educational Psychology, 88 (4),* 601–638.

Vernon, S. A., & Ferreiro, E. (1999). Writing development: A neglected variable in the consideration of phonological awareness. *Harvard Educational Review, 69 (4),* 395–415.

Vogt, W. P. (1993). *Dictionary of statistics and methodology: A nontechnical guide for the social sciences.* Thousand Oaks, CA: Sage.

Wagner, R. K., & Torgesen, J. K. (1987). The nature of phonological processing and its causal role in the acquisition of reading skills. *Psychological Bulletins, 101 (2),* 192–212.

Wagner, R. K., Torgesen, J. K., Laughton, P., Simmons, K., & Rashotte, C. A. (1993). Development of young readers' phonological processing abilities. *Journal of Educational Psy-chology, 85 (1),* 83–103.

Wagner, R. K., Torgesen, J. K., & Rashotte, C. A. (1994). Development of reading related phonological processing abilities: New evidence of bi-directional causality from a latent variable longitudinal study. *Developmental Psychology, 30 (1),* 73–87.

Wagner, R. K., Torgesen, J. K., & Rashotte, C. A. (1999). *Comprehensive Test of Phonological Processing.* Austin, TX: PRO-ED.

Wagner, R. K., Torgesen, J. K., Rashotte, C. A., Hecht, S. A., et al. (1997). Changing relations between phonological processing abilities and word-level reading as children develop from beginning to skilled readers: A 5-year longitudinal study. *Developmental Psychology, 33 (3),* 468–479.

Wallace, G., & Hammill, D. D. (1994). *Comprehensive Receptive and Expressive Vocabulary Test.* Austin, TX: PRO-ED.

Watkins, M. W., & Kush, J. C. (1994). Wechsler subtest analysis: The right way, the wrong way, or no way? *School Psychology Review, 23,* 640–651.

Watson, C., & Willows, D. M. (1995). Information-processing patterns in specific reading disability. *Journal of Learning Disabilities, 28 (4),* 216–231.

Webster, R. E. (1979). Visual and aural short-term memory capacity deficits in mathematics disabled students. *Journal of Educational Research, 72 (5),* 277–283.

Wechsler, D. (1991). *Wechsler Intelligence Scale for Children–Third Edition.* San Antonio, TX: The Psychological Corporation.

Wechsler, D. (1997). *Wechsler Adult Intelligence Scale–Third Edition.* San Antonio, TX: The Psychological Corporation.

Wepman, J., Cruickshank, W., Deutsch, D., Morency, A., & Strother, C. (1975). Learning disabilities. In N. Hobbs (Ed.), *Issues in the classification of children* (Vol. 1). San Francisco: Jossey-Bass.

Wilkinson, G. S. (1993). *Wide Range Achievement Test* (3rd ed.). Itasca, IL: Riverside.

Williams, J., Zolten, A. J., Rickert, V. I., Spence, G. T., et al. (1993). Use of nonverbal tests to screen for writing dysfluency in school-age children. *Perceptual & Motor Skills, 76 (3, Pt 1),* 803–809.

Wilson, B. C. (1992). The neuropsychological assessment of the preschool child: A branching model. In I. Rapm & S. I. Segalowitz (Eds.), *Handbook of neuropsychology: Child neuropsychology* (vol. 6, pp. 377–394).

Wimmer, H., Mayringer, H., & Landerl, K. (1998). Poor reading: A deficit in skill-automatization or a phonological deficit? *Scientific Studies of Reading, 2 (4),* 321–340.

Wolf, M. (1991). Naming-speed and reading: The contribution of the cognitive neurosciences. *Reading Research Quarterly, 26 (2),* 123–141.

Woodcock, R. (1989). *Emulation of the WISC-R type standard scores for users of the WJ-R.* Unpublished manuscript.

Woodcock, R. W. (1990). Theoretical foundations of the WJ-R measures of cognitive ability. *Journal of Psychoeducational Assessment, 8,* 231–258.

Woodcock, R. W. (1993). An information processing view of *Gf-Gc* theory. *Journal of Psychoeducational Assessment* [Monograph Series: WJ-R Monograph], 80–102.

Woodcock, R. W. (1994). Measures of fluid and crystallized intelligence. In R. J. Sternberg (Ed.), *The encyclopedia of human intelligence* (pp. 452–456). New York: Macmillan.

Woodcock, R. W. (1997). *Woodcock Diagnostic Reading Battery.* Itasca, IL: Riverside.

Woodcock, R. W. (1998). *Woodcock Reading Mastery Tests-Revised/Normative Update.* Circle Pines, MN: American Guidance Service.

Woodcock, R. W., & Johnson, M. B. (1989). *Woodcock-Johnson Psycho-Educational Battery–Revised.* Chicago: Riverside.

Woodcock, R. W., & Mather, N. (1989, 1990). WJ-R tests of cognitive ability—Standard and supplemental batteries: Examiner's manual. In R. W. Woodcock & M. B. Johnson (Eds.), *Woodcock-Johnson Psycho-Educational Battery–Revised.* Chicago: Riverside.

Woodcock, R. W., McGrew, K. S., & Mather, N. (2001). *Woodcock-Johnson III Tests of Achievement.* Itasca, IL: Riverside.

Woodcock, R. W., McGrew, K. S., & Werder, J. K. (1994). *Mini Battery of Achievement.* Itasca, IL: Riverside .

Yopp, H. K. (1988). The validity and reliability of phonemic awareness tests. *Reading Research Quarterly, 23 (2),* 159–177.

Young, A., & Bowers, P. G. (1995). Individual difference and text difficulty determinants of reading fluency and expressiveness. *Journal of Experimental Child Psychology, 60 (3),* 428–454.

Ysseldyke, J. (1990). Goodness of fit of the Woodcock-Johnson Psycho-Educational Battery–Revised to the Horn-Cattell *Gf-Gc* theory. *Journal of Psychoeducational Assessment, 8,* 268–275.

Yuill, N., Oakhill, J., & Parking, A. (1989). Working memory, comprehension ability and the resolution of text anomaly. *British Journal of Psychology, 80,* 351–361.

Zachary, R. A., & Gorsuch, R. L. (1985). Continuous norming: Implications for the WAIS—R. *Journal of Clinical Psychology, 41 (1),* 86–94.

Index